Introduction to Molecular Structure and Spectroscopy

This book is part of
The Allyn and Bacon Chemistry Series
and was developed under the co-consulting editorship of
Daryle H. Busch and Harrison Shull

Introduction to Molecular Structure and Spectroscopy

William A. Guillory

The University of Utah

Allyn and Bacon, Inc.

Boston · London · Sydney · Toronto

Library of Congress Cataloging in Publication Data

Guillory, William A
Introduction to molecular structure and spectroscopy.
(The Allyn and Bacon chemistry series)
Includes bibliographies.
1. Spectrum analysis. 2. Molecular theory. I. Title.

QC451.G86 535′.84 76-55708
ISBN 0-205-05718-7

To my friend and teacher Dolphus E. Milligan
and my wife Laura

Contents

Preface

This textbook is the result of a course in spectroscopy and molecular structure that I have taught to advanced undergraduates and first-year graduate students. It assumes as background a sound course in undergraduate physical chemistry, some exposure to quantum chemistry, and knowledge of a few rudiments of matrix algebra and group theory.

It is designed not only as a textbook for a course in spectroscopy, but also as a resource for the chemist, physicist, biologist, biochemist, technician, geologist, and others who would like to understand more clearly the theory of a particular spectroscopic technique. At every opportunity, the relation between spectroscopic information and molecular structure is discussed. It is intended that the text should bridge the gap between material presented in an introductory physical chemistry course and a particular spectroscopy treated at an advanced level, for example, Herzberg's *Infrared Spectroscopy of Polyatomic Molecules* or Wilson, Decius, and Cross's *Molecular Vibrations*. Any mathematical rigor is used only as necessary, although we must remember that rigorous mathematical techniques are ultimately essential for dealing adequately with many of the quantum mechanical problems that are encountered in spectroscopy. I hope that my colleagues will excuse any lack of mathematical sophistication; I felt that at this level it was perhaps more important to provide a *basis* for appreciating the more mathematically elegant approaches. For those who prefer a more mathematically rigorous approach, the text is ideal in the sense of being not only complementary to lectures of this nature, but also largely nonredundant for presentation to a reasonably sophisticated group. Perhaps the most important reason for writing this textbook is that I believe that understanding spectroscopy will be essential in the next decade or so in resolving fundamental scientific problems, particularly in physics and chemistry.

The problems are for the most part nonredundant, so that a careful choice must be made of those believed to be most important. In many cases, they are written as an extension of the chapter in further illustrating important principles that space limitations prevented in the written text. I strongly believe in problem solving as a means of really testing one's understanding of the important principles covered in a chapter. In practically all cases, I have tried to make the textual material self-contained in providing adequate discussion for solving the problems. Some selected problems in each chapter, however, do require recourse to other, more advanced material for their solution. My recommendation is to attempt them all, particularly if you are primarily interested in a specific spectroscopic technique.

I should welcome and encourage the criticisms (pro or con) of my colleagues and students and would appreciate their noting any errors. I should also like to express my gratitude to my colleagues at Drexel University and the University of Utah who made helpful suggestions during the writing of this manuscript. I am particularly indebted to Professor Emeritus Eugene Rosenbaum at Drexel, who read the entire manuscript and made valuable suggestions throughout the writing of the text.

I should further like to express my sincere appreciation to my secretary, Anne Stewart, for typing the manuscript. Finally, I thank my family, Laura and Danny, without whose encouragement and understanding this work would not have been possible.

William A. Guillory

Physical Constants

Speed of light in vacuum	c	2.99776×10^{10} cm/sec
Electronic charge	e	4.8024×10^{-10} $cm^{3/2}g^{1/2}$/sec (esu) 1.602×10^{-11} coulomb (emu)
Planck's constant	h $\hbar = \dfrac{h}{2\pi}$	6.623×10^{-27} erg-sec 1.054×10^{-27} erg-sec
Boltzmann's constant	k	1.3803×10^{-16} erg/K
Avogadro's constant	N_0	6.0225×10^{23} $mole^{-1}$
Electron rest mass	m_e	9.1091×10^{-28} g 5.48597×10^{-4} amu
Proton rest mass	m_p	1.67252×10^{-24} g 1.00728 amu
Bohr magneton	μ_β	0.927×10^{-21} erg/gauss
Nuclear magneton	μ_N	5.0505×10^{-24} erg/gauss
Proton moment	μ_p	1.41049×10^{-23} erg/gauss
Bohr radius	a_0	5.2960×10^{-9} cm
Gas constant	R	1.9872 cal/K-mole 8.3144×10^{7} ergs/K-mole
Electronic *g* factor	g_e	2.002319
Nuclear *g* factor (proton)	g_n	5.58490

Chapter 1

Electric Phenomena

Since the electrical properties of atomic and molecular systems are so important in the interaction leading to absorption and emission of radiation, we shall briefly review some of the elementary concepts involving electric phenomena. Especially important is the electric dipole moment (induced or permanent) of an atomic or a molecular species. The techniques and methods of calculating and estimating this fundamental property are our primary interest in this chapter.

A. DIPOLE MOMENT

The interaction between electromagnetic radiation and atomic or molecular species that gives rise to resonance phenomena, such as electronic and vibrational absorption, is intimately related to the dipole moment of that species. A bond formed between atoms having different electronegativities will result in net charge separation, and consequently a permanent electric dipole. Although strictly speaking, the dipole moment of a molecule involves the summation over all the electronic and nuclear coordinates,

$$\mu = \sum_i q_i r_i, \tag{1-1}$$

in practice it is assumed that the nuclear coordinates are fixed and that the inner-shell electrons have a spherical charge distribution. Thus, the main effects presumably arise from the electronic cloud of the bonding and nonbonding valence electrons. If the charge distribution of a diatomic molecule is represented by point charges $\pm q$, separated by some distance r, then the electric dipole moment (a vector) is given as

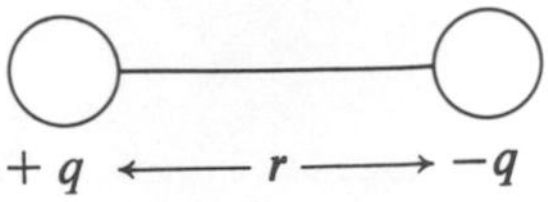

$$\mu = qr \text{ esu-cm,} \tag{1-2}$$

where we assume the chemists' convention that the electric dipole vector points from the positive to the negative charge.

If NaCl in the vapor state were a purely ionic diatomic molecule with an experimental internuclear separation of 2.3 Å, the permanent dipole moment would be $\mu_0 = 11 \times 10^{-18}$ esu-cm. The unit 10^{-18} esu-cm is defined as a debye (D) in honor of the 1936 Nobel Prize winner in chemistry, Peter J. B. Debye. The observed dipole moment of NaCl is 9.0 D and thus indicates that there are other contributions besides the obvious one arising solely from the ionic bond character. The other contributions, which should be algebraically added to the correctly estimated primary component (11.0 D), are the self-induced moment, the bond overlap moment, and the atomic orbital hybridization moment.[1] The primary moment, which is really given by $\mu_p = qri_c$ (where i_c is the percentage ionic character) is reasonably well approximated by Eq. (1-2) because $i_c \sim 0.98$; it results from the unequal distribution of electronic charge between the bonded atoms. The bond overlap moment μ_s results from the distortions caused by overlap between unsymmetrical atomic orbitals. The atomic hybridization moment μ_h results from the fact that the charge center in a hybrid orbital does not coincide with the nuclear charge. In this particular case, only the self-induced moment μ_{ind}, which arises from the internal polarization by the electric field of the resultant moment, is significant (−2.0 D).

The dipole moment of a polyatomic molecule is the resultant obtained from the vectorial addition of the products of the time-averaged electronic and nuclear coordinates and their corresponding charges over the entire molecule. Although the dipole moment of polyatomic molecules cannot be reliably predicted at present, calculating approximate moments by the vectorial addition of the individual bond moments has been useful in some cases. This procedure will be illustrated in Section E. The validity of this procedure however, depends on the transferability of the estimated bond moments from one molecule to another. Since this moment results, strictly speaking, from the four effects discussed above it will be different for different bonding situations. In some cases this procedure can lead to totally incorrect predictions.

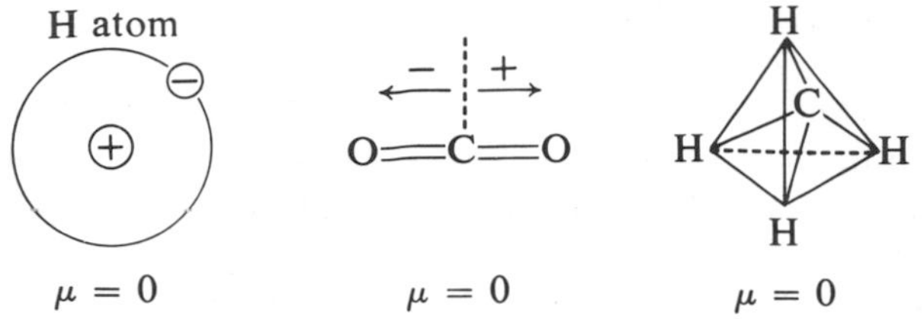

FIGURE 1-1 Spherically and symmetrically charged molecules having a zero dipole moment.

B. POLAR AND NONPOLAR MOLECULES

Neutral atoms or molecules that have a symmetrical charge distribution resulting in a permanent dipole moment of zero are called nonpolar. Examples of these are shown in Figure 1-1.

When such atoms or molecules are placed in an electric field, both the electronic and nuclear charge distributions of these species are distorted, resulting in an induced dipole moment m. For symmetrical molecules or atoms, the induced moment is directly proportional to the external field. The proportionality constant is called the polarizability α, and it consists of two contributions: the electronic and the atomic polarizabilities. The electronic polarizability α_e results from the distortion of the electronic cloud by the external field. The atomic polarizability α_a results when displacement of atomic nuclei causes slight changes in equilibrium bond angles and internuclear distances. Generally, α_e is normally 10 to 50 times greater than α_a.

Molecules having a charge separation resulting in a net permanent electric dipole vector are called polar molecules (Figure 1-2). For unsymmetrical molecules, the induced polarization will depend on the orientation of the molecule in the field since α is anisotropic. However, for our elementary consideration, we shall assume the polarizability to be isotropic and independent of molecular orientation ($\alpha_x \simeq \alpha_y \simeq \alpha_z$).

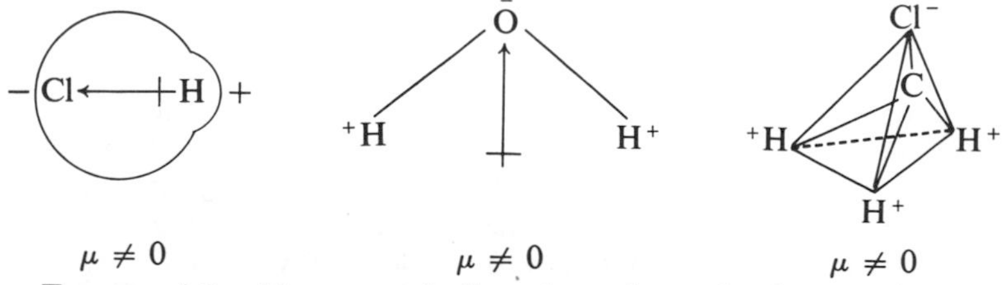

FIGURE 1-2 Unsymmetrically charged molecules having nonzero dipole moments.

C. POLARIZATION AND THE CLAUSIUS-MOSOTTI RELATION

When a nonconducting material (dielectric) is placed between the plates of a capacitor, the interaction of the electric field with the dielectric causes a separation of positive and negative charges. This effect is called polarization of the dielectric material (Figure 1-3a). This induced polarization effect occurs whether the molecules are polar or nonpolar. The external field also causes the dielectric molecules to align parallel to it. For gaseous molecules, this tendency is opposed by thermal agitation.

The presence of the dielectric decreases the electric field strength **E** and increases the capacitance C by a factor ϵ, which is the ratio $\mathbf{E}^0$(vacuum)/**E**(dielectric) and C(dielectric)/C^0(vacuum), respectively. The constant ϵ is defined as the dielectric constant. Measurements of capaci-

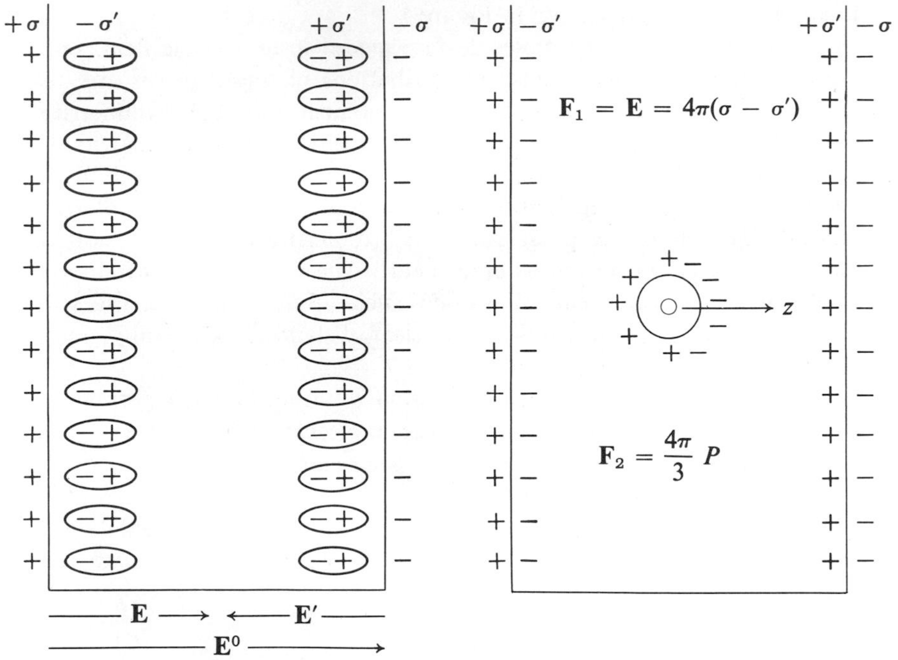

(a) (b)

FIGURE 1-3 (a) The separation of charge by the external field $\mathbf{E}^0$ (induced polarization) and the accumulation of uniform dielectric charge density σ', opposite to charge density of the capacitor plate on the inner surface. The inner medium, also containing the dielectric molecules (not shown), is electrically neutral. (b) A point molecule circumscribed in a sphere with surface charge induced by the external field **E**.

tance and evaluation of the dielectric constant allow us to calculate electric dipole moments, as will be shown in the following sections.

When a dielectric material is placed in a uniform electric field $\mathbf{E}^0$, an accumulation of charge density $\pm\sigma'$ results from the polarized dielectric along the inner surfaces of each of the capacitor plates (Figure 1-3a). Since overall charge neutrality is maintained, the uniform induced charges on the corresponding capacitor plates are equal and opposite, and the inner medium, which also contains the dielectric material, is electrically neutral. The electric field produced as a result of the presence of the dielectric is $4\pi\sigma'$, and is opposed in direction to the external field with no dielectric present, $4\pi\sigma$. The net uniform field in the presence of the dielectric is

$$\mathbf{E} = \mathbf{E}^0 - \mathbf{E}' = 4\pi\sigma - 4\pi\sigma'. \tag{1-3}$$

The question of the electrical forces that act on a single dielectric molecule naturally arises, since their algebraic sum is what really gives rise to the induced polarization. In other words, what is the nature of the local field "seen" by a single molecule in the medium? The model Clausius and Mosotti assumed was a point mass (atom) circumscribed in a sphere of dimensions that were large compared with the point mass, and small compared with the medium.[2] It is assumed that three orienting forces act on the molecule at the center of the cavity, generating three electric fields:

$$\mathbf{F} = \mathbf{F}_1 + \mathbf{F}_2 + \mathbf{F}_3. \tag{1-4}$$

The first field, $\mathbf{F}_1$, is described by Eq. (1-3), and gives rise to the induced charge about the spherical cavity shown in Figure (1-3b). The second, $\mathbf{F}_2$, results from the layer of charge on the surface of the small cavity in the z direction,[3]

$$\mathbf{F}_2 = \frac{4\pi}{3}P, \tag{1-5}$$

where P, the polarization is the dipole moment per cubic centimeter. The third, $\mathbf{F}_3$, is the electrical field due to the material within the cavity. In the case of a cubic crystal, this field has been shown to be zero, and it is assumed for gases and dilute solutions, where nearest-neighbor effects are assumed small, that the same applies. Thus, $\mathbf{F}_3$ is assumed to be zero as a reasonable approximation, and Eq. (1-4) reduces to

$$\mathbf{F} = \mathbf{E} + \frac{4\pi}{3}P. \tag{1-6}$$

This is the Clausius-Mosotti relation; it defines the local electric field to which a molecule is subjected in a dielectric medium.

1. Induced Polarization (Nonpolar Molecules)

The interaction of a nonpolar molecule with an electric field results in charge separation of the negative symmetrical electronic cloud and the positive localized atomic center of symmetry, and thus an "induced dipole moment" is produced. This induced electric moment m is proportional to the electric field strength $\mathbf{F}$ at the location of the molecule, and differs slightly from the uniform external electric field $\mathbf{E}$ owing to the presence of the polarized material,

$$m = \alpha \mathbf{F}. \quad \textbf{(1-7)}$$

The value $\mathbf{F}$ is given by Eq. (1-6), and α (cm^3), defined previously as the polarizability, is proportional to the degree to which the symmetrical charge distribution of a molecule is distorted by interaction with the external electric field. The polarizability, which has units of volume, is sometimes used as an estimate of the molecular volume of the polarized species. Thus, if n is the number of molecules per cc, the induced polarization P (dipole moment/cc) is given as

$$P = nm = n \cdot \alpha \mathbf{F} = n\alpha\left(\mathbf{E} + \frac{4\pi}{3} P\right), \quad \textbf{(1-8)}$$

where the only contribution to P in this case is that due to the induced effect P_1. For the polarized material between the capacitor plates, $\mathbf{E}'$ of Eq. (1-3) is also given as $4\pi P$. Combining this form of Eq. (1-3) with the relation given for the dielectric constant ϵ,[4]

$$\mathbf{E}^0 = \mathbf{E} + 4\pi P \quad \textbf{(1-9)}$$

and

$$\mathbf{E}^0 = \epsilon \mathbf{E}, \quad \textbf{(1-10)}$$

we obtain from Eq. (1-8), the relation

$$\frac{\epsilon - 1}{\epsilon + 2} = \frac{4\pi}{3} n\alpha. \quad \textbf{(1-11)}$$

Multiplying through by the molar volume, M (molecular weight)/ρ (density), we obtain the induced molar polarization (cc/mole) for atoms and symmetrical molecules,[5]

$$P_{\mathrm{M}} = \frac{4\pi}{3} N_0 \alpha = \frac{\epsilon - 1}{\epsilon + 2} \frac{M}{\rho}. \quad \textbf{(1-12)}$$

This equation also applies to nonpolar gases at high pressures and nonpolar liquids. Based on the discussion in Section B (where $\alpha_x \simeq \alpha_y \simeq \alpha_z$), it can also be applied to approximately symmetrical gases and liquids.

2. Orientation Polarization (Polar Molecules)

When a polar molecule is placed in a static electric field, the tendency is for the field force to align the dipole vector parallel to it. This tendency towards alignment is opposed by the thermal energy of the molecules, and thus a compromise situation results with a distribution of electric vectors at various angles ϕ to the field direction (Figure 1-4).

The potential energy due to the orientation of a dipole in an external electric field is given as

$$U = \boldsymbol{\mu} \cdot \mathbf{E}. \tag{1-13}$$

The quantity of interest is the average component of the electric moment in the direction of the field as a function of the temperature. The potential energy as a function of the angle ϕ is given as

$$U(\phi) = -\mu_0 \mathbf{F} \cos \phi, \tag{1-14}$$

where μ_0 is the permanent dipole moment and $\mathbf{F}$ is the local electric field. Theoretically at high temperatures, the Boltzmann distribution is such that there are equal contributions from $+\mu_0\mathbf{F} \cos \phi$ and $-\mu_0\mathbf{F} \cos \phi$, resulting

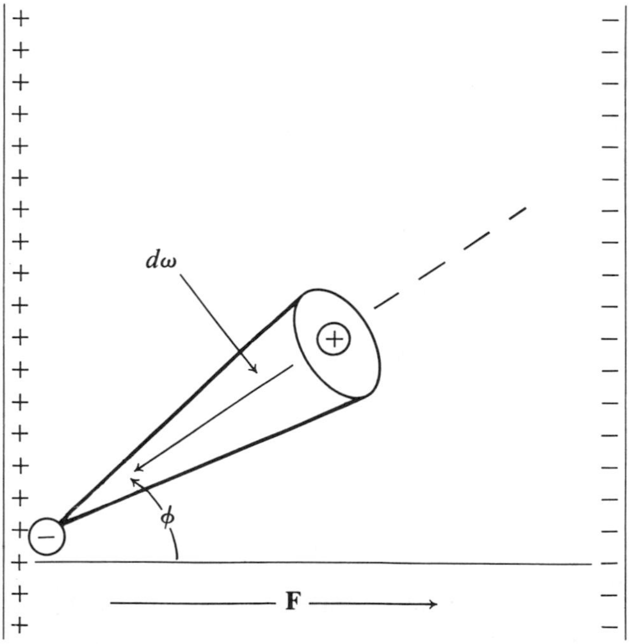

FIGURE 1-4 A dipole oriented at an angle ϕ with respect to the electric field direction. Note that the direction of the permanent dipole is from positive to negative.

in no net contribution to the total molar polarization. At lower temperatures, there will be a greater number of components with ϕ angles at less than 90° from the field direction. The number of molecules in the element of solid angle $d\omega$ as a function of angle ϕ is given as

$$n = n_0 \exp \frac{\mu_0 \mathbf{F} \cos \phi}{kT} \, d\omega. \tag{1-15}$$

Therefore, the average value of the orientation dipole moment per molecule $\overline{m}_0$ parallel to the field is

$$\overline{m}_0 = \frac{\int_0^{4\pi} n_0 \exp(\mu_0 \mathbf{F} \cos \phi / kT) \mu_0 \cos \phi \, d\omega}{\int_0^{4\pi} n_0 \exp(\mu_0 \mathbf{F} \cos \phi / kT) \, d\omega}. \tag{1-16}$$

Making the substitutions

$$\mathbf{a} = \mu_0 \mathbf{F}/kT, \; x = \cos \phi, \text{ and } d\omega = 2\pi \sin \phi \, d\phi = 2\pi \, dx, \tag{1-17}$$

we obtain

$$\frac{\overline{m}_0}{\mu_0} = \frac{\int_{-1}^{+1} e^{\mathbf{a}x} x \, dx}{\int_{-1}^{+1} e^{\mathbf{a}x} \, dx} = \frac{(e^{\mathbf{a}x}/\mathbf{a}^2)(\mathbf{a}x - 1)|_{-1}^{+1}}{(e^{\mathbf{a}x}/\mathbf{a})|_{-1}^{+1}}. \tag{1-18}$$

Simplifying gives

$$\frac{\overline{m}_0}{\mu_0} = \frac{e^{\mathbf{a}} + e^{-\mathbf{a}}}{e^{\mathbf{a}} - e^{-\mathbf{a}}} - \frac{1}{\mathbf{a}} = \coth \mathbf{a} - \frac{1}{\mathbf{a}} = L(\mathbf{a}). \tag{1-19}$$

This mathematical expression is known as the Langevin function. For values of **a** sufficiently small, $L(\mathbf{a})$ may be expanded as a power series,

$$L(\mathbf{a}) \simeq \frac{\mathbf{a}}{3} - \frac{\mathbf{a}^3}{45} + \cdots. \tag{1-20}$$

Since **a** is normally of the order of 10^{-3}, only the first term is retained, and

$$\overline{m}_0 = \frac{\mu_0 \mathbf{a}}{3} = \frac{\mu_0{}^2 \mathbf{F}}{3kT}. \tag{1-21}$$

The orientation polarization is the dipole moment per unit volume parallel to the field,

$$P_o = n\overline{m}_0 = \frac{n\mu_0{}^2 \mathbf{F}}{3kT}. \tag{1-22}$$

Combining Eqs. (1-7) and (1-21) for the total dipole moment, we obtain the total polarization P (dipole moment/cc), due to the induced and orientation effects,

$$P = P_i + P_o = n\left(\alpha + \frac{\mu_0{}^2}{3kT}\right)\left(\mathbf{E} + \frac{4\pi P}{3}\right), \tag{1-23}$$

and the total molar polarization P_{M} (cc/mole),

$$P_{\mathrm{M}} = \frac{4\pi}{3} N_0\left(\alpha + \frac{\mu_0{}^2}{3kT}\right) = \frac{M}{\rho}\cdot\frac{\epsilon - 1}{\epsilon + 2}, \tag{1-24}$$

which is known as the Debye equation. This relation applies to polar and nonpolar gases and dilute solutions of nonpolar solvents, since the derivation was based in part on the Clausius-Mosotti equation. Equation (1-24) does not hold at all when appled to pure polar liquids.

3. Distortion Polarization in an Alternating Field

An additional method for experimentally determining the dipole moment for gases and liquids is provided by one of Maxwell's electromagnetic relations, $\epsilon = n^2$, where the dielectric constant ϵ equals the square of the refractive index n. The refractive index, we recall, is the ratio of the speed of light in a vacuum to the speed of light in a given medium, $n = c/c_{\mathrm{m}}$. Since it is generally measured using visible radiation ($\sim 10^{15}$ sec^{-1}), only the electrons are able to respond to the rapidly alternating field of the probing radiation. In some cases, infrared frequency measurements or extrapolation to infrared frequencies can be made. Substituting the above relation into Eq. (1-24) and omitting the temperature-dependent orientation term, we obtain the Lorentz-Lorenz equation

$$R_{\mathrm{d}} = \frac{M}{\rho}\cdot\frac{n^2 - 1}{n^2 + 2} = \frac{4\pi N_0 \alpha}{3}, \tag{1-25}$$

where

$$R_{\mathrm{d}} = \frac{4\pi N_0}{3}(\alpha_{\mathrm{e}} + \alpha_{\mathrm{a}}). \tag{1-26}$$

The symbol R_{d} represents the molar distortion polarization. Since α_{a} is generally 10 percent or less of α_{e}, it can often be neglected, and we obtain the molar refractivity R_{e}:

$$R_{\mathrm{e}} = \frac{4\pi N_0}{3}\,\alpha_{\mathrm{e}}. \tag{1-27}$$

The induced or distortion polarization and the orientation polarization can be separately obtained by using an alternating electric field. When a substance is placed in an alternating field at high frequencies (UV-visible), only the electrons are light enough to respond to the rapidly varying electric vector and give rise to electronic polarization P_{e}. As the frequency of the field is decreased to the infrared, the atomic (nuclear) contribution causes a gradual increase in the total polarization. Thus at this point the total induced polarization consists of both the electronic and atomic effects. Further decreasing the frequency of the alternating electric field to the microwave allows the permanent electric moment to be oriented, and the additional contribution to the total polarization is obtained, P_o. Therefore, the three stages of polarization can be summarized as follows:

(a) High field frequency (ultraviolet)	$R_e = P_e$
(b) Infrared field frequency (infrared)	$R_d = P_e + P_a$
(c) Low field frequency (microwave)	$P_M = P_e + P_a + P_o$

It now becomes possible to calculate the permanent moment μ_0 by evaluating P_o from the graph, as shown in Figure 1-5. In practice, P_o is usually evaluated from dielectric-constant determinations at low frequencies, whereas P_e and P_a are obtained from refractive index measurements at infrared and ultraviolet frequencies.

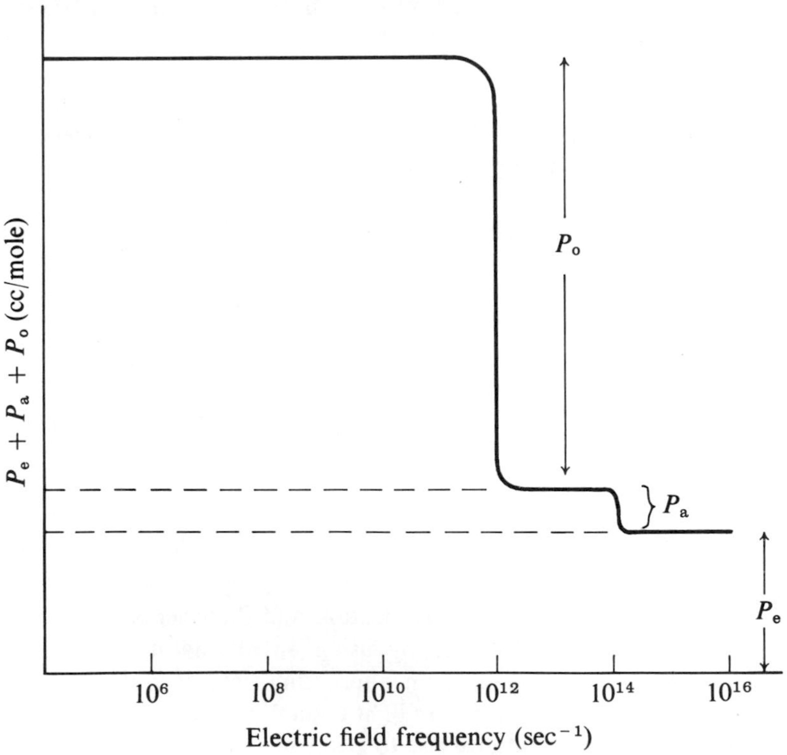

FIGURE 1-5 Schematic representation of the variation of the total molar polarization as a function of electric field frequency.

D. EXPERIMENTAL DETERMINATION OF μ_0

Since the induced polarization is temperature-dependent, Eq. (1-24) is sometimes expressed in the form

$$P_M = A + \frac{B\mu_0^2}{T}, \tag{1-24a}$$

where

$$A = \frac{4\pi N_0 \alpha}{3} \quad \text{and} \quad B = \frac{4\pi N_0}{9k}. \tag{1-28}$$

The dielectric constant is evaluated as a function of the absolute temperature, and the plot of P_M vs $1/T$ yields μ_0 from the calculated slope (Figure 1-6). The polarizability α can also be calculated from the intercept.

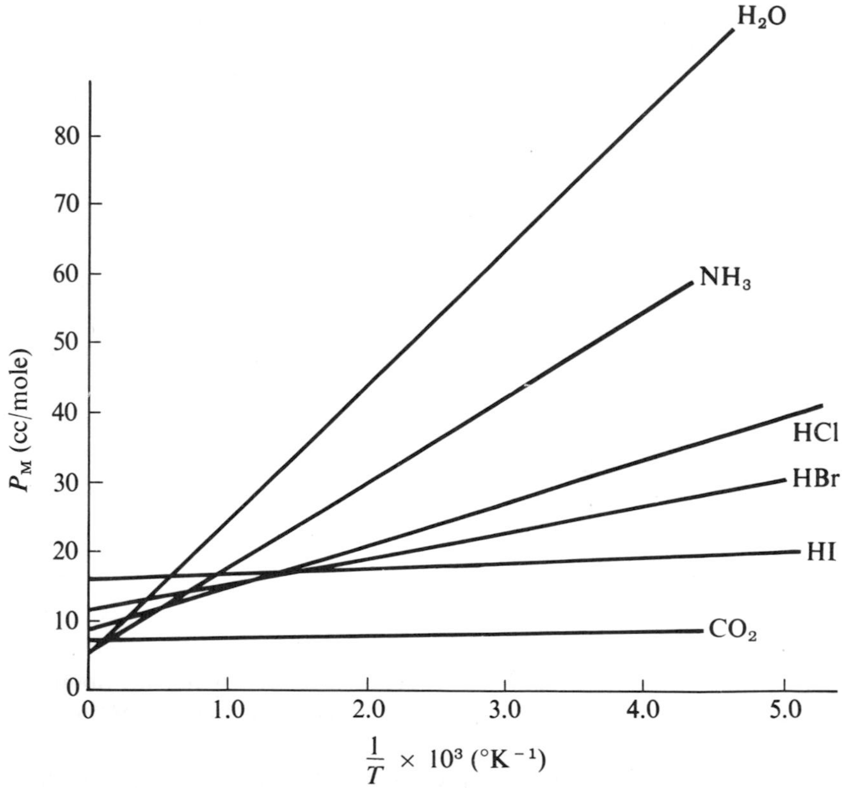

FIGURE 1-6 Plot of the total molar polarization vs the inverse of the absolute temperature for various polar and nonpolar species.

Thus, for HCl from Figure 1-6,

$$\frac{\Delta P_M}{\Delta(1/T)} = \frac{4\pi N_0 \mu_0{}^2}{9k} = 6.66 \times 10^3 \text{ cc-°K/mole} \tag{1-29}$$

and

$$\mu_0 = 1.08 \times 10^{-18} \text{ esu-cm} = 1.08 \text{ D}. \tag{1-30}$$

Similarly from the intercept,

$$\frac{4\pi N_0 \alpha}{3} = 7.84 \text{ cc/mole}, \tag{1-31}$$

and

$$\alpha = 3.1 \times 10^{-24} \text{ cm}^3. \tag{1-32}$$

The constant A, estimated from the $1/T = 0$ extrapolation, indicates that of the total molar polarization of approximately 30 cc at 333 °K, only about 8 cc is due to the induced effect. The experimentally determined HCl bond distance is 1.26 Å; if it were a completely ionic structure $H^+ \overset{1.26\text{ Å}}{\text{---}} Cl^-$, $\mu_0 = (1.26 \text{ Å})(4.80 \times 10^{-10} \text{ esu}) = 6.05$ D. Thus the ratio $\mu_{0\,HCl}/\mu_{H^+Cl^-} \simeq 1/6$, or we might say that HCl has approximately $\frac{1}{6}$ ionic character. On careful analysis of the total contributions to the dipolar effects, however, we find that

$$\mu_{obs} = 1.08 = \mu_p + \mu_s + \mu_h + \mu_{ind} = \mu_p - 0.65 - 0 - 0.83, \tag{1-33}$$

where μ_h is assumed to be zero based on quadrupole coupling calculations which shows negligible hybridization of the chlorine atom (Reference 1-4, p. 627). Estimation of μ_p from Eq. (1-33) allows the evaluation $i_c = \mu_p/q \cdot r = 0.42$, or that the ionic character of HCl is actually 42 percent. This example illustrates the inadequacy of the assumptions that fixed nuclear coordinates and spherical charge distributions from nonbonding electrons play a passive role in the net dipole moment of even simple diatomic molecules.

As pointed out previously, atomic and electronic polarizabilities determined by refractive-index measurements with infrared and visible radiation (Eqs. 1-25 and 1-27) and extrapolated to lower frequencies should be carefully compared with temperature-dependent polarization measurements where possible. This is stressed particularly for nonpolar or slightly polar species, for which the difference in the orientation and distortion effects is rather small.

An additional experimental procedure used for evaluating molecular dipole moments involves the Stark effect, which is the splitting of gas-phase rotational levels resulting from the interaction between the permanent dipole moment and an external electric field. The use of microwave spectroscopy in conjunction with this interaction has proved successful in obtaining accurate values of the dipole moments of diatomic and polyatomic molecules, particularly symmetric tops. (This application will be discussed further in Chapter 4 involving the rotational Stark effect.)

E. EVALUATING APPROXIMATE BOND AND MOLECULAR MOMENTS

When there are no theoretical or experimental data concerning the dipole moment of some polyatomic molecules, it is useful to use the method of vectorial addition of bond moments. The results obtained using this method are considered "approximate" at best within the limitations described in Section A, which are in some cases quite severe. To determine μ_0 for various bonds, data are obtained from small polyatomic molecules and a table of bonding pairs is constructed. Since the total dipole moment of a molecule is assumed to be the vectorial resultant of the individual bond moments, we assume a specific model of the species, and use the independently obtained values of the individual bond moments.

EXAMPLE 1-1: Evaluate the approximate dipole moment of the O—H bond from the resultant moment of H_2O. Given: $\mu_0 = 1.85$ D and a valence angle of 105°.

Solution: The experimentally determined dipole moment of H_2O is 1.85 Debyes. Assuming that 1.85 is the resultant of two equal μ_{OH} vectors with a valence angle of 105°, we obtain

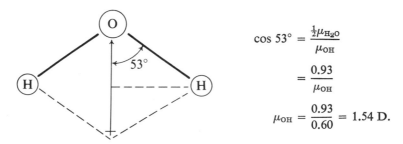

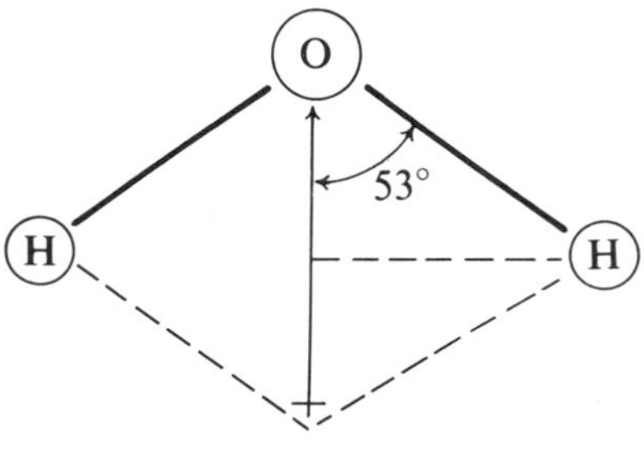

$$\cos 53° = \frac{\frac{1}{2}\mu_{H_2O}}{\mu_{OH}} = \frac{0.93}{\mu_{OH}}$$

$$\mu_{OH} = \frac{0.93}{0.60} = 1.54 \text{ D.}$$

The bond moment of O—H can be used to obtain the single bond moment of C—O from the experimentally determined dipole moment of CH_3—OH, $\mu = 1.69$ D. In this manner, we are able to construct a table of approximate bond moments as shown in Table 1-1.

TABLE 1-1. Empirically Derived Bond Moments

Bond	Dipole moment (Debyes)	Bond	Dipole moment (Debyes)
C—I	1.2	O—H	1.5
C—Br	1.4	N—H	1.3
C—Cl	1.5	F—H	1.9
C—F	1.4	Cl—H	1.0
P—H	0.4	Br—H	0.8
P—Cl	0.8	I—H	0.4
C≡N	3.0	C—O (aliphatic)	1.2
C—N	0.2	C=O	2.7
Br—Cl	0.6	F—Br	1.3
F—Cl	0.9	C—O (aromatic)	0.7

On the basis of the bond moments developed in Table 1-1, we might illustrate using this technique for estimating the dipole moments of a few molecules.

EXAMPLE 1-2: Evaluate the C═S bond moment from carbonyl sulfide (S═C═O) and use this result to obtain the dipole moment of planar thiophosgene (Cl$_2$C═S). Given: $\mu_{SCO} = 0.72$ D and $\angle$Cl—C—Cl $\simeq 112°$.

Solution: (a) $\overset{\leftarrow+\ +\rightarrow}{S═C═O}$

$$\mu_{SCO} = 0.72 = \mu_{CS} + 2.7$$
$$\mu_{CS} \simeq 2.0$$

(b) Based on the structure

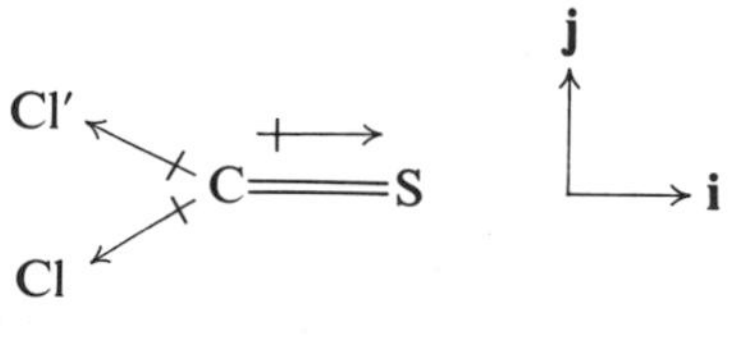

resolving the components gives

$$\mu_{CCl}' = -1.5 \cos 56°i + 1.5 \sin 56°j$$
$$= -0.84i + 1.25j$$
$$\mu_{CCl} = -0.84i - 1.25j$$
$$\mu_{CS} = 2.0i$$

Adding vectorially the i and j components, we obtain $\mu = \sqrt{(0.32)^2 + (0)^2}$. Therefore, the dipole moment is $\mu = 0.32$ D, and the experimental value is 0.29 D.

EXAMPLE 1-3: Estimate the bond moment of C—Cl and predict the approximate moment of *meta*-dichlorobenzene. The permanent moments of *ortho* and *meta*-dichlorobenzene are 2.52 and 1.72 D.

Solution: (a) Assume the accompanying structure for *o*-dichlorobenzene.

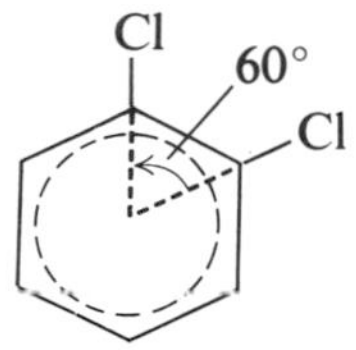

Using the law of cosines, we obtain

$$(\mu_o)^2 = \mu^2_{C-Cl} + \mu^2_{C-Cl} - 2\mu^2_{C-Cl}\cos 120°$$
$$(2.52)^2 = 2(\mu^2_{C-Cl})(1 + 0.5)$$
$$\mu_{C-Cl} = 1.48 \simeq 1.5\text{ D.}$$

(b) The dipole moment of *m*-dichlorobenzene is

$$(\mu_m)^2 = 2(\mu^2_{C-Cl})(1.0 - 0.5)$$
$$\mu_m = 1.5\text{ D,}$$

compared with the experimentally determined value 1.72 D.

F. DIPOLE MOMENT AND MOLECULAR STRUCTURE

The permanent dipole moment of a molecule can be useful in providing information about atomic orientation in space of a species, that is, symmetry. This is particularly true of symmetrical and near symmetrical molecules. In general, molecules that have a center of symmetry (are centrosymmetric) have zero dipole moments. Examples of these are shown in Table 1-2. Fairly straightforward examples are homonuclear diatomics A_2 (O_2 and N_2), symmetrical rectilinear triatomics AB_2 (CO_2 and CS_2), planar symmetric tetratomics AB_3 (BF_3 and NO_3^-), and centrosymmetric polyatomic molecules (C_2H_4, C_6H_6, and SF_6). Thus, that species such as H_2O and NH_3 both have a resultant permanent dipole moment generally confirms the respective bent and pyramidal natures of these species. Although it is perhaps obvious, we should note that substituting a dissimilar atom for a B atom in any of these centrosymmetric molecules will result in a permanent dipole moment. Examples of species having $\mu_0 = 0$ that are not so obvious are aliphatic hydrocarbons, transition metal complexes such as $Mn_2(CO)_{10}$ and the planar copper(II) phthalocyanine complex, and inorganics such as S_2Cl_2 and P_2H_4. Molecular types having nonzero dipole moments based on structural symmetry are also listed in Table 1-2.

TABLE 1-2. Symmetrical and Nonsymmetrical Molecules with and without Permanent Dipole Moments

General formula	Symmetry	$\mu_0 = 0$	Species
A_2	Linear	Yes	N_2, O_2, F_2, Cl_2
AB	Linear	No	NO, HCl, OH, CH
AB_2	Linear symmetrical	Yes	CO_2, CS_2, NO_2^+, XeF_2
AB_2	Linear unsymmetrical	No	N_2O, HCN
AB_2	Bent symmetrical	No	NO_2, H_2O, SCl_2
AB_3	Planar	Yes	BF_3, CO_3^{2-}, NO_3^-
AB_3	Pyramidal	No	NH_3, PF_3, ClO_3^-, NF_3
AB_3	T-shaped	No	BrF_3, ClF_3
AB_4	Tetrahedral	Yes	CH_4, $SnCl_4$, NH_4^+, BF_4^-
AB_4	Square planar	Yes	XeF_4, BrF_4^-, ICl_4
AB_4	Distorted (irregular) tetrahedron	No	$TeCl_4$, $TeBr_4$, SF_4
AB_5	Trigonal bipyramidal	Yes	PCl_5, $NbBr_5$, $SbCl_5$
AB_5	Square pyramidal	No	BrF_5, IF_5
AB_6	Octahedral	Yes	SF_6, $CdCl_6^{-4}$, PtF_6
AB_7	Pentagonal bipyramidal	Yes	IF_7

In extending our interest in structure, we consider the effect of an atomic or molecular group substitution on a centrosymmetric molecule or on one having no permanent moment. Substituting a chlorine atom into methane results in a polar molecule with $\mu_0 = 1.87$ D. Substituting a single chlorine atom into any position on ethane, propane, butane, and pentane gives a permanent dipole moment of approximately 2.0 D and provides validity in this case for assuming a constant-bond dipole for R—C—Cl. These observations also imply that the R group effect on the C—Cl bond moment decreases rapidly beyond the second carbon atom. The same result is observed for the bromine and iodine homologous series. If we assume for the moment that

$$\mu_{0\ \mathrm{CH_3Cl}} = \mu_{\mathrm{CH_3}} + \mu_{\mathrm{C—Cl}}, \tag{1-34}$$

where $\mu_{0\ \mathrm{CH_3Cl}} = 1.87$ D and $\mu_{\mathrm{C—Cl}} = 1.5$ D, the result is $\mu_{\mathrm{CH_3}} \simeq 0.37$ D and points in the same direction as the C—Cl vector, or $\mathrm{H_3} \xrightarrow{0.4\,\mathrm{D}} \mathrm{C}$. To test the validity of the assumption that $\mu_{\mathrm{C—Cl}} = 1.5$ D based on the calculation from *meta* and *ortho*-dichlorobenzene, we can calculate $\mu_{\mathrm{CH_3}}$ from the observed permanent moment of methanol.

The permanent dipole moments of selected molecules are summarized in Table 1-3.

TABLE 1-3. The Dipole Moments of Selected Molecules

Molecule	Dipole moment[a] (Debyes)
Chloromethane, CH_3Cl	1.87
Chloroethane, C_2H_5Cl	2.06
1-Chloropropane, C_3H_7Cl	2.05
2-Chlorobutane, C_4H_9Cl	2.05
Ammonia, NH_3	1.47
Methanol, CH_3OH	1.70
Nitrogen trifluoride, NF_3	0.22
Acetic acid, $C_2H_4O_2$	1.74
Ethanol, C_2H_5OH	1.69
Toluene, C_7H_8	0.36
Phenol, C_6H_6O	1.45
Chlorobenzene, C_6H_5Cl	1.70
o-Chloronitrobenzene, $C_6H_4ClNO_2$	4.64
m-Chloronitrobenzene, $C_6H_4ClNO_2$	3.73
p-Chloronitrobenzene, $C_6H_4ClNO_2$	2.83
Hydrogen bromide, HBr	0.80
Nitric oxide, NO	0.07
Ozone, O_3	0.52
Phosphorus trichloride, PCl_3	0.78
Phosgene, CCl_2O	1.19
Tellurium tetrachloride, $TeCl_4$	2.57

[a] 298 °K.

EXAMPLE 1-4: Estimate the magnitude and direction of the vectorial moment of —CH_3 based on $\mu_{C—O} = 1.2$, $\mu_{OH} = 1.5$, and $\mu_{CH_3OH} = 1.70$ D. Assume the valence angle of oxygen to be 110°.

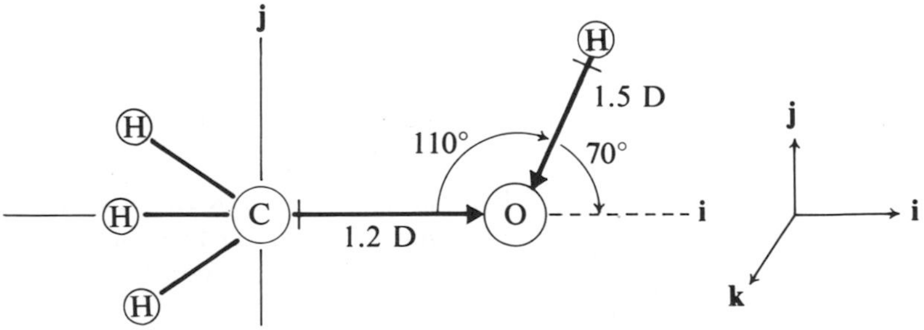

Solution: Assume the planar geometry for methanol as in the preceding diagram, with the exception of the $-CH_3$ group. We resolve the various **i** and **j** components.

$$\begin{aligned}\mu_{OH} &= -1.5 \cos 70°\mathbf{i} - 1.5 \sin 70°\mathbf{j} = -0.513\mathbf{i} - 1.40\mathbf{j}\\ \mu_{C-O} &= 1.2\mathbf{i}\\ \mu_{CH_3} &= x\mathbf{i}\\ \mu_{total} &= (0.687 + x)\mathbf{i} - 1.40\mathbf{j}\end{aligned}$$

Solving for $x = \mu_{CH_3}$, we obtain

$$\begin{aligned}\mu_{CH_3OH} = 1.70 &= [(0.687 + x)^2 + (1.40)^2]^{1/2}\\ &= (x^2 + 1.37x + 0.47 + 1.95)^{1/2}\\ x = -1.67 \quad &\text{or} \quad x = +0.30\end{aligned}$$

The first value for x is an obviously incorrect result. The second value is within the accuracy observed for μ_{CH_3}, and does tend to corroborate the previous result of 0.37 D, considering the degree of uncertainty.

Despite the difficulties we have mentioned that are associated with assuming individual bond moments for dipole moment calculations, we should not hesitate to use this procedure in the absence of other data in approaching problems involving structure. One of the most obvious applications of dipole moments that does not require quantitative data is determining the structure of isomeric compounds. Separation and structural determination of the chloroethylenes could reasonably well be made by dipole moment determinations alone. The dipole moment of

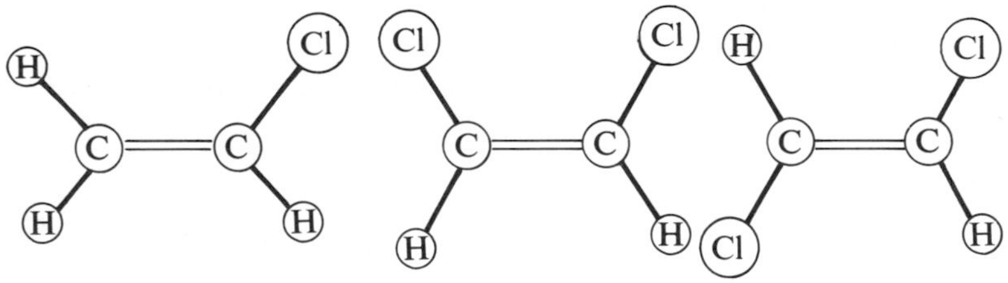

cis *trans*

$\mu = 1.45$ D $\mu = 1.87$ D $\mu = 0$

chloroethylene is essentially the resultant of a C—Cl and a C—H bond at 180°, and should be reasonably close to the C—Cl bond moment of 1.5 D. The other two structures are easily distinguished by the presence or absence of a resulting moment. Examples such as these are straightforward, but other cases for which it would be desirable to separate geometrical isomers, such as PCl_3F_2, might be more difficult. Considering the following trigonal bipyramidal configurations, only (a) would have a zero dipole moment. The other two could reasonably well be estimated, however, using bond moments.

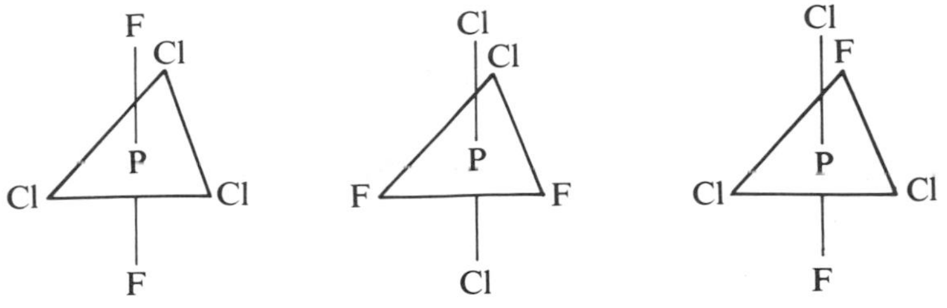

(a) (b) (c)

A final area of structural interest is one for which the dipole moment varies as a function of temperature. Such behavior is characteristic of molecules having a bond about which one part of the molecule can rotate relative to the other. As a result, we observe increased torsional motion with the absorption of heat energy. As an example, nitromethane $H_3C—NO_2$ has a barrier to rotation about the C—N bond of 0.006 Kcal. With a barrier this low, the molecule can easily be assumed to be freely rotating at 300 °K. As a result, the vector components of the oxygen atoms perpendicular to the molecular axis will average to zero. On the other hand, the acetic acid molecule has a barrier that is considerably greater and does not show free rotation about the C—O bond at 300 °K.

EXAMPLE 1-5: Evaluate the approximate dipole moment of the planar *trans*-acetic acid molecule. Assume the contribution from the CH_3 group to be negligible.

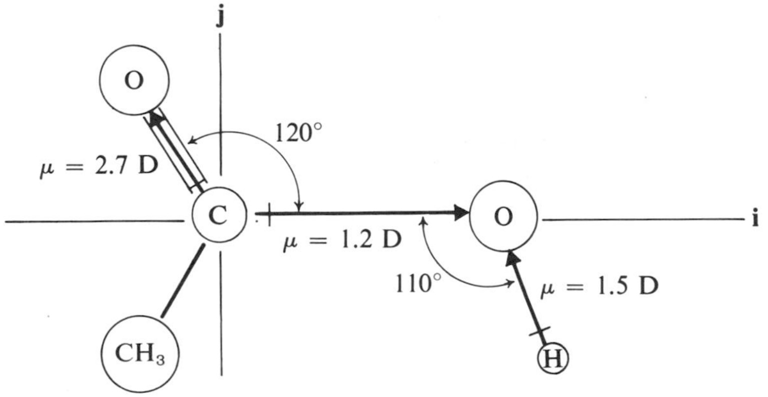

Solution: Resolving the **i** and **j** components gives

$$\mu_{C—O} = +1.2\mathbf{i}; \mu_{C=O} = -2.7 \cos 60°\mathbf{i} + 2.7 \sin 60°\mathbf{j} = -1.35\mathbf{i} + 2.33\mathbf{j};$$
$$\mu_{OH} = -1.5 \cos 70°\mathbf{i} + 1.5 \sin 70°\mathbf{j} = -0.513\mathbf{i} + 1.409\mathbf{j}.$$

Thus, for the *trans* configuration,

$$\sum_i \mu_i = -0.663\mathbf{i} + 3.73\mathbf{j}$$

or

$$\begin{aligned}\mu_{trans} &= \sqrt{(0.633)^2 + (3.73)^2} \\ &= 3.78 \text{ D}\end{aligned}$$

As an exercise, you might show that $\mu_{cis} = 1.14$ D (Problem 1-4). The experimentally observed gas phase value is 1.74 D (25 °C). This implies that free rotation about the C—O bond is not occurring but that the barrier favors a dihedral angle closer to the *cis* configuration.

SELECTED BIBLIOGRAPHY

1-1. Davidson, Norman. *Statistical Mechanics.* New York: McGraw-Hill Book Co., 1962.
1-2. Debye, P. *Polar Molecules.* New York: Dover Publications, 1929.
1-3. Le Fèvre, R. J. W. *Dipole Moments.* New York: John Wiley & Sons, 1953.
1-4. Gordy, W., and Cook, R. L. *Microwave Molecular Spectra.* New York: Interscience Publishers, John Wiley & Sons, 1970.
1-5. Halliday, D., and Resnick, R. *Physics.* New York: John Wiley & Sons, 1960.

GLOSSARY OF SYMBOLS

Electric Phenomena

$\boldsymbol{\mu}$	Resultant dipole moment, esu-cm
μ	Directional dipole moment, esu-cm
μ_0	Permanent dipole moment,,esu-cm
q	Electric charge, 4.8×10^{-10} esu or 1.6×10^{-19} coulomb
α	Total polarizability, cm^3
α_a	Atomic polarizability, cm^3
α_e	Electronic polarizability, cm^3
m	Induced dipole moment, esu-cm
C	Capacitance, cm or farad
$\mathbf{E}$	External electric field, volts/cm
$\mathbf{F}$	Local electric field, volts/cm
ϵ	Dielectric constant
P_i	Induced polarization, dipole moment/cc
U	Potential energy, ergs

P_o	Orientation polarization, cc/mole
P_T	Total polarization, dipole moment/cc
P_M	Total molar polarization, cc/mole
R_d	Molar distortion polarization, cc/mole
R_e	Molar refractivity, cc/mole
n	Refractive index

END NOTES

1. A full discussion and methods of calculating these bond moments are presented in Reference 1-3, p. 617.
2. The original development of this model was due to Lorentz and Lorenz.
3. Derivation of this expression is given in Appendix I.
4. In this case $\mathbf{E}^0 = \mathbf{D}$, where $\mathbf{D}$ is defined as the electric displacement. C. F. J. Bottcher, *Theory of Electric Polarization*, New York: Elsevier Publishing Co., 1952, p. 46.
5. Where N_0 is Avogadro's number.

PROBLEMS

1-1. Show that the second term in the expansion of Eq. (1-20) is negligible compared with the first for typical values of **a**, Eq. (1-17). Given: $\mathbf{F} \simeq 10^3$ volt/cm and $\mu_0 \simeq q \cdot r$ (where $r = 1$ Å) at $T \simeq 300$ °K.

1-2. The refractive index of NH_3 measured with sodium D light at 292 °K is $n = 1.000379$. Treating NH_3 as an ideal gas at standard pressure and 292 °K, calculate the molar distortion polarization. This is really a calculation of the molar refractivity. Why? Would you expect the estimated difference between R_d and R_e to be great (± 1 cc/mole) in this particular case?

1-3. The total polarization of NH_3 is 57.6 cc at 292 °K. Using the results of Problem 1-2, calculate the polarization effect due to orientation alone and in turn the permanent dipole moment. (Compare with the experimentally determined value 1.47 D.)

1-4. Estimate the dipole moment of the planar *cis* acetic acid molecule. Assume the contribution from the CH_3 group to be negligible.

1-5. Estimate the dipole moments of phenol, *p*-chlorophenol, and methyl chloride using the functional group approach, and compare with the experimentally determined values of 1.45 ± 0.07, 2.11 ± 0.11 and 1.87 ± 0.02 Debyes respectively. The oxygen atom is assumed to have a valency angle of 110°. $\mu_{OH} = 1.5$, $\mu_{C—Cl} = 1.5$, $\mu_{CH_3—C} = 0.4$, $\mu_{\phi C—O} = 0.7$. (Assume the C—H bond on the *para* position of the ring to be negligible.)

1-6. In Problem 1-5, the observed dipole moment for phenol is 1.45 Debyes and the calculated dipole moment is 1.4 Debyes. In what direction does the resultant vector point?

1-7. In the case of low-density gaseous vapors (Eq. (1-12)) where the difference between ϵ and unity is fairly small, $\epsilon + 2$ can be replaced by 3. With this assumption, derive the expression $\alpha = 2.94 \times 10^{-21}$ $(\epsilon - 1)$ cc/molecule at standard temperature and pressure.

1-8. Using the expression derived in Problem 1-7, compare the estimated values of α with those experimentally observed and calculate the percent error.

Species	ϵ	$\alpha(\text{exp}) \times 10^{24}$ cc
Ar	1.000545	1.626
CO	1.00070	1.926
CH_4	1.000944	2.699
C_6H_6	1.0028	9.890 (parallel component)
C_2H_6	1.00150	4.326 (parallel component)
C_2H_4	1.00144	3.702 (parallel component)

1-9. Calculate the dipole moment of phenol assuming free rotation about the ϕ—O bond. By this result, would you expect the barrier to rotation to be relatively high or low at 25 °C.

1-10. A parallel plate capacitor (condenser) with dimensions of area equal to 5 cm^2 and a plate separation of 2 cm subjected initially to a potential difference of 300 volts is then filled with benzene (ϵ = 2.284, t = 20 °C). Calculate the capacitance (in picofarads) and electric field with and without the dielectric present. In addition, calculate the charge density on the capacitor plate induced by the dielectric and the local field at the molecule.

1-11. Estimate the individual bond moment of P—Cl using the permanent dipole moment of PCl_3 from Table 1-3 and the angle ∠Cl—P—Cl 100°. Compare with the estimated value in Table 1-1.

1-12. Use the bond moments in Table 1-3 to estimate the CCl_2 bond angle in phosgene and compare with the experimental value of 111.3°.

1-13. Estimate the dipole moment of the —NO_2 group in nitromethane at 300 °K. The rotational barrier about the C—N bond is 0.006 Kcal/mole (1.44 cm^{-1}) and it can be assumed to be freely rotating. If this motion is frozen so that the —CNO_2 part is in a plane, would the dipole moment of nitromethane increase, decrease, or remain the same? Why? ($\mu_{CH_3NO_3}$ = 3.50 D.)

1-14. Assuming the equilibrium position of the OH bond in acetic acid to be out of the plane and corresponding to an experimental dipole moment of 1.74 D rather than a *cis* planar value of 1.14 D, calculate the angle of the OH bond with respect to the **i**, **j** plane.

1-15. The following molecules have $\mu_0 \neq 0$. Assign possible geometrical structures: CF_3, SF_4, SCl_2, and PI_3.

1-16. Calculate the percentage ionic character of KCl and HBr. Given: $r_{KCl} = 2.667$ Å and $r_{HBr} = 1.415$ Å and μ_p is 12.33 for KCl and 2.31 for HBr. The observed moment of KCl is 10.27 D and of HBr is 0.83 D. Why does the KCl primary moment come closest to its observed value and the HBr moment have a significantly different value?

Chapter 2

Absorption and Emission of Radiation

A. ELECTROMAGNETIC RADIATION

A review of the nature of electromagnetic radiation and the energy spectrum will be helpful for understanding the details of how radiation is absorbed and emitted. The electromagnetic theory, developed largely by James Clerk Maxwell, predicted that an oscillating charge producing an alternating current in a circuit would radiate energy in the form of waves through space at the velocity of light c. These waves are actually in the form of magnetic (**H**) and electric (**E**) fields oscillating perpendicularly both to the direction of propagation and to each other. A plane-polarized beam of radiation propagated in the z direction is shown in Figure 2-1. The oscillating electric field vector $\mathbf{E}_x(\omega)$ is polarized in the xz plane, while the magnetic field vector $\mathbf{H}_y(\omega)$ is polarized in the yz plane.

For the plane-polarized beam propagated in the z direction, $\mathbf{E}_x(\omega)$ and $\mathbf{H}_y(\omega)$ as a function of frequency $c\omega$, time t, and position z are given as

$$\mathbf{E}_x(\omega, t, z) = 2\mathbf{E}_x{}^0(\omega) \cos 2\pi c\omega\left(t - \frac{z}{c}\right), \qquad \textbf{(2-1)}$$

and

$$\mathbf{H}_y(\omega, t, z) = 2\mathbf{H}_y{}^0(\omega) \cos 2\pi c\omega\left(t - \frac{z}{c}\right), \qquad \textbf{(2-2)}$$

where $\omega(\text{cm}^{-1})$ is the frequency in wavenumbers and $\mathbf{E}_x{}^0$ and $\mathbf{H}_y{}^0$ are the

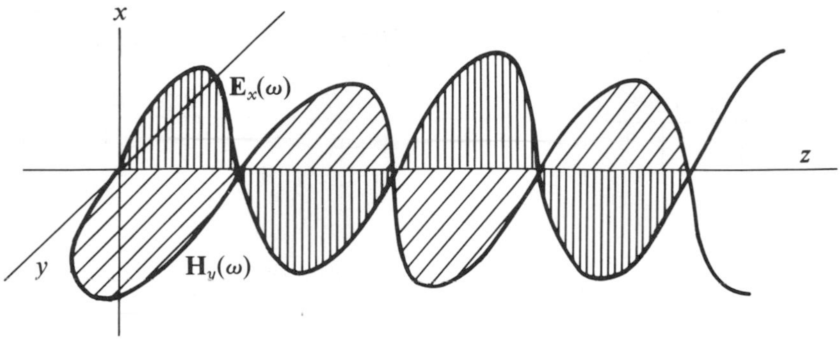

FIGURE 2-1 Classical electromagnetic plane-polarized wave propagated in the z direction with velocity c.

amplitudes of the electric and magnetic field vectors, respectively. At some fixed position along the z axis, Eqs. (2-1) and (2-2) reduce to

$$\mathbf{E}_x(\omega, t) = 2\mathbf{E}_x^0(\omega) \cos 2\pi c\omega t \tag{2-1a}$$

and

$$\mathbf{H}_y(\omega, t) = 2\mathbf{H}_y^0(\omega) \cos 2\pi c\omega t. \tag{2-2a}$$

According to Maxwell's equations, the instantaneous energy density $\rho(\omega)$ (ergs/cm^3) of the radiation field at any position in space traversed by electromagnetic radiation is

$$\rho(\omega) = \frac{\overline{\mathbf{E}^2} + \overline{\mathbf{H}^2}}{8\pi}, \tag{2-3}$$

where the bar indicates time averaging. When the electric field vector is expressed in electrostatic units (esu) and the magnetic field vector is expressed in electromagnetic units (emu), $\overline{\mathbf{E}} = \overline{\mathbf{H}}$. Therefore,

$$\rho(\omega) = \frac{\overline{\mathbf{E}^2}}{4\pi} = \frac{1}{4\pi}[\overline{\mathbf{E}_x^2}(\omega) + \overline{\mathbf{E}_y^2}(\omega) + \overline{\mathbf{E}_z^2}(\omega)]. \tag{2-4}$$

If we assume that the radiation is isotropic $[(\mathbf{E}_x(\omega) = \mathbf{E}_y(\omega) = \mathbf{E}_z(\omega)]$, then

$$\rho(\omega) = \frac{3}{4\pi}\overline{\mathbf{E}_x^2}(\omega). \tag{2-5}$$

When the square of Eq. (2-1a) is time-averaged, $\overline{\mathbf{E}_x^2}(\omega, t) = 2[\mathbf{E}_x^0(\omega)]^2$ since $\overline{\cos^2 \mathbf{a}} = \frac{1}{2}$, where $\mathbf{a} = 2\pi c\omega t$. Thus,

$$\rho(\omega) = \frac{6}{4\pi}[\mathbf{E}_x^0(\omega)]^2. \tag{2-6}$$

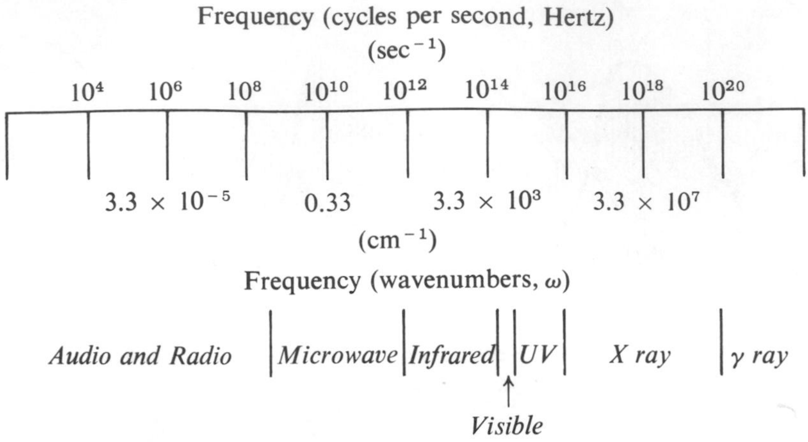

FIGURE 2-2 The electromagnetic spectrum.

The expression for the radiation energy density corresponding to a specific frequency ω_{mk} is given as

$$\rho(\omega_{mk}) = \frac{6}{4\pi} [\mathbf{E}_x{}^0(\omega_{mk})]^2. \tag{2-7}$$

The units of $\rho(\omega_{mk})$ are ergs/cm^2; expressed in words, it is energy density per volume per wavenumber interval (ergs/cm^3/cm^{-1}).

The electromagnetic spectrum ranges from the low-energy, audio region to the extremely high-energy cosmic radiation. The intermediate regions between these extremes are shown in Figure 2-2 and the spectroscopic phenomena characteristic of each are tabulated in Table 2-1.

TABLE 2-1. Spectroscopic Phenomena Characteristic of Intermediate Regions

Spectral region	Spectral phenomena	Radiating source
Radiofrequency	Nuclear magnetic resonance Nuclear quadrupole resonance	Oscillating electric circuits
Microwave	Electron spin resonance Hindered and free rotation	Oscillating electric circuits, Klystron tube
Infrared	Molecular vibration	Light sources
Visible and ultraviolet	Electronic transitions (valence electrons)	Light sources
X Rays	Electronic transitions (closed-shell electrons)	X-ray tubes
γ Rays	Nuclear transitions	Radioactivity and cosmic rays

The extremely high-energy radiation corresponding to X rays and γ rays results from transitions involving electrons in the inner closed shell of atoms and from nuclear transitions, respectively. (The spectroscopy of these regions will not be covered in this text.) The spectral regions corresponding to valence electronic transitions and molecular vibrations and rotations are characteristic of absorption and emission phenomena between virtually unperturbed quantized energy levels, whereas magnetic resonance spectroscopy (nmr and esr) is performed between degenerate energy levels that are split by an external magnetic field. Discussion and application of these spectroscopic techniques will be covered in some detail.

B. THE TIME-DEPENDENT SCHRÖDINGER EQUATION

In the quantum mechanical discussion of stationary energy levels (electronic, vibrational, etc.), we are primarily concerned with systems whose properties are independent of time, that is, the energy levels of atomic and molecular systems that are time-independent stationary states. To consider events that occur in very short time spans, that is, absorption and emission of radiation, collisions, energy transfer, and so on, we must consider the Schrödinger equation and concern ourselves with the time-dependent part of the wavefunction. The complete wavefunction for an unperturbed system is given as

$$\Psi_k{}^0 = \psi_k{}^0 e^{-iE_k t/\hbar}, \qquad \hbar = \frac{h}{2\pi}, \tag{2-8}$$

and the corresponding solution for the energy is obtained from the Schrödinger equation,

$$\hat{H}^0\Psi^0 = \hat{E}\Psi^0. \tag{2-9}$$

Replacing $\hat{E}$ with its time-dependent operator, we obtain

$$\hat{H}^0\Psi^0 = -\frac{h}{2\pi i}\frac{\partial\Psi^0}{\partial t}. \tag{2-10}$$

Assuming that the system experiences a perturbing interaction, we can write the Hamiltonian during this time as

$$\hat{H}^0 + \hat{H}'(t) = -\frac{h}{2\pi i}\frac{\partial}{\partial t}. \tag{2-11}$$

If we assume the wavefunction for the perturbed system to be a linear combination of the unperturbed wavefunctions (Eq. (2-8)), then

$$\Psi = \sum_k a_k(t)\Psi_k{}^0. \tag{2-12}$$

The product $a_k a_k^*$ represents the probability that the system will be found in the unperturbed kth stationary state for a given duration. The sum $\sum a_k a_k^*$ is normalized, such that the total probability over all states k is unity. Performing the indicated operations on Ψ (Eq. (2-11)), we obtain

$$\hat{H}^0 \sum_k a_k(t)\Psi_k^0 + \hat{H}'(t) \sum_k a_k(t)\Psi_k^0 = -\frac{h}{2\pi i}\sum_k \Psi_k^0 \frac{da_k(t)}{dt} - \frac{h}{2\pi i}\sum_k a_k(t)\frac{\partial \Psi_k^0}{\partial t}, \quad \textbf{(2-13)}$$

where the first and last terms cancel according to Eq. (2-10), and we are left with

$$\sum_k \frac{da_k(t)}{dt}\Psi_k^0 = -\frac{2\pi i}{h}\sum_k a_k(t)\hat{H}'(t)\Psi_k^0. \quad \textbf{(2-14)}$$

Since the Ψ_k^0's form a set of orthonormal wavefunctions, we multiply through by the complex conjugate Ψ_m^{0*}, and integrate over all space. We then obtain

$$\sum_k \frac{da_k(t)}{dt}\int \Psi_m^{0*}\Psi_k^0\, d\tau = -\frac{2\pi i}{h}\sum_k a_k(t)\int \Psi_m^{0*}\hat{H}'(t)\Psi_k^0\, d\tau. \quad \textbf{(2-15)}$$

All terms in the left integral must equal zero except for $m = k$, and that integral is unity according to the orthogonality theorem. Thus, substituting m for k in the derivative, we obtain

$$\frac{da_m(t)}{dt} = -\frac{2\pi i}{h}\sum_k a_k(t)\int \Psi_m^{0*}\hat{H}(t)\Psi_k^0\, d\tau. \quad \textbf{(2-16)}$$

If we assume that the total probability is contributed solely by the ground state coefficient ($a_0(0) = 1$) before the perturbation has occurred and a short time thereafter, then Eq. (2-16) becomes

$$\frac{da_m(t)}{dt} = -\frac{2\pi i}{h}\int \Psi_m^{0*}\hat{H}'(t)\Psi_k^0\, d\tau. \quad \textbf{(2-17)}$$

If the unperturbed wavefunctions, Eq. (2-8), are expressed as a product of the time-independent and time-dependent parts, we obtain[1]

$$\frac{da_m(t)}{dt} = -\frac{2\pi i}{h}\exp\left[(E_m - E_k)\frac{2\pi i t}{h}\right]\langle m^0|\hat{H}'|k^0\rangle. \quad \textbf{(2-18)}$$

At this point, our problem reduces to either solving the integral on the right or at least proving it to be zero or finite. The physical interpretation applied to the integral is: If it is zero, the corresponding transition is "forbidden"; and if it is finite, the transition is "allowed." This interpretation follows from the fact that integration of the left side of

Eq. (2-18) resulting in a finite value for $a_m(t)$ means that $a_m^*(t)a_m(t)$ is the probability that the perturbation carried the system from state E_k to E_m.

It is generally assumed that the major interaction between an atom or molecule and the electromagnetic field of radiation leading to absorption or emission occurs between the instantaneous electric dipole $\boldsymbol{\mu}$ (Eq. (1-1)) of the species and the oscillating electric field vector **E**. Thus, the perturbing Hamiltonian $\hat{H}'(t)$ for the interaction of the radiation field polarized in the x direction and the electric dipole may be written

$$\hat{H}'(t) = \mathbf{E}_x(\omega, t)\cdot\mu_x. \qquad \textbf{(2-19)}$$

In spite of the fact that the oscillating field varies periodically with time, its wavelength in the ultraviolet, infrared, and microwave regions is generally so large ($\sim$2000 Å to 10^8 Å) compared with atomic or molecular dimensions (5–10 Å) that as a first approximation it can be considered constant over the space occupied by the species. For the x component of the electric field vector, we have in terms of frequency and time (Eq. (2-1a)),

$$\mathbf{E}_x(\omega, t) = 2\mathbf{E}_x{}^0(\omega)\cos 2\pi c\omega t = \mathbf{E}_x{}^0(\omega)(e^{2\pi ic\omega t} + e^{-2\pi ic\omega t}), \qquad \textbf{(2-20)}$$

since $\cos \mathbf{a} = \frac{1}{2}(e^{i\mathbf{a}} + e^{-i\mathbf{a}})$. Substituting Eqs. (2-19) and (2-20) into Eq. (2-18) above, we obtain

$$\frac{da_m(t)}{dt} = -\frac{2\pi i}{h}\left\{\exp\left[2\pi i\left(\frac{E_m}{h} - \frac{E_k}{h} + c\omega\right)t\right]\right.$$
$$\left. + \exp\left[-2\pi i\left(\frac{E_k}{h} - \frac{E_m}{h} + c\omega\right)t\right]\right\} \times \mathbf{E}_x{}^0(\omega)\langle m^0|\mu_x|k^0\rangle. \qquad \textbf{(2-21)}$$

The expression $\langle m^0|\mu_x|k^0\rangle$ is called the transition moment integral, or matrix, and provides the basis for first-order electric dipole selection rules for atomic and molecular systems.

Integrating Eq. (2-21) from time zero where $a_m(0) = 0$ to time t and $a_m(t)$, we obtain

$$a_m(t) = \langle m^0|\mu_x|k^0\rangle\mathbf{E}_x{}^0(\omega)\left\{\frac{1 - \exp[2\pi i(E_m/h - E_k/h + c\omega)t]}{E_m - E_k + hc\omega}\right.$$
$$\left. + \frac{1 - \exp[2\pi i(E_m/h - E_k/h - c\omega)t]}{E_m - E_k - hc\omega}\right\}. \qquad \textbf{(2-22)}$$

For $a_m(t)$ to be significant, it is necessary that one of the denominators within the braces be very small (approach zero), since the product $\langle m^0|\mu_x|k^0\rangle\mathbf{E}_x{}^0(\omega)$ is small for a single frequency.[2] Thus, assuming that

$$E_m - E_k + hc\omega \simeq 0, \qquad \textbf{(2-23)}$$

then

$$E_k - E_m \simeq hc\omega,$$

and we obtain the Bohr condition for emission from state m to state k. Equating the other denominator to zero, we obtain the Bohr condition for absorption from state k to m,

$$E_m - E_k = hc\omega. \tag{2-24}$$

C. THE EINSTEIN ABSORPTION AND EMISSION COEFFICIENTS

Since $a_m{}^*(t)a_m(t)$ is the quantum mechanical probability that the system is in the mth state at time t for a single frequency, integration over the entire radiation field for ω gives the probability that a transition occurred during the time t exposed. Although only a narrow frequency range ($hc\omega \simeq E_m - E_k$) will contribute significantly to this integration, the limits are taken from $-\infty$ to $+\infty$ since the definite integral finally obtained, Eq. (2-27), is well-known. Considering the absorption condition, the first fraction in the braces of Eq. (2-22) becomes negligible. On multiplying with the complex conjugate, we obtain

$$a_m{}^*(t)a_m(t) = \langle m^0|\mu_x|k^0\rangle^2 \int_{-\infty}^{+\infty} [\mathbf{E}_x{}^0(\omega)]^2 \left[\frac{1 - e^{-2\pi i t u'}}{u}\right]\left[\frac{1 - e^{2\pi i t u'}}{u}\right] d\omega, \tag{2-25}$$

where

$$u = E_m - E_k - hc\omega \qquad \text{and} \qquad u' = \frac{E_m}{h} - \frac{E_k}{h} - c\omega.$$

If we carry through the multiplication indicated, and make use of the relation $2 \cos \mathbf{a} = (e^{i\mathbf{a}} + e^{-i\mathbf{a}})$, Eq. (2-25) becomes

$$a_m{}^*(t)a_m(t) = \langle m^0|\mu_x|k^0\rangle^2 \int_{-\infty}^{+\infty} [\mathbf{E}_x{}^0(\omega)]^2(2)\left[\frac{1 - \cos 2\pi t u'}{u^2}\right] d\omega. \tag{2-26}$$

Further simplification is achieved using the relation $2 \sin^2 \mathbf{a} = 1 - \cos 2\mathbf{a}$, and we obtain

$$a_m{}^*(t)a_m(t) = 4\langle m^0|\mu_x|k^0\rangle^2 \int_{-\infty}^{+\infty} [\mathbf{E}_x{}^0(\omega)]^2 \frac{\sin^2 \pi t(E_m/h - E_k/h - c\omega)}{(E_m - E_k - hc\omega)^2} d\omega. \tag{2-27}$$

Assuming $\mathbf{E}_x{}^0(\omega)$ constant over the range near the Bohr condition, we obtain

$$a_m{}^*(t)a_m(t) = \frac{4\pi^2}{h^2c} (\mu_x)_{mk}{}^2[\mathbf{E}_x{}^0(\omega)]^2 t, \tag{2-28}$$

using the definite integral

$$\int_{-\infty}^{+\infty} \frac{\sin^2 \mathbf{a}}{\mathbf{a}^2} \, d\mathbf{a} = \pi, \tag{2-29}$$

and

$$(\mu_x)_{mk}{}^2 = \langle m^0|\mu_x|k^0\rangle^2. \tag{2-30}$$

Since the transition probability is additionally directly proportional to the radiation field density $\rho(\omega)$ and the time duration t of the perturbation,

$$a_m{}^*(t)a_m(t) = B_{mk}\rho(\omega)t, \tag{2-31}$$

where B_{mk}, the proportionality constant, is the Einstein coefficient for induced absorption. In the original derivation by Einstein, it was assumed that B_{mk} was equal to the coefficient for induced emission. This assumption was later proved true by quantum mechanics and experiment. Therefore,[3]

$$B_{m \leftarrow k} = B_{k \leftarrow m}. \tag{2-32}$$

Thus, substituting Eq. (2-6) into Eq. (2-31), and equating Eqs. (2-28) and (2-31), we obtain

$$B_{mk} = \frac{8\pi^3}{3h^2c} (\mu_x)_{mk}{}^2. \tag{2-33}$$

For the general three-dimensional case

$$B_{mk} = \frac{8\pi^3}{3h^2c} (\mu)_{mk}{}^2, \tag{2-34}$$

where

$$(\mu)_{mk}{}^2 = (\mu_x)_{mk}{}^2 + (\mu_y)_{mk}{}^2 + (\mu_z)_{mk}{}^2. \tag{2-35}$$

In addition to induced emission, an atom or molecule in an excited state can spontaneously emit radiation. For a system at thermal equilibrium and characterized by a Boltzmann distribution, the coefficient for induced absorption B_{mk} can be related to the coefficient characterizing spontaneous emission $A_{k \leftarrow m}$. The principle of microscopic reversibility states that as a consequence of the thermal equilibrium among the many energy levels, equilibrium must also be maintained by any two energy states m and k. For the purpose of obtaining an expression for A_{km}, we assume for the moment that the only processes contributing to excitation and relaxation are radiation-induced absorption and emission and spontaneous emission. This system is shown schematically in Figure 2-3. The rate at which molecules (or atoms) are pumped into level m via absorption is

$$\text{Rate}_{m \leftarrow k} = \frac{dN_m}{dt} = N_k B_{mk} \rho(\omega_{mk}), \tag{2-36}$$

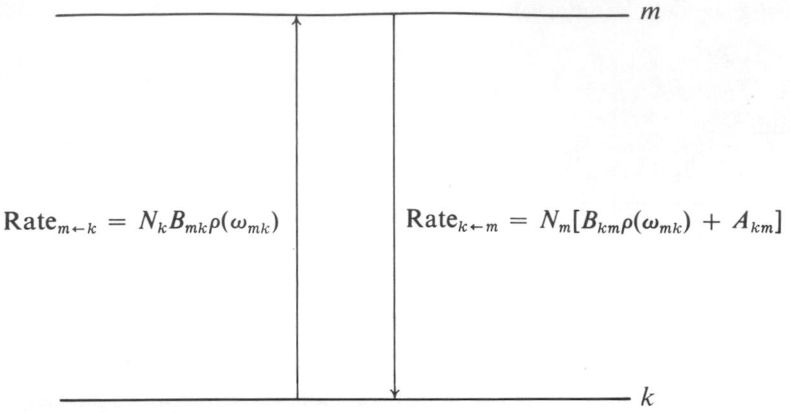

FIGURE 2-3 Thermodynamic equilibrium between the nondegenerate microscopic energy states k and m.

whereas the rate of populating into level k via stimulated and spontaneous emission from m is

$$\text{Rate}_{k \leftarrow m} = \frac{dN_k}{dt} = N_m [B_{km} \rho(\omega_{mk}) + A_{km}]. \tag{2-37}$$

At equilibrium,

$$\text{Rate}_{m \leftarrow k} = \text{Rate}_{k \leftarrow m}. \tag{2-38}$$

Therefore,

$$\frac{N_m}{N_k} = \frac{B_{mk} \rho(\omega_{mk})}{B_{km} \rho(\omega_{mk}) + A_{km}}. \tag{2-39}$$

Equating the Boltzmann relation for two nondegenerate energy states,

$$\frac{N_m}{N_k} = \exp \frac{-hc\omega_{mk}}{kT} \tag{2-40}$$

to Eq. (2-39) and rearranging, we obtain

$$\rho(\omega_{mk}) = \left(\frac{A_{km}}{B_{mk}}\right)\left(\exp \frac{hc\omega_{mk}}{kT} - 1\right)^{-1}. \tag{2-41}$$

By analogy with Planck's radiation law

$$\rho(\omega_{mk}) = (8\pi hc\omega_{mk}{}^3)\left(\exp \frac{hc\omega_{mk}}{kT} - 1\right)^{-1}, \tag{2-42}$$

and equating the preexponential factors, we obtain

$$A_{km} = 8\pi hc\omega_{mk}{}^3 B_{mk}. \tag{2-43}$$

Replacing B_{mk} with Eq. (2-34), we obtain

$$A_{km} = \frac{64\pi^4\omega_{mk}^{\ 3}}{3h}\cdot(\mu)_{mk}^{\ 2}, \tag{2-44}$$

where A_{km} (sec^{-1}) is an intrinsic first-order decay constant. Thus, the natural or spontaneous radiative lifetime of an excited state is obtained from the inverse of A_{km},

$$\tau = \frac{1}{A_{km}}. \tag{2-45}$$

Emission can occur spontaneously from numerous closely spaced quantized states associated with an absorption band, however, and therefore most experimental determinations of τ represent an average of $\sum_i 1/A_{km_i}$ for a given excited system. By using highly monochromatic sources (lasers) for excitation of atomic or molecular systems at very low pressures ($\sim$1 millitorr), it is also possible to observe lifetimes indicative of specific atomic and molecular energy levels.

Since A_{km} is proportional to the third power of the frequency, spontaneous emission processes are very important at high frequencies, in the visible and ultraviolet, but of negligible importance in the microwave and radiofrequency regions. As a result of the extremely long radiative lifetimes in the microwave and radiofrequency regions relative to other relaxation processes, spectroscopy in these regions is performed primarily in the absorption mode.

EXAMPLE 2-1: Calculate the rotational radiative lifetime for the $J = 1$ state of HCl in the ground vibrational and electronic state. The square of the transition moment integral for a rotational transition $J = 0 \rightarrow J = 1$ will be shown to be $(\mu)_{mk}^{\ 2} = \langle m|\hat{\mu}_x|k\rangle^2 = \mu_0^{\ 2}/3$; $\mu_0 = 1.03$ Debyes (1 D $= 10^{-18}$ esu-cm) and $\omega(J = 0 \rightarrow J = 1) = 20$ cm^{-1}.

Solution: The radiative lifetime is calculated using Eq. (2-45), but A_{km} must first be evaluated. From Eq. (2-44),

$$A_{km} = \frac{64\pi^4\omega_{mk}^{\ 3}}{3h}\cdot(\mu)_{mk}^{\ 2} = \frac{(64)(3.14)^4}{(3)(6.62\times 10^{-27}\text{ erg-sec})}\cdot\omega_{mk}^{\ 3}(\mu)_{mk}^{\ 2}$$

$$A_{km} = 3.13\times 10^{29}\omega_{mk}^{\ 3}(\mu)_{mk}^{\ 2} = (3.13\times 10^{29})(20)^3\left(\frac{1.06\times 10^{-36}}{3}\right)$$

$$A_{01} = 8.85\times 10^{-4}\text{ sec}^{-1}.$$

According to Eq. (2-45)

$$\tau = 1.13\times 10^{3}\text{ sec.}$$

The derivations of B_{mk} and A_{km} presented apply only to nondegenerate energy states. For transitions that occur between two degenerate levels

($E_k < E_m$) having degeneracies g_k and g_m, the Einstein coefficients are given as

$$B_{mk} = \frac{8\pi^3}{3h^2c} \frac{\sum (\mu)^2_{m_ik_j}}{g_k} \tag{2-46}$$

and

$$A_{km} = \frac{64\pi^4\omega_{mk}{}^3}{3h} \frac{\sum (\mu)^2_{m_ik_j}}{g_m}, \tag{2-47}$$

where the summations are carried over all possible combinations between the sublevels i and j.[4]

D. MAGNETIC DIPOLE AND ELECTRIC QUADRUPOLE TRANSITIONS

In addition to the emission and absorption of radiation that results from an oscillating electric dipole, emission and absorption can also occur by the interaction of the radiation field with oscillating magnetic dipole and electric quadrupole moments. These second-order effects are extremely weak compared with first-order electric dipole transitions, and are important only when $\langle m^0|\hat{\mu}|k^0\rangle = 0$. Because of their low intensity and presence only as second-order effects, they are usually referred to as forbidden transitions. In the case of magnetic dipole transitions, absorption or emission occurs as a result of the oscillating magnetic-moment interaction with the magnetic vector of the radiation field (Figure 2-1). An example of a magnetic dipole absorption is the so-called atmospheric bands of O_2 corresponding to the ${}^1\Sigma_g{}^+ \leftarrow {}^3\Sigma_g{}^-$ transition. They occur just within the visible at about 7600 Å and have an average radiative lifetime of 7.15 sec.

In the case where a collection of charges have orientations resulting in zero dipole moments, these arrangements may show electric quadrupole moments as illustrated in Figure 2-4. The electric quadrupole moment **Q** is given as

$$\mathbf{Q} = \sum_i q_i \mathbf{r}_i \mathbf{r}_i. \tag{2-48}$$

In Figures 2-4a and 2-4c, where all the charges are along the same direction, Eq. (2-48) simplifies to

$$\mathbf{Q}_x = \sum_i q_i x_i^2. \tag{2-49}$$

If the oscillating radiation field over the dimensions of the atomic or molecular species is not considered constant and the magnetic dipole

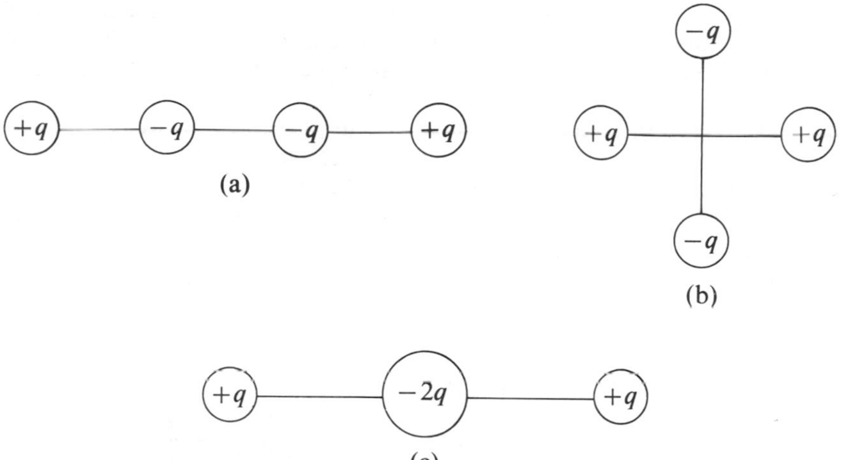

FIGURE 2-4 Three examples of an electric quadrupole moment.

interaction is not neglected, then the resulting Einstein coefficient for absorption is

$$B_{mk} = \frac{8\pi^3}{3h^2c}\left\{|\langle m^0|\hat{\boldsymbol{\mu}}|k^0\rangle|^2 + \left|\left\langle m^0\left|\frac{q}{2m_e c}\,\hat{\mathbf{r}} \times \hat{\mathbf{p}}\right|k^0\right\rangle\right|^2 + \frac{3\pi^3{\omega_{mk}}^2}{10}\,|\langle m^0|\hat{\mathbf{Q}}|k^0\rangle|^2\right\}, \tag{2-50}$$

where the second term in brackets characterizes the magnetic effect and the third term the quadrupole effect. Substituting the corresponding operators into Eq. (2-50) results in

$$B_{mk} = \frac{8\pi^3}{3h^2c}\left\{\left|\left\langle m^0\left|\sum_i q_i\mathbf{r}_i\right|k^0\right\rangle\right|^2 + \left|\left\langle m^0\left|\left(\frac{q}{2m_e c}\sum_i \mathbf{r}_i\right) \times \left(\frac{h}{2\pi i}\sum_i \frac{\partial}{\partial \mathbf{r}_i}\right)\right|k^0\right\rangle\right|^2 + \frac{3\pi^3{\omega_{mk}}^2}{10}\left|\left\langle m^0\left|\sum_i q_i\mathbf{r}_i\mathbf{r}_i\right|k^0\right\rangle\right|^2\right\}. \tag{2-51}$$

The expression in braces also replaces the transition moment matrix squared in Eqs. (2-46) and (2-47) in order to obtain the total contribution to the Einstein coefficients for absorption and emission. In general, the intensity ratio of the three contributions, electric dipole: magnetic dipole: electric quadrupole, is roughly $1:10^{-5}:10^{-7}$.

EXAMPLE 2-2: Using Eq. (2-51), estimate the relative magnitudes of the electric dipole, magnetic dipole, and electric quadrupole transition intensities, and substantiate the statement that they are roughly $1:10^{-5}:10^{-7}$.

Solution: Since the three contributions inside the braces in Eq. (2-51) are all multiplied by the same constant $(8\pi^3/3h^2c)$, we need merely to consider the relative ratio of these three factors to obtain their relative intensities.

Assuming r to be 1 Å and $\lambda_{mk} \simeq 6000$ Å, the first, second, and third terms are reasonably well approximated by

$$\{\langle m^0|k^0\rangle q\cdot r\}^2 \simeq (q\cdot r)^2 = \{(4.8\times 10^{-10}\text{ esu})(1\times 10^{-8}\text{ cm})\}^2$$
$$= 2.3\times 10^{-35}\text{ cgs-esu unit,}$$

$$\left|\left\langle m^0\left|\left(\frac{q}{2m_ec}\sum_i \mathbf{r}_i\right)\times\left(\frac{h}{2\pi i}\sum_i\frac{\partial}{\partial\mathbf{r}_i}\right)\right|k^0\right\rangle\right|^2$$
$$= \left|\left\langle m^0\left|\sum_i \mathbf{r}_i\times\sum_i\frac{\partial}{\partial\mathbf{r}_i}\right|k^0\right\rangle\cdot\frac{q\cdot\hbar}{2m_ec}\right|^2 \simeq \left(\frac{q\cdot\hbar}{2m_ec}\right)^2$$
$$= \left\{\frac{(4.8\times 10^{-10}\text{ esu})(1.05\times 10^{-27}\text{ erg-sec})}{(2)(9.11\times 10^{-28}\text{ g})(3\times 10^{10}\text{ cm/sec})}\right\}^2$$
$$= 8.5\times 10^{-41}\text{ cgs-esu unit,}$$

and

$$\frac{3\pi^3\omega_{mk}^2}{10}\left|\left\langle m^0\left|\sum_i q_i\mathbf{r}_i\mathbf{r}_i\right|k^0\right\rangle\right|^2$$
$$\simeq \frac{3\pi^3\omega_{mk}^2}{10}\times(qr^2)^2\langle m^0|k^0\rangle^2 \simeq \frac{3\pi^3\omega_{mk}^2}{10}(qr^2)^2$$
$$= \frac{(3)(3.14)^3}{10}(1.67\times 10^4\text{ cm}^{-1})^2(4.8\times 10^{-10}\text{ esu})(1\times 10^{-16}\text{ cm}^2)^2$$
$$= 6.0\times 10^{-42}\text{ cgs-esu unit.}$$

These contributions are in the ratio $1:3.7\times 10^{-6}:2.6\times 10^{-7}$.

E. SPECTRAL LINE WIDTHS

One conclusion that follows from the Bohr condition, Eqs. (2-23) and (2-24), is that only a relatively small frequency range $d\omega_{mk}$ is effective in producing a spectral transition. This frequency range usually defines the line width (or more precisely the absorption width), and is affected by several contributions, depending on the wavelength region and experimental conditions. The main contributors are the natural line width, pressure broadening, and Doppler broadening.

The natural width of an atomic or molecular transition is limited in frequency spread solely by the spontaneous emission lifetime of the excited state. It is assumed that the species is completely isolated and free of perturbing effects such as radiation fields and other molecular or atomic interactions. The energy spread is related to the uncertainty in the lifetime by the well-known uncertainty principle,

$$\Delta E \cdot \Delta t \simeq \frac{h}{2\pi}. \tag{2-52}$$

The corresponding frequency spread is

$$\Delta\omega = \frac{\Delta E}{hc} \simeq \frac{1}{2\pi c \Delta t}. \tag{2-53}$$

The uncertainty in the lifetime Δt is reasonably well approximated by τ, Eq. (2-45); therefore,

$$\Delta\omega \simeq \frac{A_{mk}}{2\pi c} = \frac{32\pi^3 \omega_{mk}{}^3}{3hc} \cdot (\mu)_{mk}{}^2, \tag{2-54}$$

and

$$\Delta\omega_N \simeq 16.65 \times 10^{17} \omega_{mk}{}^3 (\mu)_{mk}{}^2. \tag{2-55}$$

This expression represents the natural half-width of a spectral line; the natural half-width is defined as the frequency interval corresponding to $\epsilon_{\max}/2$ as illustrated in Figure (2-7). For absorptions "allowed" by first-order electric dipole transitions rules in the microwave ($\sim$1 cm^{-1}), infrared ($\sim$2000 cm^{-1}), and visible ($\sim$15,000 cm^{-1}) regions, the corresponding natural half-widths are of the order of 10^{-15}, 10^{-8}, and 10^{-5} cm^{-1}. Except for electronic transitions, natural line broadening makes a negligible contribution under most experimental conditions.

In the case where a binary collision terminates the life of a particular excited state, then the time between collisions is very important with respect to pressure broadening. The mean time between collisions is given as $1/Z$, where Z is the collision frequency per molecule per second. From kinetic molecular theory,

$$Z = 3.37 \times 10^{10} \sigma_1 \sigma_2 \left(\frac{M_1 + M_2}{M_1 M_2}\right)^{1/2} \cdot \frac{P}{\sqrt{T}} \sec^{-1}, \tag{2-56}$$

where σ_i is the collision diameter in angstroms, M_i is the molecular weight in grams/mole, P the total pressure in atmospheres, and T the temperature in degrees Kelvin. Substituting $t = 1/Z$ into Eq. (2-53), we obtain

$$\Delta\omega_P \simeq \frac{Z}{2\pi c} = \frac{Z}{18.84 \times 10^{10}} \text{ cm}^{-1}. \tag{2-57}$$

Using typical values for Z—M = 30 g/mole, σ = 2 Å, P = 1 atm, and T = 300 °K—then $Z = 1.87 \times 10^9$ collisions per sec, or $t = 1/Z = 5.35 \times 10^{-10}$ sec. The pressure-broadened half-width is in turn $\sim 10^{-2}$ cm^{-1}.

For similar calculations at 0.10, 0.01, and 0.001 atm, the corresponding half-widths are 10^{-3}, 10^{-4}, and 10^{-5} cm^{-1}. In general, above 1 mmHg total pressure, this effect is usually the dominant one.

The final major contributor to a broadened spectral absorption or emission is the effect that results from the motion of the molecules relative to the radiation field. For a molecule moving in the direction of the exciting radiation source, the Doppler-shifted absorption frequency is given as

$$\omega = \omega_{mk}\left(1 + \frac{v}{c}\right), \tag{2-58}$$

where ω is the actual absorption frequency and ω_{mk} is the stationary absorption frequency. The quantity $\omega_{mk}v/c$ is referred to as the Doppler shift. For the case where a molecule is moving away from the radiating source, the Doppler shift in Eq. (2-58) is negative. For molecules moving normal to the source direction, there is no shift. The Doppler half-width is given as

$$\Delta\omega_{\text{D}} = \frac{\omega_{mk}}{c}\left(\frac{2NkT\ln 2}{M}\right)^{1/2} = 3.57 \times 10^{-7}\left(\frac{T}{M}\right)^{1/2}\omega_{mk}, \tag{2-59}$$

where T is degrees Kelvin, M is molecular weight in grams/mole, and ω_{mk} is the band center frequency in cm^{-1}. Substituting typical values into Eq. (2-59)—$M = 30$ g/mole, $T = 300$ °K—the Doppler half-widths for absorptions in the microwave (~ 1 cm^{-1}), infrared (~ 3000 cm^{-1}), and visible (15,000 cm^{-1}) regions are 10^{-6}, 3×10^{-4}, and 1.5×10^{-2} cm^{-1}. The Doppler shift increases with the square root of the temperature, while the pressure-broadening effect has an inverse square root temperature dependence.

F. LASERS (LIGHT AMPLIFICATION BY THE STIMULATED EMISSION OF RADIATION)

Since some of the fundamental principles of laser operation are directly related to certain inherent properties of stimulated emission, it appears appropriate to at least introduce this subject here and expand its discussion and use throughout the remainder of the text. The word *LASER* is an acronym derived from the parenthetical phrase in the section title. The essential process in laser operation is that stimulated emission is the predominant mode of decay between a given set of energy levels. That is, excited-state molecules (or atoms) are *induced* to emit radiation in a definite relation to each other, and not in the random manner characteristic of spontaneous emission. This mode of radiation emission leads in one way or another to the four important properties of lasers—*high intensity, high directionality, monochromaticity*, and *coherence*. We shall discover shortly that these properties are interdependent.

To obtain an idea of one of the most important restraints placed on obtaining laser action (sometimes called oscillation), let us consider again the two-level system of Figure 2-3. For the system at thermal equilibrium, Eq. (2-38) can be expressed as

$$\frac{dN_m}{dt} = N_k B_{mk} \rho(\omega_{mk}) - N_m B_{km} \rho(\omega_{mk}) - N_m A_{km} \simeq 0. \qquad \textbf{(2-60)}$$

According to Eq. (2-32), we can denote the Einstein B coefficients with a single subscript mk; therefore Eq. (2-60) can be rearranged to give

$$\frac{A_{km}}{B_{mk}\rho(\omega_{mk})} = \frac{N_k - N_m}{N_m} = \frac{N_k}{N_m} - 1. \qquad \textbf{(2-61)}$$

This expression can be related to the ratio of the number of molecules spontaneously emitting (N_{sp}) and stimulated to emit (N_{st}) per second, which are the two terms of Eq. (2-37),

$$\frac{N_{\text{sp}}}{N_{\text{st}}} = \frac{A_{km}}{B_{mk}\rho(\omega_{mk})}. \qquad \textbf{(2-62)}$$

Equating (2-62) and (2-61) and substituting Eq. (2-40), we obtain for the nondegenerate two-level system

$$\frac{N_{\text{sp}}}{N_{\text{st}}} = \exp\frac{hc\omega_{mk}}{kT} - 1. \qquad \textbf{(2-63)}$$

In order to achieve oscillation, or lasing action, $N_{\text{st}} \gg N_{\text{sp}}$. For a visible transition, where $c\omega_{mk} \simeq 5 \times 10^{14}$ Hz, at $T \sim 300$ °K, $\exp(hc\omega_{mk}/kT) \simeq \exp(80)$, or $N_{\text{sp}} \gg N_{\text{st}}$. Thus, the temperature required to achieve even $N_{\text{sp}} \simeq N_{\text{st}}$ for this visible transition is ~34,000 °K, which for obvious reasons is impractical. On the other hand, when this expression is applied to a microwave transition, where $c\omega_{mk} \simeq 10^{10}$ Hz, then $hc\omega_{mk}/kT = 1.6 \times 10^{-3}$, and the exponential can be expanded as $e^x = 1 + x + \frac{1}{2}x^2 + \ldots$. Application to Eq. (2-63) gives

$$\frac{N_{\text{sp}}}{N_{\text{st}}} = 1.6 \times 10^{-3} \qquad \textbf{(2-64)}$$

or $N_{\text{st}} \gg N_{\text{sp}}$; Eq. (2-64) should be interpreted to mean that as a consequence of the significantly smaller energy separation of the two energy levels, the spontaneous emission lifetime becomes very much longer (Section 2C) and if a critical concentration of excited state molecules and the proper experimental conditions exist, stimulated emission can be the predominant process. Such a consideration led to the development in late 1953 of the first oscillating system, using radiation in the microwave region, due to the inversion motion of the ammonia molecule. This was called a *MASER*, where the word *microwave* is used in place of *light*. Since oscillation has now been achieved over a significant portion of the electromagnetic spectrum, however, the term *laser* is the adopted or established acronym. The conclusion to be drawn from the first calculation involving the visible transition is that for a system that is subject to Boltzmann statistics, the attempt to make N_{st} competitive with N_{sp} would require extremely high temperatures, and we should seek alternative (non-Boltzmann) means of significantly populating the upper state as well as amplifying the radiation field.

Since 1953, lasing action has been achieved in a variety of ways and a variety of systems, which have in all cases involved a greater upper-state population, compared with the lower state. Such a condition of a non-Boltzmann distribution is called a *population inversion*. The various procedures by which molecules (or atoms) are energized to the upper state are called pumping processes, that is, electric discharge, energy transfer, laser or high-intensity light irradiation, and so on. Basically, laser operation involves creating an inverted population between two states of an active medium in a period that is short relative to the spontaneous-emission lifetime of the upper state (as well as other processes that may deplete the upper state). A very weak intensity internal (spontaneous emission) or external radiation signal of frequency ω_{mk} initiates the so-called *cascade effect*, since it stimulates the emission of excited-state molecules. Stimulating emission is effectively an amplifying process, since two photons of exactly the same frequency result from the single act of stimulated emission. These two photons can propagate this process, and in turn a chain process occurs. The cascade effect occurs because these photons are propagated within the laser cavity at the speed of light, and in practically all cases the entire stimulated process occurs long before significant spontaneous emission begins. The basic design of a laser is shown in Figure 2-5.

When an excited molecule (or atom) is stimulated to emit, it does so exclusively in the direction of the propagating stimulator (photon). Since the buildup of oscillation occurs only along the direction of those photons that are propagating normal to the reflecting cavity mirrors, the directional nature of the laser beam is fixed along this cavity axis. As a result, the theoretical cross section of the beam is determined by the cross-sectional dimensions of the laser cavity. One of the end mirrors is usually reflectively coated so that only a fractional "leakage" of the laser radiation occurs. Thus, the properties of directionality and intensity

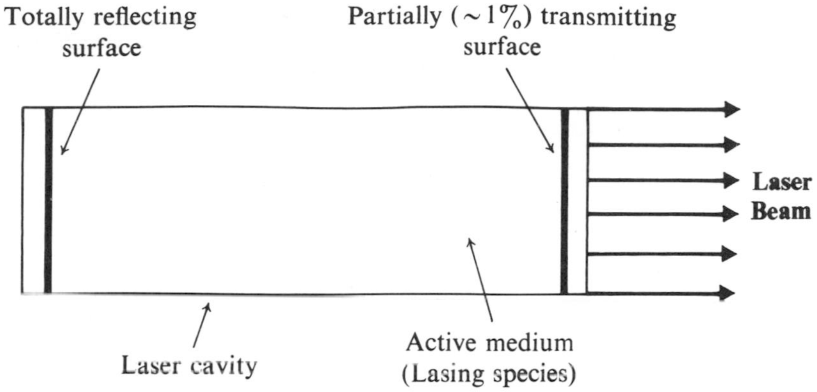

FIGURE 2-5 Basic design of a laser.

result from this aspect of stimulated emission, contrasted with spontaneous emission, which occurs over an exponential period and in all directions. The other remarkable characteristic of stimulated emission is that the stimulated radiation is in phase with the stimulator, and as a result, laser sources are extremely coherent. So that lasing intensity can be built up and maintained, the number of wavelengths traversed between the cavity mirrors by the radiations must be an exact integral number. Thus, tuning the mirror or mirrors to obtain an exact number of waves produces extremely sharp or monochromatic lines. In general, the more accurate the tuning (the more highly coherent the resonant cavity), the more monochromatic the radiation.

In spite of there being ever increasing numbers and types of lasers besides those in existence now, laser operation generally falls into two categories—continuous-wave (cw) and pulsed. A continuous-wave laser is one that *lases* continually, since the pumping conditions for amplification (oscillation) can be maintained above the threshold level. A well-known example is the He—Ne laser, whose energy-level diagram is shown in Figure 2-6. In this particular case, a population inversion between the 2*s* and 2*p* levels of excited-state Ne atoms is produced by the near resonant energy transfer from metastable 2^3S He atoms. The 2^3S state of He results from the electric discharge through a gaseous mixture containing approximately 10 percent Ne and 90 percent He at a total pressure of 1 torr. In spite of the fact that only a fractional amount of the 2^3S state is produced directly from the discharge, He atoms of higher excited states undergo relaxation processes ultimately leading to this long-lived (metastable) excited state. Oscillation occurs between several of the 2*s* and 2*p* levels of Ne as shown. The emitted frequencies correspond to infrared transitions at 1.118, 1.153, 1.160, 1.199, and 1.207 μ, the strongest being the

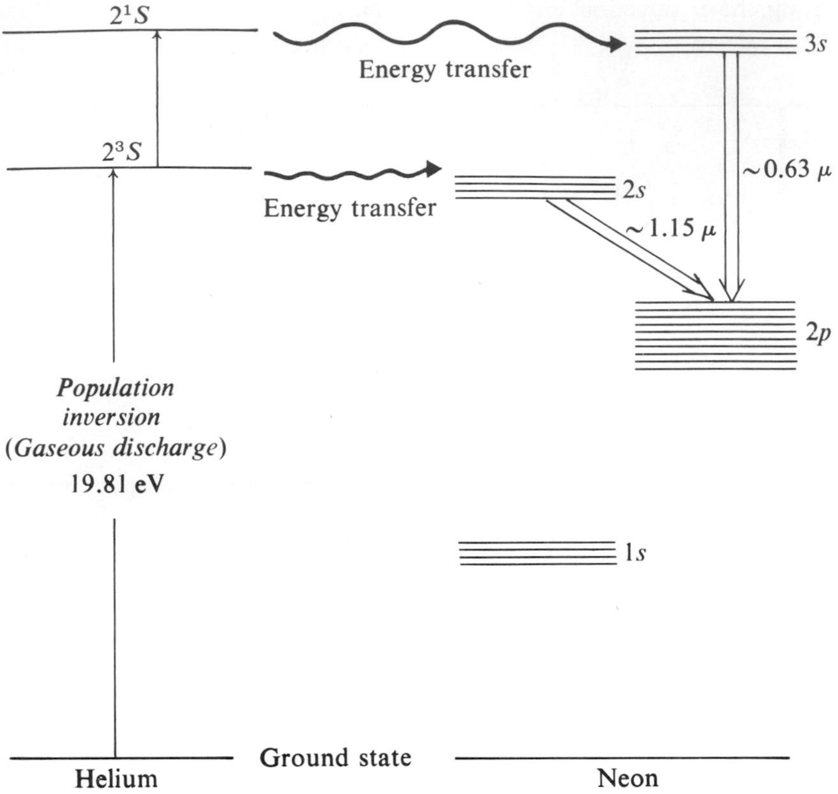

FIGURE 2-6 Energy-level diagram and operation of the He—Ne gaseous laser. The 1*s*, 2*p*, 2*s*, and 3*s* levels correspond to excited states of the Ne atom.

1.153 μ. (We shall describe, as an example of a pulsed system, the operation of a CO_2 laser in Chapter 6.)

G. DIPOLE AND OSCILLATOR STRENGTHS

In classical electromagnetic theory it was originally assumed that an electron was a three-dimensional harmonic oscillator that could interact with electromagnetic radiation of the proper frequency with resulting electronic excitation. This assumption provided a convenient means of estimating the Einstein coefficient for induced absorption and emission B_{mk} (Eq. (2-34)), since $(\mu)_{mk}^2$ could be easily evaluated using harmonic oscillator wavefunctions. For the one-dimensional harmonic oscillator along the x direction involving excitation of a single-valence electron, we have

$$(\mu_x)_{10} = \langle\psi_1|\mu_x|\psi_0\rangle = \langle\psi_1|qx|\psi_0\rangle, \tag{2-65}$$

where

$$\psi_0 = \left(\frac{\alpha}{\pi}\right)^{1/4} e^{-\alpha x^2/2} \quad \text{and} \quad \psi_1 = \left(\frac{4\alpha^3}{\pi}\right)^{1/4} x e^{-\alpha x^2/2}. \tag{2-66}$$

Thus,

$$(\mu_x)_{10} = \left(\frac{4\alpha^4}{\pi^2}\right)^{1/4} q \int_{-\infty}^{+\infty} x^2 e^{-\alpha x^2}\, dx \tag{2-67}$$

$$= \left(\frac{4\alpha^4}{\pi^2}\right)^{1/4} \cdot q \cdot \frac{1}{2}\sqrt{\frac{\pi}{\alpha^3}}$$

$$= \left(\frac{1}{4}\right)^{1/4} \frac{q}{\alpha^{1/2}},$$

where

$$\int_{-\infty}^{+\infty} x^2 e^{ax^2}\, dx = \frac{1}{2a}\left(\frac{\pi}{a}\right)^{1/2}. \tag{2-68}$$

Since $\alpha = 4\pi^2 c\omega m_e/h$, and if we assume an isotropic three-dimensional harmonic oscillator,

$$(\mu)_{10}{}^2 = \frac{3q^2h}{8\pi^2 c\omega m_e}. \tag{2-69}$$

The quantity $3h/8\pi^2 c\omega m_e$ is sometimes referred to as the dipole strength D_{mk}, and is in units of cm^2.[5] If Eq. (2-69) is substituted into Eq. (2-34), the *classical* coefficient for induced absorption and emission is given as

$$B_{mk} = \frac{\pi q^2}{hc^2\omega m_e}. \tag{2-70}$$

For complex atoms, the electrons were assumed to be a system of coupled oscillators; thus the value of B_{mk} summed over all the absorptions should be an integral multiple of $\pi q^2/hc^2\omega m_e$ (Kuhn-Thomas sum rule). This integer, which according to this classical approach should equal the number of electrons involved in transitions, was formerly defined as the oscillator strength, f. In fact, the total oscillator strength of an absorption is taken to be the effective number of oscillators placed into motion on exposure to a radiation field of frequency ω_{mk}. Its practical use today, however, is in determining relative absorption and emission band intensities and in evaluating important spectroscopic terms. (Both these procedures will be illustrated in the following section.)

H. INTEGRATED ABSORPTION COEFFICIENT

The concept of oscillator strength as a measure of relative band intensity can be conveniently realized, since B_{mk} is directly proportional to the intrinsic absorptivity of the atomic or molecular species undergoing excitation (Eq. (2-46)). The differential loss of radiation intensity due to an absorbing species of transition energy $hc\omega$ is directly proportional to the concentration of particles in the initial state N_K (molecules/cm³), the density of exciting frequencies $\rho(\omega)$, and the differential radiation path dl,

$$-dI = B_{mk}N_k\rho(\omega)hc\omega\, dl. \tag{2-71}$$

This equation can be related to the observed loss in intensity due to an absorption of a solute in a nonabsorbing medium (Beer's law),[6]

$$-dI = \alpha(\omega)IM\, dl, \tag{2-72}$$

where $\alpha(\omega)$ is the molar absorption coefficient, I the intensity of radiation, M the molar concentration of the solute, and dl the differential distance. Since absorption spectra usually consist of bands that occur over a range of frequencies and are not necessarily Gaussian in shape, the absorptivity is more accurately obtained by integrating $\alpha(\omega)$ over the entire band:

$$A(\text{experimental}) = \int_{\text{band}} \alpha(\omega)\, d\omega\ \text{cm}^{-2}M^{-1}, \tag{2-73}$$

where A is defined as the integrated absorption coefficient.

Substituting the expression for the radiation flux (ergs/cm²·sec),

$$I = c\rho(\omega), \tag{2-74}$$

and the appropriate concentration conversion factor into Eq. (2-71), we obtain[7]

$$-dI = B_{mk}\frac{N_0M}{1000} I\, h\omega\, dl. \tag{2-75}$$

Comparing Eqs. (2-72) and (2-75), and equating both to the absorption coefficient $\alpha(\omega)$, we obtain

$$\frac{-dI}{IM\, dl} = \alpha(\omega) = \frac{N_0}{1000}h\omega B_{mk}. \tag{2-76}$$

Substituting a less rigorous form of B_{mk} from Eq. (2-46), where the initial ground state is assumed to be nondegenerate ($g_k = 1$) and the $(\mu)^2_{m_ik_j}$'s are assumed to be equal, we obtain the integrated absorption expression

$$\int_{\text{band}} \alpha(\omega)\, d\omega = \frac{8\pi^3 g_m}{3h^2c}(\mu)_{mk}{}^2\frac{N_0}{1000}h\omega_{\text{max}}, \tag{2-77}$$

where the integration over ω is taken approximately to be the band center, ω_{max}. For the classical approximation involving the three-dimensional harmonic oscillator discussed in the preceding section (Eq. (2-69)), the integrated absorption coefficient is

$$A(\text{classical}) = \frac{\pi q^2 N_0}{1000 c^2 m_e}, \tag{2-78}$$

where $g_m = 1$, and $\omega_{max} \simeq \omega$.

At present, the oscillator strength is used qualitatively to indicate the relative intensities of various transitions, primarily in the visible, UV, and vacuum UV. It is defined as the ratio of the experimentally observed integrated absorption coefficient (Eq. (2-73)) to the one classically predicted (Eq. (2-78)),

$$f = 4.32 \times 10^{-9} \int_{\text{band}} \epsilon(\omega)\, d\omega, \tag{2-79}$$

where for the base 10 logarithmic absorption coefficient, $\epsilon(\omega) = \alpha(\omega)/2.303$ has been substituted. The symbol $\epsilon(\omega)$ is defined as the molar extinction coefficient and has units of $\text{cm}^{-1}M^{-1}$; it is the spectroscopic absorptivity most used in chemical spectroscopy. Physicists often use the spectral absorption coefficient P_ω in units of $\text{cm}^{-1}\cdot\text{atm}^{-1}$, which is easily convertible to $\epsilon(\omega)$ by the $RT(M^{-1}\ \text{atm})$ factor. We see from Eq. (2-79) that the oscillator strength is directly proportional to the integrated area corresponding to an absorption or an emission band. The value of $\int \epsilon(\omega)\, d\omega$ for a rather strong electronic absorption is of the order of 10^8 to 10^9, so that upper-limit electronic absorptions have oscillator strengths near unity. Values of this magnitude are characteristic of $\pi \rightarrow \pi^*$ and high-energy vacuum UV Rydberg transitions, that is, H_2, ${}^1\Sigma_u^- \leftarrow {}^1\Sigma_g^+$ (~1110 Å), $f \simeq 0.60$.

On the other hand, relatively weak absorption bands arising from rare-earth ions and transitional-metal ions range from approximately 10^{-6} to 10^{-8} and 10^{-6} to 10^{-2}, respectively. In spite of the weakness of these transitions, many of them give rise to the colors often observed in the visible region from metal complexes (Fe^{2+}, Co^{3+}, Ni^{2+}) at relatively low concentrations. This observation indicates not so much the nature of the transition as the extreme sensitivity of the eye as a detector. For a single electron undergoing one or more transitions, the Kuhn-Thomas sum rule states

$$\sum_i f_i = 1. \tag{2-80}$$

Although the integral $\int \epsilon(\omega)\, d\omega$ is totally an experimental quantity, difficulties often arise in its determination because of the uncertainty in band shape, band overlap, absorption "wings," and so on. One of the simplest approaches that has been used quite generally in resolving these problems is assuming a Gaussian band contour. Then the integrated intensity can be related to the extinction coefficient at the absorption maximum ϵ_{max} and the half-width $\Delta\omega_{1/2}$ by the following relation:

$$A = \int_{\text{band}} \epsilon(\omega)\, d\omega = \epsilon_{max}(1.0645)\Delta\omega_{1/2}. \qquad \textbf{(2-81)}$$

These quantities are illustrated in Figure 2-7.

Of the relatively strong transitions discussed previously, the half-widths are of the order of 1000 to 5000 cm^{-1}, and $\epsilon_{max} \simeq 10^4$ to 10^5 $M^{-1}cm^{-1}$. The relatively weak visible absorptions have $\Delta\omega_{1/2} \simeq 100$ cm^{-1} and $\epsilon_{max} \simeq 10$ $M^{-1}cm^{-1}$. The class of extremely weak absorption bands corresponding to singlet-triplet transitions have $\epsilon_{max} \simeq 10^{-3}$ to 10^{-4} $M^{-1}cm^{-1}$.

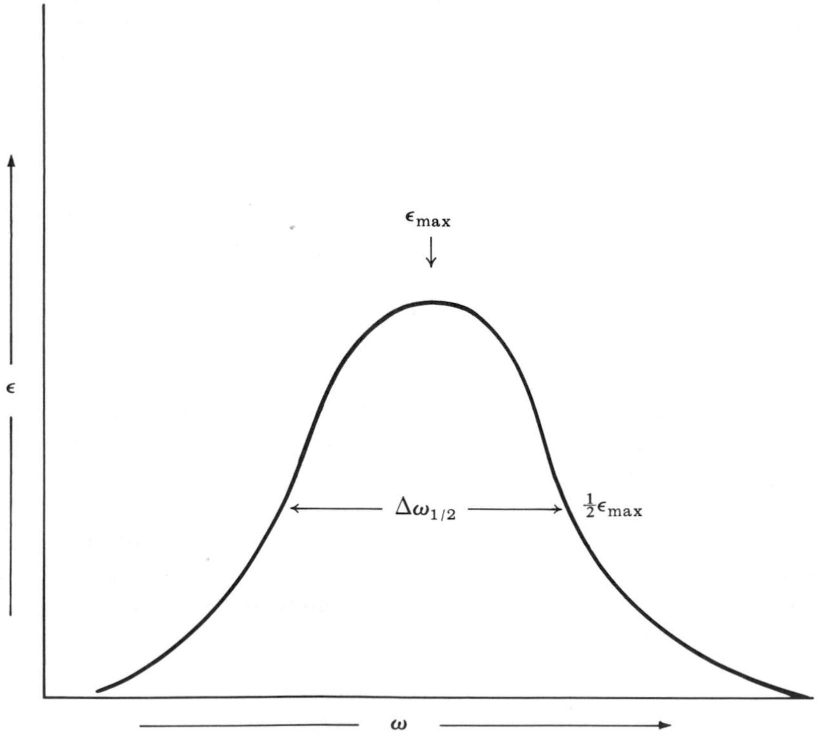

FIGURE 2-7 A Gaussian absorption band, where the integrated intensity is $A = \epsilon_{max}(1.0645)\ \Delta\omega_{1/2}$.

EXAMPLE 2-3: Calculate the oscillator strengths of the following acetaldehyde absorptions:

$$n \rightarrow \pi^*(\lambda_{\max} \simeq 2900 \text{ Å}),\ \epsilon_{\max} \simeq 15\ M^{-1}\text{cm}^{-1},\ \Delta\omega_{1/2} \simeq 600 \text{ cm}^{-1}$$
$$\pi \rightarrow \pi^*(\lambda_{\max} \simeq 1816 \text{ Å}),\ \epsilon_{\max} \simeq 10^4\ M^{-1}\text{cm}^{-1},\ \Delta\omega_{1/2} \simeq 2000 \text{ cm}^{-1}$$

Compare the f values and comment on the nature of these absorptions in higher aliphatic homologs of the aldehydes.

Solution: The oscillator strengths of these transitions can be evaluated by using Eq. (2-79), after $\int \epsilon(\omega)\, d\omega$ is obtained from Eq. (2-81). For the $n \rightarrow \pi^*$ transition,

$$\int_{\text{band}} \epsilon(\omega)\, d\omega = \epsilon_{\max}(1.0645)\, \Delta\omega_{1/2} = (15\ M^{-1}\text{cm}^{-1})(1.0645)(600 \text{ cm}^{-1})$$
$$= 9.6 \times 10^3\ M^{-1}\text{cm}^{-2}$$

and

$$f_{n\rightarrow\pi^*} = 4.32 \times 10^{-9} \int_{\text{band}} \epsilon(\omega)\, d\omega$$
$$= (4.32 \times 10^{-9})(9.6 \times 10^3)$$
$$= 4.1 \times 10^{-5}.$$

For the $\pi \rightarrow \pi^*$ transition,

$$\int_{\text{band}} \epsilon(\omega)\, d\omega = (10^4\ M^{-1}\text{cm}^{-1})(1.0645)(2 \times 10^3 \text{ cm}^{-1})$$
$$= 2 \times 10^7\ M^{-1}\text{cm}^{-2}$$

and

$$f_{\pi\rightarrow\pi^*} = (4.32 \times 10^{-9})(2 \times 10^7)$$
$$= 0.86.$$

These transitions involve the carbcnyl electrons and are considered to be relatively isolated from the rest of the molecule, so that the same approximate frequencies and intensity ratios would be expected for higher aliphatic homologs. This is indeed found to be the case.

An equivalent way of defining the oscillator strength f is by taking the ratio of the quantum mechanical integrated intensity (Eq. (2-77)) to the classical expression (Eq. (2-78)). The result is

$$f_{mk} = \frac{8\pi^2 m_e c \omega_{mk} g_m}{3hq^2} (\mu)_{mk}{}^2. \tag{2-82}$$

This relation provides the basis for evaluating important spectroscopic terms based on the experimentally determined oscillator strength as defined by Eq. (2-79).

The transition moment integral can be calculated from Eq. (2-82) by rearranging:

$$(\mu)_{mk}{}^2 = \frac{3hq^2}{8\pi^2 m_e c} \cdot \frac{f_{mk}}{g_m \omega_{mk}} = 2.12 \times 10^{-30} \frac{f_{mk}}{g_m \omega_{mk}} \text{ erg-cm}^3. \quad \textbf{(2-83)}$$

The dipole strength D_{mk}, whose magnitude is proportional to the intrinsic absorptivity of a transition, is obtained by simply factoring q^2 from $(\mu)_{mk}{}^2$ and cancelling:

$$D_{mk} = \frac{3h}{8\pi^2 m_e c} \cdot \frac{f_{mk}}{g_m \omega_{mk}} = 9.26 \times 10^{-12} \frac{f_{mk}}{g_m \omega_{mk}} \text{ cm}^2. \quad \textbf{(2-84)}$$

The less rigorous Einstein coefficients for a transition from a nondegenerate level m in emission in one case and from level k in absorption in the other, which combine respectively with final degenerate sublevels g_k and g_m, are

$$A_{km} = \frac{64\pi^2 \omega_{mk}{}^3 g_k}{3h} (\mu)_{mk}{}^2 = 3.13 \times 10^{29} g_k \omega_{mk}{}^3 (\mu)_{mk}{}^2 \text{ sec}^{-1} \quad \textbf{(2-85)}$$

and

$$B_{mk} = \frac{8\pi^3 g_m}{3h^2 c} (\mu)_{mk}{}^2 = 6.28 \times 10^{43} g_m (\mu)_{mk}{}^2 \text{ sec-gm}^{-1}, \quad \textbf{(2-86)}$$

where it is assumed that the $(\mu)^2_{m_i k_j}$'s are equal.

I. NUMERICAL EXAMPLES AND LIFETIME CALCULATIONS

EXAMPLE 2-4: Estimate the approximate collison-free lifetime of the first vibrational state (v = 1) of HCl ($\mu_{0\,\mathrm{HCl}} = 1.03$ D, $\omega = 2885\ \mathrm{cm}^{-1}$, $r_e = 1.28$ Å).

Solution: For a fundamental vibration, the transition moment integral Eq. (2-30) is given as

$$(\mu)_{10} = \langle \psi_1 | \hat{\mu}_x | \psi_0 \rangle = \left\langle \psi_1 \left| \left(\frac{\partial \mu}{\partial x}\right) x \right| \psi_0 \right\rangle \simeq \left(\frac{\partial \mu}{\partial x}\right) \langle \psi_1 | x | \psi_0 \rangle.$$

Estimating the dipole derivative near the equilibrium distance gives

$$\left(\frac{\partial \mu}{\partial x}\right)_{x=x_e} \simeq \frac{1.03 \times 10^{-18} \text{ esu-cm}}{1.28 \times 10^{-8} \text{ cm}} = 0.81 \times 10^{-10} \text{ esu}.$$

From Eqs. (2-65) and (2-67), we obtain

$$(\mu)_{10} = (0.81 \times 10^{-10} \text{ esu}) \left(\frac{1}{4}\right)^{1/4} \frac{1}{\alpha^{1/2}},$$

where

$$\alpha = \frac{4\pi^2 c\omega\mu_r}{h},$$

$$\mu_r = \text{reduced mass of HCl},$$

$$(\mu)_{10} = (0.81 \times 10^{-10})\left(\frac{1}{4}\right)^{1/4}\left(\frac{h}{4\pi^2 c\omega\mu_r}\right)^{1/2}$$

$$= (0.81 \times 10^{-10})\left(\frac{1}{1.414}\right)\left(\frac{6.62 \times 10^{-27}}{4 \times 9.8 \times 3 \times 10^{10} \times 2885 \times 1.6 \times 10^{-24}}\right)^{1/2}$$

$$= 6.3 \times 10^{-20},$$

$$(\mu)_{10}^2 = 39.70 \times 10^{-40} \text{ erg-cm}^3.$$

The Einstein coefficient for spontaneous emission (Eq. 2-85) is

$$\begin{aligned} A_{01} &= 3.13 \times 10^{29}\omega^3(\mu)_{10}^2 \text{ sec}^{-1} \\ &= 3.13 \times 10^{29}(2885)^3(39.70 \times 10^{-40}) \\ &= 29.83 \text{ sec}^{-1}, \end{aligned}$$

or an approximate radiative lifetime

$$\tau = \frac{1}{A_{01}} = 3.35 \times 10^{-2} \text{ sec}.$$

EXAMPLE 2-5: The phosphorescence lifetime τ_p of condensed CH_3—[C≡C]$_3$—CH_3 is observed at 77 °K to be 0.5 sec from the first triplet state T_1 (v′ = 0, v″ = 0) at 22,320 cm^{-1}. Calculate the oscillator strength and the frequency uncertainty of the T_1(v′ = 0, v″ = 0) state.

Solution: The combination of Eqs. (2-83), (2-47), where the $(\mu)^2_{m_i k_j}$'s are equal, and (2-45) gives the following result for $f_{S_0 \leftarrow T_1}$:

$$\begin{aligned} f_{S_0 \leftarrow T_1} &= [(3.13 \times 10^{29})(2.12 \times 10^{-30})\omega_{mk}{}^2\tau_p]^{-1}g_m \\ &= [0.664)(22{,}320)^2(0.5)]^{-1} \times 3 \\ &= 1.9 \times 10^{-8}, \end{aligned}$$

where g_m is the multiplicity of the initial state m. The uncertainty in the frequency spread is obtained by Eq. (2-53), since in these low-temperature condensed phase experiments neither pressure nor Doppler broadening is important. Therefore,

$$\Delta\omega_N = \frac{1}{2\pi c\Delta t} = \frac{1}{18.84 \times 10^{10}\tau_p} = [(18.84 \times 10^{10})(0.5)]^{-1}$$

$$= 1.06 \times 10^{-11} \text{ cm}^{-1}.$$

According to the Heisenberg uncertainty principle, this is an expected result, since the longer the lifetime of the state, the more accurate the determination of the energy of the state. Obviously, other factor(s), like instrument limitation, will establish the limitation in resolution in this case, rather than the natural half-width.

EXAMPLE 2-6: The experimentally determined oscillator strength f of a singlet-singlet visible absorption at 15,000 cm^{-1}(6666 Å) is 0.02. Evaluate $(\mu)_{mk}^2$, D_{mk}, A_{km}, and the spontaneous radiative lifetime.

Solution: (a) According to Eq. (2-83),

$$(\mu)_{mk}^2 = (2.12 \times 10^{-30}) \frac{2 \times 10^{-2}}{(1)(1.5 \times 10^4)} = 2.82 \times 10^{-36} \text{ erg-cm}^3.$$

(b) The dipole strength (Eq. 2-84) is

$$D_{mk} = (9.26 \times 10^{-12}) \frac{2.0 \times 10^{-2}}{(1)(1.5 \times 10^4)} = 1.23 \times 10^{-17} \text{ cm}^2.$$

(c) The Einstein coefficient for spontaneous emission (Eq. 2-85) is

$$A_{km} = (3.13 \times 10^{29})(1)(1.5 \times 10^4)^3(2.82 \times 10^{-36}) = 30 \times 10^5$$
$$= 3.0 \times 10^6 \text{ sec}^{-1}$$

or a radiative lifetime

$$\tau = \frac{1}{A} = 3.3 \times 10^{-7} \text{ sec} = 0.33\ \mu\text{sec}.$$

SELECTED BIBLIOGRAPHY

2-1. Allen, L. *Essentials of Lasers.* New York: Pergamon Press, 1969.

2-2. Calvert, J. C., and Pitts, J. N. *Photochemistry.* New York: John Wiley & Sons, 1967.

2-3. Fishlock, D. *A Guide to the Laser.* New York: American Elsevier Publishing Co., 1967.

2-4. Gordy, W., and Cook, R. L. *Microwave Molecular Spectra.* New York: Interscience Publishers, 1970.

2-5. Heavens, O. S. *Lasers.* New York: Charles Scribner's and Sons, 1971.

2-6. Herzberg, Gerhard. *Atomic Spectra and Atomic Structure.* New York: Dover Publications, 1945.

2-7. Herzberg, Gerhard. *Diatomic Molecules.* New York: Van Nostrand Reinhold Co., 1950.

2-8. Sandorfy, C. *Electronic Spectra and Quantum Chemistry.* Englewood Cliffs, N.J.: Prentice-Hall, 1964.

GLOSSARY OF SYMBOLS

Absorption and Emission of Radiation

$\rho(\omega)$ Radiation density, erg/cm^3
$\rho(\omega_{mk})$ Radiation intensity, erg/cm^2

$c\rho(\omega)$	Radiation flux, erg/cm²-sec
$\nu(\text{sec}^{-1}) =$	c(cm/sec)ω(cm^{-1}), frequency
B_{mk}	Einstein coefficient for absorption, sec/gm
$\epsilon(\omega)$	Molar extinction coefficient, cm$^{-2}M^{-1}$
$\alpha(\omega)$	Molar absorption coefficient, cm$^{-2}M^{-1}$
$\mathbf{H}$	Magnetic field vector
H	Hamiltonian
Ψ	Total wavefunction
ψ	Time-independent wavefunction
E	Energy
A_{km}	Einstein coefficient for spontaneous emission, sec^{-1}
$(\mu)_{mk}$	Transition moment integral
m_e	Mass of the electron, 9.1×10^{-28} gm
$\mathbf{Q}$	Electric quadrupole moment
ω	Frequency, cm^{-1}
$\Delta\omega_N$	Natural half-width, cm^{-1}
$\Delta\omega_P$	Pressure-broadened half-width, cm^{-1}
$\Delta\omega_D$	Doppler half-width, cm^{-1}
A	Integrated absorption coefficient
f	Oscillator strength
q	Electric charge
μ_r	Reduced mass, gm

ENDNOTES

1. For convenience we have substituted the shorthand notation for the integral

$$\langle m^0|\hat{H}'|k^0\rangle = \int \psi_m{}^{0*}\hat{H}'(t)\psi_k{}^0\,d\tau.$$

2. $\langle m^0|\mu_x|k^0\rangle \simeq 10^{-17}$ cgs-esu units.
3. The convention used for the subscript designation is that the first letter corresponds to the final state and the second to the initial state.
4. In most cases, "all possible combinations" refers to those sublevels that are allowed to combine by the appropriate selection rules (i.e., electric dipole, etc.).
5. In some cases (rotational and vibrational transitions), the square of the electronic charge q^2 is not so easily factored from the square of the transition moment integral. Some authors therefore define the dipole strength as simply the transition moment integral squared $(\mu)_{mk}{}^2$ (Eq. 2-35).
6. The integrated form of Beer's law is given as $I_0/I = \exp(-\alpha Ml)$, and is related to the molar extinction coefficient ϵ by $I_0/I = 10^{-\epsilon Ml}$, $\epsilon = \alpha/2.303$.
7. $N_k\left(\frac{\text{molecules}}{\text{cc}}\right) = N_0\left(\frac{\text{molecules}}{\text{mole}}\right)\left(\frac{\text{liter}}{1000\text{ cc}}\right)\left(M\frac{\text{mole}}{\text{liter}}\right) = \frac{N_0M}{1000}.$

PROBLEMS

2-1. In the derivation of Planck's radiation law, Eq. (2-36), $\rho(\omega_{mk}) = n_\omega \bar{E}$, $\bar{E}$ is the mean energy associated with any vibration. Show that $\bar{E} = hc\omega/[\exp(hc\omega/kT)] - 1$ (where $n_\omega = 8\pi\omega^2$).

2-2. Assuming for the moment that spontaneous emission is the only decay mode from excited state m, show that the inverse of A_{km} (Eq. 2-45) is the time for the initial number of excited molecules to decrease to $1/e$.

2-3. Using the result of Problem 2-2, show that the average or mean life of an excited molecule in state m relative to spontaneous emission is τ. (This calculation is an illustration of the so-called relaxation time in first-order decay processes.)

2-4. The experimentally determined oscillator strength f of the $^2\Sigma \leftarrow {}^2\Pi$ electronic transition of the OH radical having a band center of 32,600 cm^{-1} is 1.2×10^{-3}. Calculate $(\mu)_{mk}{}^2$, D_{mk}, A_{km}, and the spontaneous radiative lifetime. The multiplicity for the ground state ($^2\Pi$) is 4 and the multiplicity for the excited state ($^2\Sigma$) is 2, and the possible allowed combinations, where the $(\mu)^2_{m_ik_j}$'s are equal, is 6.

2-5. The experimentally determined integrated band intensity $\int P_\omega \, d\omega$ of C_2 corresponding to a temperature of 2877 °K for the $^1\Pi_u \leftarrow {}^1\Sigma_g{}^+$ electronic band is 5.0×10^5 $cm^{-2}atm^{-1}$. Evaluate the oscillator strength f.

2-6. If the experiment involving Example 2-5 were carried out for the gas phase at a total pressure of 10^{-3} atm and at 300 °K, estimate the number of collisions that would occur over the phosphorescent lifetime of CH_3—[C≡C]$_3$—CH_3. (Assume $\sigma \sim 5$ Å). Assuming collisional quenching to be unimportant (which is not the case) for the moment, which of the three line-broadening processes would be most important?

2-7. Verify the assumption made near the Bohr condition that the term $\langle m^0|\mu_x|k^0\rangle E_x{}^0(\omega)$ is "very small" for a single frequency.

***2-8.** The magnetic dipole transition $^1\Sigma_g{}^+ \leftarrow {}^3\Sigma_g{}^-$ of the atmospheric band of molecular oxygen has a radiative lifetime of 7.15 sec, about a factor of 10^2 to 10^3 greater than normally expected according to Example 2-2. Consider the various magnetic dipole transition rules, and suggest a reason for this factor.

***2-9.** Discuss stimulated emission vs spontaneous emission in terms of properties like monochromaticity, directionality, coherence, collimation, and intensity. How are these properties important to laser operation?

Chapter 3

Atomic Spectroscopy

The study and interpretation of atomic spectra over the last half-century or so has been very helpful in resolving complex molecular spectra. Many of the basic concepts involving quantization of the energy and the motion of electrons are more easily developed using atomic systems; these concepts also apply very closely to molecular systems. The electronic energy and electronic motion of atoms (and molecules) are quantized (exist in discrete energy states), as Max Planck first proposed, and transitions between them are experimentally observed as an everyday occurrence by most practicing spectroscopists. These quantized phenomena lead in a natural way to characteristic numbers, called quantum numbers.

The general solution of a two-body problem involving hydrogenlike atoms can be used to illustrate the natural origin of these characteristic numbers. Since the Hamiltonian operator can be expressed as two rigorously separate parts,

$$\hat{H} = \hat{H}_{\text{cm}} + \hat{H}_{\text{int}}, \tag{3-1}$$

corresponding to the translation of the center of mass and the internal energy of the two-body system (in this case the electronic energy), the Schrödinger equation becomes

$$\left[-\frac{h^2}{8\pi^2(m_1 + m_2)}\nabla^2(x, y, z) - \frac{h^2}{8\pi^2\mu}\nabla^2(r, \theta, \phi)\right]\Psi + U\Psi = E\Psi. \tag{3-2}$$

Solution of the center-of-mass equation, which has no angular dependence, leads to the well-known translation energy of the two-body system.

Substituting the Laplacian operator ∇^2 in spherical polar coordinates gives for the internal energy

$$\frac{-h^2}{8\pi^2\mu}\left[\frac{1}{r^2}\frac{\partial}{\partial r}\left(r^2\frac{\partial\psi}{\partial r}\right) + \frac{1}{r^2\sin^2\theta}\frac{\partial^2\psi}{\partial\phi^2} + \frac{1}{r^2\sin\theta}\frac{\partial}{\partial\theta}\left(\sin\theta\frac{\partial\psi}{\partial\theta}\right)\right] + [U(r) - E_{\text{el}}]\psi = 0, \quad \text{(3-3)}$$

where

$$\psi(r, \theta, \phi) = \psi(r)\psi(\theta)\psi(\phi). \quad \text{(3-4)}$$

We consider the nucleus to be located at the origin having a charge Ze and thus the potential energy is $-Ze^2/r$. Substituting Eq. (3-4) into Eq. (3-3) and successively effecting a separation of variables, we obtain three equations whose solutions require small integers,

$$\frac{1}{\psi(\theta)}\cdot\frac{\partial^2\psi(\phi)}{\partial\phi^2} = -m^2, \quad \text{(3-5)}$$

$$\frac{1}{\psi(\theta)\sin\theta}\frac{\partial}{\partial\theta}\left(\sin\theta\frac{\partial\psi(\theta)}{\partial\theta}\right) - \frac{m^2}{\sin^2\theta}\psi(\theta) = -\ell(\ell + 1), \quad \text{(3-6)}$$

and

$$\frac{1}{\psi(r)}\frac{\partial}{\partial r}\left(r^2\frac{\partial\psi(r)}{\partial r}\right) + \frac{8\pi^2\mu}{h^2}\left(E_{\text{el}} + \frac{Ze^2}{r}\right) = \ell(\ell + 1). \quad \text{(3-7)}$$

The small integers resulting from the solution of Eqs. (3-5), (3-6), and (3-7) respectively are m, ℓ, and n; their physical meanings are summarized as follows:

- n — the principal quantum number, defines the energy; it has no restriction on the integral values, $n = 1, 2, 3, \ldots$.
- ℓ — the azimuthal quantum number, defines the orbital angular momentum or the shape of the electron cloud; integral values of $\ell = 0, 1, 2, \ldots, (n - 1)$.
- m_ℓ — the magnetic quantum number, illustrates the "space degeneracy" of equal ℓ states with different spatial orientations; integral values of $m_\ell = 0, \pm 1, \ldots, \pm \ell$.
- m_s — the spin quantum number, characterizes the spin angular momentum of the electron about its own axis; although the spin quantum number does not result from the Schrödinger solutions above, it does appear naturally in relativistic wave mechanics and is restricted to half-integral values of $\pm\frac{1}{2}$.

For a system containing more than one or two electrons, the energy separation between n states is quite large, and therefore electrons occupying different n levels tend to be quite distant on the average. On the other hand, electrons occupying the same n state tend to weakly interact in both a repulsive and an attractive manner. The attractive interaction however falls off rapidly with increasing atomic size (number). The quantum numbers m_ℓ characterizing the orbital angular momentum and m_s characterizing the spin angular momentum in an external perturbing field provide the complete description of the electronic energy and electronic motion of an atom.

In the case of complex atomic systems where the potential functions in particular become difficult to evaluate, we must resort to various approximation methods. One such method is the "central field approximation." It essentially assumes as a starting point that atoms can be treated to a fairly good approximation by regarding the electrons as moving in a central field and not as interacting. In the interpretation of spectra where some electronic interaction is required, it is treated as a perturbation. In effect, the electron or electrons of interest "see" a potential field consisting of a massive nuclear charge Ze, partially screened by the spherical or symmetrical field of the other electrons. This approach has been fairly successful in interpreting many cases of complex spectra. (A full discussion of its derivation and application is given in Reference 3-1.)

A. ELECTRONIC TERM SYMBOLS

One method of describing the electronic configuration of an atom is by identifying the n and ℓ quantum numbers. For H, it is $1s^1$ and for the free carbon atom it is $1s^2 2s^2 2p_x{}^1 2p_y{}^1 2p_z$. Besides being cumbersome, this description only gives the approximate energy state or states, since the two electrons in the triply degenerate p orbital can have several m_ℓ and m_s combinations leading to different nonperturbed energy states. The descriptions used to characterize more specifically the energy states in atomic spectroscopy are called electronic term symbols.

The electronic term symbol provides an accounting of the energy and the orbital and spin angular momentum states by using the various resultant quantum number symbols that define these motions. For small atoms, the symbol also contains a quantum number for the coupling between the orbital and spin angular momentum resultants. The term symbol is generally written $^{2S+1}L_J$, where the superscript, $2S + 1$, is referred to as the multiplicity of an atomic state, and S is the quantum number defining the total spin angular momentum **S**,

$$\mathbf{S} = \sqrt{S(S + 1)}\hbar. \qquad \textbf{(3-8)}$$

The symbols L and J are the quantum numbers characterizing the total orbital angular momentum **L**, and the total angular momentum **J**:

$$\mathbf{L} = \sqrt{L(L + 1)}\hbar, \qquad \textbf{(3-9)}$$

and

$$\mathbf{J} = \sqrt{J(J + 1)}\hbar. \qquad \textbf{(3-10)}$$

The evaluation of the term symbol for a particular state depends on the manner in which the individual electrons couple. The electronic coupling of relatively light atoms (Russell-Saunders) and heavy atoms (*jj*) will be illustrated below.

1. Russell-Saunders Coupling (*LS* Coupling)

In the case of complex atoms, the (several) electrons are assumed as a first approximation to be moving in a spherically symmetric electric field, and individually characterized by n_i and ℓ_i quantum numbers. Thus, each electron is assumed to retain an angular momentum quantum number, ℓ_i. However, the movements of the electrons are not, in fact, independent of each other, and therefore rather strong electric and magnetic interactions do occur, depending on the proximity of the electrons. If the electrons are relatively close on the average, as is the case for small atoms, the individual angular momenta $\boldsymbol{\ell}_i$ will vectorially add in such a way as to create a precessional motion about the resultant angular momentum **L** (Figure 3-1).

According to the coupling strength, several different orientations of the $\boldsymbol{\ell}_i$'s are possible, as long as they give rise to (integral) quantized L states. Thus, for the case of two electrons,

$$L = (\ell_1 + \ell_2), (\ell_1 + \ell_2 - 1), (\ell_1 + \ell_2 - 2), \ldots, |\ell_1 - \ell_2|, \quad \textbf{(3-11)}$$

where a negative angular momentum has no physical meaning. In the case of an $s(\ell = 0)$ angular momentum state, the electronic cloud mapped out is spherically symmetric about the nucleus, thus the total net angular

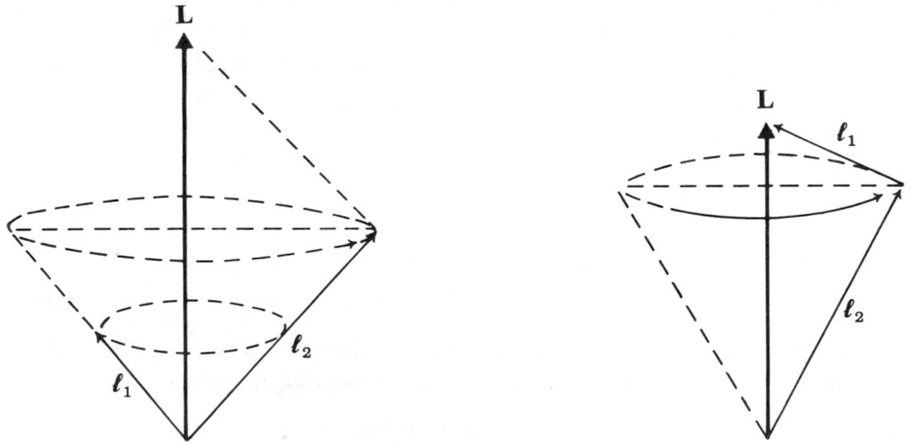

FIGURE 3-1 Precessional motion of two electrons ($\boldsymbol{\ell}_1$ and $\boldsymbol{\ell}_2$) about the resultant orbital angular momentum **L**.

momentum vector $\mathbf{L}$ is zero (where $L = \ell_i$). This angular momentum state is given the designation S as a term symbol. The quantum numbers characterizing p, d, and f electrons are respectively $\ell = 1$, $\ell = 2$, and $\ell = 3$. Vectorial addition of the ℓ_i's for complex atoms resulting in L values of 0, 1, 2, 3, and so on are given the symbols $S, P, D, F, \ldots$ respectively. The following L states are obtained for two electron configurations using Eq. (3-11).

Electron configuration	L states	Term symbol
$s\ p$	1	P
$p\ p$	2 1 0	$D\ P\ S$
$p\ d$	3 2 1	$F\ D\ P$

For the case of three or more electrons, vectorial addition is successively performed by combining the cumulative L values with each new ℓ_i for an electron.

EXAMPLE 3-1: Obtain the angular momentum states for the atom having $\ell_1 = 1$, $\ell_2 = 2$, and $\ell_3 = 3$ nonequivalent valence electrons.

Solution: For electrons 1 and 2, $L_{12} = 3, 2, 1$; thus the combination of these individually with ℓ_3 gives

$$
\begin{array}{ccccccc}
I & H & G & F & D & P & S \\
\end{array}
$$
$$
L_{123} \begin{cases} 6, & 5, & 4, & 3, & 2, & 1, & 0 \\ & 5, & 4, & 3, & 2, & 1 \\ & & 4, & 3, & 2 \end{cases}
$$

Here we see that several equivalent terms of L may exist. Thus we obtain $I(1)$, $H(2)$, $G(3)$, $F(3)$, $D(3)$, $P(2)$, and $S(1)$, where the number of equivalent terms are indicated in parentheses. Thus, the total orbital angular momentum quantum number of the atom is represented by the resultant L.

In the same manner that we have considered each of the electrons in the field of the others to possess an intrinsic orbital angular momentum, we find that the corresponding assumption is also true for the spin property (Goudsmit and Uhlenbeck assumption). Again, because of the electric interaction of the electrons in close proximity, rather strong coupling of the $\mathbf{s}_i$ vectors results. Therefore, only the resultant S has meaning with respect to the total spin angular momentum of the atom, where $S = \sum_i s_i$. For two electrons,

$$S = (s_1 + s_2), (s_1 + s_2 - 1), (s_1 + s_2 - 2), \ldots, |s_1 - s_2|. \quad \text{(3-12)}$$

In this case s_i can only be $+\frac{1}{2}$ or $-\frac{1}{2}$; therefore, S must be either 0 or 1,

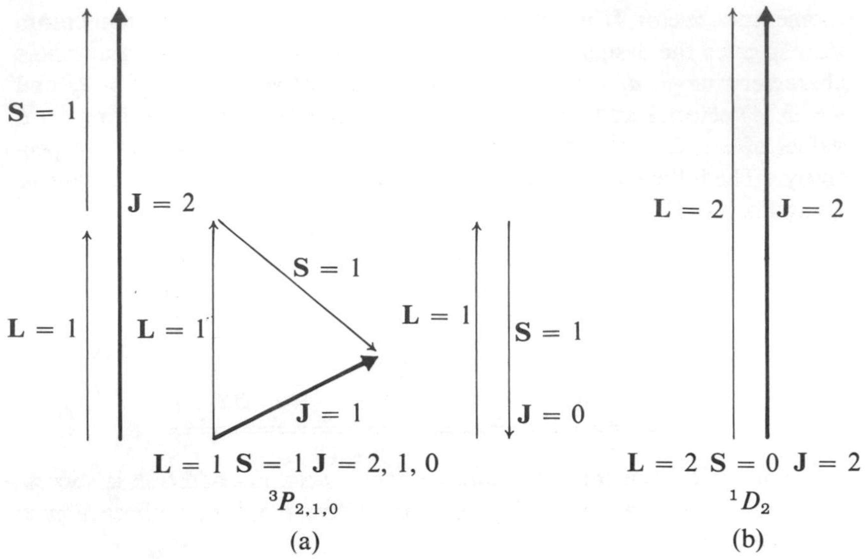

FIGURE 3-2 The vectorial addition of two equivalent p electrons resulting in S, P, and D states. (The ^1S state is not shown, since it has no net **L** or **S** vector.)

corresponding to a "singlet" [2(0) + 1] or a "triplet" [2(1) + 1] spin state. For systems containing more than two electrons, the $\mathbf{s}_i$'s must be vectorially added as demonstrated above for L.

In spite of the relatively large electric coupling that exists between the individual ℓ_i's and $\mathbf{s}_i$'s, they are also weakly coupled to each other by a magnetic dipole interaction. The total spin and orbital angular momenta **S** and **L** precess about a resultant **J**, the total angular momentum. The various states of J produced, depending again on the manner in which L and S add vectorially, are given by

$$J = (L + S), (L + S - 1), (L + S - 2), \ldots, |L - S|. \quad \textbf{(3-13)}$$

The various **J** states resulting from the vectorial addition of two equivalent p electrons is shown in Figure 3-2. Since the coupling interaction is so weak in this case, the various **J** states will result in a rather closely spaced multiplet for given **L** and **S** combinations. Therefore, the total description for an atom exhibiting Russell-Saunders coupling is given generally as $^{2S+1}L_J$.

EXAMPLE 3-2: What is the ground state electronic term symbol of the free boron atom?

Solution: The electronic configuration of B is $1s^22s^22p^1$; for the two electrons in the filled $n = 1$ level, the net angular momenta are **L** = 0, **S** = 0, and

$\mathbf{J} = 0$. So we see that as a general rule in deriving term symbols, a closed electronic shell makes no contribution to the $\sum_i s_i$ or $\sum_i \ell_i$.

For the three remaining $2s^2 2p^1$ electrons $\ell_1 = \ell_2 = 0$ and $\ell_3 = 1$. Thus, $L = \sum_i l_i = 1$, $S = \sum_i s_i = \frac{1}{2}$, and $J = \frac{3}{2}$ and $\frac{1}{2}$. The electronic term symbol (multiplet) is $^2\mathrm{P}_{3/2,1/2}$.

The spin-orbit interaction Hamiltonian for a single electron with $\ell \neq 0$, which gives rise to the term multiplet, is

$$\hat{H}_{\mathrm{so}} = \frac{1}{2m_e c^2}\frac{1}{r}\frac{\partial U(r)}{\partial r}\mathbf{L}\cdot\mathbf{S} = \xi(r)\mathbf{L}\cdot\mathbf{S}, \tag{3-14}$$

where $\mathbf{L}\cdot\mathbf{S}$ is the scalar product of the angular momenta vectors Eqs. (3-8) and (3-9), and $\xi(r)$ is a measure of the spin-orbit coupling. For hydrogenlike atoms, such as H, He^+, and Li^{2+},

$$U(r) = \frac{-Ze^2}{r} \qquad \text{and} \qquad \xi(r) = \frac{Ze^2}{2m_e^2 c^2 r^3}.$$

The spin-orbit interaction (multiplet splitting) energy is

$$E_{\mathrm{so}} = \frac{1}{\hbar^2}\int \psi'_{n,\ell,m_\ell,m_s}\hat{H}_{\mathrm{so}}\psi_{n,\ell,m_\ell,m_s}\,d\tau, \tag{3-15}$$

where $\hbar^2$ has been introduced in anticipation of normalizing $\mathbf{L}\cdot\mathbf{S}$ to a dimensionless parameter. Since $\xi(r)$ depends only on r, we can express E_{so} as the product of two integrals,

$$E_{\mathrm{so}} = \frac{1}{\hbar^2}\int \psi'_{n,\ell}(r)\xi(r)\psi_{n,\ell}(r)r^2\,dr \times \int \psi'_{\ell,m_\ell,m_s}(\theta,\phi)\mathbf{L}\cdot\mathbf{S}\psi_{\ell,m_\ell,m_s}(\theta,\phi)\sin\theta\,d\theta\,d\phi, \tag{3-16}$$

where

$$\int_0^\infty \psi'_{n,\ell}(r)\xi(r)\psi_{n,\ell}(r)r^2\,dr = A_{n,\ell}, \tag{3-17}$$

which is called the spin-orbit coupling constant for the levels $n\ell$. For hydrogenlike atoms,

$$A_{n,\ell} = \frac{Z^4 e^2 \hbar^2}{2m_e^2 c^2 a^3 n^3}\frac{1}{\ell(\ell+1)(\ell+\frac{1}{2})}\ \text{ergs}, \tag{3-18}$$

where a is the Bohr radius. Since $\mathbf{J} = \mathbf{L} + \mathbf{S}$, $\mathbf{J}^2 = \mathbf{L}^2 + \mathbf{S}^2 + 2\mathbf{L}\cdot\mathbf{S}$. Thus,

$$\mathbf{L}\cdot\mathbf{S} = \frac{\mathbf{J}^2 - \mathbf{L}^2 - \mathbf{S}^2}{2} = \frac{\hbar^2}{2}[J(J+1) - L(L+1) - S(S+1)], \tag{3-19}$$

and we obtain for E_{so}

$$E_{\mathrm{so}} = \tfrac{1}{2}A_{n,\ell}[J(J+1) - L(L+1) - S(S+1)]. \tag{3-20}$$

Since all the members of a given multiplet have the same L and S quantum numbers, ΔE_{so} for $J \rightarrow J + 1$ is

$$\Delta E_{so} = A_{n,\ell}(J + 1), \qquad \textbf{(3-21)}$$

where J is the lower state quantum number. This expression for ΔE_{so}, which is proportional to the multiplet splitting, is called the Landé interval rule. When the rule is applied to Example 3-2, $\Delta E_{so}(J = \frac{1}{2} \rightarrow J = \frac{3}{2}) = \frac{3}{2}A_{2,1}$. Since $\Delta E_{so} = 16.0\ \text{cm}^{-1}$, $A_{2,1} = 10.7\ \text{cm}^{-1}$.

For the many-electron case

$$\hat{H}_{so} = \sum_i \xi(r_i)\mathbf{L}_i \cdot \mathbf{S}_i, \qquad \textbf{(3-22)}$$

over all i electrons. This Hamiltonian includes only the interaction of each spin with its own orbital motion. It ignores orbit-orbit, spin-other-orbit, and spin-spin interactions. Proceeding in the manner above, we obtain in this case

$$E_{so} = \tfrac{1}{2}A_{n,L,S}[J(J + 1) - L(L + 1) - S(S + 1)], \qquad \textbf{(3-23)}$$

where the spin-orbit coupling constant is dependent on n, L, and S.

In a similar manner to Example 3-2, we can derive several term states for the carbon atom having two equivalent p electrons; since $L = 2$, $S = 1$, and $J = 3$, we obtain ${}^1S$, ${}^3P$, and ${}^1D$. In order to decide which is the ground state and what is the ordering of the multiplet J states for any one term, we cite Hund's rules:

1. For states with the same L, the one with the highest S is lowest in energy.
2. Of the states above with the same S, the one with the highest L is lowest in energy.
3. For multiplet J states: When a shell (or subshell) is less than half-full, states of low J are lower in energy; when a shell is more than half-full, states with higher J are lower in energy.[1]

With these rules applied in order, the lowest state is the ${}^3P_{2,1,0}$; and of these three angular momentum states for a subshell less than half-filled, we have the ground state ordering

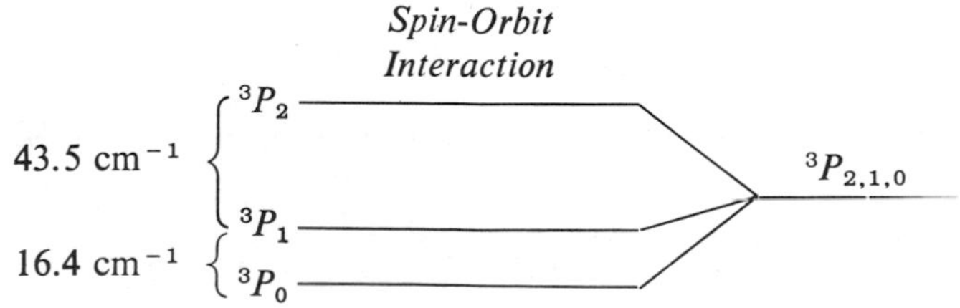

and separated by 16.4 and 43.5 cm^{-1} as shown. According to Eq. (3-23), the predicted ratio of the energy separations is 1:2, whereas the observed ratio is 16.4:43.5. This comparison provides a quantitative measure of the validity of the assumptions implicit in Eq. (3-22). Using Hund's rules for the boron example above, we find that the doublet ordering is

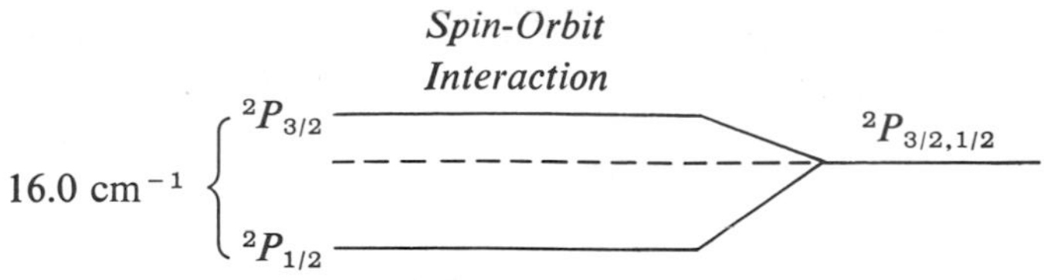

In order to decide which of the possible electronic term states exist, by applying the Pauli principle to those derived from the various L and S combinations, we must consider the summations $M_L = \sum_i m_{\ell_i}$ and $M_S = \sum_i m_{s_i}$ and avoid redundant configurations. In the case of carbon above, the vectorial additions of $L_{12} = 2, 1, 0$ and $S_{12} = 1, 0$ result in six possible states ^3D, ^3P, ^3S, ^1D, ^1P, and ^1S. For two equivalent p electrons, we can conveniently generate the possible states (and substates) by considering in turn those states with the highest total angular momentum (maximizing J), being careful to avoid redundancies. In this analysis, M_L replaces L and M_S replaces S in the generation of the various angular momentum states. The substates for each of the *allowed* term states above are generated by permuting the two equivalent electrons among the three p orbitals (np_{m_ℓ}).

If we consider first the state of greatest total angular momentum ^3D, there is no way to generate this configuration within the restriction of the Pauli principle. We conclude therefore that this state does not exist. On the other hand, the ^1D state ($L = +2$, $S = 0$) with its five substates are generated by the combinations $M_L = +2, +1, 0, -1, -2$ and $M_S = 0$.

M_L	$2p_{+1}$	$2p_0$	$2p_{-1}$	
+2	↑↓	—	—	
+1	↑	↓	—	
0	↑	—	↓	$M_S = 0$
−1	—	↑	↓	
−2	—	—	↑↓	

We should note that configurations such as $\underline{\uparrow\downarrow}$ and $\underline{\downarrow\uparrow}$ are considered to be identical on account of the indistinguishability of electrons in a single orbital. The five substates generated from the ^1D state are exactly those split by an external field (Zeeman or Stark effect).

The nine substates produced from the ^3P state ($L = +1$ and $S = 1$) having the combinations $M_L = +1, 0, -1$ and $M_S = +1, 0, -1$ are

	$2p_{+1}$	$2p_0$	$2p_{-1}$	M_S
$M_L = +1$	$\uparrow$	$\uparrow$	—	$+1$
	$\downarrow$	$\downarrow$	—	-1
	$\downarrow$	$\uparrow$	—	0
$M_L = 0$	$\uparrow$	—	$\uparrow$	$+1$
	$\downarrow$	—	$\downarrow$	-1
	$\downarrow$	—	$\uparrow$	0
$M_L = -1$	—	$\uparrow$	$\uparrow$	$+1$
	—	$\downarrow$	$\downarrow$	-1
	—	$\downarrow$	$\uparrow$	0

In this analysis, it is immaterial which configuration we use in the case of $M_L = -1$, $M_S = 0$ for the ^1D or ^3P ,as long as both are accounted for. Since there is no different way to generate a ^1P state ($L = +1$, $S = 0$) that would not be redundant with those above, we conclude that it also does not exist.

Finally, of the two S states, only the ^1S provides a different configuration from those above:

	$2p_{+1}$	$2p_0$	$2p_{-1}$	
$M_L = 0$	—	$\uparrow\downarrow$	—	$M_S = 0$

and no ^3S state exists. Thus, the possible states are $^1D_2$, $^3P_{2,1,0}$, and $^1S_0$. When these five electronic states are subjected to an external magnetic field, splitting of the degenerate J levels occurs to reveal these independent quantum states. The degeneracies for the $^1D_2$, $^3P_2$, $^3P_1$, $^3P_0$, and $^1S_0$ are 5, 5, 3, 1, and 1 respectively, for a total of 15. The degeneracy is given as $2J + 1$ for each J state. In the $^1D_2$ case $S = 0$ ($J = L$), and the quintet simply corresponds to the various M_L orientations between $+L$ and $-L$ shown above, whereas for the $^1S_0$ state $L = S = J = 0$ and it exhibits no external field splitting. (These concepts, which form the basis of the Zeeman effect, will be discussed in more detail in Section 3C.) As a general rule, the number of independent M_J states is dictated by the smaller angular momentum state (quantum number) of S or L, so that when $L > S$, there are $2S + 1$ states, and when $L < S$, there are $2L + 1$ states.

EXAMPLE 3-3: Derive all the possible electronic states for the electronic configuration. . . $2p^6 3s^2 3p^3$. From these, determine the states possible and the ground state according to the Pauli principle and Hund's rules.

Solution: (a) For three p electrons $\ell_1 = \ell_2 = \ell_3 = 1$. (In deriving terms, closed subshells can be omitted from consideration since $S = \sum_i s_i = 0$, $M_L = \sum_i m_{\ell_i} = 0$.)

Vectorial addition of electrons 1 and 2 gives $L_{12} = 2, 1, 0$; and vectorial addition of the third electron to L_{12} yields

$$L_{123}\begin{cases} 3, & 2, & 1, & \\ & 2, & 1, & 0 \\ & & 1, & \end{cases}$$
$$\overline{F(1),\ D(2),\ P(3),\ S(1)}$$

and correspondingly for the spin $S_{12} = 1, 0$; $S_{123} = \frac{3}{2}, \frac{1}{2}, \frac{1}{2}$.[2] Thus, there are

$$\begin{array}{llll} ^4F(1), & ^4D(2), & ^4P(3), & ^4S(1) \\ ^2F(1), & ^2D(2), & ^2P(3), & ^2S(1) \\ ^2F(1),^2 & ^2D(2), & ^2P(3), & ^2S(1) \end{array}$$

where the numbers in parentheses represent the number of equivalent terms in the case of three nonequivalent p electrons, which is *not* the case here. (b) According to the Pauli principle, no two electrons can have the same four quantum numbers (if the configuration were $3p\,4p\,5p$, then all twelve states would be possible). Since there is no way to permute three equivalent p electrons (with $m_\ell = 1$ each) to create a F state, no F states can exist. There is, additionally, no way to generate ^4D and ^4P states (three unpaired spins) with three equivalent p electrons; thus, of the quartic states, only the ^4S state is possible.

Since all three p electrons are in the same principal quantum shell and have the same azimuthal quantum number, $\ell = 1$, they form a triply degenerate set with m_ℓ values of $+1$, 0, and -1. The other possible states are conveniently generated by using the procedure illustrated above for the p^2 configuration; of the remaining states above, those possible are the $^2D_{5/2}$, $^2D_{3/2}$, $^2P_{3/2}$, and $^2P_{1/2}$, each of which is a single, nonredundant term. In order to decide which is the ground state, we simply apply Hund's rules. Therefore, $^4S_{3/2}$ state is of lowest energy (ground state).

2. *jj* Coupling

In the case of relatively large atoms, where the valence electrons are on the average further apart, separate $\boldsymbol{\ell}_i$ and $\mathbf{s}_i$ couplings between the individual electrons are considerably weaker. In fact, the spin-orbit magnetic interaction ($\boldsymbol{\ell}_i$ and $\mathbf{s}_i$) of each of the individual electrons is sufficiently large that a resultant $\mathbf{j}_i$ for each of them is a better description. Thus, the total angular momentum $\mathbf{J}$ is formed by the vectorial addition of the individual $\mathbf{j}_i$'s, $\sum_i j_i = J$. For the case of two electrons,

$$J = (j_1 + j_2), (j_1 + j_2 - 1), \ldots, |j_1 - j_2|. \tag{3-24}$$

There are actually few cases of pure *jj* coupling; instead, many more cases exist that are best described by the intermediate situation between

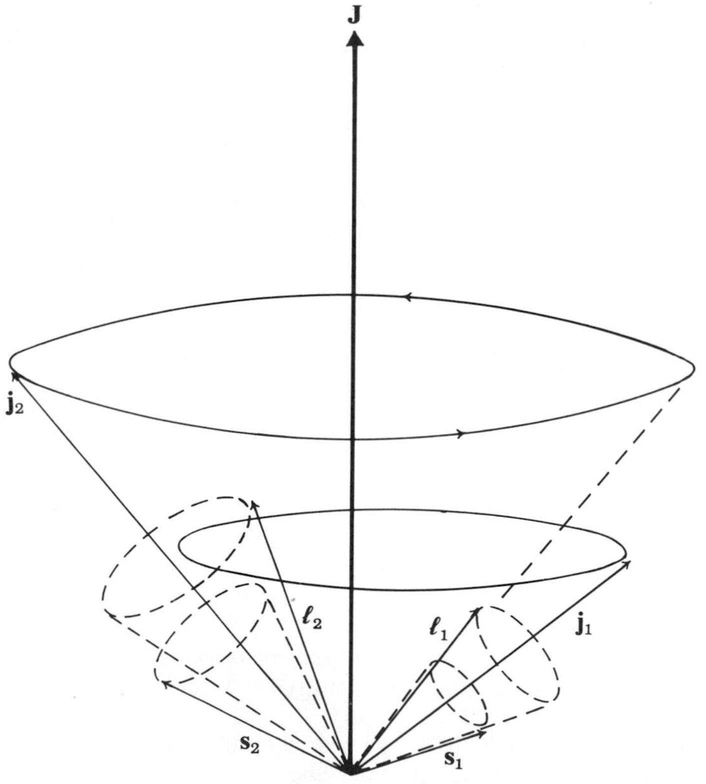

FIGURE 3-3 *jj* coupling for two electrons.

jj and *LS* coupling. Since the total angular momentum vector **J** is a constant of the motion and independent of either coupling situation, the same number of states are obtained, but with a variable energy, as one goes from *jj* to *LS* coupling.

EXAMPLE 3-4: Obtain the energy states for an *sp* configuration for both *LS* and *jj* coupling. Illustrate on an energy diagram, by a dotted line, the variable intermediate energy region.

Solution: (a) For *LS* coupling, an *sp* configuration will lead to the following states:

$$^3P_{2,1,0} \qquad \text{and} \qquad ^1P_1$$

For *jj* coupling, the *s* electron has $\ell_1 = 0$ and $s_1 = \frac{1}{2}$; thus $j_1 = \frac{1}{2}$ only. And the *p* electron has $\ell_2 = 1$ and $s_2 = \frac{1}{2}$; thus $j_2 = \frac{3}{2}$ and $\frac{1}{2}$. The total angular momentum vector is

$$J = \tfrac{3}{2} \tilde{+} \tfrac{1}{2} \qquad \text{and} \qquad \tfrac{1}{2} \tilde{+} \tfrac{1}{2}$$

(where $\tilde{+}$ indicates vector addition); thus the total angular momentum states are $J = 2$, 1, and 1, 0.

(b) The diagram herewith illustrates *LS* coupling on the left and *jj* coupling on the right.

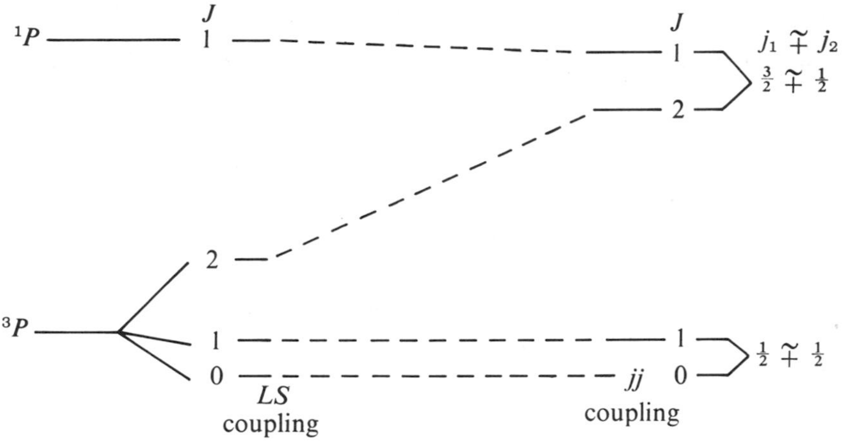

B. SELECTION RULES IN ATOMIC SPECTRA

At this point, the question of transitions between the various atomic states naturally arises. Since the absorption or emission of radiation results from the interaction of the oscillating electric-field vector of radiation with the instantaneous electric dipole moment of the atom or molecule, it is possible to generate a set of first-order electric dipole selection rules. As shown previously, Eq. (2-35), the intensity of a transition is directly proportional to the square of the transition moment matrix

$$|\langle\psi_m|\hat{\mu}|\psi_k\rangle|^2,$$

which for a complex atom is given as

$$\left|\left\langle \psi_m \left| \sum_i q\mathbf{r}_i \right| \psi_k \right\rangle\right|^2. \tag{3-25}$$

Thus, if this integral is zero, as a first-order effect the transition is "forbidden"; if the integral is nonzero, the transition is described as "allowed."

For one-electron atoms, Eq. (3-25) simplifies to

$$|\langle\psi_m|\hat{\mu}|\psi_k\rangle|^2 = q^2\{\langle\psi_m|x|\psi_k\rangle^2 + \langle\psi_m|y|\psi_k\rangle^2 + \langle\psi_m|z|\psi_k\rangle^2\}, \tag{3-26}$$

where the volume element in spherical coordinates is $d\tau = r^2 \sin\theta\, dr\, d\theta\, d\phi$, and the x, y, and z components are

$$\begin{aligned} x &= r\sin\theta\cos\phi \\ y &= r\sin\theta\sin\phi \\ z &= r\cos\theta. \end{aligned} \tag{3-27}$$

Considering first the z component of Eq. (3-26), we obtain for the final and initial quantum states $\psi'_{n\ell m_\ell}$ and $\psi_{n\ell m_\ell}$, respectively:

$$\begin{aligned} \langle\psi_m|z|\psi_k\rangle = \int_0^\infty \psi'_{n\ell}(r) r^3 \psi_{n\ell}(r)\, dr \int_0^\pi \psi'_{\ell m_\ell}(\theta)\psi_{\ell m_\ell}(\theta)\sin\theta\cos\theta\, d\theta \\ \times \int_0^{2\pi} \psi'_{m_\ell}(\phi)\psi_{m_\ell}(\phi)\, d\phi. \end{aligned} \tag{3-28}$$

The eigenfunctions for the ϕ integral have the general form $(2\pi)^{-1/2}e^{im_\ell\phi}$, thus

$$(2\pi)^{-1}\int_0^{2\pi} e^{i\phi\Delta m_\ell}\, d\phi, \tag{3-29}$$

which is zero if the exponential is not equal to unity, and if $\Delta m_\ell = 0$.[3] Thus, for radiation polarized in the z direction, transitions are allowed only for $m_\ell' = m_\ell$. Such transitions are described as π components. In a similar manner, the x and y terms respectively of the ϕ integral are

$$(2\pi)^{-1}\int_0^{2\pi} e^{i\phi m_\ell'}\cos\phi\, e^{-i\phi m_\ell}\, d\phi \quad \text{and} \quad (2\pi)^{-1}\int_0^{2\pi} e^{i\phi m_\ell'}\sin\phi\, e^{-i\phi m_\ell}\, d\phi, \tag{3-30}$$

where

$$\cos\phi = \tfrac{1}{2}(e^{i\phi} + e^{-i\phi}) \qquad \text{and} \qquad \sin\phi = \tfrac{1}{2i}(e^{i\phi} - e^{-i\phi}).$$

Substituting the $\cos\phi$ relation into the x integral yields

$$(4\pi)^{-1}\left\{\int_0^{2\pi} e^{i\phi(m_\ell' - m_\ell + 1)}\, d\phi + \int_0^{2\pi} e^{i\phi(m_\ell' - m_\ell - 1)}\, d\phi\right\}. \qquad \textbf{(3-30a)}$$

Again, the integral vanishes unless $\Delta m_\ell = \pm 1$. These transitions, excited by radiation polarized in the xy plane (circularly polarized radiation), are called σ components. A similar result is obtained for the y integral (Problem 3-3).

The other two integrals of Eq. (3-28) are more involved mathematically, and will not be evaluated here. The r integral, which can be solved using generating functions, results in no restriction on n transitions, $\Delta n = 0, 1, 2, 3, \ldots$. The θ integral, which leads to an associated Legendre function, is solved by using a recursion relation.[4] The selection rule on ℓ is $\Delta\ell = \pm 1$. This selection rule will be derived below using a symmetry argument.

One very general criterion in determining whether Eq. (3-25) will be zero or not has to do with the symmetry of the states involved. The eigenfunctions describing the various atomic states are either symmetric or antisymmetric to an inversion through the origin of the coordinates. That is, the wavefunction either changes sign or does not change sign when this symmetry operation is performed, and is accordingly described as "odd" or "even." For the case of hydrogenlike wavefunctions (Appendix II), it can be shown for an example that those states corresponding to $\ell = 0, 2, 4, \ldots$ are even and to $\ell = 1, 3, 5, \ldots$ are odd.

EXAMPLE 3-5: Show that the wavefunctions for the $n = 3$, $\ell = 1$ and 2 states for the "hydrogenlike" states in spherical coordinates are odd and even, respectively. From Appendix II, $\psi(\theta, \phi) = \psi(\theta)\psi(\phi)$.

$$n = 3, \ell = 1, m = +1, \psi(\theta, \phi) = (\tfrac{3}{4}\pi)^{1/2} \sin\theta \cos\phi.$$
$$n = 3, \ell = 2, m = +1, \psi(\theta, \phi) = (\tfrac{15}{4}\pi)^{1/2} \sin\theta \cos\theta \cos\phi.$$

Solution: The general effect of an inversion in spherical coordinates is to change $\theta \to (180° - \theta)$ and $\phi \to (180° + \phi)$. Thus, $\sin\theta$ does not change sign, but $\cos\theta$, $\cos\phi$, and $\sin\phi$ all change signs on inversion through the center of symmetry.

For $\ell = 1$, $(\tfrac{3}{4}\pi)^{1/2}(\overset{+}{\sin}\,\theta)(\overset{-}{\cos}\,\theta)$ $-$ odd.

For $\ell = 2$, $(\tfrac{15}{4}\pi)^{1/2}(\overset{+}{\sin}\,\theta)(\overset{-}{\cos}\,\theta)(\overset{-}{\cos}\,\phi)$ $+$ even.

From Eq. (3-25), the product to be integrated will be odd if ψ_m^* and ψ_k are both even or both odd, since $\mathbf{r}_i$ changes sign on inversion. The integration of this product effectively sums over equal negative and positive contributions, and the resulting integral is zero. The integral is, however, nonzero if the transition occurs between even and odd states. This general selection rule for dipole radiation, which applies not only to spherical systems, but whenever there is a center of symmetry, is called the Laporte rule,

$$\mathrm{u} \leftrightarrow \mathrm{g}, \ \mathrm{u} \not\leftrightarrow \mathrm{u}, \ \mathrm{g} \not\leftrightarrow \mathrm{g}, \tag{3-31}$$

where g (*gerade*) and u (*ungerade*) represent even and odd states, respectively, and $\leftrightarrow$ and $\not\leftrightarrow$ represent allowed and forbidden transitions. If an atom has more than one electron, the symmetry of the total wavefunction is approximated as the product of the various one-electron wavefunctions. Thus, the total wavefunction will be *gerade* or *ungerade* depending on whether $\sum_i \ell_i$ is even or odd. The result for one-electron transitions is $\Delta\ell$ must be ± 1.

Using the approximation of an isolated atom with the product of hydrogenlike wavefunctions representing the total wavefunction of the atom in a given state, first-order electric dipole selection rules for transitions involving the total wavefunction have been derived. They are:

1. $\Delta L = \pm 1, 0$ for multiple electron jumps and $\Delta\ell = \pm 1$, which follows from the Laporte rule for one-electron jumps.
2. $\Delta S = 0$; this rule results from the fact that the spin part of the wavefunctions in the transition moment integral forms an orthonormal set, and the product of two spin states of different multiplicity summed over all space is zero. This rule is sometimes called the prohibition of intercombination (an exception to this rule is the intense Hg 2537 Å line, $^1S_0 \leftarrow {}^3P_1$).
3. $\Delta J = 0, \pm 1$, except that $J = 0 \not\rightarrow J = 0$; this rule holds for both the LS and jj type of coupling since J is well defined in both cases.
4. $\Delta M_J = 0, \pm 1$, except that $M_J = 0 \not\rightarrow M_J = 0$, if $\Delta J = 0$; this rule obviously has meaning only when the atom is subjected to moderate external magnetic (Zeeman effect) or electric (Stark effect) fields.

EXAMPLE 3-6: Applying first-order electric dipole selection rules, derive the lowest excited state for Li, which involves an allowed transition to the ground state.

Solution: Ground state lithium is $1s^2 2s$ or $^2S_{1/2}$, where $J = \pm\frac{1}{2}$ are the orientations in an external field. Since $L = 0$, this is not a true "doublet" multiplet.

The lowest excited state is $1s^2 2p$, which leads to a $^2P_{1/2,3/2}$ multiplet (a true doublet). Since emission to the ground state $^2S_{1/2}$ will correspond to

$\Delta S = 0$, $\Delta\ell = -1$, and $\Delta J = 0$ and -1, these transitions correspond to the lowest allowed excited state emission processes. They are the well-known red doublet of lithium, shown in the accompanying diagram.

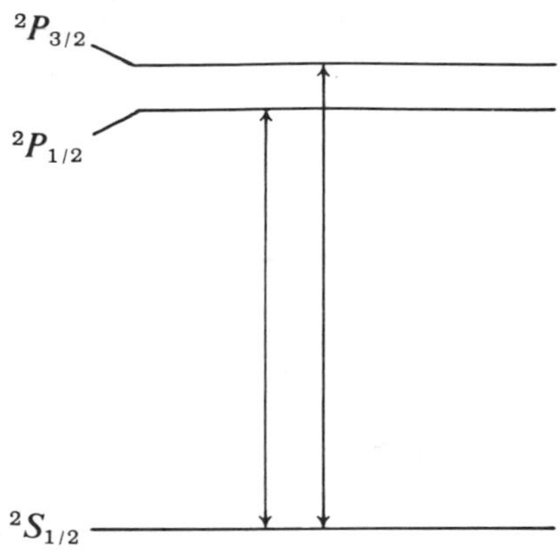

We have pointed out previously, in addition to the first-order electric dipole transition rules, weaker second-order quadrupole and magnetic dipole transitions. The selection rules governing these transitions are summarized herewith:

Quadrupole Selection Rules: $\Delta J = 0, \pm 1, \pm 2$, and $J' + J'' \geqslant 2$, where J' is the upper state and J'' the lower state.

$$\Delta L = 0, \pm 1, \pm 2, \text{ except that } L = 0 \not\rightarrow L = 0 \text{ and } \Delta S = 0.$$

Magnetic Dipole Selection Rules: $\Delta J = 0, \pm 1$, except that $J = 0 \not\rightarrow J = 0$.

$$\Delta L = 0, \pm 1.$$
$$\Delta S = 0.$$

Application of the first-order electric dipole selection rules to an atomic energy level system showing both *LS* and *jj* type coupling is shown in Figure 3-4. The energy-level diagram is that of the neutral germanium atom. Since it has an electronic configuration ($\cdots 4s^2 4p^2$) similar to the carbon configuration, exemplified previously, the ground state is $^3P_{0,1,2}$. Although the multiplet splitting of this state is very close to *LS* coupling, the upper electronic states are nearer to *jj* coupling. Thus, the term symbol designations are used more as a form of bookkeeping rather than to indicate the actual coupling. As a result, the observed transitions (indicated by solid lines) reflect one-electron *jj* transition rules ($\Delta J = \pm 1$, 0, and $\Delta S = 0$). The broken lines indicate forbidden transitions.

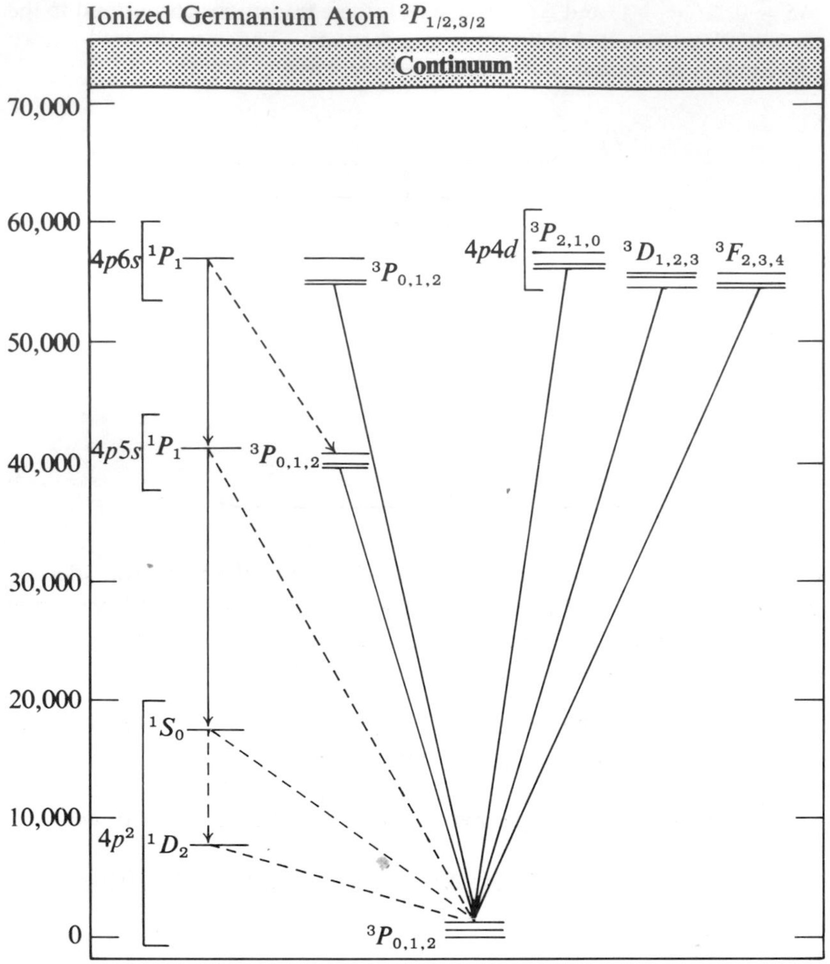

FIGURE 3-4. Energy-level diagram of the neutral germanium atom. The allowed (——) and forbidden (- - - -) transitions correspond to first-order electric dipole *jj* selection rules between the multiplet levels. Note the "inverted" J ordering of the $4p4d$ (^3P) configuration.

C. THE ZEEMAN EFFECT

In deriving electronic term symbols, constructing a **J** value was determined by the vectorial addition of a single **L** and **S** state. Recall, however, that the **L** and **S** states are degenerate, and such degeneracies if characterized by magnetic vectors should manifest themselves in an external magnetic field. The classical expression for the interaction energy of a magnetic vector with an external magnetic field is

$$E' = -\boldsymbol{\mu}\cdot\mathbf{H}, \tag{3-32}$$

where $\boldsymbol{\mu}$ is the total magnetic moment and $\mathbf{H}$ is the external magnetic field. For an atom, the total magnetic moment is the sum of those due to spin and rotation of the electrons:

$$\boldsymbol{\mu} = \boldsymbol{\mu}_{\mathbf{L}} + \boldsymbol{\mu}_{\mathbf{S}}. \tag{3-33}$$

According to classical physics, a spinning or rotating electronic charge will have a magnetic vector oriented along the rotation axis and opposite in direction to the spin or angular momentum vector $\mathbf{L}$ or $\mathbf{S}$ (due to the negatively charged electron). These are illustrated in Figure 3-5.

The magnetic moment of a rotating charge is classically expressed as the product of $q/2mc$ and the angular momentum. Thus for $\mu_{\mathbf{L}}$ we have

$$\mu_{\mathbf{L}} = -\frac{q}{2m_e c}\mathbf{L} \tag{3-34}$$

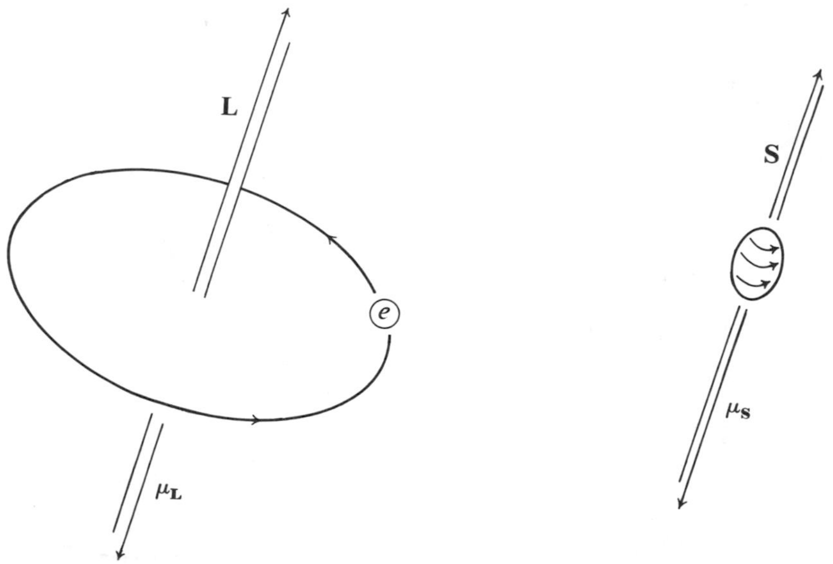

FIGURE 3-5 The angular ($\mu_{\mathbf{L}}$) and spin ($\mu_{\mathbf{S}}$) magnetic moments of a single electron generated by the rotational motion of the electronic charge. Note that they point in opposite directions to the angular and spin moments because of the negatively charged electron.

and for μ_S

$$\mu_S = -\frac{2q}{2m_e c}\,\mathbf{S}, \tag{3-35}$$

where the spin moment is twice as large as would be expected. As we shall see shortly, this important property gives rise to the "anomalous" Zeeman effect and is highly important in magnetic dipole transitions. As we previously stated, the total magnetic moment results from the vectorial addition of μ_L and μ_S illustrated in Figure 3-6. Since the spin magnetic moment is twice the magnitude of **S**, the resulting total magnetic moment μ does not lie along **J**. As a result, μ precesses about **J** and is not a constant of the total angular momentum. The interaction between this precession (oscillation) of the atomic magnetic dipole and the magnetic vector of the radiation field (Figure 2-1) results in magnetic dipole absorption and emission.

The precession of μ about **J** effectively averages to zero all components of μ except the one directed along **J**, $\bar{\mu}_J$, which is a constant of the total angular momentum. At moderate magnetic fields, the precession

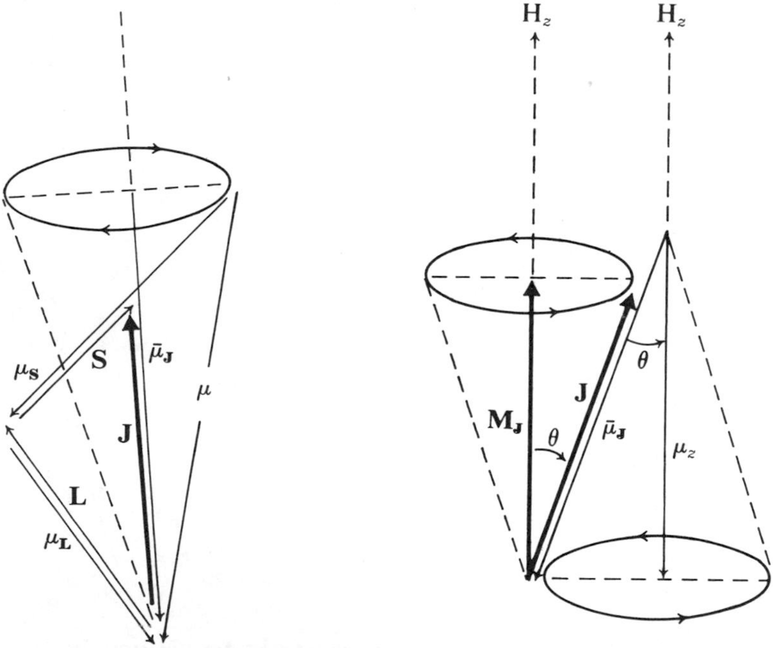

FIGURE 3-6 (a) Vectorial addition of the μ_L and μ_S to give μ, which does not lie along **J**, since μ_L = **L** and μ_S = 2**S**. μ precesses about **J** to produce the average component μ_J. (b) Precession of μ_J about the external field H_z producing the field component μ_z.

of μ about **J** is generally faster than the Larmor precession of **J** about the magnetic field. Therefore it is this average component ($\bar{\mu}_\mathbf{J}$) that interacts with the external magnetic field, and Eq. (3-32) becomes for the field oriented along the z direction

$$E' = -\mu_z \cdot \mathbf{H}_z = \bar{\mu}_\mathbf{J} \cos\theta\, \mathbf{H}_z, \qquad \textbf{(3-36)}$$

where

$$\cos\theta = \frac{\mathbf{M_J}}{\mathbf{J}} = \frac{M_J}{\sqrt{J(J+1)}} \quad \text{and} \quad \mu_\mathbf{J} = -\frac{q}{2m_e c}\,\mathbf{J}. \qquad \textbf{(3-37)}$$

M_J is the projection of J along the magnetic field direction z, and illustrates the space degeneracy of J. Note that J does not lie along the field axis but is oriented with respect to a specific angle θ, which corresponds to integral or half-integral quantized values of the M_J and J quantum numbers. The space degeneracy (quantization) for the $J = 1$ and $J = 2$ states is shown in Figure 3-7.

The total magnetic vector oriented along the field direction is $\mu_z = -\bar{\mu}_\mathbf{J} \cos\theta$, and is also given as (Eq. 3-37),

$$\mu_z = -\frac{q}{2m_e c}\,\mathbf{M_J} = -\frac{q\hbar}{2m_e c}\,M_J. \qquad \textbf{(3-38)}$$

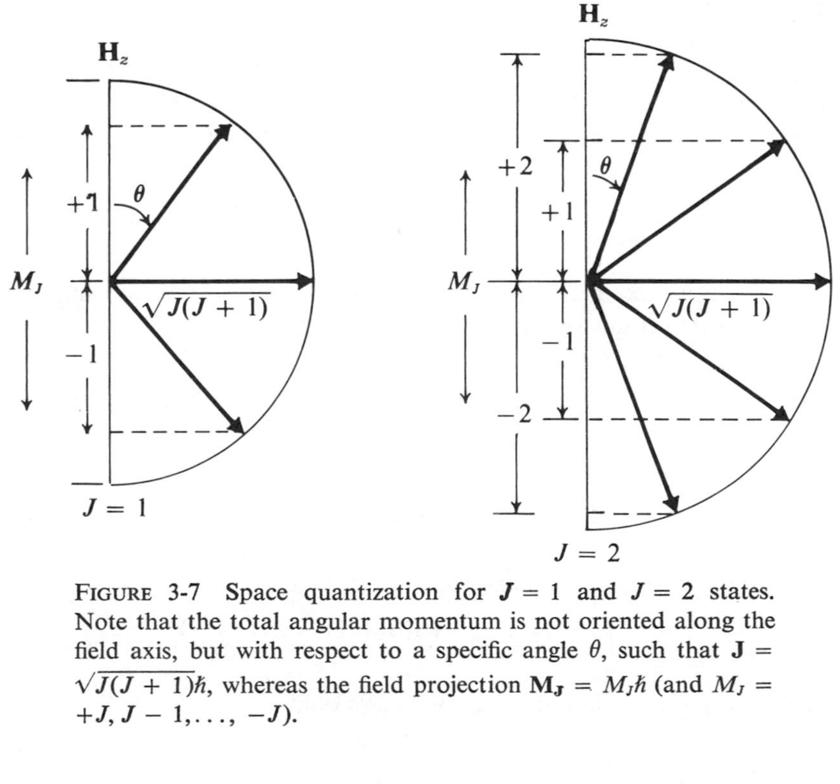

FIGURE 3-7 Space quantization for $J = 1$ and $J = 2$ states. Note that the total angular momentum is not oriented along the field axis, but with respect to a specific angle θ, such that $\mathbf{J} = \sqrt{J(J+1)}\hbar$, whereas the field projection $\mathbf{M_J} = M_J\hbar$ (and $M_J = +J, J-1, \ldots, -J$).

Substituting Eq. (3-38) into Eq. (3-36), we obtain for the interaction energy

$$E' = \frac{q\hbar}{2m_e c}\mathbf{H}_z M_J. \qquad \textbf{(3-39)}$$

The quantity $q\hbar/2m_e c$, defined as the Bohr magneton μ_β, is 0.927×10^{-20} erg-gauss^{-1}.

Let us consider for the moment applying Eq. (3-38) to the special cases of $S = 0$ and $L = 0$, first, the case of zero spin state, $S = 0$ and $J = L$, then according to Eqs. (3-38) and (3-34), $-\mu_z = \mu_\beta M_J$ as shown. The application of an external magnetic field will simply cause a splitting of the various space-fixed L configurations. On the other hand, for the case of a zero orbital angular momentum state, $L = 0$ and $J = S$, we obtain from Eqs. (3-35) and (3-38), $\mu_z = -2\mu_\beta M_J$. This example suggests that the general form of Eq. (3-38) should be

$$\mu_z = -\mu_\beta g M_J, \qquad \textbf{(3-38a)}$$

where the factor g introduced here is a constant for a particular J state. Its magnitude depends on the values of L and S and it is called the Landé g factor.

The generalized value of g can be determined from a reexamination of Figure 3-6a. The components of $\mu_\mathbf{L}$ and $\mu_\mathbf{S}$ along J (Eqs. (3-34) and (3-35)) give the resultant $\bar{\mu}_\mathbf{J}$:

$$\bar{\mu}_\mathbf{J} = [\sqrt{L(L+1)}\cos(\mathbf{L},\mathbf{J}) + 2\sqrt{S(S+1)}\cos(\mathbf{S},\mathbf{J})]\mu_\beta, \qquad \textbf{(3-40)}$$

where we have dropped the minus sign since the direction of the magnetic moments are all the same in this analysis. If the bracketed expression is equated to $g\sqrt{J(J+1)}$, we obtain

$$g\sqrt{J(J+1)} = [\sqrt{L(L+1)}\cos(\mathbf{L},\mathbf{J}) + 2\sqrt{S(S+1)}\cos(\mathbf{S},\mathbf{J})]. \qquad \textbf{(3-41)}$$

The cosine expressions can be obtained from Figure 3-6a using the law of cosines for this vector triangular system (Appendix V). We obtain for these two expressions

$$S(S+1) = L(L+1) + J(J+1) - 2\sqrt{L(L+1)}\sqrt{J(J+1)}\cos(\mathbf{L},\mathbf{J}) \qquad \textbf{(3-42)}$$

and

$$L(L+1) = S(S+1) + J(J+1) - 2\sqrt{S(S+1)}\sqrt{J(J+1)}\cos(\mathbf{S},\mathbf{J}). \qquad \textbf{(3-43)}$$

Substituting into Eq. (3-41) and solving for g yields

$$g = 1 + \frac{J(J+1) + S(S+1) - L(L+1)}{2J(J+1)}. \qquad \textbf{(3-44)}$$

Substituting Eq. (3-38a) into Eq. (3-36), we obtain

$$E' = \mu_\beta \mathbf{H}_z g M_J. \qquad \textbf{(3-45)}$$

The energy of any state in the presence of the field is

$$E = E^0 + E', \tag{3-46}$$

where E^0 and E' are the field-free and field-split energy states. For transitions between states having identical g values in the presence of the field

$$\Delta E = \Delta E^0 + \Delta E' = \Delta E^0 + \mu_\beta \mathbf{H}_z g \cdot \Delta M_J. \tag{3-47a}$$

Applying the selection rules summarized in the previous section for ΔM_J, we get

$$\Delta E = \Delta E^0 \qquad \pi \text{ components}; \tag{3-48a}$$

$$\Delta E = \Delta E^0 \pm \mu_\beta \mathbf{H}_z g \quad \sigma \text{ components}. \tag{3-48b}$$

For singlet states ($S = 0$), $g = 1$ (Eq. (3-44)), and the splitting is the same for all J states. As a result, transitions occurring between these Zeeman-split levels will simply give rise to three components: those corresponding to $\Delta M = -1, 0, +1$. The reason for this simplified behavior can be understood by examining Figure 3-6. If $S = 0$, then the magnitude of $L = \mu_\mathbf{L} = \mu_\mathbf{J} = J = \mu$. In this case μ does lie along $\mathbf{J}$, and no "anomalously" large $\mu_\mathbf{S}$ vector is involved. This type of splitting

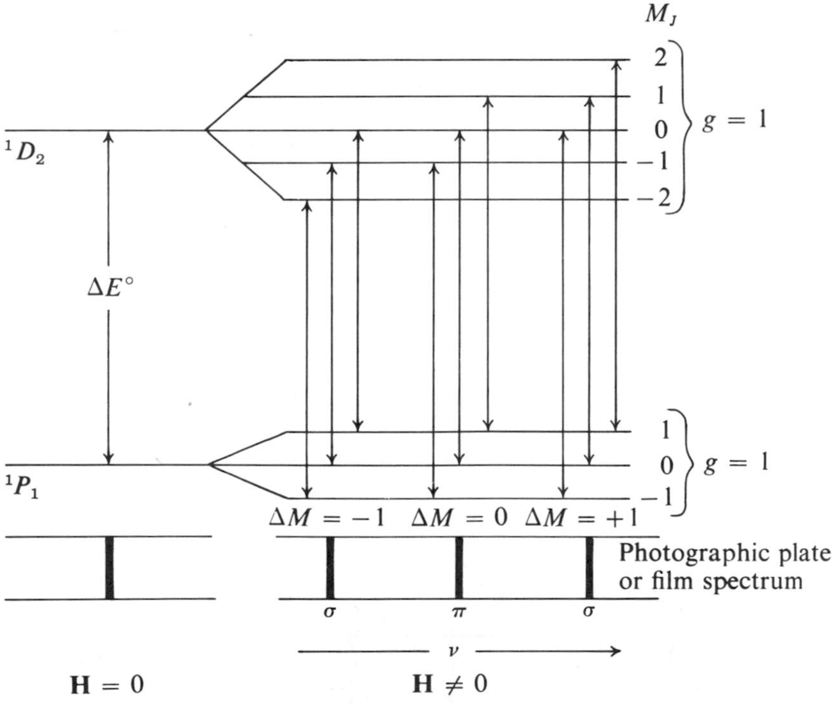

FIGURE 3-8 "Normal" Zeeman splitting for the transition $^1P_1 \rightarrow {}^1D_2$ gives rise to the simplified three-line spectrum.

is called the "normal" Zeeman effect. The transitions between the field split $^1P_1 \rightarrow {}^1D_2$ states are shown in Figure 3-8 and illustrate the normal Zeeman pattern. Notice also that the transitions $\Delta M_J = 0$ coincide with the zero-field transition ΔE^0.

When the spin of the various J states is not zero, then vectorial addition of the $\mu_{\mathbf{L}}$ and $\mu_{\mathbf{S}}$ components gives rise to a μ component that does not lie along **J**. According to Eq. (3-44), g is not unity, and therefore the splitting of a given J state is not determined by M_J alone but by the product $M_J g$. As a result, transitions in a magnetic field between states of different g will contain as many lines as are allowed transitions. This effect, which results from the apparent anomalously large spin magnetic moment is called the "anomalous Zeeman effect." The transition energy in this case is

$$\Delta E = \Delta E^0 + \mu_\beta \mathbf{H}_z \Delta(M_J g). \qquad \textbf{(3-47b)}$$

EXAMPLE 3-7: Illustrate the anomalous Zeeman splitting and the allowed transitions for the lithium "red doublet." Calculate the frequency shift and direction for the $M_J'' = -\frac{1}{2} \rightarrow M_J' = +\frac{1}{2}$ transition in a 10^4 gauss magnetic field.

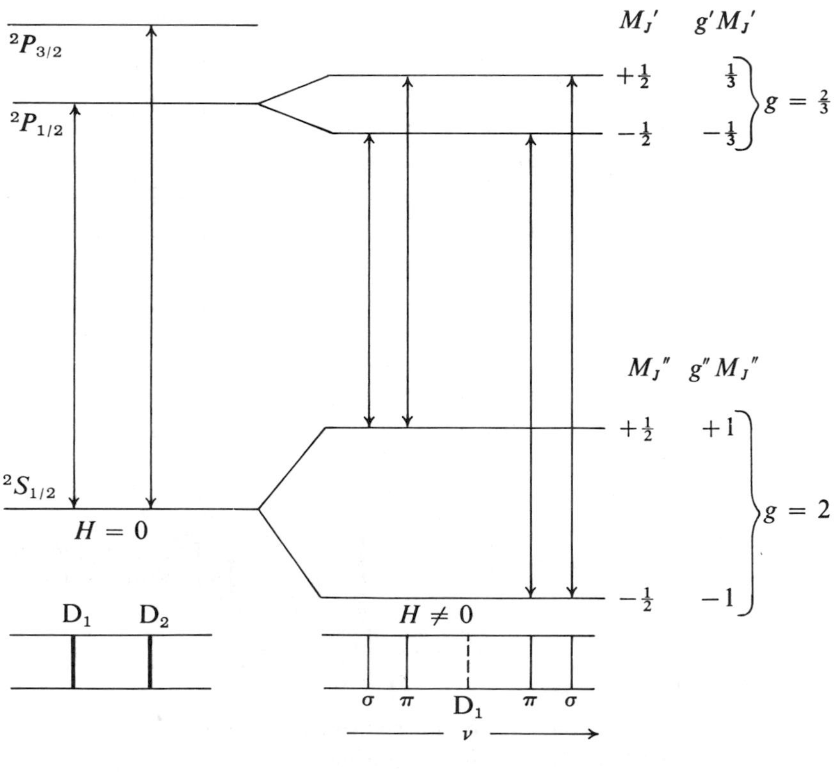

Solution: The shifted frequency corresponding to a σ transition above is given by the second term on the right of Eq. (3-47b).

$$\begin{aligned}\Delta E_s &= \mu_\beta H_z \Delta(gM_J) = \mu_\beta \mathbf{H}_z(g'M_J' - g''M_J'') \\ &= (0.927 \times 10^{-20}\ \text{erg/gauss})(10^4\ \text{gauss})(\tfrac{1}{3} + 1) \\ &= 1.236 \times 10^{-16}\ \text{erg.}\end{aligned}$$

$$\Delta\nu_s = \frac{\Delta E_s}{h} = \frac{1.236 \times 10^{-16}\ \text{erg}}{6.62 \times 10^{-27}\ \text{erg-sec}} = 1.867 \times 10^{10}\ \text{sec}^{-1}\ \text{upfield.}$$

D. THE PASCHEN-BACK EFFECT

At moderate magnetic field strengths (10^3 to 10^4 gauss), the J vector resulting from the weak LS coupling precesses about the external field (Figure 3-6). The angular velocity of this precessional motion is directly proportional to the magnetic field strength, and characterized by the interaction energy of Eq. (3-45):

$$\omega = 2\pi\nu = \frac{E'}{\hbar M_J} = g\frac{q\mathbf{H}_z}{2m_e c} = g\omega_L\ \text{radians}\quad \text{sec}^{-1}, \tag{3-49}$$

where ω_L is defined as the Larmor angular velocity, and correspondingly $\omega_L = 2\pi\nu_L$, thus

$$\nu_L = \frac{q\mathbf{H}_z}{4\pi m_e c} = 1.409 \times 10^6\ \mathbf{H}_z\ \text{cycle sec}^{-1}\ \text{(Hz)}, \tag{3-49a}$$

where ν_L is called the Larmor frequency. As the magnetic field strength increases, so does the precessional motion of **J** about $\mathbf{H}_z$ and the magnetic splitting of the space-fixed **J** states (Figure 3-7). When the magnetic splitting exceeds the multiplet splitting (resulting from spin-orbit interaction), the **L** and **S** vectors are unable to remain weakly coupled about the rapidly rotating **J** vector. As a result, they uncouple and separately precess about the external field producing space-fixed M_S and M_L states. The space-fixed M_L states have values $+L, L - 1$ to $-L$, and each of these $2L + 1$ states are further split into $+S, S - 1, \ldots, -S$ components $(2S + 1)$. The selection rules for transitions between these split states are as before, $\Delta M_L = \pm 1, 0$ and $\Delta M_S = 0$. This splitting at very large magnetic fields is called the Paschen-Back effect. The $^3S \rightarrow {}^3P$ transitions occurring for the Paschen-Back splitting is shown in Figure 3-9. The spectrum obtained consists of three closely spaced triplets corresponding to the transitions $\Delta M = -1, 0$, and $+1$. In fact, the transitions due to $\Delta M = 0$ (π components) are practically superimposed due to the symmetrical splitting of the $M_L = 0$ state, which in turn practically equals

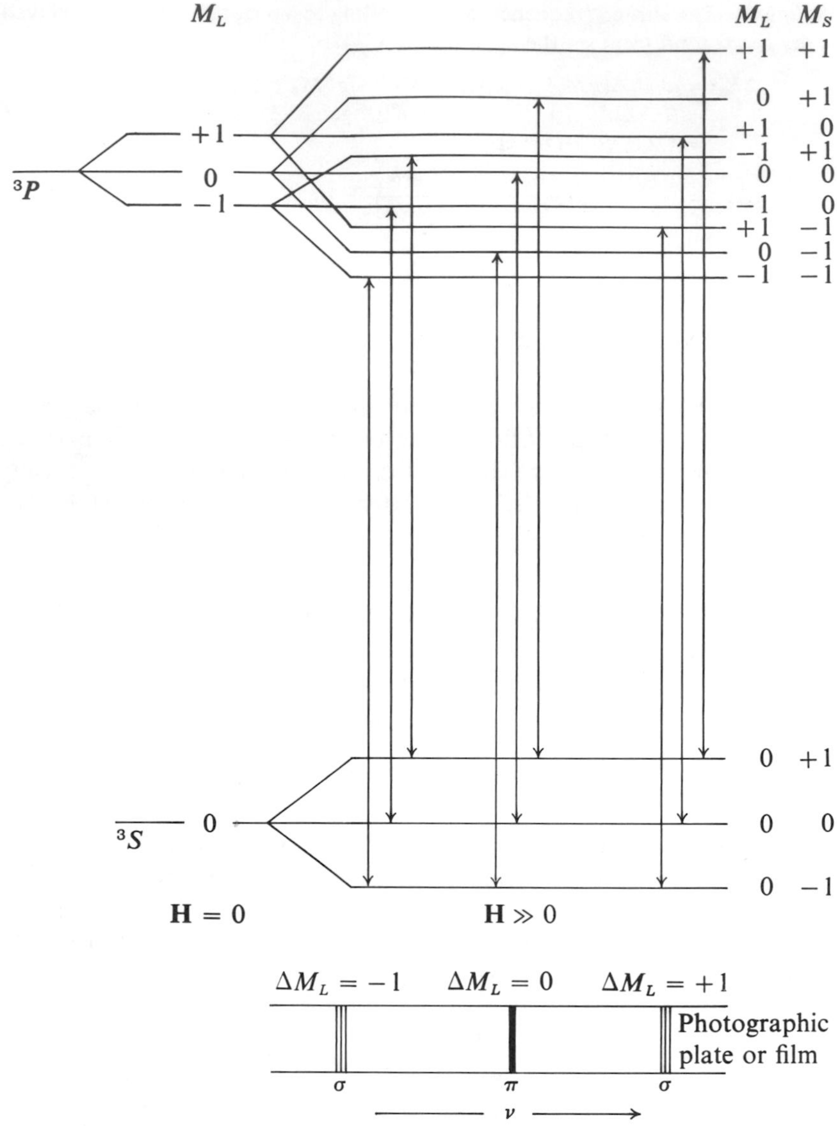

FIGURE 3-9 Paschen-Back effect for the $^3S \rightarrow {}^3P$ transitions in a strong magnetic field resulting in three sets of triplets.

the splitting of the ^3S lower state (approximately the "normal" Zeeman splitting). The other two components of the ^3P state ($M_L = +1$ and -1) are unsymmetrically split since a small degree of LS interaction still occurs. Apart from the triplet splitting, the spectrum is very similar to that of the normal Zeeman effect. The energy splitting for the various states (omitting the *LS* interaction) according to Eqs. (3-32), (3-33), (3-34), and (3-35) is

$$\Delta E' = \mu_\beta \mathbf{H}_z M_L + 2\mu_\beta \mathbf{H}_z M_S, \tag{3-50}$$

where the spin angular momentum is twice the orbital angular momentum.[5]

EXAMPLE 3-8: Calculate the Larmor frequency of a free oxygen atom subjected to an external magnetic field of 10^4 gauss. Also calculate the magnetic energy splitting of the $^2D_{3/2}$ state, and compare with the multiplet splitting (of $^2D_{5/2,3/2}$) of 2.75 cm^{-1}. Would you expect the magnetic field spectrum between these levels to be of the *LS* or the Paschen-Back type (approximately normal Zeeman)?

Solution: (a) The Larmor frequency, which depends solely on the magnetic field strength, is given by Eq. (3-49a):

$$\begin{aligned}\nu_L &= 1.409 \times 10^6 \mathbf{H}_z \text{ gauss}^{-1}\text{ sec}^{-1} = (1.409 \times 10^6)(10^4)\\ &= 1.409 \times 10^{10} \text{ sec}^{-1}\text{, or}\\ &= \frac{1.409 \times 10^{10}\text{ sec}^{-1}}{3.0 \times 10^{10}\text{ cm-sec}^{-1}} = 0.469 \text{ cm}^{-1}.\end{aligned}$$

This result indicates that the precessional motion occurs at microwave frequencies at this field strength.

(b) The magnetic energy splitting ($\Delta M_J = +1$) according to Eq. (3-45), assuming *LS* coupling, is

$$\begin{aligned}\Delta\tilde{E}'(\text{cm}^{-1}) &= \frac{\Delta E'}{hc} = \frac{\mu_\beta}{hc}\Delta M_J g \mathbf{H}_z\\ &= \frac{(0.93 \times 10^{-20}\text{ erg-gauss}^{-1})\mathbf{H}_z g}{(6.62 \times 10^{-27}\text{ erg-sec})(3 \times 10^{10}\text{ cm-sec}^{-1})}\\ \Delta\tilde{E}'(\text{cm}^{-1}) &= 0.47 \times 10^{-4} g \mathbf{H}_z \text{ gauss}^{-1}\text{ cm}^{-1}.\end{aligned}$$

Substituting $g = \frac{4}{5}$ for the $^2D_{3/2}$ state and $\mathbf{H}_z = 10^4$ gauss, we obtain

$$\Delta\tilde{E}'(\text{cm}^{-1}) = 0.376 \text{ cm}^{-1}.$$

Since $\Delta\tilde{E}'_{\text{splitting}} < \Delta\tilde{E}_{\text{multiplet}}$, *LS* coupling is still predominant and should be reflected in the magnetic field spectrum.

E. THE STARK EFFECT

The interaction of a static external electric field with an atom first causes a separation of charge (polarization) resulting in an induced electric dipole moment. The interaction of the electric field and this induced electric dipole causes a resulting shift in the field free-energy levels. In relatively moderate electric fields, the shifted energy levels can be calculated using perturbation methods. In an electric field, the change in energy is equal to the product of the induced dipole and the electric field, $m_e \cdot \mathbf{E}$. The induced dipole is $m_e = \alpha\mathbf{E}$, where α is the polarizability of the various J states. Thus, the change in energy caused by an electric field is proportional to the square of the electric field, and is a second-order effect. The J states, having slightly different polarizabilities, lead to the various M_J states,

$$M_J = J, J - 1, J - 2, \ldots -J. \tag{3-51}$$

In this case, however, states differing only in the sign of M_J correspond to simply reversing the directions of motion of all the electrons, and do not affect the magnitude of the induced dipole moment. Therefore, equivalent M_J states differing only in sign will be shifted by the same magnitude and in the same direction by external electric fields. The number of split states for a given J is $J + \frac{1}{2}$ and $J + 1$ for half-integral and integral J states. The M_J ordering for a given J splitting is from the lowest $\pm M_J$ to the highest with increasing energy. The Stark splitting of the lithium "red doublet" is shown in Figure 3-10. The selection rules for M_J are the same as in the Zeeman effect $\Delta M_J = 0$ and ± 1. As illustrated, the second-order effect for atoms is negative and results in the shifting of split levels to lower energy.

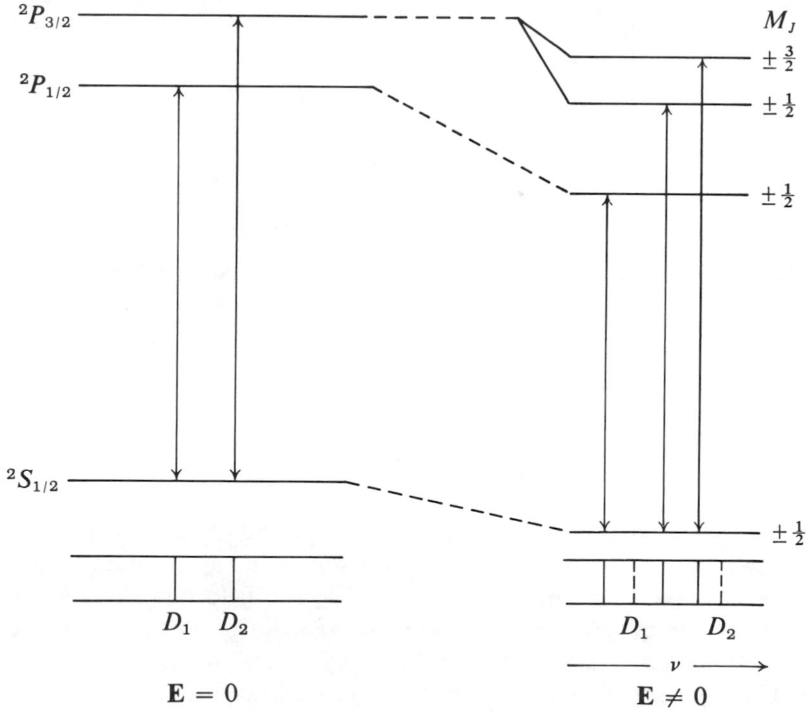

FIGURE 3-10 Stark effect splitting and allowed transitions for the lithium "red doublet" in an electric field.

In general, it is found that Stark atomic spectra provide less information in terms of the spectral analysis than does the Zeeman experiment. The Stark effect does provide, however, the most accurate method for determining molecular dipole moments (Section 4G-3).

SELECTED BIBLIOGRAPHY

3-1. Condon, E. U., and Shortley, G. H. *The Theory of Atomic Spectra.* New York: Cambridge University Press, 1964.
3-2. Herzberg, Gerhard. *Atomic Spectra and Atomic Structure.* New York: Dover Publications, 1945.
3-3. Penner, S. S. *Quantitative Molecular Spectroscopy and Gas Emissivities.* Reading, Mass.: Addison-Wesley Publishing Co., 1959.
3-4. Pilar, Frank L. *Elementary Quantum Chemistry.* New York: McGraw-Hill Book Co., 1968.
3-5. Sandorfy, C. *Electronic Spectra and Quantum Chemistry.* Englewood Cliffs, N.J.: Prentice-Hall, 1964.
3-6. White, Harvey E. *Introduction to Atomic Spectra.* New York: McGraw-Hill Book Co., 1934.

GLOSSARY OF SYMBOLS

Atomic Spectroscopy

$\hat{H}$	Hamiltonian operator
$\mathbf{S}$	Spin angular momentum
$\mathbf{L}$	Orbital angular momentum
$\mathbf{J}$	Total angular momentum
$\boldsymbol{\mu}_\mathbf{J}$	Magnetic moment along $\mathbf{J}$
$\boldsymbol{\mu}_\mathbf{L}$	Orbital magnetic moment
$\boldsymbol{\mu}_\mathbf{S}$	Spin magnetic moment
μ_β	Bohr magneton
ν_L	Larmor precessional frequency

ENDNOTES

1. In the case where the subshell is half-filled, $L = 0$, and no spin orbit coupling exists; then $J = S$, and hence there is no multiplet J structure.
2. This spin state and row of term symbol states are to be distinguished from the apparently similar set, since they are derived from a different vectorial addition.

3. This is easily proved by substituting the approximate relation $e^{i\mathbf{a}} = \cos \mathbf{a} + i \sin \mathbf{a}$ into the integral and integrating the resulting sine and cosine functions from 0 to 2π; both integrals are zero (with the quantization restriction that Δm_ℓ be integral).
4. Reference 3-4, p. 164.
5. The small energy perturbation resulting from the LS interaction is AM_SM_L (where A is a constant), thus for $M_L = 0$, the splitting that occurs is symmetrical since this term is zero. In the cases where $M_L \neq 0$, the fine splitting is a measure of the LS interaction.

PROBLEMS

3-1. Derive the three lowest electronic multiplet states for the free oxygen atom. Deduce the ground state and the J ordering.

3-2. Evaluate the total number of independent quantum states resulting from those possible, deduced in Example 3-3. Also evaluate the statistical weight (degeneracy) of each spin-orbit split state.

3-3. Derive the selection rules for the y component of the magnetic quantum number m_ℓ.

3-4. Using the "hydrogenlike" wavefunctions listed in Appendix II, show that the single electron transition $n = 1, \ell = 0, m = 0 \rightarrow n = 3, \ell = 2, m = +1$ is forbidden by a first order dipole transition. Would it be allowed either as a quadrupole or magnetic transition? Why?

3-5. Using a symmetry argument along with Eqs. (2-49) and (3-8), show that an electric dipole effect and an electric quadrupole effect for the same transition are mutually exclusive.

3-6. Making the trigonometric substitution $e^{i\mathbf{a}} = \cos \mathbf{a} + i \sin \mathbf{a}$ into either integral of Eq. (3-30a), show that the integral is zero unless the exponential is unity.

3-7. a. Determine the ground-state term symbol of the beryllium atom and the term symbol of the lowest excited state to which an "allowed" transition will occur following the atomic selection rules.

b. Show how the two states are split by an external magnetic field.

c. How many different lines are observed and what are the ratios of intensities when fine structure is resolved in an external magnetic field?

3-8. Illustrate the anomalous Zeeman splitting and the allowed transitions for the ${}^2S_{1/2} \rightarrow {}^2P_{3/2}$ system of the D_2 lithium "red doublet."

3-9. Derive the electronic term states for the configuration $\cdots 2s3s4d$ having three nonequivalent electrons.

3-10. Draw the Paschen-Back splittings and transitions for the ${}^2S \rightarrow {}^2P$ system characteristic of ns^1 configurations.

3-11. Calculate the Larmor frequency and the magnetic splittings for the ${}^3P_1$ state of the ${}^3P_{0,1,2}$ multiplet of Be for $\mathbf{H}_z \sim 10^3$. For a total multiplet splitting of the first ${}^3P$ level of 3.03 cm^{-1}, estimate the magnetic field strength where LS coupling begins to break down.

3-12. The oxygen atom, O, has a ground-state term symbol $^3P_{2,1,0}$, indicating three closely spaced electronic states and closely spaced excited states $^3D_{3,2,1}$.

a. Draw these multiplet states according to increasing energy.

b. Using the atomic selection rules, indicate *all* allowed transitions by solid lines and nonallowed transitions by dotted lines.

c. Draw the Zeeman magnetic field splittings and transitions between any two of these allowed J transitions using the notation of part b. Illustrate these on a plate spectrum and indicate the order of increasing frequency.

3-13. At what approximate frequency and region of the electromagnetic spectrum does the Larmor precession of J about **H** break down for the free lithium atom with a $^2P_{3/2,1/2}$ multiplet splitting of ~ 0.3 cm^{-1}? Compare with sodium, which has a multiplet splitting of ~ 17 cm^{-1}; thus a field of 30,000 gauss in this case is still a "weak" field.

Chapter 4

Rotational Spectroscopy

When we previously considered the total Hamiltonian for atomic systems, simplification of the energy expression resulted from the various assumptions concerning the potential energy—for example, central field approximation. As we might expect, the total Hamiltonian characterizing the energy of molecular systems contains more terms that are unknown, and also these are more difficult to estimate. In spite of these difficulties, Born and Oppenheimer examined this problem in 1927, and showed that to a very good approximation, the energy characterizing the electronic motion could be separated from the energy characterizing the nuclear motions (vibration and rotation) of a molecular system. The Schrödinger equation (Eq. (2-9)) describing the electronic energy of a molecular system is

$$\left[-\frac{h^2}{8\pi^2 m}\sum_i \nabla_i^2 + \sum_{i,i'}\frac{\mathbf{e}^2}{r_{ii'}} + \sum_{i,j}\frac{Z\mathbf{e}^2}{r_{ij}} + \sum_{j,j'}\frac{ZZ'\mathbf{e}^2}{r_{jj'}}\right]\Psi_{\text{el}} = E_{\text{el}}\Psi_{\text{el}}, \qquad \textbf{(4-1)}$$

where i refers to the electrons and j to the nuclei. The first term of the Hamiltonian is just the kinetic energy of the system; the second, third, and fourth terms are potential energy expressions corresponding to electron-electron, nuclear-electron, and nuclear-nuclear interactions. This equation will be considered later in the chapter dealing with electronic spectroscopy. The equation describing the nuclear energy of the system is

$$\left[-\frac{h^2}{8\pi^2}\sum_j \frac{\nabla_j^2}{m_j} + U(j, j')\right]\Psi_{\text{n}} = E_{\text{n}}\Psi_{\text{n}}, \qquad \textbf{(4-2)}$$

where the first and second terms on the left are simply the kinetic and potential energies of the nuclear motion in the field of the electrons, and Ψ_{n} represents the total nuclear wavefunction.

A. DIATOMIC MOLECULES

When Eq. (4-2) is applied to a diatomic molecule, the potential energy expression simplifies to $U(r)$, since it is characterized by the single internuclear distance. Near the bottom of the potential energy curve, where no significant population of vibrational states of quantum number greater than $\mathbf{v} = 0$ exists at ordinary termperatures, this expression is suitably represented as a Taylor series expansion,

$$U(r) = U_{r=r_e} + (r - r_e)\left(\frac{\partial U}{\partial r}\right)_{r=r_e} + \tfrac{1}{2}(r - r_e)^2\left(\frac{\partial^2 U}{\partial r^2}\right)_{r=r_e} + \cdots \quad (4\text{-}3)$$

The first derivative at a minimum is zero and the $U_{r=r_e}$ term is taken as the origin of the potential energy.[1] Thus, Eq. (4-3) reduces to the Hooke's law potential,

$$U(r) = \tfrac{1}{2}kq^2, \quad (4\text{-}4)$$

where

$$k = \left(\frac{\partial^2 U}{\partial r^2}\right)_{r=r_e} \quad \text{and} \quad q = r - r_e \quad (4\text{-}5)$$

and the Hamiltonian is given as

$$\left[-\frac{h^2}{8\pi^2}\left(\frac{\nabla_1{}^2}{m_1} + \frac{\nabla_2{}^2}{m_2}\right) + \tfrac{1}{2}kq^2\right]\Psi_n = E_n\Psi_n. \quad (4\text{-}6)$$

This equation can be conveniently solved as a general two-body problem (exactly as the hydrogen atom), if it is transformed to center of mass and cartesian displacement coordinates. Two separate equations are obtained from this transformation. One in center-of-mass coordinates represents the translational or kinetic energy of the $(m_1 + m_2)$ system; the other, which is of interest here, represents the internal energy due to the motion of the nuclei,

$$\left[-\frac{h^2}{8\pi^2\mu}\cdot\nabla^2 + \tfrac{1}{2}kq^2\right]\Psi_n = E_n\Psi_n, \quad (4\text{-}7)$$

where μ is the reduced mass of the nuclei m_1 and m_2, ∇^2 and Ψ_n are the Laplacian operator and wavefunction respectively in cartesian displacement coordinates, and E_n is the vibration-rotation energy. Since the potential energy (Eq. (4-4)) is a spherically symmetric function, this equation is conveniently solved by further transformation of both the Laplacian operator and the wavefunction to spherical polar coordinates,

$$\nabla^2 = \frac{1}{r^2}\frac{1}{\partial r}\left(r^2\frac{\partial}{\partial r}\right) + \frac{1}{r^2 \sin\theta}\frac{\partial}{\partial\theta}\left(\sin\theta\frac{\partial}{\partial\theta}\right) + \frac{1}{r^2\sin^2\theta}\frac{\partial^2}{\partial\phi^2}. \quad (4\text{-}8)$$

If it is assumed that there is no interaction between the rotational and the vibrational motions,

$$\Psi_n = \frac{\psi(r - r_e)}{r}\psi(\theta)\psi(\phi). \tag{4-9}$$

The angular part of the total wavefunction $\psi(\theta)\psi(\phi)$ will have the same solutions as those for the hydrogen atom, and $\psi(r - r_e)/r$, the same as those for the harmonic oscillator. Thus, we obtain the rigid-rotor–harmonic-oscillator approximation energy expression

$$E_n = (v + \tfrac{1}{2})h\nu_e + \frac{J(J+1)h^2}{8\pi^2 I_e}, \tag{4-10}$$

where I_e is the moment of inertia μr_e^2 corresponding to the internuclear minimum in the parabolic potential (Figure 4-1). If the potential energy expression $U(r)$ is represented by the so-called Morse potential,

$$U(r) = D_e[1 - e^{-\beta(r - r_e)}]^2, \tag{4-11}$$

then slight extension of the bond (nonrigid rotor) is allowed while the molecule is rotating. This potential function is also shown in Figure 4-1. The term D_e is called the spectroscopic dissociation energy and $\beta = \nu_e(2\pi^2\mu/cD_eh)^{1/2}$ is an empirical constant characteristic of the molecule. Using Eq. (4-11) in place of Eq. (4-4), we obtain an additional correction term for the energy expression of Eq. (4-10):

$$-\frac{J^2(J+1)^2h^4}{128\pi^6\nu_e^2 I_e^3}, \tag{4-12}$$

which is called the *centrifugal distortion*.

Since microwave and far-infrared spectroscopists often use energy units of megacycles per second (Mcps),[2] or wavenumbers (cm^{-1}), we shall use these units in the energy expression derived. For the nonrigid hypothetical vibrationless state corresponding to a diatomic molecule with the equilibrium internuclear separation of r_e, the rotational energy is expressed as

$$E\,(\text{MHz}) = \frac{E}{h} = \frac{J(J+1)h}{8\pi^2 I_e} - \frac{J^2(J+1)^2h^3}{128\pi^6\nu_e^2 I_e^3}$$

$$= J(J+1)B_e - J^2(J+1)^2D_e. \tag{4-13}$$

Defining

$$\tilde{B}_e = \frac{B_e}{c} = \frac{h}{8\pi^2 I_e c} \quad \text{and} \quad \tilde{D}_e = \frac{D_e}{c} = \frac{4\tilde{B}_e^3}{\omega_e^2}, \tag{4-14}$$

we obtain

$$\tilde{E}\,(\text{cm}^{-1}) = J(J+1)\tilde{B}_e - J^2(J+1)^2\tilde{D}_e. \tag{4-15}$$

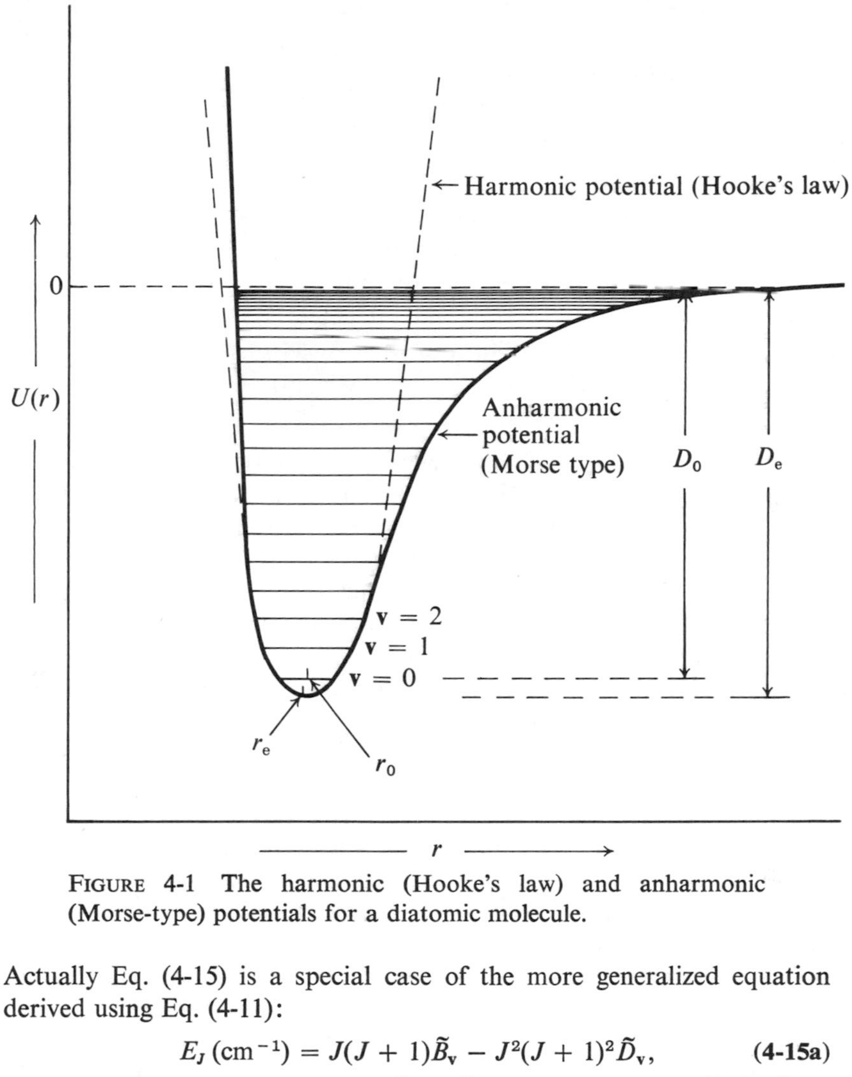

FIGURE 4-1 The harmonic (Hooke's law) and anharmonic (Morse-type) potentials for a diatomic molecule.

Actually Eq. (4-15) is a special case of the more generalized equation derived using Eq. (4-11):

$$E_J\,(\text{cm}^{-1}) = J(J+1)\tilde{B}_{\mathbf{v}} - J^2(J+1)^2\tilde{D}_{\mathbf{v}}, \qquad \textbf{(4-15a)}$$

where $\mathbf{v}$ is the vibrational state, $\tilde{B}_{\mathbf{v}} = \tilde{B}_e - \alpha_e(\mathbf{v} + \frac{1}{2})$, and $\tilde{D}_{\mathbf{v}} = \tilde{D}_e + \beta_e(\mathbf{v} + \frac{1}{2})$. The α_e and β_e are small constant terms that correct for vibration-rotation interaction of a particular vibrational state.

B. SYMMETRY AND STATISTICS

Now that we have obtained the energy expression characterizing the rotational levels of a diatomic molecule, what then are the selection rules controlling the absorption and emission of radiation in the microwave region? As we have previously shown (Eq. (2-35)), these rules are determined by the nature of the transition moment integral

$$\langle m|\hat{\mu}_{\text{rot}}|k\rangle. \tag{4-16}$$

In this section, we consider those restrictions which are governed by symmetry considerations alone of ψ_k and ψ_m.

Examination of the total wavefunction for molecular states indicates that it must be either symmetric or antisymmetric to the exchange of all elementary particles (nuclei and electrons). This exchange is carried out by the inversion symmetry operation (i) (Chapter 5), whereby all particles are inverted through the origin into their negative coordinates. If the total wavefunction is given as

$$\psi_{\text{total}} = \psi_{\text{e}}\psi_{\text{v}}\psi_{\text{r}}, \tag{4-17}$$

where the subscripts signify the electronic, vibrational, and rotational wavefunctions, we can examine what the effect will be on each individual term of the product. The inversion operation for an electronic wavefunction is equivalent to a rotation of the molecule through 180 degrees about an axis perpendicular to the internuclear axis, followed by a reflection at a plane perpendicular to this rotational axis and passing through the internuclear axis. The first operation leaves ψ_{e} unaffected, since the electronic coordinates relative to the nuclei are unaltered, whereas the second, which affects only the electrons, changes sign for Σ^- states and is unchanged in sign for Σ^+ states.[3] Most linear molecules in their ground electronic states have term symbols $^1\Sigma^+$, e.g., $H_2(^1\Sigma_g{}^+)$, where the superscript plus indicates that the electronic wavefunction is symmetric with respect to the reflection operation perpendicular to a plane through the molecular axis. In fact, most molecules, linear or polyatomic, that have an even number of electrons resulting in singlet states are generally symmetric to electronic inversion in their ground electronic states. The ground vibrational wavefunctions of linear molecules are also symmetric since the nuclear separations or magnitudes are unchanged in sign on the simple exchange of nuclei. The result in the case of linear molecules is that the symmetry of the total wavefunction on inversion depends on the symmetry of ψ_{r}. This wavefunction is found to be of symmetric (+) or antisymmetric (−) parity respectively, for even or odd J states of a + electronic state, i.e., Σ^+, and the reverse for − electronic states, i.e., Σ^-. Thus, for Eq. (4-16) to be nonzero in this case of alternating J state symmetries, it must have the form

$$\langle m\,(\text{even})|\hat{\mu}\,(\text{odd})|k\,(\text{odd})\rangle, \tag{4-18}$$

which is analogous to the Laporte atomic selection rules,

$$+ \leftrightarrow - \quad + \not\leftrightarrow + \quad - \not\leftrightarrow -. \tag{4-19}$$

Such an alternation of J states $(+, -, +, \cdots)$ coupled with the symmetry requirements of Eq. (4-19) results in the selection rule $\Delta J = \pm 1$, but does not exclude $\Delta J = \pm 3, \pm 5$, and so on.

For linear molecules having a center of symmetry i (Chapter 5), ψ_{total} must also be totally symmetric for the simple *exchange of nuclei.* The total wave function in this case must also include the nuclear wave function ψ_n,

$$\psi_{\text{total}} = \psi_e \psi_r \psi_v \psi_n. \tag{4-17a}$$

The symmetry of ψ_{total} will now depend on the product $\psi_r \psi_n$. This product will be symmetric or antisymmetric depending on whether the exchange of nuclei involves particles with half-integral (fermions) or integral (bosons) nuclear spin states; it is *symmetric* for bosons and *antisymmetric* for fermions. In the case of linear molecules of this type having zero nuclear spin states, $\mathbf{I} = 0$ (where $\mathbf{I}$ is the nuclear spin angular momentum), we have two situations to consider. For ψ_e symmetric, the symmetry of ψ_{total} simply depends on the symmetry of ψ_r,[4] and for ψ_e antisymmetric, the symmetry of ψ_{total} depends on $\psi_e \psi_r$. The symmetries of ψ_r in various Σ (or Π angular momentum states) electronic states with respect to the exchange of identical nuclei are

	Σ_g^+	Σ_u^+	Σ_g^-	Σ_u^-
Even J's	Symmetric	Antisymmetric	Antisymmetric	Symmetric
Odd J's	Antisymmetric	Symmetric	Symmetric	Antisymmetric

In the cases of the *homonuclear* diatomics $C_2(^1\Sigma_g^+)$ and $S_2(^3\Sigma_g^-)$, each of which is a molecule consisting of atoms for which $I = 0$, the total wavefunction must be symmetric to inversion (exchange) of the nuclei. According to the restrictions of the previous paragraph, odd J states that are antisymmetric for C_2 are not permitted, and therefore *do not exist.* In a like manner, even J states for S_2 *do not exist.* These statements are actually confirmed by the observed electronic band spectra of these diatomics. The existent and nonexistent rotational levels can be schematically represented:

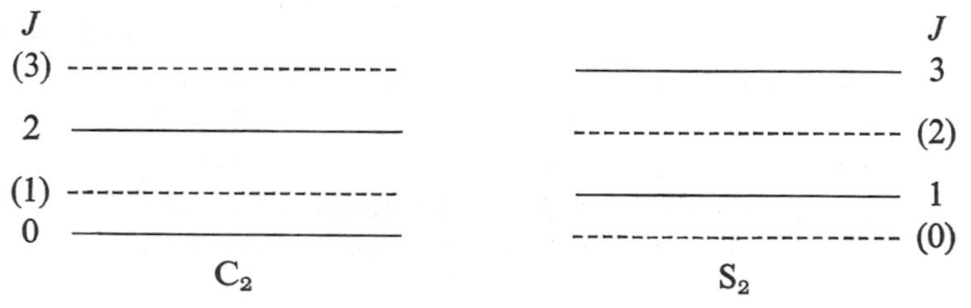

Let us consider briefly a case where $I \neq 0$ for the nuclei that are exchanged. Each of the nuclei in D_2 has an integral spin state of unity (bosons); they thus add vectorially, producing total nuclear spin states of $T = 2, 1$, and 0. The electronic state is a ${}^1\Sigma_g{}^+$, where the g and + designations inform us that ψ_e is symmetric with respect to rotation, reflection, and inversion. The vibrational wavefunction for this linear molecule is also symmetric as discussed above; therefore we need only be concerned with the exchange of nuclei affecting $\psi_r\psi_n$, which must be symmetric for bosons. Since (for bosons) even nuclear spin (T) states are symmetric to nuclear exchange and odd states are antisymmetric, only the combinations of even J and even T spin states, and odd J and odd T spin states can exist.[5] The statistical weights of these states will be dictated by the multiplicity of the total even and odd states T ($g_T = 2T + 1$) as well as by the usual $2J + 1(g_J)$ rotational multiplicity. These are exemplified for D_2 in Figure 4-2. The dotted lines represent nonexistent, or *missing*, rotational states while the solid lines represent states confirmed from observed transitions along with their total statistical weight g_τ. Even though pure rotational and vibrational transitions are forbidden

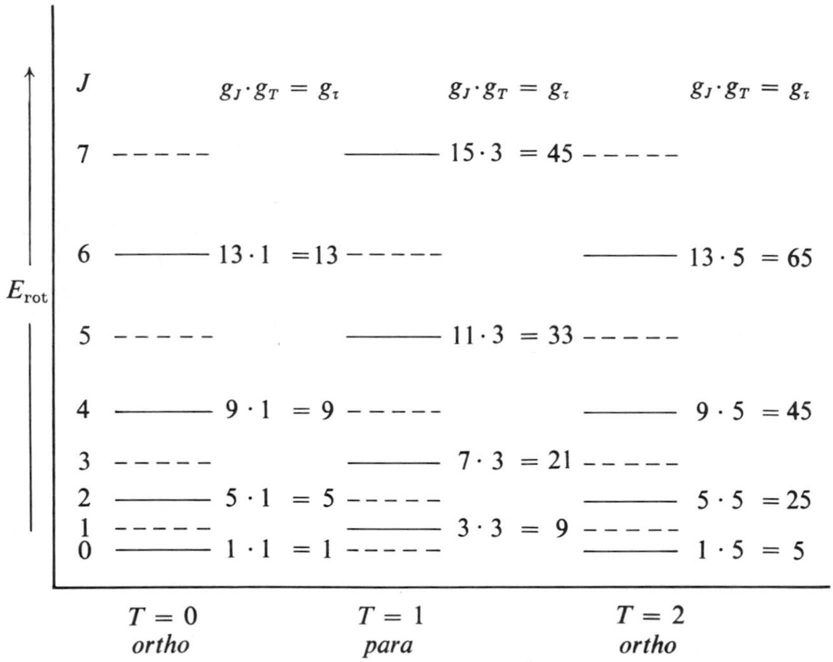

FIGURE 4-2 Statistical weights of the rotational levels for *para* ($T = 1$) and *ortho* ($T = 0, 2$) D_2 ($g_\tau = g_J g_T$). The dashed lines represent "missing" rotational levels.

for homonuclear diatomics, the alternation of intensities resulting from the statistical weights of the various rotational states is observed in electronic band spectra.

C. SELECTION RULES

Although the symmetry requirements for rotational transitions, Eq. (4-19), involve even ↔ odd states, this rule does not impose any restriction on the quantum jumps $\Delta J = \pm 1, \pm 3, \ldots$. To derive these restrictions, we must examine in more detail the transition moment integral, Eq. (4-16), with particular emphasis on the mathematical form of its components. Rotational absorption results from the interaction of the varying electric-field component of radiation with one or more of the appropriate oscillating (rotating) permanent dipole moment components x, y, or z. Since the rotational dipole moment operator involves only linear coordinates, it is given as

$$\hat{\boldsymbol{\mu}}_{\text{rot}} = \boldsymbol{\mu} = \mu_x + \mu_y + \mu_z. \tag{4-20}$$

Substituting Eq. (4-20) into Eq. (4-16), we obtain

$$\langle m|\hat{\boldsymbol{\mu}}_{\text{rot}}|k\rangle = \langle m|\mu_x|k\rangle + \langle m|\mu_y|k\rangle + \langle m|\mu_z|k\rangle. \tag{4-21}$$

For a transition to be forbidden, each of these three terms must be zero. Substituting the appropriate wavefunctions into Eq. (4-21) and applying the nonzero restriction will allow us to generate rotational selection rules.

1. Diatomics

For a heteronuclear diatomic molecule, the qualitative description of the dipole moment $\mu(r)$ as a function of the internuclear distance r is shown in Figure 4-3. In the region of r_e, where $\mu(r)$ is a maximum, the nuclear dipole moment $\mu(r)$ can be expanded in a Taylor series:

$$\mu(r) = \mu_e + \left(\frac{\partial \mu}{\partial r}\right)_e (r - r_e) + \frac{1}{2}\left(\frac{\partial^2 \mu}{\partial r^2}\right)_e (r - r_e)^2 + \cdots. \tag{4-22}$$

If only the first two terms are retained, then $\boldsymbol{\mu}$ expressed in spherical polar coordinates is given as

$$\boldsymbol{\mu} = \mu_x + \mu_y + \mu_z = \mu(r)[\sin\theta\cos\phi + \sin\theta\sin\phi + \cos\theta]. \tag{4-23}$$

Thus, if the molecule is oriented along the x axis, it has no y or z dipolar components,[6] and

$$\langle m|\mu_x|k\rangle = \int \psi_m^* \left[\mu_e + \left(\frac{\partial \mu}{\partial r}\right)_e (r - r_e)\right] \sin\theta\cos\phi\, \psi_k\, d\tau. \tag{4-24}$$

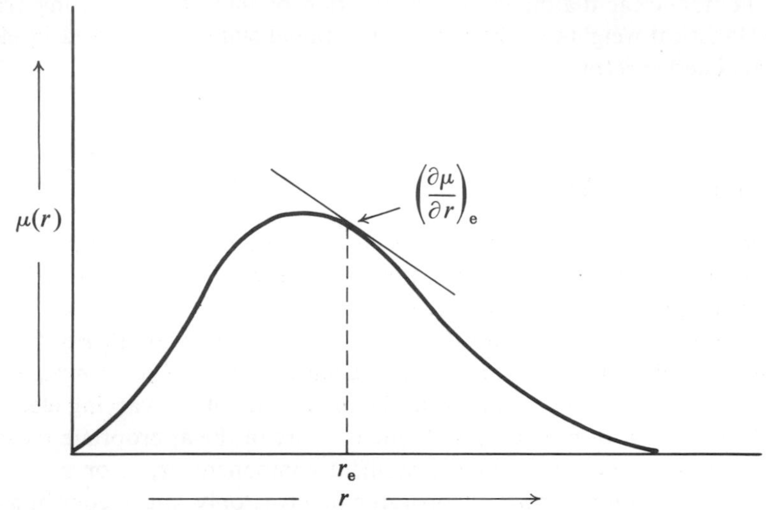

FIGURE 4-3 Qualitative description of the dipole moment as a function of internuclear distance and the dipole derivative at r_e.

The wavefunction within an electronic state k is given as

$$\psi_k = \psi_R(\theta, \phi)\,\frac{\psi_v(r - r_e)}{r} = \psi_J(\theta)\psi_{J,M}(\phi)\,\frac{\psi_v(r - r_e)}{r}, \tag{4-25}$$

where J, M, and $\mathbf{v}$ refer to the usual quantum numbers, and the volume element $d\tau = r^2 \sin\theta\, d\theta\, d\phi\, dr$. Substituting Eq. (4-25) for $\psi_m{}^*$ and ψ_k into Eq. (4-24), we obtain for the x integral

$$\begin{aligned}\langle m|\mu_x|k\rangle = &\int_0^\pi \psi_m{}^*(\theta)\psi_k(\theta)\sin^2\theta\, d\theta \\ &\times \int_0^{2\pi} \psi_m{}^*(\phi)\psi_k(\phi)\cos\phi\, d\phi \int_0^\infty \psi_m{}^*(r - r_e) \\ &\times \left[\mu_e + \left(\frac{\partial\mu}{\partial r}\right)_e (r - r_e)\right]\psi_k(r - r_e)\, dr.\end{aligned} \tag{4-26}$$

This equation can be separated into two parts, by performing the indicated multiplication, thus:

$$\begin{aligned}\langle m|\mu_x|k\rangle = \mu_e\Bigg[&\int_0^\pi \psi_m{}^*(\theta)\psi_k(\theta)\sin^2\theta\, d\theta \\ &\times \int_0^{2\pi} \psi_m{}^*(\phi)\psi_k(\phi)\cos\phi\, d\phi \int_0^\infty \psi_m{}^*(r - r_e)\psi_k(r - r_e)\, dr\Bigg] \\ &+ \left(\frac{\partial\mu}{\partial r}\right)_e\Bigg[\int_0^\pi \psi_m{}^*(\theta)\psi_k(\theta)\sin^2\theta\, d\theta \int_0^{2\pi} \psi_m{}^*(\phi)\psi_k(\phi)\cos\phi\, d\phi \\ &\times \int_0^\infty \psi_m{}^*(r - r_e)[r - r_e]\psi_k(r - r_e)\, dr\Bigg].\end{aligned} \tag{4-27}$$

At this point we are primarily interested in the first bracketed term on the right. Since the vibrational states within a given electronic level form a set of orthonormal wavefunctions, $\psi_m^*(r - r_e)$ must equal $\psi_k(r - r_e)$ to remain nonzero (orthogonality theorem), and the remaining θ and ϕ integrals will generate the selection rules for pure rotational transitions. One requirement that is obvious from inspection is that the diatomic molecule must possess a permanent dipole moment in order to give rise to pure rotational transitions. Thus, homonuclear diatomic molecules will not absorb radiation (be "rotationally active") in the microwave region. In fact, possession of a permanent moment is also a requirement for any molecule to be rotationally active, so that symmetrical linear molecules (H_2, CO_2, C_2H_2, etc.) and spherical tops (CH_4, SF_6, etc.) are rotationally inactive. The allowed solutions of the ϕ and θ integrals of Eq. (4-21) will be analogous to the treatment of atomic selection rules and will remain nonzero only for the transitions

$$\Delta M = 0, \pm 1 \qquad \text{and} \qquad \Delta J = \pm 1. \tag{4-28}$$

EXAMPLE 4-1: Show that the rotational transition $J = 0 \rightarrow J = 2$ is "forbidden" and $J = 0 \rightarrow J = 1$ is "allowed" in microwave spectroscopy. Given:

$$\psi_{0,0}(\theta, \phi) = \left(\frac{1}{\sqrt{2}}\right)\left(\frac{1}{\sqrt{2\pi}}\right); \qquad \psi_{1,1}(\theta, \phi) = \left(\frac{\sqrt{3}}{2}\sin\theta\right)\left(\frac{1}{\sqrt{\pi}}\cos\phi\right);$$

$$\psi_{2,0}(\theta, \phi) = \left[\frac{\sqrt{10}}{4}(3\cos^2\theta - 1)\right]\left(\frac{1}{\sqrt{2\pi}}\right)$$

Solution: (a) Assuming the molecule has a permanent dipole moment, we have from the first term of Eq. (4-27) for $J = 0 \rightarrow J = 2$,

$$\langle 2|\mu_x|0\rangle = \mu_e \int_0^\pi \frac{\sqrt{2}}{2}\frac{\sqrt{10}}{4}(3\cos^2 - 1)\sin^2\theta\, d\theta \int_0^{2\pi}\left(\frac{1}{2\pi}\right) \cos\phi\, d\phi.$$

Since the integration of the $\cos\phi$ function from 0 to 2π is zero, then $\langle 2|\mu_x|0\rangle = 0$. Thus, the intensity of this transition is also zero as a first-order effect: $I \propto \langle 2|\mu_x|0\rangle^2 = 0$.

(b) For the transition $J = 0 \rightarrow J = 1$,

$$\langle 1|\mu_x|0\rangle = \mu_e \int_0^\pi \frac{\sqrt{3}}{2}\frac{\sqrt{2}}{2}\sin^3\theta\, d\theta \int_0^{2\pi}\frac{1}{\sqrt{2\pi}}\frac{1}{\sqrt{\pi}}\cos^2\phi\, d\phi$$

$$= \mu_e \frac{\sqrt{3}}{4\pi}\int_0^\pi \sin^3\theta\, d\theta \int_0^{2\pi}\cos^2\phi\, d\phi$$

$$= \mu_e \frac{\sqrt{3}}{4\pi}\left[\frac{-1}{3}\cos\theta(\sin^2\theta + 2)\right]_0^\pi \left[\frac{1}{2}\sin\phi\cos\phi + \frac{1}{2}\phi\right]_0^{2\pi}$$

$$= \mu_e \frac{1}{\sqrt{3}}$$

and

$$I \propto \langle 1|\mu_x|0\rangle^2 = \frac{\mu_e^2}{3}$$

(recall Example 2–1).

2. Diatomic Energy States

Since $\Delta J = \pm 1$, the energy expression for absorption (Eq. (4-10)) for $J \rightarrow J + 1$, is given as

$$\begin{aligned} \Delta E &= (J + 1)(J + 2)B_e - J(J + 1)B_e \\ &= 2B_e(J + 1) \end{aligned} \qquad \textbf{(4-10a)}$$

where J is the initial state involved in the transition. Thus, for J transitions within a given vibrational level, the microwave frequencies would occur as shown in Figure 4-4. Application of Eq. (4-15), which includes the centrifugal distortion term, gives rise to the dotted line positions at slightly lower frequencies.

In the actual experimental determination of B_e we normally observe absorption processes within the $\mathbf{v} = 0$ level. If the species is not strongly anharmonic, then $B_e \simeq B_0(r_e \simeq r_0)$; if the potential function is significantly anharmonic near the bottom of the potential curve ($\mathbf{v} = 0$), then Eq. (4-15a) must be used with the corrected form of B_0 and D_e.[7]

EXAMPLE 4-2: Calculate the frequencies of the three lowest rotational transitions of ICl (ignoring centrifugal distortion) in MHz and cm^{-1}, where $r_e = 2.32$ Å.

Transition	ΔE
$J = 0 \rightarrow J = 1$	$2B_e$
$J = 1 \rightarrow J = 2$	$4B_e$
$J = 2 \rightarrow J = 3$	$6B_e$
$J = 3 \rightarrow J = 4$	$8B_e$

(a)

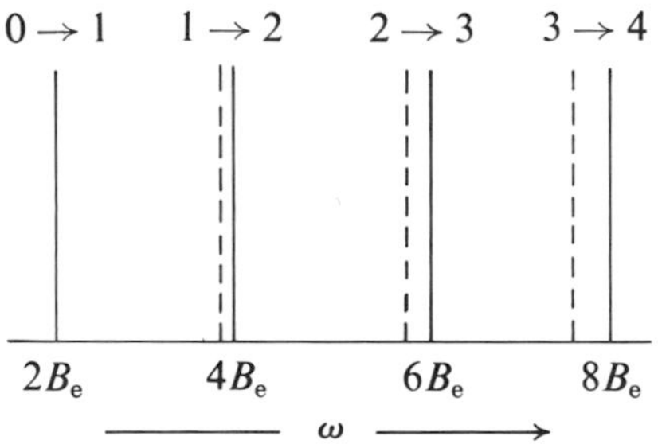

(b)

FIGURE 4-4 (a) Rotational energies for various $\Delta J = \pm 1$ transitions. (b) Relative spacing of the observed microwave spectrum is $2B_e$. The dotted lines represent the actual line positions if the centrifugal distortion is taken into account (Eq. (4-15)).

Solution: Since

$$\tilde{B}\,(\mathrm{cm}^{-1}) = \frac{h}{8\pi^2 I_e c} = \frac{27.989 \times 10^{-40}}{I_e(g = \mathrm{cm}^2)}$$

and

$$I_e = \mu r_e^{\,2} = \frac{(126.90)(35.45)}{(162.35)(6.02 \times 10^{23})}(2.32 \times 10^{-8})^2,$$

$$= 26.8 \times 10^{-39}\ \mathrm{g\text{-}cm}^2$$

$$\tilde{B}_e = \frac{27.989 \times 10^{-40}}{26.8 \times 10^{-39}} = 0.108\ \mathrm{cm}^{-1}$$

The three lowest lines will occur at $2B_e$, $4B_e$, and $6B_e$. Thus:

Transition	$\Delta E\,(\mathrm{cm}^{-1})$	ΔE (MHz)
$J = 0 \rightarrow J = 1$	0.216	6,480
$J = 1 \rightarrow J = 2$	0.432	12,960
$J = 2 \rightarrow J = 3$	0.648	19,440

D. LINEAR POLYATOMIC MOLECULES

Like a diatomic molecule, a linear rotating molecule has quantized energy levels that result from its rotation about the perpendicular axes of inertia. The energy expression can be obtained by using operator mechanics and the Schrödinger equation (Eq. (2-9)). The classical Hamiltonian for a linear rigid rotor in spherical polar coordinates is

$$\hat{H} = -\frac{h^2}{8\pi^2 I}\left[\frac{1}{\sin\theta}\frac{\partial}{\partial\theta}\left(\sin\theta\frac{\partial}{\partial\theta}\right) + \frac{1}{\sin^2\theta}\frac{\partial^2}{\partial\phi^2}\right], \tag{4-29}$$

and the classical energy expression for this free rotor that has no electronic angular momentum is

$$\epsilon = K = \frac{\mathbf{P}^2}{2I}, \tag{4-30}$$

where K is the kinetic energy of rotation, $\mathbf{P}$ is the total angular momentum, and I is the moment of inertia,

$$I = \sum_i m_i r_i^{\,2}. \tag{4-31}$$

Substituting Eq. (4-30) into Eq. (2-9) and multiplying by the complex conjugate yields

$$\psi^* \hat{H} \psi = \psi^* \epsilon \psi = \frac{\psi^* \mathbf{P}^2 \psi}{2I}. \tag{4-32}$$

Using operator mechanics in this case, we find that the Hamiltonian $\hat{H}$ and $\mathbf{P}^2/2I$ are identical with the exception of the $1/2I$ factor; thus rearranging Eq. (4-32) and integrating, we obtain[8]

$$\epsilon\langle\psi|\psi\rangle = \langle\psi|\hat{H}|\psi\rangle = \frac{\langle\psi|\mathbf{P}^2|\psi\rangle}{2I}. \tag{4-33}$$

Substituting the rotational wavefunctions $\psi(\theta, \phi)$ and noting that space integration of $\langle\psi|\psi\rangle = 1$, we obtain for the rotational energy per molecule

$$\epsilon = \frac{J(J+1)h^2}{8\pi^2 I}, \tag{4-34}$$

where for the nonzero matrix elements,

$$\langle\psi|\mathbf{P}^2|\psi\rangle = J(J+1)\frac{h^2}{4\pi^2}. \tag{4-35}$$

Rotational energy states have degeneracies of $2J + 1$ and therefore exhibit space quantization when the molecule is placed in an external magnetic or electric field similar to the atomic electronic angular momentum (Figure 3-7). For the energy projection along a z-directed external perturbing field,

$$\epsilon_z = M_J^2 \frac{h^2}{8\pi^2 I}, \tag{4-36}$$

where M_J can assume values of $+J, J-1, \ldots, -J$. Substitution of the appropriate wavefunctions for linear polyatomic molecules into Eq. (4-16) again requires a permanent dipole moment for pure rotational absorption and

$$\Delta J = \pm 1 \qquad \text{and} \qquad \Delta M_J = \pm 1, 0. \tag{4-37}$$

For absorption from J to $J + 1$, we obtain from Eq. (4-34),

$$\Delta\epsilon(\text{cm}^{-1}) = 2\tilde{B}(J+1), \tag{4-38}$$

where J = lower state. What we in fact calculate directly from experimental observations in most cases is B_0, the rotational constant of the $\mathbf{v} = 0$ vibrational state. A very good illustration of this situation is given by BrCN (Figure 4-5), for which

$$I = \sum_i m_i r_i^2 = m_{\text{Br}} r_{\text{Br}}^2 + m_{\text{C}} r_{\text{C}}^2 + m_{\text{N}} r_{\text{N}}^2, \tag{4-39}$$

where the additional relations $r_{\text{BrC}} = r_{\text{Br}} + r_{\text{C}}$, $r_{\text{CN}} = r_{\text{N}} - r_{\text{C}}$, and $r_{\text{BrN}} = r_{\text{Br}} + r_{\text{N}}$ allow conversion of Eq. (4-39) to

$$I = \frac{m_{\text{Br}} m_{\text{C}} r_{\text{BrC}}^2 + m_{\text{C}} m_{\text{N}} r_{\text{CN}}^2 + m_{\text{Br}} m_{\text{N}} r_{\text{BrN}}^2}{m_{\text{Br}} + m_{\text{C}} + m_{\text{N}}}. \tag{4-40}$$

At first sight, it might appear that there are three unknown distances, but since $r_{\text{BrN}} = r_{\text{BrC}} + r_{\text{CN}}$, there are really only two. As a basic mathemati-

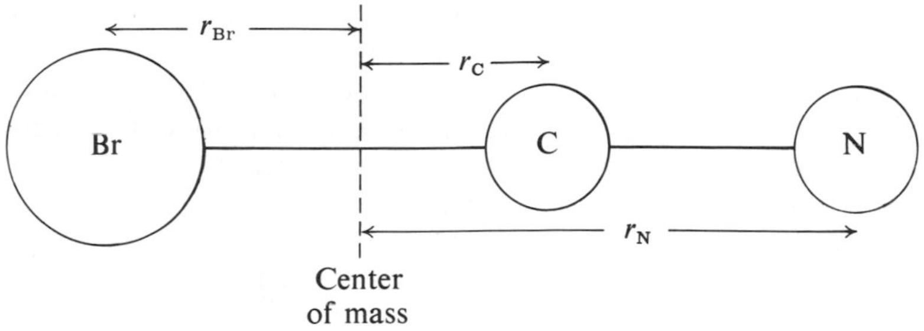

FIGURE 4-5 Structural parameters for the BrCN molecule. The relation locating the center of mass is $m_{Br}r_{Br} = m_C r_C + m_N r_N$.

cal relation, two unknowns require two equations for their solution (microwave spectrum of two isotopically different BrCN molecules), and we can show that $r_{BrC} = 1.790$ Å and $r_{CN} = 1.159$ Å (Problem 4-8). The general application of this procedure can also be made to more complex linear polyatomics, such as H—C≡C—F, which requires the results from three isotopically different molecules for the solution of the three unknown bond distances. In general, we require the microwave

TABLE 4-1. Structural Parameters of Selected Linear Molecules

Species	B_e,[a] MHz	α_e MHz	r_e, Å[b] r_{12}	r_{23}	r_{34}	ω_e, cm^{-1}
^{6}LiF	45,230.56	722.417	1.5639	...	...	964.24
$Na^{35}Cl$	6,537.41	48.711	2.3609	...	...	364.60
KI	1,824.98	8.027	3.0478	...	...	186.53
$Cs^{79}Br$	1,081.33	3.720	3.0722	...	...	149.50
$^{12}C^{32}S$	24,584.37	177.550	1.5349	...	...	...
$^{70}Ge^{32}S$	5,689.61	23.030	2.0121	...	...	...
$^{120}Sn^{34}S$	3,912.68	14.050	2.2090	...	...	...
$^{118}Sn^{78}Se$	1,991.79	5.263	2.3256	...	...	...
$H^{12}C^{14}N$	44,315.98	...	1.0659	1.1531	...	...
$F^{12}C^{14}N$	10,554.20	...	1.262	1.159	...	...
$^{32}S^{12}C^{130}Te$	1,559.93	...	1.557	1.904	...	...
$^{16}O^{12}C^{32}S$	6,081.49	...	1.1601	1.5602	...	...
$F^{12}C^{12}CH$	9,706.19	...	1.279	1.198	1.053	...
$^{35}Cl^{12}C^{12}CH$	5,684.24	...	1.637	1.204	1.055	...
$H^{12}C^{12}CD$	29,725.24	...				...

SOURCE: Gordy and Cook [Reference 4-3], by permission.

[a] The B_e entries are actually B_0 for the triatomics and tetratomics.

[b] We use the convention here 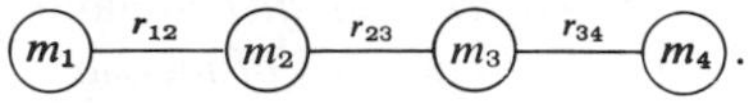.

determination of as many isotopic species as there are unknown unique bond lengths and angles. Such determinations assume that bond lengths and angles are virtually unaffected by substituting a lighter or heavier nucleus into a molecule. It presumes the molecular electronic structure, which is practically identical in such cases, to be by far the most important factor in controlling these parameters.

Actually Eq. (4-40) is an example of a general expression for the moment of inertia of any linear polyatomic molecule,

$$I = \frac{\frac{1}{2}\sum_i \sum_j m_i m_j r_{ij}^2}{\sum_i m_i}. \tag{4-41}$$

The structural parameters of some selected linear molecules evaluated from microwave experiments are shown in Table 4-1.

E. MOMENTS OF INERTIA

The molecular structural parameters obtained from rotational spectroscopy, bond lengths and bond angles, are evaluated from the experimentally observed rotational transitions. These transition energies can be related to the various inertial moments via Eqs. (4-52), (4-53), (4-54), and (4-57) (to be discussed in the following sections). Before evaluating these structural parameters, we shall briefly develop the classical expressions for the inertial moments in the molecule-fixed coordinate system.

For a rigid body (for example a molecule) composed of a collection of masses (nuclei) m_i, the moment of inertia about a given arbitrary axis of rotation j is

$$I_j = \sum_{i=1}^{N} m_i r_i^2, \tag{4-42}$$

where r_i is the perpendicular distance from the mass m_i to the j axis. We define the origin at the center of mass of the molecule-fixed coordinate system, since the inertial moments of interest are obtained from analyzing the rotational spectrum with respect to this coordinate system. In the case of a nonlinear polyatomic molecule, rotation can occur about three mutually perpendicular axes that may or may not be equivalent. If we plot a quantity $1/\sqrt{I_j}$ on each side of the origin for each of the three mutually perpendicular axes, the locus of these points is the surface of the so-called momental ellipsoid. The three axes of the ellipsoid are defined as the *principal axes of inertia*, and the corresponding inertial moments as the *principal moments of inertia* I_x, I_y, and I_z.

The choice of the principal axes for reasonably symmetric molecules is straightforward. In general, the highest symmetry axis (or any axis C_n, $n > 1$) coincides with a principal axis. An axis perpendicular to a plane of symmetry will also generally be a principal axis. For molecules having little or no symmetry (and also those having a high degree of symmetry), the three principal moments can be generated from the equation that characterizes the surface of the momental ellipsoid,

$$I_{xx}x^2 + I_{yy}y^2 + I_{zz}z^2 - 2I_{xy}xy - 2I_{yz}yz - 2I_{xz}xz = 1, \quad \textbf{(4-43)}$$

where the moments of inertia I_{xx}, I_{yy}, I_{zz} and products of inertia I_{xy}, I_{yz}, and I_{xz} are defined for an arbitrary set of cartesian coordinates in the molecule-fixed system with its origin at the center of mass. These elements are defined:

$$\begin{aligned} I_{xx} &= \sum_i m_i(y_i^2 + z_i^2) & I_{xy} &= \sum_i m_i x_i y_i \\ I_{yy} &= \sum_i m_i(x_i^2 + z_i^2) & I_{yz} &= \sum_i m_i y_i z_i \\ I_{zz} &= \sum_i m_i(x_i^2 + y_i^2) & I_{xz} &= \sum_i m_i x_i z_i. \end{aligned} \quad \textbf{(4-44)}$$

Equation (4-43) can be expressed in matrix form as $\tilde{\mathbf{X}}\mathbf{I}\mathbf{X} = 1$, where $\mathbf{X}$ is a column matrix having elements x, y, z, and $\tilde{\mathbf{X}}$ is the corresponding transpose of $\mathbf{X}$. The symbol $\mathbf{I}$ represents the moment of inertia tensor, whose elements (Eq. (4-44)) can be arranged into a square symmetrical matrix,

$$\mathbf{I} = \begin{vmatrix} I_{xx} & -I_{yx} & -I_{zx} \\ -I_{xy} & I_{yy} & -I_{zy} \\ -I_{xz} & -I_{yz} & I_{zz} \end{vmatrix}. \quad \textbf{(4-44a)}$$

The values of this matrix's elements depend not only on the origin but also on the orientation of the x, y, z coordinate system. If the coordinates in this arbitrarily chosen set (x, y, z) are rotated such that they coincide with the principal axes, then this linear transformation can be represented in matrix notation as $\mathbf{A} = \mathbf{YX}$, where $\mathbf{A}$ is a column matrix having the elements a, b, c, and $\mathbf{X}$ is the column matrix defined above, and $\mathbf{Y}$ is a square 3×3 orthogonal transformation matrix, whose elements are essentially the direction cosines of the abc axes in the xyz system (see pp. 192–93). As a result of this transformation, the transformed moment of inertia $\mathbf{I}_{abc} = \tilde{\mathbf{Y}}\mathbf{I}\mathbf{Y}$, where $\tilde{\mathbf{Y}}$ is the transpose of $\mathbf{Y}$. The new moment of inertia $\mathbf{I}_{abc}$ obtained by this so-called similarity transformation is diagonal. The elements along the diagonal are the principal moments of inertia I_a, I_b, and I_c. They are equivalent to those we have previously defined as I_x, I_y, and I_z. Thus, I_x, I_y, and I_z are respectively the same as I_{xx}, I_{yy}, and I_{zz} when $I_{xy} = I_{yz} = I_{xz} = 0$. The reason for the principal moment redundancy is that I_x, I_y, or I_z can be arbitrarily chosen along any of the three mutually perpendicular axes, but for the case of classifying molecules, we will apply the convention $I_a < I_b < I_c$, as discussed in Section F.

EXAMPLE 4-3: Calculate the principal moments of inertia I_x, I_y, and I_z for NH_3, $r_{N-H} = 1.014$ Å and ϕ HNH = 107.5°.

Solution: The procedure we use in this case is to locate the center of mass and evaluate each principal moment by use of Eq. (4-44). Through well-known trigonometric functions, useful geometrical parameters are evaluated and shown in the diagram herewith.

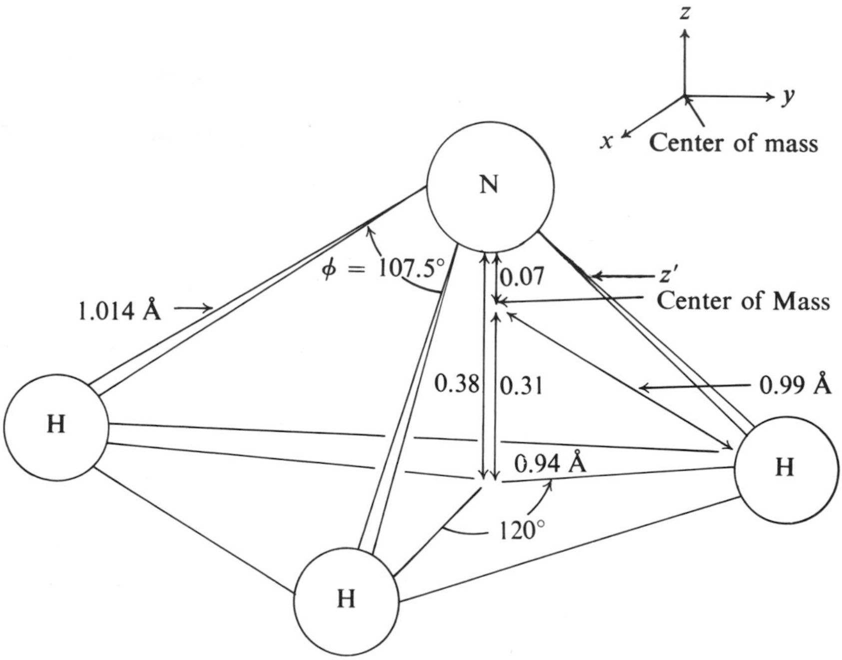

(a) Location of the center of mass.

$$m_N z' = 3m_H(R - z')$$

where z' is the distance the N atom is from the center of mass along the z axis and $R = 0.38$ Å. Thus

$$14z' = 1.14 - 3z'$$
$$z' = 0.07 \text{ Å}.$$

(b) Using familiar trigonometric relations, we are able to evaluate the necessary parameters shown in the NH_3 diagram above. Thus,

$$I_z = \sum_i m_i z_i^2 = 3m_H(0.94 \times 10^{-8} \text{ cm})^2$$

and

$$I_z = \frac{2.658 \times 10^{-16}}{6.02 \times 10^{23}} = 4.25 \times 10^{-40} \text{ g-cm}^2.$$

For the x axis,

$$I_x = [m_H(0.99)^2 + 2m_H(0.563)^2 + m_N(0.07)^2] \times 10^{-16}$$

and

$$I_x = \frac{1.62 \times 10^{-16}}{6.02 \times 10^{23}} = 2.69 \times 10^{-40} \text{ g-cm}^2.$$

For the y axis,

$$I_y = [m_H(0.31)^2 + 2m_H(0.877)^2 + m_N(0.007)^2] \times 10^{-16}$$

and

$$I_y = \frac{1.643 \times 10^{-16}}{6.02 \times 10^{23}} = 2.70 \times 10^{-40} \text{ g-cm}^2.$$

It should be noted that the independent calculation of I_x and I_y provides a check, since the two non-unique moments should be equal for symmetrical tops. In this particular example I_z, which is the unique axis, is greater than I_y or I_x. According to the convention we shall adopt in the next section, $I_z = I_c$, and we classify NH_3 as an oblate symmetric top (Section F).

The task of evaluating structural parameters from microwave determinations of B_0 and in turn I_b for relatively simple and symmetrical molecules is made easier by the use of closed expressions for the various moments. Examples of these are summarized and illustrated in Table 4-2.

F. NONLINEAR POLYATOMIC MOLECULES

In discussing the various types of nonlinear polyatomic molecules, we find it convenient to separate them into three different classes according to the degree of symmetry they possess. More specifically, on the basis of the equivalency of the various inertial moments.

Spherical Tops		$I_a = I_b = I_c$, CH_4, CCl_4, SF_6, cubane
Symmetric Tops	Prolate	$I_a < I_b = I_c$, CH_3Cl, CF_3Cl
	Oblate	$I_a = I_b < I_c$, BF_3, C_6H_6, NO_3^-
Asymmetric Tops		$I_a \neq I_b \neq I_c$, H_2O, H_2CO, $(CH_3)_2O$

A species having all three principal moments equal is defined as a spherical top, and any molecule having an n-fold axis, where $n \geqslant 3$, with any two equivalent principal moments is defined as a symmetric top. A molecule

TABLE 4-2. Moments of Inertia of Some Simple Symmetrical Molecules

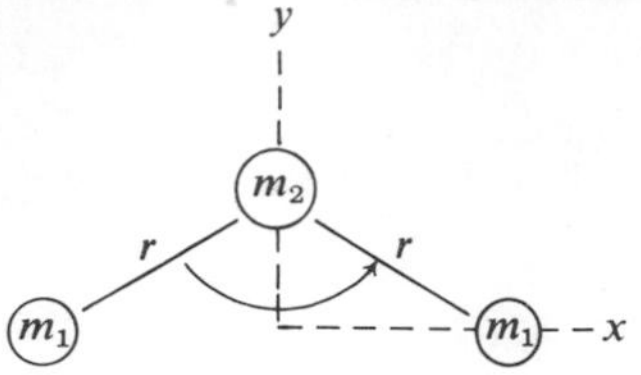 Symmetrical	$I_y = \frac{2m_1m_2}{2m_1 + m_2} r^2 \cos^2 \frac{\theta}{2}$ $I_x = 2m_1r^2 \sin^2 \frac{\theta}{2}$ $I_z = I_x + I_y$
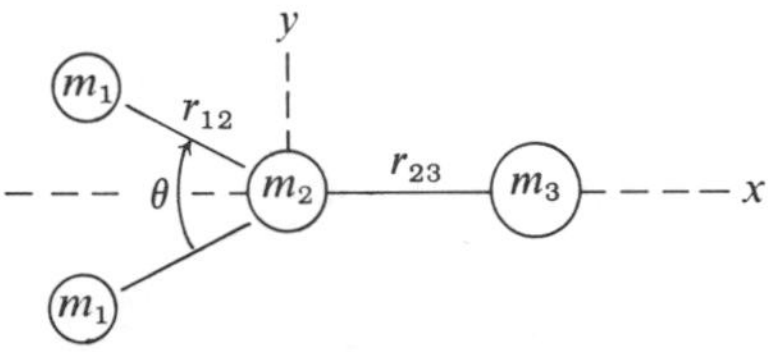 Planar	$I_x = 2m_1r_{12}{}^2 \sin^2 \theta$ $I_y = \frac{1}{2m_1 + m_2 + m_3} \Big[m_3(2m_1 + m_2)$ $+ 2m_1(m_2 + m_3)r_{12}{}^2 \cos^2 \frac{\theta}{2}$ $+ 4m_1m_3r_{23}{}^2r_{12}{}^2 \cos \frac{\theta}{2} \Big]$ $I_z = I_x + I_y$
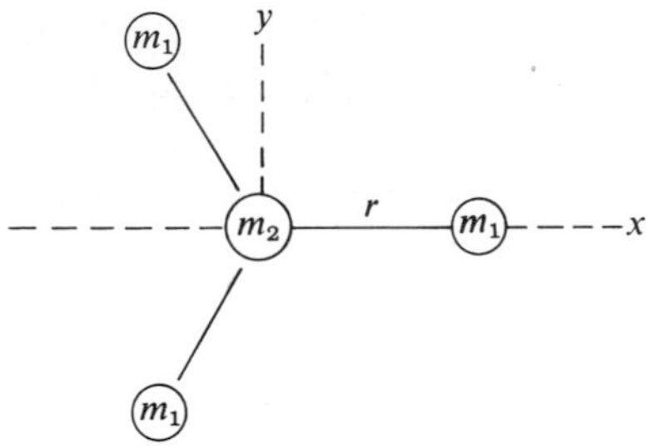 Planar symmetrical	$I_z = 3m_1r^2$ $I_x = I_y = \frac{3}{2}m_1r^2$ $I_z = I_x + I_y$[a]
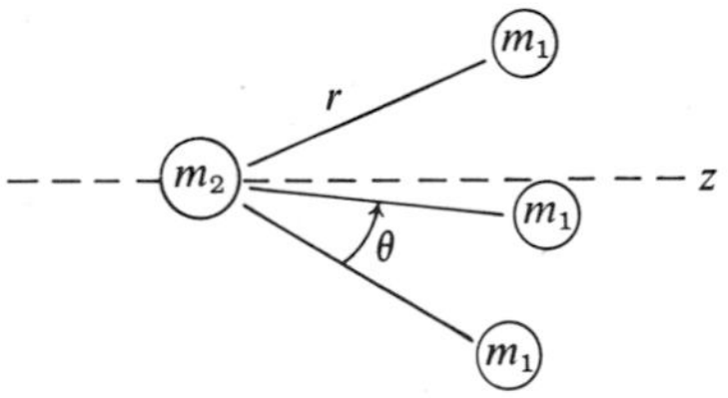 Pyramidal	$I_z = 2m_1r^2(1 - \cos \theta)$[b] $I_x = I_y = m_1r^2(1 - \cos \theta)$ $+ \frac{m_1m_2r^2}{3m_1 + m_2}(1 + 2 \cos \theta)$
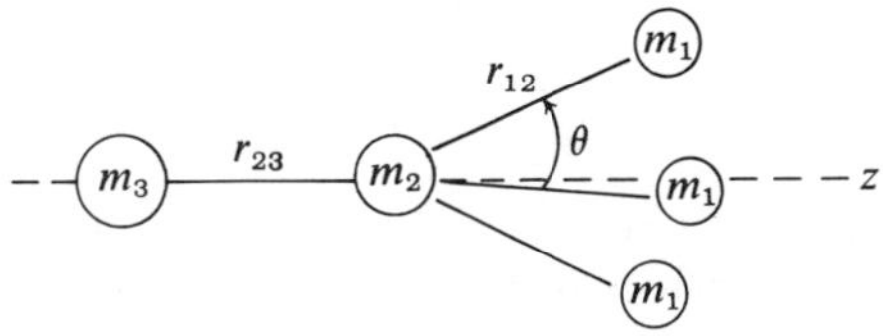 Axial symmetric	$I_z = 4m_1r_{12}{}^2 \sin^2 \frac{\theta}{2}$[b] $I_x = I_y = 2m_1r_{12}{}^2 \sin^2 \frac{\theta}{2}$ $+ \frac{3m_1}{3m_1 + m_2 + m_3}(m_2 + m_3)r_{12}{}^2$ $\times \left(1 - \frac{4}{3} \sin^2 \frac{\theta}{2}\right)$ $+ \frac{m_3r_{23}}{3m_1 + m_2 + m_3}\Big[(3m_1 + m_2)r_{23}$ $+ 6m_1r_{12}\left(1 - \frac{4}{3} \sin^2 \frac{\theta}{2}\right)\Big]^{1/2}$

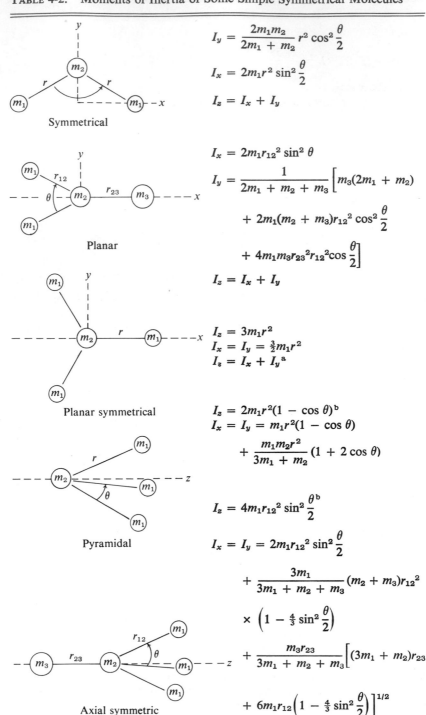

[a] A general relation for planar molecules is $I_z = I_x + I_y$.
[b] C_3 symmetry axis.

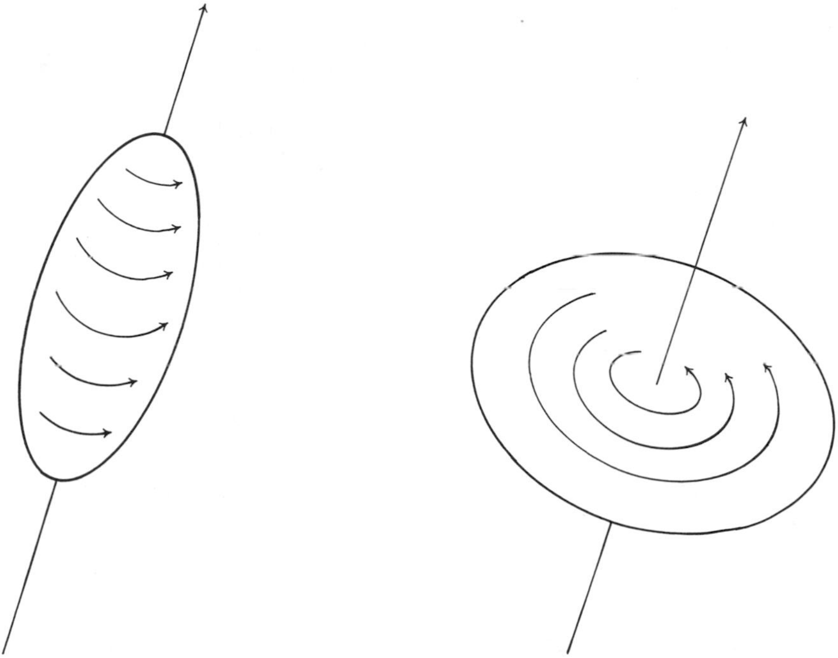

I_a (Minor axis of rotation) I_c (Major axis of rotation)

(a) (b)

FIGURE 4-6 Distribution of the electronic cloud about the minor (I_a) and major (I_c) axes of rotation for the (a) prolate and (b) oblate tops, respectively.

such as CH_3F that has a "football-shaped" electronic charge distribution about the minor unique axis (I_a) is called a prolate top, and one having a "pancake-shaped" electronic distribution about the major unique axis (I_c) is called an oblate top. The electronic distribution about the unique symmetry axes for the oblate and prolate tops are shown in Figure 4-6. Those species having different inertial moments about all three main axes are defined as asymmetric tops. The general convention used in this case is $I_a < I_b < I_c$. This classification obviously includes most of the known molecules in existence.

1. Spherical Top Molecules

The classical expression for the energy of a spherical top rigid rotor is

$$\epsilon = \frac{\mathbf{P}_a^2}{2I_a} + \frac{\mathbf{P}_b^2}{2I_b} + \frac{\mathbf{P}_c^2}{2I_c} = \frac{\mathbf{P}^2}{2I}, \tag{4-45}$$

where $I_a = I_b = I_c = I$. Again we have

$$\epsilon = \frac{\langle\psi|\mathbf{P}^2|\psi\rangle}{2I} = \frac{J(J+1)h^2}{8\pi^2 I}, \tag{4-46}$$

and I is the moment of inertia about any one of the three equivalent axes. Since a general requirement for pure rotational absorption is the possession of a permanent dipole moment, absorption by spherical tops is "forbidden" by electric dipole selection rules. However, rotational transitions superimposed on electronic or vibrational transitions or both are observed for these cases, and follow the selection rules $\Delta J = \pm 1, 0$ and $\Delta M = \pm 1, 0$.

2. Symmetric Top Molecules

The classical expression for the energy of a polyatomic rigid rotor is given as

$$\epsilon = \frac{\mathbf{P}_a^2}{2I_a} + \frac{\mathbf{P}_b^2}{2I_b} + \frac{\mathbf{P}_c^2}{2I_c}, \tag{4-47}$$

where $\mathbf{P}_i$ is the angular momentum about the various molecule-fixed axes. For the prolate top $I_b = I_c$, and I_a is the unique and minor symmetry axis. Thus,

$$\epsilon = \frac{\mathbf{P}_a^2}{2I_a} + \frac{1}{2I_b}(\mathbf{P}_b^2 + \mathbf{P}_c^2). \tag{4-48}$$

The total squared angular momentum is given as

$$\mathbf{P}^2 = \mathbf{P}_a^2 + \mathbf{P}_b^2 + \mathbf{P}_c^2 \quad \text{and} \quad \mathbf{P}_c^2 + \mathbf{P}_b^2 = \mathbf{P}^2 - \mathbf{P}_a^2. \tag{4-49}$$

Replacing $\mathbf{P}_b^2 + \mathbf{P}_c^2$ in Eq. (4-48), we obtain

$$\epsilon = \frac{\mathbf{P}_a^2}{2I_a} + \frac{\mathbf{P}^2}{2I_b} - \frac{\mathbf{P}_a^2}{2I_b} = \frac{\mathbf{P}^2}{2I_b} + \mathbf{P}_a^2\left(\frac{1}{2I_a} - \frac{1}{2I_b}\right). \tag{4-50}$$

Making use of the quantum mechanical results for the total squared angular momentum, $\mathbf{P}^2 = J(J+1)h^2/4\pi^2$, and the separate quantization of the component along the unique symmetry axis $\mathbf{P}_a^2 = K^2h^2/4\pi^2$, we obtain for the energy

$$\epsilon = \frac{J(J+1)h^2}{8\pi^2 I_b} + \left(\frac{K^2h^2}{4\pi^2}\right)\left(\frac{1}{2I_a} - \frac{1}{2I_b}\right). \tag{4-51}$$

If we define

$$A_0 = \frac{h}{8\pi^2 I_a} \quad \text{and} \quad B_0 = \frac{h}{8\pi^2 I_b}, \tag{4-52}$$

then

$$\epsilon_{JKM} = h[B_0J(J + 1) + K^2(A_0 - B_0)], \tag{4-53}$$

where J is the quantum number characterizing the total angular momentum of the molecule and K is the angular momentum about the unique axis. The total and unique angular momenta for the prolate symmetric top (CH_3F) is illustrated in Figure 4-7. The quantum number K can have any value from 0, ± 1, $\pm 2, \ldots$ to $\pm J$. Since K can assume both negative

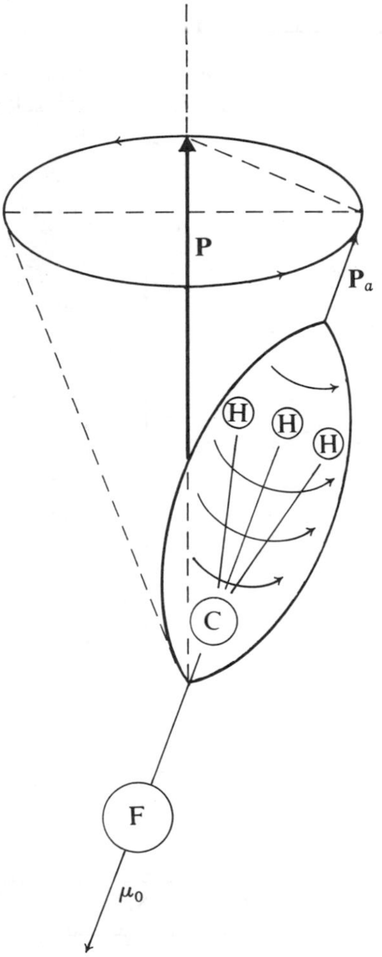

FIGURE 4-7 Precession of the unique quantization of $\mathbf{P}_a$ about the total angular momentum $\mathbf{P}$ of a prolate top, CH_3F. The lone component of the permanent dipole moment is oriented along the unique axis and opposite in direction to the unique angular momentum.

and positive values (except in the $K = 0$ case), each value of K is twofold degenerate. This degeneracy is never manifested in an external field since K appears as a squared term in Eqs. (4-53) and (4-54). The quantum number M refers to the normal degeneracy of J, which is split by an external field into $2J + 1$ components along the space-fixed axes, so that the field-free total degeneracy of a given rotational level for $K \neq 0$ is $2(2J + 1)$.

Similarly we can show that the energy expression for an oblate top is (Problem 4-10)

$$\epsilon_{JKM} = h[B_0J(J + 1) + K^2(C_0 - B_0)]. \qquad \textbf{(4-54)}$$

As in calculating for linear molecules, the dipole transition integral for genuine symmetric top molecules leads to the selection rules $\Delta J = 0$,

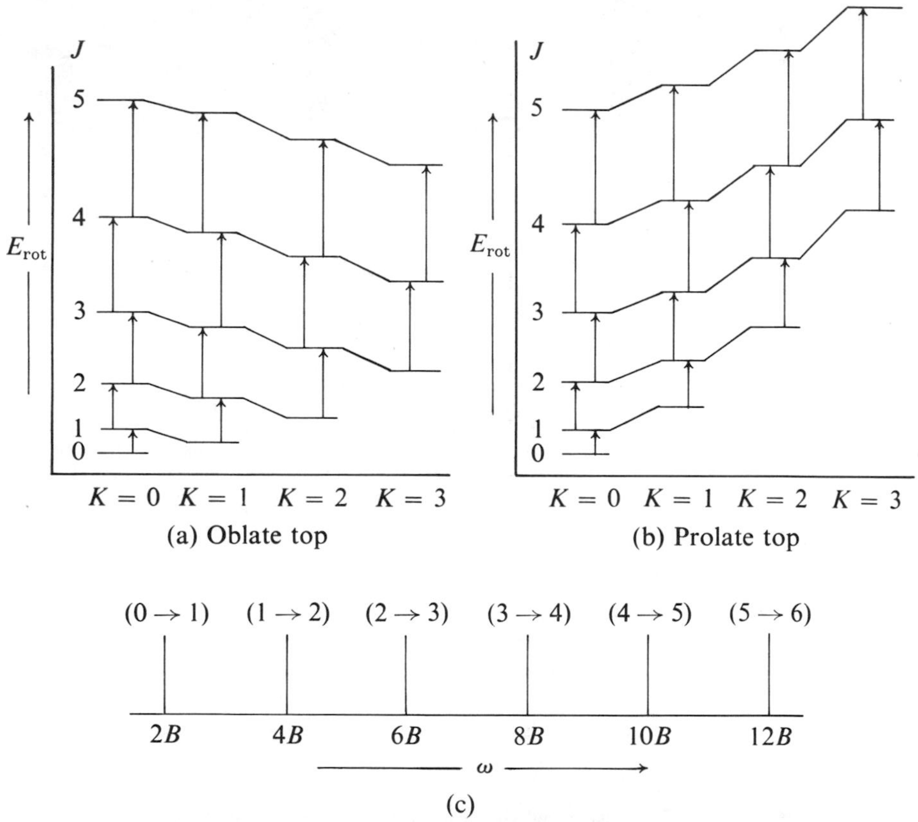

FIGURE 4-8 Energy levels and allowed vertical transitions of the (a) oblate and (b) prolate symmetric tops. (c) Since $\Delta K = 0$ in both cases, the transitions between the various K levels will be equally spaced, $2B$, $4B$, $6B$, and so on.

± 1 and $\Delta M = 0, \pm 1$ (where $\Delta J = 0$ and $\Delta M = 0, \pm 1$ are trivial selection rules in non–external field situations).[9] Since all symmetric top molecules by symmetry possess a unique axis along which the lone component of the dipole vector is oriented, interaction with the radiation electric field vector occurs only for this rotating dipole component (Figure 4-7). As a result, the selection rule governing transitions along this axis is $\Delta K = 0$. The energy-level diagrams for the oblate and prolate tops are shown in Figure 4-8; also shown are the allowed transitions corresponding to the selection rules $\Delta J = \pm 1$ and $\Delta K = 0$. For the transition $J \rightarrow J + 1$ and $\Delta K = 0$,

$$\Delta\epsilon_{JKM} = 2hB_0(J + 1), \tag{4-55}$$

where J refers to the lower quantum state. This equation allows the calculation of only I_b from the observed rotational spectrum (Eq. (4-52)). Such a result indicates the need for data on isotopic species. In general, we need B_0 values of as many different isotopically substituted species as there are unknown structural parameters (bond lengths and angles) of a molecule.

3. Asymmetric Top Molecules

Molecules having $I_a \neq I_b \neq I_c$ are called asymmetric tops, for instance, H_2O and CH_2O. In these cases only the total angular momentum, $\mathbf{P}^2 = J(J + 1)\hbar^2$, and the field-split levels of J, $\mathbf{P}_z{}^2 = M_J{}^2\hbar^2$, are quantized, so that only J and M_J are "true" quantum numbers. As a result, it is not possible to derive an equation in closed form for the rotational energy of an asymmetric rotor as we did for the spherical and symmetric tops. Correspondingly, the rotational spectra of these molecules are fairly complex. Part of the complexity arises from the increased number of rotational states. In the symmetric tops, the degenerate $\pm K$ states $(J + 1)$ exist as single rotational levels; in asymmetric tops, this degeneracy is removed and we observe $2J + 1$ levels for a given J state.

An approach used for deriving an approximate energy expression for low J states, however, is based on the assumption that an asymmetric rotor varies in its degree of asymmetry between the prolate and oblate forms at the two extremes. Thus, we define an asymmetry factor κ,

$$\kappa = \frac{2B_0 - A_0 - C_0}{A_0 - C_0}, \tag{4-56}$$

which is a measure of the degree of asymmetry. According to Eq. (4-56), the limiting values of κ are for the prolate top -1 $(B_0 = C_0)$, for the oblate top + 1 ($A_0 = B_0$), and for the most asymmetric case 0. The gradual change in energy that occurs in going from the prolate to the oblate case is shown in Figure 4-9. The notation $J_{K_{-1}K_1}$ is not a true quantum number but indicates the ordering of the K sublevels, which are no longer degenerate. Originally, they were indexed by the pseudo-quantum number τ, which assumed values from $-J$ to $+J$. The expression for $\tau = K_{-1} - K_1$, where K_{-1} represents the values of the true K quantum number of the prolate top and K_1 of the oblate top. Again, we empha-

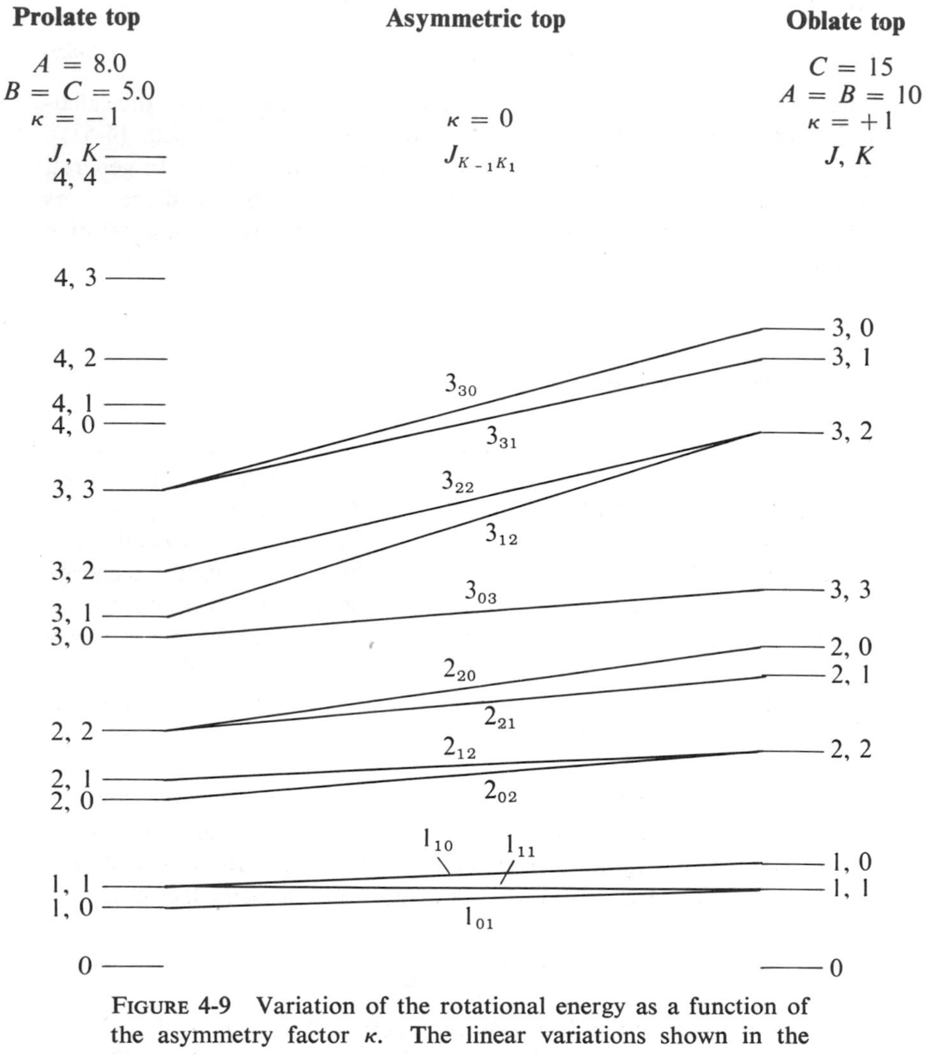

FIGURE 4-9 Variation of the rotational energy as a function of the asymmetry factor κ. The linear variations shown in the illustration are only approximate.

size that in terms of the asymmetric rotor τ, K_1, and K_{-1} are not quantum numbers.

The rotational energy expression for low J asymmetric-rotor states is

$$E = \tfrac{1}{2}(A + C)J(J + 1) + \tfrac{1}{2}(A - C)E_\tau^J(\kappa), \tag{4-57}$$

where $E_\tau^J(\kappa)$, defined as the reduced energy, can be imagined as resulting from a molecule with inertial constants of 1, κ, and -1. As such, the expression for $E_\tau^J(\kappa)$ derived in closed form is

$$E_\tau^J(\kappa) = FJ(J + 1) + (G - F)K^2 + H[f(J, K \pm 1)]^{1/2}, \tag{4-58}$$

where

$$f(J, K \pm 1) = \{\tfrac{1}{4}[J(J + 1) - K(K \pm 1)][J(J + 1) - (K \pm 1)(K \pm 2)]\}. \tag{4-59}$$

Of the six ways of identifying the a, b, c molecular axes with the coordinate system axes x, y, z, two are cited in Table 4-3. These correspond to the regions very near the extremes of κ equal to $+1$ or -1. The expressions for F, G, H and κ in these regions are also summarized in Table 4-3. For the case of an asymmetric rotor near $\kappa = +1$ (Case II), we obtain for $E_\tau^J(\kappa)$ from Table 4-3

$$E_\tau^J(\kappa) = J(J + 1) - 2K_1^2, \tag{4-60}$$

and substituting Eq. (4-60) into Eq. (4-57), we find that the rotational energy is just that for an oblate symmetric top:

$$E = J(J + 1)A - K_1^2(A - C), \tag{4-61}$$

TABLE 4-3. Summary of the Coefficients in the Evaluation of $E_\tau^J(\kappa)$ in the Regions near $\kappa = +1$ and -1

	Case I ($\kappa = -1$)	Case II ($\kappa = +1$)
x	b	b
y	c	a
z	a	c
F	$\frac{1}{2}(\kappa - 1)$	$\frac{1}{2}(\kappa + 1)$
G–F	$-\frac{1}{2}(\kappa - 3)$	$-\frac{1}{2}(\kappa + 3)$
H	$-\frac{1}{2}(\kappa + 1)$	$\frac{1}{2}(\kappa - 1)$

SOURCE: Gordy and Cook [Reference 4-3, p. 171], by permission.

TABLE 4-4. Explicit solutions of the Reduced Energy $E_\tau^J(\kappa)$

$J_{K_{-1}K_1}$	$E_\tau^J(\kappa)$
0_{00}	0
1_{10}	$\kappa + 1$
1_{11}	0
1_{01}	$\kappa - 1$
2_{20}	$2[\kappa + (\kappa^2 + 3)^{1/2}]$
2_{21}	$\kappa + 3$
2_{11}	4κ
2_{02}	$2[\kappa - (\kappa^2 + 3)^{1/2}]$
3_{30}	$5\kappa + 3 + 2(4\kappa^2 - 6\kappa + 6)^{1/2}$
3_{31}	$2[\kappa + (\kappa^2 + 15)^{1/2}]$
3_{21}	$5\kappa - 3 + 2(4\kappa^2 + 6\kappa + 6)^{1/2}$
3_{22}	4κ
3_{12}	$5\kappa + 3 - 2(4\kappa^2 - 6\kappa + 6)^{1/2}$
3_{13}	$2[\kappa - (\kappa^2 + 15)^{1/2}]$
3_{03}	$5\kappa - 3 - 2(4\kappa^2 + 6\kappa + 6)^{1/2}$

SOURCE: H. C. Allen, Jr., and Paul C. Cross, *Molecular Vib-Rotors.* New York: John Wiley and Sons, p. 30. By permission.

where $A = B$. The corresponding expression for the prolate symmetric top is obtained using the coefficients for Case I (Problem 4-13):

$$E = J(J + 1)C - K_{-1}^2(A - C), \qquad \textbf{(4-62)}$$

where $C = B$. Therefore, for slightly asymmetric rotors with κ's near $+1$ or -1 respectively, we apply the coefficients corresponding to Case II and Case I for obtaining the total rotational energy expression.

In the case of rigid rotors that are significantly asymmetric ($\kappa \simeq 0$), explicit expressions for the reduced energy $E_\tau^J(\kappa)$ for low J values have been derived as a function of τ. These terms, which are tabulated in Table 4-4, can be substituted directly into Eq. (4-57) to obtain the total rotational energy.

The selection rules for asymmetric tops are $\Delta J = 0, \pm 1$. In practice, each asymmetric rotor is taken as an individual case and handled according to the nonequivalence of its inertial moments. The Stark effect has been extremely useful in the rotational analysis of these molecules.

EXAMPLE 4-4: Given the structural parameters ($r_{CF} = 1.30$ Å and $\theta_{FCF} = 104.9°$) of the CF_2 radical in the gas phase, calculate the asymmetry factor κ, and predict whether the spectrum will be similar to an oblate top or a prolate top, or neither.

Solution: Since κ is given by Eq. (4-56), we must first evaluate A_0, B_0, and C_0 according to Eq. (4-52). Using the data from Table 4-2 and those given, we find

$$m_1 = m_F = 18.9984 \text{ amu}, \ \theta(\text{F—C—F}) = 104.9°,$$
$$m_2 = m_C = 12.0000 \text{ amu}, \ \text{C—F} = 1.30 \text{ Å}.$$

(a)

$$\begin{aligned} I_y &= \left(\frac{2m_1m_2}{2m_1 + m_2}\right) r^2 \cos^2\frac{\theta}{2} \\ &= \left(\frac{2(18.9984)(12.0000)}{2(18.9984) + 12.0000}\right)(1.30)^2(0.371) \\ &= 5.7180 \text{ amu-Å}^2. \\ I_x &= 2m_1r^2 \sin^2\frac{\theta}{2} = (2)(18.9984)(1.30)^2(0.629) \\ &= 40.3910 \text{ amu-Å}^2. \\ I_z &= I_x + I_y = 40.3910 + 5.7180 \\ &= 46.1090 \text{ amu-Å}^2. \end{aligned}$$

According to the convention, $I_a < I_b < I_c = I_y < I_x < I_z$.

(b) The various rotational constants are

$$A = \frac{h}{8\pi^2 I_a} = \frac{5.05376 \times 10^5 \text{ MHz}}{I_a(\text{amu-Å}^2)} = \frac{5.05376 \times 10^5}{5.7180} = 88{,}383.35 \text{ MHz}.$$

$$B = \frac{5.05376 \times 10^5}{40.3910} = 12{,}512.094 \text{ MHz}.$$

$$C = \frac{5.05376 \times 10^5}{46.1090} = 10{,}960.463 \text{ MHz}.$$

Since $A > B \sim C$, this molecule is a near prolate top. In order to decide which of the asymmetric relations best describe the energy levels, we calculate the asymmetry factor (Eq. (4-56)),

$$\kappa = \frac{2B - A - C}{A - C} = \frac{2(12{,}512.09) - 88{,}383.35 - 10{,}960.46}{88{,}383.35 - 10{,}960.46}$$
$$= -0.96.$$

Since the value of κ is so close to -1.00, the molecule can be treated as an approximate prolate top. Thus the energy states are best represented by Eq. (4-57) along with the parameters in Table 4-3, Case I.

The calculated energy levels of a pure prolate top, if we assume $A_0 = 88{,}383$ MHz and $B_0 = 12{,}512$ MHz, we obtain from Eq. (4-53),

$$\epsilon_{JK} = [B_0J(J + 1) + K^2(A_0 - B_0)].$$

Therefore

$$\epsilon_{10} = (12{,}512)(2) + 0 = 25{,}024 \text{ MHz};$$
$$\epsilon_{11} = (12{,}512)(2) + (1)(88{,}383 - 12{,}512) = 100{,}895 \text{ MHz}.$$

For the near prolate symmetric top, we obtain from Eqs. (4-57), (4-58), (4-59), and Case I, Table 4-3:

$J = 1, K = 0$

$$E_\tau^J(\kappa) = \tfrac{1}{2}(-1.96)(2) - 0 - 0$$
$$= -1.96$$

and

$$\epsilon_{10} = \tfrac{1}{2}(88{,}383 + 10{,}960)(2) + \tfrac{1}{2}(88{,}383 - 10{,}960)(-1.96)$$
$$= 23{,}468 \text{ MHz.}$$

$J = 1, K = 1$

$$E_\tau^J(\kappa) = 0.02$$

and

$$\epsilon_{11} = 99{,}343 + 774$$
$$= 98{,}569 \text{ MHz}$$

J, K		*Prolate Top*	*Asymmetric Prolate Top*
1, 1	100,895 MHz	———	
			——— 98,569 MHz
1, 0	25,024 MHz	———	
			——— 23,468 MHz

These results illustrate the approximate nature of Figure 4-9, where we used straight lines between various *JK* states. The actual prolate asymmetric states decrease relative to the pure prolate states before increasing toward the $\kappa = 0$ position.

G. MICROWAVE SPECTROSCOPY

1. Experimental

The absorption of radiation due to pure rotational transitions, internal rotations, and so on occurs in the wavelength range of a few centimeters. Spectroscopy performed in this region of the electromagnetic spectrum is referred to as microwave spectroscopy. A schematic diagram of a microwave spectrometer is shown in Figure 4-10. The source used in this region is a phase-coherent oscillator, that is, a Klystron tube, which emits a band width so narrow that it is essentially monochromatic. Therefore, dispersion of the radiation with a grating or a prism as in infrared or ultraviolet spectrometers is unnecessary. The source can be tuned over a wide frequency range by varying the sweep voltage from a power supply. The radiation generated is most advantageously transmitted through a metallic rectangular wave guide, so that maximum use can be

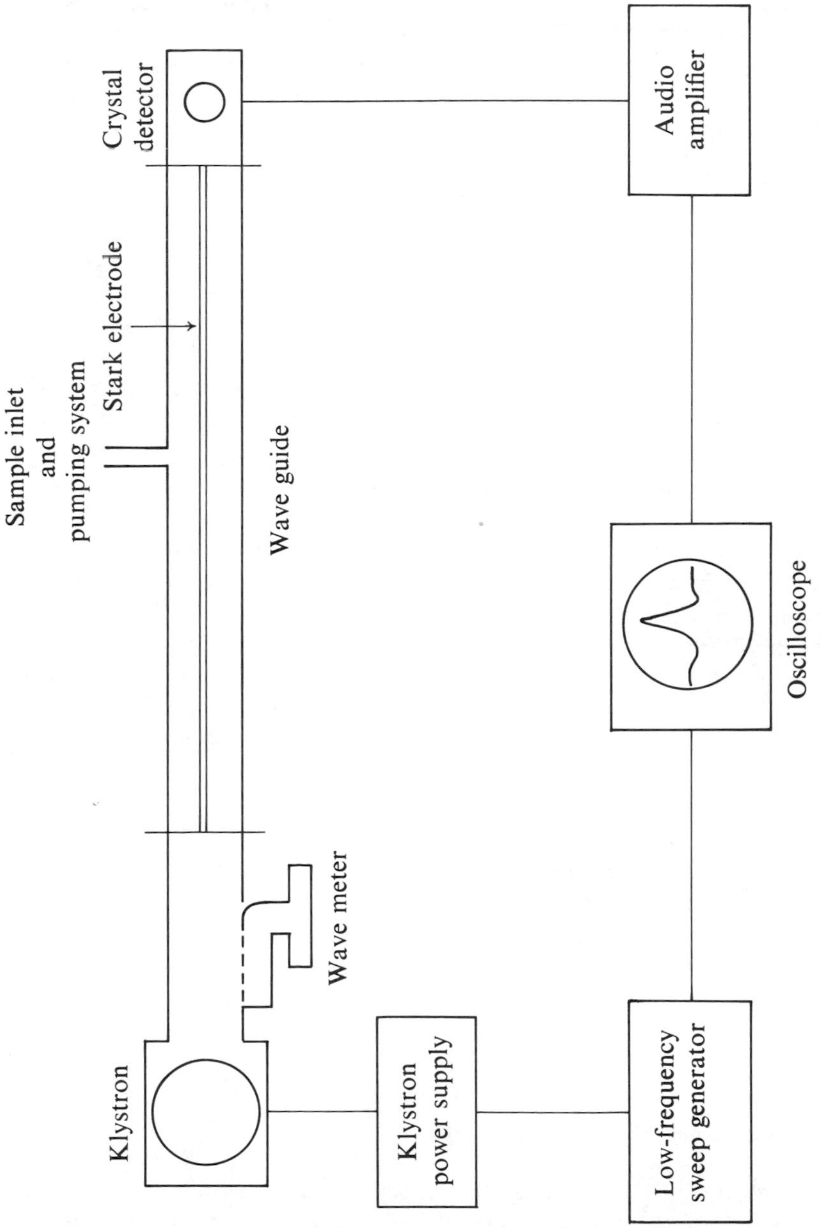

FIGURE 4-10 Schematic diagram of a microwave spectrometer.

made of the directional nature of electric and magnetic field effects. These will be illustrated in Sections G3 and G4. The material to be studied, which is normally a gas at relatively low pressure, is contained in the wave guide. The radiation that is not absorbed passes through the sample and is measured by a crystal detector or a bolometer. The detected signal is amplified and transmitted to an oscilloscope for visual display. When the source is tuned over an absorption, the intensity at the detector is reduced and we observe a corresponding "dip" in the oscilloscopic display. The frequency of the absorption is measured by comparison with a calibrated oscillator frequency.

A useful modification of the ordinary microwave spectrometer has been the insertion of parallel brass electrodes inside of the wave guide. These flat metal strips are insulated from the metallic wave guide with Teflon or some other appropriate dielectric, and are capable of producing either a constant or a modulated electric field. The interaction of the electric field with the permanent electric dipole moment of the species under investigation results in the splitting of the degenerate rotational levels. This interaction is an example of the Stark effect in rotational spectroscopy. The parallel metal strip arrangement also uses the fact that the external electric field can be generated either parallel or perpendicular to the varying electric field component of the microwave (source) radiation. Thus this directional flexibility permits transitions between specific Stark-split rotational levels in the perpendicular or the parallel orientation. To obtain an improved signal-to-noise ratio, the external electric field is turned on and off (modulated) at roughly 10^5 times per second (~ 100 kilocycles), and the resulting absorption frequency is measured using phase-sensitive detection. This technique is often referred to as Stark modulation rotational spectroscopy. Stark effect rotational spectroscopy has provided the most accurate electric dipole moment data on gaseous molecules, and is extremely helpful in the assignment of rotational transitions, particularly for asymmetric rotors.

It should be remarked that recent advances in solid state sources and detectors as well as in high-speed computing techniques are making it possible to study and interpret complex spectra, particularly those of asymmetric rotors.

2. Determining Molecular Geometry

As previously pointed out, the experimental determination of pure rotational frequencies allows us to obtain one or more moments of inertia of a species under consideration. The inertial moments are in turn directly related to the internuclear bond distances and bond angles.

TABLE 4-5. Observed Rotational Constants of Selected Symmetric and Asymmetric Rotors

Species	A_0 (MHz)	B_0 (MHz)	C_0 (MHz)	D_J (KHz)[a]	D_{JK} (KHz)[a]
CH_3F	...	25,536.148	...	60.4	439.26
$CH_3{}^{35}Cl$	...	13,292.86	...	18.1	198
CH_3CN	...	9,198.899	...	3.81	176.9
CF_3CCH	...	2,877.948	...	0.24	6.3
$CH_3{}^{198}Hg^{35}Cl$	...	2,077.48	...	0.241	21.0
$(CH_3)_3CH$	...	7,789.45	...	11	...
$(CH_3)_3C—C{\equiv}C^{35}Cl$	...	890.482	...	0.03	...
$^{28}SiH_3NCS$	...	1,516.018	...	<0.3	41.9
$C_7H_{13}N$	...	2,431.4	...	4	<15
CH_3OCl	42,064.35	6,296.88	5,670.62	...	...
$CH_2(CN)_2$	20,882.137	2.942.477	2,616.774	...	...
$(CH_3)_2O$	38,788.5	10,056.6	8,886.9	...	...
C_6H_5F	5,663.54	2,570.64	1,767.94	...	...
CH_3COF	11,039.28	9,685.65	5,322.05	...	...
$(CH_3)_2CO$	10,165.60	8,514.95	4,910.17	...	...
$CH_2CH{=}CH$	30,063.7	21,825.6	13,795.7	...	...
C_4H_4O(furan)	9,446.96	9,246.61	4,670.88	...	...
$(CH_3)_2C{=}CH_2$	9,133.32	8,381.75	4,615.99	...	...
$CH_2CH_2CH_2O$	12,045.2	11,734.0	6,730.7	...	...

SOURCE: Gordy and Cook [Reference 4-3], by permission.
NOTE: Species without A_0 and C_0 entries are symmetric tops.
[a] First-order centrifugal distortion constants in kilohertz units. For prolate and oblate tops, the nonrigid rotor energy expression is $\Delta\epsilon = 2B(J + 1) - 4D_J(J + 1)^3 - 2D_{JK}(J + 1)K^2$ for $J \rightarrow J + 1$ and $K \rightarrow K$.

The rotational constants of selected symmetric and asymmetric rotors obtained from mcrowave experiments are listed in Table 4-5. How to use these data in determining structural parameters is exemplified below.

EXAMPLE 4-5: The microwave absorptions of $P^{35}Cl_3$ and $P^{37}Cl_3$ for the $J = 0 \rightarrow J = 1$ transitions were observed at 5234.2 and 4975.0 megahertz (MHz), respectively. For this oblate symmetric top, calculate the valence bond angle and the P—Cl bond distance according to the accompanying diagram.

Solution: For the pyramidal oblate symmetric top, PCl_3 (all identical chlorines), the only unknown molecular parameters are $\theta_{Cl—P—C}$, and $r_{P—Cl}$. Since $\Delta K = 0$ for symmetric top transitions, Eq. (4-54) reduces to

$$\Delta\epsilon = 2h[B_0(J + 1)] \text{ ergs} \qquad \textbf{(4-63)}$$

for $J \to J + 1$. Converting to megahertz gives

$$\Delta\epsilon' = \frac{\Delta\epsilon}{h} = 2[B_0(J + 1)] \text{ MHz.} \tag{4-63a}$$

Substituting the microwave absorptions $\Delta\epsilon'$ for excitation from $J = 0$ results in $B_0 = 2617.1$ MHz for $P^{35}Cl_3$ and $B_0 = 2487.5$ MHz for $P^{37}Cl_3$.

The moment of inertia about the b axis for an oblate top can be expressed as (Table 4-2)

$$I_b = m_1r^2(1 - \cos\theta) + \frac{m_1m_2r^2}{3m_1 + m_2}(1 - 2\cos\theta), \tag{4-64}$$

where $I_b = h/8\pi^2B$. Rearranging Eq. (4-64) gives

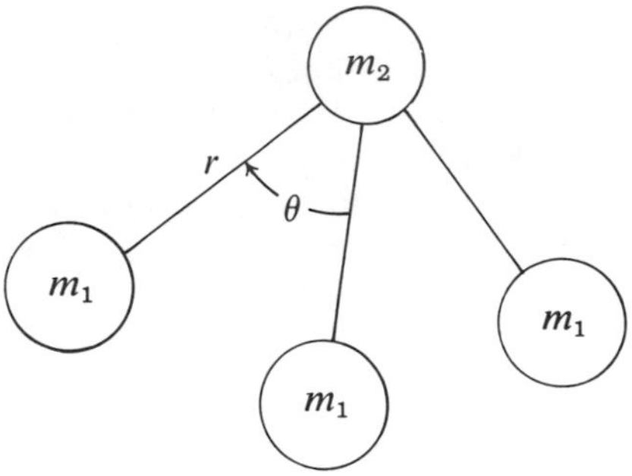

m_2 = phosphorus and m_1 = chlorine

$$\frac{I_b}{r^2} = \left[m_1 + \frac{m_1m_2}{3m_1 + m_2}\right] + \left[\frac{2m_1m_2}{3m_1 + m_2} - m_1\right]\cos\theta. \tag{4-65}$$

Taking the ratio of this expression for the two isotopically substituted molecules yields

$$\frac{I_b}{I_b'} = \frac{B_0'}{B_0}$$

$$= \frac{\{m_1 + [m_1m_2/(3m_1 + m_2)]\} + \{[2m_1m_2/(3m_1 + m_2)] - m_1\}\cos\theta}{\{m_1 + [m_1m_2/(3m_1 + m_2)]\}' + \{[2m_1m_2/(3m_1 + m_2)] - m_1\}'\cos\theta}, \tag{4-66}$$

where the prime refers to the $P^{37}Cl_3$ molecule. Substituting the following data,

$P^{35}Cl_3$	$B_0 = 2617.1$ MHz,	$^{35}Cl = 34.96885$ amu
$P^{37}Cl_3$	$B_0 = 2487.5$ MHz,	$^{37}Cl = 36.96590$ amu
		$^{31}P = 30.97376$ amu

we obtain

$$\frac{2487.5}{2617.1} = \frac{(42.939) + (-19.027)\cos\theta}{(45.036) + (-20.825)\cos\theta},$$

$$\cos\theta = -0.1790,$$

$$\theta = 100°19'.$$

Substituting θ into Eq. (4-65), we obtain

$$r^2 = 4.143 \times 10^{-16}\ \text{cm}^2,$$
$$r = 2.035 \times 10^{-8}\ \text{cm} = 2.035\ \text{Å}.$$

3. The Stark Effect

Classically, the first-order interaction energy between the permanent electric dipole moment of a molecule and an external electric field is given as

$$\epsilon^{(1)} = \boldsymbol{\mu}\cdot\mathbf{E}. \tag{4-67}$$

In the case of linear or symmetric top molecules with no nuclear spin, the electric dipole moment μ is constant, and oriented along the unique molecular symmetry axis, as shown in Figure 4-11. Quantization of this motion is characterized by the quantum number K, and the **K** vector in turn precesses about the total angular momentum vector **J**. In the case where $\epsilon_{\text{rot}} > \epsilon_{\text{Stark}}$, **K** is so strongly coupled to **J** compared with the

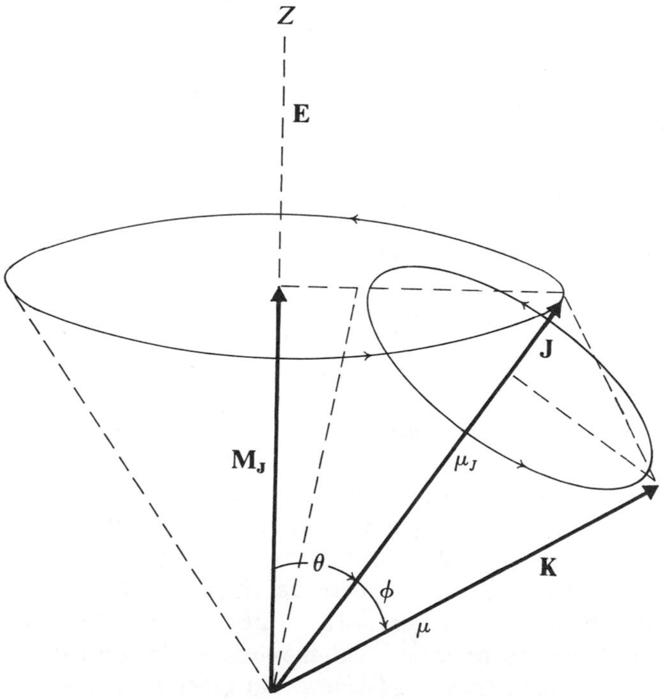

FIGURE 4-11 Vector model of a linear or a symmetric top molecule in an electric field (Stark effect).

coupling of **J** to the external field, that all the states of μ relative to **J** are averaged to zero except for the component along **J**, $\mu_{\mathbf{J}}$. Thus, the first-order interaction energy of μ_J along the field direction is given as

$$\epsilon^{(1)} = -\mu_J \mathbf{E} \cos\theta, \tag{4-68}$$

where **E** is the electric field oriented along the space-fixed axis Z (Figure 4-11). The cosine of the angle between the field component $\mathbf{M_J}$ and the **J** component of the electric moment μ_J is[10]

$$\cos\theta = \frac{\mathbf{M_J}}{\mathbf{J}} = \frac{M_J}{\sqrt{J(J+1)}}, \tag{4-69}$$

and

$$\mu_J = \mu\cos\phi = \mu\frac{\mathbf{K}}{\mathbf{J}} = \frac{\mu K}{\sqrt{J(J+1)}}. \tag{4-70}$$

Thus, substituting Eqs. (4-70) and (4-69) into (4-68), we obtain

$$\epsilon^{(1)} = -\frac{\mu K M_J \mathbf{E}}{J(J+1)}. \tag{4-71}$$

For linear molecules (special case of a symmetric top where $K = 0$) and the $K = 0$ levels of symmetric top rotors, $\epsilon^{(1)} = 0$, and no first-order Stark displacements or splittings exist.

For symmetric top levels where $K \neq 0$, the energy-level splittings for the transitions $\Delta J = +1$, $\Delta K = 0$, and $\Delta M_J = 0$ are[11]

$$\Delta\epsilon^{(1)} = -\mu\mathbf{E}KM_J\left[\frac{1}{(J+1)(J+2)} - \frac{1}{J(J+1)}\right], \tag{4-72}$$

where J equals the lower state. On simplifying, we find

$$\Delta\epsilon^{(1)} = \frac{2\mu\mathbf{E}KM_J}{J(J+1)(J+2)}, \tag{4-73}$$

or

$$\Delta\nu^{(1)} = \frac{\Delta\epsilon^{(1)}}{h} = (0.5034)\mu\mathbf{E}\cdot\frac{2KM_J}{J(J+1)(J+2)}\ \text{MHz}, \tag{4-74}$$

where μ is expressed in Debyes and **E** in volts/cm. The expression $\Delta\epsilon^{(1)}/h$ represents the frequency difference ($\Delta\nu^{(1)}$) by which the π components ($\Delta M_J = 0$) are displaced from the zero field ($\mathbf{E} = 0$) transition as a result of the first-order effect. These transitions and the spectrum are shown on the right side of Figure 4-12. Directly below the energy-level transitions is shown the spectrum—with the electric field above the dividing line, and without the electric field below. In general, for the first-order Stark effect there are $(2J + 1)$ lines for $\Delta J = \pm 1$ and $2J$ lines for $\Delta J = 0$, where J refers to the lower quantum state. Thus, for the $J = 1 \rightarrow J = 2$ transition shown, there are three lines for the $\mathbf{E} \neq 0$ situation. It should

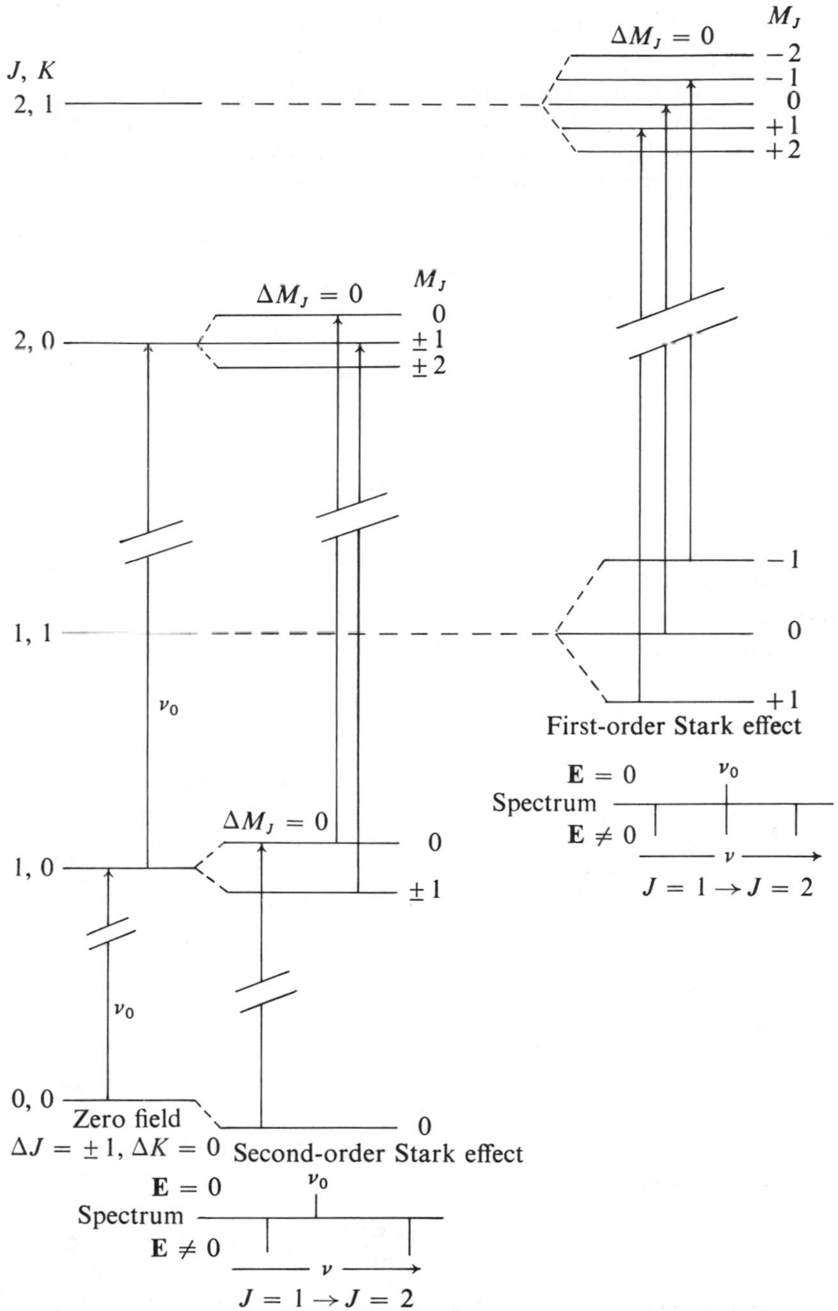

FIGURE 4-12 Energy-level diagram of a linear or a symmetric top molecule in an electric field (Stark effect).

also be noted that the lines are separated by the same frequency difference $\Delta\nu^{(1)}$, which is a general feature of first-order Stark spectra.

EXAMPLE 4-6: For the first-order Stark shift of $CH_3C{\equiv}CH$ that is 13.2 MHz in a 100-volt/cm electric field for the transition $J = 1 \rightarrow J = 2$, $K = 1 \rightarrow K = 1$, and $M_J = -1 \rightarrow M_J = -1$, calculate the electric dipole moment, assuming it to be identical in these two rotational states.

Solution: This transition of methylacetylene corresponds to the one shown in Figure 4-12 and mathematically characterized by Eq. (4-73). Applying Eq. (4-74), we obtain

$$\Delta\nu^{(1)} = 13.2 = (0.5034)\mu\mathbf{E}\cdot\frac{2KM_J}{J(J+1)(J+2)}$$

$$13.2 = (0.5034)(\mu)(100 \text{ volts/cm})(0.3333).$$

Solving for μ, we obtain

$$\mu = 0.784 \text{ Debye.}$$

Linear or symmetric top molecules with $K = 0$, which do not exhibit first-order Stark displacements, are observed to undergo second-order Stark splitting at electric fields of a couple of thousand volts/cm. The second-order Stark perturbation energy for a symmetric top molecule is

$$\epsilon^{(2)} = \sum_{J'} \frac{|\langle J, K, M_J|H_{\mathbf{E}}|J', K, M_J\rangle|^2}{E_{J,K} - E_{J',K}}. \tag{4-75}$$

The solution of this equation, which is obtained using second-order perturbation theory, is given as

$$\epsilon^{(2)} = \frac{\mu^2\mathbf{E}^2}{2hB}\left\{\frac{(J^2 - K^2)(J^2 - M_J^2)}{J^3(2J-1)(2J+1)} - \frac{[(J+1)^2 - K^2][(J+1)^2 - M_J^2]}{(J+1)^3(2J+1)(2J+3)}\right\}. \tag{4-76}$$

For linear molecules and symmetric tops where $K = 0$, Eq. (4-76) reduces to

$$\epsilon^{(2)} = \frac{\mu^2\mathbf{E}^2}{2hB}\left\{\frac{[J(J+1) - 3M_J^2]}{J(J+1)(2J-1)(2J+3)}\right\}. \tag{4-77}$$

Since the $J = 0$ level is nondegenerate ($M_J = 0$), instead of splitting it is simply displaced by

$$\epsilon^{(2)} = -\frac{\mu^2\mathbf{E}^2}{6hB}. \tag{4-78}$$

The displacement of the $J = 0$ level is shown on the left side of Figure 4-12. For the π transition from this level to $J = 1$, $K = 0$ in the presence of an electric field ($\Delta M_J = 0, J = 0 \rightarrow J = 1, \Delta K = 0$), the observed microwave frequency is shifted from the unperturbed line (ν_0) by

$$\Delta\nu^{(2)} = \frac{\Delta\epsilon}{h} = \frac{8}{15}\frac{\mu^2\mathbf{E}^2}{h^2\nu_0} = \frac{0.1352\mu^2\mathbf{E}^2}{\nu_0}\ \text{MHz}, \quad \textbf{(4-79)}$$

where ν_0 is expressed in MHz, μ in Debyes, and **E** in volts/cm.

EXAMPLE 4-7: Calculate the expected second-order frequency shift of CH_3F for the π component of the $J = 0 \rightarrow J = 1$ and $K = 0$ transition when subjected to an electric field of 2000 volts/cm. From independently obtained data, $B_0(J = 0 \rightarrow J = 1) = 25{,}536.2$ MHz and $\mu = 1.857$ Debyes.

Solution: Since CH_3F is a prolate symmetric top, Eq. (4-55) applies to the π component transition. Ignoring centrifugal distortions for the moment, we find that according to Eq. (4-55)

$$\Delta\epsilon' = \nu_0 = 2[B_0(J + 1)] = 2B_0$$

for $J =$ lower state. Thus,

$$\nu_0 = (2)(25{,}536.2) = 51{,}072.4\ \text{MHz}.$$

Substituting ν_0 into Eq. (4-79) gives

$$\Delta\nu^{(2)} = \frac{(0.1352)(1.857)^2(2000)^2}{(51{,}072.4)} = 36.5\ \text{MHz}.$$

For the normally $2J + 1$ degenerate rotational levels ($J > 0$), the second-order Stark splitting now depends on M_J^2, as shown in Eqs. (4-76) and (4-77). As a result, the rotational levels are split into *pairs* of degenerate levels ($\pm M_J$), with the exception of $M_J = 0$, which is nondegenerate (Figure 4-12). Summing the $\pm M_J$ and $M_J = 0$ states accounts for the $2J + 1$ rotational degeneracy. The second-order splitting is also considerably smaller than the first-order splitting, as shown in Figure 4-12. As a result, using normal first-order electric fields (~ 100 volts/cm), the contribution from the second-order effect is ordinarily less than 1 percent. Thus, the shifted frequency is very adequately represented solely by $\Delta\nu^{(1)}$ in this electric field region.

At electric fields of ~ 1000 volts/cm, the second-order effect does contribute to the shifted frequencies. The second-order transitions for the π components of a symmetric top for the $J = 1 \rightarrow J = 2$ transition are shown on the left side of Figure 4-12. For the transition $\Delta M_J = 0$, $J \rightarrow J + 1$, $J \neq 0$, the second-order frequency shift is given as

$$\Delta\nu^{(2)} = \frac{2\mu^2\mathbf{E}^2}{h^2\nu_0}\left\{\frac{3M_J^2(8J^2 + 16J + 5) - 4J(J + 1)^2(J + 2)}{J(J + 2)(2J - 1)(2J + 1)(2J + 3)(2J + 5)}\right\}. \quad \textbf{(4-80)}$$

Note in the field-on, field-off spectrum (Figure 4-12) that the two shifted lines are not equidistant from the zero-field line (ν_0). This occurs since M_J is inside the bracketed expression of Eq. (4-80), whereas it is a simple multiple in Eq. (4-74).

As was the case for pure rotational spectra, the asymmetric-rotor Stark effect is not only complicated but different for each molecule, depending on the degree of asymmetry. (A detailed discussion of these cases is too involved for the scope of this presentation.) However, simplification does occur when asymmetric rotors have approximately linear or symmetric symmetry, for example, in HNCO and H_2CO. Formaldehyde, which is an approximate oblate symmetric top has been studied using the Stark effect in the $n \rightarrow \pi^*$ electronic transition of the 3390-Å band.[12] The resolution and assignments of the rotational splittings were sufficient to obtain the excited state electric dipole moment. For the π component in the first-order effect, using Eq. (4-71) is justified since the Stark splitting is much greater than the asymmetry splitting. Thus, the rotational energy difference for the upper and lower electronic states in a π transition is given as

$$\Delta\epsilon = \frac{2KM_J\mathbf{E}}{J(J+1)(J+2)}(\mu' - \mu), \tag{4-81}$$

where μ' is the electric dipole moment of the electronically excited state. This equation has been used for determining $(\mu' - \mu)$; since $\mu = 2.34$ D is known from independent microwave studies of the ground electronic state, Freeman and Klemper were able to obtain the rather surprising result that $\mu' = 1.48$ D.

4. The Zeeman Effect

Most ground electronic state molecules have closed electronic shells and hence have $^1\Sigma$ ground states. Magnetic moments can be generated in these molecules, however, either by rotation or by the application of an external magnetic field. The latter effect, which is due to the magnetic susceptibility of the species, is proportional to the magnetic field strength and usually negligible compared with the rotation-induced magnetic moment. The interaction of an external magnetic field **H** with the rotational magnetic moment is the specific Zeeman effect we will discuss presently. The interaction of a magnetic field with a magnetic moment resulting from unpaired electrons (electronic angular momentum) will be discussed in Chapter 8, Resonance Phenomena. The magnetic fields necessary for observation of these spectroscopic transitions (Electron Paramagnetic Resonance) are of the order of a few gauss, compared with several kilogauss for the rotation-induced Zeeman splittings.

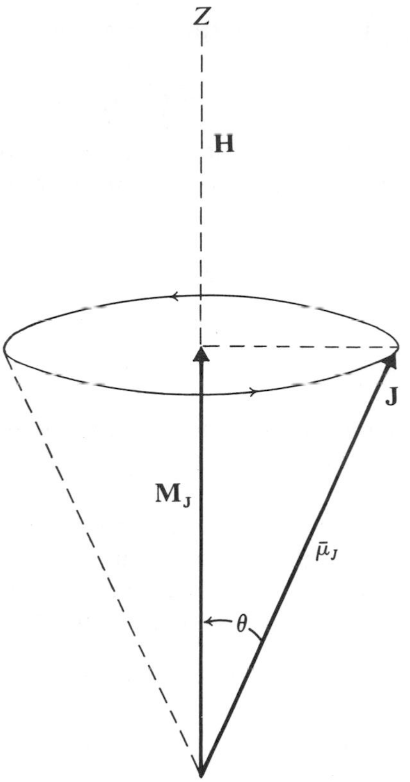

FIGURE 4-13 The first-order Zeeman interaction of the average rotation-induced magnetic moment with an external magnetic field.

The classical Hamiltonian for the interaction of an external magnetic field **H** with the rotation-induced magnetic moment $\boldsymbol{\mu}$ is

$$H' = -\boldsymbol{\mu}\cdot\mathbf{H}. \tag{4-82}$$

The corresponding vector diagram is shown in Figure 4-13. Since the average component of the magnetic moment $\bar{\mu}_J$ oriented along the molecular axis precesses about the external field **H**, then

$$H' = -\bar{\mu}_J\mathbf{H}\cos\theta, \tag{4-83}$$

where

$$\cos\theta = \frac{M_J}{\sqrt{J(J+1)}}. \tag{4-84}$$

Substituting Eq. (4-84) into Eq. (4-83), we obtain

$$H' = -\bar{\mu}_J\mathbf{H}\frac{M_J}{\sqrt{J(J+1)}}. \tag{4-85}$$

The average component of the magnetic moment introduced here without proof is

$$\bar{\mu}_J = g_J \mu_N \sqrt{J(J+1)}, \qquad \textbf{(4-86)}$$

where g_J is called the rotational g factor, or spectroscopic splitting factor, and μ_N is the nuclear magneton (5.051×10^{-24} erg/gauss). Replacing the expression for $\bar{\mu}_J$ into Eq. (4-85), we obtain

$$H' = -g_J \mu_N \mathbf{H} M_J. \qquad \textbf{(4-87)}$$

According to Eq. (2-9),

$$\epsilon'(M_J) = -g_J \mu_N \mathbf{H} M_J. \qquad \textbf{(4-88)}$$

Although this is a general expression that applies to linear, symmetric, and asymmetric rotors, the functional forms will differ by the various expressions for g_J.

In the case of linear molecules g_J is simply a constant. Although it is technically a function of the rotational state J, the resolvable frequency shift from the zero-field line is of the order of magnitude of the line width. The selection rules for transitions among the split M_J states are

$$\Delta M_J = 0 \ (\pi \text{ components}) \qquad \textbf{(4-89)}$$

and

$$\Delta M_J = \pm 1 \ (\sigma \text{ components}). \qquad \textbf{(4-90)}$$

The selection rules $\Delta M_J = 0$ and $\Delta M_J = \pm 1$ apply respectively to transitions for which the Zeeman magnetic field is parallel or perpendicular to the oscillating electric field vector of the microwave source radiation. Thus, the π and σ components are again mutually exclusive.

The corresponding shifted components for the $\Delta J = +1$ transition according to Eqs. (4-88), (4-89), and (4-90) are

$$\Delta\nu(\pi) = \frac{\Delta\epsilon'(M_J)}{h} = 0 \qquad \textbf{(4-91)}$$

and

$$\Delta\nu(\sigma) = \frac{\Delta\epsilon'(M_J)}{h} = \pm\frac{g_J \mu_N \mathbf{H}}{h}. \qquad \textbf{(4-92)}$$

Therefore, we observe a single unshifted component for the **H** parallel and a doublet for **H** perpendicular as shown in Figure 4-14 for a $J = 1 \rightarrow J = 2$ transition. Together they form the Zeeman triplet. Since the rotational g_J factors are equal within experimental error, even the higher rotational state transitions (which have greater populations, hence intensities) will have this simple triplet pattern. These rotational g_J factors may be

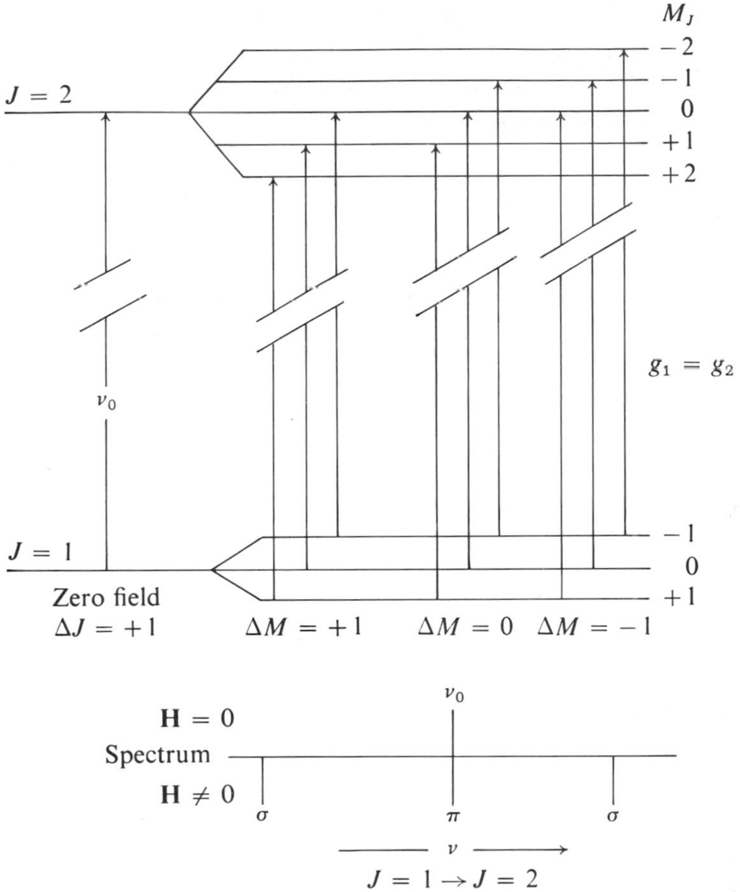

FIGURE 4-14 The Zeeman triplet of $J = 1 \rightarrow J = 2$ transition for a linear molecule. (Note that the M_J ordering assumes a positive g_J factor.)

positive or negative and in general must be experimentally determined. Note the analogy with the "normal" atomic Zeeman effect.

EXAMPLE 4-8: Calculate the energy and frequency shift for the σ components of the $J = 0 \rightarrow J = 1$ transition of $^{12}C^{32}S$ when they are subjected to a 5-kilogauss magnetic field ($g = -0.272$). Sketch the Zeeman splittings and indicate the allowed transitions.

Solution: According to Eq. (4-88), the energy shift for the σ components is

$$\begin{aligned}\Delta\epsilon'(\sigma) &= -g_J\mu_N\mathbf{H}\Delta M_J \\ &= -(-0.272)(5.05 \times 10^{-24} \text{ erg/gauss})(5.0 \times 10^3 \text{ gauss})(1) \\ &= 6.87 \times 10^{-21} \text{ erg}\end{aligned}$$

and the frequency shift according to Eq. (4-92) is

$$\Delta\nu(\sigma) = \frac{g_J\mu_N \mathrm{H}}{h} = \frac{6.87 \times 10^{-21}\ \text{erg}}{6.62 \times 10^{-27}\ \text{erg-sec}} = 1.04 \times 10^6\ \text{sec}^{-1}$$

$$= 1.04\ \text{MHz}.$$

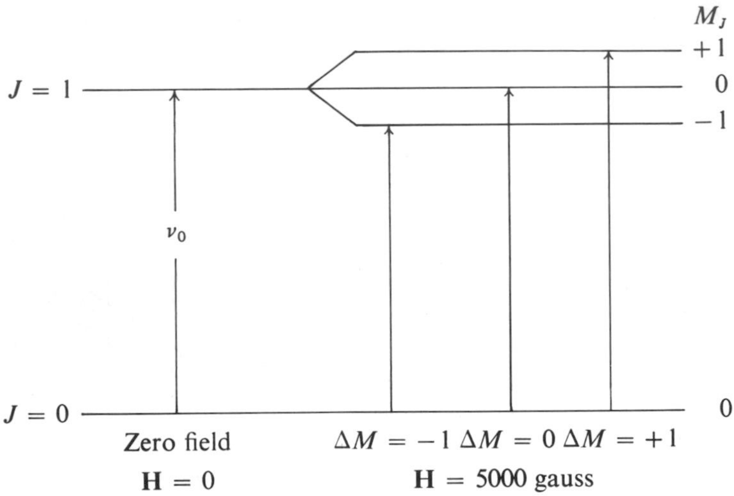

Note the M_J ordering since g is negative in this case.

In the cases of symmetric and asymmetric rotors, the g_J factor is no longer a constant and becomes a function of J and K for the former and J and τ for the latter. The nonequivalence of the g_J factors of the J and $J + 1$ states makes possible a significantly more complicated spectrum than the simple Zeeman triplet observed for the linear case.

5. Restricted and Torsional Internal Rotation

Quite often the vibrational motions of some molecules have very low force constants, corresponding to relatively low frequency motions about bonds that are usually of single-bond order or less. In such cases, the molecule does not execute simple harmonic motion, but instead, the absence of a significant resisting potential allows one part of the molecule to twist and turn relative to the other part. Such motions are referred to as torsional, or restricted, rotations. Examples are H_3C—CH_3, CH_3—OH, and (CH_3)—O—(CH_3). For simplicity, we consider the case of coaxial tops, where only two symmetrical groups rotate about a common or identical bond. If two separate inertial moments of each group are defined as I_1 and I_2, then the "reduced moment of inertia" is defined as

$$I_r = \frac{I_1 I_2}{I_1 + I_2}. \tag{4-93}$$

For coaxial tops, the potential energy of rotation will be a function of the azimuthal angle ϕ as the two groups are rotated about the common bond. For an example, we might consider molecules of the general type $Y_3C—CX_3$, illustrated in Figure 4-15. One period of rotation involves

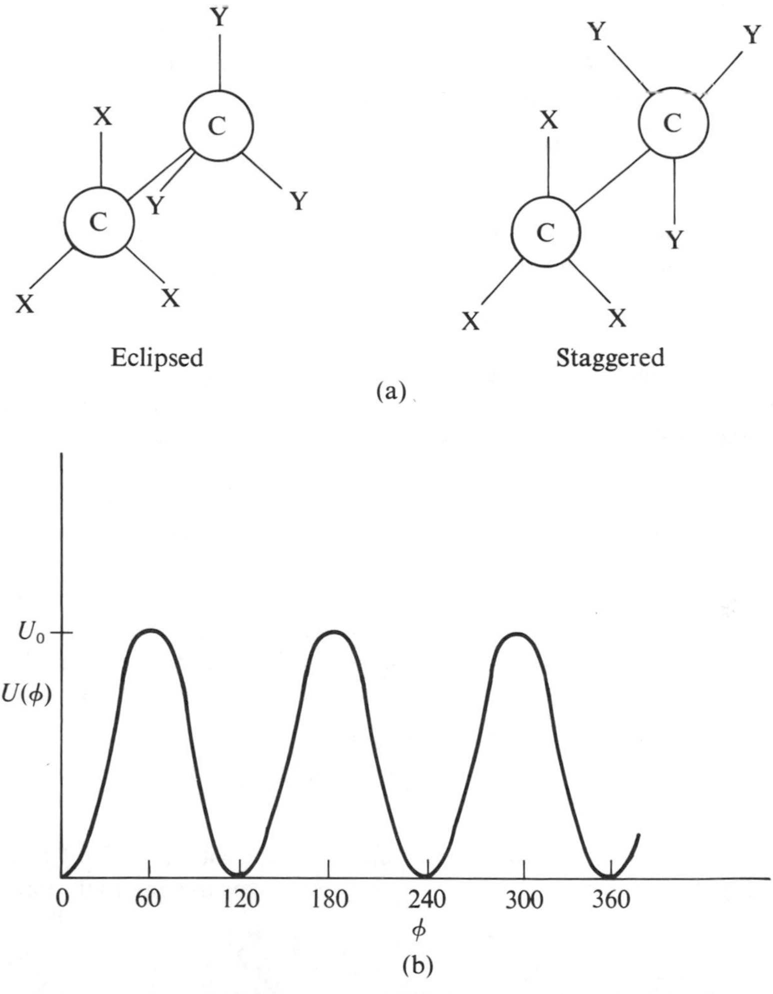

FIGURE 4-15 (a) Staggered and eclipsed positions of molecules containing the symmetrical coaxial tops CX_3 and CY_3. (b) Variation of the potential energy of rotation as a function of the azimuthal rotational angle ϕ.

three minima and three maxima in potential energy. When the CX_3 and CY_3 groups are at staggered positions, the potential energy $U(\phi) = 0$ is a minimum (0°, 120°, 240°, and 360°). When the groups assume eclipsed positions relative to each other, there is a maximum resistance to rotation, and $U(\phi) = U_0$ (60°, 180°, and 300°). This value of the potential energy is specific for a particular molecule and is called the barrier height. Since the total number of internal degrees of freedom must be constant, $3N - 6$ for nonlinear polyatomic molecules and $3N - 5$ for linear molecules, the internal rotation motion is considered to be the loss of a vibrational motion. If the interaction of this motion with the other rotational and vibrational modes is assumed to be negligible, the separable Schrödinger equation describing this motion is

$$-\frac{h^2}{8\pi^2 I_r}\frac{\partial^2\psi(\phi)}{\partial\phi^2} + [U(\phi) - \epsilon]\psi(\phi) = 0. \qquad \textbf{(4-94)}$$

The expression for the potential energy that best describes this periodic behavior as a function of the azimuthal angle ϕ is a modified Fourier series,

$$U(\phi) = \tfrac{1}{2}U_0(1 - \cos n\phi), \qquad \textbf{(4-95)}$$

where n, an integer, is related to the symmetry of the molecule. For the example of Figure 4-15, $n = 3$. The periodic function has minima corresponding to ϕ at 0, $\pm 2\pi/n$, $\pm 4\pi/n$, and so on, and maxima at $\pm\pi/n$, $\pm 3\pi/n$, and so on. The solution of (4-94) depends critically on the exact form of $U(\phi)$, or more specifically on U_0 and the absolute temperature. We consider for the moment the two extremes of a high barrier ($U_0 \gg \epsilon$) and a low barrier ($U_0 \ll \epsilon$).

In the case of a low barrier or a highly excited molecule ($\epsilon > U_0$), the internal motion is essentially a free rotation. In this case, the cosine term of Eq. (4-95) averages to zero for a complete period, and Eq. (4-95) reduces to $U(\phi) = \frac{1}{2}U_0$. The Schrödinger expression (Eq. (4-94)) simplifies to

$$\frac{\partial^2\psi}{\partial\phi^2} + \frac{8\pi^2 I_r}{h^2}(\epsilon - \tfrac{1}{2}U_0)\psi = 0. \qquad \textbf{(4-96)}$$

This is a familiar differential equation (compare with Eq. (3-5)) whose solutions lead to the quantized energy expression for free internal rotation

$$\epsilon_j = \frac{h^2 n^2 j^2}{8\pi^2 I_r}, \qquad j = 0, \pm 1, \pm 2, \ldots, \qquad \textbf{(4-97)}$$

where n is the symmetry factor and j the rotational quantum number.[13] Molecules such as CH_3NO and CH_3BF_2 with barrier heights of 6.03 and 13.77 cal/mole, respectively, are examples of practically free rotors at room temperature ($RT \simeq 600$ cal/mole). They also correspond to an internal potential energy expression with a sixfold barrier, $n = 6$.

For the case where the potential barrier is very high, such as ethane or acetaldehyde, the cosine term of Eq. (4-95) can be expanded as

$$\cos n\phi = 1 - \frac{n^2\phi^2}{2} + \frac{n^4\phi^4}{4!} - \cdots, \qquad n\phi \ll 1. \tag{4-98}$$

Retaining only the first two terms and substituting into Eq. (4-95) gives

$$U(\phi) = U_0 \frac{n^2\phi^2}{4},$$

which is similar in form to a simple harmonic potential; thus the energy is

$$\epsilon_{\mathbf{v}} = \frac{nh}{2\pi}\left(\frac{U_0}{2I_r}\right)^{1/2}(\mathbf{v} + \tfrac{1}{2}), \qquad \mathbf{v} = 0, 1, 2, \ldots. \tag{4-99}$$

The fundamental frequency of torsional oscillation is given as

$$\nu = \frac{n}{2\pi}\left(\frac{U_0}{2I_r}\right)^{1/2}. \tag{4-100}$$

This frequency is also equal to the $\mathbf{v} = 0 \rightarrow \mathbf{v} = 1$ transition frequency (with splitting ignored for the moment), and provides one of the principal sources for evaluating internal rotational barriers by far infrared and Raman spectroscopy.

The potential-energy curve for hexachloroethane has a barrier height of 10.8 kcal/mole and is a good example of a torsional harmonic oscillator. The potential curve will have three minima and three maxima ($n = 3$) in a 360° rotation, and is illustrated in Figure 4-16. In the limit of an infinite barrier, each of the **v** states is threefold degenerate, since harmonic oscillation in any of the three potential wells corresponds to three equivalent configurations (Figure 4-15). However, for a barrier of finite height and width, the quantum mechanical probability of one configuration converting to the other is finite, even though the initial configuration may not possess sufficient energy to surmount the barrier U_0. This phenomenon is called *tunneling*. In classical mechanics, this conversion is, of course, strictly forbidden. The effect of tunneling is to cause a splitting of the degenerate **v** levels into one nondegenerate A state and one doubly degenerate E state. As the **v** levels approach the barrier height, the splitting becomes greater due to the breakdown of the harmonic oscillator approximation and approaches the case of a degenerate free rotor. For the combination of low temperature and high barriers, Eq. (4-99) reasonably well characterizes the torsional oscillation of a molecule in the lower levels, where the splitting is relatively small.

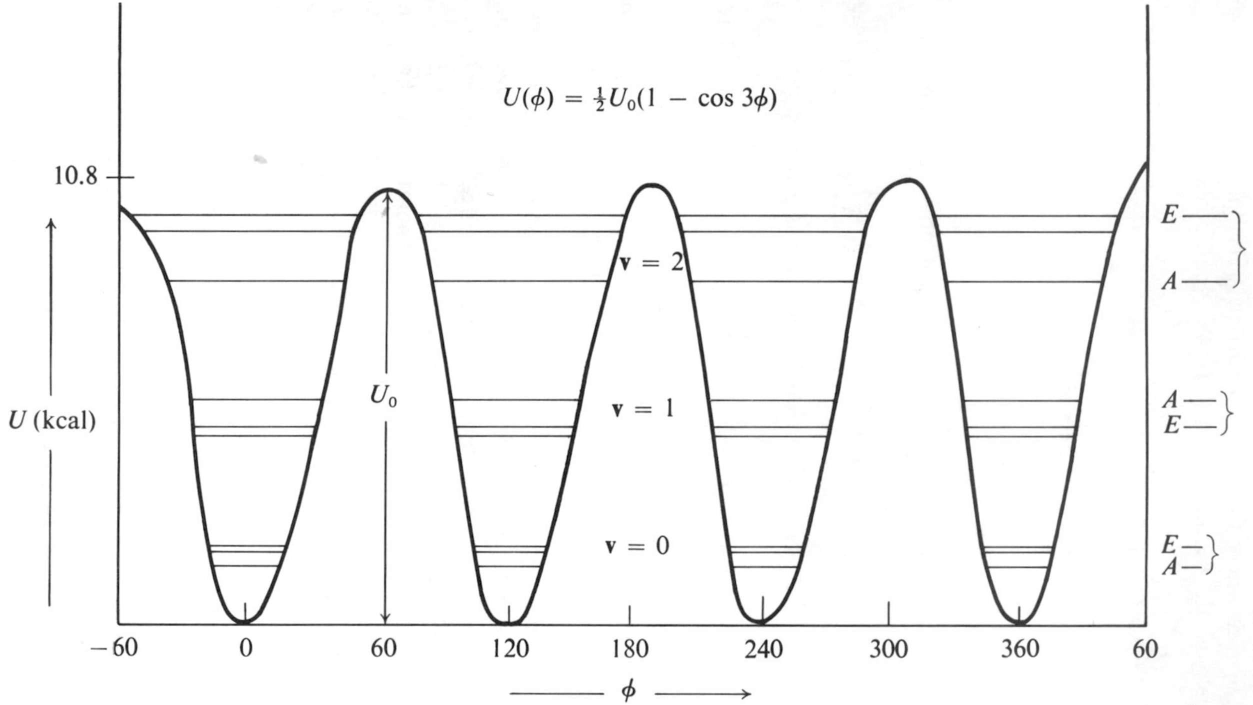

FIGURE 4-16 Potential energy of C_2Cl_6 as a function of torsional angle ϕ. Each torsional energy level (v = 0, 1, 2, . . .) is split into three sublevels, one nondegenerate A state and one doubly degenerate E state.

EXAMPLE 4-9: The reported barrier height of hexachloroethane is 10.8 kcal/mole; calculate the fundamental torsional frequency of oscillation.

Solution: Since the fundamental torsional frequency of oscillation corresponds to the periodic motion in the $\mathbf{v} = 0$ state with a barrier height in this case of 10.8 kcal, then Eq. (4-100) very adequately characterizes this frequency. Using the structure shown herewith and the pyramidal relation from Table 4-2, we obtain

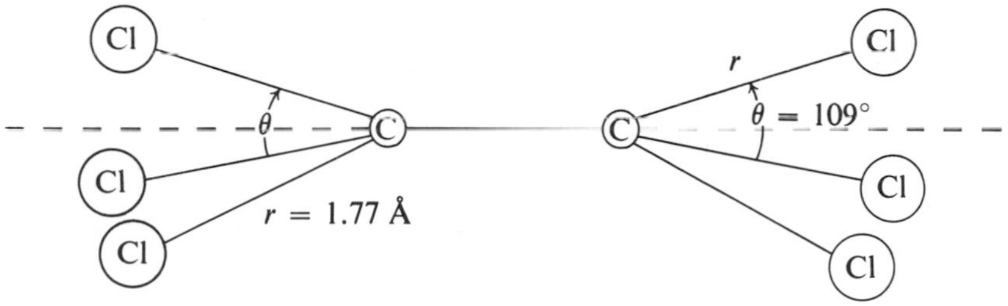

$$I_r = \frac{I(CCl_3)I(CCl_3)}{I(CCl_3) + I(CCl_3)} = \frac{I(CCl_3)}{2},$$

where

$$I(CCl_3) = 2m_{Cl}r_{CCl}^2(1 - \cos\theta)$$
$$= (2)(34.9688)(1.77)^2(1 - \cos 109°) = 290.46 \text{ amu-Å}.$$

Since

$$I(\text{g-cm}^2) = \frac{I(\text{amu-Å}^2)}{0.6023 \times 10^{40}},$$

$$I(CCl_3) = \frac{290.46}{0.6023 \times 10^{40}} = 482.25 \times 10^{-40} \text{ g-cm}^2$$

and

$$2I_r = 482.25 \times 10^{-40} \text{ g-cm}^2.$$

With the appropriate data substituted into Eq. (4-100),

$$\omega = \frac{\nu}{c} = \frac{n}{2\pi c}\left(\frac{U_0}{2I_r}\right)^{1/2}$$

$$= \frac{3}{(2)(3.14)(3 \times 10^{10} \text{ cm/sec})}$$

$$\times \left[\frac{(10.8 \times 10^2 \text{ cal/mole}) \dfrac{4.187 \times 10^7 \text{ erg/cal}}{6.02 \times 10^{23} \text{ molecules/mole}}}{482.25 \times 10^{-40} \text{ g-cm}^2}\right]^{1/2}$$

$$= 62.9 \simeq 63 \text{ cm}^{-1}.$$

In the intermediate case of the coaxial symmetrical top, where Eq. (4-99) does not adequately represent the energy levels, on substitution of the general potential function Eq. (4-95) into Eq. (4-94) a differential equation in the form of Mathieu's equation is obtained. For the threefold potential barrier, we obtain an equation in the form

$$\frac{d^2y}{dx^2} + (b - S\cos^2 x)y = 0, \tag{4-101}$$

where y is a Mathieu function, b is an eigenvalue, S is a dimensionless parameter called the reduced barrier height, and $x = \frac{1}{2}(3\phi + \pi)$, the boundary condition for the periodic function. The energy solutions for a given torsional quantum number $\mathbf{v}$ result in two sublevel energy expressions: one for the nondegenerate A state and one for the degenerate E state. The energy expression is

$$E_{\mathbf{v}\sigma} = \frac{n^2}{4} Fb_{\mathbf{v}\sigma}, \tag{4-102}$$

where $n = 3$, F is a constant for a molecular type that is related to the reduced inertial moment, and b is as defined above. The subscripts $\mathbf{v}$ and σ are indices characterizing the principal torsional quantum number and the A or E state, respectively. For a torsional absorption in the far infrared or the microwave, we obtain from Eq. (4-102)

$$\Delta E_{\mathbf{v}\to\mathbf{v}'} = 2.25F(b_{1\sigma} - b_{0\sigma}) = 2.25F(\Delta b)_\sigma, \tag{4-103}$$

where $(\Delta b)_0$ corresponds to the difference between two states of similar symmetry, that is, A or E type. Assuming that F can be obtained from known structural parameters, the value of $(\Delta b)_\sigma$ can be used to generate a corresponding S value from Eq. (4-101). The barrier height is finally obtained using this S value in the relation

$$U_0 = 2.25FS. \tag{4-104}$$

The use of these relations in the evaluation of the potential energy curve for a threefold barrier of acetaldehyde is illustrated in the accompanying example.

EXAMPLE 4-10: Calculate the potential energy barrier and the approximate splitting between the E and A states of the $\mathbf{v} = 1$ level of CH_3CHO, assuming the splitting of the $\mathbf{v} = 0$ state to be negligible. Given: $F = 7.696\ \text{cm}^{-1}$, S (A state) $= 23.84$, $(\Delta b)_A = 8.663$, and $(\Delta b)_E = 8.536$.

Solution: (a) According to Eq. (4-104), the potential barrier is given as

$$\begin{aligned} U_0 &= 2.25FS = (2.25)(7.696\ \text{cm}^{-1})(23.84) = 412.8\ \text{cm}^{-1} \\ &= 1180\ \text{cal}. \end{aligned}$$

(b) To obtain the $\mathbf{v} = 1$ state splitting we must now obtain the energy for the transitions indicated below.

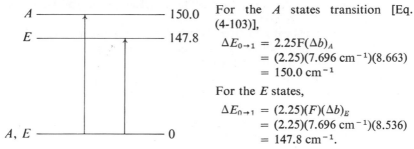

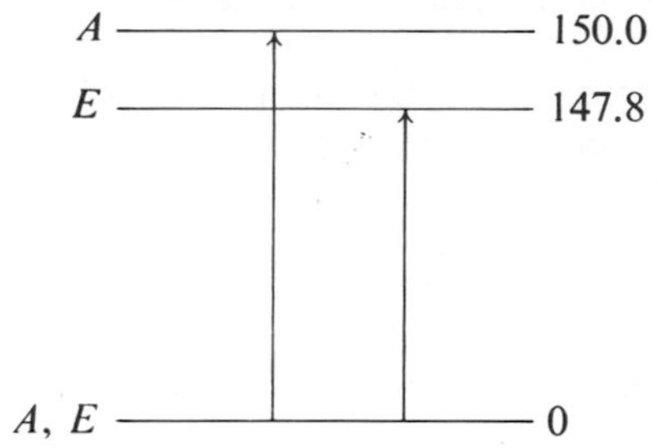

For the A states transition [Eq. (4-103)],

$$\Delta E_{0\to1} = 2.25\text{F}(\Delta b)_A = (2.25)(7.696\ \text{cm}^{-1})(8.663) = 150.0\ \text{cm}^{-1}$$

For the E states,

$$\Delta E_{0\to1} = (2.25)(F)(\Delta b)_E = (2.25)(7.696\ \text{cm}^{-1})(8.536) = 147.8\ \text{cm}^{-1}.$$

The splitting is therefore $\Delta E = 150.0 - 147.8 = 2.2\ \text{cm}^{-1}$.

SELECTED BIBLIOGRAPHY

4-1. Davidson, Norman. *Statistical Mechanics.* New York: McGraw-Hill Book Co., 1962.

4-2. Finch, A., Gates, P. N., Radcliffe, K., Dickson, F. N., and Bentley, F. F. *Chemical Applications of Far Infrared Spectroscopy.* London and New York: Academic Press, 1970.

4-3. Gordy, W., and Cook, R. L. *Microwave Molecular Spectra.* New York: Interscience Publishers, John Wiley & Sons, 1970.

4-4. Margenau, H., and Murphy, G. M. *The Mathematics of Physics and Chemistry.* New York: Van Nostrand Reinhold Co., 1964.

GLOSSARY OF SYMBOLS

Rotational Spectroscopy

$U(r)$	Potential energy, ergs, MHz, cm^{-1}, etc.
α_e	Rotation-vibration interaction constant, MHz
$D_\mathbf{v}$	First-order centrifugal stretching term, ergs, MHz, cm^{-1}, etc.
I	Moment of inertia, g-cm^2
$\mathbf{P}$	Total angular momentum
κ	Asymmetry factor, unitless
τ	Pseudo–quantum number, $K_{-1} - K_1$
$E_\tau^J(\kappa)$	Reduced energy, ergs, MHz, cm^{-1}, etc.
$\mathbf{K}$	Unique rotational angular momentum
$\mathbf{J}$	Total angular momentum
$\mathbf{H}$	Magnetic field, gauss
$\mathbf{E}$	Electric field, volts/cm
g_J	Rotational g factor
I_r	Reduced moment of inertia, g-cm^2
$U(\phi)$	Potential energy of rotation
μ_N	Nuclear magneton, 5.051×10^{-24} erg/gauss

ENDNOTES

1. The symbol r_e refers to the equilibrium internuclear distance at the potential minimum (Figure 4-1).
2. The cycle/sec is defined as a Hertz (Hz). Although both cps and Hz are commonly used interchangeably, we shall use Hz throughout the text.
3. These states are defined in Chapter 7, Section A.
4. Rotational wavefunctions of linear molecules have the same angular dependence (θ and ϕ parts) as the rotational wavefunctions derived for atomic systems, summarized in Appendix II.
5. In the case of fermions, odd nuclear spin states (T's) are symmetric and even states are antisymmetric.
6. We assume that no unpaired electrons exist that could possibly result in a component perpendicular to the molecular axis, such as the case of the diatomic radical NO.
7. The symbol r_0 refers to the average internuclear distance of the $\mathbf{v} = 0$ vibrational level.
8. Since $\hat{H}$ and $\mathbf{P}^2$ differ simply by a constant factor, eigenfunctions of $\hat{H}$ will also be eigenfunctions of $\mathbf{P}^2$.
9. Genuine symmetric tops are those determined by symmetry (a molecule having at least $n > 3$ for an n-fold axis) as opposed to an "accidental" symmetric top, where $I_a \simeq I_b$ or $I_b \simeq I_c$. Symmetry axes are discussed in Chapter 5.
10. $\mathbf{J} = \sqrt{J(J+1)}\hbar$ is a quantum mechanical result for rotational energy levels most simply obtained using raising and lowering operators and introduced here without proof. Diccussion can be found in Reference 4-3, p. 14.
11. The selection rules $\Delta M_J = 0$ (π components) and $\Delta M_J = \pm 1$ (σ components) apply respectively to transitions for which the Stark electric field is parallel or perpendicular to the oscillating electric field vector of the source radiation. Thus, the π and σ components are mutually exclusive.
12. D. E. Freeman and W. Klemperer, *J. Chem. Phys.* **40**:604 (1964).
13. Technically, the potential energy ($\frac{1}{2}U_0$) should be added to ϵ_J when it is not negligibly small.

PROBLEMS

4-1. Estimate the percentage of centrifugal distortion within the first vibrational level for the $J = 10$ levels of the light diatomic ^{6}LiF and the heavy diatomic Cs^{79}Br. Use the data in Table 4-1. What factor or factors appear to be most important in determining the magnitude of the distortion constant?

4-2. Using the data in Table 4-1, calculate I_e and r_e corresponding to the theoretical inertial moment of the diatomic molecule KI having an equilibrium internuclear separation at the minimum of the potential curve. Given: $^{39}K = 38.962$ amu, $^{127}\text{I} = 126.904$ amu, and $h/8\pi^2 =$ 505,376 amu-Å-MHz.

4-3. Calculate B_0, α_e, and r_0 for the nonrigid rotor DI. Given: $D_0 = 0.60$ MHz, $B_e = 98{,}446$ MHz, $\Delta E = 195{,}067.866$ MHz for the $J = 0 \rightarrow J = 1$ (ω_0 state) transition; D = 2.014 amu, and $^{127}\text{I} = 126.904$ amu.

4-4. Rotational intensities are important in interpreting diatomic spectra. Two isotopes of N_2 (shown in the accompanying diagram) both having $^1\Sigma_g{}^+$ electronic ground states also have the following nuclear spins per atom.

$$^{15}\text{N}{\equiv}\text{N}^{15} \qquad\qquad ^{14}\text{N}{\equiv}\text{N}^{14}$$
$$I = \tfrac{1}{2} \quad I = \tfrac{1}{2} \qquad\qquad I = 1 \quad I = 1$$

With rotational populations ignored for the moment, the following rotational intensity patterns would be observed from electronic absorption spectroscopy.

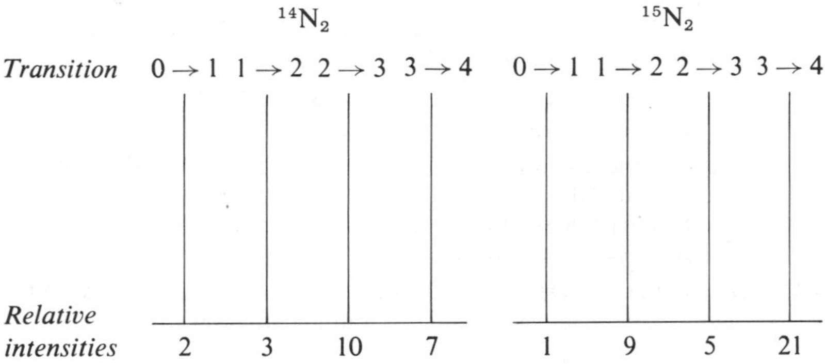

Using a rotational energy level diagram (Figure 4-2), develop a clear case for the assignment of each diatomic to its corresponding spectrum.

4-5. Derive the expression for $\langle m|\mu_z|k\rangle$ and using the wavefunctions $\psi_{0,0}$ and $\psi_{1,1}(\psi_{J,M})$ from Appendix II, show that $\Delta M \neq \pm 1$ and $\Delta J \neq \pm 1$ along the z direction.

4-6. A diatomic interhalogen molecule recovered as a reaction side product was observed to give a 0.7142-cm^{-1} line in the microwave for the $J = 0 \rightarrow J = 1$ transition. Independent solid state data revealed an approximate bond length of 1.76 Å. What is the diatomic molecule?

$$B\,(\text{cm}^{-1}) = \frac{16.858}{I\,(\text{amu-Å}^2)}.$$

4-7. Consider the rotation of a diatomic molecule about its center of mass. The Hamiltonian and the wavefunction are given:

$$H(\phi) = \frac{P_\phi{}^2}{2I} \qquad \text{and} \qquad \psi = N_\phi \exp(im\,\phi)$$

where I is the moment of inertia and m is the rotational quantum number.

a. Given the angular momentum operator $P_\phi = (h/2\pi i)(\partial/\partial\phi)$, obtain the rotational energy of a diatomic molecule.
b. Evaluate the expectation value for the energy of a rigid rotor. (*Hint:* The expectation value of G is $\langle G \rangle = \langle \psi | \hat{G} | \psi \rangle$ and $E = -(\hbar^2/2I)(\partial^2/\partial\phi^2)$.
c. Show how the relative rotational energy spacings vary as a function of both mass and internuclear distance for a heavy and a light homonuclear diatomic molecule.

4-8. Given Eq. (4-39) and the relations

$$r_{BrC} = r_{Br} + r_C = r_N - r_C, \quad r_{BrN} = r_{Br} + r_N, \quad r_{BrN} = r_{BrC} + r_{CN},$$

derive Eq. (4-40).

4-9. Given the rotational constants B_0 for the isotopic molecules of BrCN below, show that $r_{BrC} = 1.790$ Å and $r_{CN} = 1.156$ Å. (This problem requires a calculator.)

$^{79}Br^{12}C^{14}N$	4,120.198 MHz	$^{81}Br^{12}C^{14}N$	4,096.788 MHz
$^{79}Br^{13}C^{14}N$	4,073.373 MHz	$^{81}Br^{13}C^{14}N$	4,049.608 MHz

$^{79}Br = 78.9182$ $\quad$ $^{12}C = 12.0000$ $\quad$ $^{14}N = 14.0031$
$^{81}Br = 80.9163$ $\quad$ $^{13}C = 13.0033$

4-10. Show that $\epsilon = h[B_0(J+1)J + (C_0 - B_0)K^2]$ for the oblate top, where $I_a = I_b < I_c$; I_c is the unique and major axis of rotation.

4-11. Calculate the equilibrium N—F bond length and FNF bond angle of the pyramidal NF_3 molecule. $B_e = 10{,}761.91$ MHz for $^{14}NF_3$ and $B_e = 10{,}710.63$ MHz for $^{15}NF_3$; $^{19}F = 18.9984$ amu, $^{14}N = 14.0031$ amu, and $^{15}N = 15.0001$ amu.

4-12. Evaluate the expressions for the three moments of inertia relative to the center of mass of the planar tetratomic molecule shown herewith.

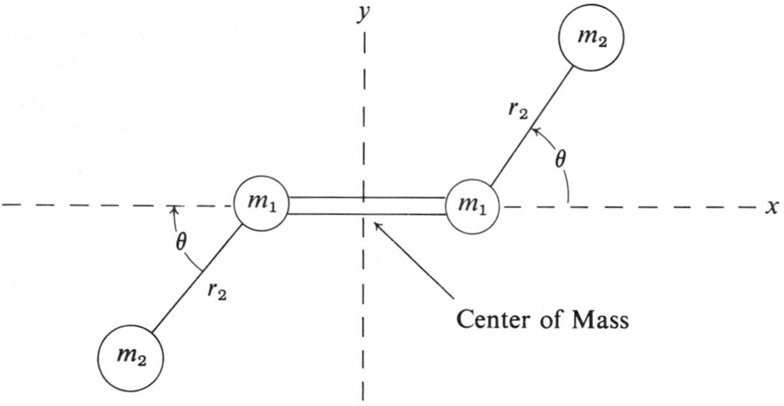

Calculate the values of the moments I_x, I_y, and I_z for the *trans*-difluorodiazine molecule, FN═NF, and show whether this asymmetric top is near-prolate, near-oblate, or intermediate. Given: $r_{N-F} = 1.384$ Å, $r_{N=N} = 1.25$ Å, and $\theta_{NNF} = 114.5°$; $^{19}F = 19.9984$ amu and $^{14}N = 14.0031$ amu.

4-13. The explicit expressions for $E_\tau^J(\kappa)$ of the $J_{K_{-1}K_1}$ states are $\kappa + 1$, 0, and $\kappa - 1$ for 1_{10}, 1_{11}, and 1_{01}. Calculate the energy levels and plot on a diagram the energy separations for the $CH_2CH{=}CH$ molecule (A_0 = 30,063.7 MHz, B_0 = 21,825.6 MHz, and C_0 = 13,795.7 MHz). Compare with those of a pure prolate symmetric top with A_0 = 30,063.7 MHz and B_0 = 21,825.6 MHz.

4-14. Sketch the first-order Stark diagram for the σ components of the $J = 1 \rightarrow J = 2$, $\Delta K = 0$, $\Delta M_J = \pm 1$ transitions and illustrate the spectrum for $\mathbf{E} = 0$ and $\mathbf{E} \neq 0$. (Assume the splitting of the lower state to be triple the splitting of the upper state).

4-15. Calculate the frequency shift in the second-order Stark effect for the $J = 1 \rightarrow J = 2$, $M_J = 1 \rightarrow M_J = 1$ transition from the field-free transition $J = 1 \rightarrow J = 2$ for LiCl. Given: B_e = 22,116.25 MHz, α_e = 291.760 MHz, $\mu_{v=0}$ = 7.119 D, $\mathbf{E}$ = 2000 volts/cm. (*Hint:* $\mu^2\mathbf{E}^2/2h^2B$ is $0.1268\mu^2\mathbf{E}^2/B$, where μ is in Debyes, $\mathbf{E}$ is in volts/cm, and B is in MHz.

4-16. Calculate the first-order Stark shift in a 150-volt/cm electric field for the $J = 1 \rightarrow J = 2$, $K = 1 \rightarrow K = 1$, $M_J = 1 \rightarrow M_J = 1$ transition of the CH_3I molecule. Given: μ = 1.618 D and $[2KM/J(J + 1)(J + 2)]$ = 0.3333.

4-17. Evaluate the energy levels of the $J = 1$ state of the asymmetric rotor CH_3OCl and plot on a diagram the energy separations. (A_0 = 42,064 MHz, B_0 = 6297 MHz, and C_0 = 5670 MHz.) Compare with those of a pure prolate top with A_0 = 42,064 MHz and B_0 = 6297 MHz.

4-18. Assuming the rotational g_J factors to be equivalent for the $J = 1$ and $J = 2$ rotational states of $D^{79}Br$, calculate the percentage shift of the σ components for the $J = 1 \rightarrow J = 2$ rotational transition in the presence of a magnetic field of 10 kilogauss; $\nu_0(J = 0 \rightarrow J = 1)$ is 254,704.68 MHz. Compare this result with the half-width pressure broadening $\Delta\omega_p$ at a total pressure of 0.10 mm (assume $\sigma_{D^{79}Br} \simeq 3$ Å); $g_J = 0.181$.

4-19. Illustrate the sixfold potential-energy diagram as a function of ϕ for nitromethane, CH_3NO_2, and calculate the rotational frequency for

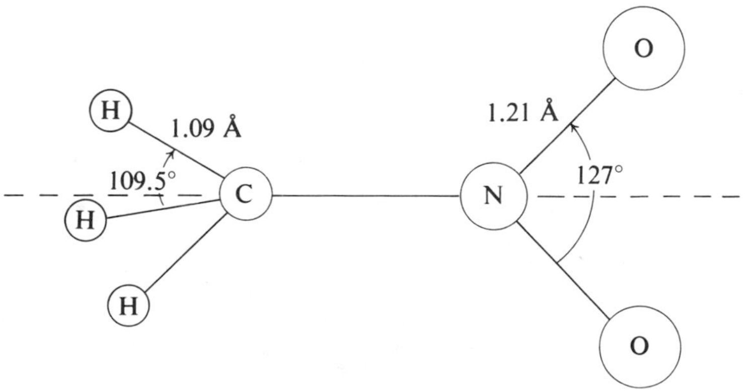

the $j = 0 \rightarrow j = 1$ transition assuming free rotation. Given: $m_O =$ 15.9949 amu. (Use Table 4-2 for calculating I_r from the structure herewith.) Would you use infrared or microwave spectroscopy to observe this transition?

4-20. Hexafluoroethane, C_2F_6, has an estimated torsional absorption ($\mathbf{v} = 0 \rightarrow \mathbf{v} = 1$) at approximately 78 cm^{-1}. Assuming the high barrier approximation to be appropriate in this case, estimate the barrier height in kilocalories. Given: $r_{CF} = 1.348$ Å, $\theta_{FCF} = 108°$, and $m_F = 18.9984$ amu. (*Hint:* Use Table 4-2 for calculating I_r.)

4-21. Assuming the high barrier approximation, estimate the torsional absorption frequency in wavenumbers for the $\mathbf{v} = 0 \rightarrow \mathbf{v} = 1$ transition of $H_3C—CF_3$. Given: $r_{CH} = 1.078$ Å, $\theta_{HCH} = 109.5°$, $m_H = 1.0078$ amu, and the data for $—CF_3$ is the same as in (4-20); $U_0 = 3.48$ kcal/mole.

4-22. Construct the rotational energy-level diagram of the O_2 molecule in its ground electronic state ($^3\Sigma_g^-$) as done for D_2 (Figure 4-2). ^{16}O ($I = 0$).

Chapter 5

Molecular Symmetry

Today there is hardly an area of modern chemistry or science in general in which we are not involved with the relative orientation of the atoms in a molecule, that is, their symmetry. The number and kinds of rotations and vibrations that are described by atomic displacements from equilibrium distances and angles can be predicted from symmetry considerations alone. The importance of symmetry to electronic, infrared, microwave, Raman, and resonance spectroscopy cannot be overstated, and in many cases symmetry provides the simplifying features essential to solving problems that arise.

A. SYMMETRY ELEMENTS AND OPERATIONS

A *symmetry element* is a property of a molecular species, such as a point, a line, or a plane, about which symmetry operations can be carried out. A *symmetry operation* is a movement of the atoms in a molecular species in such a way that when the movement is completed, the species will have a configuration equivalent to the one it had prior to the operation. There are five types of symmetry elements, each corresponding to a particular symmetry operation. These are listed in Table 5-1. These symmetry elements and operations are inextricably related and will be exemplified in the following sections.

1. Identity

The identity operation E is not an operation at all. It involves no movement of the atomic constituents and is sometimes referred to as a

TABLE 5-1. Relation of Symmetry Elements to Symmetry Operations

Symmetry element	Symbol[a]	Symmetry operation
Identity	E	No atomic movement
Proper axis of symmetry	C_n	Rotation about the proper axis
Plane of symmetry	σ_j	Reflection through the plane
Center of symmetry	i	Inversion of all the atoms through the center
Improper or alternating axis of symmetry	S_n	Rotation about a proper axis followed by reflection through a plane perpendicular to the proper axis

[a] The subscripts of the symmetry symbols C_n and S_n represent the order of the proper rotation axes for that particular operation, whereas the subscript j indicates a dihedral, a vertical, or a horizontal plane.

pseudo operation. The usefulness of this element or concept becomes very important when we apply group-theoretical methods to solving general scientific problems, and also problems of a spectroscopic nature (relative to this text). Any single operation E or series of operations for which the final configuration is identical with the original one is also the identity.

2. Proper Axis of Symmetry

A proper axis of symmetry corresponds to an imaginary line in a molecular species about which rotational motions will result in equivalent configurations. This element and its corresponding operation are illustrated below for the triangular plane BF_3 molecule. The axis passing through the B atom and perpendicular to the molecular plane is described as threefold, since three rotations in a clockwise or counterclockwise direction will return the molecule to the original, or *identical*, configuration. The three fluorine atoms, all in the molecular plane, are labeled 1, 2, and 3 simply to differentiate between equivalent and identical configurations. We do realize, however, that such labeling of identical atoms is in fact impossible, but for our example it is useful in illustrating symmetry properties. In addition to the three clockwise rotations illustrated herewith, different equivalent configurations result from counterclockwise rotation, so that

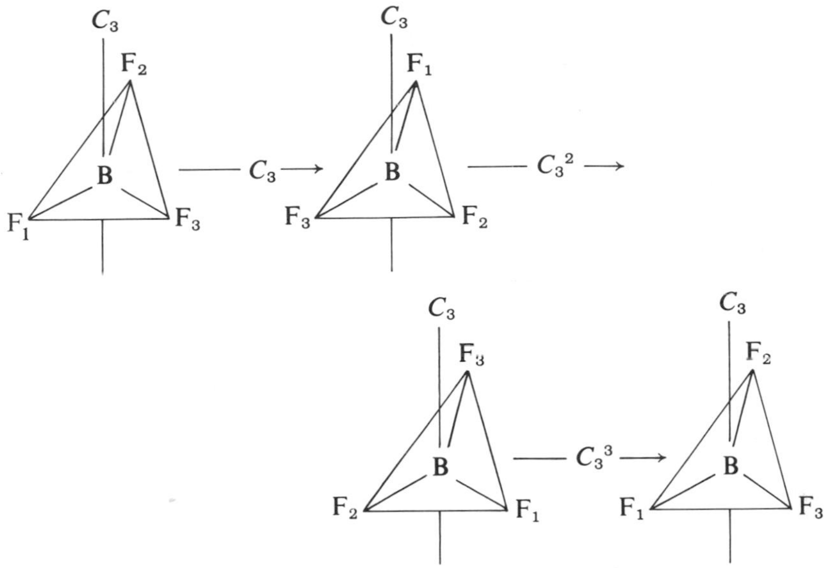

although there is only one rotational axis (symmetry element), there are two symmetry operations C_3 and C_3'. The general subscript n is simply the ratio of a complete, 360° revolution to the smallest angular rotation that will produce an equivalent configuration. In this case $360°/120° = 3$. The superscript attached to C indicates the number of separate rotations in the course of a complete revolution. Thus, the final rotation C_3^3 is the same as E, or in general $C_n^n \equiv E$.

In addition to the one threefold rotation axis, BF_3 also has three twofold rotation axes in the molecular plane along each of the B—F bonds. They are correspondingly labeled C_2, C_2', and C_2''. Other examples illustrating proper rotation axes are a singly substituted tetrahedral molecule, for example GeH_3Cl, with a unique threefold axis; a bent symmetrical triatomic, for example H_2O, with a twofold axis; and a square planar molecular type, for example ICl_4, with a unique fourfold rotation axis. This fourfold rotation axis in ICl_4 is also a twofold C_2 axis oriented along the z direction. In addition, there are also two sets of twofold rotation axes C_2' and C_2'' in the molecular plane, as illustrated in Figure 5-1. The two sets are distinguished by the fact that two of the twofold axes are oriented along the A—B bonds, whereas the other two are oriented 45° to the A—B bonds. Benzene is an example of a species having even higher symmetry. You might convince yourself that it contains $2C_6$, $2C_3$, and a C_2 nonredundant operations along the sixfold axis and $3C_2'$ and $3C_2''$ nonredundant operations in the molecular plane.

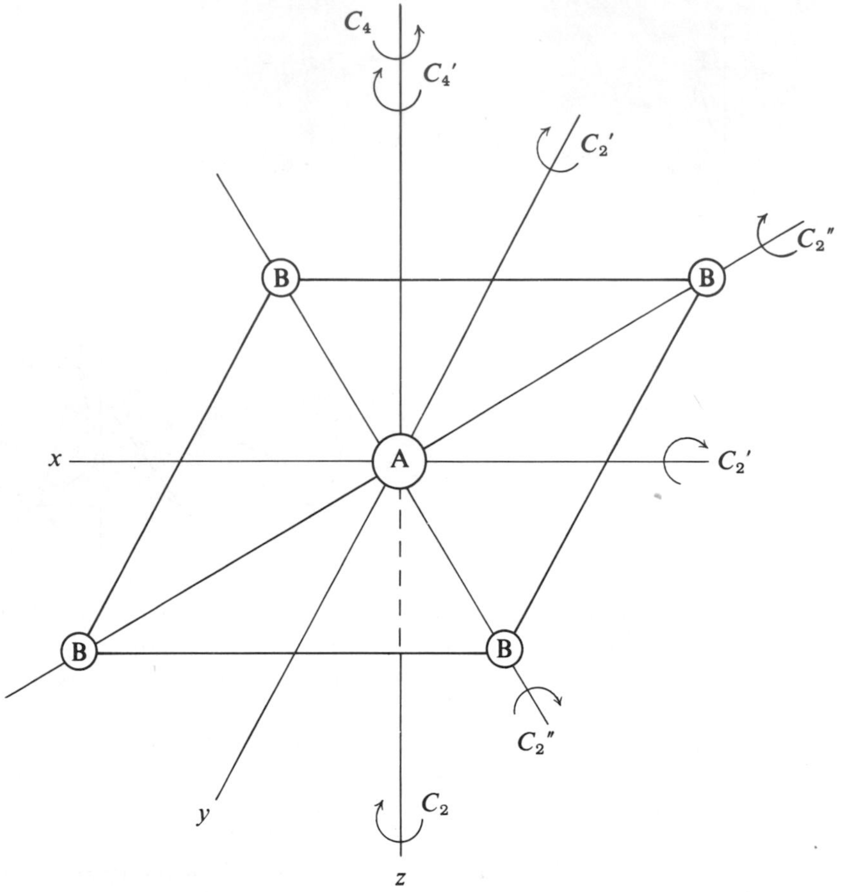

FIGURE 5-1 Illustration of the three types of proper rotation axes of an AB_4 square planar molecule. Note that the two twofold rotation axes in the molecular plane form two sets, those along the A—B bonds and those at 45° to the A—B bonds.

3. Plane of Symmetry

A plane of symmetry is perhaps best described in terms of the requirement of a mirror image. A species with a symmetry plane must have equivalent atoms on each side of the plane directly across from each other, or all atoms in the plane, or both. The operation consists of moving all identical atoms on both sides through the plane, at an angle normal to the plane, an equal distance corresponding to the position held by its identical counterpart. This operation is called reflection through the plane. The

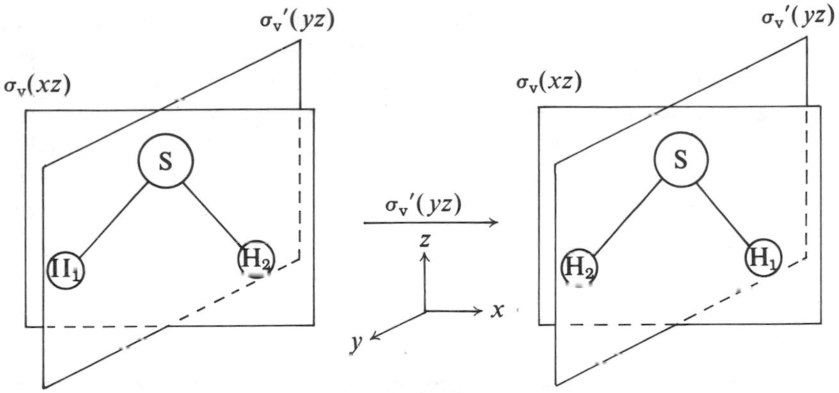

FIGURE 5-2 Reflection through the vertical *yz* plane exchanges the labeled H atoms only, since the S atom is in the plane.

H_2S molecule has two vertical planes of symmetry, which are illustrated in Figure 5-2. By convention, the highest-fold proper axis is considered vertical, and any plane containing that axis is considered to be vertical, σ_v. Correspondingly, a symmetry plane perpendicular to the highest-fold proper axis is considered to be horizontal, σ_h. Reflection through the *yz* vertical plane involves the exchange of the two hydrogen atoms labeled 1 and 2, but does not involve movement of the sulfur atom, which is in the symmetry plane. In general then, any atom that lies in the symmetry plane does not require a counterpart and does not *move* when the reflection operation is performed. We should note however that of the vectors (x, y, and z) associated with the S atom, the *out-of-plane* vector, x in this case, is reversed to $-x$. Reflection through the xz plane leaves all three atoms unmoved since they are all in the xz plane, but all three atomic y vectors are reversed in direction to $-y$. We may also note from this example that this element generates a single operation or movement. As a result, performing $\sigma_v'(yz)$ twice or any even number of times simply returns the molecule to its original configuration and is in essence the identity operation E, that is, $\sigma^n \equiv E$, where n = even. When n is odd, the resulting configuration is one identical with the single $\sigma_v'(yz)$ operation.

Other examples of molecular types having symmetry planes range from the relatively low-symmetry linear symmetrical O═C═O and unsymmetrical N═N═O molecules with an infinite number of vertical planes in both cases and one horizontal plane σ_h in the former, to species such as NH_3, BF_3, and benzene. In the case of NH_3, which is a pyramidal type, there are three vertical planes, each having N and a separate H in its plane that bisects the other HNH triangular face. If we flatten out the pyramidal type just discussed, we obtain the triangular plane BF_3, which contains four symmetry planes. One is a horizontal molecular plane

σ_h, and the other three are similar vertical planes, as in NH_3, σ_v, σ_v', σ_v''. A relatively highly symmetrical species like benzene has one horizontal (molecular) plane σ_h and six vertical planes. Of the six vertical planes, three are coincident with the C_2 axes along the C—H bonds and are labeled $3\sigma_v$; the other set of vertical planes that bisect the dihedral angles between $3\sigma_v$ are labeled $3\sigma_d$ and are called dihedral planes. One clue in identifying symmetry planes is to look along proper axes; more often than not they are contained in a symmetry plane.

4. Center of Symmetry

Center of symmetry, another symmetry element, is a point in a molecule through which all the atoms must pass in going from (x, y, z) to $(-x, -y, -z)$. This point in the molecule is the center and the operation is inversion of its atomic components.[1] If there is an atom occupying this point, it obviously does not move. So that equivalent configurations for this operation can be achieved, the atoms that are inverted must exist in equivalent pairs. In fact, the only way a molecule with the i element can have an odd number of atoms is for one atom to be at the center of symmetry. Fairly obvious examples of molecules having an inversion center i are linear symmetric types such as O═C═O and H—C≡C—H; ethylenic types such as $H_2C{=}CH_2$ and *trans*-XHC═CHX; square planar types such as XeF_4 and $PtCl_4^{2-}$; benzene; and octahedral types such as SF_6 and PtF_6. Like the reflection plane, the i element corresponds to a single movement of atoms and $i^n \equiv E$ when n is even.

5. Improper or Alternating Axis of Symmetry

In some cases, it is possible to obtain, by combining two of the operations already discussed, equivalent configurations that are impossible to achieve by applying any single one. The operation corresponding to the improper axis S_n is proper rotation about a C_n axis followed by reflection through a plane perpendicular to the rotation axis. Here again n corresponds to the order of the proper rotation axis. Two trivial cases of improper axes are S_1 and S_2. In the case of $XHC{=}CH_2$, rotation of 360° about the axis through the double bond

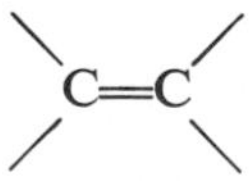

and perpendicular to the molecular plane, followed by reflection through the molecular plane, is an S_1 operation. Since the first operation is equivalent to E, the S_1 operation is equivalent to the single σ operation.

For a general S_2 operation, a $C_2(z)$ operation about the z axis transforms a general atom or point from (x, y, z) to $(-x, -y, z)$, which followed by reflection through a plane perpendicular to z results in $(-x, -y, -z)$. This transformation is identical with the i operation. Thus, since both S_1 and S_2 are identical with other single operations, they are by agreement given the σ symbol (S_1) and the i symbol (S_2).

An example of a species having an odd ($n = 3$) alternating axis is the eclipsed form of ethane, illustrated in Figure 5-3. The S_3 axis is of

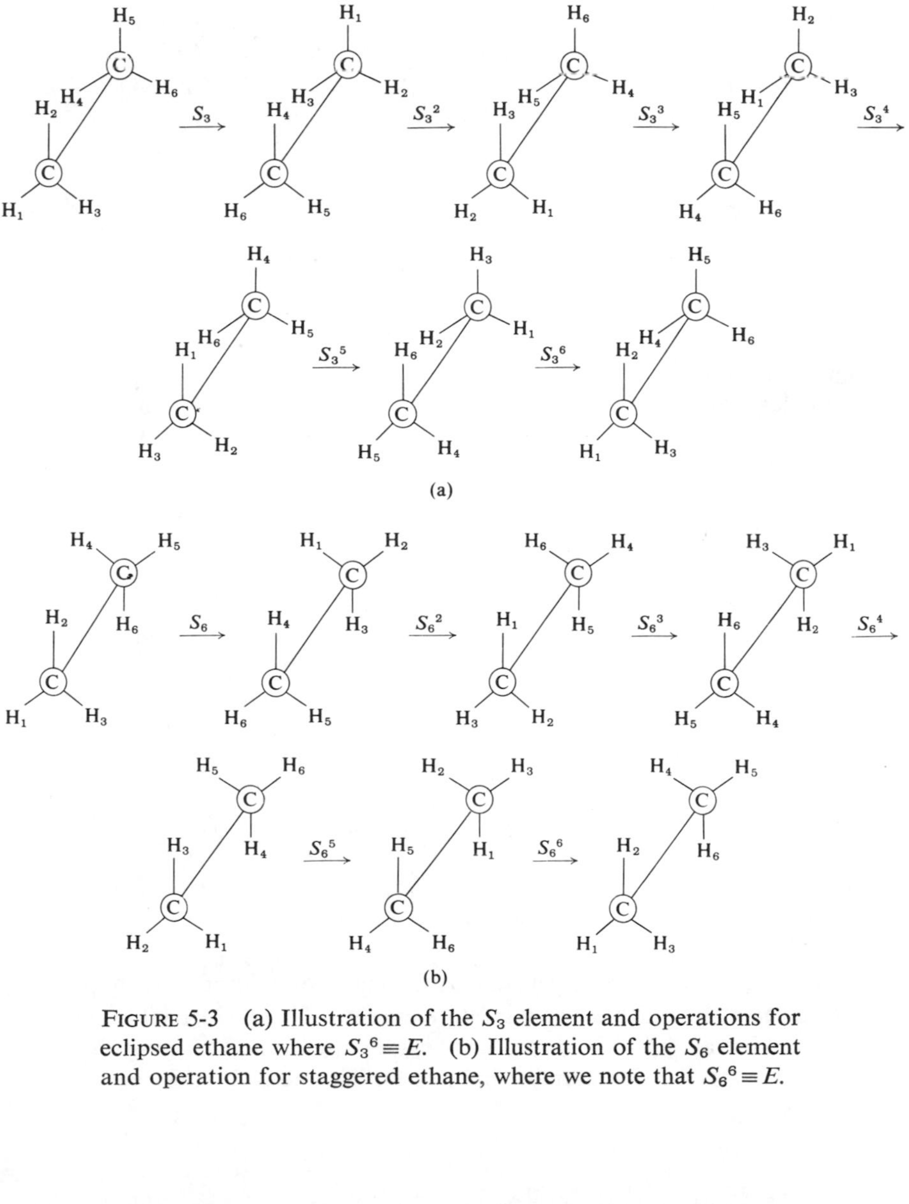

FIGURE 5-3 (a) Illustration of the S_3 element and operations for eclipsed ethane where $S_3{}^6 \equiv E$. (b) Illustration of the S_6 element and operation for staggered ethane, where we note that $S_6{}^6 \equiv E$.

course superimposed on the C_3 as the successive S_3 operations are performed. We note in Figure 5-3a that the S_3^3 operation is not equivalent to the identity operation; thus three successive S_3 operations do not return the molecule to its original configuration. However, continuing through S_3^6, we do obtain the original configuration. In general we find, for odd alternating axes, $S_n^{2n} \equiv E$. The staggered form of ethane is an example of an even alternating axis, S_6, illustrated in Figure 5-3b. In this case, a rotation of 60° followed by reflection through the plane perpendicular to S_6 will generate equivalent configurations. As shown in Figure 5-3b, successive application of S_6 through S_6^6 does return the molecule to its original configuration. Thus, for even alternating axes, $S_n^n \equiv E$.

Other obvious examples of S_3 and S_4 axes are found in NO_3^- and XeF_4, and less obvious are the $6S_4$ axes of methane.

B. PRODUCTS OF SYMMETRY OPERATIONS AND MULTIPLICATION TABLES

Now that we have become relatively adept at recognizing and cataloguing symmetry operations, we can compile sets for relatively small molecules. We shall see shortly that this complete set will have all the properties of a mathematical group and can therefore be treated as such. To ensure that we have collected all the symmetry operations, we obtain the binary products of all the symmetry operations with each other. Any product generated must also be an operation of the group. The product written $AB = C$ means that C is the product of B times A. Where A, B, and C are symmetry operations, we mean that the B operation is performed first (multiplication right to left), followed by the A operation, and the resulting change corresponds to a single group operation C. As an example, recall the H_2S molecule illustrated in Figure 5-2, for which we indicated the presence of two symmetry planes $\sigma_v(xz)$ and $\sigma_v'(yz)$. The effect of their product is first to exchange the H atoms as shown in Figure 5-2 ($\sigma_v'(yz)$), and second to leave all atoms unmoved ($\sigma_v(xz)$), which is equivalent to a $C_2(z)$ operation. We write this product as

$$\sigma_v(xz)\sigma_v'(yz) = C_2(z). \qquad \textbf{(5-1a)}$$

Thus, we have in principle generated this operation without having prior knowledge of its inclusion as a group member. This is a trivial example used to illustrate how binary products can be useful in generating a complete symmetry set for more complicated molecules. In this particular

TABLE 5-2. Multiplication Table for the H_2S Molecule (C_{2v} Point Group)

	E	$C_2(z)$	$\sigma_v(xz)$	$\sigma_v'(yz)$
E	E	$C_2(z)$	$\sigma_v(xz)$	$\sigma_v'(yz)$
$C_2(z)$	$C_2(z)$	E	$\sigma_v'(yz)$	$\sigma_v(xz)$
$\sigma_v(xz)$	$\sigma_v(xz)$	$\sigma_v'(yz)$	E	$C_2(z)$
$\sigma_v'(yz)$	$\sigma_v'(yz)$	$\sigma_v(xz)$	$C_2(z)$	E

case, the order of multiplication is immaterial, and gives the same result:

$$\sigma_v(xz)\sigma_v'(yz) = \sigma_v'(yz)\sigma_v(xz) = C_2(z). \qquad \textbf{(5-1b)}$$

In such cases, the symmetry operations are said to *commute*. In general most group products are not commutative. The binary products of all the group operations can be conveniently generated and summarized by the application of row × column multiplication. Such a collection is called a multiplication table and is shown in Table 5-2 for the H_2S molecule (C_{2v} point group) with elements E, $C_2(z)$, $\sigma_v(xz)$, and $\sigma_v'(yz)$. On inspecting Table 5-2, we find that it is symmetrical ($\mathbf{x}_{ij} = \mathbf{x}_{ji}$), or more specifically, all binary products are commutative. Groups of this nature are called Abelian.

A more involved example is the nonplanar $(PtCl_4)^{2-}$ ion (C_{4v} point group), which has the symmetry *elements* E, C_4, C_2 (coincident with C_4), σ_v, and σ_d. The complete set of nonredundant symmetry *operations* corresponding to these elements includes E, C_4, C_4^3, C_2, σ_v, σ_v', σ_d, and σ_d'. In this case, the counterclockwise operation C_4' is equivalent to C_4^3 and $(C_4')^3$ to C_4. The C_2 operation about the unique fourfold axis

TABLE 5-3. Multiplication Table for the Nonplanar $(PtCl_4)^{2-}$ Ion (C_{4v} Point Group)

	E	C_4	C_4^3	C_2	σ_v	σ_v'	σ_d	σ_d'
E	E	C_4	C_4^3	C_2	σ_v	σ_v'	σ_d	σ_d'
C_4	C_4	C_2	E	C_4^3	σ_d	σ_d'	σ_v'	σ_v
C_4^3	C_4^3	E	C_4^2	C_4	σ_d'	σ_d	σ_v	σ_v'
C_2	C_2	C_4^3	C_4	E	σ_v'	σ_v	σ_d'	σ_d
σ_v	σ_v	σ_d'	σ_d	σ_v'	E	C_2	C_4^3	C_4
σ_v'	σ_v'	σ_d	σ_d'	σ_v	C_2	E	C_4	C_4^3
σ_d	σ_d	σ_v	σ_v'	σ_d'	C_4	C_4^3	E	C_2
σ_d'	σ_d'	σ_v'	σ_v	σ_d	C_4^3	C_4	C_2	E

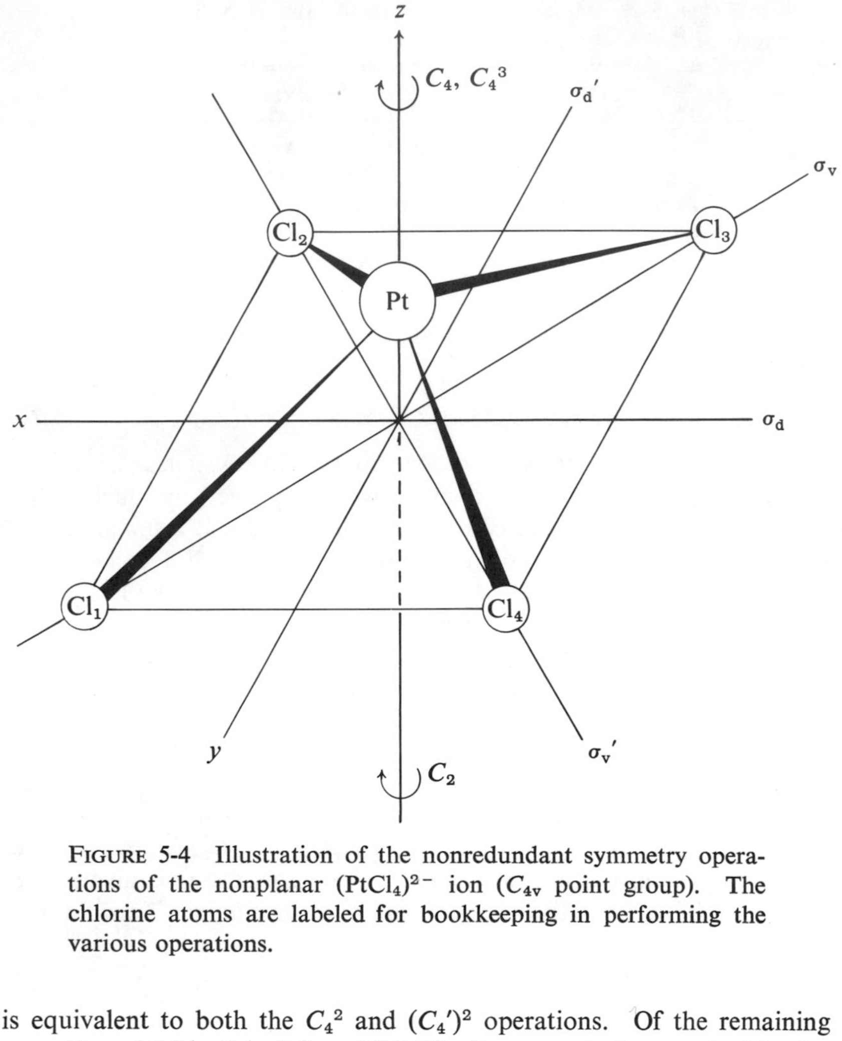

FIGURE 5-4 Illustration of the nonredundant symmetry operations of the nonplanar $(PtCl_4)^{2-}$ ion (C_{4v} point group). The chlorine atoms are labeled for bookkeeping in performing the various operations.

is equivalent to both the C_4^2 and $(C_4')^2$ operations. Of the remaining operations $(C_4')^4$, C_4^4, C_2^2, and $(C_2')^2$, all are equivalent to the identity operation. Thus, the symmetry elements are shown in Figure 5-4 and the corresponding binary products of the nonredundant symmetry operations are summarized in Table 5-3. On examining Table 5-3, we note that it is not symmetric, and is therefore non-Abelian. As an example,

$$\sigma_d'\sigma_v' = C_4 \neq C_4^3 = \sigma_v'\sigma_d' \tag{5-2}$$

and

$$\sigma_d'C_4 = \sigma_v' \neq \sigma_v = C_4\sigma_d'. \tag{5-3}$$

C. PROPERTIES OF A GROUP

At this point, we summarize the criteria for a mathematical group and demonstrate that the symmetry group operations we have discussed thus far satisfy these requirements. Then we shall be in a position to use the theorems of group theory for solving problems involving molecular structure and spectroscopy from a symmetry point of view (no pun intended).

A *group* is a collection, or set, of elements $A, B, C, \ldots$, and binary operations satisfying the following rules.

Closure: The elements C generated by all possible binary products AB must also be members of the group. This property has been demonstrated above with the multiplication tables.

Associativity: The binary products AB times C must equal A times BC, or $(AB)C = A(BC)$. This rule is also satisfied by obvious symmetry operation products performed above.

Identity Element: There must exist in the group an element E that has the following property: $EA = A = AE$. We alluded to the necessity for this element earlier, and it now becomes obvious as a requirement of the group.

Inverses: For every element A in the group, there must exist in the group an element A^{-1} (read "A inverse") that has the following property: $AA^{-1} = E = A^{-1}A$. Examining the multiplication tables generated above shows that this property corresponds to the E elements generated by the various "row × column" products.

The number of elements in a group is called the *order* of the group, and given the symbol g. In the two cases illustrated, C_{2v} and C_{4v}, we have groups of order four and eight, respectively. Of the elements in a group, we can easily distinguish "sets" of certain "types," for example, σ_v's, σ_d's, and C_2's. Elements A and B of a group that are related by the operation

$$X^{-1}AX = B \qquad \textbf{(5-4)}$$

are said to be *conjugate*, where X is any other element in the group. Such an operation is called a *similarity transformation*. A complete set of conjugate elements composes a *class*. This complete set of elements can be generated by applying Eq. (5-4) to all the elements A in the group by all the group operations X. As an example, let us generate the various classes corresponding to the nonplanar $(PtCl_4)^{2-}$ ion (C_{4v} point group). Using Table 5-3, we find that the elements and their inverses correspond to the row and column symmetry operations respectively that give rise to the identity operation E in the table. Thus, C_4 is the inverse of C_4^3;

that is, $X = C_4^3$ and then $X^{-1} = C_4$. Using Table 5-3 for the binary products, we obtain for C_4 and σ_v:

$$\begin{aligned}
EC_4E &= C_4 & E\sigma_vE &= \sigma_v \\
C_4C_4C_4^3 &= C_4 & C_4\sigma_vC_4^3 &= \sigma_v' \\
C_2C_4C_2 &= C_4 & C_2\sigma_vC_2 &= \sigma_v \\
\sigma_vC_4\sigma_v &= C_4^3 & \sigma_v\sigma_v\sigma_v &= \sigma_v \\
\sigma_v'C_4\sigma_v' &= C_4^3 & \sigma_v'\sigma_v\sigma_v' &= \sigma_v \\
\sigma_dC_4\sigma_d &= C_4^3 & \sigma_d\sigma_v\sigma_d &= \sigma_v' \\
\sigma_d'C_4\sigma_d' &= C_4^3 & \sigma_d\sigma_v\sigma_d' &= \sigma_v \\
&\{C_4, C_4^3\} & &\{\sigma_v, \sigma_v'\}
\end{aligned} \qquad (5\text{-}5)$$

Applying this procedure to all the elements in the group, we find that the classes for this point group are $\{E\}$, $\{C_4, C_4^3\}$, $\{C_2\}$, $\{\sigma_v, \sigma_v'\}$, and $\{\sigma_d, \sigma_d'\}$. We should also note here a general theorem, that the number of elements in any class must be an integral divisor of the group order.

D. SYMMETRY CLASSIFICATION (POINT GROUP DESIGNATION)

Molecular species can be systematically classified according to the number and types of symmetry elements and operations they possess. In all the symmetry operations we have considered, a point in the molecular species at which all the elements intersect is left invariant. As a result, this complete set of nonredundant symmetry operations possessing all the properties of a mathematical group is called a point group. Molecules that have a high degree of symmetry (T_h, O_h, I_h) or a low degree of symmetry (C_s, C_1, C_i) have fairly obvious point group designations; for example, SF_6 is O_h, and Cl_2O is C_s.

The assignment of a molecular species to a particular point group can be conveniently determined with the aid of the flow chart shown in Figure 5-5.

1. First one determines whether the molecule belongs to one of the special groups that are highly symmetrical: T_d (tetrahedral symmetry, CH_4 and P_4), O_h (octahedral symmetry, SF_6 and cubane), or I_h (icosahedral and dodecahedral symmetry, $B_{12}H_{12}^{-2}$). If the molecule is linear and possesses a horizontal plane, it is $D_{\infty h}$ (O═C═O and H—C≡C—H); if it does not have a horizontal plane, it is $C_{\infty v}$(N═N═O).
2. If the molecule is not assigned to a special group and does not have a proper axis of symmetry C_n, it is either C_s (has a plane of symmetry only, pyramidal GeH_2Cl), C_i (has a center of symmetry only, HFClC—CHFCl), or C_1 (has no symmetry element except for the trivial identity operation, H_3C—CFClBr).

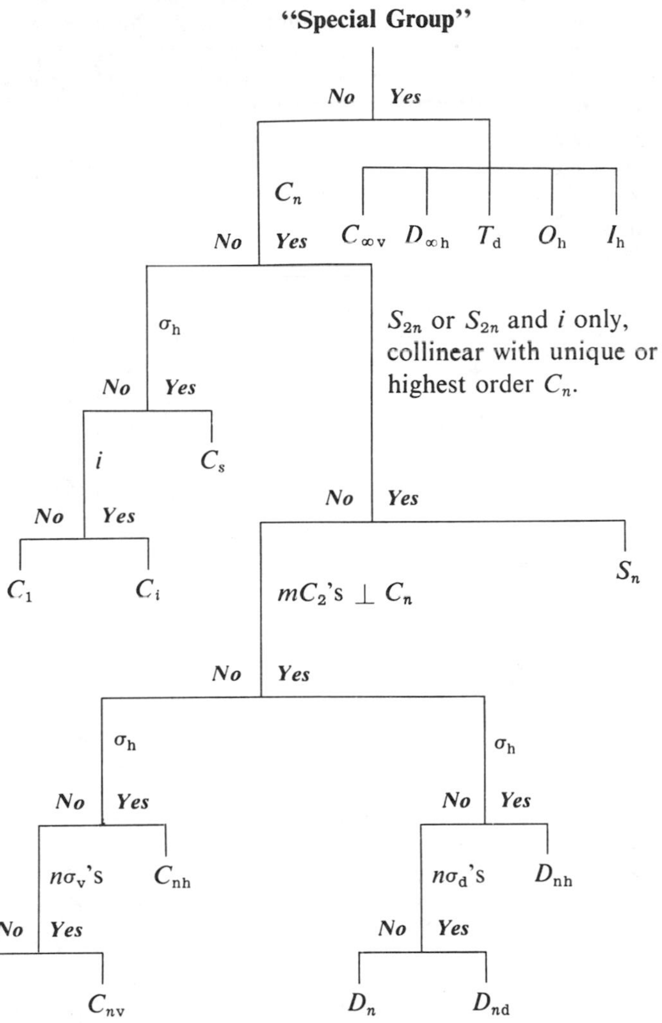

FIGURE 5-5 Flow chart for point group designations, $m = n$ for all dihedral (D) groups. (Taken from Milton Orchin and H. H. Jaffe, "Symmetry Point Groups and Character Tables," *J. Chem. Educ.* 47 (1970), 377.

3. Proceeding down the chart, molecules with only an improper axis of rotation collinear with the unique C_n axis are designated S_n, $n > 3$, and even only (S_4, 1,3,5,7-tetrabromocyclooctatetraene, tub form); those having m twofold rotation axes perpendicular to the unique C_n axis are designated D groups (dihedral group). In the case of all D groups $m = n$.

4. If the D molecule does not possess a horizontal or a vertical plane (σ_d), it is simply a D_n point group (D_2, biphenyl); if it does not possess a horizontal plane, but does have n vertical planes, it is D_{nd} (D_{3d}, staggered ethane). If it does have a horizontal plane (perpendicular to C_n), it is a D_{nh} point group (D_{3h}, NO_3^-).
5. If the species does not have m twofold rotation axes perpendicular to C_n, but does have a horizontal plane, it is designated C_{nh} (C_{2h}, *trans*-XHC=CHX). If it does not have a horizontal plane, it is designated either C_n (no n-fold vertical planes, C_3, CF_3—CH_3) or C_{nv} (has n-fold vertical planes of symmetry, C_{2v}, H_2O).

Consider the linear unsymmetrical molecule nitrous oxide, N=N=O. It does belong to one of the obvious point groups above. It has an axis

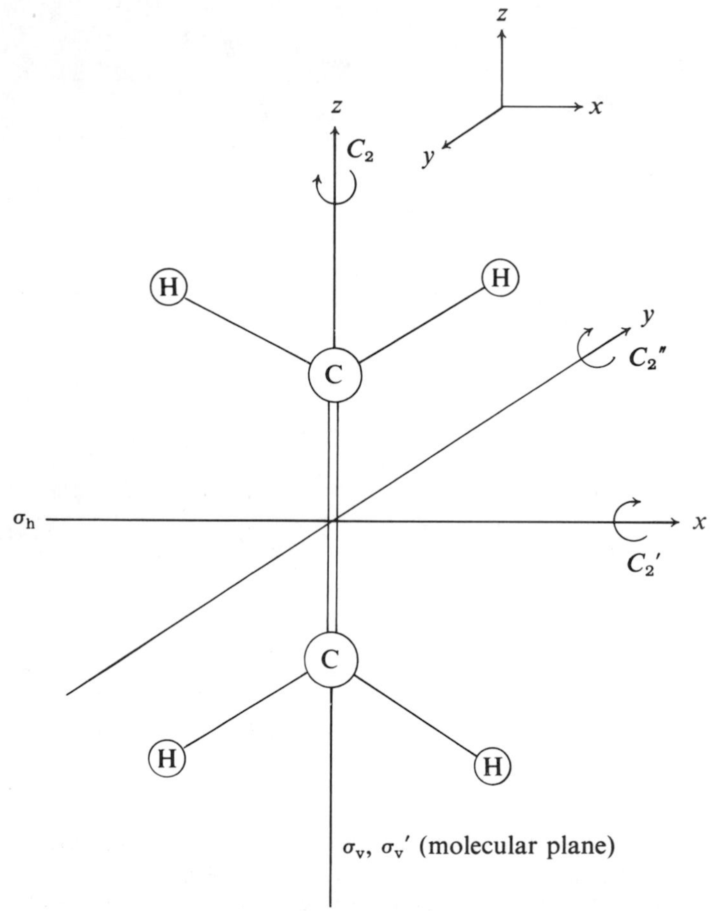

FIGURE 5-6 Symmetry elements and operations for ethylene, which has a D_{2h} point group.

of symmetry collinear with the molecular axis of the molecule. Thus, rotation about this axis produces an infinite number of equivalent configurations, C_∞. In a like manner, there are an infinite number of vertical planes corresponding to each rotation about the axis; hence the $C_{\infty v}$ point group designation.

Additional symmetry operations, according to the flow chart, are exemplified by the planar ethylene molecule, $H_2C{=}CH_2$, and shown in Figure 5-6. This molecule is characterized by three perpendicular proper axes of symmetry, C_2, C_2', and C_2'', with the unique axis collinear with the molecular axis. It also contains an alternating axis S_2 collinear with the unique C_2 axis, which is equivalent to the i element (center of symmetry). A molecule possessing a C_2 proper axis and a set of $m(=n)$ two-fold axes (C_2' and C_2'') perpendicular to it is designated a D_n group. The remaining symmetry elements are the three planes of symmetry σ_h, σ_v, and σ_v'. Finally, since the molecule contains at least one plane of symmetry normal to the unique axis, the point group designation is D_{nh}, where for ethylene $n = 2$ and the designation is D_{2h}.

Using a similar procedure, we can show that CO_2 has a $D_{\infty h}$ point group and H_2O a C_{2v} point group.

E. REPRESENTATIONS OF SYMMETRY OPERATIONS

We have established that a symmetry operation or a product of symmetry operations corresponds to the coordinate transformation of some or all constituent atoms of a species. This transformation can be mathematically *represented* by considering the general transformation of a single point or atom of the species. For a $C_2(z)$ operation, the corresponding change is $(x, y, z) \rightarrow (-x, -y, z)$. In matrix notation this transformation is represented as

$$\underbrace{\begin{bmatrix} -1 & 0 & 0 \\ 0 & -1 & 0 \\ 0 & 0 & 1 \end{bmatrix}}_{\text{Transformation matrix}} \begin{bmatrix} x \\ y \\ z \end{bmatrix} = \begin{bmatrix} -x \\ -y \\ z \end{bmatrix}, \qquad \textbf{(5-6)}$$

where the 3×3 diagonal matrix is called the *transformation matrix*. Application of this operation to the C_{2v} H_2S molecule corresponds to the transformation shown in Figure 5-7. In a like manner, we find that

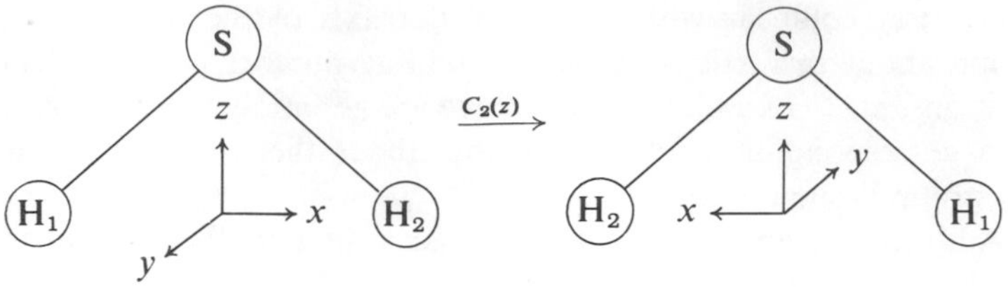

FIGURE 5-7 $C_2(z)$ operation on a general point or an atom of the H_2S molecule.

applying this procedure to the other operations of the C_{2v} molecule generates the following transformation matrices:

$$\begin{matrix} E & \sigma_v(xz) & \sigma_v(yz) \\ \begin{bmatrix} 1 & 0 & 0 \\ 0 & 1 & 0 \\ 0 & 0 & 1 \end{bmatrix}, & \begin{bmatrix} 1 & 0 & 0 \\ 0 & -1 & 0 \\ 0 & 0 & 1 \end{bmatrix}, & \begin{bmatrix} -1 & 0 & 0 \\ 0 & 1 & 0 \\ 0 & 0 & 1 \end{bmatrix}. \\ (x, y, z) \rightarrow (x, y, z) & (x, y, z) \rightarrow (x, -y, z) & (x, y, z) \rightarrow (-x, y, z) \end{matrix} \quad (5\text{-}7)$$

In this example, we have used unit vectors along the x, y, and z directions as the *basis* for the representation of the group. The corresponding matrices generated also constitute a representation of the group. We might ask the question, "What are the representations corresponding to the coordinates, their binary products, and atomic motions when they are subjected to the various symmetry operations of the group?" The matrix property of fundamental importance to us in this context is the trace of the irreducible transformation matrix for the symmetry operation performed. An irreducible transformation matrix (representation) is one that cannot be further reduced (block factored) by applying a similarity transformation, Eq. (5-4). The trace of the matrix—or the character, in group-theoretical language—is simply the sum of the diagonal elements. In the example above, all the representations are irreducible and one-dimensional; therefore each of the 3×3 transformation matrices is a block diagonal matrix consisting of three one-dimensional matrices (1×1). The characters of these representations (trivial in this case) are simply the diagonal elements themselves. Thus for the x, y, and z coordinates, we have from Eqs. (5-6) and (5-7) the various symmetry representations summarized in Table 5-4. These sets of characters that are generated from the transformation matrix for each symmetry operation are also called *symmetry species*, or *irreducible representations* (Γ_i's). For the x coordinate, the character corresponding to each group operation is the a_{11} element of each 3×3 matrix and hence it transforms as Γ_1. In a like manner, y transforms as Γ_2 and z as Γ_3. In addition to the x, y, and z

representations, only one additional irreducible representation is generated by their binary products (x^2, xy, xz, and so on), that corresponding to xy.

As you have probably recognized by now, the definition of a basis is not unique and in fact is limited only by our ingenuity in devising as many as possible. The choice of a basis then is completely arbitrary. We may choose, for example, to use the negative or positive unit vector as a basis for characterizing how the various symmetry operations affect rotational and translational motions, where -1 has the net effect of reversing the direction of motion and $+1$ of leaving it unaffected. Applying each symmetry operation to the translation in the x direction T_x leaves the motion unaffected in the cases of E and $\sigma_v(xz)$, but reverses it for $C_2(z)$ and $\sigma_v'(yz)$, as shown in Figure 5-8. In each case, the ± 1 unit vectors are considered to be 1×1 matrices with a set of characters corresponding to Γ_1 in Table 5-4, and therefore T_x "transforms as the x coordinate does." In fact, for any group, regardless of dimension, the translational motion in a given direction transforms exactly like the corresponding coordinate. A similar application to the rotational motion about the z direction R_z generates a set that transforms like Γ_4; it is also illustrated in Figure 5-8. The other rotational motions R_x and R_y about the x and y axes transform like Γ_2 and Γ_1, respectively. Up to this point, we have considered all the coordinates, their binary products, and all the motions except for the vibrational modes, and therefore we can be relatively sure that we have probably generated all the irreducible representations possible. As a general check, we can use a theorem from group theory, introduced here without proof:

The number of group-irreducible representations is equal to the number of classes.

There are four classes in the C_{2v} group and four Γ_i's generated.

A slightly more involved example illustrating both the vectorial and group-theoretical procedures in obtaining the irreducible representations is the C_{3v} nitrogen trifluoride molecule, NF_3. Since this group contains three classes, there are only three different irreducible representations.

TABLE 5-4. Irreducible Representations for the C_{2v} Point Group

Irreducible representation	E	$C_2(z)$	$\sigma_v(xz)$	$\sigma_v'(yz)$	
Γ_1	1	-1	1	-1	x, xz
Γ_2	1	-1	-1	1	y, yz
Γ_3	1	1	1	1	z, x^2, y^2, z^2
Γ_4	1	1	-1	-1	xy

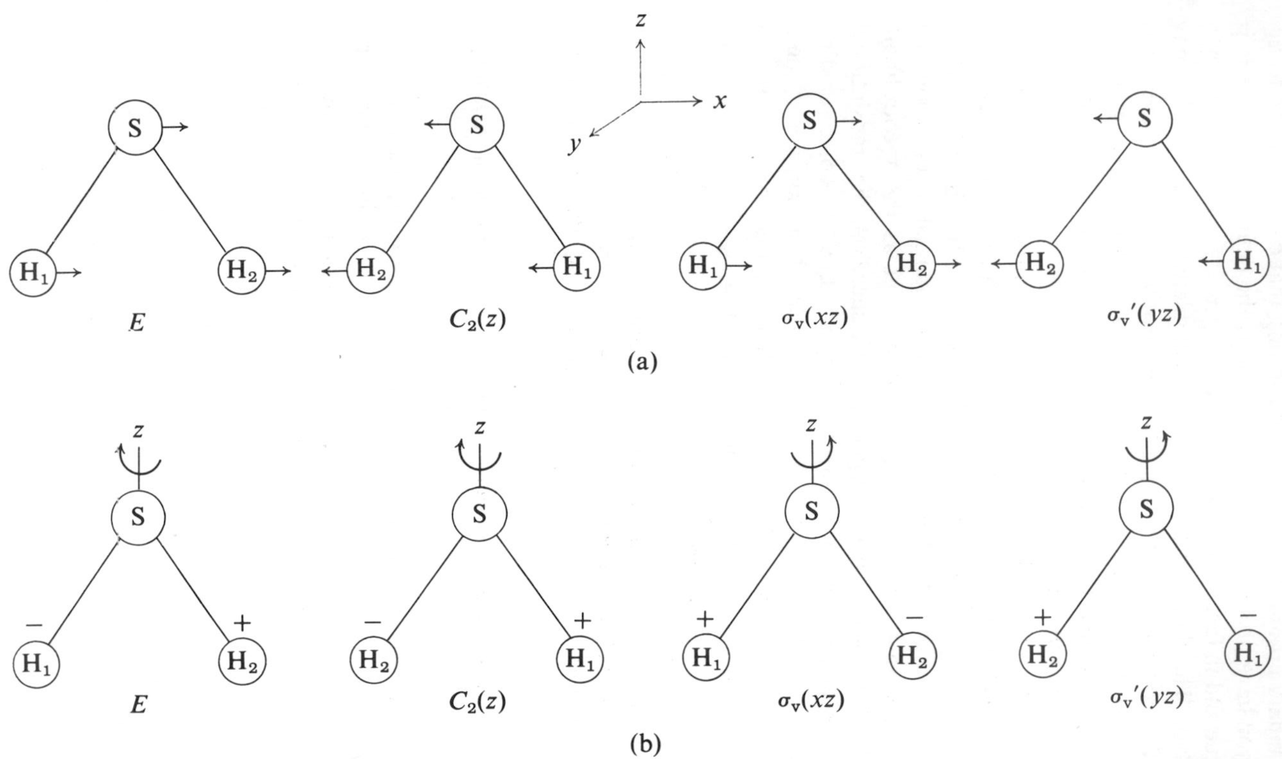

FIGURE 5-8 Summarization of the directional effect on translation in the x direction on T_x and rotation about the z axis R_z by the various group operations: (a) T_x is reversed by $C_2(z)$ and $\sigma_v'(yz)$ and unaffected by E and $\sigma_v(xz)$. (b) R_z is reversed by $\sigma_v(xz)$ and $\sigma_v'(yz)$ and unaffected by E and $C_2(z)$. The signs + and − indicate motion towards and away from the reader normal to the plane of the page.

TABLE 5-5. Irreducible Representations for the C_{3v} Point Group

Irreducible representation	E	C_3	C_3^2	σ_v	σ_v'	σ_v''	
Γ_1	1	1	1	1	1	1	z, T_z
Γ_2	1	1	1	−1	−1	−1	R_z
Γ_3	2	−1	−1	0	0	0	x, y, T_x, T_y

The most obvious of the three is the one similar to Γ_3 in Table 5-4, which is *symmetric* under all the operations of the group. The nonredundant symmetry operations of C_{3v} are E, C_3, C_3^2, σ_v, σ_v', and σ_v'', where the proper rotations and the vertical planes of symmetry make up two of the three classes and the lone E operation is the other. This irreducible representation, shown in Table 5-5 as Γ_1, having all $+1$ characters, is called the *totally symmetric representation.* It corresponds in this case

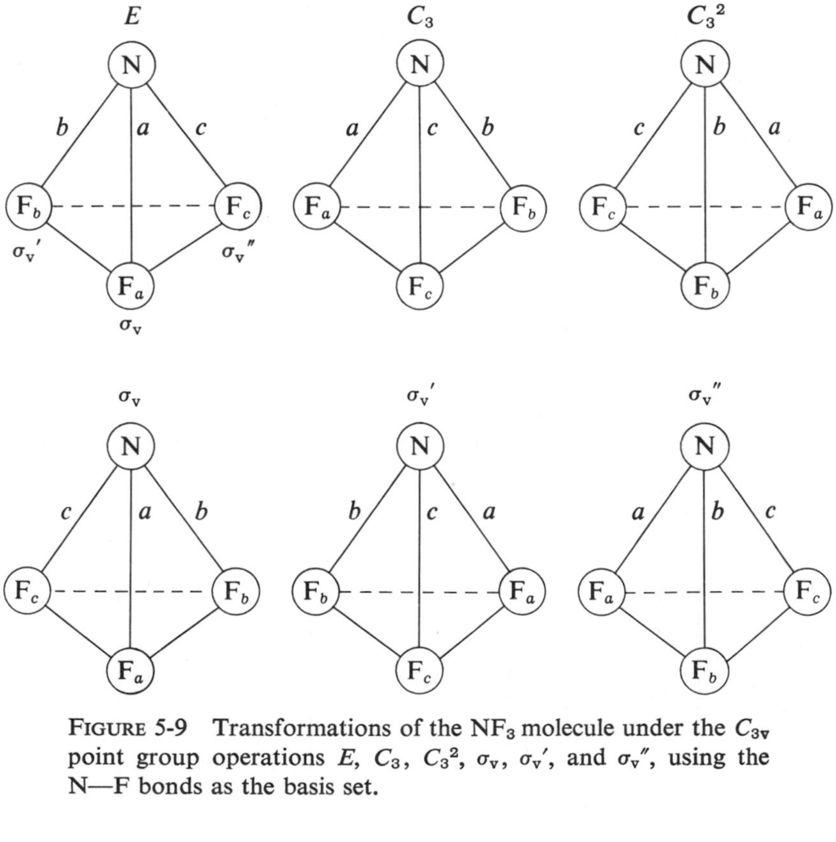

FIGURE 5-9 Transformations of the NF_3 molecule under the C_{3v} point group operations E, C_3, C_3^2, σ_v, σ_v', and σ_v'', using the N—F bonds as the basis set.

to the z coordinate, or translation in that direction. A second irreducible representation Γ_2 can be generated by rotation about the z axis, R_z. In this case R_z is unaffected by E, C_3, and C_3^2, but is reversed by all three reflections through the vertical planes.

To illustrate further the arbitrariness of the basis representation, we will generate the third irreducible representation, using the three N—F bonds as a basis set, as illustrated in Figure 5-9. The bonds corresponding to E are designated a, b, and c, coincident with the respective planes of symmetry σ_v, σ_v', and σ_v''. As the various group operations are performed, the labeled bonds are carried into one another. As shown previously, we can represent these transformations using matrix notation, where $\{a_{11} \quad a_{21} \quad a_{31}\}$ denotes a 1×3 column matrix. According to Figure 5-9, we have for each operation:

$$\mathrm{E}\{a \quad b \quad c\} = \{a \quad b \quad c\} \qquad \sigma_v\{a \quad b \quad c\} = \{a \quad c \quad b\}$$

$$\begin{bmatrix} 1 & 0 & 0 \\ 0 & 1 & 0 \\ 0 & 0 & 1 \end{bmatrix}\begin{bmatrix} a \\ b \\ c \end{bmatrix} = \begin{bmatrix} a \\ b \\ c \end{bmatrix} \qquad \begin{bmatrix} 1 & 0 & 0 \\ 0 & 0 & 1 \\ 0 & 1 & 0 \end{bmatrix}\begin{bmatrix} a \\ b \\ c \end{bmatrix} = \begin{bmatrix} a \\ c \\ b \end{bmatrix}$$

$$\mathrm{C}_3\{a \quad b \quad c\} = \{c \quad a \quad b\} \qquad \sigma_v'\{a \quad b \quad c\} = \{c \quad b \quad a\}$$

$$\begin{bmatrix} 0 & 0 & 1 \\ 1 & 0 & 0 \\ 0 & 1 & 0 \end{bmatrix}\begin{bmatrix} a \\ b \\ c \end{bmatrix} = \begin{bmatrix} c \\ a \\ b \end{bmatrix} \qquad \begin{bmatrix} 0 & 0 & 1 \\ 0 & 1 & 0 \\ 1 & 0 & 0 \end{bmatrix}\begin{bmatrix} a \\ b \\ c \end{bmatrix} = \begin{bmatrix} c \\ b \\ a \end{bmatrix} \tag{5-8}$$

$$\mathrm{C}_3^2\{a \quad b \quad c\} = \{b \quad c \quad a\} \qquad \sigma_v''\{a \quad b \quad c\} = \{b \quad a \quad c\}$$

$$\begin{bmatrix} 0 & 1 & 0 \\ 0 & 0 & 1 \\ 1 & 0 & 0 \end{bmatrix}\begin{bmatrix} a \\ b \\ c \end{bmatrix} = \begin{bmatrix} b \\ c \\ a \end{bmatrix} \qquad \begin{bmatrix} 0 & 1 & 0 \\ 1 & 0 & 0 \\ 0 & 0 & 1 \end{bmatrix}\begin{bmatrix} a \\ b \\ c \end{bmatrix} = \begin{bmatrix} b \\ a \\ c \end{bmatrix}.$$

By performing a similarity transformation (Eq. (5-4)) on each of the three-dimensional transformation matrices generated, we are able to effect a reduction of each to block-diagonal form. The matrix $\mathbf{X}$ and its inverse $\mathbf{X}^{-1}$ used to effect this matrix operation[2] are

$$\mathbf{X} = \begin{bmatrix} \frac{1}{\sqrt{3}} & 0 & \frac{2}{\sqrt{6}} \\ \frac{1}{\sqrt{3}} & \frac{1}{\sqrt{2}} & \frac{-1}{\sqrt{6}} \\ \frac{1}{\sqrt{3}} & \frac{-1}{\sqrt{2}} & \frac{-1}{\sqrt{6}} \end{bmatrix} \quad \text{and} \quad \mathbf{X}^{-1} = \begin{bmatrix} \frac{1}{\sqrt{3}} & \frac{1}{\sqrt{3}} & \frac{1}{\sqrt{3}} \\ 0 & \frac{1}{\sqrt{2}} & \frac{-1}{\sqrt{2}} \\ \frac{2}{\sqrt{6}} & \frac{-1}{\sqrt{6}} & \frac{-1}{\sqrt{6}} \end{bmatrix}. \tag{5-9}$$

The block diagonal matrices generated are

$$\mathbf{X}^{-1}\mathbf{E}\mathbf{X} = \begin{bmatrix} 1 & 0 & 0 \\ 0 & 1 & 0 \\ 0 & 0 & 1 \end{bmatrix} \qquad \mathbf{X}^{-1}\sigma_v\mathbf{X} = \begin{bmatrix} 1 & 0 & 0 \\ 0 & -1 & 0 \\ 0 & 0 & 1 \end{bmatrix}$$

$$\mathbf{X}^{-1}\mathbf{C}_3\mathbf{X} = \begin{bmatrix} 1 & 0 & 0 \\ 0 & -\frac{1}{2} & \frac{\sqrt{3}}{2} \\ 0 & -\frac{\sqrt{3}}{2} & -\frac{1}{2} \end{bmatrix} \qquad \mathbf{X}^{-1}\sigma_v'\mathbf{X} = \begin{bmatrix} 1 & 0 & 0 \\ 0 & \frac{1}{2} & -\frac{\sqrt{3}}{2} \\ 0 & -\frac{\sqrt{3}}{2} & -\frac{1}{2} \end{bmatrix}$$

$$\mathbf{X}^{-1}\mathbf{C}_3^2\mathbf{X} = \begin{bmatrix} 1 & 0 & 0 \\ 0 & -\frac{1}{2} & -\frac{\sqrt{3}}{2} \\ 0 & \frac{\sqrt{3}}{2} & -\frac{1}{2} \end{bmatrix} \qquad \mathbf{X}^{-1}\sigma_v''\mathbf{X} = \begin{bmatrix} 1 & 0 & 0 \\ 0 & \frac{1}{2} & \frac{\sqrt{3}}{2} \\ 0 & \frac{\sqrt{3}}{2} & -\frac{1}{2} \end{bmatrix}. \tag{5-10}$$

As indicated by the dashed squares, we have generated one one-dimensional matrix and one two-dimensional matrix for each transformation. Since the similarity transformations have reduced the three-dimensional matrices to a form that cannot be further reduced, the resulting matrices are said to form a set of *irreducible* transformation matrices. They equally well form a representation of the operations performed, exactly like the original set. One set of matrices along the diagonal is the totally symmetric irreducible representation Γ_1; the other is a two-dimensional irreducible representation. The characters for each of these (sum of the diagonal elements) form the third irreducible representation shown in Table 5-5.

On closer examination of Table 5-5, there are some features we should note and state in general form as actual theorems of group theory. One is that the characters for each member of a class are identical, and the second, that the irreducible representations Γ_1, Γ_2, and so on are orthogonal.

The characters of all the operations of the same class are identical for a given representation.

The vectors corresponding to the characters generated for different irreducible representations of a given group are orthogonal. Mathematically this statement is expressed as

$$\sum_R \chi_k(R)\chi_\ell(R) = 0, \qquad \text{if } k \neq \ell, \tag{5-11}$$

where R represents a symmetry operation and χ_k and χ_ℓ are the corresponding characters of this operation from different irreducible representations.

F. CHARACTER TABLES

Information concerning the manner in which the various molecular motions (translation, vibration, and rotation) are affected by symmetry operations and also about properties of various energy states can be predicted from the character tables. First, we briefly examine the contents of these tables and then consider how to apply this information to solving some simple examples.

The character tables for any molecular species having C_{2v} or D_{3d} symmetry are shown in Figure 5-10, for example, SO_2 and staggered ethane. A set of character tables most useful for structural chemistry purposes is listed in Appendix III. The symbols C_{2v} and D_{3d} are so-called

C_{2v}	E	$C_2(z)$	$\sigma(xz)$	$\sigma'(yz)$		
A_1	1	1	1	1	$z, (T_z)$	x^2, y^2, z^2
A_2	1	1	−1	−1	R_z	xy
B_1	1	−1	1	−1	$x, (T_x), R_y$	xz
B_2	1	−1	−1	1	$y, (T_y), R_x$	yz

D_{3d}	E	$2C_3$	$3C_2$	i	$2S_6$	$3\sigma_d$		
A_{1g}	1	1	1	1	1	1		$x^2 + y^2, z^2$
A_{2g}	1	1	−1	1	1	−1	R_z	
E_g	2	−1	0	2	−1	0	R_x, R_y	$x^2 - y^2, xy, xz, yz$
A_{1u}	1	1	1	−1	−1	−1		
A_{2u}	1	1	−1	−1	−1	1	$z, (T_z)$	
E_u	2	−1	0	−2	1	0	$x, y, (T_x, T_y)$	

FIGURE 5-10 Character tables for the point group C_{2v} and D_{3d}.

Schoenfliess symbols for the point group designations. The general point group designation for any species has been discussed in Section 5D. The symbols below this designation are in fact the irreducible representations that we have previously described as Γ_i's in Tables 5-4 and 5-5. The symbols A and B, E, and T individually signify one-, two-, and three-dimensional irreducible representations. The A designation is used for representations that are symmetric to rotation about the principal C_n axis, and B for those that are antisymmetric; for C_{2v} those characters having $+1$ or -1 for $C_2(z)$, respectively, and for D_{3d}, those one-dimensional representations with $+1$ or -1 characters for C_3, respectively. The subscripts, 1 or 2, designate which representations are symmetric or antisymmetric about a C_2 axis perpendicular to the unique axis or to a molecular plane if no C_2 exists. In the case of C_{2v}, we use the $\sigma(xz)$ molecular plane criterion for the 1 or 2 designation while the perpendicular C_2 axis is used for D_{3d}. If the species under consideration has a center of symmetry i, then these symbols are further designated with a "g" for a symmetric character or a "u" for an antisymmetric character. In the cases where a horizontal plane of symmetry σ_h either is the only operation (C_s) or is among the group operations, the Schoenfliess symbol may also contain a prime (′) designation for a symmetric character or a double prime (″) for an antisymmetric character.

The numbers in the central part of the tables represent the characters of the irreducible transformation matrix for the symmetry operation performed. (These have been discussed at length in the preceding section.) We can see now why these are called character tables. The unique irreducible representation (A, A_1, A_g, or A') having $+1$ characters for all symmetry operations is referred to as the totally symmetric representation.

The third column of the character table indicates how the rotational, translational, and general coordinates transform under the group operations. For example, for the translation of H_2S in the z direction, performing all four symmetry operations (E, $C_2(z)$, $\sigma(xz)$, and $\sigma'(yz)$) will leave the z vector unchanged, and hence it will have all $+1$ characters and be of A_1 symmetry. We say then that translation in the z direction T_z transforms like the z coordinate. In a like manner, performing the group operations on the rotation about the z axis will produce a set of characters that transform like A_2. It will be shown in the following section that the vibrational modes that transform like the x, y, and z coordinates are the ones that are "allowed" by first-order electric dipole selection rules.

The last column of the character table represents the squares and binary products of the x, y, and z coordinates. The vibrational modes that transform as these products and squares do will lead to active transitions by Raman spectroscopy. This occurs because the components of the polarizability tensor transform in the same way as these square and binary products do, and is a fundamental condition necessary for allowed transitions in Raman spectroscopy.

G. SYMMETRY OPERATIONS AND MOLECULAR MOTIONS

A final relation from group theory that allows the evaluation of how many times an irreducible representation appears in a reducible representation. It is

$$n^{(\Gamma_i)} = \frac{1}{g} \sum_k g_k \chi_k^{(\Gamma_i)} \chi_k. \tag{5-12}$$

Where Γ_i refers to the ith irreducible representation (A_1, E, etc.), g is the group dimension (number of group operations), g_k is the class dimension (number of class operations), $\chi_k^{(\Gamma_1)}$ is the character of the kth operation belonging to the Γ_ith irreducible representation, and χ_k is the character of the kth reducible representation. The χ_k characters are generated like those of the irreducible representations, with all $3N$ cartesian displacement coordinates used as a basis set in this case. Since the total reducible representation Γ_t for the motions of a gaseous molecule, where

$$\Gamma_t = \sum_{i=1}^{g} n^{(\Gamma_i)} \Gamma_i, \tag{5-13}$$

contains the number and types of irreducible representations that transform like the translational, rotational, and vibrational motions, then

$$\Gamma_t = \Gamma_{3N} = \Gamma_{\text{trans}} + \Gamma_{\text{rot}} + \Gamma_{\text{vib}}. \tag{5-14}$$

The simplest transformation matrix for a given molecule is that corresponding to the identity operation E. For a bent symmetrical triatomic, this operation leaves all the displacement vectors unaltered and the resulting transformation matrix simply has $+1$'s for all the diagonal elements and zero for all off-diagonal elements. As a result, $\chi_E = 9$

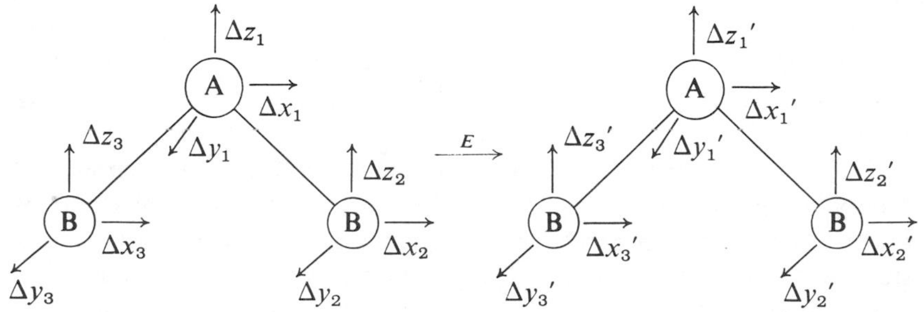

for the reducible representation. In general, for a molecule consisting of N atoms $\chi_E = 3N$.

$$\begin{bmatrix} \Delta x_1 \\ \Delta y_1 \\ \Delta z_1 \\ \Delta x_2 \\ \Delta y_2 \\ \Delta z_2 \\ \Delta x_3 \\ \Delta y_3 \\ \Delta z_3 \end{bmatrix} \begin{bmatrix} 1 & 0 & 0 & 0 & 0 & 0 & 0 & 0 & 0 \\ 0 & 1 & 0 & 0 & 0 & 0 & 0 & 0 & 0 \\ 0 & 0 & 1 & 0 & 0 & 0 & 0 & 0 & 0 \\ 0 & 0 & 0 & 1 & 0 & 0 & 0 & 0 & 0 \\ 0 & 0 & 0 & 0 & 1 & 0 & 0 & 0 & 0 \\ 0 & 0 & 0 & 0 & 0 & 1 & 0 & 0 & 0 \\ 0 & 0 & 0 & 0 & 0 & 0 & 1 & 0 & 0 \\ 0 & 0 & 0 & 0 & 0 & 0 & 0 & 1 & 0 \\ 0 & 0 & 0 & 0 & 0 & 0 & 0 & 0 & 1 \end{bmatrix} = \begin{bmatrix} \Delta x_1' \\ \Delta y_1' \\ \Delta z_1' \\ \Delta x_2' \\ \Delta y_2' \\ \Delta z_2' \\ \Delta x_3' \\ \Delta y_3' \\ \Delta z_3' \end{bmatrix} \qquad \text{(5-15)}$$

In a symmetry operation in which an atom replaces one of an equivalent type, the transformation for atom a replacing atom b is

$$q_a = \sum_{b=1}^{3} R_{ab} q_b, \qquad \text{(5-16)}$$

where $q_a = \Delta x_a$, Δy_a, and Δz_a. Since the new position that atom a occupies contains only q_b displacement coordinates, then $b \neq a$, and all diagonal elements $R_{aa} = 0$. Thus, the contribution of atom a to χ_k is zero. In general, any atom whose *position* is changed by a symmetry operation contributes zero to the kth character of the reducible representation. Therefore, in generating the characters for the totally reducible representation using cartesian displacement coordinates as a basis set, we need be concerned only with those atoms that are unshifted by the various symmetry operations.

To obtain the transformation matrices for the unshifted atoms, we must determine both the change in direction and the magnitude of their atomic displacement vectors along the coordinate system axes. The characters $(\Delta x_{11} + \Delta y_{11} + \Delta z_{11})$ of each atom are added (algebraically) to obtain χ_k. With the exception of C_n^i and S_n^i, the contributions to the character for each unshifted atom are relatively easy to generate using $+1$ elements for unchanged vectors and -1 elements for 180°-direction-changed displacement vectors. For an unshifted atom contained in a plane of symmetry, two of the displacement vectors (in the plane) will contribute $+1$ each, while the other normal to the plane will change direction by 180° and contribute -1, when the operation is performed. Thus χ_σ is in general $+1 + 1 - 1 = +1$ for each unshifted atom. For the inversion operation, the only possible unshifted atom (at the center) has all its displacement vectors changed by 180°, and $\chi_i = -1 - 1 - 1 = -3$. These results along with those of C_n^i and S_n^i for the contribution to the character for each unshifted atom are summarized in Table 5-6.[3]

TABLE 5-6. Character Contribution to Γ_k for Each Unshifted Atom

Symmetry operation	Contribution
E	$+3$
C_n^i	$1 + 2\cos\frac{2\pi i}{n}$
σ	$+1$
i	-3
S_n^i	$-1 + 2\cos\frac{2\pi i}{n}$

Application of the C_n^i relation in Table 5-6 to a C_2^1 and a C_3^1 operation would be $1 + 2\cos\pi = -1$ and $1 + 2\cos(2\pi/3) = 0$, respectively.

Application of the appropriate contributions in Table 5-6 to NF_3 (Figure 5-9) gives $\chi_E = 3N = (3)(4) = 12$, $\chi_{C_3^1} = \chi_{C_3^2} = 1 + (2)(-\frac{1}{2}) = 0$, and $\chi_{\sigma_v} = +1(2)$. In the first case we have four unshifted, in the second only one (nitrogen), and in the third two (a vertical plane containing N and F) atoms.

The total reducible representation generated for the $3N$ degrees of freedom of the C_{3v} nonlinear gaseous species NF_3 is summarized as

$$\begin{array}{cccc} & \underline{E} & \underline{2C_3} & \underline{3\sigma_v} \\ \Gamma_{3N}(\chi_k) & 12 & 0 & 2 \end{array}.$$

Applying Eq. (5-12) in conjunction with the C_{3v} character table (Appendix III) generates the following distribution:

$$\begin{aligned} n^{(A_1)} &= \tfrac{1}{6}[(1)(1)(12) + (2)(1)(0) + (3)(1)(2)] = 3 \\ n^{(A_2)} &= \tfrac{1}{6}[(1)(1)(12) + (2)(1)(0) + (3)(-1)(2)] = 1 \qquad \textbf{(5-16a)} \\ n^{(E)} &= \tfrac{1}{6}[(1)(2)(12) + (2)(-1)(0) + (3)(0)(2)] = 4. \end{aligned}$$

Thus, the total reducible representation decomposed into its irreducible representations is given as

$$\Gamma_{3N} = 3A_1 + A_2 + 4E. \qquad \textbf{(5-17)}$$

Once the point group and symmetry elements of a molecule are known, we can use them in conjunction with the character table to predict very useful information about spectroscopic and structural theory from symmetry considerations alone. Although symmetry properties can generally be applied in a wide variety of chemical problems, we should like to illustrate their application for "allowed" and "forbidden" vibrational transitions. A vibrational wavefunction for a single mode can be expressed as the product of three terms: a constant or normalizing term, $N_{\mathbf{v}}$; an exponential, $\exp(-\frac{1}{2}\gamma q)$; and a Hermite polynomial, in $\gamma^{1/2}q$, where

$$N_{\mathbf{v}} = \left[\left(\frac{\gamma}{\pi}\right)^{1/2} \frac{1}{2^{\mathbf{v}}(\mathbf{v}!)}\right]^{1/2}, \tag{5-18}$$

and

$$\gamma = \frac{4\pi^2\nu}{h}, \tag{5-19}$$

and $\mathbf{v}$ designates the vibrational quantum number. The generalized vibrational wavefunction for a polyatomic molecule in the ground state with k vibrational modes is given as

$$\psi_0 = N_0 \exp\left(-\frac{\gamma_1 q_1^{\,2}}{2} - \frac{\gamma_2 q_2^{\,2}}{2} - \frac{\gamma_3 q_3^{\,2}}{2} - \cdots - \frac{\gamma_k q_k^{\,2}}{2}\right), \tag{5-20}$$

where the first Hermite polynomial is unity, $H(\gamma^{1/2}q) = 1$, and $N_0 = [(\gamma_1/4)(\gamma_2/4)(\gamma_3/4)\cdots(\gamma_k/4)]^{1/4}$. This wavefunction is completely or totally symmetric to all symmetry operations, since all the nondegenerate q_k's transform as $\pm q_k$, and the various $(\pm q_k)^2$ terms are unaltered in sign. Doubly and triply degenerate ground state wavefunctions transform like sums of $(\pm q_k)^2$ terms, and are therefore also totally symmetric. The symmetries of the excited vibrational state wavefunctions differ only by the nature of the corresponding Hermite polynomial, since it is the only term of the product having a variable power of the transformed displacement coordinate q_k. These polynomials along with the first few vibrational state wavefunctions are listed in a table in Appendix IV. The wavefunctions of the first three states of a single vibrational mode are

$$\psi_0 = \left(\frac{\gamma}{\pi}\right)^{1/4} \exp(-\tfrac{1}{2}\gamma q^2), \tag{5-21}$$

$$\psi_1 = \left(\frac{\gamma}{4\pi}\right)^{1/4} 2\gamma^{1/2}q \exp(-\tfrac{1}{2}\gamma q^2), \tag{5-22}$$

$$\psi_2 = \left(\frac{\gamma}{64\pi}\right)^{1/4} (4\gamma q^2 - 2) \exp(-\tfrac{1}{2}\gamma q^2). \tag{5-23}$$

Thus, the symmetry of the excited state will simply be the symmetry of the corresponding Hermite polynomial, or more specifically of q or q^2, where even $\mathbf{v}$ states (0, 2, etc.) are symmetric and odd $\mathbf{v}$ states (1, 3, etc.) are antisymmetric.

We have shown previously, Eq. (2-35), that the fundamental requirement for an active electric-dipole absorption is that at least one of the integrals,

$$\int \psi_m{}^* \hat{\mu} \psi_k \, d\tau = \int \psi_m{}^* \hat{\mu}_x \psi_k \, d\tau_x + \int \psi_m{}^* \hat{\mu}_y \psi_k \, d\tau_y + \int \psi_m{}^* \hat{\mu}_z \psi_k \, d\tau_z, \tag{5-24}$$

must be totally symmetric, since integration over total configuration space will be zero for odd or antisymmetric integrands. In this expression, $\psi_m{}^*$ is the vibrational wavefunction of the excited state and ψ_k of the ground state and they are functions of the nuclear coordinates. The appropriate dipole moment operators, $\hat{\mu}_x$, $\hat{\mu}_y$, $\hat{\mu}_z$, are summations over the N atoms of the species having effective charge $\mathbf{e}_\beta$.

$$\mu_x = \sum_{\beta=1}^{N} \mathbf{e}_\beta x_\beta, \qquad \mu_y = \sum_{\beta=1}^{N} \mathbf{e}_\beta y_\beta, \qquad \mu_z = \sum_{\beta=1}^{N} \mathbf{e}_\beta z_\beta. \tag{5-25}$$

To determine the selection rules for infrared absorption, the nonzero requirement of each of these integrals may be tested by performing a set of symmetry operations on them. Since these operations involve simply a change of coordinates, the integrals should remain unchanged or symmetric. The effect of a symmetry operation R on the $(\mu_x)_{mk}$ integral will be to transform $\psi_m{}^*$ and $\hat{\mu}_x$ only, since ψ_k (the ground state) is totally symmetric:[4]

$$\psi_m{}^* \xrightarrow{\Gamma_i} \sum_i R_i \psi_m{}^* \tag{5-26}$$

and

$$\mu_x \xrightarrow{\Gamma_j} \sum_j R_j \mu_x, \tag{5-27}$$

where R_i and R_j are summed over all symmetry operations in the group. Thus, for the x component averaged over the g group operations,

$$(\mu_x)_{mk} = \int \psi_m{}^* \mu_x \psi_k \, d\tau_x \xrightarrow{\Gamma_i\Gamma_j} \frac{1}{g}\left(\sum_{ij} R_i R_j\right) \int \psi_m{}^* \mu_x \psi_k \, d\tau_x. \tag{5-28}$$

Since the product of the symmetry operations can be represented simply by the direct product of the irreducible representations,

$$\sum_{ij} R_i R_j = \Gamma_i \times \Gamma_j = \sum_{ij} \chi_i(R) \chi_j(R). \tag{5-29}$$

According to Eq. (5-11), this summation will be zero unless $i = j$, in which case

$$\frac{1}{g}\left(\sum_{ij} R_i R_j\right) = \frac{1}{g}\left(\sum_{ij} \chi_i(R) \chi_j(R)\right) = 1, \tag{5-30}$$

which is the "totally symmetric species." In such a case the integral remains nonzero. We apply the same procedure to the y and z components. Therefore, for a "symmetry allowed" infrared transition from a ground vibrational state, the μ_x, μ_y, or μ_z components must transform exactly like the wavefunction of the excited state $\psi_m{}^*$ under all the symmetry operations of the group. Stated simply, at least one of the products $\psi_m{}^*\mu_x$, $\psi_m{}^*\mu_y$, or $\psi_m{}^*\mu_z$ must transform like the totally symmetric representation.

The effect of a symmetry operation R on μ_x, μ_y, or μ_z (Eq. (5-27)) will simply be first to exchange atoms of equivalent charge (altering the summation), and secondly to transform the x, y, and z components of the βth atom in the same manner that they generally transform in the character tables. Thus, the symmetry properties of μ_x, μ_y, and μ_z will be the same as for the corresponding general x, y, and z coordinates. Since first vibrational excited states with $H_1 = 2\gamma^{1/2}q$ also transform like the generalized x, y, and z coordinates, *fundamental* vibrations will be active in the infrared for those modes having irreducible representations that transform like the x, y, and z coordinates. These are shown in the third column of the character table.

For Raman scattering, we find that the dipole moment operator $\hat{\mu}$ in Eq. (5-24) is the dipole moment $\mathbf{P}$ induced by the incident radiation field $\mathbf{E}$,

$$\hat{\mu} = \mathbf{P} = \boldsymbol{\alpha}\mathbf{E}, \tag{5-31}$$

where $\boldsymbol{\alpha}$, defined previously as the polarizability, is a tensor. The general expression for the product $\boldsymbol{\alpha}\mathbf{E}$, according to matrix algebra for an anisotropic molecule, more clearly characterizes the nature of $\boldsymbol{\alpha}$ (a 3×3 matrix):

$$\hat{\mu} = \begin{bmatrix} P_x \\ P_y \\ P_z \end{bmatrix} = \boldsymbol{\alpha}\mathbf{E} = \begin{bmatrix} \alpha_{xx} & \alpha_{xy} & \alpha_{xz} \\ \alpha_{yx} & \alpha_{yy} & \alpha_{yz} \\ \alpha_{zx} & \alpha_{zy} & \alpha_{zz} \end{bmatrix} \begin{bmatrix} \mathbf{E}_x \\ \mathbf{E}_y \\ \mathbf{E}_z \end{bmatrix}. \tag{5-32}$$

Substituting Eq. (5-31) into (5-24), we obtain

$$\int \psi_m{}^*\mathbf{P}\psi_k \, d\tau = \mathbf{E}\int \psi_m{}^*\boldsymbol{\alpha}\psi_k \, d\tau. \tag{5-33}$$

A nonzero value of this integral will depend, as before, on the transformation properties of the $\psi_m{}^*\boldsymbol{\alpha}$ product under a set of group operations. Since ψ_k is totally symmetric, then this product must be totally symmetric also. Thus, at least one of the components of the polarizability $\boldsymbol{\alpha}$ must transform like $\psi_m{}^*$. For fundamental transitions in the Raman effect, we find that this condition is satisfied for symmetry species that transform like any one of the components x^2, xy, zx, and so on, corresponding to α_{xx}, α_{xy}, α_{zx}, and so on. These are shown in the last column of the character tables.

EXAMPLE 5-1: Show that all the fundamental vibrations for the C_{2v} H_2S molecule are "symmetry allowed" both in the infrared and the Raman, given the total reducible representation

$$\Gamma_{3N} = 3A_1 + A_2 + 3B_1 + 2B_2.$$

Solution: The total reducible representation for the $3N$ degrees of freedom is

$$\Gamma_{3N} = \Gamma_{\text{trans}} + \Gamma_{\text{rot}} + \Gamma_{\text{vib}},$$

where from the C_{2v} character table (Appendix III),

$$\Gamma_{\text{rot}} = A_2 + B_1 + B_2 \quad \text{and} \quad \Gamma_{\text{trans}} = A_1 + B_1 + B_2;$$

thus if these are subtracted from Γ_{3N},

$$\Gamma_{\text{vib}} = 2A_1 + B_1.$$

Since both of these symmetry species transform exactly like either z, x^2, y^2, z^2 or xz, x for all operations of the group (that is, A_1 like z and B_1 like x), all three fundamentals will be infrared- and Raman-active.

Furthermore, by performing the four group operations on each of the vibrations illustrated below, we can prove to ourselves that two are totally symmetric (ν_1 and ν_2) and one (ν_3) antisymmetric to the $C_2(z)$ and $\sigma_v'(yz)$ symmetry operations.

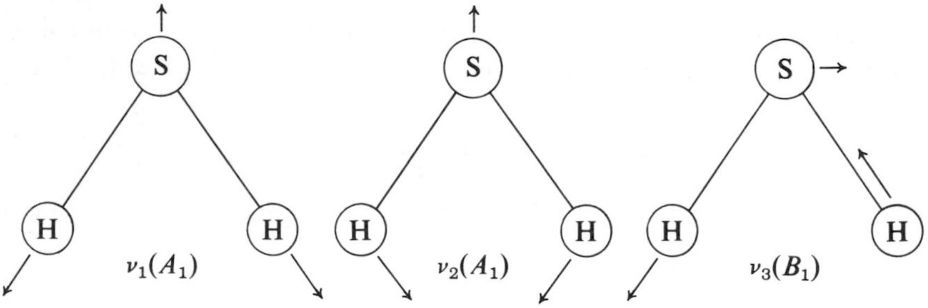

EXAMPLE 5-2: Using the D_{2h} character table (Appendix III), determine which of the twelve ethylene vibrations are Raman- or infrared-active or both. Given Table 5-7:

Solution: Using the D_{2h} character table, we can make the following assignments: ν_1, ν_2, ν_3, ν_5, ν_6, and ν_8 are all Raman-active, whereas ν_7, ν_9, ν_{10}, ν_{11}, and ν_{12} are all infrared-inactive.

We note one interesting result here, no infrared-active vibration is Raman-active, and vice versa. This mutually exclusive property is one

TABLE 5-7. Molecular Vibrational Assignments of Ethylene

Irreducible representation	Assignment	Approximate description
A_g	ν_1	CH_2 sym-stretch
	ν_2	CC stretch
	ν_3	CH_2 scissors
A_u	ν_4	CH_2 twist
B_{1g}	ν_5	CH_2 antisym-stretch
	ν_6	CH_2 rock
B_{1u}	ν_7	CH_2 wag
B_{2g}	ν_8	CH_2 wag
B_{2u}	ν_9	CH_2 antisym-stretch
	ν_{10}	CH_2 rock
B_{3u}	ν_{11}	CH_2 sym-stretch
	ν_{12}	CH_2 scissors

that is generally observed for molecules having a center of symmetry (principle of mutual exclusion).

SELECTED BIBLIOGRAPHY

5-1. Cotton, F. Albert. *Chemical Applications of Group Theory*, 2d ed. New York: Wiley-Interscience, 1971.

5-2. Jaffe, H. H., and Orchin, Milton. *Symmetry in Chemistry*. New York: John Wiley & Sons, 1967.

5-3. Perrin, Charles L. *Mathematics for Chemists*. New York: Wiley-Interscience, 1970.

5-4. Wilson, E. Bright, Jr., Decius, J. S., and Cross, Paul C. *Molecular Vibrations*. New York: McGraw-Hill Book Co., 1955. (Classic.)

ENDNOTES

1. This operation is sometimes called *reflection at the origin*.
2. Note that X^{-1} is simply the transpose of $X(X_{ij} = X_{ji}^{-1})$. This property is general for unitary matrices only.
3. These contributions are worked out in detail in Wilson, Decius, and Cross [Reference 5-4, p. 102].
4. $(\mu_x)_{mk} = \int \psi_m{}^*\mu_x\psi_k \, d\tau_x$.

PROBLEMS

5-1. Illustrate the total number and types of nonredundant proper rotations of the benzene molecule, and using the character tables (Appendix III) group them into classes.

5-2. Using a rectangular box, as illustrated below, locate and perform the successive symmetry operations corresponding to S_4 in allene and prove the statement that $S_n^n \equiv E$, for n = even.

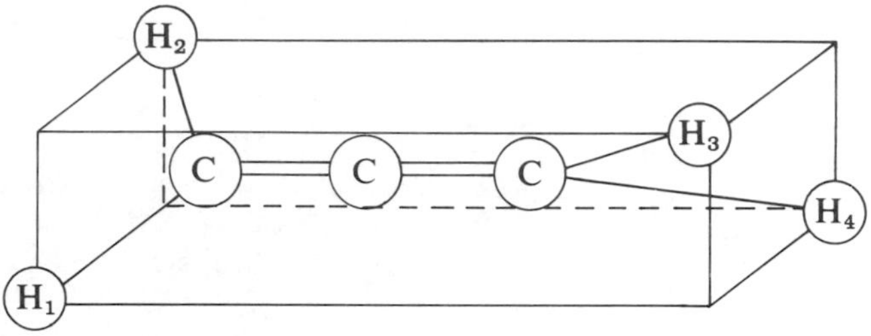

5-3. Obtain the products of each of the following operations using the transformation of a general point (x, y, z). Indicate which of the binary products commute.

a. $\sigma_v(xz)\sigma_v(yz)$. b. $C_2(z)\sigma_h(x, y)$. c. $C_2(x)C_2(y)$.
d. $\sigma_v(xz)C_2(y)$. e. $\sigma_h(xy)\sigma_v(xz)i$. f. $\sigma_v(yz)iC_2(z)$.

5-4. Construct the multiplication table for the allene molecule using only the nonredundant symmetry operations. Using this table, obtain the different classes corresponding to this D_{2d} molecule. Is the group Abelian?

5-5. Determine the number and types of symmetry elements and the corresponding point group designation of the following molecular species:

a. HCN. b. Planar vinyl radical (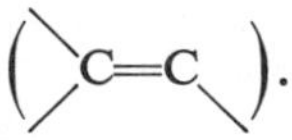).

c. *p*-Chlorobenzene. d. Cyanogen (N≡C—C≡N).
e. $C_2H_5^-$ (planar). f. $XeOF_4$ (tetragonal pyramid).
g. $X_2C{=}CH_2$. h. Tetrahedral P_4.

5-6. By performing the symmetry operations as in Figure 5-8, show that R_x and R_y for H_2S transform like Γ_2 and Γ_1 respectively, as shown in Table 5-4.

5-7. Show that the total reducible representation for the $3N$ degrees of freedom of H_2S in Example 5-1 is $\Gamma_{3N} = 3A_1 + A_2 + 3B_1 + 2B_1$. Given:

	E	$C_2(z)$	$\sigma_v(xz)$	$\sigma_v'(yz)$
$\Gamma_{3N}(\chi_k)$	9	-1	3	1

5-8. Determine the symmetry elements and operations for the diborane molecule illustrated herewith, and hence the point group designation.

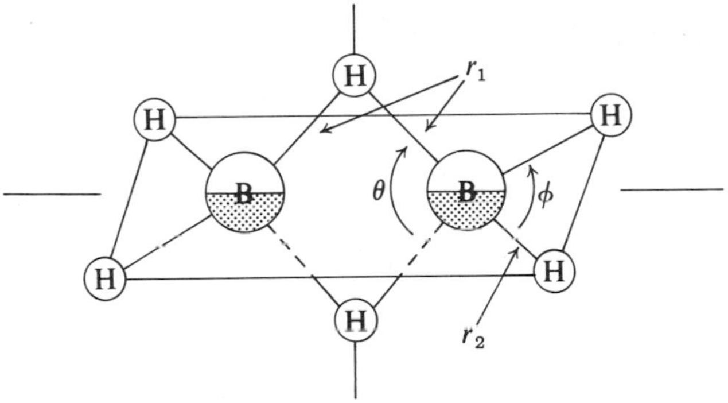

5-9. Using a symmetry argument, convince yourself that a molecule with a center of symmetry (i) cannot have a dipole moment. Develop a general argument for the requirement of a dipole moment in any molecule. (*Hint:* Performance of symmetry operations does not affect physical molecular properties).

5-10. For the SiF_4 molecule, the vibration representation is

$$\Gamma_{vib} = A_1 + E + 2T_2,$$

where each E is a doubly (two vibrational modes) degenerate representation and each T a triply (three vibrational modes) degenerate representation.

a. Of the total vibrational modes possible, determine which are infrared-active and which are Raman-active. $\nu_1(A_1)$, $\nu_2(E)$, ν_3 and $\nu_4(T_2)$.

b. How many *different* vibrational absorptions would you expect to see in the infrared and in the Raman?

Chapter 6

Vibrational Spectroscopy

Although vibrational spectroscopy is a relatively matured field in both theory and application, it remains one of the most useful spectroscopic tools in basic research. In new areas of research, the laser has probably had the greatest effect in enlarging the scope of vibrational spectroscopic techniques for probing phenomena that have previously been inaccessible. Examples are laser-induced energy-transfer processes, vibrational spectra of excited states, and various new Raman scattering processes induced by high-powered lasers, such as hyper, stimulated, and inverse Raman spectroscopy. We also expect, as a significant instrumental advance, the commercial availability of a tunable infrared laser spectrophotometer, capable of covering most of the absorption-rich regions. Such an instrument would allow us to do away with gratings and other optical alignment devices, and would significantly simplify the overall design and use of the spectrophotometer.

In this chapter we stress some of the fundamental principles in the understanding and interpretation of infrared spectra. The material covered is comprehensive and therefore reference is often made to more advanced texts of interest. The emphasis throughout is on providing continuity from basic material learned in undergraduate physical chemistry to the more advanced treatment of vibrational spectroscopy in such textbooks as Herzberg [Reference 6-3] and Wilson, Decius, and Cross [Reference 6-5]. Finally, we conclude with a glimpse at some of the recent applications of infrared lasers in chemistry and the stepwise process of determining a valence bond molecular force field in order to map a potential-energy surface.

A. DIATOMIC MOLECULES

1. The Harmonic Oscillator

When we derived the energy expression for the rigid rotor in Chapter 4 (Eq. (4-10)), we also obtained the energy of a quantized nonrotating simple harmonic oscillator:

$$E_{\mathrm{v}}\,(\mathrm{cm}^{-1}) = (\mathbf{v} + \tfrac{1}{2})\omega_{\mathrm{e}}. \tag{6-1}$$

This model pictured the vibration of a diatomic molecule as the movement of the two atoms towards and away from each other about an equilibrium separation r_e and characterized by simple harmonic motion. This motion is illustrated in Figure 6-1, using the spring-and-ball model of the diatomic molecule. The potential energy $U(r)$ used in that derivation (Eq. (4-4)) is the well-known quadratic expression (Hooke's law potential) having the familiar parabolic shape illustrated in Figure 4-1. The classical expression obtained for the nonquantized vibrational frequency in wavenumber units is

$$\omega\,(\mathrm{cm}^{-1}) = \frac{1}{2\pi c}\left[\frac{k}{\mu_{\mathrm{r}}}\right]^{1/2}, \tag{6-2}$$

which is equal to ω_e in Eq. (6-1); μ_r is the reduced mass of the diatomic $m_1 m_2/(m_1 + m_2)$ and k is defined as the force constant, expressed in millidynes/Å, or 10^5 dynes/cm. The right side of this expression is sometimes referred to as the *fundamental* vibration frequency. For the quantized oscillator (Eq. (6-1)), even in the $\mathbf{v} = 0$ state, the molecule is still vibrating with one-half this energy. This residual vibrational energy that remains even to approximately 0 °K is termed the *zero-point energy.*

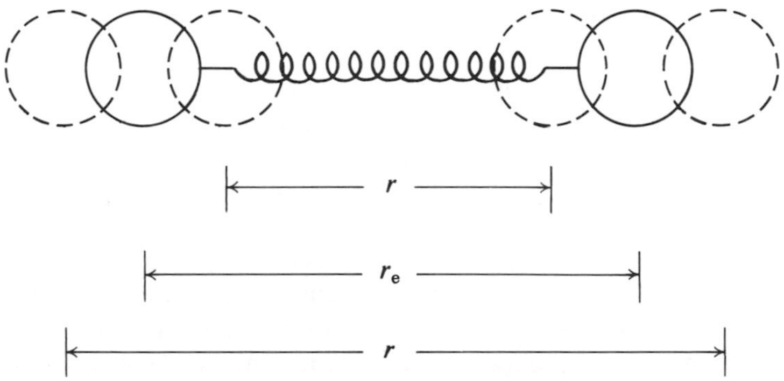

FIGURE 6-1 A diatomic molecule executing simple harmonic motion. The strength of the spring (bond strength), is proportional to the magnitude of the force constant k.

2. Selection Rules for Infrared Transitions

As before, we are naturally led to considering the restrictions involving transitions between the various vibrational states. To obtain the transitions allowed by first-order dipole selection rules, we make use of the second bracketed term of Eq. (4-27),

$$\left(\frac{\partial\mu}{\partial r}\right)_{e}\left\{\int_0^{\pi} \psi_m^*(\theta)\psi_k(\theta)\sin^2\theta\, d\theta \int_0^{2\pi} \psi_m^*(\phi)\psi_k(\phi)\cos\phi\, d\phi \right.$$
$$\left.\int_0^{\infty} \psi_m^*(r - r_e)[r - r_e]\psi_k(r - r_e)\, dr\right\}. \qquad \textbf{(6-3)}$$

The first two integrals have been evaluated and the selection rules obtained are $\Delta M = 0, \pm 1$, and $\Delta J = \pm 1$. For simplicity, we substitute q for the general displacement coordinate $r - r_e$ in the third integral, and thus we obtain

$$\int_{-\infty}^{+\infty} \psi_m^*(q)\psi_k(q)q\, dq, \qquad \textbf{(6-4)}$$

where $dq = dr$ and the limits on the integral are now from $-\infty$ to $+\infty$. On examining the orthonormal set of vibrational wavefunctions listed in Appendix IV, we can use the general property of the recursion formula by which the Hermite polynomials were generated,

$$\psi_{\mathbf{v}}(q)q = c\psi_{(\mathbf{v}+1)}(q) + c'\psi_{(\mathbf{v}-1)}(q), \qquad \textbf{(6-5)}$$

where c and c' are constants. Substituting Eq. (6-5) into (6-4) for the quantum state $\mathbf{v} = k$, we obtain

$$c\int_{-\infty}^{+\infty} \psi_m^*(q)\psi_{(k+1)}(q)\, dq + c'\int_{-\infty}^{+\infty} \psi_m^*(q)\psi_{(k-1)}(q)\, dq. \qquad \textbf{(6-6)}$$

According to the orthogonality relationship, these two integrals will remain nonzero if $m = k + 1$ for the first integral and $m = k - 1$ for the second. Since m and k correspond to any $\mathbf{v}$ wavefunction, we express the general vibrational selection rules for a (heteronuclear) diatomic as $\Delta\mathbf{v} = \pm 1$. In addition to the vibrational selection rules, there is an additional restriction placed on homonuclear types. The coefficient $(\partial\mu/\partial r)_e$ (Eq. (6-3)), which is the rate of change of the dipole moment with r at the equilibrium internuclear separation, must also be nonzero. Since a homonuclear diatomic has a zero dipole moment at all separations, $(\partial\mu/dr)_e = 0$, and no rotation-vibration spectrum is observed for these diatomics. This quantity is difficult to evaluate experimentally and may be either negative or positive, depending on the slope corresponding to r_e.

EXAMPLE 6-1: Show that the transition $\mathbf{v} = 0 \rightarrow \mathbf{v} = 2$ is not an "allowed" first-order dipole transition.

Solution: Using the wavefunctions from Appendix IV, we have

$$\psi_0 = \left(\frac{\gamma}{\pi}\right)^{1/4} \exp(-\tfrac{1}{2}\gamma q^2) \qquad \text{and} \qquad \psi_2 = \left(\frac{\gamma}{4\pi}\right)^{1/4} (2\gamma q^2 - 1) \exp(-\tfrac{1}{2}\gamma q^2).$$

Substituting ψ_0 and ψ_2 into Eq. (6-4) yields

$$\left(\frac{\gamma^2}{4\pi^2}\right)^{1/4} \int_{-\infty}^{+\infty} (2\gamma q^2 - 1) q \exp(-\gamma q^2)\, dq.$$

Expanding and evaluating the various integrals, we obtain

$$\left(\frac{\gamma^2}{4\pi^2}\right)^{1/4} \left[2\gamma \int_{-\infty}^{+\infty} q^3 \exp(-\gamma q^2)\, dq - \int_{-\infty}^{+\infty} q \exp(-\gamma q^2)\, dq\right] = 0.$$

Both integrals are zero since the integration of odd functions over all space effectively sums equal positive and negative portions. This result predicts a first-order transition probability of zero.

3. The Anharmonic Oscillator

Thus far we have considered the vibrational motion of a diatomic to be of a purely harmonic nature; we know, however, that is only an approximation justified for infinitesimal amplitudes. For small displacements from the minimum in the potential curve, the energy expression Eq. (4-3) can be expanded to include higher-order anharmonic cubic and quartic terms,

$$U(r) = aq^2 - bq^3 + cq^4 + \cdots, \tag{6-7}$$

where q is the general displacement coordinate corresponding in this case to $r - r_e$, and b and c are the anharmonic force constants. Substituting Eq. (6-7) into Eq. (4-2) and solving gives the resulting energy expression for the anharmonic oscillator,

$$E_{\mathrm{v}}\,(\mathrm{cm}^{-1}) = \omega_e(\mathbf{v} + \tfrac{1}{2}) - \omega_e x_e(\mathbf{v} + \tfrac{1}{2})^2 + \omega_e y_e(\mathbf{v} + \tfrac{1}{2})^3 + \cdots, \tag{6-8}$$

where ω_e is the hypothetical vibrational frequency for the r_e internuclear separation (infinitesimal amplitude). In this expression $\omega_e \gg \omega_e x_e \gg \omega_e y_e$. The second term is practically always positive; although the third coefficient may be positive or negative, it is generally small. As $\mathbf{v}$ becomes large, $\omega_e x_e(\mathbf{v} + \frac{1}{2})^2$ makes a greater contribution to the energy; it finally becomes large enough that the energy difference between it and the first term is so small that the $\mathbf{v}$ states are effectively continuous (Figure 4-1).

If we assume that the anharmonic wavefunctions are not significantly different from the wavefunctions of the harmonic oscillator, then the $\Delta\mathbf{v} = \pm 1$ selection rules can be applied to Eq. (6-8). We also find that the original dipole moment expression for $\mu(r)$, Eq. (4-22), should be expanded to include higher-order terms for sufficiently anharmonic oscillators. On including these higher-order terms, we obtain allowed transitions for $\Delta\mathbf{v} = \pm 2, \pm 3, \pm 4, \ldots$, with rapidly decreasing intensity. These transitions are called *overtones*. For a harmonic oscillator, these transitions would be exact multiples (2, 3, or 4) of the fundamental vibration frequency. For the anharmonic oscillator however, they are practically always less than a multiple of the fundamental frequency.

In the case of a transition from the ground vibrational level $\mathbf{v} = 0$ to any upper vibrational state $\mathbf{v}$, excluding the cubic term we have, according to Eq. (6-8),

$$\Delta E_{\mathrm{v}}\,(\mathrm{cm}^{-1}) = \mathbf{v}\omega_{\mathrm{e}} - \mathbf{v}(\mathbf{v}+1)\omega_{\mathrm{e}}x_{\mathrm{e}} = \omega_{\mathrm{obs}}. \tag{6-9}$$

For HCl, the observed frequency for the $\mathbf{v} = 0 \rightarrow \mathbf{v} = 1$ and $\mathbf{v} = 0 \rightarrow \mathbf{v} = 2$ (second harmonic) transitions are 2886 and 5668 cm^{-1}, respectively. Substituting these data into Eq. (6-9) and solving the two simultaneous equations, we obtain $\omega_{\mathrm{e}} = 2990\ \mathrm{cm}^{-1}$ and $\omega_{\mathrm{e}}x_{\mathrm{e}} = 52\ \mathrm{cm}^{-1}$. The magnitude of $\omega_{\mathrm{e}}x_{\mathrm{e}}$ is quite large in this case, indicating that the HCl vibrational levels are very anharmonic. Typical values of $\omega_{\mathrm{e}}x_{\mathrm{e}}$ range from about 10 to less than 1 cm^{-1}. Therefore, for most molecules the difference between $\mathbf{v}\omega_{\mathrm{e}}$ and ω_{obs} is relatively small.

The fundamental vibration frequency of a specific diatomic molecule, Eq. (6-2), is equivalent to the frequency of the $\mathbf{v} = 0 \rightarrow \mathbf{v} = 1$ transition of a quantized harmonic oscillator. Using this experimental observation, we are able to calculate the magnitude of the force constant k. The force constant for a particular bond type and bond order is experimentally observed to be remarkably constant from one molecule to another. As a result, the corresponding vibrational absorption frequency is also only slightly shifted in many cases. This behavior has provided the basis for the assumption of transferring bond frequencies from one polyatomic molecule to another. This practice should be used with extreme caution, since the vibrations of a polyatomic molecule technically involve the displacements of all the constituent atoms and are a sensitive function of the bond environment. Typical force constants for selected "diatomics" are summarized in Table 6-1.

EXAMPLE 6-2: Given the force constant $k \simeq 17.0$ mdyn/Å for the "diatomic type" C≡N, estimate the approximate "C≡N stretch" in methyl cyanide and comment briefly on the usefulness of this approximation.

Solution: Using Eq. (6-2), we obtain

$$\omega\,(\mathrm{cm}^{-1}) = \frac{1}{2\pi c}\left(\frac{k}{\mu_{\mathrm{r}}}\right)^{1/2} = 5.323 \times 10^{-12}\left(\frac{k}{\mu_{\mathrm{r}}}\right)^{1/2}$$

TABLE 6-1. Approximate Stretching Force Constants for Selected Bonds

Bond	Molecule	k (mdyn/Å)
H—F	HF	9.67
H—Cl	HCl	5.15
H—Br	HBr	4.11
H—I	HI	3.16
H—O	H_2O	7.8
H—S	H_2S	4.3
H—Se	H_2Se	3.3
H—N	NH_3	6.5
H—C	CH_3X	4.7
H—C	C_2H_4	5.1
H—C	C_6H_6	5.1
F—C	CH_3F	5.6
Cl—C	CH_3Cl	3.4
Br—C	CH_3Br	2.8
C═C	C_6H_6	7.62
C—C	...	4.5–5.6
C═C	C_2H_4	9.5–9.9
C≡C	...	15.6–17.0
N—N	...	3.5–5.5
N═N	...	13.0–13.5
N≡N	N_2	22.9
O—O	...	3.5–5.0
C—N	...	4.9–5.6
C═N	...	10–11
C≡N	...	16.2–18.2
C—O	...	5.0–5.8
C═O	...	11.8–13.4

SOURCE: Wilson, Decius, and Cross [Reference 6-5, p. 175], by permission

where for C≡N,

$$\mu_r = \frac{(12.00)(14.00)}{(26.00)(6.02 \times 10^{23})} = 1.0733 \times 10^{-23} \text{ g/molecule};$$

$$k = 17.0 \times 10^5 \text{ dyn/cm}.$$

Thus, we obtain

$$\begin{aligned} \omega &= (5.323 \times 10^{-12})\left(\frac{17.0 \times 10^5}{10.73 \times 10^{-23}}\right)^{1/2} \\ &= (5.323 \times 10^{-12})(3.978 \times 10^{14}) \\ &= 2118 \text{ cm}^{-1}. \end{aligned}$$

Examination of the CH_3CN spectrum shows that there is a fundamental frequency that occurs at 2267 cm^{-1}, and none within 687 cm^{-1} of this one. Thus, we conclude that in selected cases, this approach can be useful in identifying bonds of the molecule, but not the frequency of absorption.

4. Rotation-Vibration Spectra

For transitions occurring between different vibrational states, we also have concurrent transitions between specific rotational states within each of these vibrational levels. The selection rules for vibration-rotation transitions are just those derived above from Eq. (6-3), $\Delta\mathbf{v} = \pm 1$ and $\Delta J = \pm 1$. If we assume for the moment that the energy is adequately represented by a vibrating rotor having no rotation-vibration interaction, then

$$\tilde{E}\,(\text{cm}^{-1}) = (\mathbf{v} + \tfrac{1}{2})\omega_e + J(J+1)\tilde{B}_\mathbf{v}, \qquad \textbf{(6-10)}$$

where ω_e has been defined previously and $\tilde{B}_\mathbf{v}$ is the rotational constant of a particular vibrational state $\mathbf{v}$. For a transition between two vibrational states, we obtain

$$\Delta\tilde{E}\,(\text{cm}^{-1}) = \omega_0 + J'(J'+1)\tilde{B}_\mathbf{v}' - J''(J''+1)\tilde{B}_\mathbf{v}'', \qquad \textbf{(6-11)}$$

where ω_0 is the frequency corresponding to the transition between the rotationless ($J'' = 0 \rightarrow J' = 0$) states of each vibrational level, and the prime and double prime refer to the upper and lower vibrational states. Applying each of the rotational selection rules $\Delta J = +1$ and $\Delta J = -1$ separately yields

$$\Delta\tilde{E}\,(\text{cm}^{-1})_R = \omega_0 + 2\tilde{B}_\mathbf{v}' + (3\tilde{B}_\mathbf{v}' - \tilde{B}_\mathbf{v}'')J + (\tilde{B}_\mathbf{v}' - \tilde{B}_\mathbf{v}'')J^2, \qquad \textbf{(6-12)}$$

and

$$\Delta\tilde{E}\,(\text{cm}^{-1})_P = \omega_0 - (\tilde{B}_\mathbf{v}' + \tilde{B}_\mathbf{v}'')J + (\tilde{B}_\mathbf{v}' - \tilde{B}_\mathbf{v}'')J^2, \qquad \textbf{(6-13)}$$

where J has replaced J'', and corresponds to the lower rotational quantum state in both equations. The R equation (generates the R branch), corresponding to $J \rightarrow J+1$, and the P equation (P branch), corresponding to $J \rightarrow J-1$, have minimum J values of 0 and 1. The energy-level diagram of a typical vibration-rotation band and the resulting spectrum is shown in Figure 6-2. In the case where there is significant rotation-vibration interaction and $\tilde{B}_\mathbf{v}'' > \tilde{B}_\mathbf{v}'$, the energy spacings $\Delta\tilde{E}$ of the R branch transitions can lead to eventual convergence because the negative third and fourth terms on the right of Eq. (6-12) become dominant at high J values. The $R(J'')$ transition at which these negative terms cause a reversal of the transition energy is called the *band head.* On the other

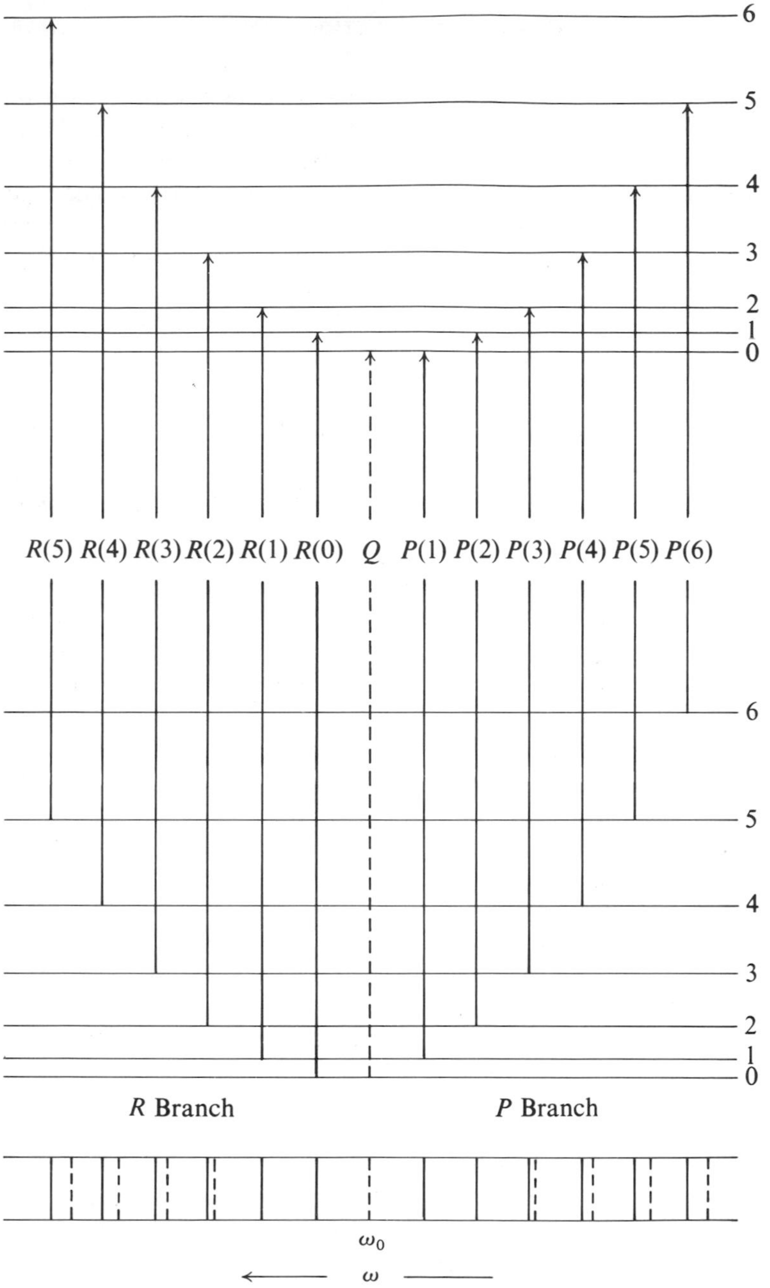

FIGURE 6-2 Energy-level diagram and spectrum of a rotation-vibration band of a diatomic molecule. The missing middle transition is the forbidden Q branch. An exaggerated illustration of the rotation-vibration spectrum resulting when $\tilde{B}_v'' > \tilde{B}_v'$ (dotted line) indicates eventual convergence of the R branch and increased spacing of the P branch.

hand, the second and third terms on the right of Eq. (6-13) are both negative and cause the P branch transition energy spacings to become greater at high J values. Transitions between these levels are illustrated by the dotted lines of Figure 6-2 (excluding the dotted line ω_0 corresponding to the forbidden Q branch). It should be emphasized that the occurrence of this effect at such low J values as shown in Figure 6-2 is highly unlikely, and is exaggerated for the illustration.

In the cases where the vibration-rotation interaction is negligible, or for relatively low J states where $\tilde{B}_v'' \simeq \tilde{B}_v'$, Eqs. (6-12) and (6-13) simplify to

$$\Delta\tilde{E}\,(\text{cm}^{-1})_R = \omega_0 + 2\tilde{B} + 2\tilde{B}J \qquad \textbf{(6-12a)}$$

and

$$\Delta\tilde{E}\,(\text{cm}^{-1})_P = \omega_0 - 2\tilde{B}J. \qquad \textbf{(6-13a)}$$

The application of these equations to the observed vibration-rotation spectrum adequately characterizes the solid-line spectrum of Figure 6-2. The fundamental vibration-rotation band of HCl gas is illustrated in Figure 6-3. The doublets are due to the presence of both $H^{35}Cl$ and $H^{37}Cl$ in a 3:1 ratio. Two important features of this band are the transition-energy (band) spacings and the intensity distribution. The absorption spacings are simply those of the rotational levels, which are inversely proportional to the reduced masses μ_r (see Eq. (4-13)). For hydrogen-containing diatomics, μ_r is very small, and thus we obtain relatively large rotational energy-level spacings. On examining Figure 6-3 more closely, we note the decreased spacings of the R branch and the increased spacings of the P branch as characterized by Eqs. (6-12) and (6-13). If we assume for the moment that the transition-moment integral (Eq. (4-16)) for the lower-vibrational-state rotational levels are approximately constant, then the intensity of a $P(J'')$ or an $R(J'')$ transition will be directly proportional to the population of the lower J'' state. Applying the Boltzmann distribution law to the rotational states of HCl yields

$$\frac{N_J}{N_0} = \frac{g_J}{g_0} \exp \frac{-(E_J - E_0)}{RT}, \qquad \textbf{(6-14)}$$

where $g_J = 2J + 1$, and the subscripts J and 0 refer to the upper and ground rotational states (within the $\mathbf{v} = 0$ level). The plot of N_J/N_0 versus J is shown in Figure 6-4 at 300 °K, where we observe that the peak in the rotational distribution corresponds to the J state peaks of the P and R branches; and the complete distribution gives rise to the characteristic "Boltzmann-shaped envelope."

EXAMPLE 6-3: The spacings between the lower rotational absorption lines of Figure 6-3 are approximately 20.3 cm^{-1}; use this data to estimate the

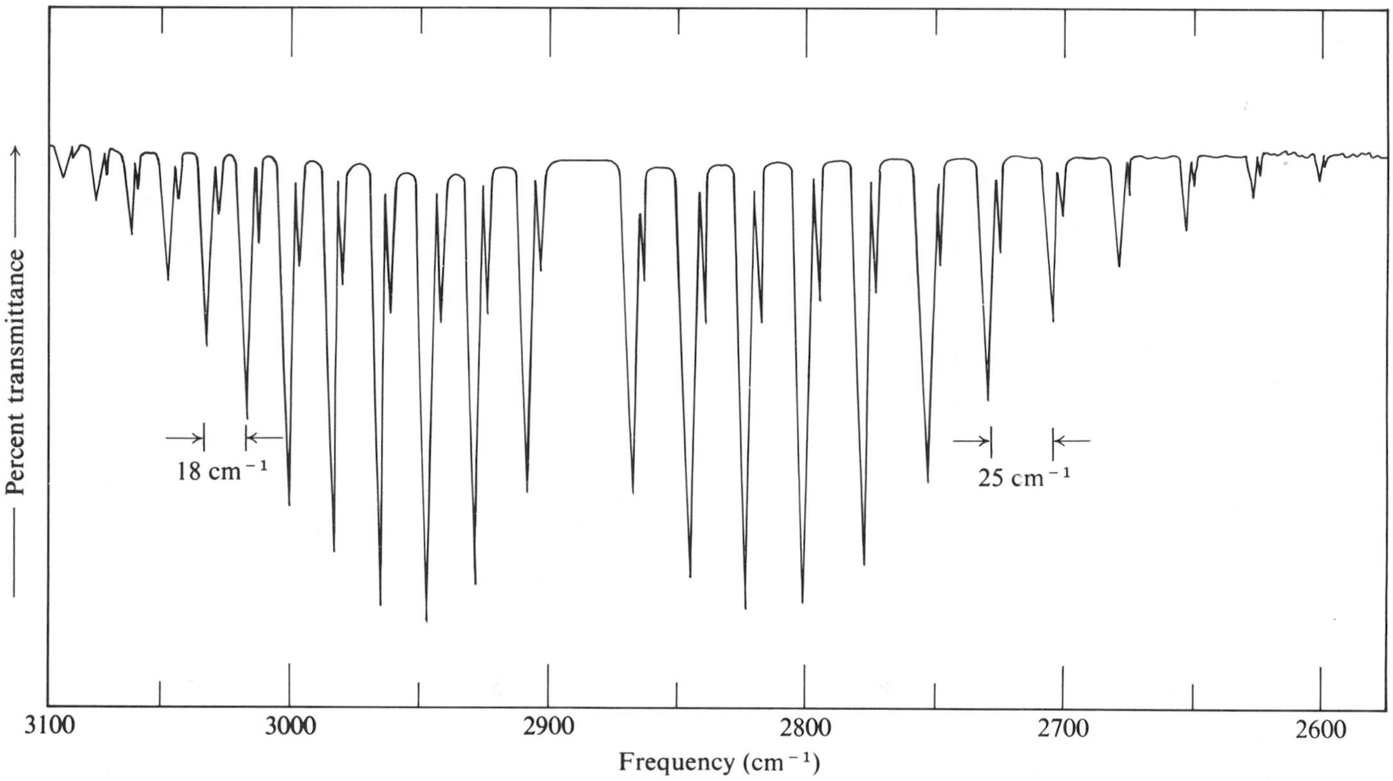

FIGURE 6-3 Rotation-vibration spectrum of HCl gas at 5 torr in a 10-cm path cell at 300 °K. Note the decreased spacings of the *R* branch and the increased spacings of the *P* branch as characterized by the Eqs. (6-12) and (6-13). The doublets are due to the presence of both $H^{35}Cl$ and $H^{37}Cl$ in a 3:1 ratio.

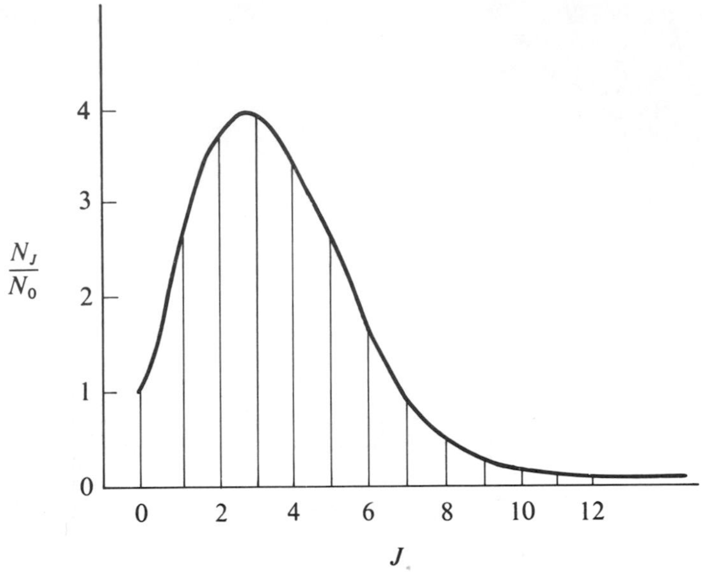

FIGURE 6-4 Relative populations of the rotational energy levels for HCl gas at 300 °K. (Taken from J. C. Davis, Jr.–*Advanced Physical Chemistry—Molecules, Structure and Spectra*–Copyright © 1965, The Ronald Press Company, New York.

lone structural parameter of HCl, r_0. (Assume rotation-vibration interaction to be negligible).

Solution: Since Eq. (6-13a) characterizes any given P branch transition, we have for any two rotational levels that are adjacent

$$\Delta\tilde{E}\,(\text{cm}^{-1})_{P(J)} - \Delta\tilde{E}\,(\text{cm}^{-1})_{P(J+1)} = 2\tilde{B}[(J+1) - J]$$

$$20.3\ \text{cm}^{-1} = \frac{2h}{8\pi^2 I_0 c} = \frac{(2)27.989 \times 10^{-40}}{I_0}$$

$$I_0 = 2.76 \times 10^{-40}\ \text{g-cm}^2 = \mu r_0^{\,2}$$

where

$$\mu_r = \frac{m_{\text{Cl}} m_{\text{H}}}{m_{\text{Cl}} + m_{\text{H}}} \frac{1}{6.02 \times 10^{23}} = 1.616 \times 10^{-24}\ \text{g},$$

and

$$r_0 = 1.30\ \text{Å}.$$

B. POLYATOMIC MOLECULES

We should like to obtain the expression for the total vibrational energy of a nonrotating molecule with its center of mass at the origin of the coordinate system. For a polyatomic molecule containing N atoms, there are $3N$ degrees of freedom, or displacement coordinates, describing the motion of the nuclei. These displacements of the various nuclei in phase give rise to the translational, rotational, and vibrational motions of a molecule. We must, however, make a careful choice of these coordinates—such that the Schrödinger equation, generated from the classical expressions for the kinetic T and potential U energies, can be reasonably solved. To accomplish this choice, we begin with a discussion of *normal modes of vibration* and *normal coordinates.* As we shall see shortly, using these coordinates provides the simplifying features for evaluating the total vibrational energy. Following examination of the procedure for obtaining selection rules for vibration-rotation transitions, we shall consider examples of their application for both simple and moderately complex molecules.

1. Normal Modes of Vibration

To generate the coordinates referred to above, we locate the center of mass at the origin

$$\sum_i m_i x_i = 0, \qquad \sum_i m_i y_i = 0, \qquad \sum_i m_i z_i = 0$$

and fix the coordinates describing the rotation about the three mutually perpendicular axes in space

$$\sum_i m_i(y_i z_i - z_i y_i) = 0, \qquad \sum_i m_i(z_i x_i - x_i z_i) = 0, \qquad \sum_i m_i(x_i y_i - y_i x_i) = 0.$$

In applying these conditions, we have a model of a nontranslating and nonrotating molecule with origin at the center of mass. Although applying these six restraints leaves $3N - 6$ ($3N - 5$ for linear polyatomics) independent displacement coordinates for describing the vibrational motion, we shall carry through the treatment using all $3N$ coordinates and eliminate these six at a convenient point in the discussion. The kinetic energy of the $3N$ modes expressed in cartesian displacement coordinates—Δx_1, Δy_1, Δz_1, $\Delta x_2, \ldots, \Delta x_k$, Δy_k, $\Delta z_k, \ldots, \Delta x_N$, Δy_N, Δz_N—is[1]

$$2T = \sum_{k=1}^{N} m_k[\dot{x}_k^2 + \dot{y}_k^2 + \dot{z}_k^2], \tag{6-15}$$

where $\Delta x_k = x_k - x_{ke}$, $\Delta y_k = y_k - y_{ke}$, $\Delta z_k = z_k - z_{ke}$, and so on; x_k, y_k, and z_k are the coordinates of the kth atom in terms of the translating system, and x_{ke}, y_{ke}, and z_{ke} their equilibrium positions. So that the kinetic energy can be expressed in homogeneous quadratic form with no constant (m_k), we define a new set of mass-weighted cartesian displacement coordinates, $q_1, q_2, \ldots, q_{3N}$ as

$$q_1 = \sqrt{m_1}\Delta x_1, q_2 = \sqrt{m_1}\Delta y_1, q_3 = \sqrt{m_1}\Delta z_1, q_4 = \sqrt{m_2}\Delta x_2, \ldots, q_{3N}. \tag{6-16}$$

The reason for this choice of coordinates will become obvious shortly. Thus, the kinetic energy is given as

$$2T = \sum_{i=1}^{3N} \dot{q}_i^2. \tag{6-17}$$

The corresponding potential energy for small displacements about the nuclear equilibrium positions is[2]

$$U(q) = U_e + \sum_{i=1}^{3N} \left(\frac{\partial U}{\partial q_i}\right)_e q_i + \frac{1}{2}\sum_{i=1}^{3N}\sum_{j=1}^{3N}\left(\frac{\partial^2 U}{\partial q_i \partial q_j}\right)_e q_i q_j + \cdots. \tag{6-18}$$

The first term on the right is zero by choice of the origin of energy in the equilibrium configuration ($U_e = 0$), and the second is zero because it is a first derivative at a minimum, $(\partial U/\partial q_i)_e = 0$. Equation (6-18) reduces to

$$U(q) = \frac{1}{2}\sum_{i=1}^{3N}\sum_{j=1}^{3N}\left(\frac{\partial^2 U}{\partial q_i \partial q_j}\right)_e q_i q_j = \frac{1}{2}\sum_{i=1}^{3N}\sum_{j=1}^{3N} f_{ij} q_i q_j, \tag{6-19}$$

where second derivatives are just the potential constants

$$f_{ij} = \left(\frac{\partial^2 U}{\partial q_i \partial q_j}\right)_e, \qquad \text{with } f_{ij} = f_{ji}. \tag{6-20}$$

Substituting Eqs. (6-19) and (6-17) into Lagrange's equations of motion for the generalized coordinate q_j,

$$\frac{d}{dt}\left(\frac{\partial T}{\partial \dot{q}_j}\right) + \frac{\partial U}{\partial q_j} = 0, \qquad j = 1, 2, \ldots, 3N, \tag{6-21}$$

we obtain[3]

$$\ddot{q}_j + \sum_{i=1}^{3N} f_{ij} q_i = 0, \qquad j = 1, 2, \ldots, 3N. \tag{6-22}$$

These are a set of $3N$ simultaneous second-order differential equations having solutions q_i. For simple harmonic motion, one form of the solution is

$$q_i = A_i \cos(\lambda^{1/2} t + \phi), \tag{6-23}$$

where A_i is the amplitude, λ is a constant, t is time, and ϕ is a phase constant. Taking the double time derivative of the $i = j$ solution, we obtain

$$\dot{q}_j = \frac{dq_j}{dt} = A_j\lambda^{1/2}\sin(\lambda^{1/2}t + \phi)$$

and **(6-24)**

$$\ddot{q}_j = \frac{d^2q_j}{dt^2} = -A_j\lambda\cos(\lambda^{1/2}t + \phi).$$

Substituting Eqs. (6-23) and (6-24) into (6-22), we obtain

$$-A_j\lambda + \sum_{i=1}^{3N} f_{ij}A_i = 0,$$

which rearranges to

$$\sum_{i=1}^{3N} (f_{ij} - \delta_{ij}\lambda)A_i = 0, \qquad j = 1, 2, \ldots, 3N, \tag{6-25}$$

where δ_{ij} is the Kronecker delta symbol; $\delta_{ij} = 0$ if $i \neq j$ and unity for $i = j$, since the λ term is nonzero only for the $i = j$ coordinates of the summation. Equation (6-25) is a set of $3N$ simultaneous linear homogeneous equations in the unknown amplitudes A_i. For a nontrivial solution, the determinant of the A_i coefficients must be zero, $\det|f_{ij} - \delta_{ij}\lambda| = 0$,

$$\begin{vmatrix} f_{11} - \lambda & f_{12} & \cdots & f_{1,3N} \\ f_{21} & f_{22} - \lambda & & \\ \vdots & & \ddots & \vdots \\ f_{3N,1} & & \cdots & f_{3N,3N} - \lambda \end{vmatrix} = 0. \tag{6-26}$$

This is the so-called secular equation of $3N$ degree in λ having $3N$ roots. Six of these roots will be zero, and the secular equation will be reduced to $3N - 6$ (or $3N - 5$ for linear polyatomics) degree. These zero λ's result from the six original constraints we placed on the system, corresponding to locating the center of mass at the origin and fixing the coordinates describing the rotational degrees of freedom (see beginning of this section). The remaining $3N - 6$ roots are the genuine vibrational degrees of freedom. The constant $\lambda = 4\pi^2\nu^2 = 4\pi^2c^2\omega^2$ and for a particular root λ_m, we can obtain a particular solution of A_{im}, where the m subscript is identified with λ_m. The general solutions of these equations, however, do not uniquely fix the A_{im}'s, but only their ratios. To obtain a unique set of A_{im}'s, we define

$$A_{im} = K_m\ell_{im}, \qquad i = 1, 2, \ldots, 3N - 6, \tag{6-27}$$

where K_m is simply a proportionality constant relating corresponding members of the sets A_{im} and ℓ_{im}. The ℓ_{im} amplitudes are normalized such that

$$\sum_{i=1}^{3N-6} \ell_{im}^2 = 1. \tag{6-28}$$

A set of $3N - 6$ equations from Eq. (6-26) can be generated (for the genuine vibrations) for each $3N - 6$ root, λ_m, and the set of amplitudes (coefficients) ℓ_{im} and the coefficient K_m determined for each root. Thus, we obtain unique solutions for Eq. (6-22),

$$q_i = K_m \ell_{im} \cos(\lambda_m^{1/2} t + \phi_m), \qquad i = 1, 2, \ldots, 3N - 6, \tag{6-29}$$

where each λ_m corresponds to a set of $3N - 6$ amplitudes $K_m \ell_{im}$. For a given root λ_m, the three ℓ_{im}'s generated for each nucleus are proportional to the corresponding mass-weighted cartesian displacement coordinates and can therefore be used to construct the *net* vectors describing the relative directions and magnitudes in which the nuclei are displaced for a given normal mode of vibration ω_m.

The physical significance of Eq. (6-29) is extremely important in understanding the nature of these vibrational motions. Each atom in the molecule oscillating about its equilibrium position does so in simple harmonic motion with a frequency of $\lambda_m^{1/2}/2\pi$. The atoms vibrate in phase and are constrained to move back and forth along straight lines. Although the frequency of each coordinate is the same for a given λ_m, the amplitudes are generally different. This means that even though some atoms undergo greater displacements from their equilibrium positions than others, they all reach their maximum and minimum displacements simultaneously. The $3N - 6$ vibrational modes having these properties are called the *normal modes of vibration*.

The normal modes of vibration of the HCN molecule are shown in Figure 6-5. The actual relative displacement amplitudes of the nuclei are indicated by the arrow lengths. As a result of these mass-weighted coordinates, the relatively light hydrogen nucleus is greatly displaced in each of the vibrations relative to carbon and nitrogen. The carbon and nitrogen atoms, on the other hand, are comparably displaced. We also note that this molecule has two vibrations that are equivalent in terms of nuclear displacements and frequency (ω_{2a} and ω_{2b}). Such normal modes correspond to two identical solutions (roots) among the $3N - 5$ (in this case) obtained from the secular equation. These are called *degenerate* vibrational modes. In the case where two or more independent modes have the same vibrational frequency (degeneracies), the most general solution is that represented by a sum over the $3N - 6$ normal modes,

$$q_i = \sum_{m=1}^{3N-6} A_{im} \cos(\lambda_m^{1/2} + \phi_m), \qquad i = 1, 2, \ldots, 3N - 6. \tag{6-30}$$

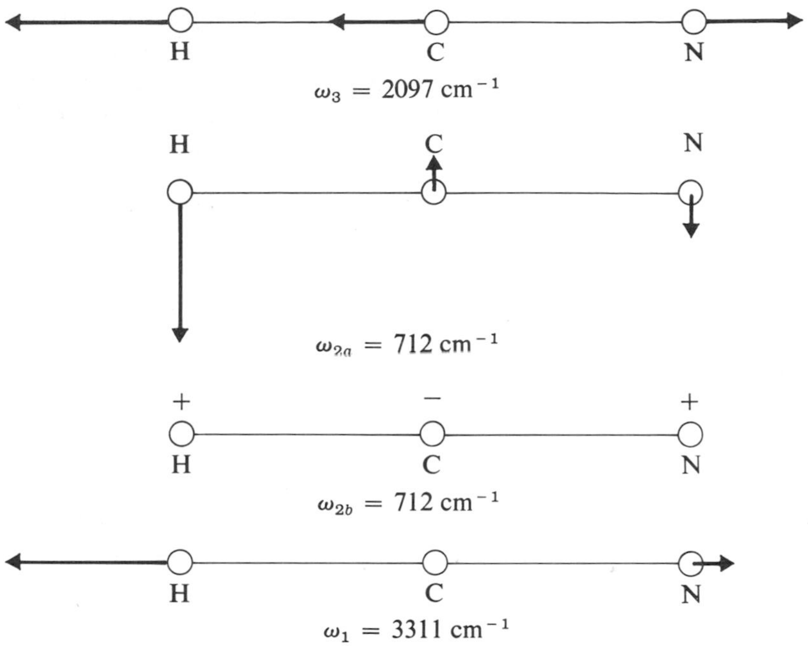

FIGURE 6-5 The normal modes of vibration of the HCN molecule, including the actual relative amplitudes of the nuclei. The bending vibration in and perpendicular to the plane of the page is degenerate. (From *Molecular Spectra and Molecular Structure*, Vol. II by G. Herzberg © 1945 by Litton Educational Publishing Inc. Reprinted by permission of Van Nostrand Reinhold Company.)

If the degenerate modes are superimposed in phase, the resulting motion of the nuclear displacements is also a normal mode of vibration. In general, if degenerate normal modes are superimposed out of phase or if independent normal modes of different frequency are superimposed, the resulting motion of the nuclei is *not* a normal mode of vibration.

2. Vibrational Energy of a Polyatomic Molecule

To obtain the expression for the energy of a polyatomic molecule, we proceed by setting up the Hamiltonian H in terms of the classical kinetic and potential energies, substituting the appropriate operators, and solving for the energy according to the Schrödinger equation (Eq. (2-9)). In the previous section, the expression we obtained for the potential energy, Eq. (6-19), contained cross terms, $q_i q_j$. In order that we may use the method of separation of variables as a means of solving the multidimensional Schrödinger equation, we must define a set of coordinates such that the potential-energy and kinetic-energy expressions contain no cross terms. This is the point we made earlier about the importance of the coordinate choice. We can accomplish this end by defining a new set of coordinates in terms of the mass-weighted cartesian displacement coordinates we obtained in the previous section (Eq. (6-29)) by the linear transformation,

$$Q_k = \sum_{i=1}^{3N-6} \ell_{ik} q_i, \qquad k = 1, 2, \ldots, 3N-6, \tag{6-31a}$$

or in matrix notation,

$$\mathbf{Q} = \mathbf{l}\mathbf{q}. \tag{6-31b}$$

The $\mathbf{Q}$ and $\mathbf{q}$ column vectors are matrices having $3N - 6$ elements, whereas the transformation matrix is of dimension $3N - 6 \times 3N - 6$, having elements ℓ_{ik}. The Q_k's are called *normal coordinates* and the ℓ_{ik}'s are chosen in such a way that the transformed expressions for the potential and kinetic energies are the sum of squared terms,

$$2T = \sum_{k=1}^{3N-6} \dot{Q}_k^2 \quad \text{and} \quad 2U = \sum_{k=1}^{3N-6} \lambda_k Q_k^2, \tag{6-32a}$$

or in matrix notation

$$2T = \dot{\mathbf{Q}}'\dot{\mathbf{Q}} \quad \text{and} \quad 2U = \mathbf{Q}'\boldsymbol{\Lambda}\mathbf{Q}, \tag{6-32b}$$

where $\dot{\mathbf{Q}}'$ and $\mathbf{Q}'$ are row vectors (matrix transposes) of $\dot{\mathbf{Q}}$ and $\mathbf{Q}$. This is equivalent to substituting the q_i's for the inverse transformation,

$$q_i = \sum_{k=1}^{3N-6} (\ell_{ik})^{-1} Q_k, \qquad i = 1, 2, \ldots, 3N-6,$$

or (6-33)

$$\mathbf{q} = \mathbf{l}^{-1}\mathbf{Q},$$

into Eqs. (6-17) and (6-19). It follows then that Eq. (6-31) is also an orthogonal transformation,[4] since for the kinetic energy and potential energy expressions (Eq. (6-32b)),

$$2T = \dot{\mathbf{q}}'\dot{\mathbf{q}} = (\mathbf{l}^{-1}\dot{\mathbf{Q}})'(\mathbf{l}^{-1}\dot{\mathbf{Q}}) = \dot{\mathbf{Q}}'(\mathbf{l}')'\mathbf{l}^{-1}\dot{\mathbf{Q}} = \dot{\mathbf{Q}}'\dot{\mathbf{Q}}$$

where (6-34a)

$$(\mathbf{l}')'\mathbf{l}^{-1} = \mathbf{l}\mathbf{l}^{-1} = \mathbf{E},$$

and

$$2U = \mathbf{q}'\mathbf{F}\mathbf{q} = (\mathbf{l}^{-1}\mathbf{Q})'\mathbf{F}(\mathbf{l}^{-1}\mathbf{Q}) = \mathbf{Q}'\mathbf{l}\mathbf{F}\mathbf{l}^{-1}\mathbf{Q} = \mathbf{Q}'\boldsymbol{\Lambda}\mathbf{Q}$$

where (6-34b)

$$\mathbf{l}\mathbf{F}\mathbf{l}^{-1} = \boldsymbol{\Lambda}.$$

The symbol **E** represents the identity matrix (diagonal unit vector matrix), **F** is the $3N - 6 \times 3N - 6$ symmetric matrix of elements f_{ij}, and $\mathbf{\Lambda}$ is a diagonal matrix.

The Hamiltonian can now be written as

$$H = T + U = \tfrac{1}{2} \sum_{k=1}^{3N-6} \hat{\dot{Q}}_k^2 + \tfrac{1}{2} \sum_{k=1}^{3N-6} \lambda_k \hat{Q}_k^2, \qquad \textbf{(6-35)}$$

where the corresponding operators are

$$\hat{\dot{Q}}_k = \frac{h}{2\pi i} \frac{\partial}{\partial Q} \quad \text{and} \quad \hat{Q}_k = Q_k. \qquad \textbf{(6-36)}$$

Substituting Eq. (6-36) into (6-35), and in turn, into the Schrödinger expression (Eq. (2-9)), we obtain

$$-\frac{h^2}{8\pi^2} \sum_{k=1}^{3N-6} \frac{\partial^2 \psi_{\mathbf{v}}}{\partial Q_k^2} + \frac{1}{2} \sum_{k=1}^{3N-6} \lambda_k Q_k^2 \psi_{\mathbf{v}} = E_{\mathbf{v}} \psi_{\mathbf{v}}. \qquad \textbf{(6-37)}$$

As a result of the summations of Eq. (6-35), $\psi_{\mathbf{v}}$ is simply the product of the $\psi_{\mathbf{v}_k}$'s for the noninteracting normal modes,

$$\psi_{\mathbf{v}} = \psi_{\mathbf{v}_1}(Q_1)\psi_{\mathbf{v}_2}(Q_2) \cdots \psi_{\mathbf{v}_{3N-6}}(Q_{3N-6}). \qquad \textbf{(6-38)}$$

Substituting Eq. (6-38) into (6-37), we obtain $3N - 6$ separable equations of the general form

$$-\frac{h^2}{8\pi^2} \frac{\partial^2 \psi_{\mathbf{v}_k}(Q_k)}{\partial Q_k^2} + \frac{1}{2} \lambda_k Q_k^2 \psi_{\mathbf{v}_k} = E_k \psi_{\mathbf{v}_k}. \qquad \textbf{(6-39)}$$

This differential equation is similar to the familiar one-dimensional harmonic oscillator equation, whose solutions have the general form (Appendix IV)[5]

$$\psi_{\mathbf{v}_k}(Q_k) = H_{\mathbf{v}_k}(\gamma_k^{1/2} Q_k) N_{\mathbf{v}_k} \exp(-\tfrac{1}{2}\gamma_k Q_k^2), \qquad \textbf{(6-40)}$$

corresponding to the total vibrational energy,

$$E_{\mathbf{v}}\,(\text{cm}^{-1}) = [(\mathbf{v}_1 + \tfrac{1}{2})\omega_1 + (\mathbf{v}_2 + \tfrac{1}{2})\omega_2 + (\mathbf{v}_3 + \tfrac{1}{2})\omega_3 + \cdots + (\mathbf{v}_{3N-6} + \tfrac{1}{2})\omega_{3N-6}]. \qquad \textbf{(6-41)}$$

In this expression $\mathbf{v}_k$ is the quantum number of the kth vibrational mode and ω_k is its corresponding *fundamental* frequency of vibration (this frequency will be defined momentarily). When all the vibrational modes of a molecule are in their $\mathbf{v}_k = 0$ quantum states, the residual energy given by Eq. (6-41) is called the zero-point energy, $\Sigma_k \frac{1}{2}\omega_k$. For the H_2S molecule with $\omega_1 = 2615\ \text{cm}^{-1}$, $\omega_2 = 1183\ \text{cm}^{-1}$, and $\omega_3 = 2626\ \text{cm}^{-1}$, the zero-point energy is

$$E_{\mathbf{v}}\,(\text{cm}^{-1}) = \tfrac{1}{2}(2615) + \tfrac{1}{2}(1183) + \tfrac{1}{2}(2626) = 3212\ \text{cm}^{-1}. \qquad \textbf{(6-42)}$$

The vibrational energy levels of the H_2S molecule above the zero-point level based on these harmonic frequencies are shown in Figure 6-6. The levels in Figure 6-6 that involve $\mathbf{v}_k = 1$, and the other two levels having zero quantum numbers, (010), (100), (001), are called *fundamental* levels. Those having two or more quanta, $n\mathbf{v}_k (n \geqslant 2)$, and the other levels having zero quanta, are called *overtone* levels. Those having more than one $\mathbf{v}_k$ nonzero are called *combination* levels. For transitions between the zero-point level and those types just described, the corresponding frequencies are called fundamental, overtone, and combination transition frequencies. Transition frequencies that excite a molecule from an initially excited vibrational state to a higher vibrational level are called *difference* transition frequencies.

In the general case, two or more normal modes of vibration that correspond to the same vibrational frequency are said to be *degenerate*. An example of a doubly degenerate vibration is shown in Figure 6-5 for the HCN bending mode. The quantum state designation for the molecule, $(\mathbf{v}_1, \mathbf{v}_{2a}, \mathbf{v}_{2b}, \mathbf{v}_3)$, is more generally written $(\mathbf{v}_1, \mathbf{v}_{2a,b}, \mathbf{v}_3)$, since the vibrational excitation of the doubly degenerate mode corresponds to a single frequency,

$$(\mathbf{v}_{2a} + \mathbf{v}_{2b})\omega_2 = \mathbf{v}_{2a,b}\omega_2. \tag{6-43}$$

Thus, for $\mathbf{v}_{2a,b} = 1$, this single quantum of vibrational excitation may be either $(\mathbf{v}_{2a} = 1, \mathbf{v}_{2b} = 0)$ or $(\mathbf{v}_{2a} = 0, \mathbf{v}_{2b} = 1)$; hence the vibrational energy level (0, 1, 0) is doubly degenerate. In a like manner, the level (0, 2, 0) can have the distributions $(\mathbf{v}_{2a} = 2, \mathbf{v}_{2b} = 0)$, $(\mathbf{v}_{2a} = 0, \mathbf{v}_{2b} = 2)$, or $(\mathbf{v}_{2a} = 1, \mathbf{v}_{2b} = 1)$, and is therefore triply degenerate. For molecules with higher symmetry, the frequency of occurrence of degenerate modes of vibration is much greater and occurs in the form of both doubly degenerate (E symmetry designation) and triply degenerate (T symmetry designation) vibrations. The general class of tetrahedral molecules (T_d symmetry), such as methane, serves as an excellent example; of its four fundamental modes of vibration, two are triply degenerate (ω_3 and ω_4), one is doubly degenerate (ω_2), and one nondegenerate (ω_1). As we shall see in Section 6F, this symmetry property provides essential simplification of the secular equation, allowing a reasonable evaluation of the potential energy force field (force constants) of a molecule.

The widely accepted procedure for numbering the normal modes of vibration is first to separate them into subgroups having the same symmetry properties (characters) as the irreducible representations of the molecular point group. Within each of these subgroups, the numbering is in order from the highest to the lowest frequency vibration. The highest frequency vibration belonging to the totally symmetric representation is labelled ω_1, and successively through the subgroup. After all the symmetric vibrations have been assigned number designations, the anti-

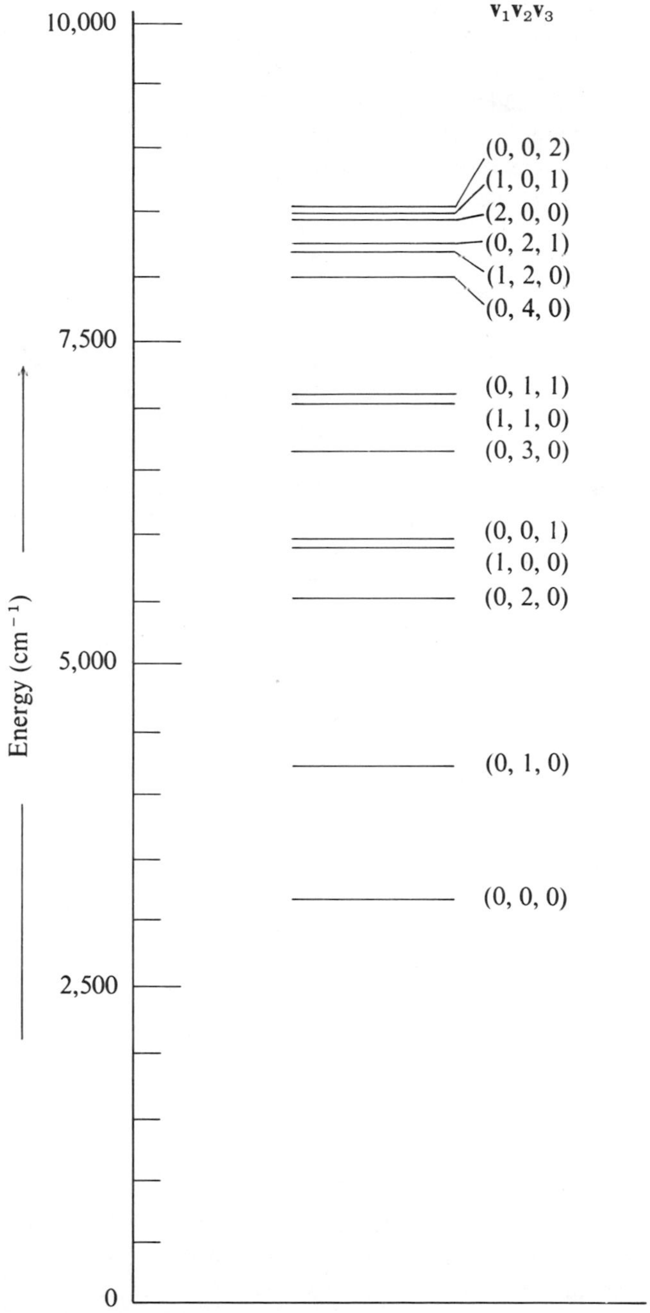

FIGURE 6-6 Vibrational energy levels of the H_2S molecule based on the nondegenerate fundamental frequencies $\omega_1 = 2615 \text{ cm}^{-1}$, $\omega_2 = 1183 \text{ cm}^{-1}$, and $\omega_3 = 2626 \text{ cm}^{-1}$.

symmetric modes are in turn labeled from highest to lowest frequency. In the case of linear triatomic molecules, the long-standing practice of assigning ω_2 to the doubly degenerate bend is used; ω_1 is assigned to the symmetric stretch and ω_3 to the antisymmetric stretch.

As the number of vibrations of a molecule increases, we expect a corresponding increase in the probability that two (or more) vibrations will "accidentally" have the same approximate frequency. If the two energy levels involved belong to the same symmetry species (irreducible representation), then a resonance interaction will occur. This phenomenon is called *accidental degeneracy*. The resonance interaction causes the two levels, which would normally occur rather close in energy, to be shifted to lower and higher energies (repel each other). The extent of this split is inversely proportional to the closeness of the energies that the two unperturbed levels would theoretically have in the absence of the resonance interaction. The first case of accidental degeneracy was observed in CO_2, and interpreted by Enrico Fermi. The doubly degenerate bending frequency at 667.5 cm^{-1} would theoretically have its first overtone at approximately 1335 cm^{-1}, which is almost in exact resonance with the unperturbed symmetric stretching fundamental at 1333 cm^{-1}. The *observed* absorption frequencies corresponding to the resonance split levels are 1388.15 cm^{-1} for the bending overtone ($2\omega_2$) and 1285.40 cm^{-1} for the symmetric stretch (ω_1). As a result of Fermi's initial interpretation of this effect of accidental degeneracy, it is also called Fermi resonance.

3. Selection Rules for Infrared Transitions

To determine the electric-dipole selection rules for the rotation-vibration spectra of polyatomic molecules, we must ascertain the restrictions that allow us to obtain nonzero values of the various integrals and terms of the transition moment matrix

$$\langle m|\hat{\mu}|k\rangle = \int \psi_m{}^*\mu_X\psi_k\,d\tau + \int \psi_m{}^*\mu_Y\psi_k\,d\tau + \int \psi_m{}^*\mu_Z\psi_k\,d\tau. \qquad \textbf{(6-44)}$$

For transitions within a given electronic state, the wavefunction and volume element are given as

$$\psi = \psi_r\psi_v \qquad \text{and} \qquad d\tau = d\tau_r\,d\tau_v. \qquad \textbf{(6-45)}$$

In the discussions to follow, we shall also find it convenient for bookkeeping to indicate the final state by a single prime (′) and the initial state by a double prime (″).

The coordinates X, Y, and Z above refer to the space-fixed axes whose origin is located at the center of mass and moves (translates) with the molecule. The rotation of the molecule is on the other hand characterized by the rotating coordinate system x, y, and z; these coordinates make up the molecule-fixed axes. To obtain Eq. (6-44) in terms of this coordinate system, we must first obtain the relation between the two coordinate systems. A molecule with dipole moment components in the molecule-fixed system μ_x, μ_y, μ_z will have a component along the space-fixed Z axis of

$$\mu_Z = \mu_x \Phi_{Zx} + \mu_y \Phi_{Zy} + \mu_z \Phi_{Zz}, \tag{6-46}$$

where Φ_{Fg} is defined as the direction cosine; $F = X$, Y, or Z, and $g = x$, y, or z. For all three components, we should have a 3×3 matrix in Φ_{Fg}.[6] The symbol Φ_{Fg} is called the direction cosine because it is equal to the cosine of the angle between a given pair of F and g axes. Substituting Eqs. (6-46) and (6-45) into the Z integral of Eq. (6-44) yields

$$\int \psi_{\mathrm{r}'}{}^*\Phi_{Zx}\psi_{\mathrm{r}''}\,d\tau_{\mathrm{r}} \int \psi_{\mathrm{v}'}{}^*\mu_x\psi_{\mathrm{v}''}\,d\tau_{\mathrm{v}} + \int \psi_{\mathrm{r}'}{}^*\Phi_{Zy}\psi_{\mathrm{r}''}\,d\tau_{\mathrm{r}} \int \psi_{\mathrm{v}'}{}^*\mu_y\psi_{\mathrm{v}''}\,d\tau_{\mathrm{v}}$$
$$+ \int \psi_{\mathrm{r}'}{}^*\Phi_{Zz}\psi_{\mathrm{r}''}\,d\tau_{\mathrm{r}} \int \psi_{\mathrm{v}'}{}^*\mu_z\psi_{\mathrm{v}''}\,d\tau_{\mathrm{v}}, \tag{6-47}$$

and correspondingly we should obtain six terms for the x and y axes. In evaluating the dipole components, we must consider the fact that the electrons and nuclei are in constant motion. If however, in this summing process (Eq. (5-25)), we consider the effective atomic charges, then the effective dipole moment can be given as a Taylor expansion in terms of the normal coordinates,

$$\mu_z = \mu_z^{\mathrm{e}} + \sum_{k=1}^{3N-6} \left(\frac{\partial \mu_z}{\partial Q_k}\right)_{\mathrm{e}} Q_k + \frac{1}{2} \sum_{k=1}^{3N-6} \sum_{j=1}^{3N-6} \left(\frac{\partial^2 \mu_z}{\partial Q_k \partial Q_j}\right)_{\mathrm{e}} Q_k Q_j + \cdots, \tag{6-48}$$

where μ_z^{e} is the z component of the equilibrium dipole moment. We continue the derivation for the Z_z and μ_z integrals of Eq. (6-47); the procedure is similar for the z and y components. Substituting Eq. (6-48) into the μ_z integral of Eq. (6-47) gives

$$\mu_z^{\mathrm{e}} \int \psi_{\mathrm{r}'}{}^*\Phi_{Zz}\psi_{\mathrm{r}''}\,d\tau \int \psi_{\mathrm{v}'}{}^*\psi_{\mathrm{v}''}\,d\tau_{\mathrm{v}}$$
$$+ \int \psi_{\mathrm{r}'}{}^*\Phi_{Zz}\psi_{\mathrm{r}''}\,d\tau_{\mathrm{r}} \sum_{k=1}^{3N-6} \left(\frac{\partial \mu_z}{\partial Q_k}\right)_{\mathrm{e}} \int \psi_{\mathrm{v}'}{}^*Q_k\psi_{\mathrm{v}''}\,d\tau_{\mathrm{v}}, \tag{6-49}$$

where we have assumed the quadratic term in the expansion to be negligible. We shall soon see that for most polyatomic molecules this is not a very valid assumption. Since the total vibrational wavefunction of a polyatomic molecule given by Eq. (6-38) is the product of an orthonormal set,

$$\int \psi_{v'}^* \psi_{v''}\, d\tau_v = \prod_{k=1}^{3N-6} \int \psi_{v'_k}^*(Q_k)\psi_{v''_k}(Q_k)\, dQ_k, \qquad \textbf{(6-50a)}$$

where for $\mathbf{v}'_k = \mathbf{v}''_k$ the integral is unity, and zero for $\mathbf{v}'_k \neq \mathbf{v}''_k$. Thus, the first term of Eq. (6-49) reduces to one of the terms used to derive the selection rules for pure rotational transitions. Besides the general requirement of a permanent moment along the z axis, the rotational integral will remain nonzero only for $\Delta J = \pm 1$ and $\Delta K = 0$, where z is considered to be the unique axis of a linear or symmetric top molecule. According to our convention, μ_z^{e} is μ_a^{e} or μ_c^{e} depending on whether the molecule is a prolate or an oblate top. Similar selection rules are obtained for the Φ_{Xx} and Φ_{Yy} integrals along μ_z^{e}.

Substituting Eq. (6-38) into the second term of Eq. (6-49) yields

$$\int \psi_{r'}^* \Phi_{Zz} \psi_{r''}\, d\tau_r \left(\frac{\partial \mu_z}{\partial Q_k'}\right)_{\mathrm{e}} \int \psi_{v'_k}^*(Q_k')Q_k'\psi_{v''_k}(Q_k')\, dQ_k'$$

$$\times \prod_{k=1}^{3N-7} \int \psi_{v'_k}^*(Q_k)\psi_{v''_k}(Q_k)\, dQ_k. \qquad \textbf{(6-50b)}$$

The first factor of this product gives rise to the rotational selection rules for vibrational transitions having $(\partial\mu_z/\partial Q_k')_{\mathrm{e}} \neq 0$. They are the same as those obtained above for pure rotational transitions. The third factor involving the Q_k' integral remains nonzero only if $\Delta \mathbf{v}'_k = \pm 1$ and is zero otherwise. The last factor, which is a product of integrals, is unity, if in all $3N - 7$ cases $\Delta \mathbf{v}_k = 0$. Thus, for a set of harmonic oscillators, the *only* allowed transitions in absorption or emission are the fundamentals. Evaluation of the other eight integrals in all cases gives the same vibrational selection rules. The corresponding rotational transitions however, depend on the symmetry of the molecule. For linear and symmetric top molecules having their sole nonzero component of the permanent dipole moment along the unique z axis, vibrational displacements of the atoms parallel to this axis resulting in $(\partial\mu_z/\partial Q_k)_{\mathrm{e}} \neq 0$, and the x and y components equal to zero are called parallel vibrational modes ($\|$). Those resulting in $(\partial\mu_y/\partial Q_k)_{\mathrm{e}} \neq 0$ and $(\partial\mu_x/\partial Q_k)_{\mathrm{e}} \neq 0$ are called perpendicular vibrational modes ($\perp$). With these designations applied to the vibrational modes, we can summarize the rotation-vibration selection rules of polyatomic molecules:

Linear Molecules	parallel vibrations ($\|$)	$\Delta J = \pm 1$, $\Delta \mathbf{v} = \pm 1$
	perpendicular vibrations ($\perp$)	$\Delta J = \pm 1, 0$, $\Delta \mathbf{v} = \pm 1$

Spherical Top Molecules	$\Delta J = 0, \pm 1; \Delta \mathbf{v} = \pm 1$	
Symmetric Top Molecules	parallel vibrations ($\parallel$)	$\Delta J = \pm 1, 0; \Delta K = 0$ when $K \neq 0$, $\Delta \mathbf{v} = \pm 1$. $\Delta J = \pm 1; \Delta K = 0$ when $K = 0$, $\Delta \mathbf{v} = \pm 1$.
	perpendicular vibrations ($\perp$)	$\Delta J = \pm 1, 0;$ $\Delta K = \pm 1,$ $\Delta \mathbf{v} = \pm 1$
Asymmetric Top Molecules	$\Delta J = 0, \pm 1, \Delta \mathbf{v} = \pm 1$	

4. Rotation-Vibration Spectra

Having obtained the selection rules characterizing the rotation-vibration spectra of polyatomic molecules, we now apply these to simple and moderately complex molecules in order to obtain a "first-order" interpretation of the observed spectra.

a. Linear Polyatomic Molecules. The linear unsymmetrical triatomic N_2O is a good example of a relatively simple molecule illustrating important rotation-vibration spectral features. For a linear triatomic, there are $3 \times 3 - 5 = 4$ vibrational modes, including a doubly degenerate bending motion. Its point group designation is $C_{\infty v}$, and reference to this character table in Appendix III will show that only vibrational modes of A_1 or E_1 symmetry (irreducible representations) will be infrared-active. The normal modes of vibration, the symmetry type, and the corresponding approximate descriptions are illustrated in Figure 6-7. On applying the symmetry operations of this point group (E, C_∞^ϕ, and $\infty\sigma_v$) to the normal modes illustrated in Figure 6-7, we easily ascertain that ω_1 and ω_3 have A_1 symmetry and ω_2 has E_1 symmetry. As a result, all four vibrational modes are infrared- (and Raman-) active; because of the doubly degenerate bending mode, we expect to observe only three distinct absorptions. The infrared spectrum of N_2O illustrated in Figure 6-8 has three relatively intense absorptions at 589, 1285, and 2284 cm^{-1}. The two high-frequency absorptions both having missing Q branches indicate parallel vibrations. The lower-frequency absorption on the other hand has a strong Q branch and indicates motion of the electric dipole perpendicular to the molecular axis, that is, a perpendicular vibration. The spectral observation of these three fundamentals and their corresponding band structures is unambiguous confirmation that the molecule is linear and unsymmetrical. The other less intense absorptions in the spectrum at 1167, 2462, 2564, 2798,

Approximate Description	Symmetry Type	Normal Mode	Observed Frequency (cm^{-1})
"N═N" stretch	$A_1(\equiv\Sigma^+)$	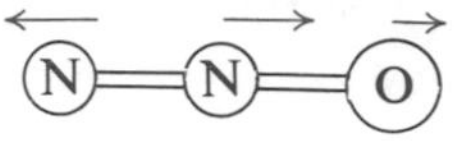	$\omega_1 = 2224\ (\parallel)$
"Doubly degenerate bend"	$E_1(\equiv\Pi)$	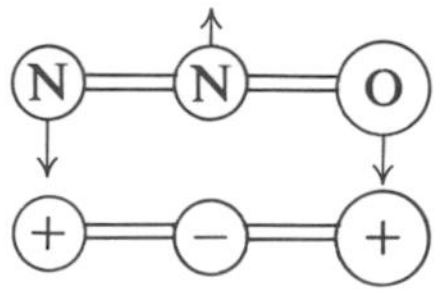	$\omega_{2a} = \omega_{2b} = 589\ (\perp)$
"N═O" stretch	$A_1(\equiv\Sigma^+)$	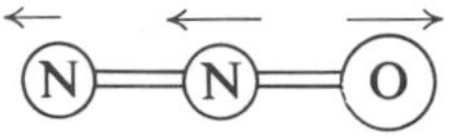	$\omega_3 = 1285\ (\parallel)$

FIGURE 6-7 Normal modes of vibration of the N_2O molecule. (From *Molecular Spectra and Molecular Structure*, Vol. II by G. Herzberg © 1945 by Litton Educational Publishing, Inc. Reprinted by permission of Van Nostrand Reinhold Company.)

3366, and 3481 cm^{-1} are due to various overtone and combination bands (Problems 6-8 and 6-9).

In the case of linear symmetrical polyatomics, such as C_2H_2, CO_2, and C_2N_2, which possess a center of symmetry i, we must additionally be concerned about the spectral effects of nuclear spin statistics (see Section 4B). These molecules have $D_{\infty h}$ symmetry and will have rotational states of alternating statistical weights. For those molecules having $I = 0$ for all atoms except possibly one at the center of symmetry, we have a case similar to a homonuclear diatomic molecule with $I = 0$. The allowed rotational states will be determined by the symmetry properties of the electronic state. For linear polyatomics having $\Sigma_g{}^+$ ground electronic states, the electronic and ground vibrational wavefunctions ($\psi_\tau = \psi_e\psi_v\psi_r$) are both symmetric (see Section 4B) and the allowed rotational states will be determined by the inversion symmetry of ψ_τ. For $I = 0$ nuclei (bosons), ψ_τ is symmetric to inversion, and thus only symmetric rotational levels can exist. For $\Sigma_g{}^+$ electronic states (practically all known linear polyatomics have Σ^+ ground electronic states), even J rotational levels are symmetric, so that molecules such as CO_2 have "missing" odd J levels. As a result, instead of an alternation in intensity, the observed rotation-vibration spectrum has missing lines corresponding to the nonexistent odd J levels (Problem 6-11). In the case of excited vibrational states, the inversion symmetry of ψ_τ (which must still be totally symmetric) is now determined by the product $\psi_v\psi_r$. The *vibrational* symmetries of the first excited levels of ω_1, ω_2, and ω_3 for CO_2 are $\Sigma_g{}^+$, Π_u, and $\Sigma_u{}^+$, respectively. The corresponding g or u

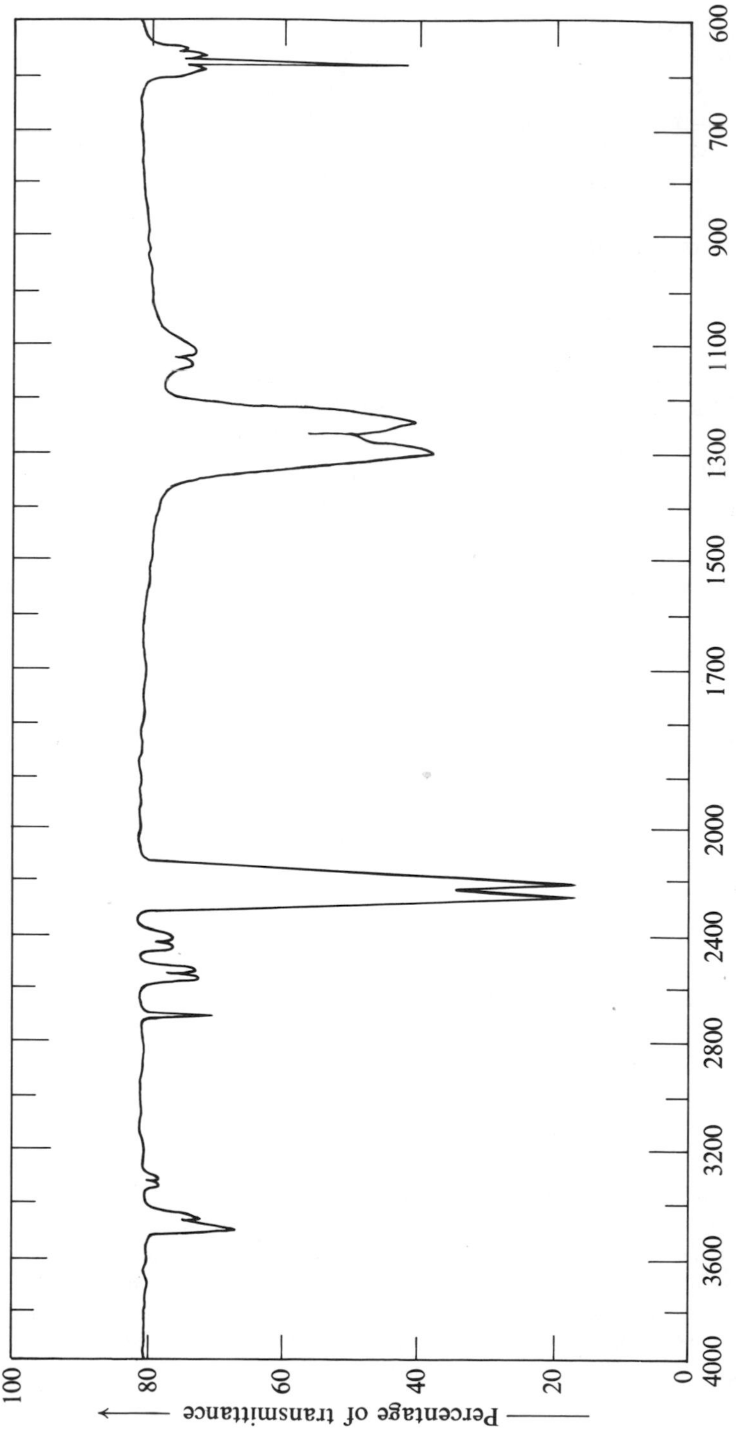

FIGURE 6-8 Infrared spectrum of 50 torr of N_2O in a 10-cm path cell.

designations indicate that the vibrational wavefunction is symmetric or antisymmetric to nuclear inversion. The existent rotational states will thus depend on those J state wavefunctions that combine with ψ_v to generate a totally symmetric ψ_τ. These combinations for Σ, Π, and Δ vibrational state symmetries have been summarized by Herzberg [Reference 6-3, p. 373]. As a result, $\mathbf{v} = 1$ for ω_1 will have only even J states, $\mathbf{v} = 1$ for ω_2 will have even and odd J states, and $\mathbf{v} = 1$ for ω_3 will have only odd J states existent.

Those molecules that have $I = 0$ for equivalent nuclei will have rotational states of nonzero alternating intensity. The effect of nuclear statistics on the resulting band structure and intensity will be illustrated for acetylene, C_2H_2. When the nuclei (i) are exchanged, only the H atoms affect the nuclear wavefunction, since $I(\mathrm{H}) = \frac{1}{2}$ and $I(^{12}\mathrm{C}) = 0$. Since H atoms, having half-integral spins, are fermions, the total wavefunction is antisymmetric, for the exchange of nuclei

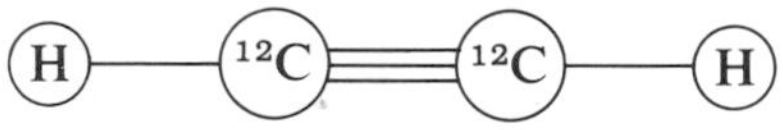

$$I = \tfrac{1}{2} \qquad I = 0 \qquad I = 0 \qquad I = \tfrac{1}{2} \tag{6-51}$$

and

$$\psi_\tau = \psi_e\psi_v\psi_r\psi_n \xrightarrow{(i)} -\psi_e\psi_v\psi_r\psi_n$$

For the ground electronic and vibrational states of C_2H_2, ψ_e and ψ_v are symmetric, thus the statistical weights of the rotational states are determined by the product transformation of $\psi_r\psi_n$. The nuclear spins of the two hydrogen atoms will combine to form three degenerate symmetric $T = 1$ ($\alpha(1)\alpha(2)$, $\beta(1)\beta(2)$, and $\alpha(1)\beta(2) + \alpha(2)\beta(1)$) and one antisymmetric $T = 0$ ($\alpha(1)\beta(2) - \alpha(2)\beta(1)$) nuclear spin states.[7] For the $^1\Sigma_g{}^+$ ground electronic state of C_2H_2, the even and odd J states are symmetric and antisymmetric, respectively. Thus, the $\psi_r\psi_n$ combinations must be ψ_r (even J) ψ_n (even T) and ψ_r (odd J) ψ_n (odd T) to be antisymmetric to nuclear exchange. The resulting odd rotational levels will have three times the nuclear statistical weight compared to the even rotational levels. The rotation-vibration spectrum of a C_2H_2 parallel band ($\omega_4 + \omega_5$) (missing Q branch) and the relative transition intensities, with the Boltzmann distribution neglected (Eq. (6-14)), are shown in Figure 6-9a. The

FIGURE 6-9 (a) Rotation-vibration spectrum of a parallel vibration of linear symmetric polyatomics such as C_2H_2. With the Boltzmann factor neglected, the relative transition intensities are proportional to the total rotational state multiplicity, $g_\tau = g_T g_J$ (in parentheses). (b) C_2H_2 parallel combination band superimposed ($\omega_4 + \omega_5$) on the Boltzmann distribution, illustrating the alternating intensity described in (a).

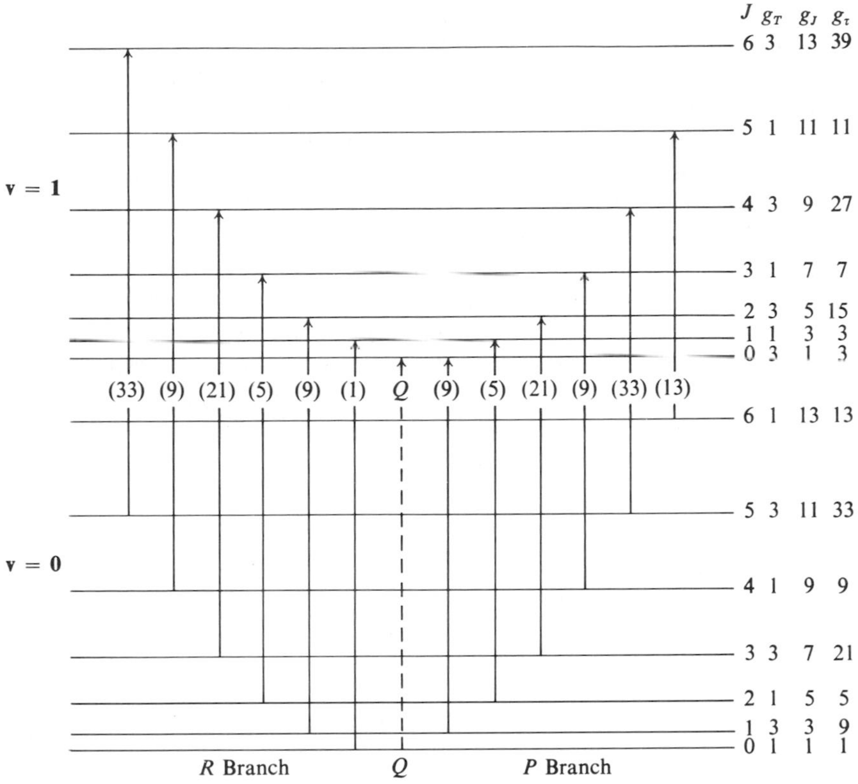
J g_T g_J g_τ
6 3 13 39
5 1 11 11
4 3 9 27
3 1 7 7
2 3 5 15
1 1 3 3
0 3 1 3
v = 1
(33) (9) (21) (5) (9) (1) Q (9) (5) (21) (9) (33) (13)
6 1 13 13
5 3 11 33
4 1 9 9
3 3 7 21
2 1 5 5
1 3 3 9
0 1 1 1
v = 0
R Branch
Q
P Branch

(a)

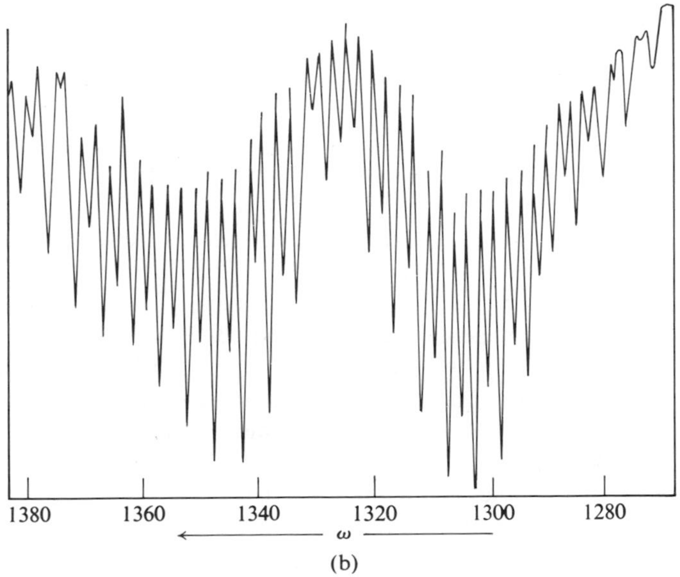
1380
1360
1340
1320
1300
1280
ω

(b)

infrared spectrum of gaseous acetylene is shown in Figure 6-10. The two intense fundamentals at 3289 and 730 cm^{-1} are easily identified as the antisymmetric "C—H stretch" and the antisymmetric "C—H bend." The less intense parallel absorption occurring at 1228 cm^{-1} is the combination band $\omega_4 + \omega_5$ previously referred to and illustrated in Figure 6-9b. The corresponding Raman spectrum contains three absorptions attributable to C_2H_2 fundamentals at 1974, 3374, and 612 cm^{-1}. These frequencies along with their corresponding seven normal modes of vibration are shown in Figure 6-11. In addition to the expected missing Q branch for parallel vibrations, we also notice that none of the fundamentals is both Raman- and infrared-active. This observation is normally unequivocal evidence that the molecule has a center of symmetry, and in this case is consistent with the assumption of a linear molecule with $D_{\infty h}$ symmetry. Examining the $D_{\infty h}$ character table (Appendix III) reveals that none of the position coordinates (x, y, or z) has the same symmetry species as its squares and binary products. This is however, a general property for molecules that possess a center of symmetry—that is, any infrared-active vibration will not be Raman-active—and is called the principle of mutual exclusion. The combination of this property and the rotational structure of vibrational bands (P, Q, R structure) provides definitive confirmation of the linear and symmetrical nature of C_2H_2.

By virtue of symmetry, linear polyatomic molecules have one or more doubly degenerate bending vibrational modes perpendicular to the molecular axis. Linear triatomics such as HCN (Figure 6-5), N_2O (Figure 6-7), and CO_2 have one ($\omega_{2a,2b}$), and tetratomics such as C_2H_2 have two ($\omega_{4a,4b}$ and $\omega_{5a,5b}$). We have noted that a linear molecule is a special case of a symmetric top where $K = 0$. For the singly excited ω_2 rotating triatomic, we have on the average a slightly bent equilibrium configuration for which the rotation about the molecular axis of the unbent molecule is $K \neq 0$. Replacing K with the quantum number ℓ, we define the absolute value of this nuclear vibrational angular momentum about the molecular axis as $\ell h/2\pi$, where ℓ varies from $\mathbf{v}_2$, $(\mathbf{v}_2 - 2), \ldots$ to $-\mathbf{v}_2$. In this case, we have $\pm \ell h/2\pi$ for the clockwise and counterclockwise rotation about the molecular axis. The interaction of this vibrational angular momentum with the ordinary rotational angular momentum breaks down the ℓ degeneracy and results in slightly split J rotational levels. This splitting is called *ℓ-type doubling*. For most molecules, this splitting is quite small, but increases with increasing J. In order to indicate the vibrational angular momentum of a linear triatomic bending mode, we use the designation $\mathbf{v}_1\mathbf{v}_2^{|\ell|}\mathbf{v}_3$. For the ground and first excited states of the bending mode we have $(0, 0^0, 0)$ and $(0, 1^1, 0)$. Since $\mathbf{v}_2 = 1$ is doubly degenerate (Section 6B-2), the split states correspond to $\pm h/2\pi$ ($\ell = \pm 1$).

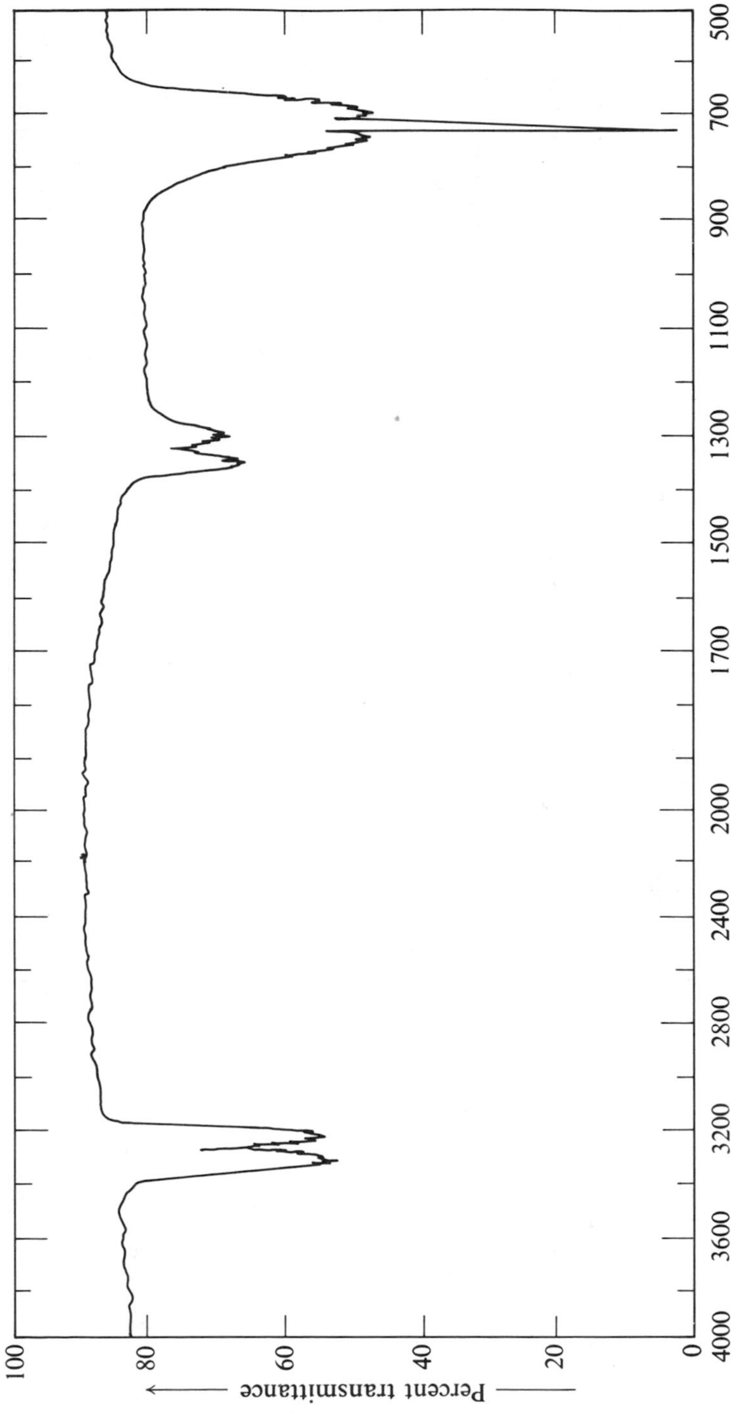

FIGURE 6-10 The infrared spectrum of 50 torr of C_2H_2 in a 10-cm path cell.

Approximation Description	Normal Mode	Observed Frequency (cm^{-1})
"Symmetric C—H stretch" (Σ_g^+)	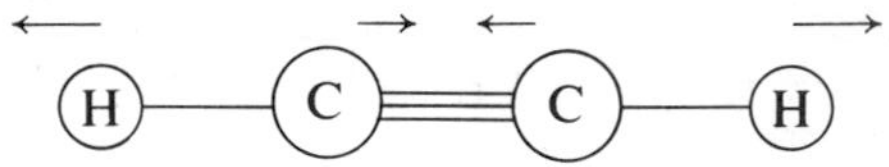	$\omega_1 = 3374$ ($\parallel$), Raman-active only
"Symmetric C≡C stretch" (Σ_g^+)	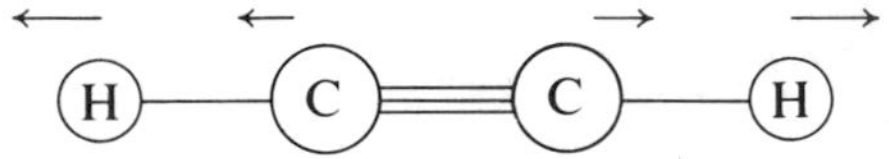	$\omega_2 = 1974$ ($\parallel$), Raman-active only
"Antisymmetric C—H stretch" (Σ_u^+)	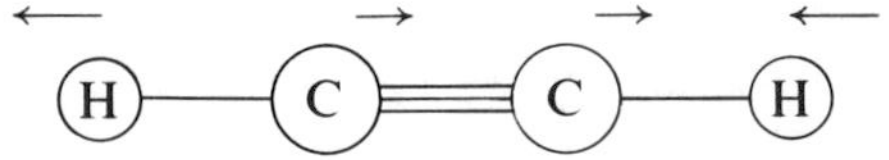	$\omega_3 = 3289$ ($\parallel$), Infrared-active only (*P* and *R* branches only)
"Symmetric C—H bend" (Π_g)	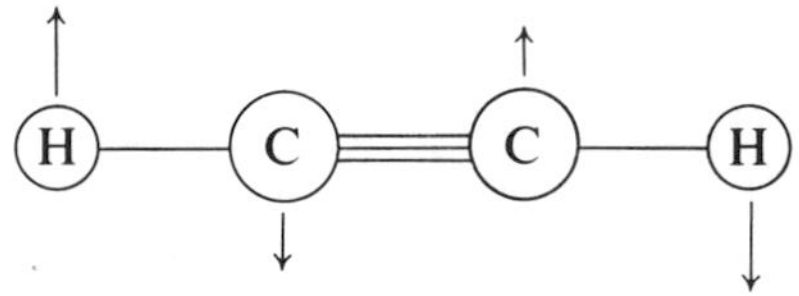	$\omega_{4a,b} = 612$ ($\perp$), Raman-active only
"Antisymmetric C—H bend" (Π_u)	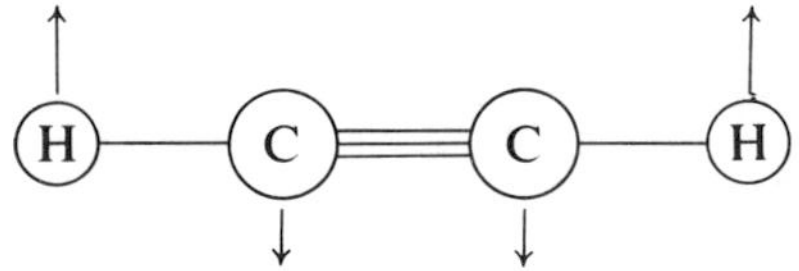	$\omega_{5a,b} = 730$ ($\perp$), Infrared-active only (*PQR* branches)

FIGURE 6-11 Normal modes of vibration of C_2H_2 having $D_{\infty h}$ symmetry. (From *Molecular Spectra and Molecular Structure*, Vol. II by G. Herzberg © 1945 by Litton Educational Publishing Inc. Reprinted by permission of Van Nostrand Reinhold Company.)

EXAMPLE 6-4: For excitation of the first overtone (0, 2, 0) of the doubly degenerate bending mode of a linear triatomic molecule in the nonharmonic approximation, show how the various vibrational perturbations split this triply degenerate state.

Solution: A linear triatomic molecule having the designation $(0, 2^{\ell}, 0)$ is triply degenerate (Section 6B-2). When this degeneracy is removed, we have vibrational angular momentum states of $+2, 0, -2\,(+\mathrm{v}, \mathrm{v}-2, \ldots, -\mathrm{v})$.

Vibrational anharmonicity first produces a splitting of the triply degenerate state into a nondegenerate ($\ell = 0$) $\Sigma(0, 2^0, 0)$ and a doubly degenerate ($\ell = 2$) $\Delta(0, 2^2, 0)$ state. Vibration-rotation interaction of the type just discussed results in an ℓ-type doubling of the various Δ states.

One of the most powerful and efficient lasers is the CO_2 laser. Operating in pulsed mode, it is capable of producing in excess of megawatts per pulse. Population inversion in this flow system (of CO_2) is achieved by an electric discharge pulsing as high as 50 Hz. The particular laser emissions and the tunability (rotational) are a direct result of the spectroscopic nature of its excited vibrational levels. The vibrational-energy-level diagram shown in Figure 6-12a illustrates the two main vibrational laser emissions at 10.6 μ and 9.6 μ. If we replace one of the end mirrors of the laser cavity with a grating, then it becomes possible to obtain oscillation on the various vibration-rotation transitions (rotational tuning).[8] These are shown in Figure 6-12b for the two types of vibrational states involved and the designations of rotational transitions. Subject to the selection rules $\Delta J = \pm 1, 0$, sym $\leftrightarrow$ sym, antisym $\not\leftrightarrow$ sym, u $\leftrightarrow$ g, and $\Sigma^+ \leftrightarrow \Sigma^+$, we see that no Q transitions are allowed, since there is alternation of the even and odd rotational states existent in the Σ_g^+ and Σ_u^+ vibrational states, respectively. When N_2 is added to CO_2, the laser intensity is increased as a result of the near resonance of the $\mathrm{v} = 1 \rightarrow \mathrm{v} = 0$ transition of N_2, which is 2330.70 cm^{-1}.

b. Nonlinear Polyatomic Molecules. For simplicity, we assume the rigid-rotor–harmonic-oscillator approximation in most of our consideration of polyatomic molecules. The selection rules, summarized in Section 6B-3, will be applied to PH_3 (symmetric top), GeH_4 (spherical top), and CH_2O (asymmetric top), and the expected rotation-vibration spectra will be compared with those experimentally observed.

The normal modes of vibration of the PH_3 molecule and their approximate designations are shown in Figure 6-13. This molecule has C_{3v} symmetry and is a prolate symmetric top. Of the six vibrational modes, there are only four fundamentals for a symmetrical pyramidal structure; two totally symmetric (A_1) vibrations and two doubly degenerate (E) vibrations. On examining these normal modes, we note that ω_1 and ω_2

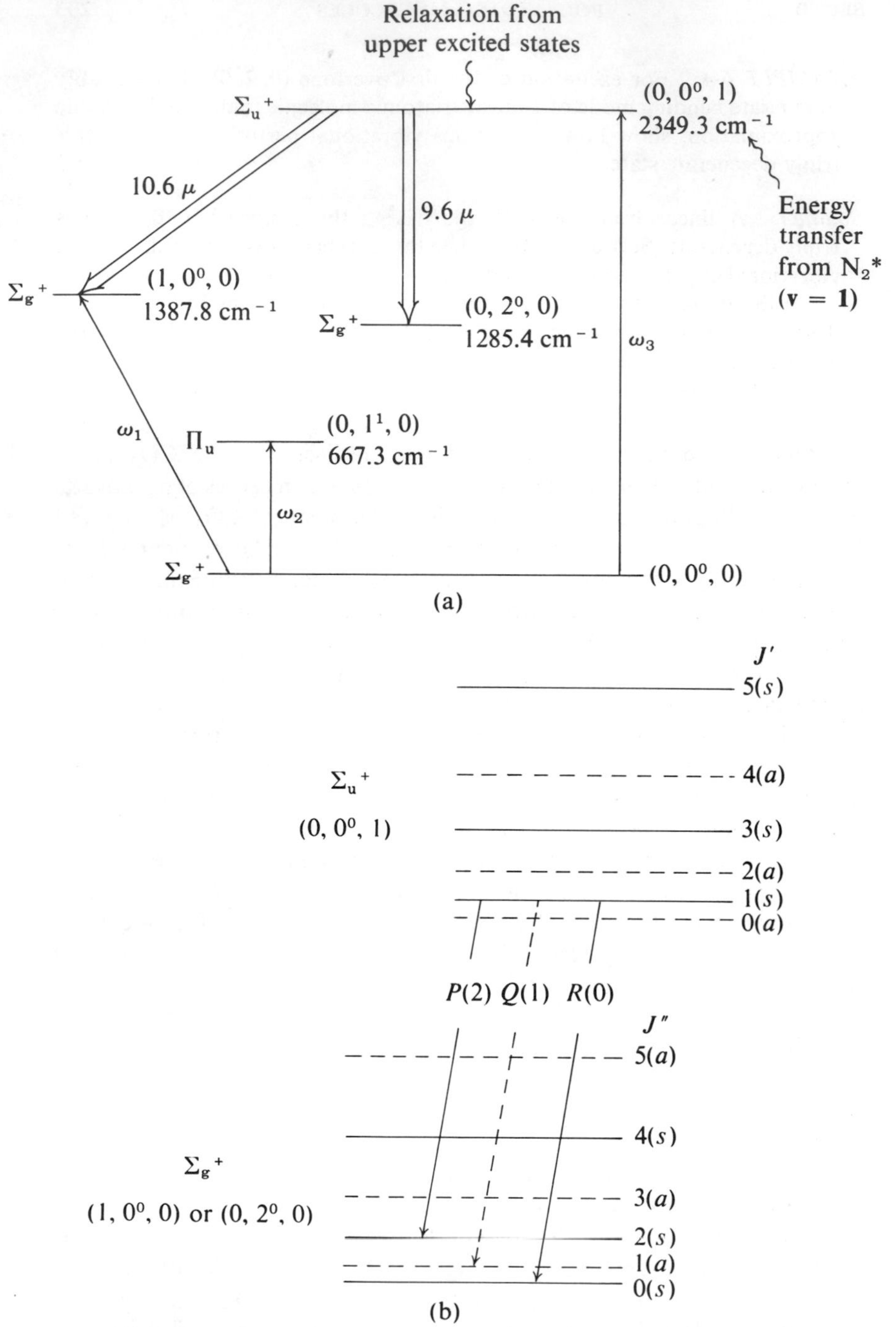

FIGURE 6-12 (a) Vibrational-energy-level diagram of CO_2 illustrating the main laser emission at 10.6 μ and 9.6 μ. (b) Two allowed vibration-rotation transitions of approximately sixty, which occur near 10.0 μ.

A_1
(Parallel Vibrations)

"Symmetric Stretch"   "Symmetric Deformation"

$\omega_1 = 2323\ \text{cm}^{-1}$ $\omega_2 = 992\ \text{cm}^{-1}$

E
(Perpendicular Vibrations)

ω_{3a} ω_{3b}

Doubly Degenerate "Antisymmetric Stretch"

$\omega_3 = 2328\ \text{cm}^{-1}$

ω_{4a} ω_{4b}

Doubly Degenerate Deformation

$\omega_4 = 1118\ \text{cm}^{-1}$

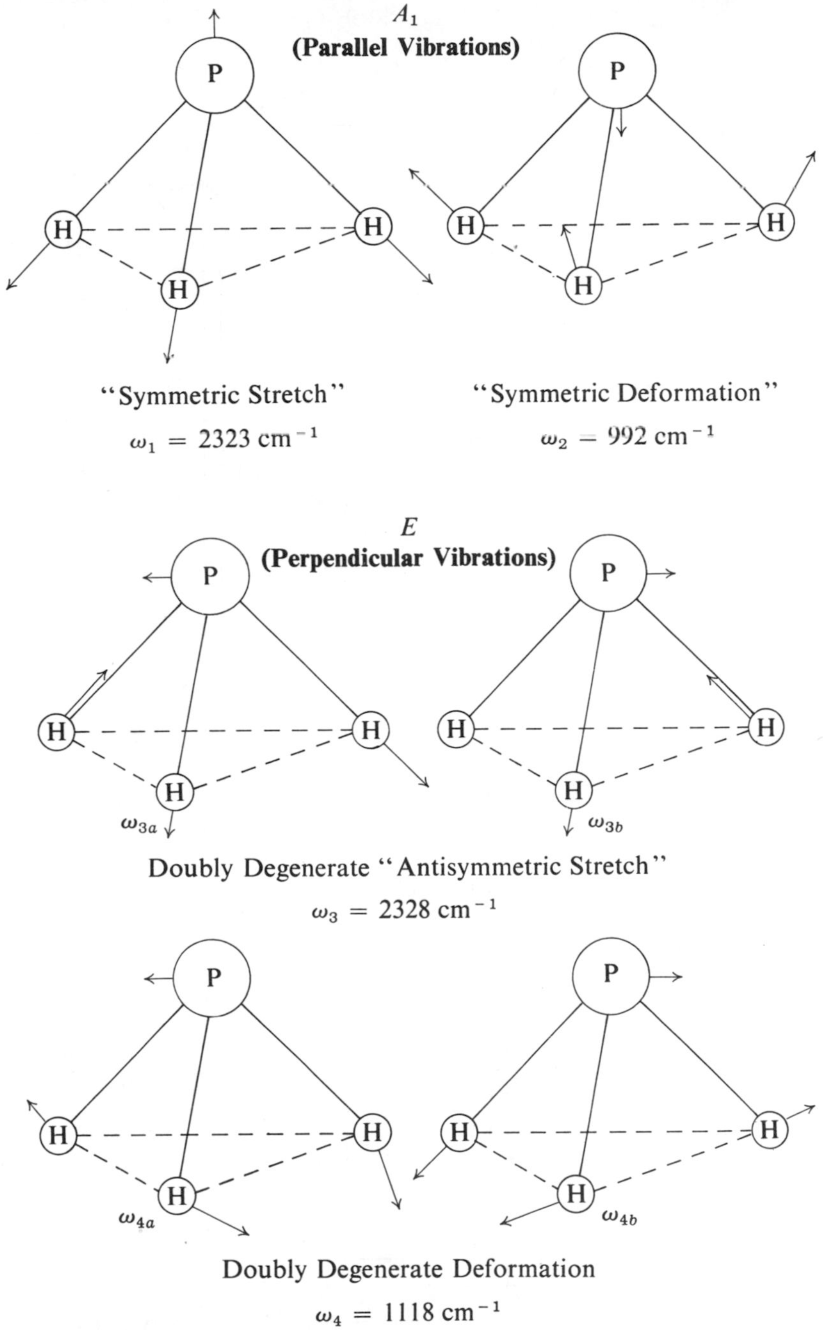

FIGURE 6-13 Normal modes of vibration of the C_{3v} phosphine molecule. (From *Molecular Spectra and Molecular Structure*, Vol. II by G. Herzberg © 1945 by Litton Educational Publishing, Inc. Reprinted by permission of Van Nostrand Reinhold Company.)

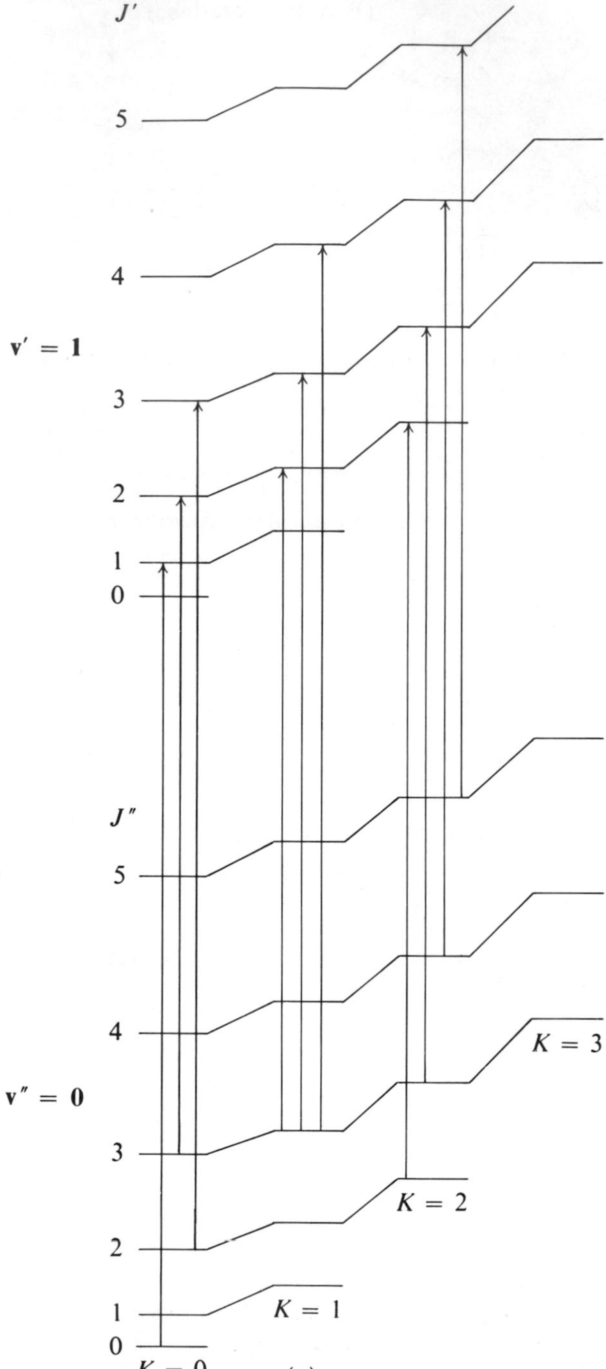

(a)

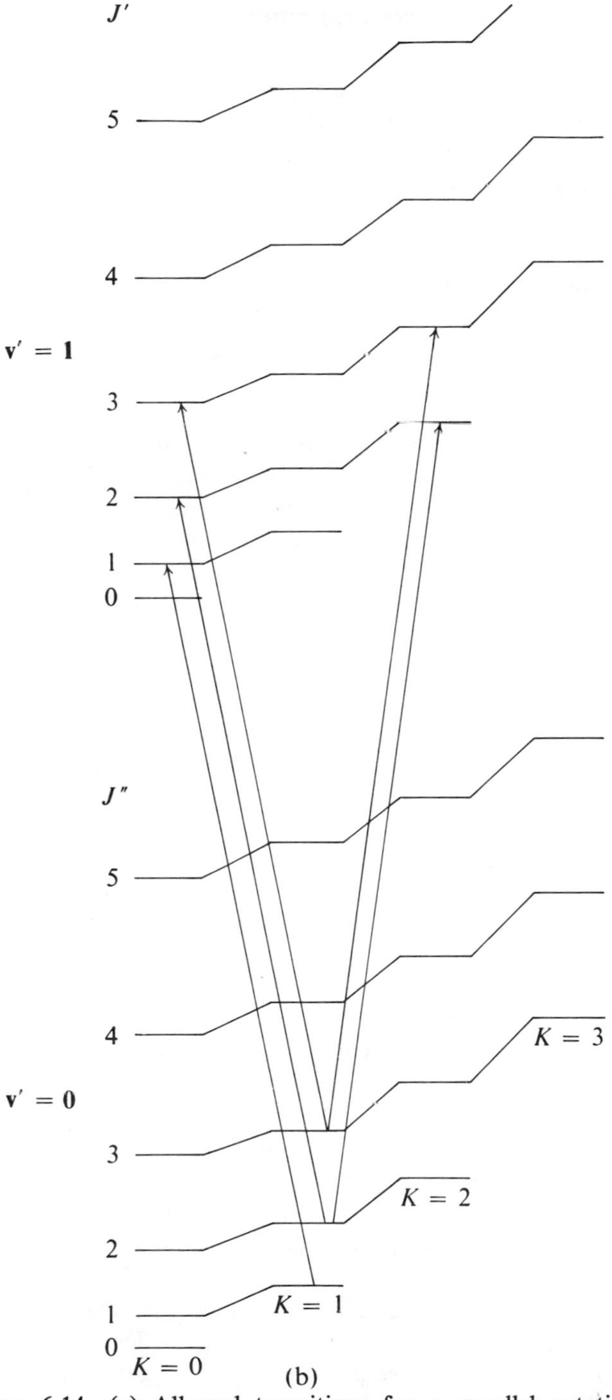

(b)

FIGURE 6-14 (a) Allowed transitions for a parallel rotation-vibration prolate symmetric top. (b) Allowed Q-type transitions for a perpendicular rotation-vibration prolate symmetric top.

are parallel vibrations, and ω_3 and ω_4 are perpendicular vibrations. Applying the appropriate selection rules in each case, we expect the rotation-vibration transitions and the resulting spectra to approximate those shown in Figures 6-14 and 6-15.

In the case of parallel vibrations ($\Delta K = 0$), for which transitions are illustrated in Figure 6-14a for the $K = 0$ level, $\Delta J = \pm 1$, and no Q-type transitions are allowed. For $K \neq 0$, $\Delta J = \pm 1$ and 0, the allowed transitions from a given J level are of the P, Q, and R types shown for $J'' = 3$ and $K = 1$. The set of transitions originating from the J'' levels ($K = 2$) are of the Q type and for a perfectly rigid rotor would all be superimposable. For the "slightly" nonrigid rotor, the transitions from the upper J'' states in all cases will have slightly lower energies and the resulting lines will be correspondingly shifted. The summarization of these transitions and the resulting rotation-vibration parallel spectrum is shown in Figure 6-15a.

In the case of perpendicular vibrations ($\Delta K = \pm 1$) where $\Delta J = \pm 1$ and 0, the most prominent feature is the Q-type transitions. In addition to the P and R lines, the approximately superimposable Q lines for a specific ΔK value occur for each J state of a given K. These transitions are shown in Figure 6-14b. We also note that for a given $\Delta K > 0$, the Q line occurs at a greater frequency than the ω_0 line, whereas for $\Delta K < 0$, it occurs at a lower frequency. The spectrum resulting from applying these selection rules to a "slightly" nonrigid rotor is shown in Figure 6-15b.

The rotation-vibration selection rules for spherical top molecules, such as GeH_4, are similar to the rules for the perpendicular vibrations of linear molecules, $\Delta \mathbf{v} = \pm 1$, $\Delta J = \pm 1, 0$, and as such, might be expected to have the same overall gross features. Of the molecules studied thus far that have T_d symmetry, the nondegenerate vibrational levels give rise to rotation-vibration spectra similar to the perpendicular linear case, but the degenerate vibrations give rise to spectral features that indicate strong rotation-vibration perturbations. Examination of the T_d point group indicates that only the vibrational modes that belong to the T_2 species will be infrared-active. These are the two triply degenerate ω_3 antisymmetric stretch and ω_4 deformation vibrations. For the $\omega_{3a,b,c}$ mutually degenerate vibrational modes, the interaction of ω_{3a} and ω_{3c} with the rotation about the z axis causes a splitting of these degenerate levels into sublevels with slightly different energies. The two split levels are actually linear combinations of the original ω_{3a} and ω_{3c} fundamental energy levels; the result is three sublevels, two equidistant above and below the original triply degenerate level, and one uninfluenced by the rotation-vibration interaction at the original nonperturbed energy. This interaction is similar to the interaction described previously, resulting in ℓ-type doubling, and is called *Coriolis interaction.* In spite of these perturbations, we find that the rotational spacing for the lower rotational transitions is roughly

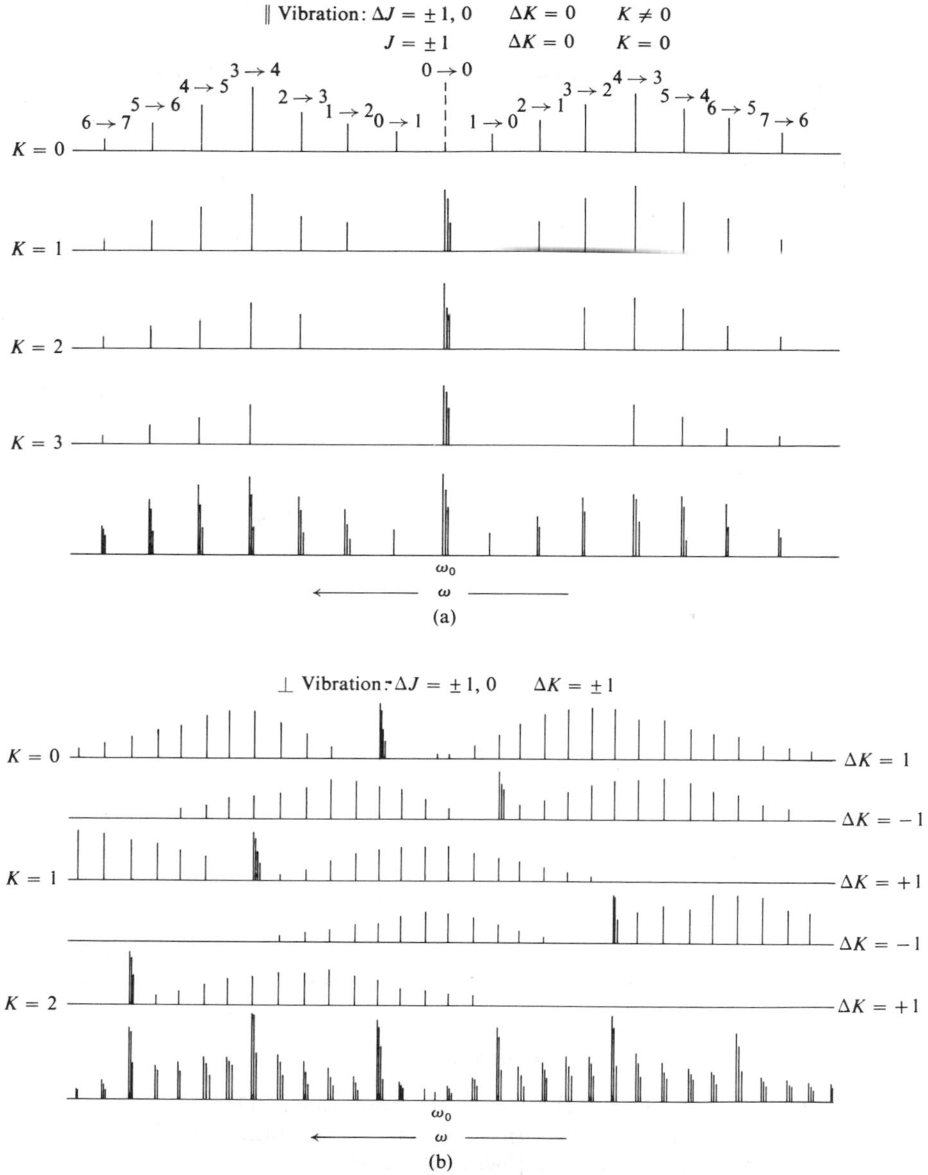

FIGURE 6-15 *K*-level (subband) transition intensities and the spectrum resulting from their superimposition (a) for a symmetric top parallel rotation-vibration band and (b) for a perpendicular rotation-vibration band.

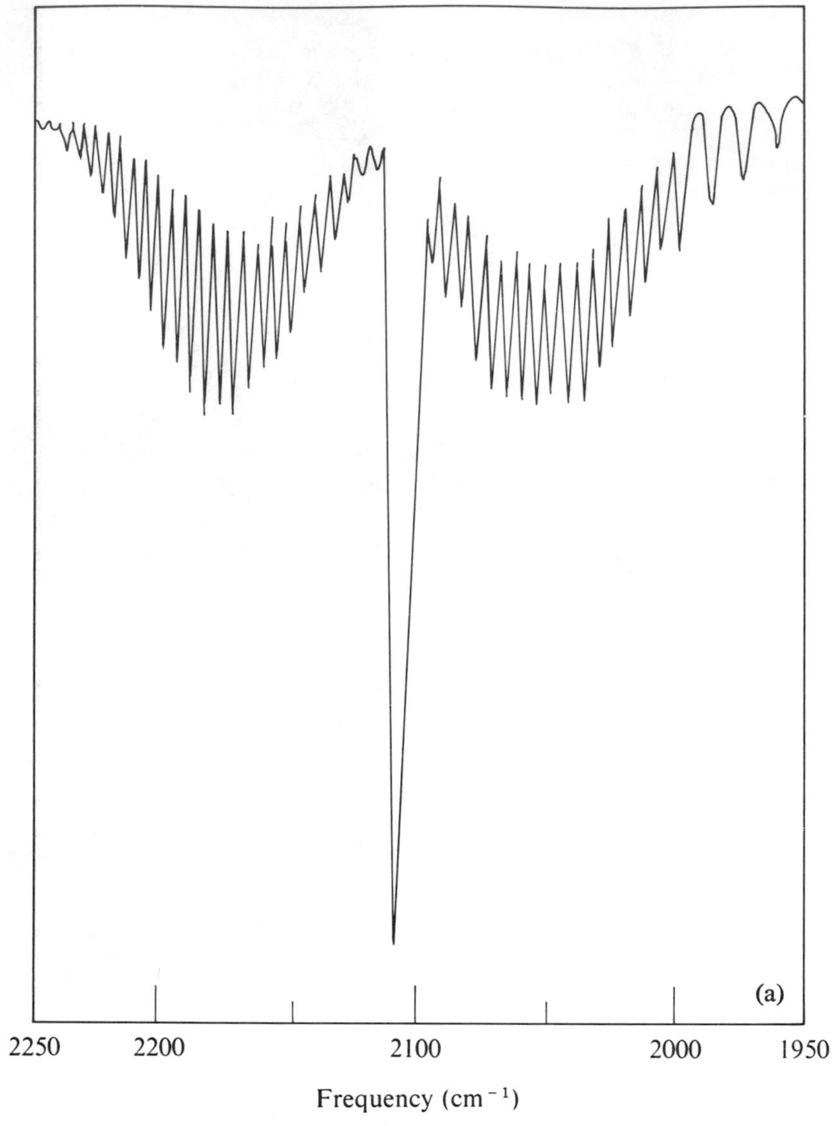

FIGURE 6-16 The GeH_4 rotation-vibration bands of (a) the triply degenerate antisymmetric stretching and (b) deformation vibrations at 15 torr through a 10-cm path length.

constant and is given by $2B(1 - \xi_i)$, where ξ_i is the Coriolis coupling constant for the ith vibration and B the rotational constant. The "allowed" rotation-vibration bands of ω_3 and ω_4 for GeH_4 are shown in Figure 6-16. The ω_3 band displays strikingly symmetrical P, Q, R

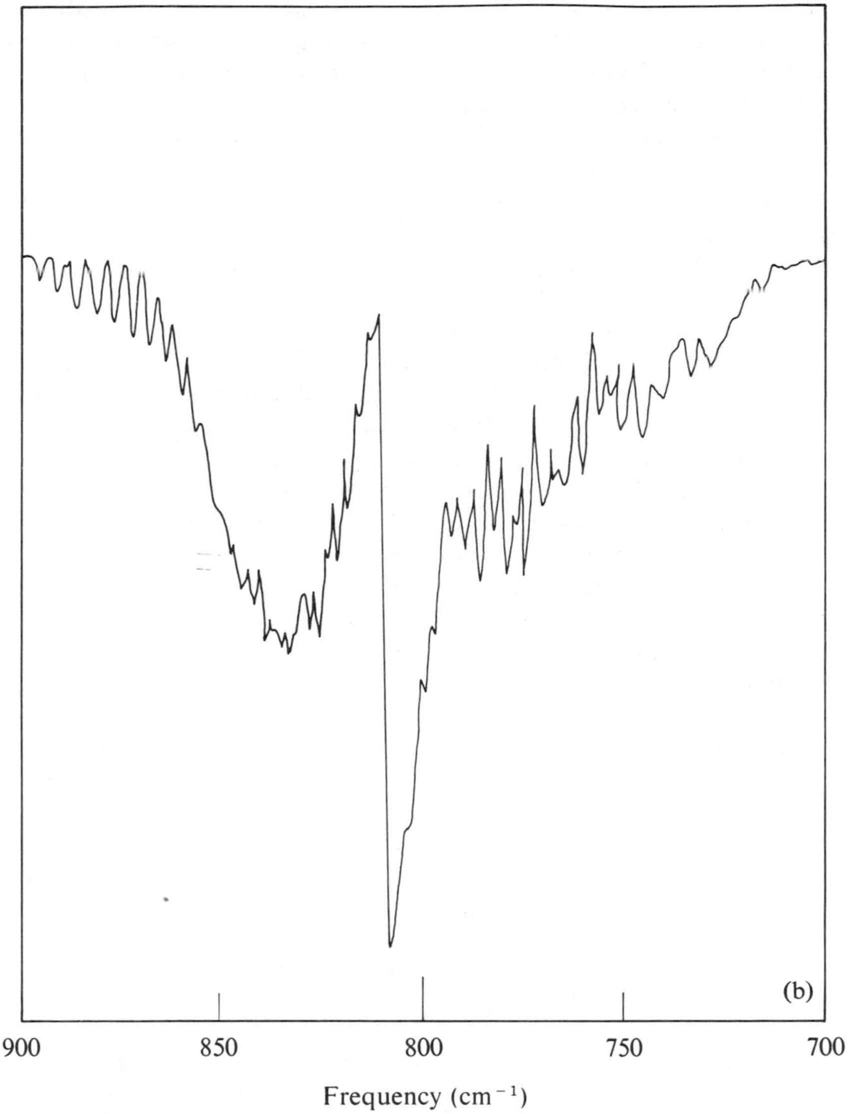

structure as in the linear cases, and this indicates a small Coriolis coupling constant. The rotational spacings are approximately 5.5 cm^{-1}. The triply degenerate deformation band on the other hand, ω_4, is strongly perturbed through a Coriolis interaction with the "inactive" doubly degenerate $\omega_2(E)$ deformation. This strong interaction is due to the close proximity (and appropriate symmetry species) of the two fundamental frequencies ($\omega_2 = 931$ cm^{-1} and $\omega_4 = 819$ cm^{-1}), and in fact has led to the infrared observation of ω_2 as a direct result of the strong mixing of the two vibrational-energy levels. As a result, the rotation-vibration spectrum is significantly unsymmetrical (perturbed) and has an approximate rotational spacing of 2.8 cm^{-1}.

The formaldehyde (CH_2O) molecule is a good example of a relatively small asymmetric top containing no degenerate fundamentals. Actually CH_2O has two components of its inertial moment that are approximately equal, and is by "accident" a slightly asymmetric rotor (or a nongenuine prolate symmetric top). All six normal modes of vibration are infrared- (and Raman-) active, and are shown in Figure 6-17. The observed infrared bands and the normal mode assignments of CH_2O provide an excellent illustration of the rules for frequency assignments ω_i described in Section 4B-2. The modes described as the "CH_2 symmetric stretch," "CO stretch," and "CH_2 scissors bend" are symmetric to all the symmetry operations of the C_{2v} point group (E, $C_2(z)$, $\sigma_v(xz)$, $\sigma_v'(yz)$), and therefore belong to the totally symmetric A_1 irreducible representation. The corresponding frequencies are listed in order of the decreasing numerical value. Those modes described as "CH_2 antisymmetric stretch" and "CH_2 rock" transform as the B_1 irreducible representation does, and are labeled ω_4 and ω_5. The remaining mode, the "CH_2 wag," is the only out-of-plane vibration, and it transforms like B_2 with the designation ω_6.

A further point to be made concerning the vibrational normal modes of the methylene group is that the $=CH_2$ group motions are regarded as if the methylene group were attached to an infinite mass (the O atom in this case). In the case of "CH_2 motions," the oxygen atom does in fact have a relatively small amplitude, and such a description is probably "good" as a first approximation. It is this type of assumption that provides the basis for transferring "group motions" from one molecule to another. As noted earlier for diatomics, this practice must be used with extreme caution. A comparison of similar "CH_2 modes" in CH_2O, $H_2C{=}CCl_2$, and CH_2Cl_2 is shown in Table 6-2.

TABLE 6-2. Methylene Group Frequencies in Various Molecules

Approximate Designation	CH_2O Frequency (cm^{-1})	$H_2C{=}CCl_2$ Frequency (cm^{-1})	CH_2Cl_2 Frequency (cm^{-1})
CH_2 symmetric stretch	2783	3035	2999
CH_2 scissors	1500	1400	1467
CH_2 antisymmetric stretch	2843	3130	3040
CH_2 rock	1249	1095	898
CH_2 wag	1167	875	1268

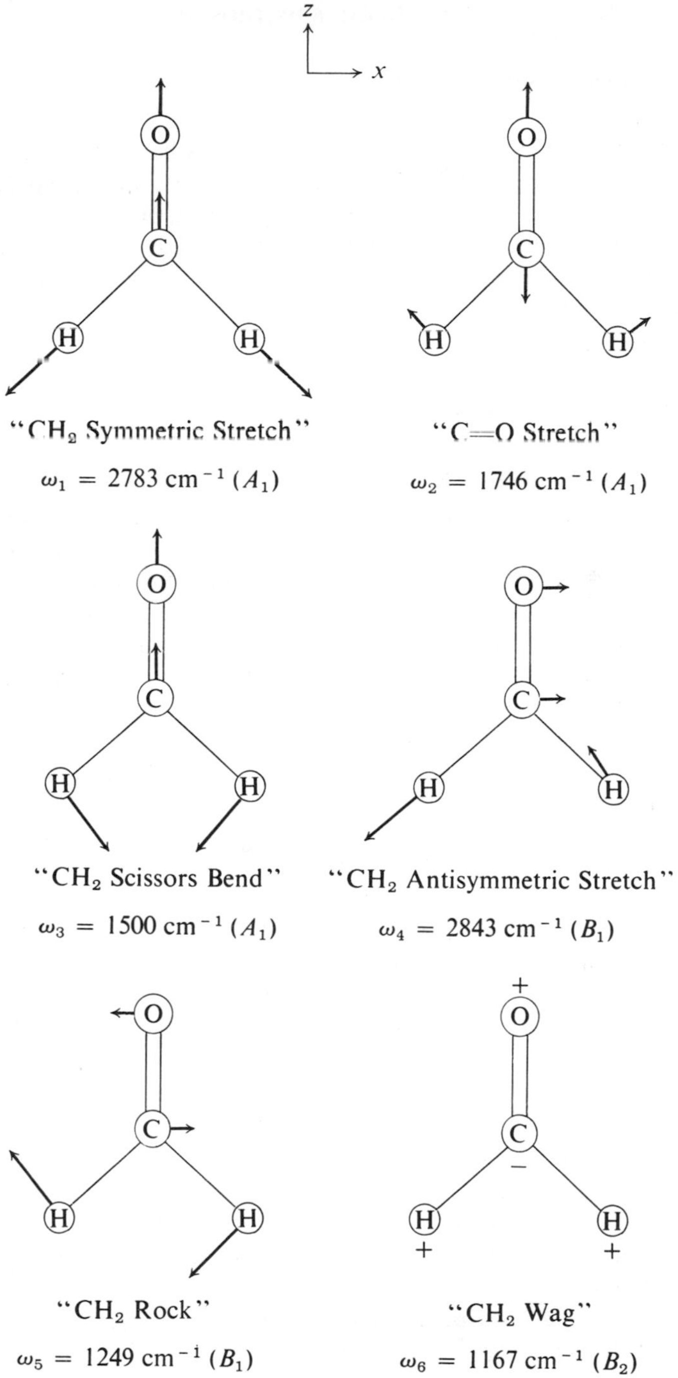

FIGURE 6-17 Normal modes of vibration of the formaldehyde molecule.

C. INFRARED SPECTROSCOPY

Starting in the 1930s, infrared spectroscopy has become one of the most useful and reliable tools for investigating physical and chemical properties of molecules. Although there are many applications, it has been applied extensively in determining molecular structure, the nature of chemical bonds, and the forces that hold atoms together in a molecule (molecular force fields).

1. Dispersion Spectroscopy

Practically all modern laboratories have commercially available infrared spectrophotometers. An optical schematic diagram of a commercially available double-beam infrared instrument that has some useful features for the experimental spectroscopist is shown in Figure 6-18. The essential components of the instrument are a relatively high intensity broad-band infrared source of radiation, a high-resolution dispersing element (monochromator), that is, a prism or a grating, and a relatively sensitive infrared detector (thermopile) along with signal-handling electronics. Since improved signal/noise (S/N) is obtained with a modulated signal, the radiation reaching the detector is usually "chopped" at some prior position. For the spectrophotometer shown in Figure 6-18, the air-cooled globar source radiation is directed through a series of stationary mirrors to the sector mirror (chopper) M-6, where it is modulated at 15 Hz and split into two beams (sample and reference). The two beams are directed through the sampling area and focused onto a second sector mirror (chopper) M-11, which modulates the beams at 30 Hz. This arrangement minimizes IR source heating of the sample, modulates at 30 Hz any radiation generated by the sample (which is subsequently discriminated against), and leaves unaffected the 15-Hz source radiation to which the electronics solely respond. The recombined source and reference beams are directed to a series of five infrared gratings, all operating in first order over the infrared from 4000 to 180 cm^{-1}. The dispersed radiation is focused onto the detector and is in turn amplified, demodulated, ratioed (double-beam mode), and recorded. The dotted components shown in Figure 6-18 are an alternative source and detector used for a far-infrared option down to 30 cm^{-1}.

General guidelines for analyzing and interpreting the infrared spectrum of a polyatomic molecule are the following:

1. In general, the more intense absorptions are probably due to fundamental vibration frequencies ("allowed" by the vibrational selection rules).

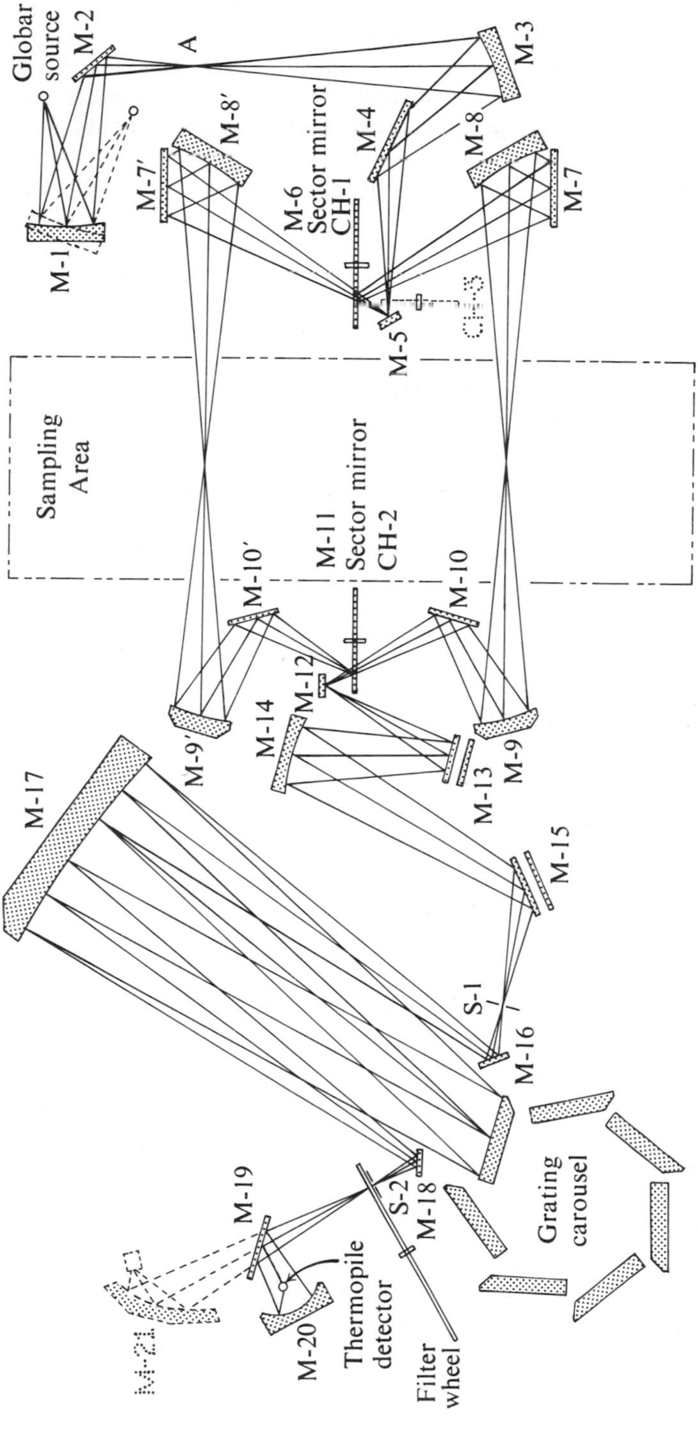

FIGURE 6-18 Optical schematic diagram of an infrared spectrophotometer. (Courtesy of the Perkin-Elmer Corporation.)

2. For a given spectrum, the higher-frequency absorption fundamentals are usually due to bond stretching motions and the lower fundamentals due to bending and deformation motions. This generalization is less valid and more difficult to apply to molecules containing a variety of light and heavy atoms.
3. For linear molecules, parallel vibrations have no *Q* branch (exception NO), but perpendicular vibrations do.
4. Overtone transitions may occur with decreasing intensity as $\mathbf{v}$ increases ("forbidden" by first-order vibrational selection rules, $\Delta\mathbf{v} = \pm 2, \pm 3, \ldots$).
5. Combination and difference transitions result from the simultaneous change of one quantum from two different vibrational modes. Combinations are generally more intense than difference transitions, since significant population of at least the first vibrational state ($\mathbf{v} = 1$) of one of the modes involved is required for the latter to occur.

These general guidelines in addition to the theory discussed in the previous section will be applied to analyzing the low-resolution infrared spectrum of BF_3, shown in Figure 6-19. This particular molecule is one that provides an added feature to the spectrum because of the natural isotopic abundance of $^{10}BF_3$ (20%) and $^{11}BF_3$ (80%). To conserve space in our present discussion, we shall assume the molecule to be a triangular plane (D_{3h} symmetry) and as such $\Gamma_{vib} = A_1' + A_2'' + 2E'$. The assignment of these irreducible representations to the normal modes of vibration of planar BF_3 is shown in Figure 6-20. On examining the D_{3h} character table (Appendix III), we note that all fundamentals are infrared-active, except for $\omega_1(A_1')$. We note a significant displacement of the boron atom in each normal mode of those that are active. As a result, we expect a significant mass effect and identical doublet absorptions in each case (except Raman-active ω_1, where B is not displaced). The absorptions occurring at 1505 and 1454 cm^{-1} are easily assigned to the doubly degenerate antisymmetric stretches ω_3 of $^{10}BF_3$ and $^{11}BF_3$, respectively. The low resolution of these bands tend to give the appearance of a missing *Q* branch. However, closer analysis reveals that these are perpendicular vibrational absorptions of the type illustrated in Figure 6-15b. The strong noncoincident *Q* absorptions are not resolved, and as a result, the net appearance is similar to that of a parallel vibration of a linear molecule. The *P* branch is less intense than the *R* branch because of a small Coriolis perturbation. This type of effect will be very pronounced as we consider the other absorptions, and will result in significant distortion of the nonperturbed band structure.

The absorption doublet that occurs at 719 and 691 cm^{-1} has been assigned to the nondegenerate out-of-plane bending mode (ω_2) of $^{10}BF_3$ and $^{11}BF_3$, respectively. In this case, we would have expected the parallel band structure for the symmetric top shown in Figure 6-15a.

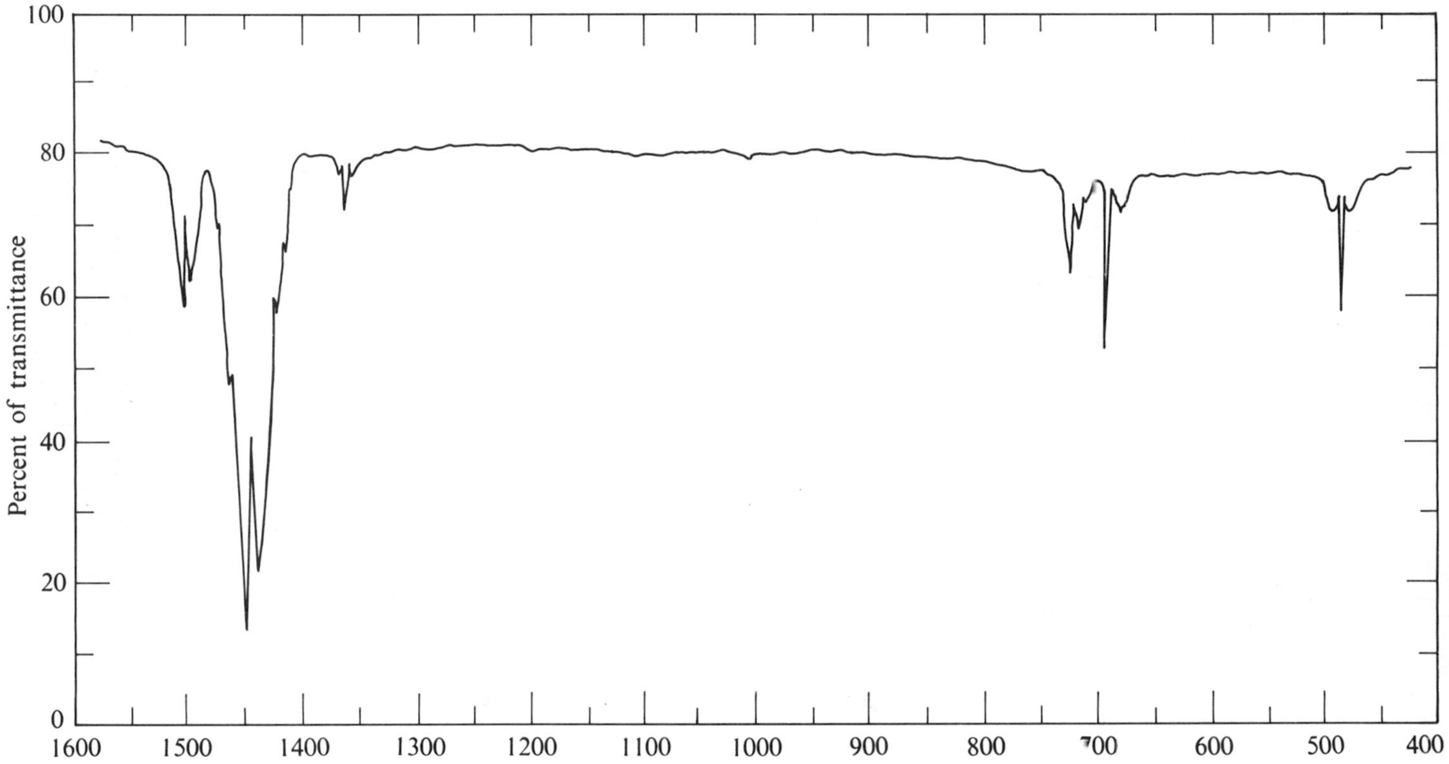

FIGURE 6-19 Infrared spectrum of 10 torr of BF_3 through a 10-cm cell.

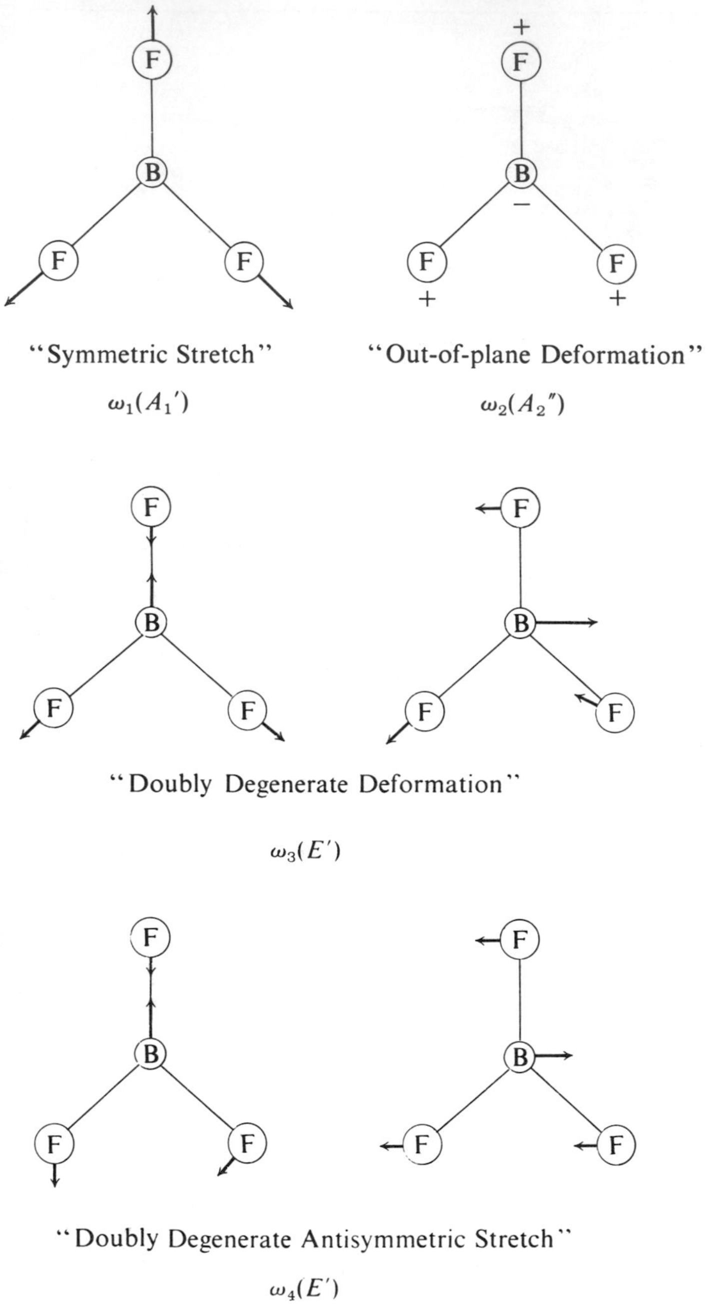

FIGURE 6-20 Actual normal modes of vibration of the D_{3h} BF_3 molecule. (From *Molecular Spectra and Molecular Structure*, Vol. II by G. Herzberg © 1945 by Litton Educational Publishing, Inc. Reprinted by permission of Van Nostrand Reinhold Company.)

TABLE 6-3. Summary of the BF_3 Assignments

Absorption Frequency (cm^{-1})			
$^{11}BF_3$		$^{10}BF_3$	Assignment
480		482	$\omega_4(E')$
691		791	$\omega_2(A_2'')$
	888		$\omega_1(A_1')$
	1359		$\omega_1(A_1') + \omega_4(E')$
1454		1505	$\omega_3(E')$

However, as a result of rather strong rotation-vibration (Coriolis) interaction, the upper and lower rotational constants (A_v and B_v) are sufficiently different that nonresolvable Q branches of the subbands converge rapidly to give a relatively narrow intense high-frequency component. The corresponding unresolved low-frequency component is consequently spread out and less intense.

The absorption doublet (observed under high resolution) at 482 and 480 cm^{-1} has been assigned to the doubly degenerate bending fundamentals (ω_4) of $^{10}BF_3$ and $^{11}BF_3$, respectively. Again, instead of the nonperturbed band structure as illustrated in Figure 6-15b, the exceptionally strong Coriolis coupling causes the Q subbands to shift near the origin. As a result, the band has a strong unresolved Q-type component, resembling that of a typical symmetric-top parallel band. These two examples of significantly perturbed band structure emphasize that we must exercise caution in interpreting low-resolution infrared spectra.

Finally, we consider the weak absorption occurring at 1359 cm^{-1}. Having eliminated the possibility that it is a fundamental, we consider possible overtones or combinations. One overtone option is too high, $2 \times 691\ cm^{-1} = 1382\ cm^{-1}$; the other too low, $2 \times 480\ cm^{-1} = 960\ cm^{-1}$. Of the combination options $\omega_1 + \omega_4$ and $\omega_1 + \omega_3$, we obtain for the unobserved totally symmetric mode $\omega_1 \simeq 1359 - 480 = 879\ cm^{-1}$, or $1359 - 691 = 668\ cm^{-1}$. Judging from the intense *single* Raman line observed at approximately 888 cm^{-1} due to ω_1, we conclude that the 1359-cm^{-1} band is due to the $\omega_1 + \omega_4$ combination. This discussion of BF_3 is summarized in Table 6-3.

2. Fourier Transform Spectroscopy (Fourier Multiplex Spectroscopy)

Fourier transform spectroscopy is capable of detecting the transitions between quantized molecular energy levels due to vibrations, the restricted and free rotations of molecular groups, and the pure rotation of gaseous molecules with large rotational energy spacings, for example HCl and

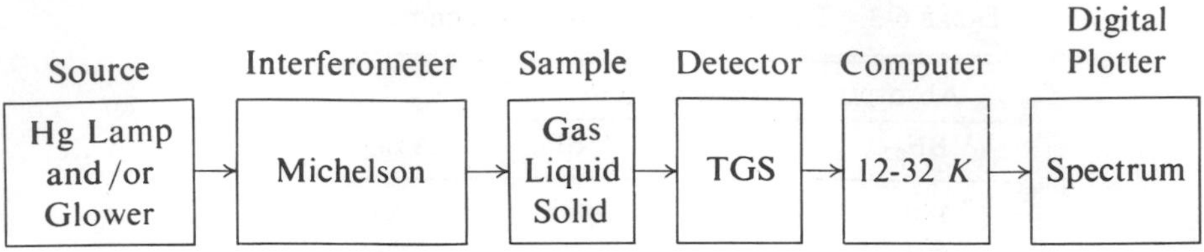

FIGURE 6-21 Schematic box diagram of the components of a Fourier transform spectrometer.

NH_3. At present, the total spectral range over which it is applied extends from the near infrared (7000 cm^{-1}) to the onset of the microwave ($\sim$10 cm^{-1}) region. The technique itself has been known and used for some time, but recently popularized because of breakthroughs in sampling and data handling.

The basic components of a Fourier transform spectrometer are shown in Figure 6-21. The source, which is normally a high-pressure mercury arc (far-infrared) or a glower operated at 1100 °C, is directed into a Michelson interferometer, where the intensity of each wavelength component is converted into a modulated (ac) audio frequency waveform. The general design of a Michelson interferometer is shown in Figure 6-22. If the source is monochromatic, a single frequency (λ/c) of radiation impinges on the beamsplitter, where ideally 50 percent is transmitted to M_2 and 50 percent reflected to M_1. When the two mirrors are equidistant from the beamsplitter, the two components of the split beam will return in phase, and reinforce each other (constructive interference). If the movable mirror M_1 is shifted a distance $\lambda/4$ from the zero position, its split component will travel a total distance back and forth of $\lambda + \lambda/2$. As a result, the $\lambda/2$ phase shift will cause it to be 180 degrees out of phase, resulting in destructive interference. The sample and the detector will "see" alternating bright and dark fields as a function of mirror movement x, as the components go in and out of phase. The intensity at the detector is mathematically given as

$$I(x) = B(\nu)\cos(2\pi x\nu), \tag{6-52}$$

where $I(x)$ is the intensity, $B(\nu)$ is the amplitude of frequency ν, and x is the mirror distance from the zero position. If the frequency of the source is about 1000 cm^{-1} and the movable mirror drive about 0.05 cm/sec, then the ac signal received at the detector is $f = (0.05)(1000) = 50$ Hz (modulated audiofrequency). If this treatment is extended to a broadband source, then the signal at the detector will be simply the summation (integral) of Eq. (6-52) over all frequencies. The signal output from the broadband source as a function of mirror displacement x is called an interferogram.

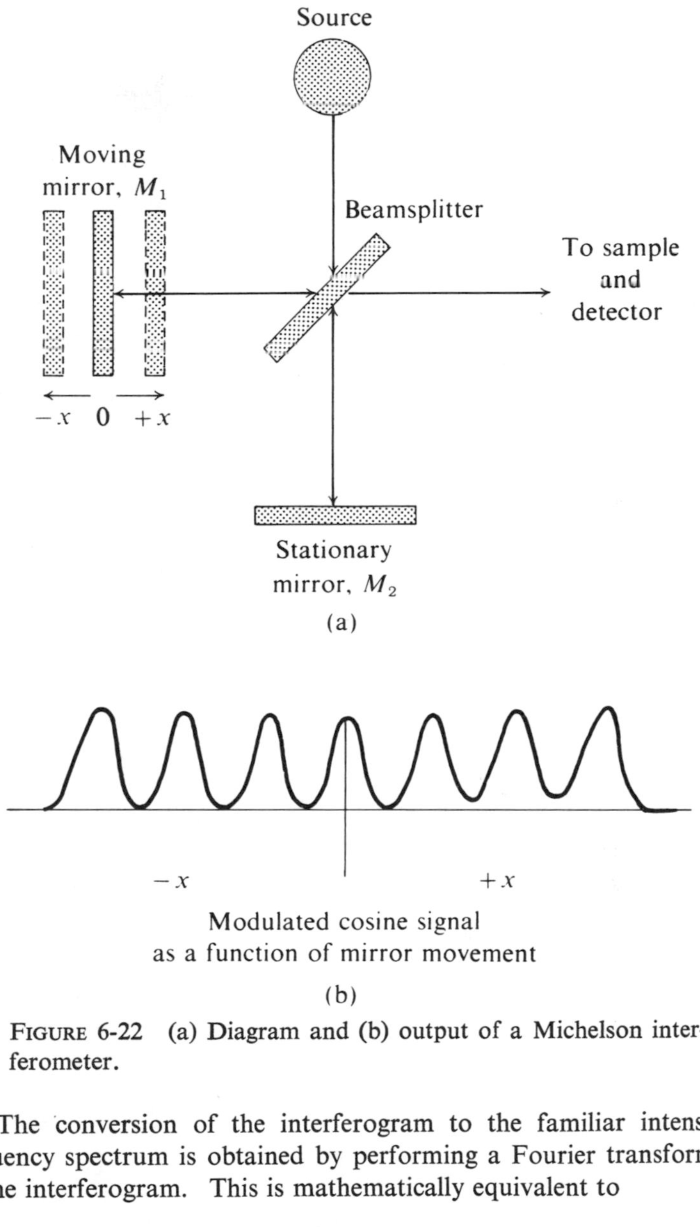

FIGURE 6-22 (a) Diagram and (b) output of a Michelson interferometer.

The conversion of the interferogram to the familiar intensity-vs-frequency spectrum is obtained by performing a Fourier transformation on the interferogram. This is mathematically equivalent to

$$B(\nu) = \int_{-\infty}^{+\infty} I(x) \cos(2\pi x \nu) \, dx, \quad \textbf{(6-53)}$$

where $B(\nu)$ represents the intensity as a function of frequency—hence the name *Fourier transform spectroscopy* (FTS). Renewed activity in this

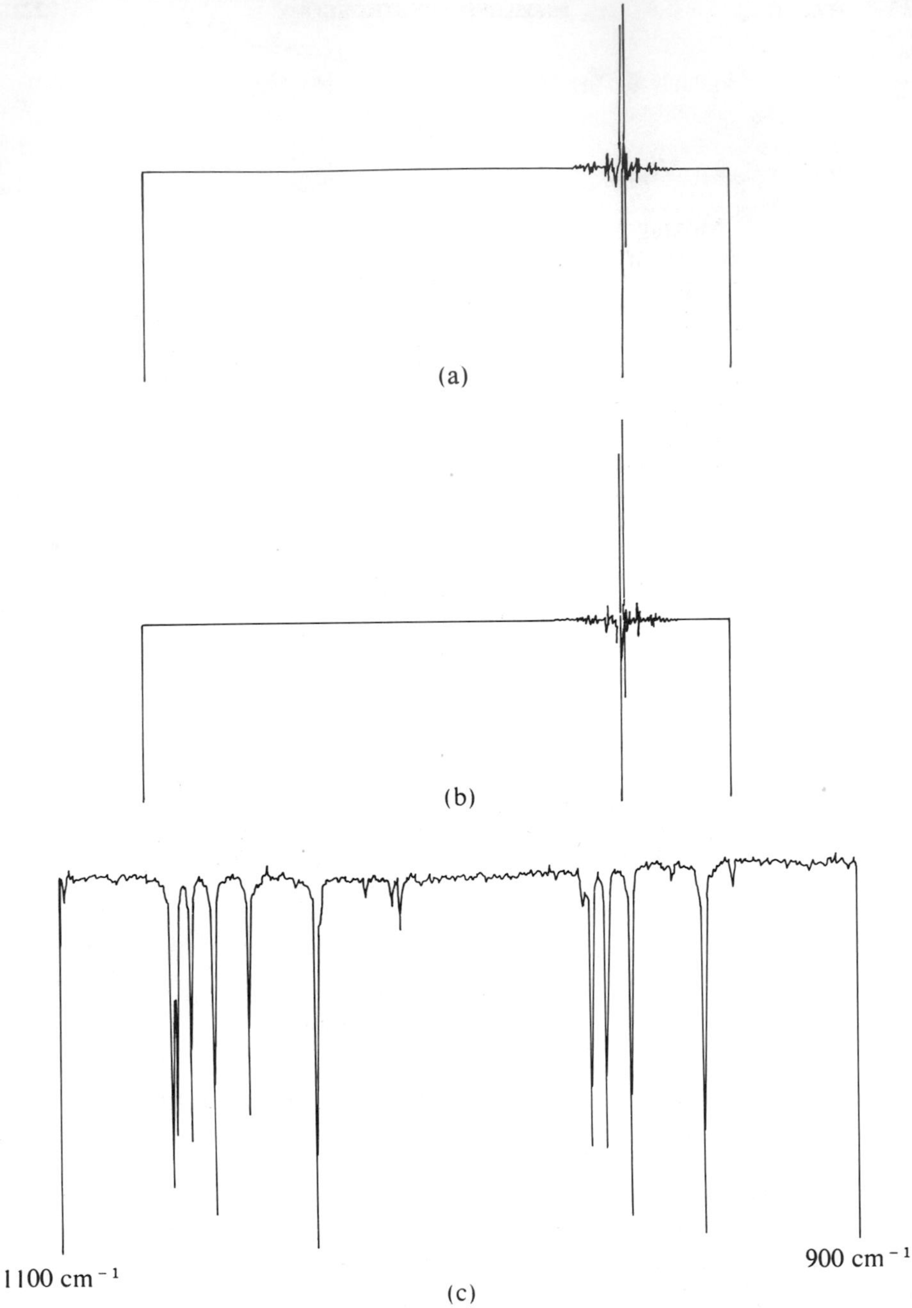

FIGURE 6-23 Interferogram (a) of a 10-cm empty cell (background) and (b) of the 2 torr sample of NH_3. (c) High-resolution ($0.1\ cm^{-1}$) spectrum ratioing of (a) and (b). (Courtesy of Digilab, Inc.)

area (particularly in the far infrared) has resulted primarily from commercially available instruments containing low-cost computers, which perform the Fourier transformation as the interferogram is recorded.

The advantages of Fourier transform spectrometers over the well-established dispersion instruments are the following:

1. Throughput. The FTS detector "sees" the full intensity of the source without an entrance slit, which grating and prism instruments use. The improvement is roughly a factor of 100.
2. Fellgett's advantage. Refers to the derivation by Fellgett, which shows that the signal-to-noise ratio (S/N) is theoretically improved by a factor of $M^{1/2}$ for an interferometer, where M is the number of resolution elements.
3. A direct result of Fellgett's advantage for a typical infrared spectrum where $M \sim 3000$, performed with an observation time of 1 sec/element, is that the dispersive instrument requires 3000 sec (50 min), whereas the interferometer requires approximately 1 min for the same S/N.

The interferograms of a sample of ammonia (2 torr) and the background through an empty 10-cm cell are shown in Figures 6-23b and 6-23a. The differences in the two interferograms, which may be difficult to visualize because of size reduction, are due to the sample absorptions at specific frequencies. After the Fourier transformation is performed, the two spectra are ratioed to give the resulting (net) spectrum shown in Figure 6-23c.

D. RAMAN SPECTROSCOPY

1. The Raman Effect

The technique of Raman spectroscopy depends on the *inelastic scattering* of radiation by a nonabsorbing medium. When a monochromatic beam of radiation passes through a gas, a liquid, or a solid, the radiation may be transmitted, absorbed, or scattered. The transmitted radiation is not important for our consideration, and we assume that the incident radiation is not in resonance with any allowed electronic transition (no absorption). The scattered radiation may be of the same frequency as the incident radiation, in which case it is called elastic, or Rayleigh, scattering. However, only one in approximately every million incident photons (10^{-6}) will be scattered with a loss or gain of energy, which is not fluorescence. This phenomenon is called "Raman scattering," or the Raman effect, after the physicist C. V. Raman, who first observed it in 1928. The inelastic-scattered radiations occur at lower (Stokes lines) and higher (anti-Stokes lines) frequencies, corresponding to the rotational or vibrational transition frequencies or both of the sample or medium. This effect therefore provides an additional means of observing the rotation or rotation-vibration spectra of simple and complex molecules.

The Raman effect results from the interaction of the oscillating induced polarization or dipole moment of the medium with the electric field vector **E** of the incident radiation. The oscillating induced polarization **P** is also caused by **E**, and is given as

$$\mathbf{P} = \boldsymbol{\alpha}\mathbf{E}, \tag{6-54}$$

where $\boldsymbol{\alpha}$, the molecular polarizability, is in general a tensor. If the medium is anisotropic, then Eq. (6-54) is

$$\mathbf{P} = \begin{bmatrix} P_x \\ P_y \\ P_z \end{bmatrix} = \begin{bmatrix} \alpha_{xx} & \alpha_{xy} & \alpha_{xz} \\ \alpha_{yx} & \alpha_{yy} & \alpha_{yz} \\ \alpha_{zx} & \alpha_{zy} & \alpha_{zz} \end{bmatrix} \begin{bmatrix} E_x \\ E_y \\ E_z \end{bmatrix}. \tag{5-30}$$

The $\boldsymbol{\alpha}$ matrix is symmetric ($\alpha_{ij} = \alpha_{ji}$), and its elements, which are constants and independent of **E** and **P**, are called the components of the polarizability tensor.

As the molecule vibrates (undergoes nuclear displacements), the charge distribution and thus the polarizability constantly varies. If we assume that this variation occurs over small displacements from the equilibrium configuration, then the polarizability for the α_{xx} component can be expanded as a Taylor series in normal coordinates,

$$\alpha_{xx} = \alpha_{xx}{}^{\mathrm{e}} + \sum_{k=1}^{3N-6} \left(\frac{\partial \alpha_{xx}}{\partial Q_k}\right)_{\mathrm{e}} Q_k + \frac{1}{2} \sum_{k=1}^{3N-6} \sum_{j=1}^{3N-6} \left(\frac{\partial^2 \alpha_{xx}}{\partial Q_k \partial Q_j}\right)_{\mathrm{e}} Q_k Q_j + \cdots, \tag{6-55}$$

where $\alpha_{xx}{}^{\mathrm{e}}$ is the induced equilibrium polarizability along the x direction by the electric field component E_x. For a normal mode executing simple harmonic motion, the normal coordinate k is

$$Q_k = Q_k{}^0 \cos 2\pi c\omega_k t, \tag{6-56}$$

where $Q_k{}^0$ is the time-independent amplitude of Q_k, and we have dropped the phase constant, which is unimportant in this discussion (compare Eq. (6-31)). Substituting Eq. (6-56) into Eq. (6-55) and retaining only the first two terms on the right, we obtain

$$\alpha_{xx} = \alpha_{xx}{}^{\mathrm{e}} + \sum_{k=1}^{3N-6} \left(\frac{\partial \alpha_{xx}}{\partial Q_k}\right)_{\mathrm{e}} Q_k{}^0 \cos 2\pi c\omega_k t. \tag{6-57}$$

Substituting this expression into Eq. (5-30), we obtain for the $\alpha_{xx}E_x$ element

$$\alpha_{xx}E_x = \alpha_{xx}E_x{}^0 \cos 2\pi c\omega_0 t = \alpha_{xx}{}^{\mathrm{e}}E_x{}^0 \cos 2\pi c\omega_0 t$$

$$+ E_x{}^0 \sum_{k=1}^{3N-6} \left(\frac{\partial \alpha_{xx}}{\partial Q_k}\right)_{\mathrm{e}} Q_k{}^0 \cos 2\pi c\omega_0 t \cos 2\pi c\omega_k t. \tag{6-58}$$

Using the trigonometric relation $\cos \mathbf{a} \cdot \cos \mathbf{b} = \frac{1}{2}[\cos(\mathbf{a} + \mathbf{b}) + \cos(\mathbf{a} - \mathbf{b})]$, we obtain

$$\begin{aligned} \alpha_{xx}E_x &= \alpha_{xx}{}^{e}E_x{}^{0} \cos 2\pi c\omega_0 t \\ &\quad + E_x{}^{0} \sum_{k=1}^{3N-6} \frac{1}{2} \left(\frac{\partial \alpha_{xx}}{\partial Q_k}\right)_e Q_k{}^{0} \\ &\quad \times [\cos 2\pi c(\omega_0 + \omega_k)t + \cos 2\pi c(\omega_0 - \omega_k)t]. \end{aligned} \tag{6-59}$$

The first term on the right characterizes the intensity of the Rayleigh line and is proportional to $\alpha_{xx}{}^{e}$; the second term characterizes the Raman intensity and is proportional to $(\partial\alpha_{xx}/\partial Q_k)_e$. Although this *classical* derivation does illustrate the Raman shifted frequencies at $\omega_0 + \omega_k$ (anti-Stokes lines) and $\omega_0 - \omega_k$ (Stokes lines), it also incorrectly implies that the two sets will occur with equal intensity. To illustrate the Raman effect, we have used this classical derivation in terms of only *one* element of the nine generated by the matrix multiplication of Eq. (5-30). The other eight elements are derived in a similar manner and must also be considered in determining a Raman allowed transition.

The actual intensities of the Stokes and anti-Stokes lines are principally determined by the Boltzmann factor characterizing the vibrational population.[9] For high-frequency vibrations, the Stokes lines are relatively intense whereas the anti-Stokes lines are extremely weak or nonexistent, since they depend on significant population of the upper vibrational levels. As a result, vibrational Raman spectroscopy is practically always performed by observation of the Stokes component.

2. Transitions in the Raman Effect

According to Eq. (5-31),

$$\int \psi_m{}^{*}\mathbf{P}\psi_k \, d\tau = \mathbf{E} \int \psi_m{}^{*}\boldsymbol{\alpha}\psi_k \, d\tau, \tag{5-31}$$

we obtain for the $\mathbf{P}$ components of Eq. (5-30)

$$\begin{aligned} [P_x]_{mk} &= E_x \int \psi_m{}^{*}\alpha_{xx}\psi_k \, d\tau + E_y \int \psi_m{}^{*}\alpha_{xy}\psi_k \, d\tau + E_z \int \psi_m{}^{*}\alpha_{xz}\psi_k \, d\tau; \\ [P_y]_{mk} &= E_x \int \psi_m{}^{*}\alpha_{yx}\psi_k \, d\tau + E_y \int \psi_m{}^{*}\alpha_{yy}\psi_k \, d\tau + E_z \int \psi_m{}^{*}\alpha_{yz}\psi_k \, d\tau; \\ [P_z]_{mk} &= E_x \int \psi_m{}^{*}\alpha_{zx}\psi_k \, d\tau + E_y \int \psi_m{}^{*}\alpha_{zy}\psi_k \, d\tau + E_z \int \psi_m{}^{*}\alpha_{zz}\psi_k \, d\tau. \end{aligned} \tag{6-60}$$

To derive the vibrational selection rules, we can use any of the integrals above since they all give the same final result. For the α_{xx} integral, on substituting the first two terms on the right of Eq. (6-55), we obtain

$$\alpha_{xx}{}^{e} \int \psi_{\mathbf{v}_k'}{}^*(Q_k)\psi_{\mathbf{v}_k''}(Q_k)\,dQ_k + \sum_{k=1}^{3N-6} \left(\frac{\partial \alpha_{xx}}{\partial Q_k}\right)_e \int \psi_{\mathbf{v}_k'}{}^*(Q_k)Q_k\psi_{\mathbf{v}_k''}(Q_k)\,dQ_k, \tag{6-61}$$

where we have replaced ψ_m and ψ_k with the upper ($\mathbf{v}_k'$) and the lower ($\mathbf{v}_k''$) vibrational state wavefunctions in normal coordinates. The first integral will be nonzero only if $\mathbf{v}_k' = \mathbf{v}_k''$, and therefore corresponds to the pure rotational Raman effect. The selection rules for rotational Raman transitions derived in a manner similar to the procedure used for infrared transitions are summarized below for linear and symmetric top molecules:[10]

Linear Molecules	$\Delta J = 0, \pm 2$	
Symmetric Top Molecules	$\Delta J = 0, \pm 2, \quad \Delta K = 0$	when $K = 0$
	$\Delta J = 0, \pm 1, \pm 2, \quad \Delta K = 0$	when $K \neq 0$

Since molecules of tetrahedral, cubic, and higher-order symmetry all have polarizability components of zero, they will not have a pure rotational Raman spectrum.

The integral of the second term of Eq. (6-61) for a polyatomic molecule will have vibrational wavefunctions of the form of Eq. (6-38), and thus

$$\int \psi_{\mathbf{v}_k'}{}^*(Q_k)Q_k\psi_{\mathbf{v}_k''}(Q_k)\,dQ_k$$
$$= \int \psi_{\mathbf{v}_k'}{}^*(Q_k')Q_k'\psi_{\mathbf{v}_k''}(Q_k')\,dQ_k' \prod_{k=1}^{3N-7} \int \psi_{\mathbf{v}_k'}{}^*(Q_k)\psi_{\mathbf{v}_k''}(Q_k)\,dQ_k. \tag{6-62}$$

As in the case of the infrared selection rules, these integrals are the same as the integrals of Eq. (6-50). The first integral on the right remains nonzero only if $\Delta \mathbf{v}_k = \pm 1$; and the product of integrals is unity if in all $3N - 7$ cases $\Delta \mathbf{v}_k = 0$ (otherwise they are zero). In addition to the requirement of $\Delta \mathbf{v} = \pm 1$ vibrational quantum jumps, at least one of the components of the polarizability derivative, $(\partial\alpha_{xx}/\partial Q_k)_e$, $(\partial\alpha_{xy}/\partial Q_k)_e$, and so on, must be nonzero. The physical picture of this derivative can be easily visualized by means of the *polarizability ellipsoid*. If the general coordinate system of the polarizability tensor is rotated in such a manner that the direction of the components of the polarization **P** corresponds to the direction of the components of the electric field **E**, then the values of α_{ij} along the three mutually perpendicular directions will have a minimum and a maximum value. A transformation of this type, which results in the orientation of the polarizability components along these mutually perpendicular principal axes, is orthogonal, and as a result all the off-diagonal elements of Eq. (5-30) are zero, $\alpha_{xy} = \alpha_{xz} = \alpha_{yz} = 0$; the components along the new (transformed) axes are simply α_x, α_y, and α_z. If we plot $1/\sqrt{\alpha_x}$, $1/\sqrt{\alpha_y}$, $1/\sqrt{\alpha_z}$ along the principal axes and form a three-dimensional surface from the locus of the points, then such a surface is called the polarizability ellipsoid. If the medium (or sample) scatters the radiation isotropically, then the induced polarization will be equal along all three perpendicular directions, and α is simply a constant,

$$\alpha = \alpha_x = \alpha_y = \alpha_z. \tag{6-63}$$

The polarizability ellipsoid of symmetrical molecules is relatively easy to construct since the principal axes are usually coincident with or perpendicular to the symmetry axes and planes, or both. The change in polarizability (and the polarizability ellipsoid) as a function of Q_k for a linear symmetric XY_2 molecule, such as CO_2 is shown in Figure 6-24. If the principal axes of the polarizability ellipsoid are oriented so that α_z lies along the molecular axis and α_x and α_y are perpendicular, then

$$\left(\frac{\partial \alpha_{xy}}{\partial Q_k}\right)_e = \left(\frac{\partial \alpha_{xz}}{\partial Q_k}\right)_e = \left(\frac{\partial \alpha_{yz}}{\partial Q_k}\right)_e = 0$$

for all three normal modes $k = 1$, 2, and 3. Furthermore, the three diagonal elements are also zero for $k = 2$ and 3 (ω_2 and ω_3), and thus these vibrations will not be Raman-active. Only the totally symmetric vibrational mode ω_1, for which

$$\left(\frac{\partial \alpha_x}{\partial Q_1}\right)_e = \left(\frac{\partial \alpha_y}{\partial Q_1}\right)_e \neq 0 \neq \left(\frac{\partial \alpha_z}{\partial Q_1}\right)_e,$$

will be active as a result of the Raman effect. Centrosymmetric molecules (having a center of symmetry), which are subject to the mutual exclusion principle, exemplify the complementary nature of infrared and Raman spectroscopy.

Applying the selection rules summarized above to a linear molecule, where a small population of the first excited vibrational state exists, results in the theoretical spectrum shown in Figure 6-25. The transition energies for a linear rigid-rotor–harmonic oscillator molecule (Eq. 4-10) are

$$\begin{aligned} \Delta E &= \omega_0 + (4J + 6)B && \text{for } \Delta J = +2,\ S \text{ branch,} \\ \Delta E &= \omega_0 && \text{for } \Delta J = 0,\ Q \text{ branch,} \\ \Delta E &= \omega_0 - (4J - 2)B && \text{for } \Delta J = -2,\ O \text{ branch, where } J \geqslant 2, \end{aligned} \tag{6-64}$$

where J refers to the initial state of the transition. The center series of lines corresponding to $\Delta v = 0$ is the rotational Raman spectrum of the molecule. The center line at ω_R is the elastically scattered Rayleigh line approximately 10^6 times more intense than the others. The successive

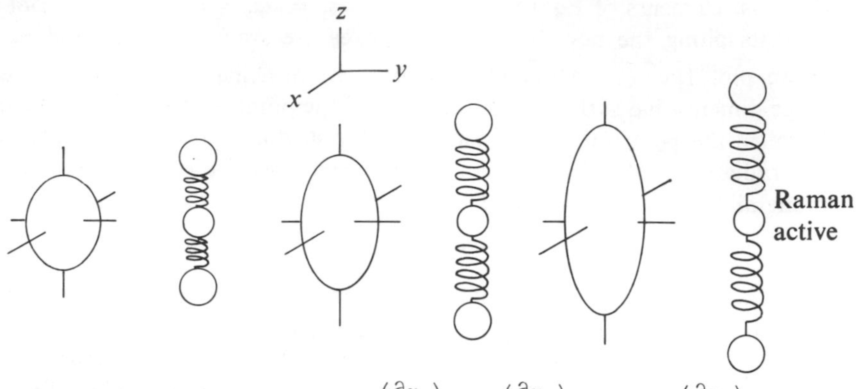

ω_1, Symmetric Stretch, $\left(\dfrac{\partial \alpha_x}{\partial Q_1}\right)_e = \left(\dfrac{\partial \alpha_y}{\partial Q_1}\right)_e \neq 0 \neq \left(\dfrac{\partial \alpha_z}{\partial Q_1}\right)_e$

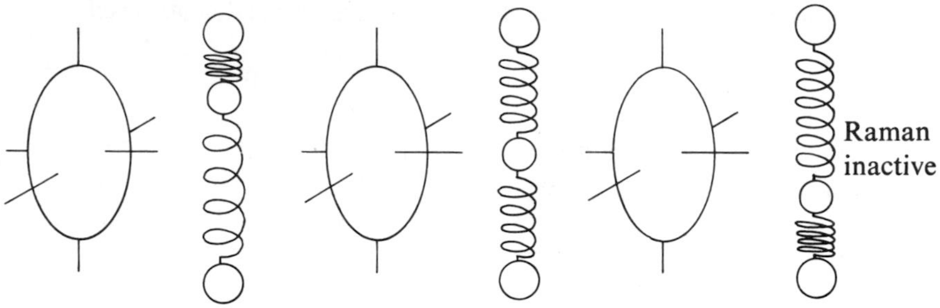

ω_3, Antisymmetric Stretch, $\left(\dfrac{\partial \alpha_x}{\partial Q_3}\right)_e = \left(\dfrac{\partial \alpha_y}{\partial Q_3}\right)_e = \left(\dfrac{\partial \alpha_z}{\partial Q_3}\right)_e = 0$

ω_2, Bending Vibration, $\left(\dfrac{\partial \alpha_x}{\partial Q_2}\right)_e = \left(\dfrac{\partial \alpha_y}{\partial Q_2}\right)_e = \left(\dfrac{\partial \alpha_z}{\partial Q_2}\right)_e = 0$

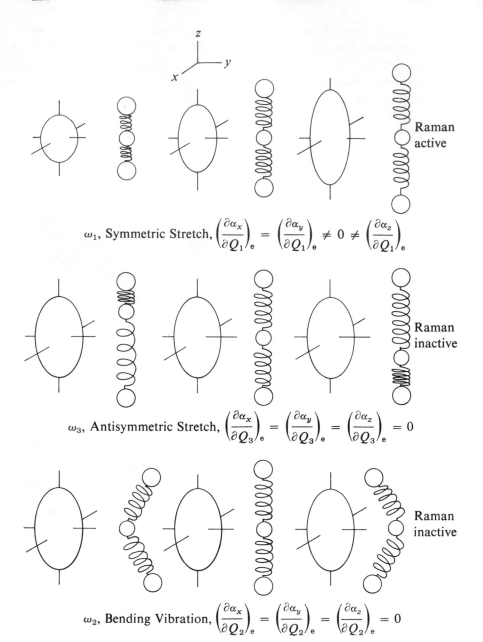

FIGURE 6-24 The change in polarizability (and the polarizability ellipsoid) as a function of the normal modes of vibration of CO_2 (according to R. S. Tobias, *J. Chem. Educ.* **44**, 40 (1967), by permission).

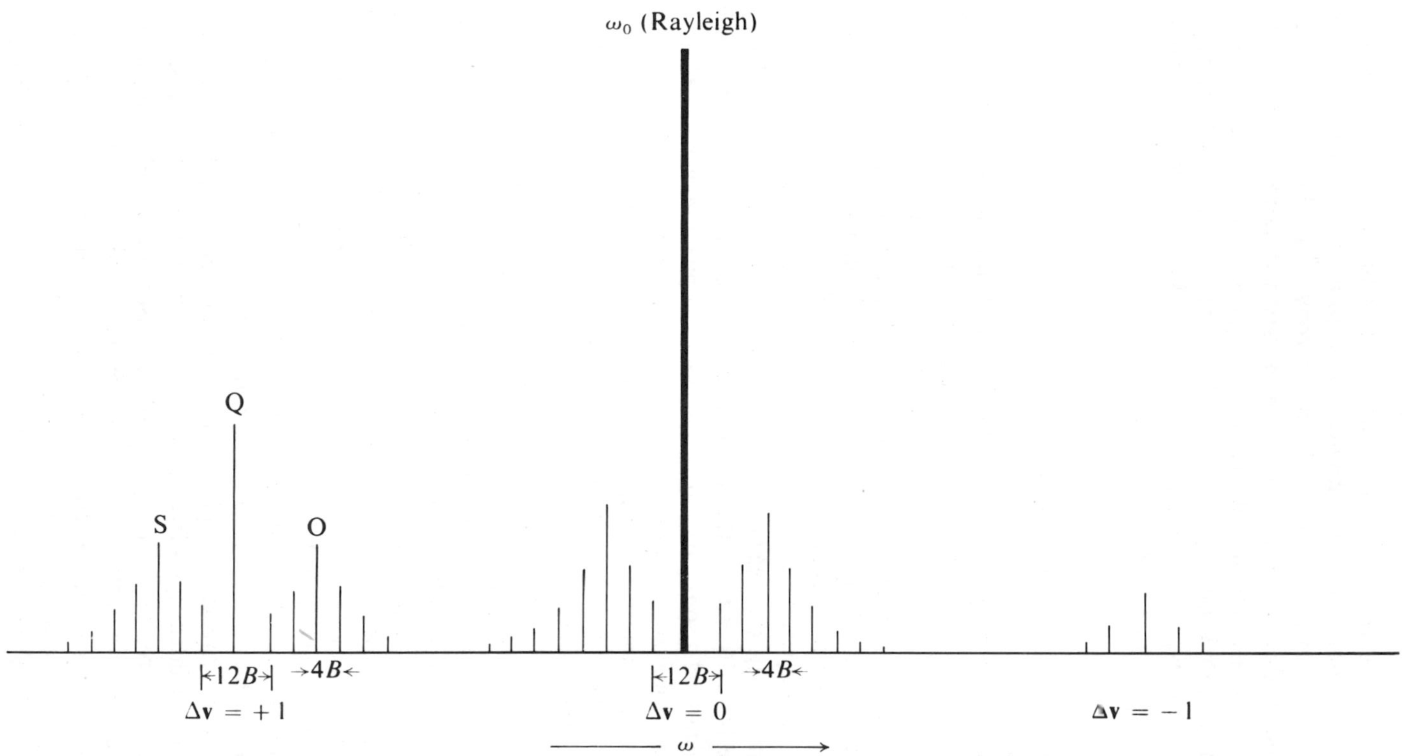

FIGURE 6-25 The theoretical rotation-vibration Raman spectrum resulting from the application of the selection rules $\Delta \mathbf{v} = 0, \pm 1$ and $\Delta J = 0, \pm 2$ to a linear molecule. Nuclear-spin statistics have been omitted in this illustration.

line spacings are $4B$, and provide a way of determining the lone structural parameter of homonuclear diatomic molecules r_0, which cannot be obtained by microwave or infrared spectroscopy. The band systems on each side of this center system are the rotation-vibration bands of the Stokes ($\Delta\mathbf{v} = +1$) and anti-Stokes ($\Delta\mathbf{v} = -1$) transitions. The transition frequencies corresponding to $\Delta J = +2$, 0, and -2 are called the S, Q, and O branches. The intensity of the anti-Stokes band is proportional to the $\mathbf{v} = 1$ excited state population.

3. Experimental Raman Spectroscopy

Raman spectroscopy as an experimental tool has, since the late 60's, experienced renewed activity with the use of visible laser sources. The disadvantages of the older principal radiation source, a high-pressure mercury arc, have been overcome with the advent of the laser. A schematic diagram of a laser Raman spectrometer is shown in Figure 6-26a. As for the infrared spectrophotometer, the chief components are the source, the dispersing element (s), the detector, and the signal-handling electronics. The tunable visible and UV sources are capable of producing a range from 10^{-3} to watts of continuous power, which is comparable to conventional resonance sources, such as a low-pressure mercury arc. In most cases however, conventional sources require filtering, which may reduce appreciably the intensity of the exciting line. The line widths of the laser sources are also smaller than the line widths of the conventional types. Perhaps the most important property of the laser source is coherence which not only reduces significantly any loss of intensity from focusing or collimating, but also allows greater efficiency in the collection of scattered radiation from the sample, since this radiation is scattered from a small localized point in the sample. These general improvements in the source characteristics have allowed higher-resolution rotation-vibration and pure rotational Raman spectra to be obtained. Whatever the laser source, it is directed into the sample, where the scattered radiation is normally collected at 90° to the incident source. The scattered radiations consisting of Rayleigh and Raman frequencies are dispersed either with a double- or a triple-grating monochromator. The dispersed radiations are directed to a photomultiplier tube and are in turn displayed as the usual intensity-vs-frequency spectrum by the appropriate signal-handling electronics. The nature of the laser source, allowing easier focusing and collimating, allows a greater intensity of the dispersed radiation to reach the detector. The rotation-vibration spectrum of the centrosymmetric benzene molecule is shown in Figure 6-26b. A molecule like this, which has twenty different (nonredundant) vibrational frequencies (30 normal modes), emphasizes more dramatically the complementary

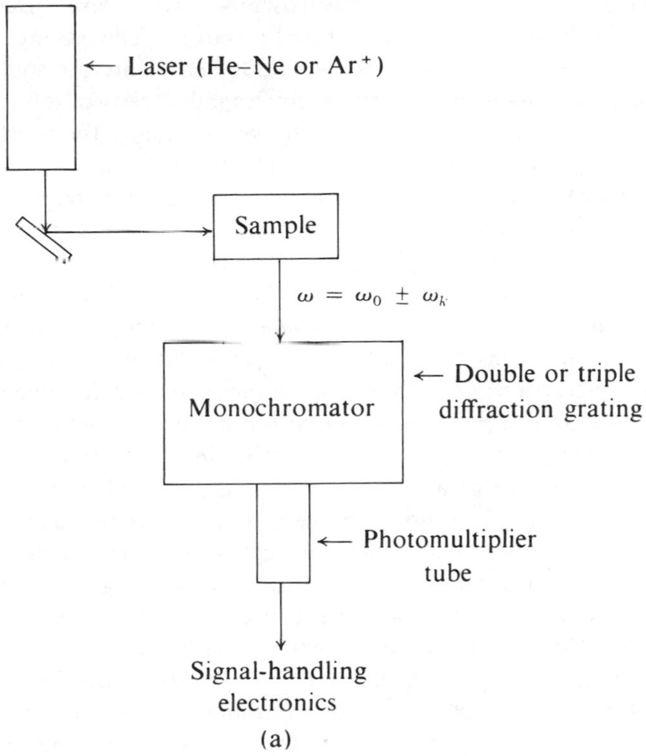

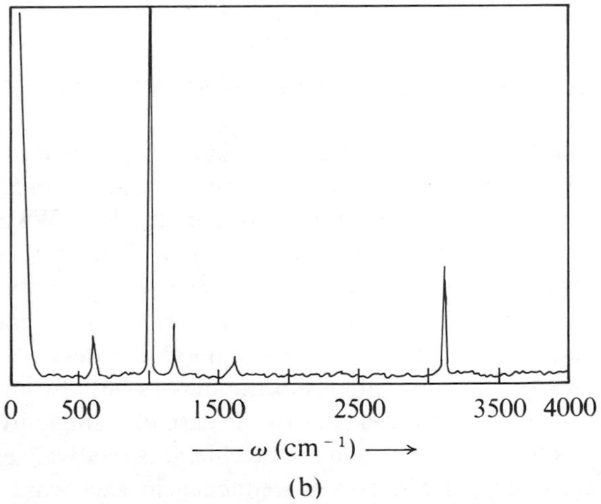

FIGURE 6-26 (a) Schematic diagram of a laser spectrometer, where ω_0 is the Raleigh frequency and ω_k the Raman frequency. (b) Rotation-vibration spectrum of the centrosymmetric benzene molecule.

nature of infrared and Raman spectroscopy. The Raman frequencies displayed in Figure 6-26b are infrared-inactive. The strong Raman-shifted frequencies occurring at 992 and 3062 cm^{-1} are the totally symmetric ring stretching and C—H stretching modes, respectively. Totally symmetric vibrational modes such as these are usually the most intense features in rotation-vibration Raman spectroscopy.

When the frequency of the incident laser source approaches an absorption (electronic) of the sample, there usually occurs a strong increase, or "resonance enhancement," of the scattering efficiency. The study of such resonance-scattering processes, in which the sample absorption may be important, is termed *resonance Raman* spectroscopy. In relating this effect to the vibrations of a molecule, we must distinguish between two regions of interaction: one characterizing the scattering of incident radiation having a frequency near but not within the strong electronic absorption of the scattering sample; and the other involving the scattering of incident radiation having a frequency within the strong electronic absorption of the sample. The former process is called pre-resonance Raman and the latter simply resonance Raman scattering.[11] In general, the pre-resonance experiments result in the significant intensity enhancement of the fundamentals, but no enhancement of overtone frequencies. On the other hand, the resonance experiments result in scattered frequencies corresponding to very high overtone progressions of fundamentals, allowing the evaluation of anharmonic constants. These overtone progressions almost exclusively correspond to totally symmetric vibrations.

E. CHARACTERISTIC GROUP FREQUENCIES

Relative to the fundamental vibrational frequencies of diatomic molecules, we noted the remarkable invariance of the vibrational force constants of certain atomic pairs in various polyatomic molecules. We also indicated that in addition to the simple stretching vibration of these "diatomic types," groups of atoms in certain molecules execute vibrational motions in concert that give rise to characteristic absorption frequencies. Strictly speaking, the vibrational frequency of a molecule depends not only on the force constants and amplitudes of the masses but also on anharmonic effects and chemical environment. In the case of a single hydrogen atom attached to N, C, S, and so on in a molecule, it is relatively easy to understand its constancy of absorption frequency in each case. Since H is always an end atom, it can only vibrate along the bond or perpendicular to it; in each case, the motion is essentially that of the H atom extended by a spring from an infinitely heavy mass. The chemical environment (localized electronic bond structure) on the other hand provides the basis for the force constant in each case, k_{N-H}, k_{C-H}, k_{S-H}, and so on. Applying these assumptions to Eq. (6-2) gives ω (cm^{-1}) = $(\frac{1}{2}\pi c)(k/m_H)^{1/2}$ for the fundamental vibration frequency in each case, which is dependent only on k_{M-H}. Characteristic M—H frequencies are shown in Table 6-4. On the other hand, when there is more than one hydrogen present either on adjacent atoms or on a common atom, such as

$$- CH_3, \quad \diagdown CH_2, \quad H_2C=CH_2,$$

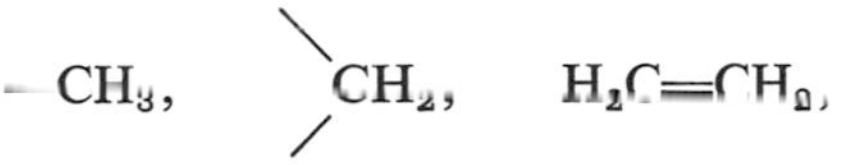

they all undergo significant bond displacements during a vibration and give rise to characteristic group frequencies. The resolved normal modes give rise to stretching motions that are described as symmetric (in phase) and antisymmetric (out of phase), while the bending motions are variously described as scissoring, wagging, twisting, and rocking motions. All these descriptions have been applied to the $=CH_2$ group in formaldehyde, Figure 6-17. The skeletal bonds of aliphatic and aromatic hydrocarbons also execute vibrational motions that give rise to approximately constant vibrational frequencies for

$$\diagup C - C \diagdown, \quad \diagup C = C \diagdown, \quad -C \equiv C-,$$

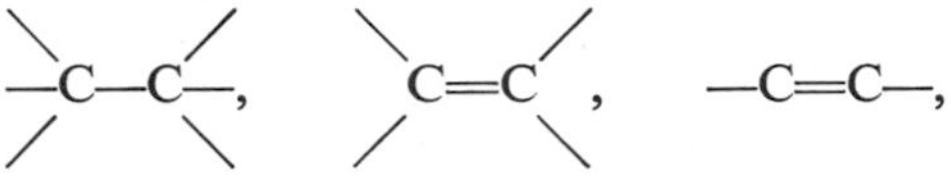

and the aromatic ring stretching. The reason for these approximate constant frequencies is that the simultaneous hydrogen displacements occur in such a manner (symmetrically) as to have the net effect of remaining unchanged during the skeletal stretches. Thus, the —C≡C— stretch in acetylene, is 1974 cm^{-1}, in methylacetylene is 2060 cm^{-1}, and in silylacetylene is 2055 cm^{-1}. Other vibrational motions that give rise to transferable frequencies are those due to heavy atoms that normally occur at relatively low frequencies. Examples are

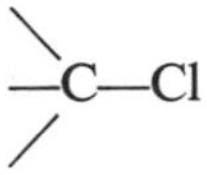

$$\diagdown C - Cl \quad \text{and} \quad \diagdown C - Br.$$

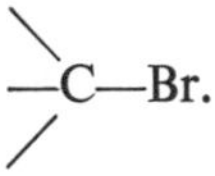

The vibrational interaction of these types of modes with the other frequencies of a given molecule is usually negligible. On the other hand, when several adjacent atoms are of comparable mass, the amplitudes of the several vibrational motions can and do lead to significant interaction, and significantly shifted absorption frequencies. For N=N=O, the "N=N" stretch is observed at 1285 cm^{-1} and the "N=O" stretch at 2224 cm^{-1}, compared with the expected characteristic "N=N" ($\sim$1800 cm^{-1}) and "N=O" (1600 cm^{-1}) frequencies. The "stretch-stretch"

TABLE 6-4. Characteristic Group Vibration Frequencies

Group	Stretching Motion (cm^{-1})	Group	Bending Motion (cm^{-1})
>N—H	3320	—CH_3 scissors	1460
—C—H (with > and < bonds)	2940	—CH_3 wag	1350
ϕ—H	3000	—C(=O)H	780
—S—H	2620	—CH_3 rock	1187
—CH_3 antisym str.	3040	>CH_2 scissors	1450
—CH_3 sym str.	2940	>CH_2 wag	1300
>C—C< (—C—C—)	1000	=CH_2 wag	880
>C=C<	1650	>CH_2 twist	1200
—C≡C—	2050	>CH_2 rock	850
—C—Cl	650	—NO_2 scissors	750
—C—Br	560	>CCl_2 scissors	280
—C—I	500	—NH_2 scissors	1623
>C=O	1750	—C≡C—H bend	700
—C≡N	2200	—C—C=O bend	500
—N≡O	1830	>C=C=C< bend	355
>N=O	1600	—NF_2 scissors	500
>N—O (—N—O)	850	H—O—H bend	1600

NOTE: Approximated to $\pm 100\ cm^{-1}$ or less in some cases.

interaction force constant for a simple valence force field in this case is 1.36 mdyn/Å, which is unusually large and accounts for the resulting shifted frequencies. If, however, the end nitrogen atom is replaced by the heavier F or Cl atom, the —N≡O gives rise again to absorption frequencies of 1845 or 1800 cm^{-1}, respectively. The approximately characteristic vibrational frequencies of several groups are summarized in Table 6-4.

This property of characteristic group frequency has been extremely useful not only to organic and inorganic chemists trying to identify stable unknowns but also to photochemists studying radical fragments. In the latter case, the unstable species is essentially "pieced together" by identifying certain bond types based on characteristic group frequencies.

F. INFRARED LASER APPLICATIONS IN CHEMISTRY

1. Laser-Induced Vibrational Fluorescence

Pulsed infrared lasers, particularly He—Ne and CO_2, have been used extensively since 1966 to study vibration to vibration ($V \rightarrow V$) as well as vibration to translation/rotation ($V \rightarrow R/T$) energy transfer processes. The experimental technique, generally described as *laser-induced vibrational fluorescence*, involves the laser excitation of a single vibrational energy level. Time-resolved fluorescence from either the initially excited vibrational level or from one or more other vibrational states excited via energy transfer is monitored by a suitable infrared detector, amplified and processed by a signal averager, and displayed on an X-Y recorder or an oscilloscope. A typical design of an experimental system used to study laser-induced vibrational fluorescence is shown in Figure 6-27.

Although much of the initial work involving studies of this nature was limited to laser pulse widths of at best ~ 1 μsec (full width half maximum), present commercially available CO_2 lasers have pulse widths of the order of nanoseconds. This factor establishes a natural limitation on how rapidly after the onset of the laser pulse observation of the system processes can be made. The importance of the laser pulse width is reflected by the fluorescence risetimes in these experiments; they can be considerably shorter than 1 μsec. Fluorescence detection from specific vibrational modes is accomplished by combining suitable detectors and interference filters. Depending on the intensity of the vibrational radiative intensity and the laser pulse rate, signal averaging may involve periods of minutes to an hour for data collecting. Intensity-vs-time is plotted on an X-Y recorder to obtain maximum resolution.

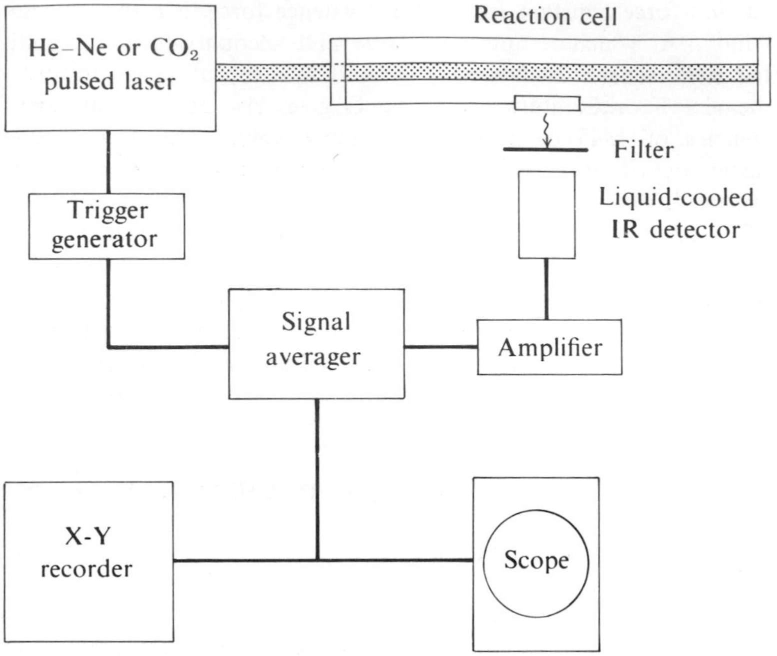

FIGURE 6-27 Schematic design of the experimental setup used to study $V \rightarrow V$ and $V \rightarrow R/T$ relaxation processes.

Although a host of workers have been very active in this research, two typical studies are those of C. Bradley Moore and co-workers and of G. W. Flynn and co-workers.[12,13] General observations that have come out of studying the vibrational relaxation of various simple polyatomic molecules are the following. This initially excited vibrational mode undergoes rapid $V \rightarrow V$ energy transfer. The initial equilibration process involving specific vibrational modes depends critically on how resonant a subsequent energy transfer process is that is initiated by the laser-excited vibrational mode and on the extent of mode coupling. As an example, the laser-excited ω_1 mode (1151 cm^{-1}) of SO_2 is so strongly coupled to the ω_3 mode (1361 cm^{-1}) that vibrational relaxation is observed to occur in approximately 135 collisions, whereas these levels are in turn weakly coupled to the bending mode ω_2 (518 cm^{-1}) and ω_2 is equilibrated with ω_1 and ω_3 in approximately 2600 collisions.[13] Following the rapid equilibration between certain vibrational modes (which actually defines a non-Boltzmann vibrational temperature), equilibration to translation and rotation occurs. Although, $V \rightarrow T/R$ is usually considerably longer (10 to 10^3) than $V \rightarrow V$ in general, in the example of SO_2 above, it occurs in about 300 collisions. This is an example of a slow $V \rightarrow V$ process.

2. Laser-Selective Chemical Reactions

As a result of the rapid progress in the development of powerful tunable infrared lasers, there has been considerable activity devoted to studying *IR-laser-selective chemical reactions.* These studies involve the selective excitation of a given vibrational mode in an attempt to (1) produce an exclusive reaction, where thermally there might be competing processes; (2) reduce the energy requirements for reaction, thereby photocatalyzing the process; (3) and possibly produce reaction paths and products that might generally be inaccessible via thermally generated Boltzmann routes. Details of these studies have been discussed in a review article.[14] The initial conditions for the successful generation of an IR-photocatalyzed process involve a highly intense monochromatic source capable of exciting a reactant molecule with relatively sharp narrow band widths, both of which are fairly easily realized. A more severe condition, however, is the conservation of selectivity in an excited vibrational mode prior to chemical reaction. In most systems studied to date, $V \rightarrow V$ relaxation and equilibration can occur in less than 50–100 collisions, whereas $V \rightarrow R/T$ generally require more than an order of magnitude longer. This situation places an additional restraint on the type of chemical reaction that can be studied, since the Boltzmann activation energy must be low enough that fewer collisions are required for reaction than for loss of vibrational selectivity. Actually, a given reaction may be catalyzed by selectivity, resulting from vibrational relaxation and equilibration, either in a single vibrational mode or in several. The period over which such vibrational equilibration exists essentially defines a non-Boltzmann vibrational temperature.

In any case, most important of all is that the photocatalytic chemical reaction rate should be faster than $V \rightarrow R/T$ relaxation, or what we observe would simply be a rapidly heated Boltzmann reaction. Many of the early experiments involving selective vibrational excitation were subsequently shown to be rapid thermal reactions, but more recent studies of the reaction of NO and vibrationally excited O_3 have apparently resulted in a photocatalytic effect as opposed to the purely thermal reaction.[15]

3. Photochemical Elimination Lasers

In a series of truly remarkable experiments, G. C. Pimentel and several co-workers recognized that HF and HCl are photoeliminated from a number of fluoroethylenic and chloroethylenic molecules in highly excited nonstatistical vibronic states.[16] Since one vibrational quantum of ground electronic state HF is roughly 11.4 kcal/mole and of HCl, 8.0 kcal/mole,

$V \rightarrow R/T$ relaxation in these systems is sufficiently long that oscillation (lasing action) is possible between the various population-inverted vibronic states. The $V \rightarrow R/T$ relaxation time within a given vibronic state is also lengthened by the large rotational spacings characteristic of these hydrogen halides (Section 6A-4). These so-called photochemical *elimination lasers* operate in the following manner. After the basic laser cavity design of Figure 2-5, a premixed sample of the active material (that is, $F_2C{=}CH_2$) diluted in argon is flash-photolyzed with a Xe flashlamp. These flashlamps generally reach peak intensity in a few microseconds and produce energies in the range 1–2 kilojoules. The vibronically excited HX molecule, which is photochemically eliminated, undergoes oscillation at the various vibrational frequencies corresponding to $\Delta \mathbf{v} = -1$ within the ground electronic vibrational manifold. More recently, M. J. Berry has used this technique to determine the relative photochemical product yields and HCl vibronic state distributions resulting from the flash-photolysis of several chloroethylenes.[16,17]

G. EVALUATING THE MOLECULAR FORCE FIELD (FG MATRIX METHOD)

One of the important aspects of studying vibrational spectroscopy is to understand the forces that hold atoms together in a molecule. The sum total of these forces in a molecule is usually referred to as the *molecular force field*, and is mathematically described by the potential energy function. Such a potential function is Eq. (6-18); evaluating the potential force constants (Eq. (6-20)) not only allows us to understand something of the forces between atoms, but in favorable cases will also provide information concerning the nature of the constituent chemical bonds. For relatively simple molecules, the procedure outlined in Section 6B-1, and the evaluation of the roots of the secular equation (Eq. (6-26)) giving numerical values of the f_{ij}'s, can be reasonably applied without extreme difficulty. In the cases of molecules containing four or more atoms, however, the more mathematically powerful method that E. Bright Wilson developed using techniques of group theory allows a considerable simplification of the secular equation.[18] We shall use this technique without proof for evaluating the secular equation of a nonlinear symmetric triatomic molecule.[19]

The secular determinantal equation derived by Wilson that we use is

$$|\mathbf{FG} - \mathbf{E}\lambda| = 0. \tag{6-65}$$

The symbol **F** represents a symmetrical matrix whose elements are linear combinations of elementary force constants derived from the potential-energy expression. The symbol **G** represents a symmetrical matrix whose elements are linear combinations of geometrical parameters (bond distances and angles) derived from the kinetic-energy expression. The symbol **E** represents a unit matrix and $\boldsymbol{\lambda}$ a diagonal matrix having elements $\lambda_i = 4\pi^2c^2\omega_i^2$. In most cases, the observed vibrational frequencies, ω_i's, are used to generate, for a particular molecule, a set of f_{ij}'s contained in the **F** matrix. The stepwise procedure we shall use in this *vibrational analysis* will be (1) constructing appropriate coordinates (internal symmetry coordinates); (2) constructing the **F** matrix; (3) constructing the **G** matrix; (4) evaluating the f_{ij}'s; and (5) determining the valence force-field potential function.

1. Internal Symmetry Coordinates

To use the simplifying techniques of group theory as they apply to the $3N - 6 \times 3N - 6$ secular equation, it is first necessary to construct internal symmetry coordinates. These are simply linear combinations of the internal coordinates. Internal coordinates ($\mathbf{s}_1$'s) are displacements from equilibrium bond lengths and angles—Δr_i's and $\Delta\theta_i$'s. Both the internal and symmetry coordinates are chosen in such a way that they also provide a basis for the various vibrational symmetry species or irreducible representations (Γ_{vib}'s.). That is, the internal symmetry coordinates constructed—$\mathbf{S}_1, \mathbf{S}_2, \ldots$—must transform like the vibrational symmetry species $\Gamma_1, \Gamma_2, \ldots$ under the group operations. Internal symmetry coordinates are easy to construct from equivalent internal coordinates, such as the two bond displacements Δr_1 and Δr_2 and the lone angle displacement $\Delta\theta$, in nonlinear symmetrical *BAB*. The three Δr_i's and the three $\Delta\theta_i$'s in pyramidal AB_3 are also two sets of equivalent internal displacement coordinates. The internal symmetry coordinates for nondegenerate vibrations can be conveniently generated using the following expression:[20]

$$\mathbf{S}_j^{(\Gamma_i)} = N \sum_k \chi_k^{(\Gamma_i)} R\mathbf{s}_1, \tag{6-66}$$

where $\mathbf{S}_j^{(\Gamma_i)}$ is the jth internal symmetry coordinate, Γ_i is the ith vibrational irreducible representation (symmetry species), N is a normalization constant, $\chi_k^{(\Gamma_i)}$ is the character of the kth operation belonging to the Γ_ith irreducible representation, and $R\mathbf{s}_1$ is the equivalent transformed coordinate resulting from the symmetry operation R. This sum needs to be applied to only as many of the group operations as are necessary to generate the different equivalent internal coordinates in each summation at least once. These prescriptions are probably best understood when applied to an example such as a nonlinear *BAB* species.

We showed in Example 5-1 that $\Gamma_{\text{vib}} = 2A_1 + B_1$, and that of the three internal symmetry coordinates generated, two must have A_1 symmetry and one must have B_1 symmetry. Thus, for the bond displacement Δr, we apply Eq. (6-66) to $\Delta r_1(\mathbf{s}_1)$, and obtain for the summation over the first two group (C_{2v}) operations ($\hat{E}\Delta r_1 + \hat{C}_2\Delta r_1$),

$$\mathbf{S}_{\Delta r}{}^{(A_1)} = N[\Delta r_1 + \Delta r_2]. \tag{6-67a}$$

Applying the normalization condition for these orthogonal internal coordinates yields

$$\begin{aligned} N^2 \int (\Delta r_1 + \Delta r_2)^2 \, d\tau \\ &= N^2\left[\int \Delta r_1{}^2 \, d\tau_1 + 2\int \Delta r_1 \, \Delta r_2 \, d\tau_{12} + \int \Delta r_2{}^2 \, d\tau_2\right] = 1 \\ &= N^2[1 + 0 + 1] = 1, \end{aligned} \tag{6-68}$$

and $N = 1/\sqrt{2}$. Using a similar procedure for the B_1 irreducible representation gives

$$\mathbf{S}_{\Delta r}{}^{(B_1)} = \frac{1}{\sqrt{2}}[\Delta r_1 - \Delta r_2]. \tag{6-67b}$$

Since the only internal coordinate remaining is $\Delta\theta$, and we require another A_1 irreducible representation, the internal symmetry coordinate is

$$\mathbf{S}_{\Delta\theta}{}^{(A_1)} = \Delta\theta. \tag{6-67c}$$

We should make a special note that the number of vibrational modes ($3N - 6$ or $3N - 5$) equals the number of internal coordinates and also the number of internal symmetry coordinates. These internal symmetry coordinates can be summarized as a system of linear equations:

$$\begin{aligned} \mathbf{S}_1 &= 0 + 0 + \Delta\theta \\ \mathbf{S}_2 &= \frac{\Delta r_1}{\sqrt{2}} + \frac{\Delta r_2}{\sqrt{2}} + 0 \\ \mathbf{S}_3 &= \frac{\Delta r_1}{\sqrt{2}} - \frac{\Delta r_2}{\sqrt{2}} + 0 \end{aligned} \tag{6-67}$$

This form will have special significance, as we shall see shortly.

2. The F Matrix

The potential energy in terms of internal symmetry coordinates is

$$2U = \sum_{ij} \mathbf{F}_{ij}\mathbf{S}_i\mathbf{S}_j, \tag{6-69}$$

where the $\mathbf{F}_{ij}$'s are the elements of the $\mathbf{F}$ matrix consisting of linear combinations of the f_{ij}'s. It is the evaluation of these elementary bond, angle, and interaction force constants that we want to obtain. An equivalent way of expressing the potential energy above, Eq. (6-69), in matrix notation is

$$2U = \mathbf{S'FS}, \tag{6-70}$$

where $\mathbf{S}$ is a column matrix and $\mathbf{S'}$ a row matrix, in terms of the internal coordinates; $\mathbf{S'}$ is the transpose of $\mathbf{S}$.[21] We need U in terms of $\mathbf{S}$ for maximum symmetry factoring and in terms of the f_{ij}'s for chemical and physical interpretation. The relation between the f_{ij}'s and $\mathbf{F}$ is

$$\mathbf{F} = \mathbf{UfU'}, \tag{6-71}$$

where $\mathbf{U}$ and its transpose $\mathbf{U'}$ are used to symmetry-factor the $\mathbf{f}$ matrix, which consists of the elements f_{ij}. The $\mathbf{f}$ matrix is generated by constructing a multiplication table of the internal coordinates as shown below for the nonlinear symmetrical *BAB*.

	Δr_1	Δr_2	$\Delta\theta$
Δr_1	f_r	f_{rr}	$f_{r\theta}$
Δr_2	f_{rr}	f_r	$f_{r\theta}$.
$\Delta\theta$	$f_{r\theta}$	$f_{r\theta}$	f_θ

(6-72)

The $\mathbf{U}$ matrix is simply the coefficients of Eq. (6-67), and its transpose $\mathbf{U'}$ in this case is simply the inverse $\mathbf{U}^{-1}$, since $\mathbf{U}$ describes a linear orthogonal transformation. Thus, $\mathbf{f}$ is symmetry-factored by applying Eq. (6-71):

$$\mathbf{F} = \begin{bmatrix} 0 & 0 & 1 \\ \frac{1}{\sqrt{2}} & \frac{1}{\sqrt{2}} & 0 \\ \frac{1}{\sqrt{2}} & \frac{-1}{\sqrt{2}} & 0 \end{bmatrix} \begin{bmatrix} f_r & f_{rr} & f_{r\theta} \\ f_{rr} & f_r & f_{r\theta} \\ f_{r\theta} & f_{r\theta} & f_\theta \end{bmatrix} \begin{bmatrix} 0 & \frac{1}{\sqrt{2}} & \frac{1}{\sqrt{2}} \\ 0 & \frac{1}{\sqrt{2}} & \frac{-1}{\sqrt{2}} \\ 1 & 0 & 0 \end{bmatrix}. \tag{6-73}$$

Ordinarily the $\mathbf{f}$ matrix would consist of nine independent force constants, but the symmetry of this molecule reduces it to only four. If we perform the indicated matrix operations of Eq. (6-73), we obtain

$$\mathbf{F} = \left[\begin{array}{cc|c} f_\theta & \sqrt{2}f_{r\theta} & 0 \\ \sqrt{2}f_{r\theta} & f_r + f_{rr} & 0 \\ \hline 0 & 0 & f_r - f_{rr} \end{array}\right]. \tag{6-74}$$

Although this example is relatively simple in some respects, it does illustrate symmetry factorization. The **f** matrix has been reduced from a 3×3 to a 2×2 and a 1×1 matrix along the diagonal.

3. The G Matrix

The **G** matrix is constructed like the **F** matrix since

$$\mathbf{G} = \mathbf{UgU}', \tag{6-75}$$

where **g** is the matrix that contains elements in terms of the atomic masses and the geometrical parameters. Carrying through the procedure as we did above for the **F** matrix, symmetry factorization of **g** gives (compare Eq. (6-74))

$$\mathbf{G} = \begin{bmatrix} g_\theta & \sqrt{2}g_{r\theta} & 0 \\ \sqrt{2}g_{r\theta} & g_r + g_{rr} & 0 \\ 0 & 0 & g_r - g_{rr} \end{bmatrix}. \tag{6-76}$$

The elements of the **G** matrix are directly obtainable from the expression for the kinetic energy

$$2T = \dot{\mathbf{S}}'\mathbf{G}^{-1}\dot{\mathbf{S}}, \tag{6-77}$$

where $\mathbf{G}^{-1}$ is the inverse **G** matrix, $\dot{\mathbf{S}}$ is the time derivative of the internal symmetry coordinate matrix, and $\dot{\mathbf{S}}'$ of the transpose. The generation of the **G** elements of Eq. (6-77) has been worked out and summarized not only for this case but also for general vibrational motions in Appendix VI of Wilson, Decius, and Cross, *Molecular Vibrations* [Reference 6-5]. For our *BAB* example:

$$\begin{aligned} g_\theta &= \frac{2[1/M_B + 1/M_A - (\cos\theta)/M_A]}{r^2} \\ g_{r\theta} &= -\left(\frac{1}{M_A r}\right)\sin\theta, \\ g_r &= \frac{1}{M_B} + \frac{1}{M_A}, \\ g_{rr} &= \frac{\cos\theta}{M_A}. \end{aligned} \tag{6-78}$$

For the H_2Se molecule, the following data allow us to evaluate the molecular force field:

$$r = 1.406\ \text{Å}$$

$$\theta = 91°$$

$$A_1 \begin{cases} \omega_1 = 2345\ \text{cm}^{-1} \\ \omega_2 = 1034\ \text{cm}^{-1} \end{cases}$$

$$M_A = M_{\text{Se}} = 78.96\ \text{amu}$$

$$B_1 \quad \omega_3 = 2358\ \text{cm}^{-1}$$

$$\begin{aligned} M_B &= M_{\text{H}} = 1.0078\ \text{amu} \\ g_\theta &= 1.0163\ \text{amu}^{-1}\ \text{Å}^{-2} \\ g_{r\theta} &= -0.0090\ \text{amu}^{-1}\ \text{Å}^{-1} \\ g_r &= 1.0049\ \text{amu}^{-1} \\ g_{rr} &= -0.0002\ \text{amu}^{-1} \end{aligned}$$

According to Eq. (6-65), the symmetry-factored secular determinant is given as

$$\begin{bmatrix} f_\theta & \sqrt{2}f_{r\theta} & 0 \\ \sqrt{2}f_{r\theta} & f_r + f_{rr} & 0 \\ 0 & 0 & f_r - f_{rr} \end{bmatrix} \begin{bmatrix} g_\theta & \sqrt{2}g_{r\theta} & 0 \\ \sqrt{2}g_{r\theta} & g_r + g_{rr} & 0 \\ 0 & 0 & g_r - g_{rr} \end{bmatrix} - \begin{bmatrix} \lambda_2 & 0 & 0 \\ 0 & \lambda_1 & 0 \\ 0 & 0 & \lambda_3 \end{bmatrix} = 0, \qquad \textbf{(6-79)}$$

which is decomposable into two parts, a two-dimensional A_1 matrix and a one-dimensional B_1 matrix. The B_1 equation relates the frequency of the antisymmetric (stretching) normal vibration to the stretching and stretching interaction force constants,

$$[f_r - f_{rr}][g_r - g_{rr}] = \lambda_3 = 4\pi^2c^2\omega_3^2 \qquad \textbf{(6-80)}$$

and

$$[f_r - f_{rr}](1.0051\ \text{amu}^{-1}) = 5.88985 \times 10^{-7}\omega_3^2\ \text{mdyn/Å-amu}, \qquad \textbf{(6-81)}$$

where ω_3 is expressed in cm^{-1} units. Substituting the frequency for ω_3 above, we obtain the force constant element

$$f_r - f_{rr} = 3.264\ \text{mdyn/Å}. \qquad \textbf{(6-82)}$$

For the A_1 two-dimensional matrix, we obtain

$$\left| \begin{bmatrix} f_\theta & \sqrt{2}f_{r\theta} \\ \sqrt{2}f_{r\theta} & f_r + f_{rr} \end{bmatrix} \begin{bmatrix} g_\theta & \sqrt{2}g_{r\theta} \\ \sqrt{2}g_{r\theta} & g_r + g_{rr} \end{bmatrix} - \begin{bmatrix} \lambda_2 & 0 \\ 0 & \lambda_1 \end{bmatrix} \right| = 0 \qquad \textbf{(6-83)}$$

On solving for Eq. (6-83), we shall generate a single equation containing two unknown force constants. Without additional vibrational data from an isotopically substituted molecule (which retains the C_{2v} symmetry), we are forced to make an approximation.

Since ω_1 and ω_2 differ by more than 1000 cm^{-1}, we can use the so-called high-frequency approximation, as a means of reducing the number of unknown force constants.[22] This is achieved by setting the low-frequency force constant f_θ to zero, which is equivalent to eliminating those rows and columns in **F** and **G** containing f_θ and g_θ. Since the expanded form of Eq. (6-83) would ordinarily involve the product of the eliminated **F** and **G** rows and their corresponding λ, then λ_2 will also vanish. Therefore Eq. (6-83) reduces to

$$[f_r + f_{rr}][g_r + g_{rr}] = \lambda_2 = 5.88985 \times 10^{-7}\,\omega_1^2. \qquad \textbf{(6-84)}$$

Substituting ω_1 and $(g_r + g_{rr})$ from above, we obtain

$$f_r + f_{rr} = 3.229 \text{ mdyn/Å}. \qquad \textbf{(6-85)}$$

Thus, the stretching and corresponding stretching interaction force constants obtained by successively adding and subtracting Eqs. (6-85) and (6-82) are $f_r = 3.246$ and $f_{rr} = 0.017$ mdyn/Å.

An equivalent form of the high-frequency approximation is to set the diagonal stretching force constant element in Eq. (6-83) to infinity. This has the effect of essentially "freezing" the high-frequency motions and thus eliminating their contribution to the kinetic and potential energy expressions. As a result, in this case, the corresponding row, column, and λ_1 will vanish. Therefore,

$$[f_\theta][g_\theta] = \lambda_2 = 5.88985 \times 10^{-7}\,\omega_2^2. \qquad \textbf{(6-86)}$$

Substituting g_θ and ω_2 from above, we obtain

$$f_\theta = 0.620 \text{ mdyn-Å}, \qquad \textbf{(6-87)}$$

which must be divided by the product of the bond distances r_1r_2(Å^2) for conversion to millidynes/Å; thus, $f_\theta/r^2 = 0.620/1.977 = 0.314$ mdyn/Å.

The molecular valence force field, Eq. (6-19), for this symmetrical AB_2 molecule is

$$2U = f_r\,\Delta r_1^2 + f_r\,\Delta r_2^2 + f_\theta(\Delta\theta)^2 + 2f_{rr}\,\Delta r_1\,\Delta r_2, \qquad \textbf{(6-88)}$$

where the $f_{r\theta}$ interaction term is assumed negligible. On collecting terms, we get

$$U = \tfrac{1}{2}f_r(\Delta r_1^2 + \Delta r_2^2) + \tfrac{1}{2}f_\theta(\Delta\theta)^2 + f_{rr}\,\Delta r_1\,\Delta r_2. \qquad \textbf{(6-88a)}$$

Substituting $f_r = 3.246$ mdyn/Å, $f_\theta = 0.620$ mdyn-Å, and $f_{rr} = 0.017$ mdyn/Å, we obtain

$$U = 1.623 \times 10^{-5}(\Delta r_1{}^2 + \Delta r_2{}^2) + 0.310 \times 10^{-11}(\Delta\theta)^2 - 0.017 \times 10^{-5}(\Delta r_1\, \Delta r_2) \text{ erg} \qquad (6\text{-}89)$$

where a mdyn/Å $= 10^{-5}$ dyn/cm and a mdyn-Å = erg/radian^2.

Expressions such as these are extremely useful in constructing potential-energy surfaces for small displacements from the equilibrium configuration. As an example, if we fix the bond angle $\Delta\theta$ in Eq. (6-89), we can construct a three-dimensional plot of the ground potential surface of H_2Se, with coordinates Δr_1 and Δr_2, and energy.

SELECTED BIBLIOGRAPHY

6-1. Davidson, Norman. *Statistical Mechanics.* New York: McGraw-Hill Book Co., 1962.

6-2. Davis, Jeff C., Jr. *Advanced Physical Chemistry.* New York: Ronald Press Co., 1965.

6-3. Herzberg, Gerhard. *Molecular Spectra and Molecular Structure, Infrared and Raman Spectra of Polyatomic Molecules.* Vol. II. Princeton, N.J.: Van Nostrand Co., 1945. (Classic.)

6-4. Levine, Ira N. *Quantum Chemistry*, Volume II: *Molecular Spectroscopy.* Boston: Allyn and Bacon, 1970.

6-5. Wilson, E. Bright, Jr., Decius, J. C., and Cross, Paul C. *Molecular Vibrations.* New York: McGraw-Hill Book Co., 1955. (Classic.)

GLOSSARY OF SYMBOLS

ω	Fundamental vibration frequency, cm^{-1}, MHz, etc.
k or f_{ij}	Vibrational force constant, millidynes/Angstrom
$\tilde{B}_v$	Rotational constant, cm^{-1}
q_i	Normal modes
Q_i	Normal coordinates
Φ_{Fg}	Direction cosine
$\mathbf{P}$	Induced polarization
α	Molecular polarizability, cm^3
$\mathbf{F}$	Force constant matrix
$\mathbf{G}$	Geometrical parameters matrix
$\mathbf{S}_i$	Internal symmetry coordinate

ENDNOTES

1. Where we note that these are derivatives of displacement coordinates,

$$\dot{x}_k = \frac{d\Delta x_k}{dt},$$

and so on.

2. Compare with Eq. (4-3).
3. For the coordinate $j = i$ in the summation of Eq. (6-17),

$$\frac{d}{dt}\left(\frac{\partial T}{\partial \dot{q}_j}\right) = \frac{d}{dt}\dot{q}_j = \ddot{q}_j,$$

and for the summation of Eq. (6-19),

$$\frac{\partial U}{\partial q_j} = \frac{1}{2}\left[\frac{\partial}{\partial q_j}\sum_{i=1}^{3N}\sum_{j=1}^{3N} f_{ij}q_iq_j\right] = \frac{1}{2}\left[2\sum_{i=1}^{3N} f_{ij}q_i\right].$$

4. $\mathbf{l}^{-1} = \mathbf{l}^{1}$.
5. H_{v} is the Hermite polynomial.
6. Excellent detailed discussion of the direction cosines is given in References 6-4, 6-5, and 4-3.
7. As in the diatomic case, even T states are symmetric for bosons and antisymmetric for fermions, and odd T states are antisymmetric for bosons and symmetric for fermions.
8. See Figure 2-5.
9. The true ratio of the intensity of the Stokes lines to the anti-Stokes lines is

$$\frac{I(\text{Stokes})}{I(\text{anti-Stokes})} = \left(\frac{\omega_0 - \omega_k}{\omega_0 + \omega_k}\right)^4 \exp\frac{E_k - E_0}{kT}.$$

10. Deriving these selection rules is considered in Reference 6-5, p. 365. The direction cosine integrals from which these selection rules are derived contain quadratic terms in these cases and have the general form

$$\int \psi_{\mathbf{r}'}{}^{*}\Phi_{Fg}\Phi_{F'g'}\psi_{\mathbf{r}''}\, d\tau_{\mathbf{r}}.$$

11. W. Kieffer and H. J. Bernstein, *Mol. Phys.* **23**, No. 5, 835 (1972).
12. R. V. Steele, Jr. and C. Bradley Moore, *J. Chem. Phys.* **60**:2794 (1974) and references cited therein.
13. F. W. Grabiner and G. W. Flynn, *J. Chem. Phys.* **60**:398 (1974), and references cited therein.
14. V. S. Letokhov, *Science* **180**:451 (1973).
15. W. Braun, M. J. Kuryls, A. Kaldor, and R. P. Wayne, *J. Chem. Phys.* **61**:461 (1975); R. J. Gordon and M. C. Lin, *Chem. Phys. Lett.* **22**:262 (1973).
16. J. A. Parker and G. C. Pimentel, *J. Chem. Phys.* **55**:857 (1971); M. J. Berry and G. C. Pimentel, *J. Chem. Phys.* **53**:3453 (1970).
17. M. J. Berry, *J. Chem. Phys.* **61**:3114 (1974).
18. E. Bright Wilson, *J. Chem. Phys.* **7**:1047 (1939).

19. The procedure used here follows the original one summarized in Reference 6-5, but also adopts the simplicity and clarity of Reference 5-1.
20. For degenerate vibrations, see Reference 6-5, p. 119.
21. The transpose of a matrix **S** is matrix **S′**, obtained by exchanging rows and columns $\mathbf{S}_{ij} = \mathbf{S}_{ji}'$.
22. Reference 6-5, p. 76.

PROBLEMS

6-1. Given the spectroscopic constants $\omega_e = 536.10$ cm^{-1} and $\omega_e x_e = 3.83$ cm^{-1} for NaF, calculate the approximate frequencies of the second, third, and fourth harmonics.

6-2. Using Table 6-1, calculate the approximate vibrational frequencies you might expect to observe for the C—H stretch in an aromatic and an aliphatic compound.

6-3. Estimate the approximate C═C stretching frequency you might expect for tetrafluoroethylene. The observed frequency is 1872 cm^{-1}. How would you account for this difference?

6-4. Given the fundamental vibration frequency of HCl as 2990 cm^{-1}, estimate the fundamental vibration frequency of DCl.

6-5. Consider a two-dimensional harmonic oscillator in the *xy* plane.

$$U = \frac{1}{2}k(x^2 + y^2) = \frac{k}{2}(r^2)$$

and

$$\nabla^2 = \frac{\partial^2}{\partial x^2} + \frac{\partial^2}{\partial y^2} = \frac{1}{r}\frac{\partial}{\partial r}\left(r\frac{\partial}{\partial r}\right) + \frac{1}{r^2}\frac{\partial^2}{\partial \phi^2}.$$

a. Set up the wave equation in plane polar coordinates and carry out the separation of variables.

b. Explain the physical significance of the separation constant associated with the angular equation and why it can take on only certain values; list the allowed values. Write the general solution to the angular equation.

6-6. For the linear OCS molecule determine the following:

a. The total number of vibrational modes that are active in the infrared.

b. Draw the normal modes of vibration and indicate which, if any, will have a *Q* branch.

c. Three absorptions are observed in the infrared spectrum of OCS. If this number differs from the total allowed, how would you explain this difference?

6-7. Use the rules outlined in the chapter (Section 6B-2) for assigning the normal modes of vibration for OCS ($C_{\infty v}$) and NF_3 (C_{3v}) to specific frequency designations ω_i based on the irreducible representations they belong to. Use can be made of Figures 6-5 and 6-13. Using the information in the accompanying chart, make the numerical assignments:

NF_3	Frequency (cm^{-1})	OCS	Frequency (cm^{-1})
Sym. stretch	1032	CO stretch	2062
Deg. stretch	907	CS stretch	859
Sym. deform	647	Bend	520
Deg. deform	492		

6-8. Assign the weak features at 1167, 2462, 2564, 2798, 3366, and 3481 cm^{-1} in the infrared spectrum of N_2O (Figure 6-8) to specific overtones and combinations.

6-9. Explain why the 1167 cm^{-1} absorption in the N_2O spectrum is for an overtone relatively intense and not an exact multiple of the bending fundamental.

6-10. Predict the intensity pattern of the rotation-vibration spectrum of the parallel vibrations of C_2N_2 assuming the classical limit in the rotational population distribution. Given $I(N) = 1$, $I(C) = 0$.

6-11. Draw the energy levels of the ground and first vibrational states of $CO_2(\omega_3)$ in its ground electronic state ($\psi_{\mathbf{v}} \overset{(i)}{\rightarrow} - \psi_{\mathbf{v}}$, for $\mathbf{v} = 1$). Also draw the spectrum resulting from the transitions $\Delta J = \pm 1$ and $\Delta \mathbf{v} = 1$. Is there any unusual feature?

6-12. For the CO_2 molecule obtain the vibrational symmetry and describe the rotation-vibration interaction that splits the doubly degenerate (0, 1, 0) state.

6-13. For GeH_4 with a rotational constant $B = 2.87$ cm^{-1}, calculate the Coriolis coupling constants for ω_3 and ω_4 and interpret the physical significance of their magnitudes on the rotation-vibration bands. The rotational spacing for the ω_3 band is 5.50 cm^{-1} and for the ω_4 band is 2.86 cm^{-1}.

6-14. Even at high BF_3 pressures, the low-resolution spectrum of the 1359 cm^{-1} band has an apparent symmetrical P, Q, R structure with a sharp single Q absorption. Explain how this observation further confirms the combination assignment of $\omega_1 + \omega_4$.

6-15. Draw the rotational Raman spectrum of $^{14}N_2$ and the rotation-vibration spectrum of ω_3 of $^{12}C^{16}O_2$, including nuclear-spin statistics.

6-16. Derive the internal symmetry coordinates for the pyramidal AB_3 molecule and illustrate the symmetry factorization of the **F** matrix.

6-17. Do the complete vibrational analysis of the bent HDSe molecule, assuming the same geometrical parameters used for H_2Se. Make any approximations necessary about the force constants. For HDSe, ω_1 (SeD stretch) = 1691, ω_2 (bend) = 912, and ω_3 (SeH stretch) = 2352 cm^{-1}. Reference 6-5, pp. 303–306, should be consulted for constructing the **G** matrix.

6-18. For the pyramidal symmetric top molecule deuterated ammonia, ND_3, determine the following:

a. The number and kinds of symmetry operations.
b. The point group designation.
c. One of the infrared vibrations is the symmetric bending motion as shown in the accompanying drawing. Deduce the characters for each symmetry operation on this motion, using the displacement vectors as a basis (+1 unaffected; −1, changed) and on such a basis determine symmetry species (A_i, B_i, E_i, etc.).

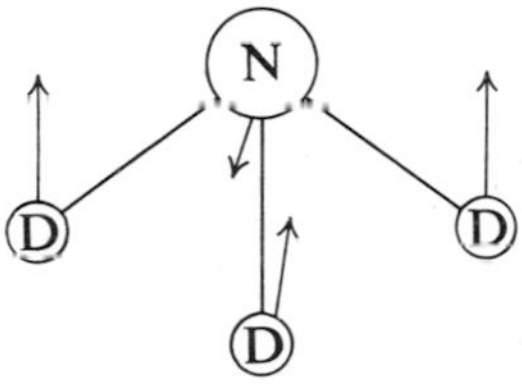

Chapter 7

Electronic Spectroscopy

The approximation of Born and Oppenheimer provides a means of separating the electronic and nuclear motions of a molecule (see beginning of Chapter 4). That approximation assumes that the time-independent wavefunction for the molecular system can be reasonably approximated as

$$\psi = \psi_e(\ldots x_i, y_i, z_i, \ldots)\psi_n(\ldots x_j, y_j, z_j, \ldots), \tag{7-1}$$

where i refers to the electrons and j to the nuclei. Using this wavefunction in the Schrödinger equation (Eq. (2-8)) and applying the general separation of variables procedure, we obtain terms for first and second derivatives of the electronic wavefunction with respect to the coordinates of the nuclei,

$$\frac{\partial\psi_e}{\partial x_j}, \frac{\partial\psi_e}{\partial y_j}, \ldots \quad \text{and} \quad \frac{\partial^2\psi_e}{\partial x_j^2}, \frac{\partial^2\psi_e}{\partial y_j^2}, \ldots$$

It is assumed that these terms are negligible or that the electronic motion occurs so rapidly relative to the nuclear motion that the nuclei are for all practical purposes fixed. This assumption, in essence, is the Born-Oppenheimer approximation, and allows applying Eq. (4-1) to the problems we shall undertake.

A. DIATOMIC MOLECULES

1. Classification of Electronic States (Term Symbols)

To determine the nature of the energy levels of molecular electronic states and the allowed electric dipole transitions between them, we must

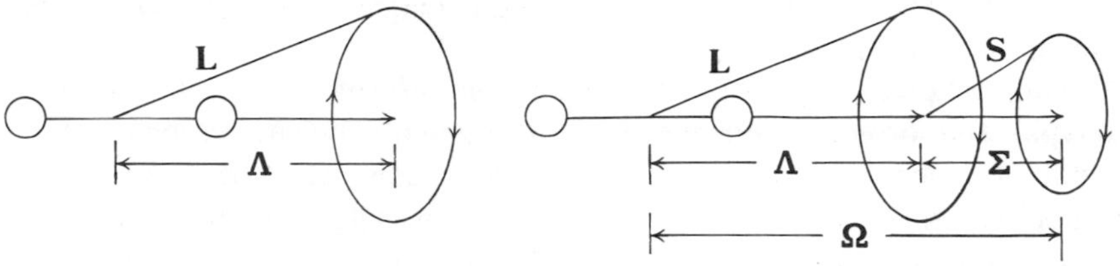

FIGURE 7-1 (a) The vector diagram illustrating the coupling of **L** about the electric field along the internuclear axis producing the axial component **Λ**. (b) Vector (or algebraic) addition of **Λ** + **Σ**, producing the total electronic angular momentum vector **Ω**.

first classify the various states, as the atomic electronic term states have been classified. The basis of this term symbol description is the electronic orbital angular momentum **L**. In a diatomic molecule, the electronic cloud has axial symmetry about the internuclear axis of the molecule. As a result **L** is not a constant of the motion (that is, not constant in direction and magnitude) but can take on certain quantized projections relative to the internal electric field along the internuclear axis from $+L, L - 1, \ldots$ to $-L$. The component of **L** along the axis, which *is* a constant of the motion, is **Λ**, and its magnitude is $\Lambda\hbar$. The vector diagram illustrating the coupling **L** about the internuclear axis is shown in Figure 7-1a. As far as the molecule is concerned, the coupling of **L** in the positive or negative direction producing $+\Lambda$ or $-\Lambda$ has the same energy. Thus, each $\mathbf{\Lambda} \neq 0$ state is doubly degenerate. There are symbols for the molecular electronic states like the atomic term symbols; states having

$$\Lambda = 0, 1, 2, 3, 4, \ldots,$$

are labeled, respectively

$$\Sigma, \Pi, \Delta, \Phi, \Gamma, \ldots.$$

As in the atomic case, the individual electronic spins vectorially add to produce integral or half-integral spin quantum numbers depending on whether there is an even or an odd number of electrons. In the case where there is net spin angular momentum, **S** may or may not have a component along the internuclear axis that can couple with **Λ**. If $\mathbf{\Lambda} \neq 0$, the electronic angular momentum will generate an internal magnetic field along the internuclear axis to which **S** can couple, producing the axial spin component **Σ** (to be distinguished from the $\Lambda = 0$, Σ state). The Σ state can take on all quantized spin orientations relative to the internal magnetic field from $+S, S - 1, \ldots$ to $-S$. If $\mathbf{\Lambda} = 0$, then **S** will not have spaced-fixed components, since no axial magnetic field is produced. The coupling of **S** to the axial magnetic field for $\mathbf{\Lambda} \neq 0$ is shown in Figure 7-1b.

For relatively light diatomics (low nuclear charge), weak coupling of spin and orbital electronic angular momenta occurs to produce a resultant component along the internuclear axis, $\mathbf{\Omega} = |\mathbf{\Lambda} + \mathbf{\Sigma}|$. The symbol $\mathbf{\Omega}$, which is a constant of the motion, is called the total electronic angular momentum vector. The number of components of an $\mathbf{\Omega}$ state will simply be equal to the spin multiplicity, $2S + 1$, since the various Ω states are generated by vector addition of a fixed $\mathbf{\Lambda}$ value with various allowed spin orientations ($\Sigma = +S, S - 1, \ldots$ to $-S$). Consequently, an electronic state with $\Lambda = 1$ and $S = 1$ ($\Sigma = +1, 0$, and -1) will have *naturally* occurring triplet components $\Lambda + 1, \Lambda + 0$, and $\Lambda - 1$ separated by the spin-orbit ($\mathbf{\Lambda}, \mathbf{S}$) interaction energy. In addition, each of these states is also doubly degenerate (and not split) by virtue of the $\pm\Lambda$ degeneracy. In a manner analogous to the atomic term symbol, the designation of an electronic state is given as $^{2S+1}\Lambda_{\Omega}$, where $2S + 1$ is the multiplicity, Λ is the electronic orbital angular momentum, and Ω is the total electronic angular momentum. Applied to the example above, we obtain the states $^3\Pi_2$, $^3\Pi_1$, and $^3\Pi_0$. The splitting of the multiplet is directly proportional to both the $\mathbf{\Lambda}$ and the $\mathbf{\Sigma}$ vectors, and as a result, the shift in energy from the unperturbed level of a given electronic state E_e is

$$\pm\, \xi_{\Lambda\Sigma}\Lambda\Sigma, \tag{7-2}$$

where $\xi_{\Lambda\Sigma}$ is the spin-orbit coupling constant. Since Λ has a fixed value for a given multiplet, the splittings are equal in magnitude. The coupling constant, however, may be either positive or negative, so that the ordering of the various Ω states may be regular or inverted, and in general must be experimentally determined. Assuming $\xi_{\Lambda\Sigma}$ to be positive for the example above, we obtain for the multiplet having regular ordering, $^3\Pi_r$.[1]

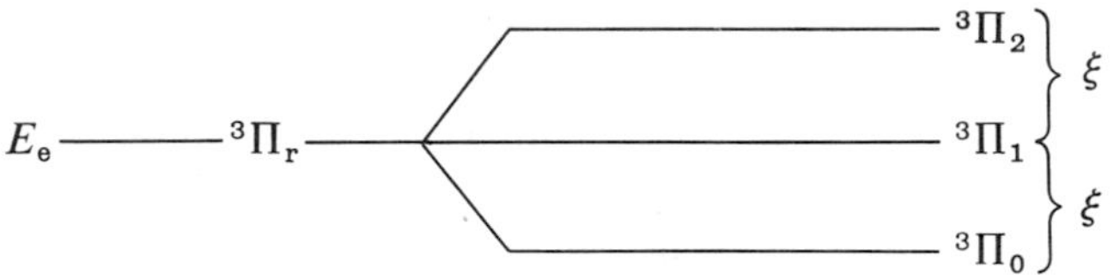

with a splitting of ξ. The order of magnitude of these coupling constants for relatively light diatomics is a few wavenumbers, but for the lowest $^3\Pi$ state of I_2, ξ is about 3975 cm^{-1}. Transitions involving this state are observed to violate the singlet-singlet multiplicity selection rule, as we observed for heavy-atom electronic transitions. Clearly, in the case of heavy-atom diatomics also, **S**, $\mathbf{\Lambda}$, and $\mathbf{\Sigma}$ vectors have all lost their meaning as quantized angular momenta, and only $\mathbf{\Omega}$ is a constant of the motion.

This situation is analogous to the change from *LS* to *jj* coupling in the atomic case. As a result, the components of a multiplet are probably best considered as separate electronic states.

In considering diatomics, we are primarily concerned with cases in which **S**, **Σ**, **Λ**, and **Ω** adequately represent the quantized electronic angular momenta. In an actual isolated molecule, however, the total molecular angular momentum results from the vectorial coupling of electronic spin angular momentum, electronic orbital angular momentum, and the nuclear rotational angular momentum. The four important types of coupling that occur are variously described as Hund's cases (a) through (d), and summarized in Herzberg [Reference 7-4]. The most frequent of these are (a) and (b), the only two that will concern us in our discussion of diatomics. In both cases, the quantized angular momenta **S** and **Λ** (when $\mathbf{\Lambda} \neq 0$) are good representations of the electronic spin and orbital angular momenta, respectively. In case (a), illustrated in Figure 7-1b, when $\mathbf{\Lambda} \neq 0$, weak coupling occurs between **Ω** and **R**, producing the *total*

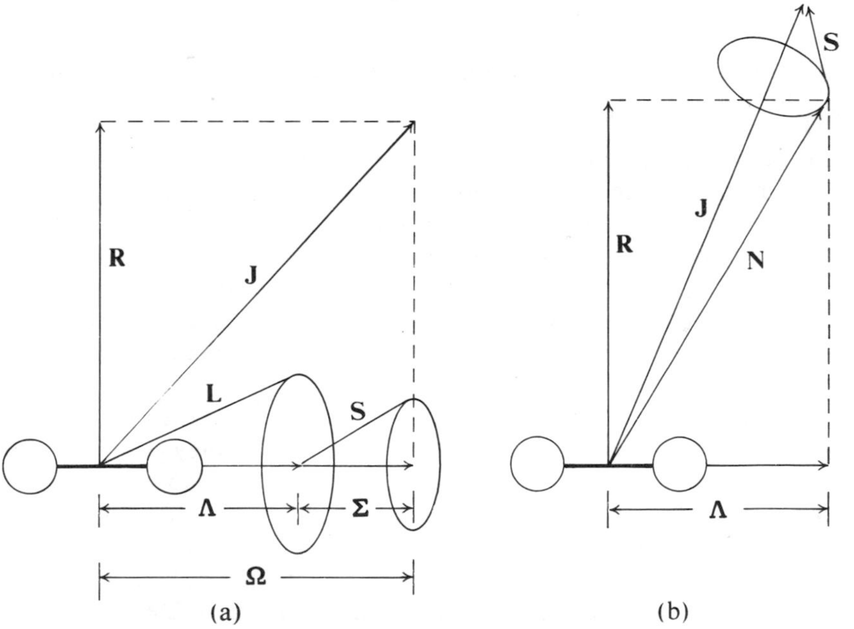

FIGURE 7-2 Vector diagram of Hund's cases (a) and (b). Case (a): Strong coupling of **L** and **S** about the internuclear axis and weak coupling of **Ω** and **R** about the total molecular angular momentum vector **J**. Case (b): **Λ** and **R** couple directly to produce **N**. **N** and **S** are in turn weakly coupled to the total molecular angular momentum vector **J**.

molecular angular momentum **J**. The vectorial component **R** of the nuclear rotational angular momentum is normal to the internuclear axis. When $\Lambda = 0$, **S** does not couple along the axis, thus **Ω** and **Σ** are not defined. If $\mathbf{S} \neq 0$, it can couple directly with **R** to form **J**. Cases like these, where **S** is either not coupled at all to the internuclear axis or very weakly coupled to it, are called Hund's case (b). In case (b), where $\boldsymbol{\Lambda} \neq 0$, **Λ** first couples with **R** to produce the resultant **N**, after which **N** in turn couples with **S** to form **J**. The vector **N** represents the total molecular angular momentum, apart from spin. The important point is that in practically all our discussions of the electronic spectra of diatomic molecules, **S**, **Σ**, **Λ**, and **Ω** are all "good" quantum numbers subject to Hund's case either (a) or (b). The two cases are illustrated in Figure 7-2. We should remark here for clarity that **J** was previously used to characterize the nuclear rotational angular momentum. This usage is valid only for molecules having $^1\Sigma$ electronic states, and characterizing such quantized rotational states by the corresponding quantum numbers J should be confined to these cases.

2. Determination of Molecular Electronic Configuration (Molecular Orbital Approach)

To classify ground and excited states of specific diatomic molecules, we must first have a means of determining the ordering of the energy levels as a function of the electronic configuration, preferably in terms of the quantum numbers discussed in the previous section.

Two basic approaches have been used in describing the molecular energy states of diatomic (and polyatomic) molecules; the valence-bond method and the molecular orbital method. In both methods, the wavefunction characterizing the electronic state is constructed from the atomic wavefunctions (hybridized or unhybridized orbitals). In the valence-bond approach, the electronic state wavefunction is taken simply as the product of the atomic wavefunctions, but in the molecular orbital (MO) approach, the atomic wavefunctions are first linearly combined to form MO's, and the product of these MO's is taken as the electronic state wavefunction. Since the MO approach has been more successful not only in predicting the ordering of electronic state manifolds as a function of energy, but also in explaining the relative magnitudes of other properties such as bond order, relative bond strength, ionization potential, and stability, we shall consider only this approach.

In this case, we assume that the two nuclei are held at some fixed distance from each other, corresponding to the internuclear distance for a specific molecule. It is also assumed that the electronic cloud about the nuclei is axially symmetric about the internuclear axis. Such a system is usually referred to as a two-center system. In addition to the spin quantum number, the other three quantum numbers used to describe the electronic configuration depend on whether the internuclear distance is very large ($r \to \infty$) or very small ($r \to 0$). At all distances, the orbital angular momentum of a single electron along the internuclear axis is adequately described by the vector $\boldsymbol{\lambda}$, whose magnitude is $\lambda\hbar$. For electrons having values of $\lambda = 0, 1, 2, 3, \ldots$, the corresponding symbols are $\sigma, \pi, \delta, \phi, \ldots$. The magnitude of λ determines the shape of the electronic cloud in space; σ states are symmetric about the internuclear axis and have zero net angular momentum, while $\lambda \neq 0$ for the other states and the molecule will have net electronic angular momentum about the internuclear axis.

For the case where r approaches zero, we assume that the state of the diatomic molecule approaches the state of the united atom. For diatomics having relatively small internuclear distances, such as H_2 and hydrides in general, the atomic quantum numbers n and ℓ are still approximately defined. The orientations of ℓ relative to the internal electric field along the internuclear axis are $\lambda = \pm|\ell|, \pm|\ell - 1|, \pm|\ell - 2|, \ldots, 0$, where the $+$ or $-$ of the absolute m_ℓ values represents the double degeneracy of the $\lambda \neq 0$ states corresponding to the positive and negative directions along the internuclear axis. The MO's corresponding to these approximate internuclear separations are symbolized as $n\ell\lambda$. Thus, the states generated for the principal quantum numbers $n = 1$, 2, and 3 in order of increasing energy are $1s\sigma$, $2s\sigma$, $2p\sigma$, $2p\pi$, $3s\sigma$, $3p\sigma$, $3p\pi$, $3d\sigma$, $3d\pi$, and $3d\delta$. The energy-level diagrams for diatomics of equal and unequal nuclear charge approaching the united atom are shown in Figure 7-3.

In the case of diatomics that have internuclear distances significantly larger than the hydrides, the united atom approximation is no longer adequate, and the MO description is approached from the other extreme, the separated atoms. The MO's are constructed from a linear combination of atomic orbitals (LCAO). In this approach, the linear combination in each case produces two MO's, one resulting in attraction and the overlap of the two AO's, the other resulting in repulsion and a nodal plane corresponding to zero electron density. The attractive overlapping MO is termed *bonding* and the repulsive one *antibonding*. Those that are antibonding are indicated by an asterisk in Figure 7-3. Qualitatively, a bonding orbital is regarded as one that makes a positive contribution toward the stability of a molecular state, whereas an antibonding orbital is regarded as contributing instability to a molecular state. Thus according to Herzberg, if the number of bonding electrons is greater than the number of antibonding electrons, we should expect a stable molecular state. If on the other hand, the number of antibonding electrons is equal to or

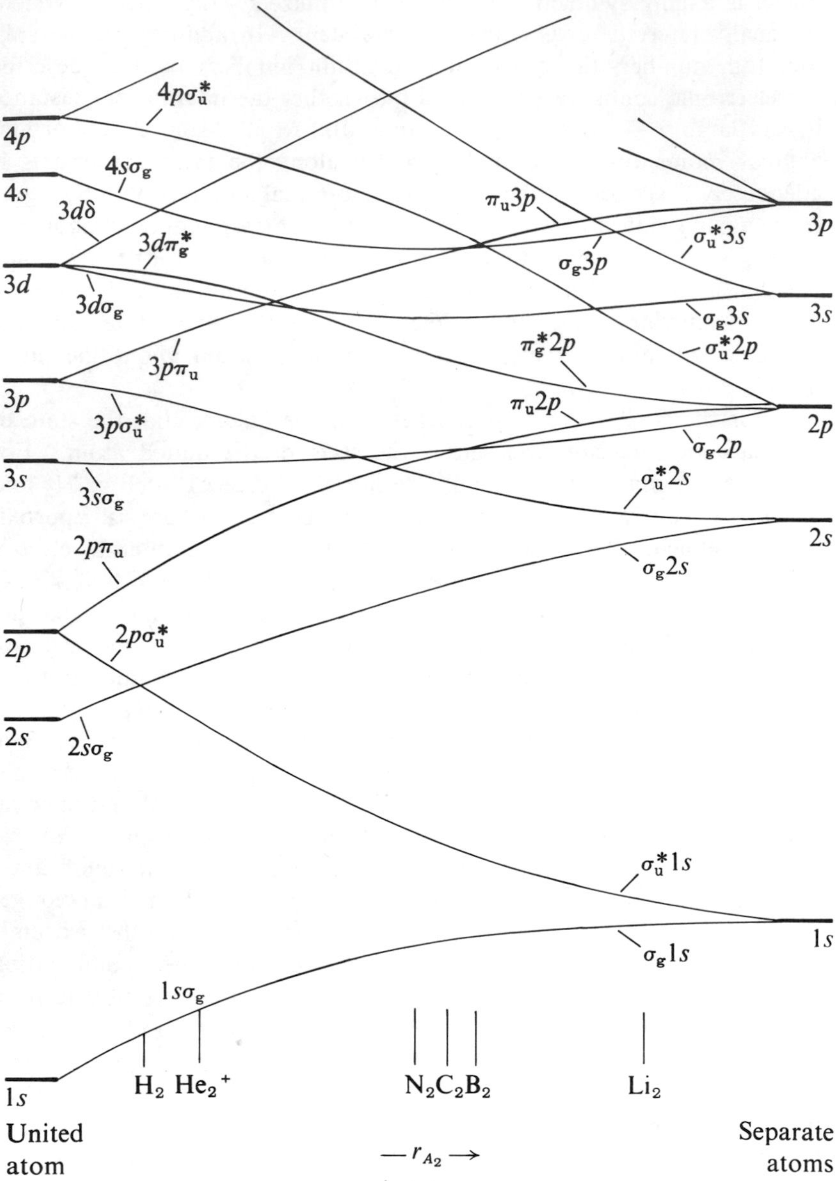

4p
4s
3d
3p
3s
2p
2s
1s
United atom
4pσu*
4sσg
3dδ
3dπg*
3dσg
3pπu
3pσu*
3sσg
2pπu
2pσu*
2sσg
1sσg
H2 He2+
N2C2B2
Li2
πu3p
σg3p
σu*3s
σg3s
σu*2p
πg*2p
πu2p
σg2p
σu*2s
σg2s
σu*1s
σg1s
3p
3s
2p
2s
1s
Separate atoms
— rA2 →

(a)

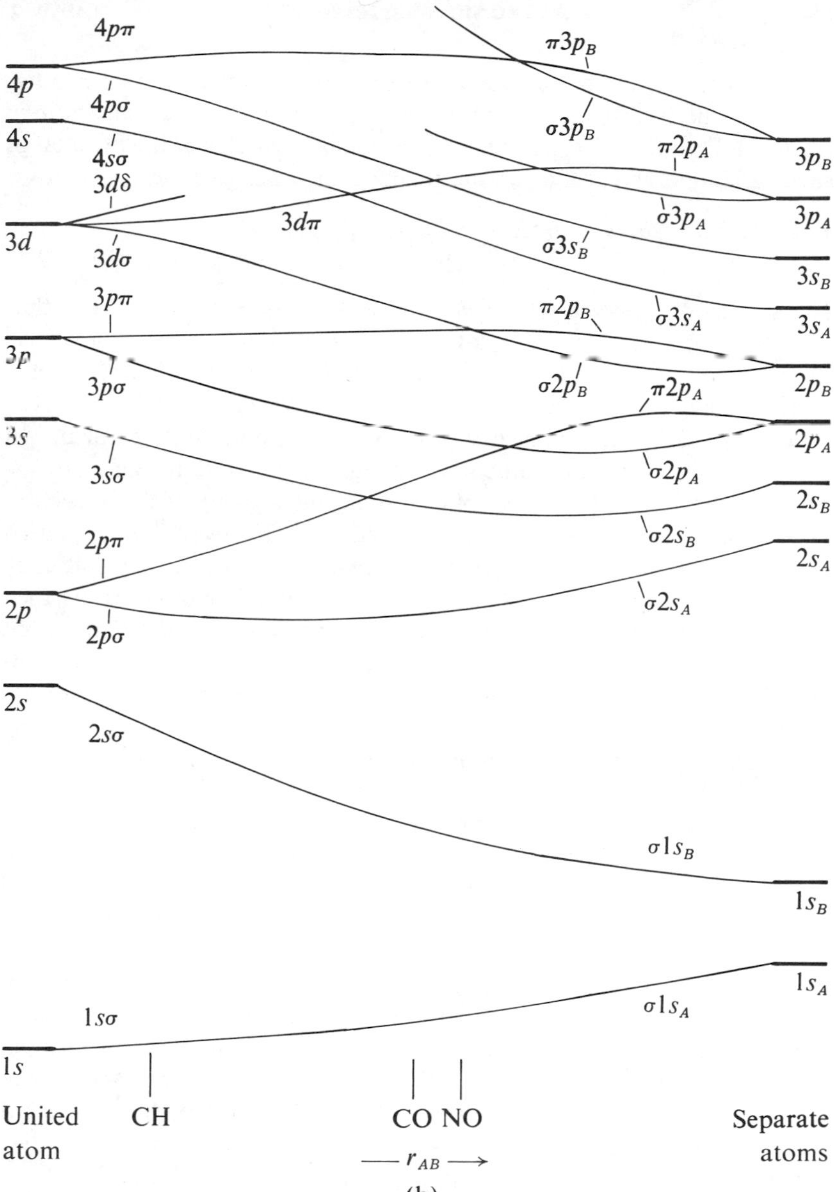

(b)

FIGURE 7-3 Correlation diagrams of the molecular orbitals for diatomics of (a) equal and (b) unequal charge derived from the united and separate atom approaches. The correlation between the MO energy levels and the internuclear separation is only approximate, and is designed to illustrate the proper sequence of the levels. (Taken from J. C. Davis [Reference 7-2, pp. 429 and 434].)

greater than the number of bonding electrons, an unstable state results. The MO's derived from the LCAO approximation for large separations are symbolized $\lambda n\ell$. For diatomics of equal nuclear charge having a large fixed value of r, the orbitals in increasing energy are given as

$$\sigma_g 1s < \sigma_u{}^* 1s < \sigma_g 2s < \sigma_u{}^* 2s < \sigma_g 2p < \pi_u 2p_y = \pi_u 2p_z < \pi_g{}^* 2p_y = \pi_g{}^* 2p_z < \sigma_u{}^* 2p. \quad (7\text{-}3)$$

The subscript g (*gerade*) or u (*ungerade*) indicates that the MO is either symmetric or antisymmetric relative to inversion through the molecular center. The designation "g" or "u" results from the symmetry of ℓ corresponding to the united atom; for even ℓ (s, d, etc.) or odd ℓ (p, f, etc.) states respectively, the symmetry of the corresponding MO is g or u. In deriving electronic term symbols, we designate a u state for an *ungerade* MO, which has an odd number of electrons, and a g state if the molecular orbital contains an even number of electrons. Those MO's designated *gerade* are symmetric to the inversion operation, and as a result they exclusively generate g states, regardless of the number of electrons they contain. These designations apply only to homonuclear diatomics (and polyatomics with a center of symmetry), whereas for heteronuclear diatomics there is no center of symmetry. Again, the transition from the united atom to separated atoms of the two diatomic types and the MO's for large internuclear distances are shown in correlation diagrams (Figure 7-3).

To derive the electronic term symbol for a particular diatomic based on the correlation diagrams, we must specify the types of coupling of the various electronic motions. For most diatomic molecules, the individual $\mathbf{s}_i$'s and $\boldsymbol{\lambda}_i$'s independently couple to form the resultants $\mathbf{S}$ and $\boldsymbol{\Lambda}$, the spin and orbital electronic angular momenta. The $\boldsymbol{\lambda}_i$'s are the individual electronic projections along the internuclear axis, so that $\boldsymbol{\Lambda}$ is the resultant along this axis. Thus, the number and types of electronic states possible will depend on the number and types of equivalent or nonequivalent electrons occupying the various MO's. Equivalent electrons are defined as those occupying one and the same MO, and hence they have the same n and ℓ quantum numbers; in the case of σ MO's that can contain only two electrons, they will also have m_ℓ in common.

In the case of equivalent electrons, the number of possible states is limited according to the Pauli principle. For two equivalent σ electrons, $\Lambda = 0$, $S = 0$, and the only state possible is the ${}^1\Sigma^+$. The + superscript appearing with this term symbol indicates that reflection of the occupied MO's in a vertical plane containing the internuclear axis is symmetric. In fact, σ orbitals are in general symmetric under the reflection operation and therefore Σ states arising exclusively from such orbitals will be +. On the other hand, Σ states that are antisymmetric to the reflection operation

TABLE 7-1. Electronic Term Symbols Resulting from Equivalent and Nonequivalent Electrons

Equivalent electrons	Electronic terms	Nonequivalent electrons	Electronic terms
σ^2	$^1\Sigma^+$	$\sigma\sigma$	$^1\Sigma^+$, $^3\Sigma^+$
π^2	$^1\Sigma^+$, $^3\Sigma^-$, $^1\Delta$	$\sigma\pi$	$^1\Pi$, $^3\Pi_r$
π^3	$^2\Pi_i$	$\sigma\delta$	$^1\Delta$, $^3\Delta_r$
π^4	$^1\Sigma^+$	$\pi\pi$	$^1\Sigma^+$, $^3\Sigma^+$, $^1\Sigma^-$, $^3\Sigma^-$, $^1\Delta$, $^3\Delta_r$
δ^2	$^1\Sigma^+$, $^3\Sigma^-$, $^1\Gamma$	$\pi\delta$	$^1\Pi$, $^3\Pi$, $^1\Phi$, $^3\Phi_r$
δ^3	$^2\Delta_i$	$\sigma\sigma\sigma$	$^2\Sigma^+$, $^2\Sigma^+$, $^4\Sigma^+$
δ^4	$^1\Sigma^+$	$\sigma\sigma\pi$	$^2\Pi$, $^2\Pi$, $^4\Pi_r$
		$\pi^2\sigma\sigma$	$^1\Sigma^+$, $^1\Sigma^-$, $^1\Delta$, $^3\Sigma^+$, $^3\Sigma^-(2)$, $^3\Delta$, $^5\Sigma^-$

SOURCE: From *Molecular Spectra and Molecular Structure*, Vol. I by G. Herzberg © 1950 by Litton Educational Publishing, Inc. Reprinted by permission of Van Nostrand Reinhold Company.
NOTE: The subscripts r and i indicate regular and inverted multiplets.

have the superscript $-$. These $+$ or $-$ superscripts apply only to Σ states. Except for those Σ states generated by σ MO's, these states do not have signs that are simply determined; various combinations used to generate them are summarized in Table 7-1. For two σ electrons that are nonequivalent, $S = 0$ and 1, and $\Lambda = 0$. Thus, we obtain a $^1\Sigma^+$ and a $^3\Sigma^+$.

For the case of three nonequivalent σ, π, δ electrons, the electronic angular momentum states generated are Φ and Π, as shown in the accompanying diagram. The two configurations shown for each state represent the double degeneracy of Λ. The vectorial addition of three electron spin states of $\frac{1}{2}$ was illustrated in Example 3-3 and the vector sum for $S_{12} = 1$ and 0, added vectorially to the third electronic spin, is $S_{123} = \frac{3}{2}, \frac{1}{2}$, and $\frac{1}{2}$.

$\Lambda = \pm 3$ $\qquad$ $\Lambda = \pm 1$

The spin state $\frac{1}{2}$ appears twice, since it results from two different vectorial additions. Thus, each Λ state (Φ and Π) will be two doublet states and one quartet state. We obtain $^2\Pi(2)$, $^4\Pi$, $^2\Phi(2)$, and $^4\Phi$, where the number in parentheses represents the number of different Λ states that occur. Electronic term symbols resulting from various combinations of equivalent and nonequivalent electrons are summarized in Table 7-1.

3. Application to Homonuclear and Heteronuclear Diatomics

Now that we have accomplished what we initially set out to do—to find a way of ordering the energy states as a function of the electronic configuration in terms of the quantum numbers S and Λ—we can apply those procedures to ascertaining the energy states of the various diatomics and compare the predicted results with experimental observations. Homonuclear diatomics are our first consideration.

Using the correlation diagram of Figure 7-3a, we obtain for the H_2^+ ion molecule the configuration $(1s\sigma_g)^1$, which gives a ground state term $^2\Sigma_g^+$. Using Herzberg's definition of bond order as $\frac{1}{2}$(number of bonding electrons minus number of antibonding electrons), the lone electron in a bonding orbital predicts a stable ground state molecule with $\frac{1}{2}$ bond order. Adding additional electrons successively to the first two orbitals in the region of the united atom, which corresponds to the approximate bond lengths of H_2, He_2^+, and He_2, we obtain $(1s\sigma_g)^2$, $(1s\sigma_g)^2(2p\sigma_u^*)^1$, and $(1s\sigma_g)^2(2p\sigma_u^*)^2$ configurations. These give corresponding ground state term symbols $^1\Sigma_g^+(H_2)$, $^2\Sigma_u^+(He_2^+)$, and $^1\Sigma_g^+(He_2)$, having bond orders of 1, $\frac{1}{2}$, and 0. As a result, all four diatomics discussed thus far, except for He_2, would be expected to have stable ground electronic states. These observations have indeed been confirmed by experimentation. If one of the two $2p\sigma_u^*$ electrons in He_2 is excited to the $2s\sigma_g$ orbital, however, a stable single-bonded diatomic should result.[2] According to Table 7-1, the electronic states possible for these two nonequivalent σ electrons are $^1\Sigma_u^+$ and $^3\Sigma_u^+$. Applying Hund's rule in this case, which is also valid for molecular states, it can be predicted that the triplet will lie lower. The existence of $He_2^*(^1\Sigma_u^+)$ has been confirmed by observing the continuous-emission spectrum to the unstable ground state from a gaseous discharge, $^1\Sigma_u^+ \rightarrow {}^1\Sigma_g^+$. Even though these four diatomics more closely approach the united atom, the various electronic terms could equally well have been derived using the MO's corresponding to intermediate values of r, and this procedure is often used. Using the MO designation, the predicted and observed properties of several homonuclear and near homonuclear diatomics are summarized in Table 7-2.

The remaining homonuclear or near homonuclear diatomics have bond distances that are more appropriately described by the MO's generated by the separate atom approach. Therefore, these MO's will be used almost exclusively in the remainder of this discussion. Adding successively two electrons each to the $(\sigma_g 2s)$ and $(\sigma_u^* 2s)$ orbitals, we obtain the electronic configurations for the diatomics Li_2 and Be_2:

$$KK(\sigma_g 2s)^2 \qquad \text{and} \qquad KK(\sigma_g 2s)^2(\sigma_u^* 2s)^2,$$

where KK indicates filled $(\sigma_g 1s)^2(\sigma_u^* 1s)^2$ orbitals. The predicted bond

TABLE 7-2. Summary of Properties of Ground Electronic State Diatomic Molecules

Species	Electronic configuration	State[a]	Bond order[b]	Dissociation energy (kcal)	Bond length (Å)	Ionization potential (eV)
H_2^+	$(\sigma_g 1s)^1$	$^2\Sigma_g^+$	$\frac{1}{2}$	61.06	1.05	...
H_2	$(\sigma_g 1s)^2$	$^1\Sigma_g^+$	1	103.24	0.742	15.6
He_2^+	$(\sigma_g 1s)^2(\sigma_u^* 1s)^1$	$^2\Sigma_u^+$	$\frac{1}{2}$	60	1.08	...
He_2	$(\sigma_g 1s)^2(\sigma_u^* 1s)^2(=KK)$	$(^1\Sigma_g^+)$	0	...	...	...
Li_2	$KK(\sigma_g 2s)^2$	$^1\Sigma_g^+$	1	25	2.672	...
Be_2	$KK(\sigma_g 2s)^2(\sigma_u^* 2s)^2(=KKLL)$	$(^1\Sigma_g^+)$	0	...	...	...
B_2	$KKLL(\pi_u 2p)^2$	$^3\Sigma_g^-$	1	69	1.589	...
C_2	$KKLL(\pi_u 2p)^4$	$^1\Sigma_g^+$	2	150	1.312	12
N_2^+, CN	$KKLL(\pi_u 2p)^4(\sigma_g 2p)^1$	$^2\Sigma_g^+$	$2\frac{1}{2}$	201, 212	1.116, 1.172	... , 14
N_2, CO	$KKLL(\pi_u 2p)^4(\sigma_g 2p)^2$	$^1\Sigma_g^+$	3	225.0, 256	1.094, 1.128	15.51, 14.1
O_2^+, NO	$KKLL(\pi_u 2p)^4(\sigma_g 2p)^2(\pi_g^* 2p)^1$	$^2\Pi_g$	$2\frac{1}{2}$	149, 150	1.123, 1.151	... , 9.5
O_2	$KKLL(\pi_u 2p)^4(\sigma_g 2p)^2(\pi_g^* 2p)^2$	$^3\Sigma_g^-$	2	117.96	1.207	12.5
F_2	$KKLL(\pi_u 2p)^4(\sigma_g 2p)^2(\pi_g^* 2p)^4$	$^1\Sigma_g^+$	1	36	1.42	17.8
Ne_2	$KKLL(\pi_u 2p)^4(\sigma_g 2p)^2(\pi_g^* 2p)^4(\sigma_u^* 2p)^2$	$(^1\Sigma_g^+)$	0	...	...	...

[a] The states in parentheses are unstable.

[b] $\frac{1}{2}$[number of bonding electrons minus number of antibonding electrons].

order of Li_2 is 1, and Li_2 has a stable ground state of term symbol $^1\Sigma_g^+$, whereas Be_2 has a zero bond order for the ground state and is unstable.

The B_2 diatomic with 10 electrons is an interesting case because its approximate internuclear bond distance corresponds to the region of $\pi_u 2p$ and $\sigma_g 2p$ crossing, and as such, the last two electrons would go into either one or the other of these two orbitals, giving significantly different ground state terms. If both were added to the $\sigma_g 2p$ orbital, B_2 would have bond order 1 and ground state term $^1\Sigma_g^+$. If the $\pi_u 2p$ doubly degenerate MO were of lower energy, however, according to Table 7-1 the resulting states would be $^1\Sigma_g^+$, $^3\Sigma_g^-$, and $^1\Delta_g$. By Hund's rule, the $^3\Sigma_g^-$ would be the lowest of the three. The latter has been confirmed by experimentation and the ground state is $^3\Sigma_g^-$.

The C_2 molecule provides a particularly appropriate example of the difficulties that may arise in the ground state assignment for bond distances corresponding to the region of energy-level crossing where even small electronic interactions can cause one of several configurations to be of lower energy. In cases such as these, the MO assignment can predict only alternatives. For C_2 having 12 electrons, one alternative is $(\pi_u 2p)^4$, and according to Table 7-1, a resulting $^1\Sigma_g^+$ ground state; the other is $(\pi_u 2p)^3(\sigma_g 2p)^1$, giving rise to $^3\Pi_u$ and $^1\Pi_u$, of which the $^3\Pi_u$ is lower. By excellent but indirect data, the $^3\Pi_u$ was thought to be the ground state; recently, however, it was proved that the $^1\Sigma_g^+$ was 610 cm^{-1} lower in energy. We also have in the case of C_2 a resulting double bond, since there are four net bonding electrons. As a result C_2 has a bond energy of 150 kcal and an internuclear separation of 1.312 Å, compared with the single-bonded B_2 of bond energy 69 kcal and internuclear separation 1.589 Å. Properties such as these are logically predictable using the MO approach.

For the case of N_2, which has 14 electrons, the ground state configuration is clearly $KKLL(\pi_u 2p)^4(\sigma_g 2p)^2$ and according to Table 7-1 has the lone ground state term $^1\Sigma_g^+$. It has a bond order of 3, and correspondingly its bond energy is 225 kcal and its internuclear bond distance is 1.098 Å. The ground N_2^+ state, resulting from the ionization of an electron from the $(\sigma_g 2p)$ orbital, has an electronic term symbol $^2\Sigma_g^+$ and a corresponding bond energy of 201 kcal and bond length of 1.116 Å.

The O_2 molecule, containing 16 electrons, presents another interesting example because of the partially filled doubly degenerate $(\pi_g{}^*2p)$ orbital. For the electronic configuration $KKLL(\pi_u 2p)^4(\sigma_g 2p)^2(\pi_g{}^*2p)^2$, there are three predicted low-lying electronic states, $^3\Sigma_g^-$, $^1\Delta_g$, and $^1\Sigma_g^+$ (Table 7-1). In agreement with Hund's rule, the $^3\Sigma_g^-$ is the ground state, and the $^1\Delta_g$ is 7918 cm^{-1} above it and the $^1\Sigma_g^+$ 13,195 cm^{-1} above it ($^3\Sigma_g^-$) (Figure 7-8). Transitions between these two states and the ground state are forbidden, in part because of the spin prohibition. Despite being forbidden, these transitions do occur very weakly, giving rise to the so-called "atmospheric bands." One of the most important electronic states of O_2, which gives rise to very strong continuous absorption from the ground state, is the $^3\Sigma_u^-$ state. This state, along with other states, results from the electronic configuration $KKLL(\pi_u 2p)^3(\sigma_g 2p)^2(\pi_g^* 2p)^3$. This absorption system gives rise to the so-called Schumann-Runge bands.

The F_2 molecule, containing 18 electrons, has an electronic configuration that fills the doubly degenerate antibonding π orbital, $KKLL(\pi_u 2p)^4(\sigma_g 2p)^2(\pi_g^* 2p)^4$, and has a resulting term symbol $^1\Sigma_g^+$. Electronic excitation to the configuration $KKLL(\pi_u 2p)^4(\sigma_g 2p)^2(\pi_g^* 2p)^3(\sigma_u^* 2p)^1$, gives rise to two states $^3\Pi_u$ and $^1\Pi_u$, of which the triplet is lower in energy. The transition, $^1\Pi \leftarrow {}^1\Sigma_g^+$, is presumably responsible for the strong continuous absorption in the visible and ultraviolet, and is a very efficient source of F atoms for photochemical purposes.

Heteronuclear diatomics can largely be treated like the homonuclear diatomics in applying molecular orbital theory. The situation is more complicated, however, since we cannot use identical atomic orbitals in constructing the MO's. A molecular orbital correlation diagram for heteronuclear diatomics is shown in Figure 7-3b, and again the ordering of the energy levels depends on the internuclear distance. For those diatomics that differ in nuclear charge by one or two units, the energy-level ordering is closely approximated by the homonuclear correlation diagram. The term states resulting in such situations are expected to be the same as those observed for the isoelectronic homonuclear diatomic. Examples of these are included in Table 7-2, for example, CN, CO, and NO. Since the MO's in such cases are not constructed from equivalent AO's nor properly described as a series having largely the character of one or the other atomic constituent, Mulliken introduced a new symbolism to describe such cases. Assuming that the lowest σ orbitals are either hydrogenlike or have very short internuclear separations (and are therefore described adequately by the left side of Figure 7-3b), Mulliken's symbolism begins with the $\sigma 2s$ orbital.

Molecular orbital	$(\sigma 1s)$	$(\sigma^* 1s)$	$(\sigma 2s)$	$(\sigma^* 2s)$	$(\sigma 2p)$	$(\pi 2p)$	$(\pi^* 2p)$	$(\sigma^* 2p)$
Mulliken	K	K	$(z\sigma)$	$(y\sigma)$	$(x\sigma)$	$(w\pi)$	$(v\pi)$	$(u\sigma)$

The MO configuration of a few first-period heteronuclear diatomics and their resulting electronic ground state terms are given below (note that we have dropped the "u, g" designation in these cases).

Species having 12 electrons: BN and BeO

$$KK(z\sigma)^2(y\sigma)^2(x\sigma)^2(w\pi)^2\ {}^3\Sigma^- \qquad \text{or} \qquad KK(z\sigma)^2(y\sigma)^2(w\pi)^3(x\sigma)^1\ {}^3\Pi$$

Species having 13 electrons: CN, CO^+, and BO

$$KK(z\sigma)^2(y\sigma)^2(w\pi)^4(x\sigma)^1\ {}^2\Sigma^+$$

Species having 14 electrons: CO

$$KK(z\sigma)^2(y\sigma)^2(w\pi)^4(x\sigma)^2\ {}^1\Sigma^+$$

Species having 15 electrons: NO

$$KK(z\sigma)^2(y\sigma)^2(w\pi)^4(x\sigma)^2(v\pi)^1\ {}^2\Pi$$

Although we have written these orbitals in such a way as to approximate the isoelectronic homonuclear species, each of these diatomics must be considered an individual case. The exact ordering (and hence the term state) in each case will depend on the degree of distortion of the homonuclear levels caused by the dissimilarities of the atomic constituents. Obviously, the greater the difference, the greater the distortion. For heteronuclear diatomics containing atoms from different periods (excluding hydrides for the moment), the ordering of the levels, and hence the manifold of term states, is extremely difficult to predict.

Practically all the diatomic hydrides are adequately described by the orbital approach of the heteronuclear united atom, with a distinction made for the extent to which orbitals are actually involved in bonding. For the simple hydride LiH, containing 4 electrons, the ground electronic configuration is $(1s\sigma)^2(2s\sigma)^2$ and the corresponding term symbol is ${}^1\Sigma^+$. The $(1s\sigma)$ orbital is essentially the inner-shell $1s$ atomic orbital of Li and the $(2s\sigma)$ is effectively the bonding molecular orbital. For BeH, the ground electronic configuration is $(1s\sigma)^2(2s\sigma)^2(2p\sigma)^1$, and the term is ${}^2\Sigma^+$. In addition to the inner-shell Be $1s$ atomic orbital, the $(2p\sigma)$ orbital containing a lone electron is also essentially atomic in nature. Only the $(2s\sigma)$ is a bonding molecular orbital. An electron contained in the valence shell that is not used in bonding is called a *nonbonding* electron. It is the excitation of this type of electron to higher principal quantum shells that results in spectra very similar to atomic Rydberg states; hence in molecular cases they are also called Rydberg transitions. Finally, in the case of HF, we have $(1s\sigma)^2(2s\sigma)^2(2p\sigma)^2(2p\pi_y)^2(2p\pi_z)^2$, corresponding to ${}^1\Sigma^+$. In this case, we have in addition to the F $1s$ atomic orbital, the $(2s\sigma)$, $(2p\pi_y)$, and $(2p\pi_z)$ nonbonding atomic orbitals; only the $(2p\sigma)$ is an effective MO resulting in the H—F bond.

4. Selection Rules

If the Born-Oppenheimer approximation is assumed, ψ_e is independent of the nuclear coordinates, and as such the total time-independent wavefunction is written

$$\psi_\tau = \psi_e \psi_v \psi_r \psi_s, \tag{7-4}$$

where the subscripts signify electronic, vibrational, rotational, and electronic spin wavefunctions. The application of the transition moment matrix, Eq. (2-35), provides a way of getting the first-order electric dipole selection rules. Thus, we obtain

$$\int \psi_\tau'^* \hat{\mu} \psi_\tau'' \, d\tau = \int \psi_e'^* \psi_v'^* \psi_r'^* \psi_s'^* \boldsymbol{\mu} \psi_e'' \psi_v'' \psi_r'' \psi_s'' \, d\tau, \tag{7-5}$$

where the total dipole moment $\boldsymbol{\mu}$ can be divided into two parts, one due to the electrons and the other due to the nuclei,

$$\boldsymbol{\mu} = \boldsymbol{\mu}_e + \boldsymbol{\mu}_n. \tag{7-6}$$

Substituting Eq. (7-6) into (7-5), we obtain

$$\int \psi_e'^* \boldsymbol{\mu}_e \psi_e'' \, d\tau_e \int \psi_v'^* \psi_v'' \, d\tau_v \int \psi_r'^* \psi_r'' \, d\tau_r \int \psi_s'^* \psi_s'' \, d\tau_s$$
$$+ \int \psi_e'^* \psi_e'' \, d\tau_e \int \psi_v'^* \psi_r'^* \boldsymbol{\mu}_n \psi_v'' \psi_r'' \, d\tau_{vr} \int \psi_s'^* \psi_s'' \, d\tau_s. \tag{7-7}$$

The ψ_e integral of the second term (and hence the second term) is zero, since the electronic wavefunctions are orthogonal.

The separate electronic spin integral is based on the approximation $\psi_{es} \simeq \psi_e \psi_s$, where we assume that the spin-orbit interaction $(\boldsymbol{\Lambda}, \mathbf{S})$ is small. This approximation is very good for light diatomics, but breaks down for the heavier species, for which spin-orbit coupling is strong. Since the spin wavefunctions for different electronic states are orthogonal, this integral vanishes unless $\psi_s'^* = \psi_s''$, or $\Delta S = 0$. Thus for electronic transitions involving diatomics (and polyatomics), only states of the same electronic multiplicity can combine.

The rotational integral of Eq. (7-7), which is the product of the angular integrals obtained in the rotation-vibration problem of Eq. (6-3), gives the same general selection rules, $\Delta J = \pm 1$ and $\Delta M = 0, \pm 1$, but without the restriction $\mu_0 \neq 0$. In addition, transitions involving electronic states having electronic angular momenta $(\boldsymbol{\Lambda} \neq 0)$ will also have allowed $\Delta J = 0$ transitions, so that P, Q, and R rotational structure is possible within a vibrational band.

The product separation of the two remaining integrals is based on the assumption that $\psi_{ev} = \psi_e(q, Q_0)\psi_v(Q)$, where q and Q are generalized electronic and nuclear coordinates; Q_0 corresponds to a fixed nuclear separation at roughly the equilibrium nuclear distance of one of the two electronic states. Substituting ψ_{ev} into Eq. (7-7), we obtain

$$\mathbf{R} = \int \psi_e'^*(q, Q_0)\mu_e\psi_e''(q, Q_0)\, d\tau_e \int \psi_v'^*\psi_v''\, d\tau_v, \tag{7-8}$$

where the first integral is called the electronic transition moment matrix and the second the *vibrational overlap integral.* The Q_0 coordinate in both electronic wavefunctions assumes that the internuclear separation is approximately constant over the duration of an electronic transition, and this assumption provides the basis for the Franck-Condon principle. Since the variation of ψ_e with Q is very small, we can define the average electronic transition moment as $\mathbf{R}_e$; this moment $\mathbf{R}_e$ determines the intensity of the band system as a whole.

The vibrational overlap integral (the square of which is called the Franck-Condon factor) contains wavefunctions that do not belong to an orthonormal set. Thus the magnitude of this integral, and hence the intensity, are determined by the vertical coincidence, or internuclear distance, of the maxima or minima of the vibrational wavefunctions of the upper and lower electronic states. Although the $\mathbf{v} = 0$ level in the ground electronic state is normally harmonic, the upper vibrational state in an electronic transition can be quite anharmonic. Therefore, for general electronic transitions (whether harmonic or anharmonic), $\Delta\mathbf{v}$ may be 0, ± 1, ± 2, ± 3, ... In electronic transitions then, there are no specific vibrational selection rules, and "allowed" vibrational transitions are determined by the magnitude of the overlap integral for a specific case. In spite of this generality of selection, $\psi_v'^*\psi_v''$ must still be totally symmetric. The relative internuclear displacements of the electronic states involved in a transition lead to three generally observed cases in electronic band spectra. These are diagrammed in Figure 7-4. The transitions are drawn as vertical lines on the potential-energy diagrams according to the Franck-Condon principle, that is, electronic transitions occur so rapidly ($\sim 10^{-15}$ sec) compared with nuclear displacements ($\sim 10^{-12}$ sec) that the nuclei are considered to be fixed over the duration of a transition.

Most diatomic molecules exhibit Case II spectra, which is why Case II is illustrated in some detail. The equilibrium internuclear distance of the $\mathbf{v}' = 0$ state is significantly shifted to the right, $r_0'' < r_0'$. The vibrational wavefunctions of the various states are also shown, and the vertical coincidence (overlap) of the $\mathbf{v}'' = 0$ and $\mathbf{v}' = 3$ maxima gives rise to the most intense vibrational transition. On either side of this transition, the intensity progressively decreases, primarily because the magnitude of $\psi''_{v=0}$ decreases on either side of r_0''. Excitation into the unbounded

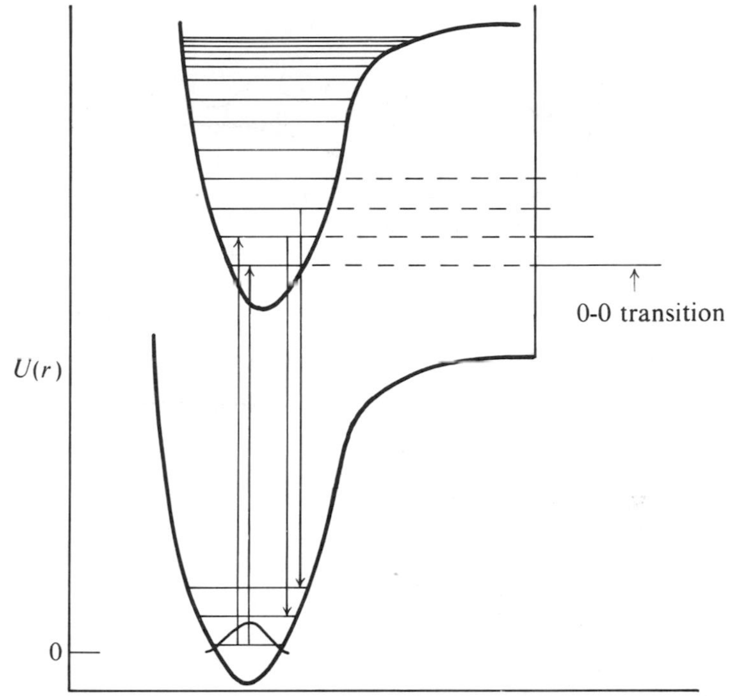

Case I

FIGURE 7-4 Case I: Coincidence of $r_0'' \simeq r_0'$ leads to discrete bound states, with no dissociation; resident time 10^{-8} sec, followed by fluorescence. Case II: $r_0'' < r_0'$ leads principally to discrete states centered higher in the vibronic state than Case I. Case III: $r_0'' \ll r_0'$ leads to a practically continuous electronic spectrum. (Taken from Calvert and Pitts [Reference 7-1, pp. 177 and 179].)

region above the limit of discrete vibrational states leads to nondiscrete, or continuous, absorption. The frequency at which this change occurs is called the convergence limit. Since the region above is unbounded, the molecule dissociates within a vibrational period. The spectral intensities for the transitions over the entire band are shown on the right of each figure. The intensity of each of the lines corresponding to a specific vibronic transition (vibration-electronic transition) is proportional to the vibrational overlap integral of Eq. (7-8).

Case I corresponds to almost exact coincidence of r_0'' and r_0' for the two electronic states. If in addition, the potential-energy curves of the two electronic states are approximately identical, then the vibrational wavefunctions of the two electronic states would form an approximate

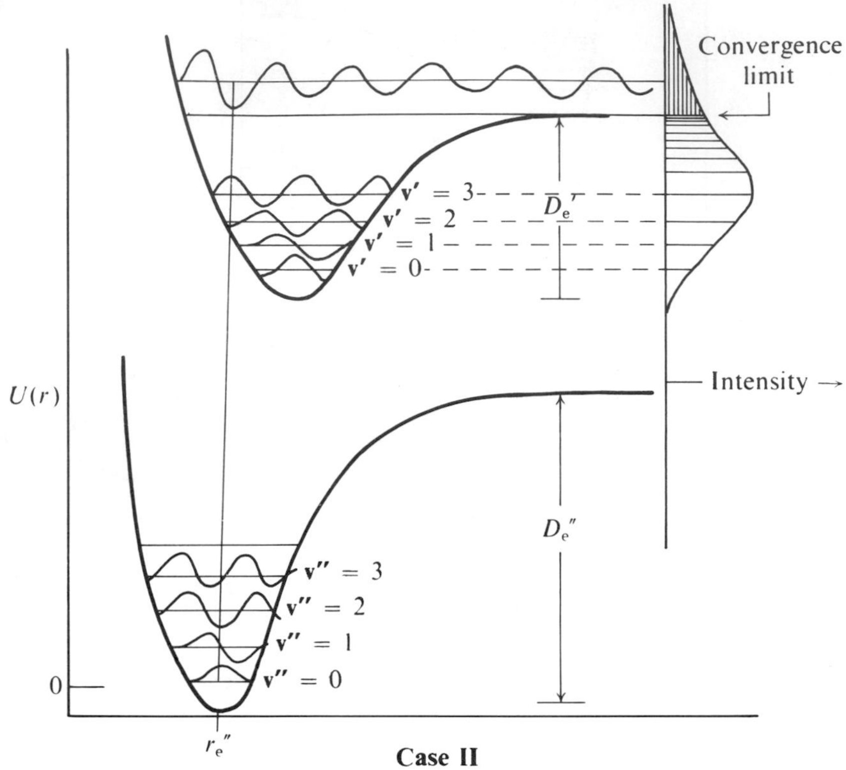

Case II

total orthonormal set. In this case, we must now place a constraint on the vibrational overlap integral, which leads to approximate selection rules. The application of the orthogonality condition to the vibrational overlap integral of Eq. (7-8) gives $\Delta\mathbf{v} = 0, \pm 1, \pm 2, \pm 3, \ldots$ for the single totally symmetric vibration of a diatomic molecule. For these symmetry-allowed transitions, the more exact the two potential-energy curves, the greater the magnitude of the vibrational overlap integral for the $\Delta\mathbf{v} = 0$ transitions. Thus, for absorption from the ground vibronic state, the $\mathbf{v}'' = 0 \rightarrow \mathbf{v}' = 0$ (0–0) transition is by far the strongest.[3] The intensity of the other vibronic transitions shown in Figure 7-4, Case I, is a measure of the nonidentical shape of the two potential-energy curves, or more specifically, the deviation from orthogonality of the vibrational wave-functions involved in the transitions. Similarly, emission transitions are approximately governed by the $\Delta\mathbf{v} = 0$ selection rule; and depending on the upper states populated, the most intense transitions will be those corresponding to this selection rule. The near ultraviolet absorption and emission bands of the CN radical are an excellent illustration of a system showing a Case I spectrum.

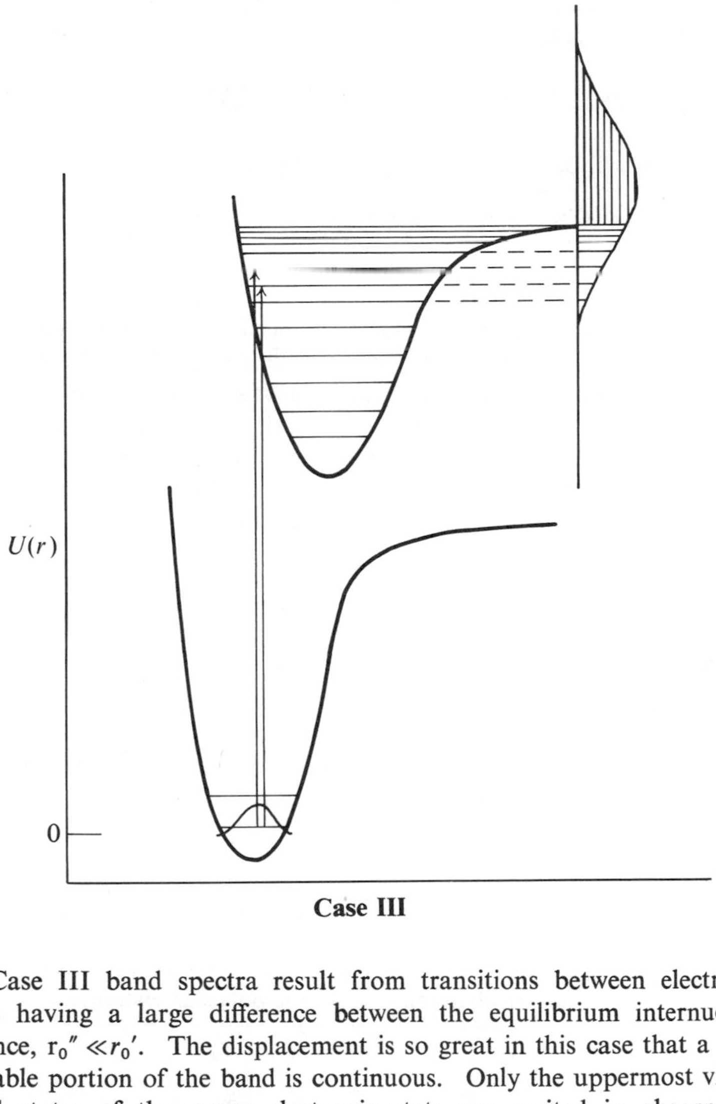

Case III

Case III band spectra result from transitions between electronic states having a large difference between the equilibrium internuclear distance, $r_0'' \ll r_0'$. The displacement is so great in this case that a considerable portion of the band is continuous. Only the uppermost vibrational states of the upper electronic state are excited in absorption. Diatomic molecules exhibiting this spectral behavior are excellent atomic sources in photochemical reactions. The Schumann-Runge near ultraviolet absorption band of O_2 is an example of a Case III spectrum (see Figure 7-8).

The average electronic transition moment of Eq. (7-8),

$$\mathbf{R}_e = \int \psi_e'^*(q, Q_0)\mu_e\psi_e''(q, Q_0)\, d\tau_e, \tag{7-9}$$

determines the allowed transitions between the various electronic states. The electronic dipole moment, summed over the electronic coordinates, is

$$\mu_e = \sum_i ex_i + \sum_i ey_i + \sum_i ez_i. \tag{7-10}$$

A transition will be allowed if any of the three combined products,

$$\psi_e'^* \sum_i x_i\psi_e'', \qquad \psi_e'^* \sum_i y_i\psi_e'', \qquad \psi_e'^* \sum_i z_i\psi_e'', \tag{7-11}$$

are totally symmetric. The selection rules governing these transitions are generally derived using the symmetry properties of the electronic states involved. These symmetry properties in turn depend on the extent of coupling between the rotational and electronic angular momenta [Reference 7-4], which is considered to be weak in these discussions. The details of these derivations will not be presented here, but the selection rules for the cases encountered most frequently will be summarized below. These are for Hund's cases (a) and (b).

$\Delta\Lambda = 0, \pm 1;$
$\Delta S = 0;$
$u \leftrightarrow g,\ u \not\leftrightarrow u,\ g \not\leftrightarrow g$ *Homonuclear diatomics* (7-12)
(Laporte rule)
$\Sigma^+ \leftrightarrow \Sigma^+, \Sigma^- \leftrightarrow \Sigma^-, \Sigma^+ \not\leftrightarrow \Sigma^-$ *(Parity rule)*.

Allowed transitions between various electronic angular momentum states of homonuclear and heteronuclear diatomics are summarized in Table 7-3.

TABLE 7-3. Allowed Electronic Transitions between Various States

Heteronuclear diatomics	Homonuclear diatomics
$\Sigma^+ \leftrightarrow \Sigma^+$	$\Sigma_g{}^+ \leftrightarrow \Sigma_u{}^+$
$\Sigma^- \leftrightarrow \Sigma^-$	$\Sigma_g{}^- \leftrightarrow \Sigma_u{}^-$
$\Pi \leftrightarrow \Sigma^+$	$\Pi_g \leftrightarrow \Sigma_u{}^+,\ \Pi_u \leftrightarrow \Sigma_g{}^+$
$\Pi \leftrightarrow \Sigma^-$	$\Pi_g \leftrightarrow \Sigma_u{}^-,\ \Pi_u \leftrightarrow \Sigma_g{}^-$
$\Pi \leftrightarrow \Pi$	$\Pi_g \leftrightarrow \Pi_u$
$\Pi \leftrightarrow \Delta$	$\Pi_g \leftrightarrow \Delta_u, \Pi_u \leftrightarrow \Delta_g$
$\Delta \leftrightarrow \Delta$	$\Delta_g \leftrightarrow \Delta_u$

SOURCE: From *Molecular Spectra and Molecular Structure*, Vol. I by G. Herzberg © 1950 by Litton Educational Publishing, Inc. Reprinted by permission of Van Nostrand Reinhold Company.
NOTE: Electronic transitions subject to spin conservation, $\Delta S = 0$.

5. Structure of Electronic Transitions

The total energy of a diatomic molecule, excluding translation, is

$$E_\tau = E_e + E_v + E_r, \tag{7-13}$$

where E_e is defined according to whether the origin of energy of the ground electronic state is zero at r_e or r_0. The terms E_v and E_r have been derived previously; they are written

$$E_v = \omega_e(v + \tfrac{1}{2}) - \omega_e x_e(v + \tfrac{1}{2})^2 + \omega_e y_e(v + \tfrac{1}{2})^3 + \cdots \tag{6-8}$$

and

$$E_r = J(J + 1)\tilde{B}_v - J^2(J + 1)^2\tilde{D}_v. \tag{4-15a}$$

Thus, for a transition between different electronic states, we obtain

$$\begin{aligned}\Delta E_\tau &= \Delta E_e + \Delta E_v + \Delta E_r \\ &= \omega_{ee} + \{[\omega_e'(v' + \tfrac{1}{2}) - \omega_e'x_e'(v' + \tfrac{1}{2})^2 + \omega_e'y_e'(v' + \tfrac{1}{2})^3] \\ &\quad - [\omega_e''(v'' + \tfrac{1}{2}) - \omega_e''x_e''(v'' + \tfrac{1}{2})^2 + \omega_e''y_e''(v'' + \tfrac{1}{2})^3]\} \\ &\quad + \{[J'(J' + 1)\tilde{B}_{v'} - J'^2(J'^2 + 1)^2\tilde{D}_{v'}] \\ &\quad - [J''(J'' + 1)\tilde{B}_{v''} - J''^2(J''^2 + 1)^2\tilde{D}_{v''}]\},\end{aligned} \tag{7-14}$$

where the single prime indicates the upper state and the double prime the lower state. The first term on the right is the difference in the electronic energy states relative to the minima in the potential curves at $r_e(\omega_{ee})$; this term is constant for a given transition. The terms within the first set of braces on the right are the differences in the vibrational and rotational energies for the upper and lower electronic states. To obtain a clear understanding of the coarse (low-resolution) and fine (high-resolution) features of an electronic spectrum, we consider the vibrational and rotational terms separately.

a. Vibrational Structure. Assuming for the moment that we are interested in the low-resolution spectrum corresponding to vibronic transitions, and that ΔE_r and the terms in $\omega_e y_e(v + \frac{1}{2})^3$ can be considered negligible, Eq. (7-14) reduces to

$$\begin{aligned}\Delta E_\tau = \omega_{ee} &+ [\omega_e'(v' + \tfrac{1}{2}) - \omega_e'x_e'(v' + \tfrac{1}{2})^2] \\ &- [\omega_e''(v'' + \tfrac{1}{2}) - \omega_e''x_e''(v'' + \tfrac{1}{2})^2].\end{aligned} \tag{7-15}$$

In electronic absorption spectroscopy, the transitions practically always originate from the $v = 0$ vibrational level of the ground state. Only in cases where the ground vibrational fundamental is small (<300 cm^{-1}) or in high-temperature systems do we have transitions occurring from higher ground vibrational levels. Transitions giving rise to such bands are called *hot bands*. For our present purposes, we assume that $\mathbf{v}'' = 0$; and Eq. (7-15) is further reduced:

$$\Delta E_\tau = \omega_{ee} + (\tfrac{1}{2}\omega_e' - \tfrac{1}{4}\omega_e'x_e') + \omega_e'\mathbf{v}' - \omega_e'x_e'\mathbf{v}'^2 - \omega_e'x_e'\mathbf{v}' - (\tfrac{1}{2}\omega_e'' - \tfrac{1}{4}\omega_e''x_e''), \quad \textbf{(7-15a)}$$

where the first and second terms in parentheses are the zero-point energies of the upper and lower electronic states. Since the lowest observed frequency (ω_{00}) in absorption corresponds to the vibronic transition $\mathbf{v}' = 0 \leftarrow \mathbf{v}'' = 0$ (the 0–0 band), we include it as a separate term in Eq. (7-15b),

$$\Delta E_\tau = \omega_{\mathbf{v}'} = \omega_{00} + \omega_e'\mathbf{v}' - \omega_e'x_e'\mathbf{v}'(\mathbf{v}' + 1), \quad \textbf{(7-15b)}$$

where

$$\omega_{00} = \omega_{ee} + (\tfrac{1}{2}\omega_e' - \tfrac{1}{4}\omega_e'x_e') - (\tfrac{1}{2}\omega_e'' - \tfrac{1}{4}\omega_e''x_e''). \quad \textbf{(7-16)}$$

If Eq. (7-15b) is applied to Figure 7-4, Case II, the spectrum would be that shown in Figure 7-5. The vibrational spacing gradually becomes smaller and smaller, until the spectrum is essentially continuous. The approximate frequency at which the discrete levels become continuous is called the *convergence limit*. A spectrum resulting from transitions having consecutive final states originating from a single initial state is called a *progression*. Figure 7-5 is a progression in $\mathbf{v}'$.

We can use the data in the accompanying table from the absorption spectrum of PN as an example of the information that can be obtained from applying Eq. (7-15b) to a $\mathbf{v}'$ progression.

Vibronic transition	$\omega_{\mathbf{v}'}$, cm^{-1}
0–0	39,699.1
1–0	40,786.8
2–0	41,858.9
3–0	42,919.0

For the successive transitions 0–0, 1–0, and 2–0, we have from Eq. (7-15b),

$$\begin{aligned} \omega_0 &= \omega_{00} = 39{,}699.1, \\ \omega_1 &= \omega_{00} + \omega_e' - 2\omega_e'x_e' = 40{,}786.8, \\ \omega_2 &= \omega_{00} + 2\omega_e' - 6\omega_e'x_e' = 41{,}858.9. \end{aligned}$$

Defining the difference $\Delta\omega_{\mathbf{v}}' = \omega_{\mathbf{v}}' - \omega_{\mathbf{v}}$, we obtain

$$\begin{aligned} \Delta\omega_1 &= \omega_1 - \omega_0 = \omega_e' - 2\omega_e'x_e' = 1087.7, \\ \Delta\omega_2 &= \omega_2 - \omega_0 = 2\omega_e' - 6\omega_e'x_e' = 2159.8. \end{aligned}$$

Through algebraic manipulation, we obtain ω_e' and $\omega_e'x_e'$. Thus, the

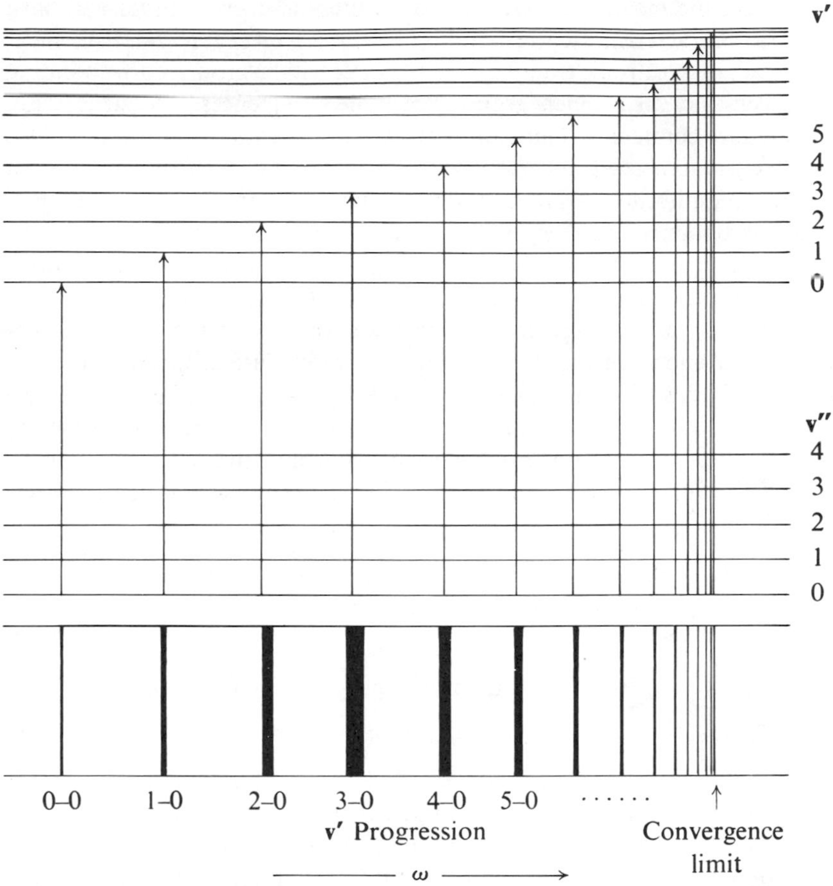

FIGURE 7-5 Electronic spectrum of **v**′ progression in absorption from the **v**″ = 0 state.

information obtained about the PN excited state from these spectral observations is summarized as:

$$\begin{aligned} \omega_{00} &= 39{,}699.1 \text{ cm}^{-1} \\ \omega_e' &= 1103.3 \text{ cm}^{-1} \\ \omega_0' &= 1087.7 \text{ cm}^{-1} \\ \omega_e' x_e' &= 7.8 \text{ cm}^{-1}. \end{aligned}$$

By a similar procedure, we could also obtain an expression for a **v**″ progression in emission (Problem 7-7). Analysis of such spectral observations provides one of the best sources of information about the higher vibrational levels, which are otherwise difficult to populate and thus inaccessible for spectroscopic information.

Diatomic molecules having similar potential-energy curves will have spectral characteristics corresponding to Case I of Figure 7-4. As such, the strongest electronic transitions that occur will be groups corresponding to a constant $\Delta\mathbf{v}_i$. Such groups are called sequences. Sequences are much more common in emission spectra than in absorption spectra, since the excited molecules generated by discharges and so forth are not in thermal equilibrium. Thus, a non-Boltzmann distribution of excited states is obtained, allowing emission from several vibronic states. The actual intensities from the emitting states, however, will still be determined by the vibrational overlap integral, with the 0–0 transition the strongest. The typical emission spectrum of a diatomic, consisting of several sequences, is shown in Figure 7-6. The line widths are proportional to the emission intensity. There is also a gradual convergence of each sequence toward the low-frequency side. Since the $\Delta\mathbf{v} = 0$ sequence is frequently the strongest in most observed spectra, we can derive a relation similar to Eq. (7-15b). If we expand Eq. (7-15) for the upper and lower states, we obtain

$$\begin{aligned}\Delta E_\tau = \omega_{ee} + \omega_e'\mathbf{v}' + \tfrac{1}{2}\omega_e' - \omega_e'x_e'\mathbf{v}'^2 - \omega_e'x_e'\mathbf{v}' - \tfrac{1}{4}\omega_e'x_e' \\ - \omega_e''\mathbf{v}'' - \tfrac{1}{2}\omega_e'' + \omega_e''x_e''\mathbf{v}''^2 + \omega_e''x_e''\mathbf{v}'' + \tfrac{1}{4}\omega_e''x_e''.\end{aligned} \tag{7-17}$$

Using Eq. (7-16) for ω_{00} and the relation $\mathbf{v}' = \mathbf{v}'' = \mathbf{v}$, we find

$$\Delta E_\tau = \omega_\mathbf{v} = \omega_{00} + \mathbf{v}(\omega_e' - \omega_e'') + \mathbf{v}(\mathbf{v} + 1)(\omega_e''x_e'' - \omega_e'x_e'), \tag{7-18}$$

where $\omega_\mathbf{v}$ refers to the frequency of the transition having identical $\mathbf{v}$ quantum numbers in the upper and lower electronic states.

For the lowest excited $^1\Pi$ state of CO, we should like to obtain the vibrational constants ω_e' and $\omega_e'x_e'$. From ground state vibrational overtone observations, $\omega_e'' = 2170.2\ \text{cm}^{-1}$ and $\omega_e''x_e'' = 13.46\ \text{cm}^{-1}$. The observed frequencies in emission for $^1\Pi \rightarrow {}^1\Sigma^+$ are 64,751.4, 64,087.6, and 63,416.1 cm^{-1}, corresponding to the 0–0, 1–1, and 2–2 transitions.

Substituting the appropriate quantum numbers into Eq. (7-18), we obtain

$$\begin{aligned}\omega_0 &= \omega_{00} = 64{,}751.4, \\ \omega_1 &= \omega_{00} + (\omega_e' - \omega_e'') + 2(\omega_e''x_e'' - \omega_e'x_e') = 64{,}087.6, \\ \omega_2 &= \omega_{00} + 2(\omega_e' - \omega_e'') + 6(\omega_e''x_e'' - \omega_e'x_e') = 63{,}416.1.\end{aligned}$$

We can now generate two equations with two unknowns:

$$\begin{aligned}\Delta\omega_1 &= \omega_1 - \omega_0 = (\omega_e' - \omega_e'') + 2(\omega_e''x_e'' - \omega_e'x_e') = -663.8, \\ \Delta\omega_2 &= \omega_2 - \omega_0 = 2(\omega_e' - \omega_e'') + 6(\omega_e''x_e'' - \omega_e'x_e') = -1335.3.\end{aligned}$$

Substituting the values for ω_e'' and $\omega_e''x_e''$, and solving for the desired unknowns, we obtain $\omega_e' = 1514.1\ \text{cm}^{-1}$ and $\omega_e'x_e' = 17.4\ \text{cm}^{-1}$.

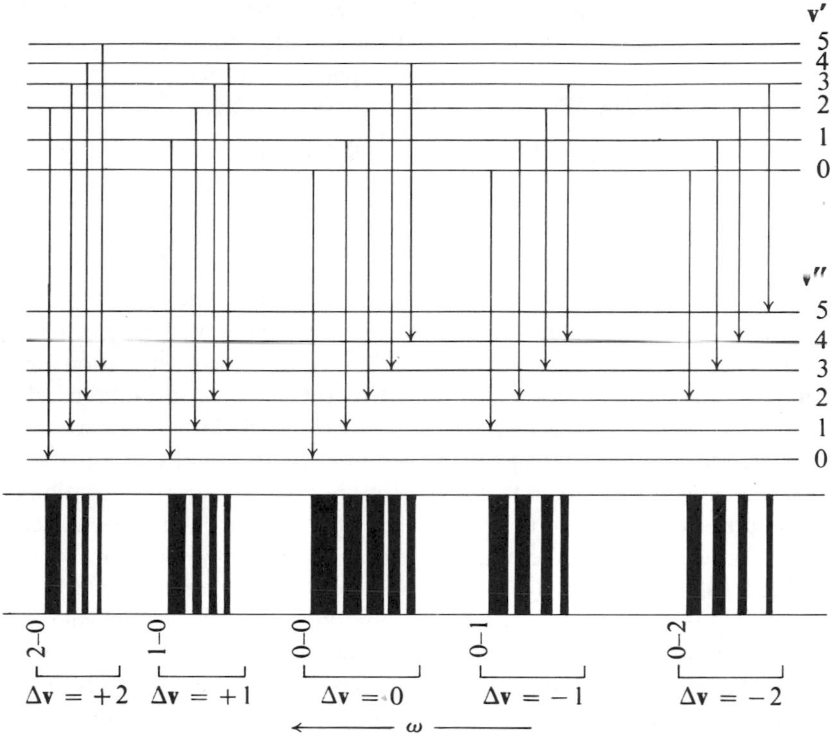

FIGURE 7-6 Electronic spectrum of several sequences observed in emission, where the line widths are proportional to the intensities. Each sequence is shaded toward the violet, since the upper electronic state converges at a faster rate than the lower electronic state. Note that the convergence of the **v**′–0 transitions represents the degree of vibrational anharmonicity in the upper electronic state, and the convergence of the 0–**v**″ transitions, the anharmonicity in the lower electronic state.

b. Rotational Structure. Now that we have at least a general idea of what the vibrational structure of an electronic transition is like, we can concern ourselves with the rotational structure of a particular vibrational band. Since the electronic and vibrational transition frequency, ω_{ev}, of a given band is constant, we can express Eq. (7-14) as

$$\Delta E_{\tau} = \omega_{ev} + [J'(J' + 1)\tilde{B}_{v'} - J''(J'' + 1)\tilde{B}_{v''}], \qquad \textbf{(7-19)}$$

where we have assumed the centrifugal distortion to be negligible. The actual details of the rotational structure depend critically on the specific states involved in a transition. In our elementary discussion, we consider two commonly observed transitions, a $^1\Sigma \leftarrow {}^1\Sigma$ and a $^1\Pi \leftarrow {}^1\Sigma$.

For $^1\Sigma \leftarrow {}^1\Sigma$ transitions, where there is zero electronic orbital angular momentum ($\Lambda = 0$) in both upper and lower states, the rotational selection rules are $\Delta J = \pm 1$. The corresponding expressions for the $R(\Delta J = +1)$ and $P(\Delta J = -1)$ branches respectively are

$$\Delta E_\tau\,(\text{cm}^{-1})_R = \omega_{\text{ev}} + 2\tilde{B}_\text{v}' + (3\tilde{B}_\text{v}' - \tilde{B}_\text{v}'')J + (\tilde{B}_\text{v}' - \tilde{B}_\text{v}'')J^2 \quad \textbf{(7-20)}$$

and

$$\Delta E_\tau\,(\text{cm}^{-1})_\text{p} = \omega_{\text{ev}} - (\tilde{B}_\text{v}' + \tilde{B}_\text{v}'')J + (\tilde{B}_\text{v}' - \tilde{B}_\text{v}'')J^2, \quad \textbf{(7-21)}$$

where J corresponds to the lower quantum state. Thus we expect a spectrum exactly analogous to the one shown in Figure 6-2. In electronic transitions, however, where the equilibrium internuclear separations are generally significantly different, thus the rotational constants of the upper and lower states ($\tilde{B}_\text{v}'$ and $\tilde{B}_\text{v}''$) are also significantly different. As a result, the terms involving differences in the rotational constants will cause the R or the P branch to converge more rapidly than the vibrational transitions converged. In most cases, the equilibrium internuclear separation is greater for the upper state than for the lower state, $r_\text{e}'' < r_\text{e}'$, and thus $\tilde{B}_\text{v}'' > \tilde{B}_\text{v}'$ (Eq. (4-14)). Upon examination of Eq. (7-20), we note that the term $(\tilde{B}_\text{v}' - \tilde{B}_\text{v}'')J^2$ is negative and $(3\tilde{B}' - \tilde{B}'')J$ may or may not be negative. In any case, the squared term becomes dominant for large J, and causes the R branch to reverse in direction, towards lower frequency. The frequency (and the transition) at which this reversal occurs defines the *band head.* Since the reversal is towards lower frequency, the band is said to be "shaded toward the red." In the case of the P branch (Eq. (7-21)), both the linear and the quadratic terms make a negative contribution. As a result, the transition frequencies simply decrease in a nonlinear fashion as a function of J. At the band center, corresponding to the 0–0 ($J' \leftarrow J''$) transition, there will be a missing line (no Q branch). These features, which are characteristic of a $^1\Sigma \leftrightarrow {}^1\Sigma$ transition, are shown in Figure 7-7. The contributions due to the Q branch shown in Figure 7-7 do not apply in this case. For given upper and lower vibrational states, Eqs. (7-20) and (7-21) are simply equations describing two parabolas, and therefore are two empirical equations that can be used not only in obtaining the rotational constants in the upper and lower states but also in assigning the J transitions (band analysis). A plot of J vs the transition frequency for the P and R branches is called a Fortrat diagram, and is also shown in Figure 7-7. Such a plot allows the branches of a vibrational band system to be clearly displayed and analyzed if zero gaps can be identified.

In the case where $r_\text{e}' < r_\text{e}''$ and $\tilde{B}_\text{v}' > \tilde{B}_\text{v}''$, the reverse of the situation described above occurs. All terms of the R branch (Eq. (7-20)) are now positive, and its transitions simply extend to higher frequencies as a

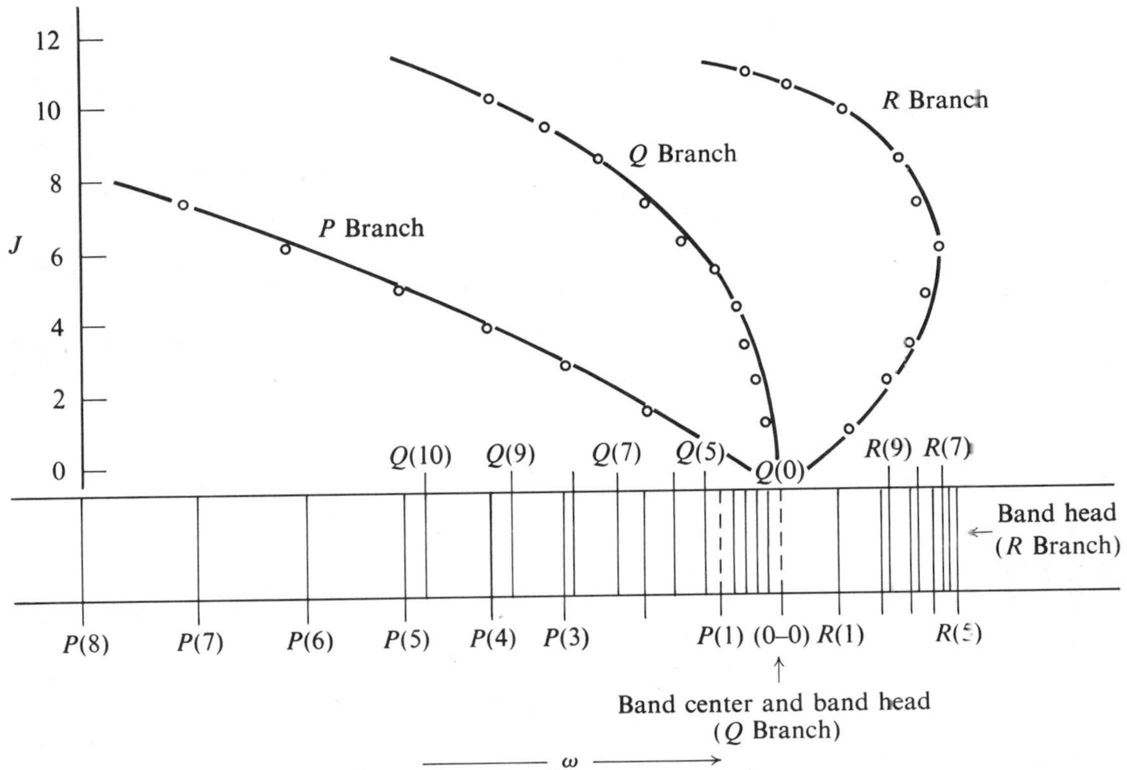

FIGURE 7-7 The rotational band structure of a $^1\Pi \leftarrow {}^1\Sigma$ electronic transition for $r_e'' < r_e'$, or $\tilde{B}' > \tilde{B}''$. Note that for the upper $^1\Pi$ state, no $J = 0$ level exists; therefore, the lowest J transition for each branch is $P(2)$, $Q(1)$, and $R(0)$. A Fortrat diagram is drawn above the spectrum, and clearly displays the P, Q, and R branches as a function of J.

function of increasing J. The P branch on the other hand will have a negative linear term in J and a positive squared term in J. In addition, the coefficient of the linear term is greater than the coefficient of the squared term, $(\tilde{B}_v' + \tilde{B}_v'') > (\tilde{B}_v' - \tilde{B}_v'')$. As a result, the P branch will initially extend to frequencies that are lower relative to the band center; as the $(\tilde{B}_v' - \tilde{B}_v'')J^2$ term becomes dominant, it will cause a band head to occur and finally become "shaded toward the violet" (high frequency).

When either of the electronic states involved in the transition has net electronic angular momentum ($\mathbf{\Lambda} \neq 0$), the rotational selection rules are $\Delta J = 0, \pm 1$. Thus we obtain Q branch transitions in addition to the P and R branches. We also have from Eq. (7-19), in addition to Eqs. (7-20) and (7-21),

$$\Delta E_\tau\,(\mathrm{cm}^{-1})_q = \omega_{ev} + (\tilde{B}_v' - \tilde{B}_v'')J + (\tilde{B}_v' - \tilde{B}_v'')J^2, \qquad \textbf{(7-22)}$$

where $J' = J'' = J$. For the case of $r_e'' < r_e'$, or $\tilde{B}_v'' > \tilde{B}_v'$, both linear and quadratic terms in J are negative. As a result, the Q branch will be "shaded towards the red," but not at the same rate as the P branch; the reason is that the linear J coefficient is the sum $(\tilde{B}_v' + \tilde{B}_v'')$ in the P branch, but the difference $(\tilde{B}_v' - \tilde{B}_v'')$ in the Q branch. The lines due to the Q branch and its Fortrat plot are shown in Figure 7-7. The general structures of the P and R branches will again be the same as discussed above for the $^1\Sigma \leftarrow {}^1\Sigma$ transition, except for some important features characteristic of $^1\Pi \leftarrow {}^1\Sigma$ transitions.

Electronic states of diatomic molecules that have net electronic angular momentum ($\mathbf{\Lambda} \neq 0$) can have $\mathbf{\Lambda}$ either couple with $\mathbf{\Sigma}$ (to produce $\mathbf{\Omega}$) when there is net spin angular momentum (states other than singlets), or couple directly to the perpendicular projection of the nuclear rotational angular momentum $\mathbf{R}$, to produce $\mathbf{J}$, the total molecular angular momentum. For the $^1\Pi$ state of interest to us here, the latter case is applicable. Therefore, the rotational states to (or from) which transitions occur in the $^1\Pi$ electronic state are designated J. Since $\mathbf{J} = |\mathbf{R} + \mathbf{\Lambda}|$, the quantum number $J \geqslant \Lambda$. Thus, in this case, the lowest J level possible is $J = 1$ ($\mathbf{R} = 0$). For diatomics with $\mathbf{\Lambda} \neq 0$, J is the quantum number characterizing the total molecular angular momentum (electronic and nuclear); for diatomics with $\Lambda = 0$ ($^1\Sigma$ states), it is the quantum number characterizing the nuclear rotational angular momentum. The important point is that there will be no $J = 0$ level in the $^1\Pi$ state. As a result, there will be no transitions corresponding to $P(1)$ or $Q(0)$. "Missing" lines, such as these observed from the band spectrum, serve as a means of identifying the $^1\Pi$ as the upper state in the absorption spectrum illustrated in Figure 7-7. These missing components are indicated by broken lines.

6. Electronic Transitions of O_2

The electronic absorption bands of the O_2 molecule not only are interesting from the point of view of their photochemistry and spectroscopy, but also provide good examples of "forbidden transitions." The potential-energy diagram of several electronic states of O_2 are shown in Figure 7-8. As shown in Table 7-1, the ground configuration of two equivalent π electrons

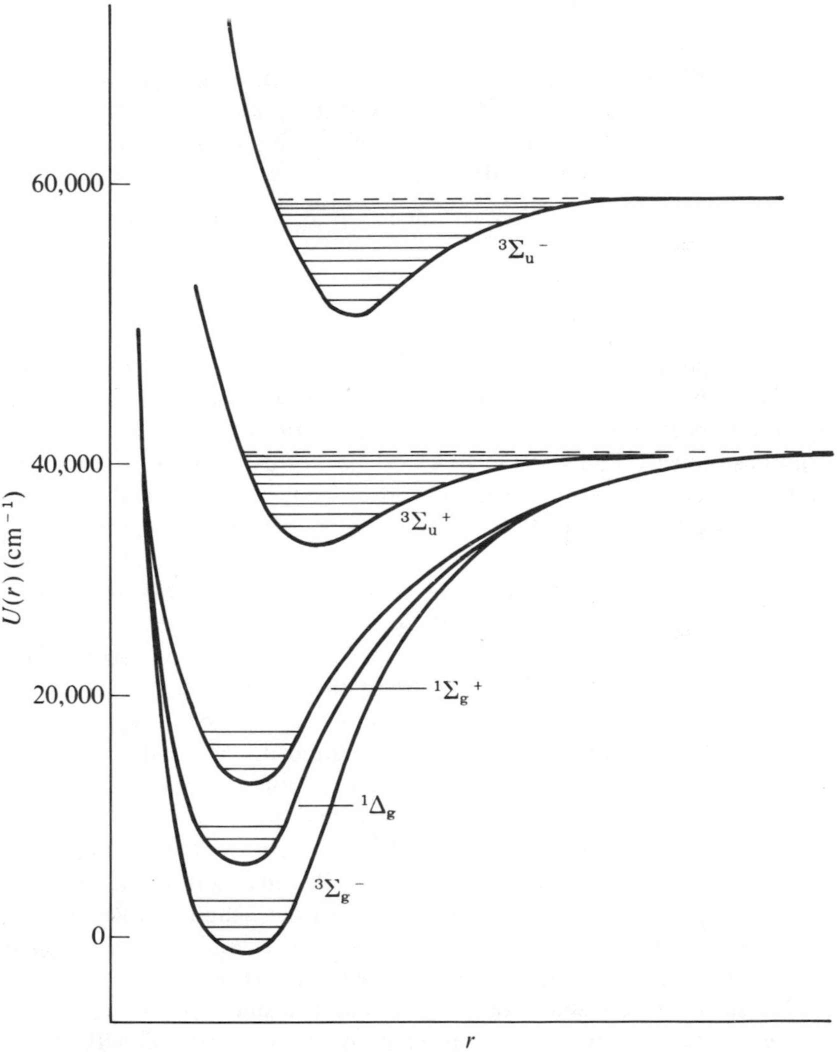

FIGURE 7-8 Potential-energy diagram of several electronic states of O_2.

gives rise to the three low-lying states, $^3\Sigma_g^-$, $^1\Delta_g$, and $^1\Sigma_g^+$. That the latter two states have energies of 7918 cm^{-1} and 13,915 cm^{-1} above the $^3\Sigma_g^-$ ground state exemplifies the splitting magnitude due to the different vectorial additions of the two units of electronic orbital angular momenta. Transitions between these two states and the ground state (Case I, Figure 7-4) violate several of the selection rules summarized in Eq. (7-12). In both cases, the electronic spin ($\Delta S = 0$) and the Laporte ($g \nleftrightarrow g$) rules are violated. In addition the $^1\Delta_g \leftarrow {}^3\Sigma_g$ transition involves a change of $\Delta\Lambda = 2$, and the $^1\Sigma_g^+ \leftarrow {}^3\Sigma_g^-$ transition involves the change $\Sigma^+ \rightarrow \Sigma^-$, both of which are prohibited by electric dipole selection rules. Transitions that are restricted by two or more selection rules (strongly forbidden) in the first-order effect provide an excellent opportunity for observing the less intense magnetic dipole transitions. The selection rules for these transitions can be summarized:

$$\begin{aligned} &\Delta\Lambda = 0, \pm 1 \ (\Delta\Lambda = 0 \text{ for singlet} \leftrightarrow \text{triplet violations only});\\ &\Delta S = 0; \qquad\qquad\qquad\qquad\qquad\qquad\qquad\qquad\qquad\qquad \textbf{(7-23)}\\ &g \leftrightarrow g,\ u \leftrightarrow u,\ u \nleftrightarrow g;\\ &\Sigma^+ \nleftrightarrow \Sigma^+, \Sigma^- \nleftrightarrow \Sigma^-, \Sigma^+ \leftrightarrow \Sigma^-. \end{aligned}$$

In a comparison with the electric dipole selection rules, the restriction involving the parity rule is removed in one case, and the restriction involving the Laporte rule is removed in both transitions. The $\Delta S = 0$ rule is rigorous, however, only so far as $\psi_{es} \simeq \psi_e\psi_s$, or as the spin-orbit interaction is extremely small. Moderate "breakdown" of this rule does occur, and the extent can be determined only by experimental observation. Collisional perturbations are important in bringing about the violation of this symmetry-derived selection rule, and are primarily responsible for the spectral observation of these atmospheric absorptions. As a measure of the degree of this breakdown for the $\Delta S = 0$ violation of the $^1\Sigma_g^+ \leftarrow {}^3\Sigma_g^-$ transition, the observed lifetime of the $^1\Sigma_g^+$ state is 7.15 sec compared with $\sim 10^{-2}$ sec for an "allowed" magnetic dipole transition (based on Section 7D-2). The other "atmospheric band" that is also due to magnetic dipole absorption is even less intense than this one, and indicates the strong violation associated with $\Delta\Lambda = \pm 2$.

The strongly absorbing $^3\Sigma_u^- \leftarrow {}^3\Sigma_g^-$ system does not violate any of the selection rules summarized in Eq. (7-12), and as a result has an oscillator strength $f \sim 0.20$. This transition is in the Schumann-Runge near ultraviolet band, which has its onset at $\sim$2000 Å and absorbs strongly to $\sim$1300 Å. This is an example of a Case III (Figure 7-4) transition, and as such is a very efficient source of O atoms, since most of its absorption envelope is continuous. These O atoms can in turn react with molecular oxygen via a three-body collision ($O + O_2 + M \rightarrow O_3 + M$) to produce ozone. This is an important photochemical reaction in the laboratory as well as in the stratosphere, where the O_3 produced acts as an efficient filter of dangerous ultraviolet radiation. The region of the electromagnetic spectrum below the wavelength of ~2000 Å and extending to ~1000 Å is called the vacuum-ultraviolet, since O_2 (and also N_2) must be removed from the absorption path. This is usually accomplished by evacuating the region between the source and the sample; hence the name "vacuum UV."

7. Photophysical Processes in Diatomic Molecules

Up to this point, we have not considered much about what happens to a diatomic molecule after electronic excitation. Actually, some of the subsequent processes directly affect the observed absorption spectra; some give rise to emission spectra, and some result in ultimate molecular fragmentation. All these processes, exclusive of those subsequent to fragmentation (which is photochemistry), that involve physical changes (electronic structure, energy transfer, etc.) of the initially excited rotational-vibronic state, are generally referred to as photophysical processes.

The electronic absorption process results in excitation of the molecule to the regions either above the convergence limit or below it. As we have seen in Figure 7-4, excitation above the convergence limit into the continuum results in molecular dissociation over a vibrational period ($\sim 10^{-12}$ sec). Processes such as these are pressure-independent. Excitation below the convergence limit at low total pressures generally results in discrete absorption bands. Figure 7-9 illustrates several of the photophysical (and dissociative) processes subsequent to excitation. Continuous absorption (CA) leading to dissociation has been mentioned. The discrete absorption (DA′) to the $\mathbf{v}' = 2$ state generally has a residence time (lifetime) of 10^{-8} sec, and returns to the ground state by either resonance fluorescence (RF) or ordinary fluorescence (F). In resonance fluorescence, the frequency of the emitted photon is exactly the same as that used in excitation, whereas the transition labeled "F" results from an initially excited molecule that has been reduced in energy from the $\mathbf{v}' = 2$ to the $\mathbf{v}' = 0$ state before emission. This reduction in energy is the result of inelastic collisions that the excited molecule has suffered before fluorescence. The time between collisions for a gaseous molecule contained in a system at 1 atm total pressure is 5×10^{-10} sec compared with a typical excited state lifetime of $\sim 10^{-8}$ sec (Section 7C-2). In order to obtain pure resonance fluorescence, the total system pressure is generally not greater than 10^{-1} to 10^{-2} torr. These inelastic energy transfer processes also have selection rules, which for diatomic molecules are $\Delta J = 0, \pm 1$ and $\Delta \mathbf{v} = \pm 1$. Therefore, energy reduction over several rotational or vibrational

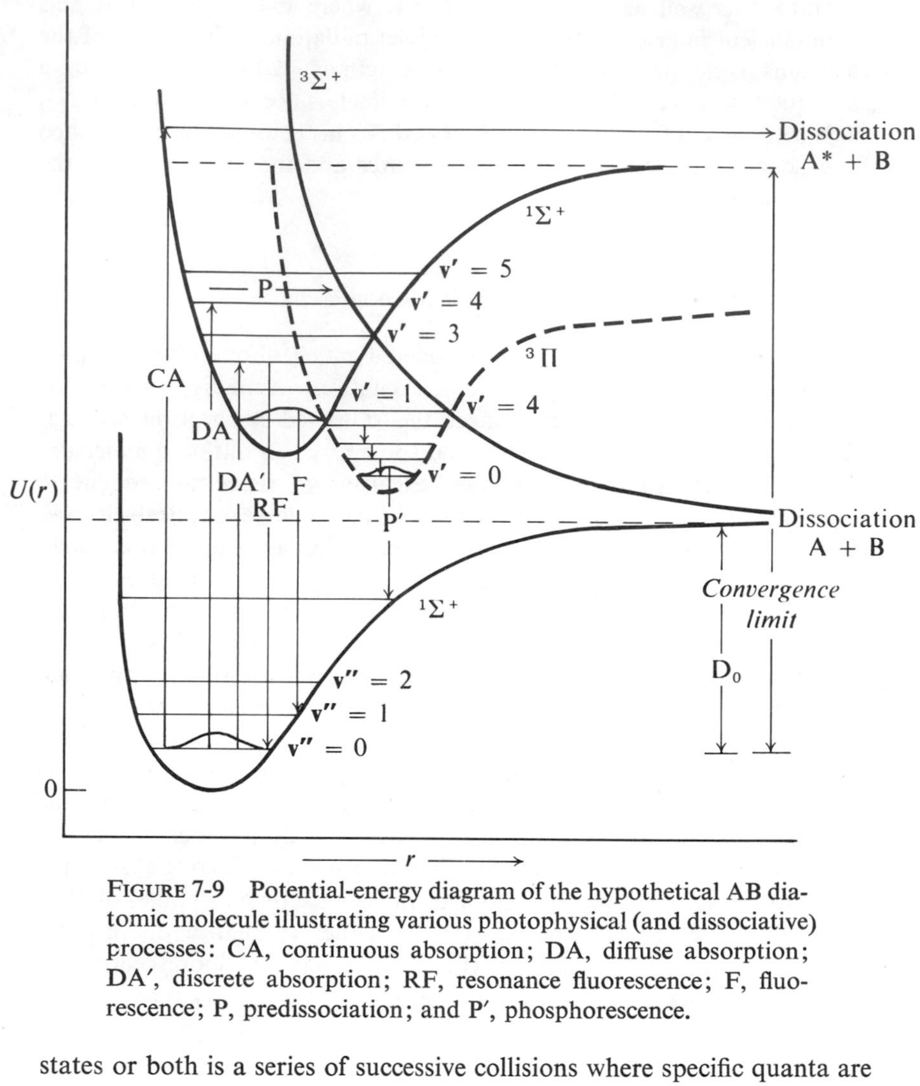

FIGURE 7-9 Potential-energy diagram of the hypothetical AB diatomic molecule illustrating various photophysical (and dissociative) processes: CA, continuous absorption; DA, diffuse absorption; DA′, discrete absorption; RF, resonance fluorescence; F, fluorescence; P, predissociation; and P′, phosphorescence.

states or both is a series of successive collisions where specific quanta are exchanged in each inelastic collision.

The excitation labeled "DA" is for diffuse absorption. In fact, above the $\mathbf{v}' = 3$ level of the excited $^1\Sigma^+$ state the rotational structure may or may not be resolved, and may range from slightly broadened lines to a complete "washout" of the rotational structure. The degree to which rotational resolution is lost is a direct result of the lifetime of the molecule in a specific excited rotational-vibronic state. In this particular example (Figure 7-9), the lifetime of the state may be terminated by three primary processes: fluorescence $^1\Sigma^+ \rightarrow {}^1\Sigma^+$, collision-induced rotation-vibration energy transfer, and a radiationless change of electronic state called intersystem crossing (ISC), $^1\Sigma^+ \rightarrow {}^3\Sigma^+$. The degree of diffuseness in each case will depend on the time (τ_t) necessary for each process to terminate the initially excited rotational-vibronic state. The broadness or uncertainty in the line frequency ($\Delta\omega$) is given by the uncertainty expression,

$$\Delta\omega\,(\text{cm}^{-1}) \simeq \frac{1}{2\pi c\,\Delta t}, \tag{2-53}$$

where c is the speed of light and $\Delta t \sim \tau_t$, the life of a specific state. For fluorescence $\tau_t = \tau_f \simeq 10^{-8}$ sec, and the uncertainty ($\sim$ broadening) in line width is 5×10^{-4} cm^{-1}. This corresponds to resolution of the order of 10 MHz. We have assumed in this calculation, however, that τ_f is the "natural lifetime" of the molecule, or more specifically, that the molecule is not perturbed in any way between excitation and (resonance) fluorescence. This assumption is obviously based on a low limiting total pressure that defines the collision frequency. If however, collisions do occur during the 10^{-8} sec lifetime, then an inelastic collision brings about an earlier termination of the occupation of a specific rotational or vibrational state or both. By the selection rules mentioned above for these energy-transfer processes and the smaller rotational energy separations, rotational exchanges are more efficient than vibrational ones. Therefore diffuseness, or in this case "pressure-broadening," of the rotational structure usually results. The most important factor in energy-transfer processes, however, is the near resonance of the exchanging energy levels. For the termination of an occupied rotational-vibronic state in a rotational period, $\tau_r \simeq 10^{-11}$ sec, $\Delta\omega \simeq 0.5$ cm^{-1}. This uncertainty corresponds to resolution of the order of 10,000 MHz. This would be classified somewhere between very diffuse and "washed out" rotational structure.

Radiationless transitions, just like those involving radiation, also have selection rules. These rules are the same as those in Table 7-3 except that $(+) \nleftrightarrow (-)$ and $g \nleftrightarrow u$. A radiationless transition between two electronic states of different multiplicity is termed *intersystem crossing* (ISC). In Figure 7-9, ISC from the excited $^1\Sigma^+$ state to the $^3\Sigma^+$ leads immediately to dissociation of the *AB* molecule, since the $^3\Sigma^+$ state is unstable at all internuclear distances. The sum total of these two processes is called *predissociation*, and labeled "P", which essentially means "dissociation before reaching the convergence limit." However, the ISC process is spin-forbidden, so that it can occur only as a result of two main occurrences. One is the partial or total breakdown of weak spin-orbit coupling, so that S is no longer a very good representation of the total electronic spin quantum number. Thus, at the internuclear distance where the potential curves intersect ($\mathbf{v}' = 2$ for excited $^1\Sigma^+$), coupling of the two states is sufficient for significant ISC. If this natural electronic state coupling does not exist to any significant extent, then ISC can be brought about by collision-induced perturbations of the two electronic states involved, resulting in significant mixing. Predissociation brought about by "natural" mixing is sometimes called spontaneous, and is pressure-independent, whereas pressure-induced predissociation is called induced. The "allowed" *internal conversion* IC $^3\Pi \rightarrow {}^3\Sigma^+$ for all $\mathbf{v}'$ states above the $\mathbf{v}' = 4$ level is also "spontaneous predissociation" with no selection rule limitation.

If either induced or natural significant mixing exists between the excited $^1\Sigma^+$ and $^3\Pi$ states, then ISC results. For ISC of vibrational states below the $\mathbf{v}' = 4$ of the $^3\Pi$ state, the molecule is reduced through successive collisions to the $\mathbf{v}' = 0$ level. To return to the ground electronic state, the molecule has to undergo a spin-forbidden transition. As a result, the emission lifetime is relatively long, $\tau_p \sim 10^{-4}$ to 10^{-3} sec, depending again on the degree of weak spin-orbit coupling ($\mathbf{\Lambda}$, S) and pressure-induced perturbations. This emission is called *phosphorescence* (P′).

B. POLYATOMIC MOLECULES

Now we will consider how electronic transitions are interpreted. As with diatomics, a suitable approach is to classify the term manifolds, predict approximately the energy ordering, and correlate these with observed electronic transitions. The molecular orbital (MO) approach will be used in defining the energy states. Our discussions of triatomic and tetratomic molecules will involve some degree of detail, but our approach to the larger polyatomic molecules will be more qualitative and more generally descriptive.

1. Classification of Electronic States (Group-Theoretical Notation)

***a. Triatomic Molecules* (XY_2).** In using the MO approach for designating the various electronic state term symbols, we must first have an approximate energy ordering of the various MO's as a function of internuclear separation, that is, a correlation diagram. Such correlation diagrams are constructed in the same way that those of the diatomic molecules are, except that three atoms are simultaneously brought together in either a linear or a bent configuration, and the MO's at the bonding separations are the linear combinations of the separate atomic orbitals (AO's). These diagrams are more approximate than the diagrams of the diatomics and must be constructed for each molecular type, for example linear XH_2 or bent XY_2. The details of these correlation diagrams have been discussed at length in Herzberg [Reference 7-5]. We will not try to duplicate them here, but will make use of the approximate MO energy ordering for various molecular types as a basis for designating the manifold of states (electronic term symbols) possible.

We begin with the linear dihydrides, H—X—H, which have relatively short bond distances (similar to XH), and as such approach more closely the case of the united atom. The approximate energy ordering and orbital descriptions are

$$1\sigma_g < 2\sigma_g < 1\sigma_u < 1\pi_u < 3\sigma_g < 2\sigma_u < 2\pi_u < 4\sigma_g < 1\pi_g \ldots, \quad (7\text{-}24)$$

where a nondegenerate (σ) state can hold 2 electrons and a doubly degenerate (π) state 4 electrons. The various MO's are simply labeled in the numerical order in which they occur as a function of the orbital energy (stability). To obtain the term symbols, all the electrons are successively placed in the orbitals, and the possible states are determined using the procedure for homonuclear diatomics and Table 7-1 where necessary. For the possible linear ground state species BeH_2, there are 6 electrons distributed as $(1\sigma_g)^2(2\sigma_g)^2(1\sigma_u)^2$, which gives the state ${}^1\Sigma_g{}^+$. If one of the $1\sigma_u$ electrons is promoted to the $1\pi_u$ level, we would have as the first excited state the electronic configuration $(1s\sigma_g)^2(2\sigma_g)^2(1\sigma_u)^1(1\pi_u)^1$. According to Table 7-1, for the general configuration $\sigma\pi$, the states possible are ${}^3\Pi_g$ and ${}^1\Pi_g$; it is expected from Hund's rule that the former would lie lower. In a similar manner, the possible linear ground states of NH_2 (9 electrons) and SiH_2 (16 electrons) with $\ldots(1\sigma_u)^2(1\pi_u)^3$ and $\ldots(\sigma_u)^2(\pi_u)^2$ valence states would be ${}^2\Pi_u$ and ${}^1\Sigma_g{}^+$, ${}^3\Sigma_g{}^-$, ${}^1\Delta_g$ (Table 7-1).

In the case of general linear XY_2 molecules (nonhydrides), it is assumed that the closed electronic shells of the three atoms retain their relatively "pure" atomic orbital characters. As a result, only the valence shell electrons are effective in linearly combining to form the various MO's. For triatomics of the first period, where the 1*s* orbitals of each of the atoms are omitted, the approximate energy ordering and orbital descriptions are

$$3\sigma_g < 2\sigma_u < 4\sigma_g < 3\sigma_u < 1\pi_u < 1\pi_g < 2\pi_u < 5\sigma_g < 4\pi_u \ldots, \quad (7\text{-}25)$$

where u and g are used only in the cases of Y—X—Y. ($D_{\infty h}$ symmetry). For the case BO_2 having 15 *valence* electrons, the electronic configuration is $(3\sigma_g)^2(2\sigma_u)^2(4\sigma_g)^2(3\sigma_u)^2(1\pi_u)^4(1\pi_g)^3$, and has a corresponding ground state term ${}^2\Pi_g$. For the excited state configuration $\ldots(3\sigma_u)^2(1\pi_u)^3(1\pi_g)^4$, we have the term state ${}^2\Pi_u$, which is the first observed excited state of linear BO_2. Linear NCN and OCO are additional examples that have the electronic configurations $\ldots(1\pi_u)^4(3\sigma_u)^2(1\pi_g)^2$ and $\ldots(3\sigma_u)^2(1\pi_u)^4(1\pi_g)^4$.[4] According to Table 7-1, for NCN the ground state is a multiplet of $^3\Sigma_g^-$, $^1\Delta_g$, $^1\Sigma_g^+$, of which the $^3\Sigma_g^-$ is the expected (Hund's rule) and observed ground state. For the completely filled CO_2 orbital configuration, the ground state is $^1\Sigma_g^+$. In the case of linear unsymmetrical XY_2 molecules, both the u, g, and the numerical orbital designations are dropped and only the orbital types and ordering are retained. The ground electronic configurations of NNO (16 valence electrons) and NCO (15 valence electrons) are $\sigma^2\sigma^2\sigma^2\sigma^2\pi^4\pi^4$ and $\sigma^2\sigma^2\sigma^2\sigma^2\pi^4\pi^3$. The corresponding states are $^1\Sigma^+$ and $^2\Pi_i$.

For nonlinear triatomic molecules, the π and σ molecular orbital designations are no longer appropriate, since the molecule has other than axial symmetry. The procedure used in the MO designations is based on the assumption that the symmetry of the total electronic wavefunction is reasonably well approximated by the direct product of the symmetry species of the occupied MO's, $\psi_e = \psi_1\psi_2\psi_3\cdots\psi_n$. As such, the electronic state term symbols will indicate the symmetry species of a specific point group. Again, the MO's are constructed from a linear combination of AO's, having either a symmetrical (Y—X—Y) or an unsymmetrical (Y—Y—X) structure. The symmetrical structure belongs to the point group C_{2v} (Appendix III) and therefore can have only electronic states (total wavefunctions, ψ_e) that transform like A_1, A_2, B_1, and B_2. The individually occupied MO's (ψ_i's) will also have the symmetry of one of these symmetry species, and are designated by the lower cases, a_1, a_2, b_1, and b_2. The C_{2v} point group has only nondegenerate representations; therefore each MO can hold only two electrons. For electronic configurations having closed MO's, the symmetry species of the electronic state is always the totally symmetric representation; in this example A_1 (C_{2v} molecules). For states having a single electron occupying an orbital with all the others closed, the electronic state designation will simply be the symmetry of the unfilled MO. The energy ordering of the MO's generated for the symmetrical bent XH_2 type is given as

$$1a_1 < 2a_1 < 1b_2 < 3a_1 < 1b_1 < 4a_1 < 2b_2 < 5a_1 < 2b_1 < 6a_1\cdots. \tag{7-26}$$

The electronic configuration of BH_2 having 7 *total* electrons is $(1a_1)^2(2a_1)^2(1b_2)^2(3a_1)^1$, and the corresponding term state is $^2A_1$; the lone unpaired electron gives rise to the doublet state. The ground state configuration of H_2O is $(1a_1)^2(2a_1)^2(1b_2)^2(3a_1)^2(1b_1)^2$, giving a resulting term symbol of $^1A_1$; for the first excited state, the configuration is $\ldots(3a_1)^2(1b_1)^1(4a_1)^1$. For these two nonequivalent electrons, the term is obtained by the direct product $\Gamma(B_1) \times \Gamma(A_1) = \Gamma(B_1)$ and the vector addition of $S_{12} = 1$ and 0. Thus, we obtain $^3B_1$ and $^1B_1$, in which the triplet state is lower in energy. The electronic states that can be generated from nonequivalent electrons are summarized in Table 7-4 for the C_{2v}

TABLE 7-4. Electronic States Generated from Equivalent and Nonequivalent Electrons

Equivalent electrons			Nonequivalent electrons		
Point group	Electronic configuration	Electronic states	Point group	Electronic configuration	Electronic states
C_{3v}	a_2	$^2A_2$	C_{2v}	a_1	$^2A_1$
	a_2^2	$^1A_1$		a_1a_1	$^3A_1$, $^1A_1$
	e	^2E		a_1a_2	$^1A_2$, $^3A_2$
	e^2	$^1A_1$, ^1E, $^3A_2$		b_1b_2	$^1A_2$, $^3A_2$
	e^3	^2E	C_{3v}	e	^2E
	e^4	$^1A_1$		a_1e	^1E, ^3E
D_{3h}	e'	$^2E'$		ee	$^1A_1$, $^1A_2$, ^1E, $^3A_1$, $^3A_2$, ^3E
	e'^2	$^1A_1'$, $^1E'$, $^2A_2'$	D_{3h}	$a_2''e'$	$^1E''$, $^3E''$
	e'^3	$^2E'$		$e'e''$	$^1A_1''$, $^1A_2''$, $^1E''$, $^3A_1''$, $^3A_2''$, $^3E''$
	e'^4	$^1A_1'$		$a_1''e'e''$	$^2A_1'(2)$, $^2A_2'(2)$, $^2E'(2)$, $^4A_1'$, $^4A_2'$, $^4E'$
	e''	$^2E''$			
	e''^2	$^1A_1'$, $^1E'$, $^3A_2'$			
	e''^3	$^2E''$			
	e''^4	$^1A_1'$			

SOURCE: From *Molecular Spectra and Molecular Structure*, Vol. III by G. Herzberg © 1966 by Litton Educational Publishing, Inc. Reprinted by permission of Van Nostrand Reinhold Company.

TABLE 7-5. Ground State Electronic Configurations and Term States as Derived from Their Observed Electronic Spectra

Species	Valence electrons	Ground state electronic configuration[a]	Valence angle	Ground term state
BeH_2	4	$K(2\sigma_g)^2(1\sigma_u)^2$	180°	$^1\Sigma_g{}^+$
BH_2	5	$K(2a_1)^2(1b_2)^2(3a_1)^1$	131°	$^2A_1$
CH_2	6	$K(2a_1)^2(1b_2)^2(3a_1)^2$	104°	$^1A_1$
NH_2	7	$K(2a_1)^2(1b_2)^2(3a_1)^2(1b_1)^1$	103°	$^2B_1$
H_2O	8	$K(2a_1)^2(1b_2)^2(3a_1)^2(1b_1)^2$	105°	$^1A_1$
H_2S	8	$KL(a_1)^2(b_2)^2(a_1)^2(b_1)^2$	92°	$^1A_1$
CN_2	14	$KKK(3\sigma_g)^2(2\sigma_u)^2(4\sigma_g)^2(1\pi_u)^4(3\sigma_u)^2(1\pi_g)^2$	180°	$^3\Sigma_g{}^-$
N_3	15	$KKK(\sigma_g)^2(\sigma_u)^2(\sigma_g)^2(\sigma_u)^2(\pi_u)^4(\pi_g)^3$	180°	$^2\Pi_g$
BO_2	15	$KKK(3\sigma_g)^2(2\sigma_u)^2(4\sigma_g)^2(3\sigma_u)^2(1\pi_u)^4(1\pi_g)^3$	180°	$^1\Pi_g$
$NO_2{}^+$	16	$KKK(3\sigma_g)^2(2\sigma_u)^2(4\sigma_g)^2(3\sigma_u)^2(1\pi_u)^4(1\pi_g)^4$	180°	$^1\Sigma_g{}^+$
NO_2	17	$KKK\ldots(3b_2)^2(1b_1)^2(5a_1)^2(1a_2)^2(4b_2)^2(6a_1)^1$	134°	$^2A_1$
$NO_2{}^-$	18	$KKK\ldots(3b_2)^2(1b_1)^2(5a_1)^2(1a_2)^2(4b_2)^2(6a_1)^2$	115°	$^1A_1$
CF_2	18	$KKK\ldots(5a_1)^2(4b_2)^2(1a_2)^2(6a_1)^2$	105°	$^1A_1$
SiF_2	18	$KKKL\ldots(a_1)^2(a_2)^2(b_2)^2(a_1)^2$	101°	$^1A_1$
SO_2	18	$KKKL\ldots(a_1)^2(a_2)^2(b_2)^2(a_1)^2$	120°	$^1A_1$
F_2O	20	$KKK\ldots(5a_1)^2(6a_1)^2(4b_2)^2(1a_2)^2(2b_1)^2$	103°	$^1A_1$

[a] The K and L orbitals are closed nonbonding atomic shells.

and C_{3v} point groups.[5] The relative orbital energies for nonhydride, symmetrically bent XY_2 molecules excluding the K shells of each of the three atoms are:

$$3a_1 < 2b_2 < 4a_1 < 3b_2 < 1b_1 < 5a_1 < 1a_2 < 4b_2 < 6a_1 < 2b_1 \cdots. \tag{7-27}$$

The ordering of the $1a_2$, $4b_2$, and $6a_1$ MO's depends critically on the valence angle. The order shown in Eq. (7-27) favors a valence angle that is roughly greater than 110°. These orbital energy variations are illustrated by the triatomics having more than 16 valence electrons listed in Table 7-5. The compounds NO_2 having a valence angle of 134° and SO_2 of 120° have the ordering shown in Eq. (7-27), whereas CF_2 and F_2O having valence angles of 105° and 103° have exchanged energy ordering of the $1a_2$ and $4b_2$ orbitals.

***b. Tetratomic Molecules* (XY_3).** Like the procedure used for the triatomics above, the ordering of the energy levels for intermediate cases is derived from the various correlation diagrams for XH_3 and nonhydride XY_3 types. The energy-level orderings for each of the four cases are shown on the extreme left and right of Figures 7-12 and 7-13. The left and extreme right ordinates of these figures correspond to the bent and planar configurations, respectively. In deriving the electronic term states from the direct product of the occupied MO's, we have in the case of C_{3v} and D_{3h} molecules an added consideration—doubly degenerate MO's. The direct product of two of these doubly degenerate MO's generates several different electronic states permuted among the spin orientations, some of which are not possible, depending on whether the electrons are equivalent or nonequivalent. For two nonequivalent doubly degenerate electrons, all the states generated are possible, as in the diatomic case. For the configuration *ee* belonging to the C_{3v} point group, the states possible are ${}^1A_1$, ${}^1A_2$, ${}^1E$, ${}^3A_1$, ${}^3A_2$, and ${}^3E$, as shown in Table 7-4. For two equivalent doubly degenerate electrons, we are first of all bound by the Pauli principle; we also have the additional restriction that the total electronic wavefunction, ψ_e, must be antisymmetric to the inversion operation. In this case of two equivalent doubly degenerate electrons, the direct product $e \times e$, produces the antisymmetric A_2 and symmetric A_1 and E states. Since the total wavefunction for electronic exchange in this case must be antisymmetric, $\psi_e \xrightarrow{i} -\psi_e$, only the *symmetric* triplet spin function can combine with the *antisymmetric* orbital function, giving ${}^3A_2$, whereas the antisymmetric singlet spin state combines with the symmetric states, producing the ${}^1A_1$ and ${}^1E$ states.[6] These are the only states possible for equivalent doubly degenerate electrons. The molecular term states possible for molecules belonging to the C_{3v} and D_{3h} point groups are summarized in Table 7-4.

For planar CH_3 with seven valence electrons, the ground electronic configuration according to Figure 7-12 is $K(2a_1')^2(1e')^4(1a_2'')^1$ and a resulting term state ${}^2A_2''$. The excited planar configuration $K(2a_1')^2(1e')^4(3a_1')^1$ has the term state ${}^2A_1'$. The nonplanar NH_3 ground configuration is $K(2a_1)^2(1e)^4(3a_1)^2$, giving rise to the totally symmetric ${}^1A_1$ state; the homologs PH_3, AsH_3, and so on, which also have C_{3v} symmetry, probably have the analogous configurations $\ldots(a_1)^2(e)^4(a_1)^2$ and term states ${}^1A_1$.

According to Figure 7-13, the ground electronic configuration of the planar species BF_3, CO_3^{2-}, and NO_3^- having 24 valence electrons is $KKKs_1s_2s_3(1a_1')^2(1e')^4(1a_2'')^2(2e')^4(1e'')^4(1a_2')^2$, which gives rise to the totally symmetric ${}^1A_1'$ state.[7] On the other hand, the distinctly pyramidal NF_3 molecule (26 valence electrons) has the electronic configuration $KKKs_1s_2s_3(1a_1)^2(1e)^4(2a_1)^2(2e)^4(3e)^4(1a_2)^2(3a_1)^2$ and a corresponding ground state term ${}^1A_1$.

The group-theoretical term states for larger polyatomic molecules are derived like the states we have discussed in this section. With the symmetry (and point group) of the molecule as a basis, the MO correlation diagram is constructed from the atomic orbitals of the constituent atoms and the united atom (or united molecule in some cases) with an "approximate" energy ordering. The electrons in appropriate number are placed in the MO's, from which the group-theoretical term state is derived. Benzene and ethylene, for example, belong to point groups D_{6h} and D_{2h}, and both have totally symmetric ground electronic states, $^1A_{1g}$ and ^1A_g.

2. Walsh Correlation Diagrams

The correlation between the orbital energies of similar molecular types (bent and planar XH_2) as a function of a given coordinate was first performed by A. D. Walsh and reported in a series of papers published in 1953. The correlation diagrams of the orbital energies of XH_2 and XY_2 as a function of the valence angle between 180° and 90° were plotted and are shown in Figures 7-10 and 7-11.

These are called *Walsh diagrams.* The two extreme valence angles represent molecules that have C_{2v} symmetry at the left and $D_{\infty h}$ at the extreme right. Such diagrams are useful in roughly predicting whether or not a given symmetrical triatomic will be linear or bent. It is important to recognize that these predictions were made long before any substantial

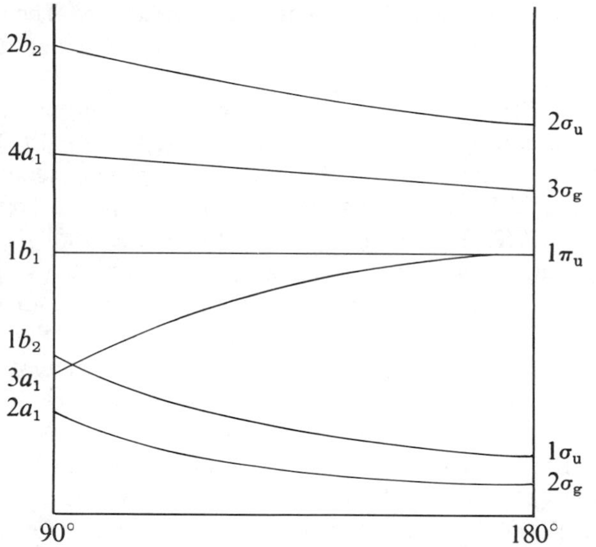

FIGURE 7-10 Walsh diagram for XH_2 molecules. Variation of the orbital energies as a function of the HXH valence angle from 90° to 180°. The atomic 1*s* X orbital is not included. (Taken from the publication by A. D. Walsh, *J. Chem. Soc.* 2260 (1953), with permission.)

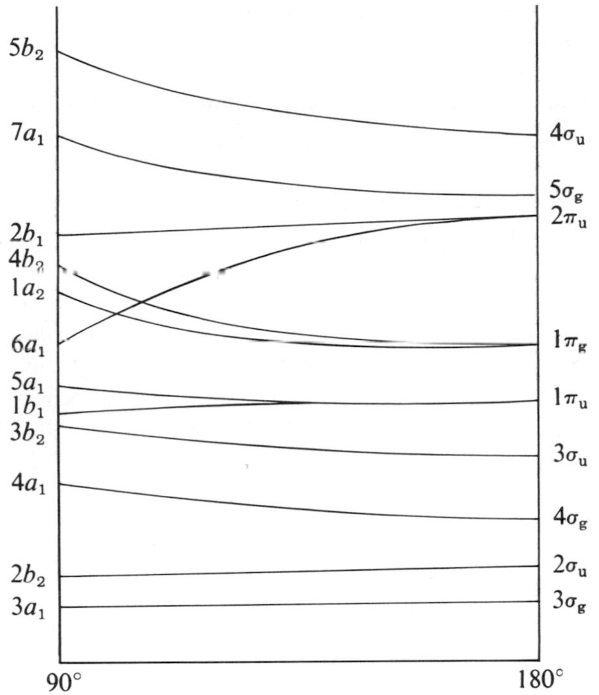

FIGURE 7-11 Walsh diagram for XY_2 molecules. Variation of the orbital energies as a function of the YXY valence angle from 90° to 180°. The atomic 1*s* X and Y orbitals are not included. (Taken from the publication by A. D. Walsh, *J. Chem. Soc.* 2266 (1953), with permission.)

experimental data base was available, and yet the predicted configurations are remarkably correct for most of the observed cases. The procedure in using these diagrams is simply to assign the appropriate number of electrons to each MO (according to the Pauli principle), proceeding up the center of the diagram, and using the direction that minimizes the orbital energy for approximating the linear or bent configuration. The triatomic BeH_2 has 4 valence electrons and a ground state configuration having the highest energy orbital $1b_2$–$1\sigma_u$ filled. The stability of this orbital favors a linear configuration, which agrees with the experimentally observed linear molecule. Excitation of this ($1\sigma_u$) electron to the $3a_1$–$1\pi_u$ orbital results in a bent (first) excited state. For CH_2 with 6 valence electrons, the steeply sloped $3a_1$–$1\pi_u$ orbital containing the two highest-energy (ground) electrons causes the molecule to be distinctly bent (104°). Excitation of one of these electrons to the next-highest orbital, $1b_1$–$1\pi_u$, now involves the cumulative effects of the two orbitals containing one electron each. The steep slope of the former and the virtual independence of the $1b_1$–$1\pi_u$ orbital energy as a function of bond angle give a structure that is less bent.

According to Figure 7-11, any symmetrical (nonhydride) XY_2 molecule containing 16 or fewer valence electrons should be linear. As shown in Table 7-5, this is indeed found to be the case for many triatomics in this category. However, when the $6a_1$–$2\pi_u$ orbital is occupied (17th valence electron), the configuration, it is predicted, will be bent, as exemplified by NO_2. When the relative energy-level configurations of Figure 7-11 are applied to NO_2^+, NO_2, and NO_2^- having 16, 17, and 18 valence electrons, the predicted configurations are linear, bent, and very bent. The observed valence bond angles for NO_2^+, NO_2, and NO_2^- are respectively 180°, 134°, and 115°, giving remarkable agreement. Further occupation of the $6a_1$–$2\pi_u$ and the $2b_1$–$2\pi_u$ orbitlas (17–20 valence electrons) both favor bent configurations. Such is the case for SO_2 (120°), CF_2 (105°), and F_2O (103°) having 18, 18, and 20 valence electrons.

The Walsh diagrams for XH_3 and XY_3 are illustrated in Figures 7-12 and 7-13. According to Figure 7-12, the species BeH_3 and BH_3, having

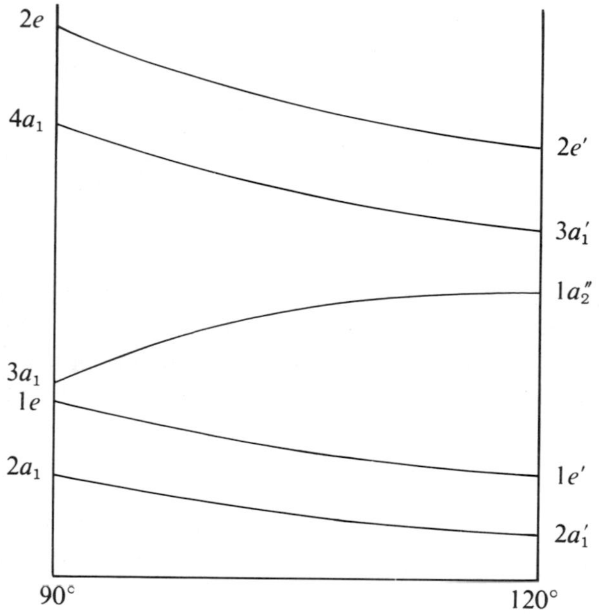

FIGURE 7-12 Walsh diagram for XH_3 molecules. Variation of the orbital energies as a function of the HXH bond angle from 90° to 120°. The 1*s* X atomic orbital is not included. (Taken from the publication by A. D. Walsh, *J. Chem. Soc.* 2296 (1953), with permission.)

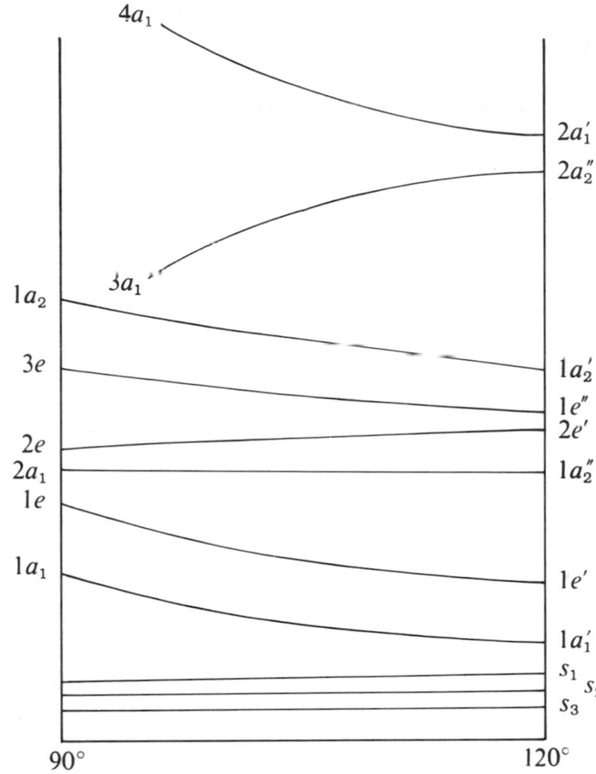

FIGURE 7-13 Walsh diagram for XY_3 molecules. Variation of the orbital energies as a function of the YXY bond angle from 90° to 120°. The atomic 1*s* X and Y orbitals are not included, but those of the 2*s* atomic orbitals are shown at the bottom of the table. (Taken from the publication by A. D. Walsh, *J. Chem. Soc.* 2303 (1953), with permission.)

ground electronic configurations $K(2a_1')^2(1e')^3$ and $K(2a_1')^2(1e')^4$, should both be planar. The ground states of these molecules have not been observed. Adding one electron to the $3a_1$–$1a_2''$ orbital corresponding to CH_3 and two electrons to a like orbital for NH_3 should result in distinctly bent configurations. This is indeed observed for NH_3 ($\angle$HNH $\sim$ 107°), although fairly substantial evidence exists confirming the planar configuration of CH_3. In this case, the approximate ordering of the orbitals at 120° is not appropriate and the next $4a_1$–$3a_1'$ orbital that favors the planar configuration probably is very significant in the resulting observed geometry.

The final Walsh diagram we consider is that correlating the XY_3 pyramidal-planar configurations reproduced from the original article in

Figure 7-13. According to this diagram, symmetrical XY_3 molecules having 24 valence electrons or fewer should be planar. This is indeed the case for a variety of species such as CO_3^{2-}, NO_3^-, BF_3, and $GaCl_3$. However, when the $2a_2''$–$3a_1$ orbital is occupied, the molecule should be bent. Numerous examples of this case also exist, a few of which are $GeCl_3$, NF_3, $BiCl_3$, and CF_3.

The structure and bonding of a variety of stable and unstable group IV species have been reviewed and findings generally confirm the predicted Walsh configurations.[8]

3. Selection Rules

The most general criterion for *allowed* electric dipole emission and absorption is

$$\int \psi'^* \mu \psi'' \, d\tau \neq 0. \qquad \textbf{(7-28)}$$

If Eq. (7-28) is zero for all components of the electric dipole operator μ, then the transition between the states ψ'^* and ψ'' is regarded as *forbidden.* Since the limits on the integral of Eq. (7-28) span total space, the direct product of the factors ψ'^*, μ, and ψ'' must be *totally symmetric*, that is, symmetric to all operations of the point group appropriate to the equilibrium configurations of the upper and lower molecular states. In group-theoretical notation,

$$\Gamma(\psi'^*) \times \Gamma(\mu) \times \Gamma(\psi'') = \Gamma \text{ (totally symmetric)}. \qquad \textbf{(7-29)}$$

Like the diatomic derivation, substituting the corresponding expressions for μ (Eq. (7-6)) and ψ (Eq. (7-4)) gives a result similar to Eq. (7-7), in this case for a polyatomic molecule. Assuming again the electronic wavefunctions to be orthogonal, the resulting expressions that determine the electronic selection rules are:

$$\mathbf{R}_x = \int \psi_e'^* \mu_e^x \psi_e'' \, d\tau_e \int \psi_v'^* \psi_v'' \, d\tau_v \int \psi_r'^* [\Phi_{Xx} + \Phi_{Yx} + \Phi_{Zx}] \psi_r'' \, d\tau_r,$$

$$\mathbf{R}_y = \int \psi_e'^* \mu_e^y \psi_e'' \, d\tau_e \int \psi_v'^* \psi_v'' \, d\tau_v \int \psi_r'^* [\Phi_{Xy} + \Phi_{Yy} + \Phi_{Zy}] \psi_r'' \, d\tau_r,$$

$$\mathbf{R}_z = \int \psi_e'^* \mu_e^z \psi_e'' \, d\tau_e \int \psi_v'^* \psi_v'' \, d\tau_v \int \psi_r'^* [\Phi_{Xz} + \Phi_{Yz} + \Phi_{Zz}] \psi_r'' \, d\tau_r, \qquad \textbf{(7-30)}$$

where Φ_{Fg}'s are the direction cosines defined previously in Section 6B-3, and μ_e^x, μ_e^y, and μ_e^z are the components of the *electronic* dipole moment operator (not the equilibrium dipole moment) in the x, y, z molecule-fixed coordinate system. Since these components contain the position coordinates as shown by Eq. (7-10), the condition placed on the electronic integrals of Eq. (7-30) is that

$$\Gamma(\psi'^{*}) \times \Gamma(\psi_e'') = \Gamma(x, y, \text{ or } z) \qquad \textbf{(7-31)}$$

for a symmetry-allowed transition. For the special case (which is quite common) where the ground electronic state is totally symmetric, then $\psi_e'^{*}$ must transform like one of the components x, y, or z.

The ground and first excited electronic states of H_2O, both having C_{2v} symmetry, are $^1A_1$ and $^3B_1$, $^1B_1$ (as derived previously). The upper state has two components that differ simply by the spin orientation. Since the ground state is totally symmetric in this case ($^1A_1$), we examine the C_{2v} character table for those symmetry species that transform like the x, y, and z components. They are

$$\Gamma(x) = B_1, \qquad \Gamma(y) = B_2, \qquad \Gamma(z) = A_1. \qquad \textbf{(7-32)}$$

Thus the A_1 and the B_1 states are allowed to combine along the x component of the electric dipole moment. As in the diatomic cases for relatively light atoms composing the polyatomic molecule, however, we have the prohibition of intercombinations, $\Delta S = 0$. Thus, $^1B_1 \leftrightarrow {}^1A_1$ and $^3B_1 \not\leftrightarrow {}^1A_1$ (spin-forbidden). Thus, for all the possible electronic state combinations (transitions) possible for a molecule having C_{2v} as the appropriate symmetry in an electronic transition, we can construct the accompanying table (Eq. (7-33)). The entries in (7-33) are generated by

C_{2v}	A_1	A_2	B_1	B_2	
	μ_z	f	μ_x	μ_y	A_1
		μ_z	μ_y	μ_x	A_2
			μ_z	f	B_1
				μ_z	B_2

(7-33)

taking the direct product between any two of the combining states, that is, $\Gamma(A_2) \times \Gamma(B_1) = \Gamma(B_2)$, and identifying the cartesian coordinate that transforms like the product representation $\Gamma(B_2) = \Gamma(y)$. Thus, the corresponding entry in the table signifies that a transition is allowed between the A_2 and B_1 states if there exists a nonzero electronic dipole component along the molecule-fixed y axis. Using the same procedure gives $\Gamma(B_2) \times \Gamma(B_1) = \Gamma(A_2)$, which does not transform like x, y, or z, and is therefore *forbidden* (f).

In the case of many electronic transitions, the initial and final electronic state configurations are of different symmetry. Consequently, it is not immediately obvious how to interpret the expression "the point group appropriate to the equilibrium configurations of the upper and lower molecular states." This point group corresponds to the point group having common symmetry operations in the two different configurations, or quite often it turns out to be simply the point group having the lower symmetry. For the NH_3 transition between the pyramidal ground state (C_{3v} symmetry) and the planar first excited state (D_{3h} symmetry) $^1A_2'' \leftarrow {}^1A_1$, the appropriate point group to use in deducing the electronic transitions is the C_{3v}. The direct product $\Gamma(A_2'') \times \Gamma(A_1) = \Gamma(A_2'')$. When the symmetry operations common to these two point groups (all those of C_{3v}: E, $2C_3$, $3\sigma_v$) are examined in the D_{3h} character table, we find that the characters are all $+1$. Thus, $\Gamma(A_2'') = \Gamma(A_1)$, the totally symmetric representation of C_{3v}, which transforms like the z coordinate. Thus, this allowed electronic transition is said to be z-polarized. Also, in this transition $\Delta S = 0$, as required by the spin selection rule.

As a final selection rule for molecules possessing a center of symmetry, we also have the so-called Laporte, or parity, rule $\mathrm{u} \leftrightarrow \mathrm{g}$, $\mathrm{g} \not\leftrightarrow \mathrm{g}$, and $\mathrm{u} \not\leftrightarrow \mathrm{u}$.

4. Transitions in Electronic Spectroscopy

As might be expected, the additional degrees of rotational and vibrational motions possible in polyatomic molecules contribute considerable complexity to the observed electronic spectrum. Even a relatively simple nonlinear triatomic molecule has three different vibrational modes and three different rotational modes, all of whose transitions are possibly superimposable on an electronic transition. Except for a few "relatively small" molecules, complete vibrational and rotational analyses have been practically impossible.[9] In spite of these complexities, we shall try to review the type of data obtainable from the spectra of these relatively small molecules and outline in general terms the approach to interpreting the spectra of larger polyatomics.

Molecular electronic transitions are generally divided into two main classifications, Rydberg and sub-Rydberg. Rydberg transitions are those involving excitation from a ground (or low-lying) state orbital to one of very high energy (whose convergence leads to ionziation) in the far and near ultraviolet. These are analogous to atomic electronic transitions, wherein the excited electron is on the average far from the nuclei. Sub-Rydberg transitions are those involving electronic excitation between typically bonding, nonbonding, and antibonding molecular orbitals. They occur primarily in the visible and near ultraviolet. Since they occur between energy levels formed as a result of molecule formation, these transitions do not involve a change in the principal quantum number, as the Rydberg type does. In some cases, however, this distinction is not so obvious since the principal quantum number is not so clearly definable for a molecular orbital as for an atomic orbital.

Electronic transitions generally occur between the MO's shown in the accompanying diagram. This illustration presents only an *approximate* ordering of the MO's contained in molecules having sigma (σ) or pi (π) orbitals, or both, and nonbonding (n) orbitals. The notation used here, which gives a better description of the chemical nature of the bonding or

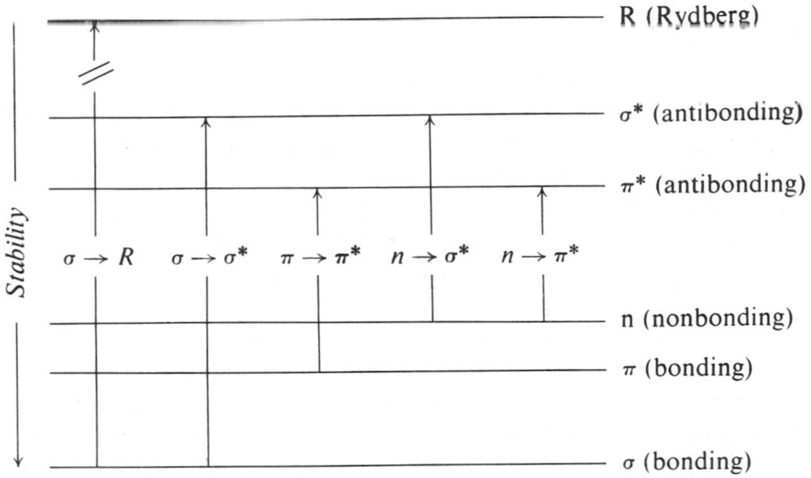

antibonding orbital than the group-theoretical notation does, is due to Kasha. This notation describes orbitals wherein the occupying electrons are more or less localized about one or two atoms. In general, electronic transitions from bonding to antibonding orbitals are classified by Mulliken as $V \leftarrow N$ transitions:

$$\sigma \rightarrow \sigma^* \quad \text{or} \quad \pi \rightarrow \pi^*.$$

Both of these types of transitions are strongly allowed. The $\pi \rightarrow \pi^*$ transition generally occurs in the visible-UV and the $\sigma \rightarrow \sigma^*$ in the far-UV. Transitions from nonbonding orbitals to higher antibonding orbitals are classified as $Q \leftarrow N$ transitions:

$$\text{n} \rightarrow \pi^* \quad \text{or} \quad \text{n} \rightarrow \sigma^*.$$

The $\text{n} \rightarrow \pi^*$ transition involves excitation from a relatively localized (about an atom) nonbonding orbital to one that is antibonding and localized over the space between two atoms. For excitation from a pure *p*-atomic orbital perpendicular to the molecular axis, the $\text{n} \rightarrow \pi^*$ transition is forbidden, whereas excitation from a nonbonding hybridized orbital in the molecular plane (which is symmetry-allowed) is relatively weak in intensity because of an unfavorable overlap integral. The $n \rightarrow \sigma^*$ transitions generally have greater intensity than the $n \rightarrow \pi^*$ and occur in the middle-to-far UV. Both the $V \leftarrow N$ and $Q \leftarrow N$ transitions are classified as sub-Rydberg. Excitation to orbitals beyond those corresponding to MO's and more appropriately described as high-energy atomic orbitals of one or more of the constituent atoms is described by Mulliken as $R \leftarrow N$ transitions, that is, Rydberg.

a. Electronic Band Structure of Some Triatomics and Tetratomics. In considering selection rules for electronic transitions, we outlined the general procedure for ascertaining the nonzero nature of the electronic integrals of Eq. (7-30). Actually, the intensity of the various bands is determined by the magnitude of the vibrational overlap integral. Ignoring the rotational integral for the moment, we find that the requirement for a nonzero value of the overlap integral is that $\psi'^*\psi_v'' \, d\tau_v$ is totally symmetric. For the bent XYZ molecule belonging to the C_s point group, there are three normal modes of vibration, all of which belong to the totally symmetric species a'. If we consider "cold absorption" ($\mathbf{v}_i'' = 0$ are the only significantly populated levels), only totally symmetric upper-state vibrational modes can combine, since all of the $\mathbf{v}_i'' = 0$ states of the ground electronic state are totally symmetric. As a result, for a symmetry-allowed electronic transition of this nature, there is generally no restriction on the change in vibrational quantum number for sequences or progressions. For the system having only $\mathbf{v}_i'' = 0$ populated, we can eliminate sequences as one complicating source of possible overlapping lines. In terms of our interpretation of an observed electronic spectrum, we consider two cases: one for which there is little change in the XYZ valence angle; the other for which the upper electronic state is linear.

In the first case, with little change in the valence angle, the point group appropriate to this electronic transition is C_s, and examining this character table reveals that excited states having A'' symmetry will be x, y-polarized (perpendicular to the molecular plane) and those having A' symmetry will be z-polarized. Since all three vibrational modes are totally symmetric (a' symmetry) in both upper and lower states, unrestricted change in the vibrational quantum number is allowed. In this case, the resulting spectrum will have progressions in all three vibrational modes of the upper state. The most important factor, however, in simplifying the electronic spectrum concerns the *relative intensities* with which these transitions occur. The relative intensities are determined by the Franck-Condon overlap integral. For transitions involving slight changes in the molecular configuration (bond distances and angles), the two potential-energy surfaces are assumed to contain a common set of orthogonal vibrational states; thus $\Delta\mathbf{v}_i = 0$ (for totally symmetric and non–totally symmetric vibrations), where the 0–0 band is by far the most intense. The separations of successive bands in each of the progressions equal the vibrational frequencies in the excited electronic state. The electronic transition of HNO, $^1A'' \leftarrow {}^1A'$, is an example of this case where the upper $^1A''$ state is only slightly changed from the ground state configuration; progressions involving all three vibrational modes have led to the evaluation of the excited state vibrational frequencies $\omega_1' = 2854$ cm^{-1}, $\omega_2' = 1420$ cm^{-1}, and $\omega_3' = 981$ cm^{-1}, compared with the ground state frequencies $\omega_1'' = 3596$ cm^{-1}, $\omega_2'' = 1562$ cm^{-1}, and $\omega_3'' = 1110$ cm^{-1}.

In the second instance, where the upper state configuration is linear, the appropriate point group is still C_s, and on the basis of the vibrational selection rules, all three vibrational modes are possible in upper-state progressions. In this case, the upper- and lower-state potential surfaces are distinctly different in their equilibrium configurations, so that we can deduce immediately that the Franck-Condon factor will be greatest for $\Delta\mathbf{v}_i \neq 0$. Since immediately after the electron jump the molecule has essentially the same bent configuration in the excited state, the upper-state equilibrium configuration (linear) is most favorably formed on the upper-state potential surface by the *symmetric displacement* of the nuclei to the new (linear) configuration. This nuclear displacement obviously corresponds to the bending vibration. As a general rule, the vibrational mode or modes associated with the change in nuclear configuration in going from one electronic state to another will have the most intense progression. We should expect, as a result, to observe an intense and extended progression in the bending vibration of the upper electronic state. The visible absorption spectrum of HCO, which is bent (120°) in the ground electronic state, is observed to have its main progression in the upper-state bending frequency. Such an observation is conclusive evidence of a significant change in the valence angle and strong evidence of a near linear excited state. Depending on the degree of spectral resolution and complexity, rotational analysis of band structure can be used to confirm the latter point.

In the case for which both upper and lower states are linear XYZ species, the two totally symmetric vibrations of the $C_{\infty v}$ group, ω_1 and ω_3, would be expected to have intense and extended progressions in the electronic absorption spectrum. The near ultraviolet absorption spectrum of NCO is an excellent example in this instance, corresponding to the transition $^2\Pi \leftarrow {}^2\Pi_i$. The progressions in the two totally symmetric frequencies have led to the evaluation of $\omega_1' = 2303$ cm^{-1} and $\omega_3' = 1047$ cm^{-1}, but spectral observations sufficient to identify the bending frequency were not obtained. The same general observations outlined here occur in the cases of linear and bent symmetrical triatomics.

The electronic spectra of tetratomic molecules are in general more complicated than those considered above, but also have some of the same overall features. For planar-nonplanar transitions, long relatively intense progressions in the totally symmetric bending vibration of the 2168–1700 Å absorption band of NH_3 indicate a large change in the HNH valence angle; rotational analysis has in fact confirmed a planar upper-state configuration. On the other hand, the absence of intense progressions in the out-of-plane bending vibration in the various vacuum-ultraviolet absorption systems of CH_3 strongly confirms the planar configuration in these excited states. The symmetrical NO_3 free radical provides an additional example of a molecule that is approximately planar in both the ground and upper states of the visible electronic band from 6650 to 5000 Å. The progression is observed to have spacings corresponding to 930 cm^{-1}, which is interpreted to be the frequency of the totally symmetric stretching vibration in the upper state, since this type of symmetric nuclear displacement conserves the planar configuration. Recently observed infrared spectra of this matrix-isolated radical have suggested the occurrence of this totally symmetric vibration at about 956 cm^{-1} in the ground state.[10] This vibrational mode is infrared-active for a species having perfect D_{3h} symmetry. The absorption is relatively weak and probably indicates a ground state molecule that is slightly nonplanar. Formaldehyde, CH_2O, is a final example of a nonplanar-planar transition that has a long intense progression in the CO stretching vibration of $\omega_2' = 1182\,cm^{-1}$. These also have less intense, shorter progressions in the out-of-plane bending vibration (ω_4'), the CH_2 scissors (ω_3'), and the CH_2 stretching vibration (ω_1'). This absorption spectrum is an excellent example of an intermediate case in which ω_1, ω_2, and ω_3 are all totally symmetric vibrations of the planar molecule and expected to be intense for a planar-planar transition whereas the non–totally symmetric out-of-plane bend occurs in the progression as a result of the Franck-Condon factor, indicating a bent upper state of C_s symmetry.

In larger molecules, excitation tends to be more localized and results in minimal configurational changes. As a result, the progressions tend to be short rather than extended. In addition, the significant increase in the number of electronic states brings about many more competitive photophysical processes (Section 7B-5), which further complicate resolution of the observed spectra.

b. Saturated Molecules. Classifying molecules termed *saturated* here specifically refers to those containing no multiple bonds, whether these molecules are organic or inorganic. Molecules included in this grouping typically have transitions that are described in the Kasha notation as $\sigma \rightarrow \sigma^*$, $n \rightarrow \sigma^*$, $\sigma \rightarrow R$, and $n \rightarrow R$. These transitions originate from relatively stable bonding and nonbonding MO's in absorption and have relatively high energy antibonding and Rydberg final states. As a result, these transitions generally occur in the vacuum-UV (far ultraviolet) region of the spectrum.

With saturated hydrocarbons, there are no n or π orbitals (or electrons), consequently the observed vacuum-UV transitions are $\sigma \rightarrow \sigma^*$ and $\sigma \rightarrow R$. The lower $\sigma \rightarrow \sigma^*$ absorption occurs over the region from 1600 Å to below 1200 Å and is broad and continuous. Although the general band structure for CH_4, C_2H_6, C_3H_8, and so on are all similar, the onset shifts to shorter wavelength (higher energy) for the lower molecular weight species (CH_4, ~1440 Å). The Rydberg transitions of these molecules, which extend below 1000 Å, lead principally to photoionization, presumably above (in energy) the Rydberg convergence limit.

Inorganic species containing no multiple or conjugated bonding, hydrides in particular, are good examples of species that may have occupied nonbonding orbitals. Thus, $n \rightarrow \sigma^*$ and $n \rightarrow R$ transitions are now possible in addition to those involving the bonding σ orbitals. The ground electronic configuration of H_2O and H_2S shown in Table 7-5 indicates that the highest occupied orbital is $(b_1)^2$, which is essentially a nonbonding p-type orbital. Excitation from this level to the high-energy Rydberg states gives rise to both discrete and continuous spectra. In general, the stability of a Rydberg state depends on whether the electron that is excited is promoted from a bonding, nonbonding, or antibonding orbital. Since these excitations generally involve resulting high-energy antibonding orbitals, origination from nonbonding or antibonding orbitals does not decrease the stability of the resulting excited state relative to the ground state. As a result, the highly excited and ionized states resulting from such transitions have structures that are similar to the ground electronic state. In this example of H_2O, for the $n \rightarrow R$ transition the excited state molecule has a slightly increased bond length of 0.06 Å and a valence angle increase, from 105° to 107°. These $n \rightarrow R$ transitions generally have very short progressions, consisting of about two or three bands. An exception to these generalizations of similarity of structure and shortness of the progression for $n \rightarrow R$ transitions is the extended NH_3 progression converging to stable planar NH_3^+. This progression has a band separation of about 900 cm^{-1}, corresponding to the symmetrical bending (umbrella) motion, which confirms the planar excited state. The ionized molecule NH_3^+ is isoelectronic with CH_3, and has a similar justification for planarity, as discussed for CH_3 in Section 7A-3. These exceptions noted in the case of NH_3 are more typical of the σ(bonding) $\rightarrow$ R transitions, wherein the ground equilibrium configuration is significantly different from the ionized excited state.

These transitions and this discussion apply equally well to unsaturated molecules, but are the only transitions observed in these cases having only occupied n and σ orbitals.

c. ***Unsaturated Hydrocarbons.*** Molecules grouped in this category are those having double or triple carbon-carbon bonds, either of a localized or delocalized nature. Our review highlights some of the important features of the observed electronic spectra of these molecules.

Ethylene is the simplest C═C compound and has an MO configura-that is expressed in the Kasha notation as

$$(1s_{\rm C})^2(1s_{\rm C}')^2(\sigma_{\rm CH}')^2(\sigma_{\rm CH}')^2(\sigma_{\rm CH})^2(\sigma_{\rm CH})^2(\sigma_{\rm CC})^2(\pi_{\rm CC})^2.$$

The characteristic ethylenic $\pi \rightarrow \pi^*$ transitions ($^1B_{1u} \leftarrow A_g$ in the case of ethylene) have intensity maxima between 1600 and 1700 Å. This transition in ethylene has a long progression with an initial spacing of 850 cm^{-1}, corresponding to the totally symmetric CC stretching mode. When this frequency is compared with the frequency of the ground state, 1623 cm^{-1}, we conclude that the CC bond has been significantly weakened. This conclusion is in fact consistent with an electron in the antibonding state, cancelling the stability of the other π-bonding electron. The excited molecule has essentially a single CC bond ($\sigma_{\rm CC}$), and free rotation about the CC bond is possible. The isomerization about the π^* excited state ethylenic CC bonds in both 1,2-dichloroethylene and 1,2-difluoroethylene has indeed been observed in matrix-isolated monochromatic photolysis experiments, and presumably occurs via the first excited singlet state.[11] Excitation of a π_u electron to the Rydberg states leads to progressions not only in the CC stretch, but also the torsional mode ($\omega_4 \sim 200$ cm^{-1}), which indicates a significant change away from the planar configuration. Other localized C═C systems in longer-chain molecules are roughly similar in terms of their observed sub-Rydberg transitions. The characteristic acetylenic $\pi \rightarrow \pi^*$ transition has its origin from the doubly degenerate $1\pi_u$ orbital. The corresponding absorptions are broad and diffuse, and have intensity maxima ~1720 Å.

Chainlike molecules containing alternating double bonds also have their occupied MO's consisting of the double-bond pi electrons. In contrast with the cases above, these pi electrons are delocalized and able to move freely the entire length of the molecule; a so-called conjugated system. This property of delocalization results in extra stability for the entire pi system and a corresponding decrease in the $\pi \rightarrow \pi^*$ transition energy. Consequently, these transition frequencies are observed to shift progressively to lower energy as the chain length increases. One very elementary approach to characterizing the pi electron energy levels along a conjugated chain is the *free electron model.* According to this approach, the pi electrons are essentially particles moving freely along the conjugated bonds, bounded only by the chain length. This situation is analogous to the one-dimensional particle in a box. The Schrödinger equation for the problem, where the potential energy is zero ($U = 0$), is given as

$$\frac{d^2\psi}{dx^2} + \frac{8\pi^2 mE}{h^2}\psi = 0. \tag{7-34}$$

The corresponding energy for the n quantized level is

$$E_n = \frac{n^2h^2}{8mL^2}, \tag{7-35}$$

where m is the electronic rest mass and L is the total chain length. Assuming the average C—C distances (of C═C and C—C) to be roughly equal for a given conjugated polyene, then as a first approximation $L = 2N\bar{r}_{CC}$, where N is the number of double bonds in the chain. Substituting this relation into Eq. (7-35), we obtain

$$E_n = \frac{n^2h^2}{32m\bar{r}_{CC}^2N^2}. \tag{7-36}$$

For a given polyene, N is equal to the quantum number of the highest filled pi level of the ground state, $N = n$; hexatriene for an example has six pi electrons and a ground state configuration as shown in the accompanying diagram.

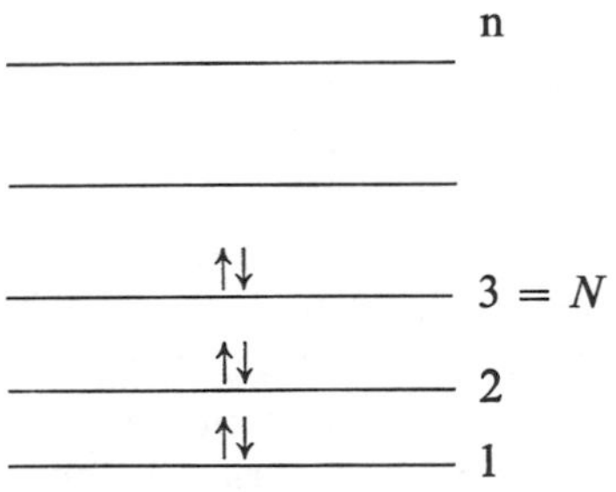

Thus for the lowest $\pi \rightarrow \pi^*$ transition, we obtain from Eq. (7-36)

$$\Delta E_{N+1\leftarrow N} = \frac{h^2}{32mr_{CC}^2}\frac{2N+1}{N^2}. \tag{7-37}$$

Since $r_{C=C} = 1.476$ Å and $r_{C-C} = 1.536$ Å in butadiene, we obtain for the average C—C distance, $\bar{r}_{CC} = 1.506$ Å. Using this value in Eq. (7-37), we obtain the data for the lowest-energy $\pi \rightarrow \pi^*$ transitions in the polyenes shown in Table 7-6. Although this rather crude approach is successful only in approximating the transition energies, it does correctly

TABLE 7-6. Calculated and Observed $\pi \rightarrow \pi^*$ Transition Frequencies for the First Four Conjugated Polyenes

Conjugated polyene	N	Lowest $\pi \rightarrow \pi^*$ transition: Observed (cm^{-1})	Calculated (cm^{-1}) (Eq. (7-37))
Ethylene	1	62,000	100,500
Butadiene	2	46,080	41,875
Hexatriene	3	39,750	26,056
Octatetraene	4	32,900	18,848

predict the shift to lower transition energies with increasing chain length.

d. ***Chromophores.*** In the systematic cataloguing of the electronic absorption spectra of numerous molecules, it has long been recognized that characteristic absorption bands could be ascribed to particular atoms or groups of atoms in polyatomic molecules. That is, the absorption bands of a related series of molecules containing a particular chemical group

$$\left(\text{for instance, } -NO_2 \text{ or } \;\rangle C{=}O\right)$$

are similar and occur in approximately the same region of the spectrum. For an example, the $n \rightarrow \pi^*$ transitions of carbonyl groups in H_2CO, HFCO, and HC≡CCHO are, in angstroms, 3500–2300, 2700–2000, and 3800–3000. The early characterizations, applied to dyes and molecules having color, led to the coining of the term *chromophores* ("color carriers") as a description. The transferability of a group absorption band and intensity over a given frequency range from one molecule to another presupposes a certain degree of remoteness and minimal interaction with other parts of the molecule. In the case for which neighboring structural groups interact sufficiently (via inductive or resonance effects, etc.), the observed absorption range of the chromophore may be significantly shifted. Such neighboring groups are called *auxochromes.* Examples of chromophores and auxochromes are shown in Table 7-7.

In organic molecules, most of the visible-UV absorption bands of chromophores are due to $n \rightarrow \pi^*$ and $\pi \rightarrow \pi^*$ absorptions. Thus, UV-visible spectra of molecules suspected of containing certain chromophoric groups can be used as a means of confirmation. Care must be exercised, however, to ensure the absence of interference in the spectral interpretation.

TABLE 7-7. Chromophores and Auxochromes

Group	Example	ω (10^3 cm^{-1})	λ (Å)	ε (l mole^{-1} cm^{-1})
C=C	$H_2C{=}CH_2$	55	1,825	250
		57.3	1,744	16,000
		58.6	1,704	16,500
		62	1,620	10,000
C≡C	$H{-}C{\equiv}C{-}CH_2{-}CH_3$	58	1,720	2,500
C=O	H_2CO	34	2,950	10
		54	1,850	Strong
C=S	$CH_3{-}C({=}S){-}CH_3$	22	4,600	Weak
—NO_2	$CH_3{-}NO_2$	36	2,775	10
		47.5	2,100	10,000
—N=N—	$CH_3{-}N{=}N{-}CH_3$	28.8	3,470	15
		> 38.5	< 2,600	Strong
		39	2,550	200
		50	2,000	6,300
		55.5	1,800	100,000
—Cl	CH_3Cl	58	1,725	—
—Br	CH_3Br	49	2,040	1,800
—I	CH_3I	38.8	2,577	—
		49.7	2,010	1,200
—OH	CH_3OH	55	1,830	200
		67	1,500	1,900
—SH	C_2H_5SH	43	2,320	160
—NH_2	CH_3NH_2	46.5	2,150	580
		52.5	1,905	3,200
—S—	$CH_3{-}S{-}CH_3$	44	2,280	620
		46.5	2,150	700
		49.3	2,030	2,300
C=C—C=C	$H_2C{=}CH{-}CH{=}CH_2$	48	2,090	25,000
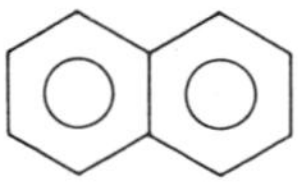		32	2,110	250
		37	2,700	5,000
		45	2,210	100,000
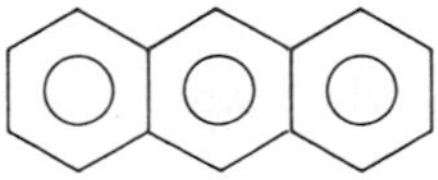		28	3,600	6,000
		40	2,500	150,000
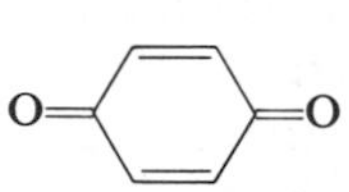		23	4,400	20
		34	3,000	1,000
		40	2,500	15,000

TABLE 7-7. (Continued)

Group	Example	ω (10^3 cm^{-1})	λ Å	ε (l mole^{-1} cm^{-1})
C=C—C=O	$H_2C{=}C{-}C({=}O){-}H$	30	3,330	20
		27.5	2,100	12,000
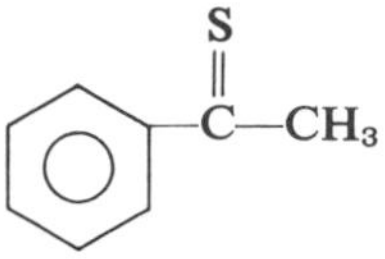		16.5	6,000	—
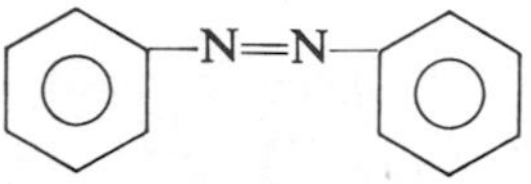		22.5	4,400	500
		31	3,200	20,000
		43	2,300	10,000

SOURCE: Bauman, *Absorption Spectroscopy*, John Wiley & Sons, 1962, p. 318, with permission.

5. Photophysical Processes in Polyatomic Molecules

The extreme complexity of electronic band spectra of large polyatomic molecules, compared with simple molecules, occurs primarily as a result of the significantly increased probability of competing photophysical processes. This increased complexity is a result of the large number of potential-energy surfaces, which can, and do, lead to numerous radiationless transitions. A modified Jablonski diagram, reproduced in Figure 7-14 from the excellent treatise on photochemistry by Calvert and Pitts [Reference 7-1], illustrates the various options open to a molecule excited to spin and symmetry-allowed upper states. Since most stable ground state molecules have their electronic spins totally paired, the lowest state is usually a singlet in a manifold of states corresponding to transitions which do not violate the "spin conversation" rule. For simplicity, only the first three are shown on the left of Figure 7-14. As with diatomic photophysical processes, both resonance fluorescence and longer (than the exciting) wavelength fluorescence from the initially excited singlet state or states are possible.

The occurrence of continuous and diffuse spectra, which are often observed, indicate dissociation, predissociation, or ionization. The unambiguous characterization of a continuous spectrum, which results from direct excitation into a continuous range of upper energy levels, is quite difficult to determine since the vibronic states of polyatomic molecules tend to be strongly predissociated. Furthermore, most electronically

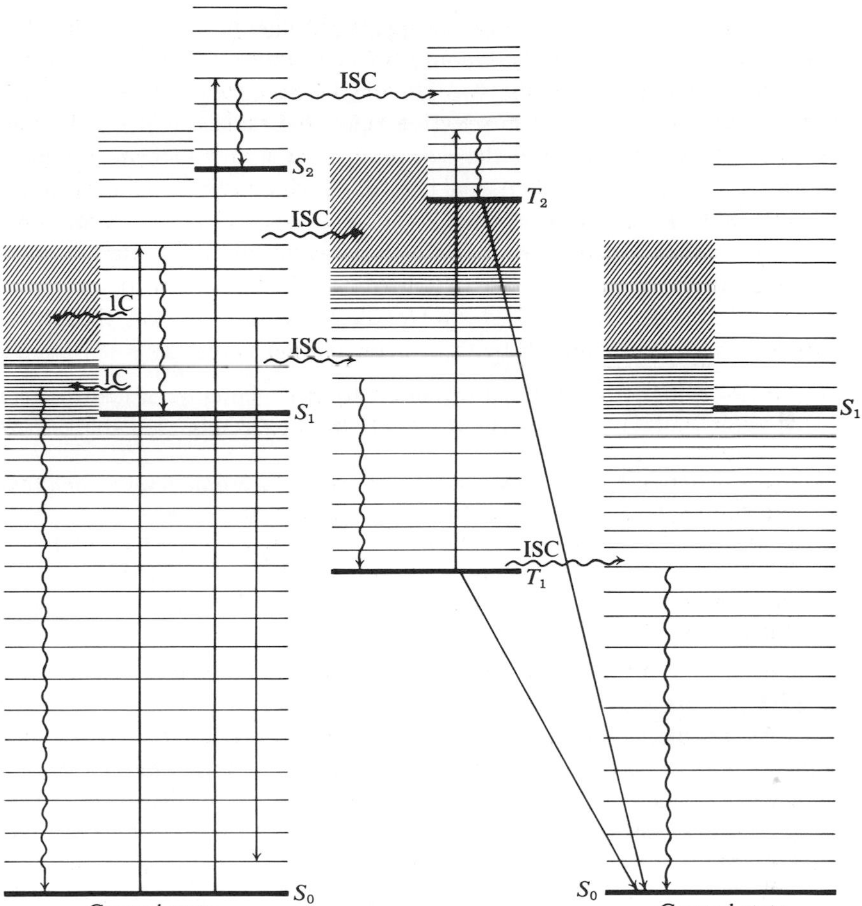

FIGURE 7-14 Modified Jablonski diagram illustrating the various photophysical processes between states of a "typical" organic molecule. The various anharmonic vibronic states, which are indicated by the horizontal lines, merge into their corresponding continua, which are indicated by the diagonal lines. Radiative transitions between states are given by solid lines, radiationless processes by wavy lines: IC = internal conversion and ISC = intersystem crossing.

excited states of these large polyatomics have the same approximate equilibrium configuration as the ground state; consequently, the vibronic progressions are rather short as a result of being predissociated long before the onset of the continuum. The continuous spectrum we are referring to here results from systems having relatively direct dissociation of the order of a vibrational period, 10^{-12} to 10^{-13} sec.

If there is a system of discrete quantized energy levels that has the same energy as that of a continuous set (a continuum), then it is possible for the wavefunctions of the two systems to be mixed. After a certain period and subject to certain selection rules, the molecule in the discrete system can cross over into the continuous set and dissociate (along a critical coordinate) in a vibrational period. Such a radiationless transition is referred to as an *Auger* process. When the process leads to decomposition, it is called predissociation. This process occurs more often in polyatomics than in diatomics, simply because of the density of potential energy surfaces. As outlined by Herzberg [Reference 7-5], these predissociative processes occur by three principal mechanisms:

1. Predissociation by electronic transition from an initially excited discrete vibronic state into the continuum of an intersecting potential-energy surface.
2. Predissociation by the transition from a discrete vibronic level to one that is continuous and belongs to the same electronic state.
3. Predissociation involving a given vibronic state that has discrete rotational levels above the dissociation limit, wherein the excess energy of the mechanically unstable rotational levels is converted to vibrational energy and subsequent dissociation.

The occurrence of diffuse spectra generally indicates one of these predissociative processes.

As we discussed for diatomic molecules, the excited molecule has several options available, subsequent to excitation into bound vibronic singlets (S_1 or S_2). Aside from the fluorescence processes discussed above, the excited molecule can undergo nonradiative electronic state transitions (IC and ISC) as well as energy-degrading relaxation processes. Vibration-rotation relaxation ($\geqslant 10^{-12}$ sec) down a given vibronic state is measurably aided by high pressure or condensed media, where the number of collisions in an electronic state lifetime ($\tau_f \sim 10^{-8}$ sec) is very large. The internal conversion process (10^{-6} to 10^{-12} sec) occurs as a result of the intrinsically close proximity of potential-energy surfaces (S_1 and S_0 or S_1 and S_2) or from a collision-induced interaction, which results in the significant quantum mechanical mixing of the similar energy states. In a like manner, the spin-forbidden radiationless transition (ISC), resulting from large intrinsic or induced Franck-Condon factors, occurs in the time range of 10^{-4} to 10^{-13} sec. If ISC is a predominant process, then relaxation to the lowest vibronic level of T_1 is very rapid. Assuming for the moment that both phosphorescence and ISC to S_0 are ineffective enough to produce a significant zero vibronic state population in T_1, then $T_2 \leftarrow T_1$ absorption is possible with an appropriate radiation source. Processes such as these, which are successive "two-photon processes" and *not* biphotonic (simultaneous absorption of two photons) processes, have been reported in the recent literature.[12] The various photophysical processes discussed in this paragraph are diagrammed in Figure 7-14.

Since lifetimes of the various electronically excited states as well as the rates of the possible photophysical processes play such an integral role relative to the nature of the observed electronic spectra, it is useful to know how to ascertain and estimate such information. For simplicity, we shall consider a three-energy-level system consisting of S_0, S_1, and T_1 (Figure 7-14). The various main processes that have been observed to occur, exclusive of vibrational relaxation and dissociation, are

$$A(S_0) + h\nu \rightarrow A^*(S_1^{\mathbf{v}}) \quad \textit{Excitation} \quad \textbf{(7-38)}$$

$$A^*(S_1^{\mathbf{v}}) \rightarrow A(S_0) + h\nu_f \quad \textit{Fluorescence} \quad \textbf{(7-39)}$$

$$A^*(S_1^{\mathbf{v}}) \rightarrow A(S_0^{\mathbf{v}}) \quad \textit{Internal Conversion} \quad \textbf{(7-40)}$$

$$A^*(S_1^{\mathbf{v}}) \rightarrow A(T_1^{\mathbf{v}}) \quad \textit{Intersystem crossing} \quad \textbf{(7-41)}$$

$$A^*(S_1^{\mathbf{v}}) + M \rightarrow A(S_0) + M^* \quad \textit{Collisional quenching} \quad \textbf{(7-42)}$$

$$A(T_1) \rightarrow A(S_0) + h\nu_p \quad \textit{Phosphorescence} \quad \textbf{(7-43)}$$

where the superscript * refers to an electronically excited molecule and **v** to an excited vibronic state. If a system containing A and M molecules is subjected to a continuous broadband radiation source that exclusively excites A over vibronic states of $S_i^{\mathbf{v}}$, the steady-state concentration of $A^*(S_1^{\mathbf{v}})$ is

$$\frac{d[A^*(S_1^{\mathbf{v}})]}{dt} = I_a - [k_f + k_{ic} + k_{isc} + k_q(M)][A^*(S_1^{\mathbf{v}})] \simeq 0, \quad \textbf{(7-44)}$$

where I_a is the number of quanta absorbed per cubic centimeter per second. For a specific quantum state i, the rate of process (7-38) is $\phi_i I_a$, and ϕ_i is the quantum efficiency for excitation. Therefore, $I_a = I_0 \sum_i \phi_i$, where I_0 is the incident radiation intensity. Since the steady-state fluorescent intensity I_f of $A^*(S_1^{\mathbf{v}})$ is defined as $k_f[A^*(S_1^{\mathbf{v}})]$, solving for $[A^*(S_1^{\mathbf{v}})]$ from Eq. (7-44), we obtain

$$I_f = \frac{k_f I_a}{k_f + k_{ic} + k_{isc} + k_q(M)}. \quad \textbf{(7-45)}$$

Since the fluorescence occurs from several vibronic states of S_1, the corresponding rate constant k_f represents an *average* over the emitting states. Although the relative competition between the terms in the denominator of Eq. (7-45) must be experimentally determined for a given system, let us assume for the moment that k_{ic} and k_{isc} are relatively small; then Eq. (7-45) can be rearranged to give:

$$Y_f = \frac{I_f}{I_a} = \frac{k_f}{k_f + k_q(M)} = \frac{1}{1 + k_q(M)/k_f}. \quad \textbf{(7-46)}$$

Y_f is defined as the *fluorescence yield.* Substituting the relation $k_f = 1/\tau_f$, and inverting, we obtain

$$\frac{1}{Y_f} = \frac{I_a}{I_f} = 1 + \tau_f k_q(M), \tag{7-47}$$

where τ_f is the intrinsic fluorescence lifetime averaged over the emitting states. An expression of this nature is called a Stern-Volmer formula. In the case where M is the sole quencher, we can obtain a measure of its quenching efficiency by evaluating k_q from the linear plot of I_a/I_f vs the concentration of M. Since we are seeking the property of a single molecule, k_q is expressed in units of cm^3/molecule-sec and approximated from simple collision theory to be $\sigma_q\bar{v}$, where σ_q (cm^2/molecule) is the effective cross section for quenching and $\bar{v}$ (cm/sec) the averge velocity. When we use Eq. (7-47), it is most convenient to plot M in units of pressure, thus recalling the relation from Section 2H, M (molecules/cm^3) = $(N_0/1000\ RT)P = (0.97 \times 10^{16})P/T$, where P is in units of torr and T in °K.

In evaluating σ_q above, we assume that τ_f either is known from independently obtained lifetime measurements or can be measured directly from a time-resolved experiment. In the latter case, the fluorescence (in the absence of quenching gas) from $A^*(S_1{}^v)$, at very low pressures, is recorded as a function of time (~nsec). In this case, only process (7-39) is applicable, and we can write for the decay of fluorescence

$$\frac{d[A^*(S_1{}^v)]}{dt} = k_f[A^*(S_1{}^v)]. \tag{7-48}$$

This is a familiar first-order differential equation, whose integrated solution is

$$\ln\,[A^*(S_1{}^v)] = k_f t + c', \tag{7-49}$$

where c is a constant of integration. Since $[A^*(S_1{}^v)]$ is proportional to the fluorescent intensity,

$$\ln I_f = k_f t + c. \tag{7-50}$$

Plotting $\ln I_f$ vs t gives k_f as the slope, which is in turn the inverse of τ_f.

EXAMPLE 7-1: The slope of a linear Stern-Volmer plot of benzene (B) fluorescence (I_a/I_f) vs added cyclobutanone (CB) quenching pressure (torr) is 0.35×10^{-3} torr^{-1} at 300 °K. Given $\tau_f = 60$ nsec, calculate the effective quenching cross section and compare with *trans*-1,3-C_5H_8 having a value 1.3 Å^2.

Solution: Applying the Stern-Volmer relation Eq. (7-47), we obtain

$$\frac{I_a}{I_f} = 1 + \tau_f k_q(M) = 1 + \tau_f k_q(0.97 \times 10^{16})\frac{P}{T}.$$

Rearranging, we obtain

$$\text{slope} = \frac{I_a/I_f}{P} = \frac{(0.97 \times 10^{16})(60 \times 10^{-9})k_q}{(300)} = 0.194 \times 10^7 k_q,$$

$$k_q = \frac{0.35 \times 10^{-3}}{0.194 \times 10^7} = 1.8 \times 10^{-10}\ \text{cm}^3/\text{molecule-sec}.$$

Since $\sigma_q = k_q/\bar{v}$, we must first calculate the relative velocity of the collision pair:

$$\bar{v} = \left(\frac{8\pi RT}{\mu}\right)^{1/2}$$

$$= \left[\frac{(8)(3.14)(8.314 \times 10^7)(300)}{36.89}\right]^{1/2}$$

$$= 1.30 \times 10^5\ \text{cm/sec}$$

where $\mu = M_B M_{CB}/(M_B + M_{CB})$. Thus

$$\sigma_q = \frac{1.8 \times 10^{-10}\ \text{cm}^3/\text{molecule-sec}}{1.3 \times 10^5\ \text{cm/sec}} = 13.8 \times 10^{-16}\ \text{cm}^2.$$

The effective collision cross section of CB, which is 13.8 Å^2, is about ten times greater than *trans*-1,3-C_5H_8.

6. Dye Lasers and Spectroscopic Applications

The material we have so far discussed is extremely important in understanding the operation of dye lasers. For example, the free-electron model of a conjugated chain is useful not only in estimating the absorption and fluorescence regions of large dye molecules but in estimating oscillator strengths and the positions of triplet states relative to singlet states. Population inversion in dye systems is generally achieved by either laser pumping or flash lamp pumping. Although flash lamp pumping is usually more efficient than laser pumping, the relatively long risetimes (>100 ns) of the former results in long laser half-widths for pulsed systems and also operational difficulties from the significant accumulation of triplet state molecules. To clarify this point concerning triplet accumulation, let us refer to Figure 7-14; although this Jablonski diagram is of a molecule with discrete rovibronic states, the superposition of the many normal modes of vibration in addition to the broadening of the rotational structure due to collisions in the liquid phase has the net effect of making the electronic state a *quasi continuum* for these large dye molecules. For the relatively slow risetime flash lamp pump, significant triplet population occurs as a result of intersystem crossing, typically $k_{isc} \sim 10^7\ \text{sec}^{-1}$ in these dye systems. The risetimes of laser pump sources, typically 5–50 nsec, practically eliminate triplet participation via ISC in the lasing sequence.

As a result of processes such as triplet-triplet absorption and triplet-triplet annihilation, in addition to the slow spin-forbidden phosphorescence $S_0 \leftarrow T_1$ transition, dye laser action to date has not been achieved from a phosphorescing state but only in fluorescence from population-inverted S_1 electronic states. Thus, significant triplet state population, resulting in fewer S_1 molecules for stimulated emission, in addition to triplet-triplet absorption (induced by the lasing frequencies) and the other T_1 processes cited above all represent loss mechanisms for the pump as well as the dye radiation.

A schematic diagram of a Hänsch-type tunable dye laser is shown in Figure 7-15.[13] The dye solution is transversely pumped by a high-powered (300–1000 kW) pulsed nitrogen laser, which is focused into the dye cell with a beam that is less than a millimeter in diameter. So that solvent schlieren in the dye cell (cuvette), which reduces the dye-laser output, can be avoided, the dye solution is usually flowed transversely through the cell with a small centrifugal pump at such a rate that the cuvette contains fresh solution for each laser shot. The schlieren effect is caused by the heat generated via radiationless transitions in the dye molecule and subsequent heat transfer to the solvent. In spite of this difficulty with dye lasers, there is a commercially available dye laser that uses a magnetically stirred nonflowing cuvette, which is quoted as avoiding such schlieren effects up to 25-Hz N_2 pumping and having a 400-kW peak power in about 5 nsec.[14] The dye laser cavity is defined between the diffraction grating and the output mirror. The lasing fluorescence beam from the dye solution is expanded twice by two lenses (performing as an inverted telescope) onto the diffraction grating; this prevents possible burning of the grating and low spectral resolution. An optional feature is the etalon, which provides even greater spectral resolution, $\sim$0.001 nm compared with $\sim$0.01 nm in its absence, but reduces the dye laser output by roughly one order of magnitude.

The intracavity quartz polarizer is used not only to polarize the lasing beam, but to maximize the horizontal component that is focused onto the ADP (ammonium dihydrogen phosphate) nonlinear doubling crystal. A natural property of these nonlinear crystals, which results from the directional nature of the induced polarization by the laser radiation field, is that the horizontally focused fundamental beam having a sufficiently high energy intensity generates a second harmonic (doubling of the fundamental frequency). If the power generated from the fundamental frequency is sufficient, the doubling crystal can be placed exterior to the laser cavity. However, the doubling crystal may also be placed in the laser cavity to give maximum conversion efficiency. In the arrangement shown in Figure 7-15 (exteriorly situated), the doubled power conversion efficiency is between 2 percent and 10 percent, whereas intracavity doubling

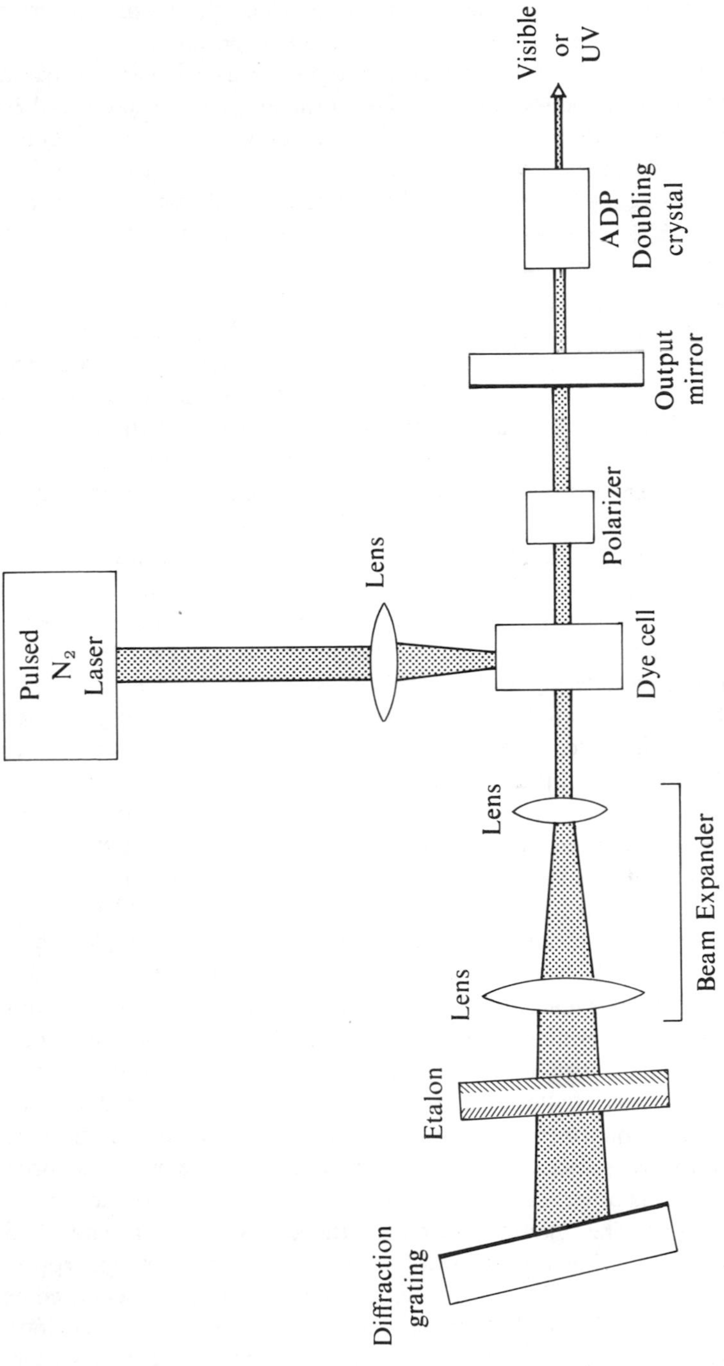

FIGURE 7-15 Schematic diagram of a Hänsch-type tunable pulsed dye laser.

uses the full power of the fundamental, since the second harmonic is proportional to the square of the fundamental power.

The operation of a continuous wave (cw) laser is very similar to the operation of the pulsed laser relative to the excited dye states and optical arrangement. One important difference, however, is the accumulation of molecules in the triplet state, which we have shown previously to be practically negligible for pulsed dye systems. The loss mechanisms associated with the triplet state (discussed above) in addition to careful design of the cavity to avoid extraneous optical losses are essential parameters in reaching the pumping threshold for an oscillation. Successful attempts to abort the long natural radiative lifetime of T_1 have involved using triplet quenchers like O_2. Another technique that has been adopted is using essentially a "jet stream" flow of the dye laser solution. Experimental observations indicate lower thresholds for oscillation, presumably as a result of the mechanical removal of triplet state molecules from the active lasing region. Continuous-wave dye lasers are generally pumped by high-powered (5–20 watts) Ar^+ or Kr^+ lasers.

Lasers have been used extensively since the late 1960s as both exciting and probing sources of high-intensity monochromatic radiation in studying elementary photophysical and photochemical processes. Although the variations in experimental design have been numerous and equally ingenious, considering a few specific examples will suffice.

One such example, which involved the use of an N_2-pumped dye laser to excite specific rovibronic electronic states, is the work of Thayer and Yardley.[15] This particular experiment was designed to determine the rates of intersystem crossing and internal conversion, under both collisional and collision-free conditions, as well as the quantum yields of fluorescence and phosphorescence. The schematic time-resolved experimental arrangement is shown in Figure 7-16. The 300-kW N_2 pulsed laser is focused into a dye solution, from which the 3821-Å line with a band width of 20 Å is used to excite almost exclusively the vibrationless S_1 state of propynal vapor. Fluorescence as well as phosphorescence lifetimes are determined from the time-resolved emission from the luminescence cell, which is detected by the photomultiplier tube, and is in turn fed to an oscilloscope for visual display or to the data handling instrumentation for time resolution. Discrimination between fluorescence and phosphorescence is based on time resolution of the two decay processes —the latter is observed to be at least two orders of magnitude longer than the former. The quantum yields, ϕ_f and ϕ_p, were experimentally determined by focusing the transmitted laser beam into an absorption cell 91.2 cm long and of 4 cm diameter and measuring the transmitted excitation intensity with a photodiode. The signal from the photodiode was amplified and fed to a duplexer, which is simply a coaxial switch that

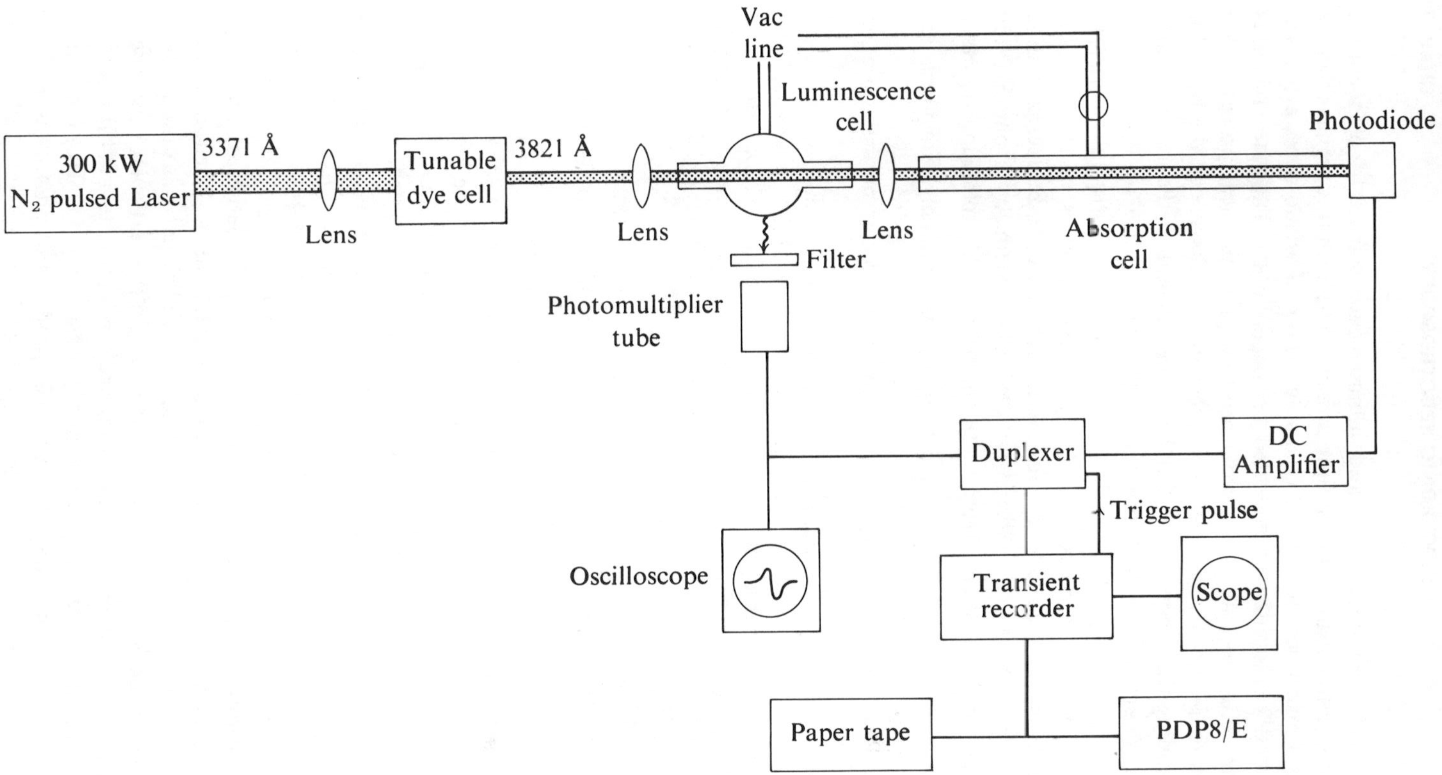

FIGURE 7-16 Experimental arrangement of Yardley et al. designed to study time-resolved fluorescence and phosphorescence of gaseous molecules.

allows both the photodiode and luminescence signals to be recorded during one transient recorder time sweep. The resulting signal received by the transient recorder could be displayed on an oscilloscope, processed by a PDP8 computer, or collected on paper tape. The rate constants for the collision-induced and collision-free photophysical processes are related to ϕ_f and ϕ_p, and thus their measurements provided the basis for determining these constants. Further experimental or theoretical details can be obtained from the footnoted publication.

E. Yeung and C. Bradley Moore used a tunable ultraviolet dye laser (spectral width <1 Å) to excite single vibronic levels of the $^1A_2$ (S_1) state of formaldehyde 4000 cm^{-1} above the zero onset.[16] Besides providing information about the collision-induced photochemistry from S_1, the collision-free lifetime data from these studies gave the following results:

1. The fluorescence lifetime decreases rapidly and smoothly with increasing vibrational excitation (refer to Section 2C).
2. The lifetimes do not vary greatly with the particular normal vibration excited.
3. The lifetimes are independent of rotational quantum number.
4. The lifetimes show a large isotopic effect (D_2CO vs H_2CO). An additional remark on this particular system is that since the S_1 levels of both H_2CO and D_2CO are so sharp and well resolved, exclusive excitation of one or the other with subsequent chemical reaction provides an excellent photochemical means for isotopic separation.

R. N. Zare and co-workers were first to use the technique of laser-induced fluorescence to detect the collisionless product energy distribution of BaO resulting from the reaction of barium atoms with oxygen in a molecular beam system.[17] The product BaO, formed in the ground $X^1\Sigma^+$ state distributed in a nonthermal manner over the various rotational-vibrational states, is excited by a tunable dye laser in the reaction zone to the $A^1\Sigma^+$ state. Fluorescence from the A state of BaO ($\sim$350 nsec), detected by a photomultiplier 5 cm from the reaction zone and signal-averaged by a boxcar integrator, is indicative of the rotational and vibrational state distribution of the nonrelaxed product. More recently, W. M. Jackson and R. J. Cody made similar use of a tunable dye laser in a photochemical system described as *laser-induced photoluminescence spectroscopy* (LIPS).[18] This experimental technique is designed to measure the quantum state of a free radical in a chemical system. The time resolution allows one to minimize the effects of collisional relaxation. The experimental design is shown in Figure 7-17. In the particular experiment Jackson et al. described, C_2N_2 at a total pressure of 0.10 torr in the reaction cell is flash-photolyzed by a vacuum-UV flash lamp (50 Hz) 0.8 joule/flash for a 2-μsec duration. The possible products of photolysis are CN radicals in the $X^2\Sigma^+$ ground state and the $A^2\Pi$ excited state. The $A^2\Pi$

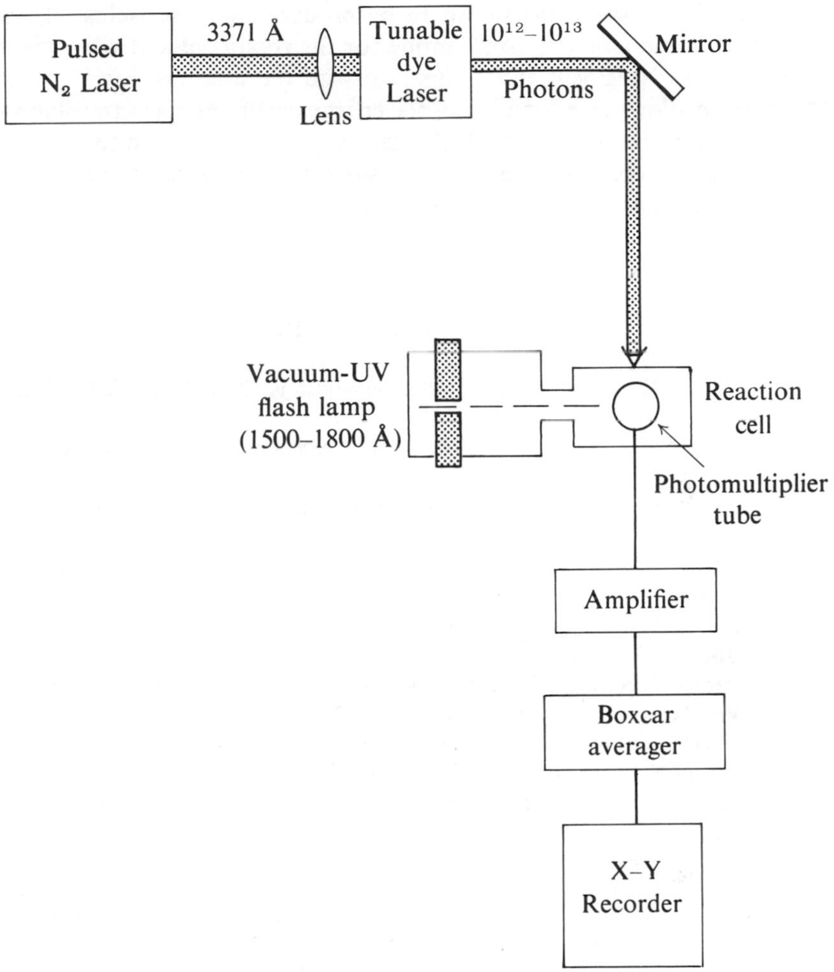

FIGURE 7-17 Schematic design of the apparatus used in the LIPS experiment.

state will either radiatively relax to the $X^2\Sigma^+$ or be collisionally quenched, depending on the condition in the reaction cell. The N_2-pumped dye laser is pulsed at some delay time after the flash lamp and excites rovibronic transitions between the $X^2\Sigma^+$ ground state and the $B^2\Sigma_g^+$ state of CN. The emission from the $B^2\Sigma_g^+$ is detected by the photomultiplier tube, processed by a boxcar averager, and displayed on an X–Y recorder. The emitted intensity from the $B^2\Sigma_g^+$ state is recorded as a function of exciting laser wavelength and therefore represents the unquenched rovibrational product distribution resulting from photolysis. In this particular experiment, the $X^2\Sigma^+$ state was shown to be produced almost exclusively in the zero vibrational level. Accounting for the rotational and vibrational energy of each fragment and comparing with the total exothermicity of the reaction allows an estimation of the energy partitioned into translation of the CN fragments. Although this technique was described for photochemically produced products, its obvious extension to carefully chosen chemical reactions appears to be imminent.

SELECTED BIBLIOGRAPHY

7-1. Calvert, J. C., and Pitts, J. M. *Photochemistry.* New York: John Wiley & Sons, 1967.

7-2. Davis, Jeff C., Jr. *Advanced Physical Chemistry.* New York: Ronald Press, 1965.

7-3. Dixon, Richard N. *Spectroscopy and Structure.* New York: John Wiley & Sons, 1965.

7-4. Herzberg, Gerhard. *Molecular Spectra and Molecular Structure—Spectra of Diatomic Molecules.* Vol. I. New York: Van Nostrand Reinhold Co., 1950. (Classic.)

7-5. Herzberg, Gerhard. *Molecular Spectra and Molecular Structure—Electronic Spectra of Polyatomic Molecules.* Vol. III. Princeton, N.J.: D. Van Nostrand Co. 1967. (Classic.)

7-6. Herzberg, Gerhard. *The Spectra and Structures of Simple Free Radicals.* Ithaca, N.Y.: Cornell University Press, 1971.

7-7. Sandorfy, C. *Electronic Spectra and Quantum Chemistry.* Englewood Cliffs, N.J.: Prentice-Hall, 1964.

7-8. Schäfer, F. P. *Topics in Applied Physics: Dye Lasers.* New York: Springer-Verlag, 1973.

7-9. Williams, Dudley. *Molecular Physics, Part A.* New York: Academic Press, 1974.

ENDNOTES

1. The subscript r indicates regular ordering of the multiplet, that is, from the lowest Ω value to the highest with increasing energy. The inverted ordering is just the opposite.
2. *Stability* in this context refers to a state with a potential well and not to the lifetime of the excited state.
3. A specific vibrational level within a given electronic state is termed a *vibronic* state ("vibrational-electronic" state).
4. Note the exchange of the $(1\pi_u)$ and $(3\sigma_u)$ orbitals for the internuclear separations of linear NCN as in the diatomic C_2 case.

5. The states resulting from point groups of higher symmetry are given in Herzberg [References 7-5 or 7-6].
6. Compare p. 198.
7. The s_1, s_2, and s_3 are the 2s atomic orbitals for the three Y atoms.
8. W. A. Guillory, G. R. Smith, and R. Isabel, *J. Mol. Struct.* **19**:473–491 (1973).
9. The author recognizes that the term "relatively small" is an ambiguous expression, but it is hoped that some feel for these molecular types will be obtained as the discussion proceeds since there is no clearly definable small molecular type.

10. M. L. Bernstein and W. A. Guillory, unpublished data.
11. W. A. Guillory and G. H. Andrews, *J. Chem. Phys.* **62**:3208 (1974).
12. F. P. Schwartz and A. C. Albrecht, *J. Phys. Chem.* **77**:2808.
13. T. W. Hänsch, *Appl. Opt.* **11**:895 (1972).
14. Molectron DL Dye Cell Series, Molectron Corporation.
15. C. A. Thayer and J. T. Yardley, *J. Chem. Phys.* **61**:2487 (1974).
16. E. S. Yeung and C. B. Moore, *J. Chem. Phys.* **58**:3988 (1973).
17. A. W. Cruse, P. J. Dagdigian, and R. N. Zare, *Faraday Disc. Chem. Soc.* **55**:277 (1973); P. J. Dagdigian, A. W. Cruse, A. Schultz, and R. N. Zare, *J. Chem. Phys.* **61**:4450 (1974).
18. W. M. Jackson and R. J. Cody, *J. Chem. Phys.* **61**:4183 (1974).

PROBLEMS

7-1. The first excited electronic state of HgH is a $^2\Pi_r$ having a $\mathbf{v}'' = 0$ to $\mathbf{v}' = 0$ splitting of approximately 3680 cm^{-1}. Calculate the spin-orbit coupling constant (assuming no nuclear rotational coupling).

7-2. For diatomic molecules having the following electronic configurations, determine the electronic state term, its multiplet (assuming weak (Λ, S) coupling), and the total degeneracy of each component of the multiplet: (a) $S = \frac{1}{2}$, $\Lambda = 1$; (b) $S = 0$, $\Lambda = 1$; (c) $S = \frac{3}{2}$, $\Lambda = 2$.

7-3. For the three nonequivalent electrons σ, σ, δ, determine the types and numbers of each Λ state possible.

7-4. Derive the electronic term symbol corresponding to the exicted state B_2 configuration $KK(\sigma_g 2s)^2(\sigma_u{}^* 2s)^1(\pi_u 2p)^2(\sigma_g 2p)^1$ that will have allowed transitions to the ground state $^3\Sigma_g{}^-$.

7-5. Using MO theory, predict the lowest stable state of Ne_2.

7-6. Write the MO ground electronic configuration for CH and deduce the corresponding term symbol.

7-7. Starting with Eq. (7-15), derive the expression for a $\mathbf{v}''$ progression similar to Eq. (7-15b), for emission from the $\mathbf{v}' = 0$ vibronic state. Such progressions are quite common in low-temperature spectra of diatomics, where relaxation to the $\mathbf{v}' = 0$ vibronic state is quite rapid.

7-8. Determine the linear electronic ground state term symbols of CH_2 and $CH_2{}^+$ and their first excited states.

7-9. For two nonequivalent e electrons in a molecule belonging to the point group C_{3v}, using group theory, derive the number and types of molecular electronic states possible. Of these states, determine which are possible for two equivalent electrons on the basis of the symmetrized and the antisymmetrized direct product.

7-10. Construct a table similar to Eq. (7-33) for the point group C_{3v} using the direct products of symmetry species and the appropriate information in the C_{3v} character table.

7-11. Discuss (predict) the expected vibrational structure of the cold electronic absorption spectra resulting from the transitions

X—Y—X → X—Y—X and X—Y—X → 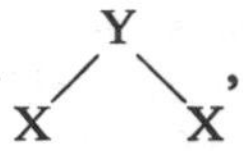,

both for the various progressions and sequences.

7-12. Calculate the $\pi \rightarrow \pi^*$ absorption frequency for benzene using the model of a particle on a ring and the appropriate structural parameters. Compare with the observed $\pi \rightarrow \pi^*$ transition frequency of 55,550 cm^{-1}. The radius of a benzene ring is ~1.3 Å.

7-13. Using the time-resolved fluorescence data herewith, calculate τ_f for the excited singlet state of benzene.

Fluorescence intensity (arbitrary units)	Time (nsec)
50	20
40	40
33	60
27	80
15	120
9	160
6	170

Chapter 8

Magnetic Resonance Spectroscopy

An atom or a molecule must possess net nuclear or electronic spin or net electronic orbital angular momenta in order to exhibit magnetic resonance spectra. These spin and orbital motions give rise to permanent magnetic dipole moments. Unlike optical spectroscopy which we have discussed to this point, magnetic resonance spectroscopy involves transitions between quantized angular momentum states (energy levels), which are degenerate in the absence of an external perturbing field. These degenerate states are split by the interaction of an external magnetic field with the permanent magnetic dipole moments. Classically, in the presence of an external magnetic field, the magnetic dipole experiences a torque (like that of the electric dipole, $\tau = \boldsymbol{\mu}_e \times \mathbf{E}$), which causes the magnetic dipole moment to precess about the magnetic field. Quantum mechanically, absorption and emission of radiation occur when an appropriate radiation source is tuned to the *resonance* frequency corresponding to the energy-level separation; hence the term *magnetic resonance spectroscopy*. Our primary concern here will involve the transitions occurring between nuclear (nuclear magnetic resonance, NMR) and electronic (electron spin resonance, ESR) spin states.

A. MAGNETIC PHENOMENA

Atoms that have net spin or orbital electronic angular momenta producing permanent magnetic dipole moments, or both, are *paramagnetic*. Those that contain no intrinsic permanent magnetic dipole moments are *diamagnetic.* These properties, paramagnetism and diamagnetism, are manifested in the bulk by the interaction of a given material with an externally applied magnetic field. The magnetic moment of paramagnetic substances reinforces an external field, whereas the induced magnetic moment of diamagnetic substances opposes the direction of an externally applied magnetic field. For completeness, we should also mention a class of metals that have very strong permanent magnetic moments even in the absence of an external magnetic field. They generally belong to the iron group, and are described as *ferromagnetic,* for example, Fe, Co, and Ni. Ferromagnetism, however, is a macroscopic phenomenon due to aggregates of atoms, in contrast to paramagnetism and diamagnetism, which are the cumulative manifestations of individual atoms.

1. Diamagnetism

Diamagnetism is the magnetism *induced* in an atom or molecule when it is subjected to an external magnetic field. In the case of a diamagnetic substance, which has no net electronic spin or orbital angular momenta, the external field causes an acceleration in the electronic orbital velocity. This increased orbital angular velocity, which is not cancelled by an equal and opposite effect, produces an electromotive force in the atom or molecule. The resulting circulating flow of current induces a magnetic dipole, which is opposite in direction to the external magnetic field.

The Hamiltonian operator for the interaction of an external magnetic field with an atom, including the electron spin interaction, is given as

$$\hat{H}' = -\frac{\mathbf{e}\mathbf{H}_z}{2m_\mathbf{e}c}(\hat{L}_z + 2\hat{S}_z) + \frac{\mathbf{e}^2\mathbf{H}_z{}^2}{8m_\mathbf{e}c^2}\sum_i (x_i{}^2 + y_i{}^2), \tag{8-1}$$

where the external field is aligned along the z axis. Applying first-order perturbation theory to a diamagnetic atom, we obtain

$$E' = \frac{\mathbf{e}^2\mathbf{H}^2}{8m_\mathbf{e}c^2}\sum_i \overline{(x_i{}^2 + y_i{}^2)}, \tag{8-2}$$

where the average of the coordinates accounts for nonspherical orbitals. For approximately spherical orbitals, $\overline{(x_i{}^2 + y_i{}^2)} = \frac{2}{3}\bar{r}_i{}^2$, and Eq. (8-2) reduces to

$$E' = \frac{\mathbf{e}^2\mathbf{H}^2}{12m_\mathbf{e}c^2}\sum_i \bar{r}_i{}^2, \tag{8-3}$$

where $\bar{r}_i{}^2$, the mean square radius of an orbital, is summed over i orbitals. The induced magnetic dipole moment per atom, $\mu_{\text{ind}} = -\partial E'/\partial H$, is

$$\mu_{\text{ind}} = -\frac{\mathbf{e}^2\mathbf{H}}{6m_\mathbf{e}c^2}\sum_i \bar{r}_i{}^2, \tag{8-4}$$

where the negative sign indicates a dipole that is opposed in direction to the external field. In fact, when a diamagnetic substance is placed in a magnetic field, the lines of force of the field are pushed outward by the substance to such an extent that the internal field is less than the field in free space.

In simple isotropic materials, the intensity of magnetization **M** (magnetic moment per unit volume) per field strength is defined as the magnetic susceptibility χ. The molar diamagnetic susceptibility is defined as

$$\chi_M = \frac{\mathbf{M}}{\mathbf{H}} = \frac{N_0 \mu_{\text{ind}}}{\mathbf{H}} = -\frac{N_0 \mathbf{e}^2}{6 m_e c^2} \sum_i \bar{r}_i^2, \tag{8-5}$$

and is expressed in the unit mole^{-1}. The calculation of atomic diamagnetic susceptibilities according to Eq. (8-5) is reasonably close to experimental observations for small atoms, but becomes increasingly inaccurate for large atoms, which have elliptical orbits.

The calculation of the diamagnetic susceptibility of a molecule is a more complicated situation, primarily because of the loss of spherical symmetry. As a result, the molecular diamagnetic susceptibility may depend significantly on the molecular orientation. The effect of large anisotropies is a mixing of ground and excited states in the determination of χ_M. The expression derived by Van Vleck of χ_M for a polyatomic molecule is

$$\chi_M = -\frac{N_0 \mathbf{e}^2}{6 m_e c^2} \sum_i \bar{r}_i^2 + \frac{N_0 \mathbf{e}^2}{2 m_e^2 c^2} \sum_{n \neq 0} \frac{|\langle 0|\hat{L}_z|n\rangle|^2}{E_n - E_0}, \tag{8-6}$$

where i is summed over all the electrons in the molecule, and 0 and n refer to the ground and excited n states. The second term of Eq. (8-6) is positive, as is the paramagnetic term, and therefore makes a significant contribution in opposition to the first term when there are low-lying excited states. For this reason, it is sometimes referred to as the second-order paramagnetic term. As might be expected, application of this expression to polyatomic molecules has been fairly limited, primarily because of the inadequacy of known excited state wavefunctions and energies. Fortunately for magnetic resonance spectroscopy systems, the diamagnetic effect is several orders of magnitude smaller than the paramagnetic effect, and is therefore important only in the absence of the latter.

2. Paramagnetism

Paramagnetic substances have net magnetism only in the presence of an external magnetic field. Each of the constituent atoms having a resultant dipole vector tends to align in such a manner as to reinforce the externally applied field. We might expect these dipoles to be aligned parallel to the field; instead, they are distributed at various orientations relative to it as a result of thermal motion. In fact, the higher the temperature, the greater the thermal motion opposing alignment, and thus a resulting decrease in paramagnetism. This behavior is observed for all paramagnetic substances.

An expression analogous to Eq. (1-24a) can be derived for the molar magnetic susceptibility as a function of absolute temperature. For a system of paramagnetic atoms subjected to an external magnetic field, the potential energy of alignment is $E' = \mu_\beta \mathbf{H} g M_J$ (Eq. (3-45)). If the energy distribution is assumed to be characterized by the Maxwell-Boltzmann law, the average magnetic moment for this sytem of atoms is

$$\bar{\mu} = \frac{\sum_{M_J=-J}^{M_J=+J} M_J g \mu_\beta \exp(M_J g \mu_\beta \mathbf{H}/kT)}{\sum_{M_J=-J}^{M_J=+J} \exp(M_J g \mu_\beta \mathbf{H}/kT)}, \tag{8-7}$$

where the magnetic moment in the field direction is $M_J g \mu_\beta$ (Eq. (3-28a)). When this system of paramagnetic atoms is subjected to even the highest attainable magnetic fields at present, the exponential terms of Eq. (8-7) are sufficiently small that they can be expanded and only the first two terms retained.[1] Thus we obtain

$$\bar{\mu} = \frac{g\mu_\beta \sum_{M_J=-J}^{M_J=+J} M_J(1 + M_J g \mu_\beta \mathbf{H}/kT)}{\sum_{M_J=-J}^{M_J=+J} (1 + M_J g \mu_\beta \mathbf{H}/kT)}. \tag{8-8}$$

Since

$$\sum_{M_J=-J}^{M_J=+J} M_J = 0, \qquad \sum_{M_J=-J}^{M_J=+1} 1 = (2J+1),$$

and

$$\sum_{M_J=-J}^{M_J=+J} M_J^2 = \frac{(2J+1)J(J+1)}{3},$$

Eq. (8-8) reduces to

$$\bar{\mu} = \frac{g^2\mu_\beta^2\mathbf{H}}{kT}\,\frac{(2J+1)(J)(J+1)}{3(2J+1)} = \frac{g^2\mu_\beta^2\mathbf{H}J(J+1)}{3kT}, \tag{8-9}$$

where g is the Landé splitting factor, μ_β the Bohr magneton, and $\mathbf{H}$ the magnetic field strength in gauss. The intensity of magnetization $\mathbf{M}$ for this system of atoms exhibiting LS coupling (Section 3A-1) is

$$\mathbf{M} = N_0\bar{\mu} = \frac{N_0 g^2\mu_\beta^2 HJ(J+1)}{3kT}, \tag{8-10}$$

and the corresponding paramagnetic molar susceptibility is

$$\chi_M = \frac{\mathbf{M}}{\mathbf{H}} = \frac{N_0 g^2 \mu_\beta^2 J(J+1)}{3kT}. \tag{8-11}$$

For a given system of atoms, $N_0 g^2 \mu_\beta^2 J(J+1)/3k$ is a constant, sometimes referred to as the *Curie constant* and written C. Thus, considering the sum total of the magnetic susceptibility (Eqs. (8-11) and (8-5)), we obtain

$$\chi_M = A + \frac{B\mu_\beta^2}{T}, \tag{8-12}$$

which is known as the *Curie law*. In Eq. (8-12), which is analogous to Eq. (1-24a), A is the temperature-independent term (Eq. 8-5), and B the coefficient of the temperature-dependent term, $N_0 g^2 J(J+1)/3k$.

Although the derivation above is made strictly for an atomic system, Eq. (8-12) has been reasonably well applied to paramagnetic substances consisting of ions that are approximately independent of neighboring ionic effects. It has also been shown to hold approximately for molecular liquids and gases, where in general, the susceptibility is independent of field orientation. Equation (8-12) does not apply to crystalline materials, since in general, most crystalline structures are anisotropic and the g factors depend on field orientation; exceptions are ionic atoms having completely symmetrical internal crystalline fields.

The property of electron paramagnetism of rare earth and transition metal ions in solution and in crystals, and the corresponding measurement of their susceptibilities, have been shown to play an important role in the interpretation of observed electron paramagnetic resonance (EPR) spectra. The measurement of this property is particularly important, since the overwhelming majority of systems studied are interpreted in terms of the electron spin angular momentum contributing most to the magnetic dipole vector, and little, if any, contributed by the orbital angular motion. In these cases, the orbital motion is presumably *quenched* by the relatively strong ionic and crystalline fields. Thus, the observed results in these cases are effectively ESR spectra.

B. MAGNETIC RESONANCE

The Hamiltonian expression representing the energy of an atom or a radical in an external magnetic field $\mathbf{H}$ having unpaired electrons and nuclei with nonzero spins is

$$\hat{H} = \sum_i g_{n_i}\mu_N \hat{\mathbf{I}}_i \mathbf{H} - h \sum_{i<j}\sum J_{ij}\hat{\mathbf{I}}_i\hat{\mathbf{I}}_j - \mu_\beta(\hat{\mathbf{L}} + 2\hat{\mathbf{S}})\mathbf{H} + h\hat{\mathbf{S}} \sum_i A_i \hat{\mathbf{I}}_i + \hat{H}_{ss}. \tag{8-13}$$

The first two terms are characteristic of NMR spectroscopy; the first is called the nuclear Zeeman term and the second the indirect nuclear spin–spin interaction term. The latter three terms are characteristic of ESR spectroscopy, and are called the electronic Zeeman, the electronic spin–nuclear spin hyperfine interaction, and the electronic spin–spin interaction terms. Operating on the appropriate wavefunction according to Eq. (2-9) by Eq. (8-13) gives rise to the corresponding energy expressions characterizing the spectra observed in NMR and ESR.

1. Electronic Orbital and Spin Angular Momenta

For simplicity of illustration, we consider the angular and spin motion of an atom having a single unpaired electron. Classically, a circulating charge generates a magnetic field similar to that produced by a magnetic dipole moment μ located at the center of the orbit, as illustrated in Figure 8-1a. The magnitude of the magnetic dipole moment (emu) is $\pi\mathbf{r}^2I/c$, where I is the current, $\mathbf{r}$ the radius of the orbit, and c the velocity of light. The current (charge flowing/time) generated by the circulating electron is $-(\mathbf{ev}/2\pi\mathbf{r})$, and therefore $\mu = -(\mathbf{evr}/2c)$. If the electronic mass is substituted in the numerator and denominator, $\mu = -(qm_e\mathbf{vr}/2m_ec) = -(q\mathbf{r} \times \mathbf{p}/2m_ec) = -(q\mathbf{L}/2m_ec)$. Since the quantum mechanical eigenvalue of $\mathbf{L} = \sqrt{\ell(\ell + 1)}\hbar$, the corresponding magnetic moment is

$$\mu_{\mathbf{L}} = -\sqrt{\ell(\ell + 1)}\,\frac{q\hbar}{2m_ec}, \tag{8-14}$$

where the constant $q\hbar/2m_ec$ has been defined previously as the Bohr magneton, $\mu_\beta = 0.927 \times 10^{-20}$ erg/gauss (Section 3C). Therefore when this species consisting of a circulating electron is placed in an external magnetic field, the magnetic moment is oriented at some angle along the field direction z and given by

$$\mu_L = -M_L\mu_\beta. \tag{8-15}$$

For the rotation of an orbiting electron, the spin angular momentum is derived in a similar manner:

$$\mu_{\mathbf{S}} = -g_e\frac{q}{2m_ec}\,\mathbf{S} = -g_e\frac{q\hbar}{2m_ec}\sqrt{S(S + 1)}, \tag{8-16}$$

where g_e is defined as the electronic "g" factor. The g factor, which is in general experimentally determined, accounts for the *effective* spin magnetic moment when there is a nonzero contribution from the orbital angular momentum. The corresponding component of spin angular momentum along an external magnetic field is

$$\mu_S = g_e\mu_\beta M_S. \tag{8-17}$$

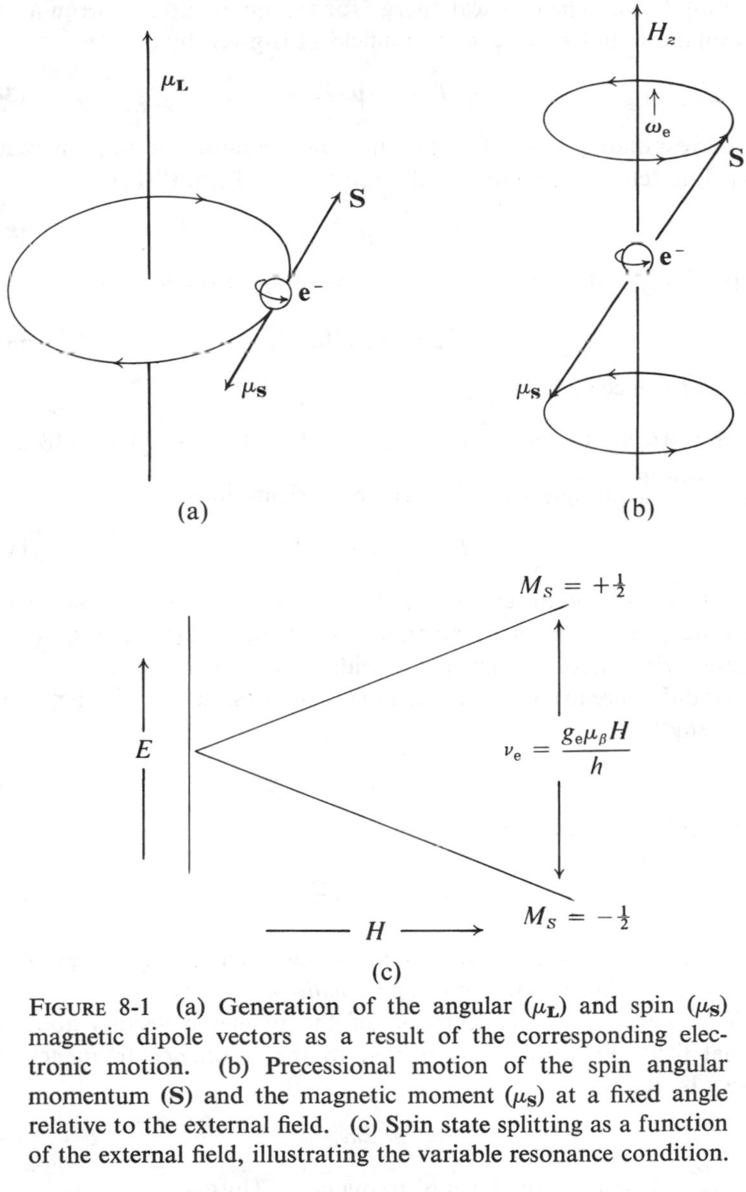

FIGURE 8-1 (a) Generation of the angular ($\mu_\mathbf{L}$) and spin ($\mu_\mathbf{S}$) magnetic dipole vectors as a result of the corresponding electronic motion. (b) Precessional motion of the spin angular momentum (**S**) and the magnetic moment ($\mu_\mathbf{S}$) at a fixed angle relative to the external field. (c) Spin state splitting as a function of the external field, illustrating the variable resonance condition.

For a single electron having no orbital angular contribution (an *s* electron), where $M_S = \pm\frac{1}{2}$, $g_e = 2.0023$, and $\mu_S \simeq \pm\mu_\beta$.

The external magnetic field exerts a torque on the magnetic dipole vector; hence, a precessional motion of the angular momentum vector at some angle relative to the external field direction will result (as illustrated in Figure 8-1b). The classical energy for the interaction between a magnetic dipole $\boldsymbol{\mu}$ and a static magnetic field $\mathbf{H}$ is given by

$$E = -\boldsymbol{\mu} \cdot \mathbf{H}. \tag{3-15}$$

The corresponding magnetic Hamiltonian operator for this interaction (when $\mathbf{L}$ is zero or negligible) is the third term of Eq. (8-13),

$$\hat{H}_e = g_e \mu_\beta \hat{\mathbf{S}} \cdot \mathbf{H}. \tag{8-18}$$

For the $\hat{\mathbf{S}}$ projection along the z axis (direction of the field, H_z),

$$\hat{H}_e = g_e \mu_\beta H \hat{S}_z. \tag{8-19}$$

By operator mechanics,

$$\hat{S}_z \psi_i(M_S = +\tfrac{1}{2}) = +\tfrac{1}{2}\psi_i \qquad \text{and} \qquad \hat{S}_z \psi_i(M_S = -\tfrac{1}{2}) = -\tfrac{1}{2}\psi_i.$$

Thus, $\hat{H}_e \psi_i = E_e \psi_i$ gives for the two spin orientations

$$E_e = \pm \tfrac{1}{2} g_e \mu_\beta H, \tag{8-20}$$

where the upper and lower signs are for $M_S = \frac{1}{2}$ and $M_S = -\frac{1}{2}$ electronic spin states. Since E_e is proportional to H, the splitting of spin states increases with increasing magnetic field, as shown in Figure 8-1c. The obvious difference in energy between the two spin states at a given magnetic field strength is

$$\Delta E_e = g_e \mu_\beta H, \tag{8-21}$$

and the corresponding frequency is

$$\nu_e = \frac{\Delta E_e}{h} = \frac{g_e \mu_\beta H}{h}. \tag{8-21a}$$

This frequency ν_e, which corresponds to the difference in energy of spin states $\pm\frac{1}{2}$, is defined as the *resonance condition*, or *frequency.*

The precessional frequency ω_e of the magnetic vectors about the external field (Figure 8-1c) is related to the resonance frequency (Eq. (8-21a)) by the relation

$$\omega_e = 2\pi\nu_e, \tag{8-22}$$

where ω_e is known as the Larmor frequency. Thus,

$$\omega_e = \frac{2\pi g_e \mu_\beta H}{h} = g_e \frac{\mu_\beta}{h} H = \gamma_e H, \tag{8-23}$$

where the proportionality constant $\gamma_e = g_e \mu_\beta / h$ is called the gyromagnetic ratio (or also the magnetogyric ratio).

2. Nuclear Spin Angular Momentum

As we mentioned in the introduction, the possession of a net spin magnetic dipole is a necessity for an atom or molecule to exhibit nuclear magnetic resonance. The origin of this magnetic dipole is a result of net nuclear spin angular momentum by one or more of the constituent atoms of a molecule. Although the vector addition of nuclear spins cannot be predicted in a simple manner, the following rules have been formulated based on observed spin angular momenta.

1. Nuclei having an even number of protons and neutrons will vectorially add to produce a net spin of zero, for example, ^{4}He, ^{16}O, and ^{12}C.
2. Nuclei having an odd number of both protons and neutrons will have integral spins, for example $^{14}N(I = 1)$, $^{2}H(I = 1)$, and $^{10}B(I = 3)$.
3. Nuclei having odd mass will have half-integral spins, for example, $^{15}N(I = \frac{1}{2})$, $^{19}F(I = \frac{1}{2})$, and $^{11}B(I = \frac{3}{2})$.

The interaction of the nuclear spin magnetic vector with an external magnetic field is similar to the interactions of the spinning electron treated above. Since the nuclear charge is positive in this case, both the spin angular momentum and magnetic dipole vectors point in the same direction. This interaction is illustrated in Figure 8-2. The nuclear spin angular momentum derived in a similar manner to a circulating charge is

$$\mu_{\mathbf{N}} = g_{\mathrm{n}} \frac{q}{2m_p c} \mathbf{I} = g_{\mathrm{n}} \frac{q\hbar}{2m_p c} \sqrt{I(I+1)}, \qquad \textbf{(8-24)}$$

where g_{n} is defined as the nuclear g factor, $q\hbar/2m_p c$ ($\equiv \mu_N$) a constant called the nuclear magneton, and I the nuclear spin quantum number. When the electronic charge (-4.80×10^{-10} esu) and the mass of the proton are substituted for q and m_p in μ_N, we obtain the constant 5.050×10^{-24} erg/gauss. The corresponding component of the spin angular momentum along the external magnetic field is

$$\mu_{\mathrm{n}} = g_{\mathrm{n}} \mu_N M_I, \qquad \textbf{(8-25)}$$

where g_{n} for the proton is 5.58490, but must in general be experimentally determined. The magnetic quantum number M_I can assume values from $-I$, $-I + 1$, to $+I$, $(2I + 1)$, and are oriented to the external field as illustrated in Figure 3-7.

The magnetic Hamiltonian operator for this interaction is the first term of Eq. (8-13), where for a single nucleus

$$\hat{H}_{\mathrm{n}} = -g_{\mathrm{n}} \mu_N \hat{\mathbf{I}} \cdot \mathbf{H}. \qquad \textbf{(8-26)}$$

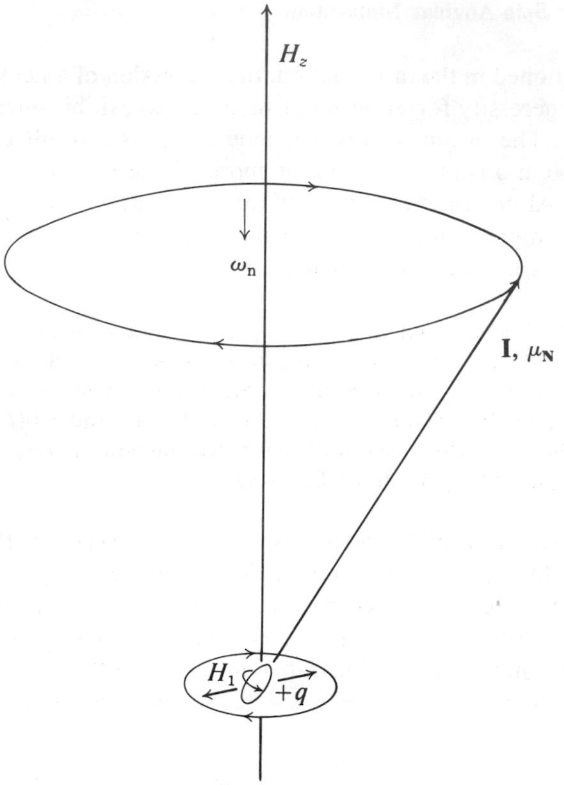

FIGURE 8-2 Precession of the nuclear spin angular momentum (I) and magnetic moment (μ_N) vectors about the externally applied magnetic field. Note that for the positively charged spinning nucleus both **I** and μ_N point in the same direction. Also shown is the smaller perpendicularly applied oscillating field H_1, necessary to achieve nuclear resonance.

The corresponding eigenvalues, determined by operator mechanics, are

$$E_n = -g_n\mu_N M_I H, \tag{8-27}$$

where there will be $2I + 1$ values of M_I for a given nuclear spin state I. In the case of a spinning proton, the energy between the spin states $M_I = +\frac{1}{2}$ and $M_I = -\frac{1}{2}$ is

$$\Delta E_n = -g_n\mu_N H, \tag{8-28}$$

and the corresponding nuclear resonance condition

$$\nu_n = -\frac{g_n\mu_N H}{h}. \tag{8-28a}$$

The Larmor precessional frequency about the external magnetic field is

$$\omega_n = 2\pi\nu_n = -\frac{2\pi g_n \mu_N H}{h} = -\gamma_n H, \tag{8-29}$$

where $\gamma_n = 2\pi g_n \mu_N / h$.

3. Transitions

Since the degenerate electronic and nuclear spin levels are split by the application of an external magnetic field, we are thus provided the opportunity to perform spectroscopy between these space-fixed levels. Since these splittings correspond to energy separations in the microwave (ESR) and radiofrequency (NMR) regions, the sources used to induce such transitions are different from those we have used in conventional optical spectroscopy. As we shall see shortly, magnetic resonance transitions between the space-fixed spin states can occur only when induced by another time-dependent field oriented perpendicularly to the external static field. In NMR spectroscopy, the resonance condition is achieved by applying a radiofrequency field oscillating at the Larmor precessional frequency perpendicular to the external static field. This linearly oscillating field is produced by applying an oscillating voltage to a coil whose axis is perpendicular to the external field. If the external field is assumed to be oriented along the z axis, the oscillating field generated along the x axis is $\mathbf{H}_x = 2\mathbf{H}_1 \cos \omega t$ (Figure 8-2). This oscillating field in turn produces a component radiofrequency field rotating (at the Larmor frequency) in the same direction as the precessing magnetic dipole in the x-y plane. Interaction of this rotating field and the precessing dipole gives rise to magnetic resonance transitions. The resonance condition in ESR spectroscopy is achieved in a similar manner except that the perpendicular time-varying $\mathbf{H}_1$ field is generated by the oscillating magnetic field component of the microwave radiation source.

The transition probabilities between the nuclear Zeeman or electron Zeeman states are determined by the interaction of the perpendicular oscillating fields (H_x or H_y) with the nuclear magnetic moment or the electronic magnetic moment. The expression for the induced transition probability between final state m and initial state k is

$$P_{mk} = \frac{2\pi}{\hbar^2} |\langle m|\hat{H}'|k\rangle|^2 \delta(\omega_{mk} - \omega), \tag{8-30}$$

where $\hat{H}'$ is the perturbation operator representing the effect of the oscillating magnetic field and $\delta(\omega_{mk} - \omega)$ is the Dirac delta function. The delta function is unity when $\omega_{mk} = \omega$ and zero when $\omega_{mk} \neq \omega$; ω_{mk} is the frequency of the resonance condition and ω is the frequency of the oscillating magnetic field. Thus, as a primary requirement for a transition to be induced, the perpendicular magnetic field must *theoretically* oscillate at exactly the frequency of the resonance condition (δ assumes an infinitely narrow line).

For electron spin resonance transitions

$$\hat{H}' = g_e \mu_\beta \mathbf{H}_1 \cdot \hat{\mathbf{S}}, \tag{8-31}$$

where H_1 is the amplitude of the oscillating magnetic field.[2] For orientation along the x axis,

$$\hat{H}' = g_e \mu_\beta H_1 \cdot \hat{S}_x. \tag{8-32}$$

Substitution into Eq. (8-30) above gives

$$P_{mk} = \frac{2\pi}{\hbar^2} g_e^2 \mu_\beta^2 H_1^2 |\langle m|\hat{S}_x|k\rangle|^2 \delta(\omega_{mk} - \omega), \tag{8-33}$$

where we can show, by operator mechanics, that the matrix element of $\hat{S}_x$ is zero unless $m = k \pm 1$ (Problem 8-3). Thus, $\Delta M_S = \pm 1$.

In the same way, we can show that the transition probability for nuclear transitions between nuclear spin states m and k is

$$P_{mk} = \frac{2\pi}{\hbar^2} g_n^2 \mu_N^2 H_1^2 |\langle m|\hat{I}_x|k\rangle|^2 \delta(\omega_{mk} - \omega), \tag{8-34}$$

where $\hat{I}_x$ in this case corresponds to the nuclear spin operator. The $\hat{I}_x$ matrix element again vanishes unless $m = k \pm 1$; thus the selection rules for induced absorption and emission from an oscillating magnetic field are $\Delta M_I = +1$ and $\Delta M_I = -1$.[3]

Applying the selection rules $\Delta M_S = \pm 1$ to Eq. (8-20) and $\Delta M_I = \pm 1$ to (8-27), we find that the transition frequencies are the same as the resonance conditions, Eqs. (8-21a) and (8-28a). Furthermore, we can induce transitions by either fixing H and varying the perpendicular oscillating field or vice versa. In practice, it is usually more convenient to use a fixed-frequency oscillating field and vary the magnetic field. For reasons that will become clear as we proceed, typical ESR and NMR external static fields are ~3,000 and ~15,000 gauss (G), respectively.

EXAMPLE 8-1: Calculate the frequency of the resonance condition for the NMR absorption of a system of hydrogen atoms in an external magnetic field of 15,000 gauss. Make a similar calculation for the ESR absorption, where the external magnetic field is 5000 gauss. Given $\mu_\beta = 0.927 \times 10^{-20}$ erg/gauss, $\mu_N = 5.050 \times 10^{-24}$ erg/gauss, $g_e = 2.0023$, and $g_n = 5.5849$.

Solution: According to Eq. (8-28a),

$$\nu_n = \frac{g_n\mu_N H}{h} = \frac{(5.585)(5.050 \times 10^{-24})(15{,}000)}{(6.626 \times 10^{-27})}$$
$$= 63.85 \times 10^6 \text{ sec}^{-1}$$
$$= 63.85 \text{ MHz.}$$

And according to Eq. (8-21a),

$$\nu_e = \frac{g_e\mu_\beta H}{h} = \frac{(2.0023)(0.927 \times 10^{-20})(5000)}{(6.626 \times 10^{-27})}$$
$$= 14.01 \times 10^9 \text{ sec}^{-1},$$
$$= 14.01 \text{ GHz (gigahertz; 1 GHz} = 10^9 \text{ Hz).}$$

Therefore, typical resonance frequencies are in the microwave for ESR, and occur in the radiofrequency region for NMR (see Figure 2-2).

On examination of Example 8-1, we see that the difference in the external fields is only a factor of 3; consequently, the factor that contributes most to the significantly different absorption frequencies is μ_i (μ_β or μ_N). This difference is almost totally a result of the much heavier proton mass; as a result of the mass ratio for electron and proton, $\mu_\beta/\mu_N = 1836$.

C. POPULATION AND RELAXATION IN NMR

In our study of optical absorption spectroscopy thus far, we have simply assumed a Boltzmann distribution between states and a replenishable excess population in the lower initial state. In these cases, the natural radiative lifetime or collisional processes or both were sufficiently effective to justify these assumptions. In the present case, NMR energy splittings are considerably smaller than the splittings previously considered. As a result, the number of excess molecules in the lower state or states is an extremely small fraction of the total distributed over the $2I + 1$ energy-split states. Using the data from Example 8-1 for a two-level system, the proton spin states are separated by $\Delta\epsilon = 4.23 \times 10^{-19}$ erg. According to the Boltzmann expression for this system of protons at 300 °K, we obtain

$$\frac{N(\text{upper})}{N(\text{lower})} = \exp - \frac{\Delta\epsilon}{kT} \simeq 1 + \frac{\Delta\epsilon}{kT} = 1 + 1.02 \times 10^{-5}, \qquad \textbf{(8-35)}$$

where the exponential expansion is justified since $\Delta\epsilon/kT \ll 1$. Thus, for every one hundred thousand nuclei in the upper level there are one hundred thousand and one in the lower. Therefore not only is it necessary for the experimental method to be extremely sensitive, but the system must be capable of maintaining this excess in the lower state in order to perform absorption spectroscopy. In the absence of effective processes replenishing the lower state at a rate sufficient to maintain its excess population, the molecules in the lower and upper states become equal in number and thus no net absorption occurs. This phenomenon is known as *saturation.*

Since we are aware that NMR experiments have been performed, we shall discuss briefly how the problem of saturation is avoided. Since the natural radiative lifetimes of these energy-level separations are extremely long ($\tau_f \gg 10^3$ sec), such a mechanism for the lower-state repopulation is impossible. In spite of the fact that nuclei are relatively well shielded, both long- and short-range magnetic interactions resulting from neighboring molecular motions are responsible for maintaining the excess lower-state population. Such mechanisms are known as *relaxation processes.* The two relaxation processes important in NMR spectroscopy are *spin-lattice* and *spin-spin* relaxations.

1. Spin-Lattice Relaxation

Spin-lattice relaxation in NMR arises from the interaction of the fluctuating magnetic fields of the surrounding molecules (lattice) and the magnetic moment of the nucleus of interest. These fluctuating magnetic fields are generated by electronic and nuclear motions of the lattice molecules as a result of translation, rotation, and vibration. The magnetic fields of the appropriate frequency associated with these motions will have components in the locality of the nucleus of interest that induce transitions to the lower spin level. The energy exchanged in this process is absorbed by the lattice and in this manner the Boltzmann distribution between the upper and lower states is maintained.

Equally important to maintaining the Boltzmann distribution is the time necessary to achieve relaxation. The relaxation time in NMR is formally defined as the time required for the excited state population to fall to $1/e = 0.37$ of its original population. Spin-lattice relaxation times are also known as longitudinal relaxation times and given the symbol T_1. These times range from 10^{-2} to 10^4 sec for solids and from 10^{-2} to 10^2 sec for liquids. In the situation where paramagnetic ions may be present in solutions, this time may be as short as 10^{-4} sec. The length of time in which these excited states are depleted will significantly affect the nature of the spectral absorptions (lines).

2. Spin-Spin Relaxation

In addition to spin relaxation resulting from the nuclear spin interaction with the lattice, spin relaxation also occurs via a mechanism involving the direct interaction of two spin states. This spin-flip process is brought about when a spinning nucleus generates a localized magnetic field at a neighboring nucleus of a different spin orientation. The magnetic field generated will correspond to the resonance condition, since it is produced by rotation of the magnetic dipole about the static magnetic field at the Larmor frequency. The net result is that the two spins will have exchanged orientations during the relaxation process. Processes such as these, in which relaxation is brought about via spin-spin interactions, are known as spin-spin relaxations. Although there is no net change between the upper- and lower-state populations, the time involved in terminating either spin state will have a pronounced effect on the uncertainty in the energy-level separation. These spin-spin relaxation times are known also as transverse relaxation times and given the symbol T_2. For solids, T_2 is usually very short, $\sim 10^{-4}$ sec, but for liquids $T_2 \simeq T_1$.

The uncertainty in the frequency of a spectral line is given by multiplying Eq. (2-53) by the speed of light c,

$$\Delta\nu = \frac{1}{2\pi\Delta t}, \tag{8-36}$$

where Δt is the relaxation time. In the case of very short relaxation times $\Delta t \simeq 10^{-4}$ sec, the uncertainty in frequency is 0.11×10^4 sec^{-1}, or 0.0011 MHz. On the other hand when the relaxation times are very long, the frequency is well defined, but the occurrence of saturation is significantly increased since the lower state is being repopulated at such a slow rate. Thus, operating somewhere between these two extremes, NMR spectroscopy is more or less divided into broadline (wideline) and high-resolution. Broadline spectra are generally characteristic of solids and some liquids that have very short relaxation times, for example, solutions containing paramagnetic ions, whereas high-resolution spectra are generally attainable from gases and liquids. When T_2 is the more important relaxation time, it can be calculated from the shape of the absorption line. The relation is

$$\frac{1}{T_2} = \Delta\nu_{1/2} \text{ Hz}, \tag{8-37}$$

where $\Delta\nu_{1/2}$ is the half-width of the line at half the absorption peak height.

D. NUCLEAR MAGNETIC RESONANCE (NMR) SPECTROSCOPY

1. Experimental

Certain experimental requirements are obvious from our review thus far of the elementary theory of NMR. Perhaps the simplest experimental arrangement for performing such observations is one involving absorption.

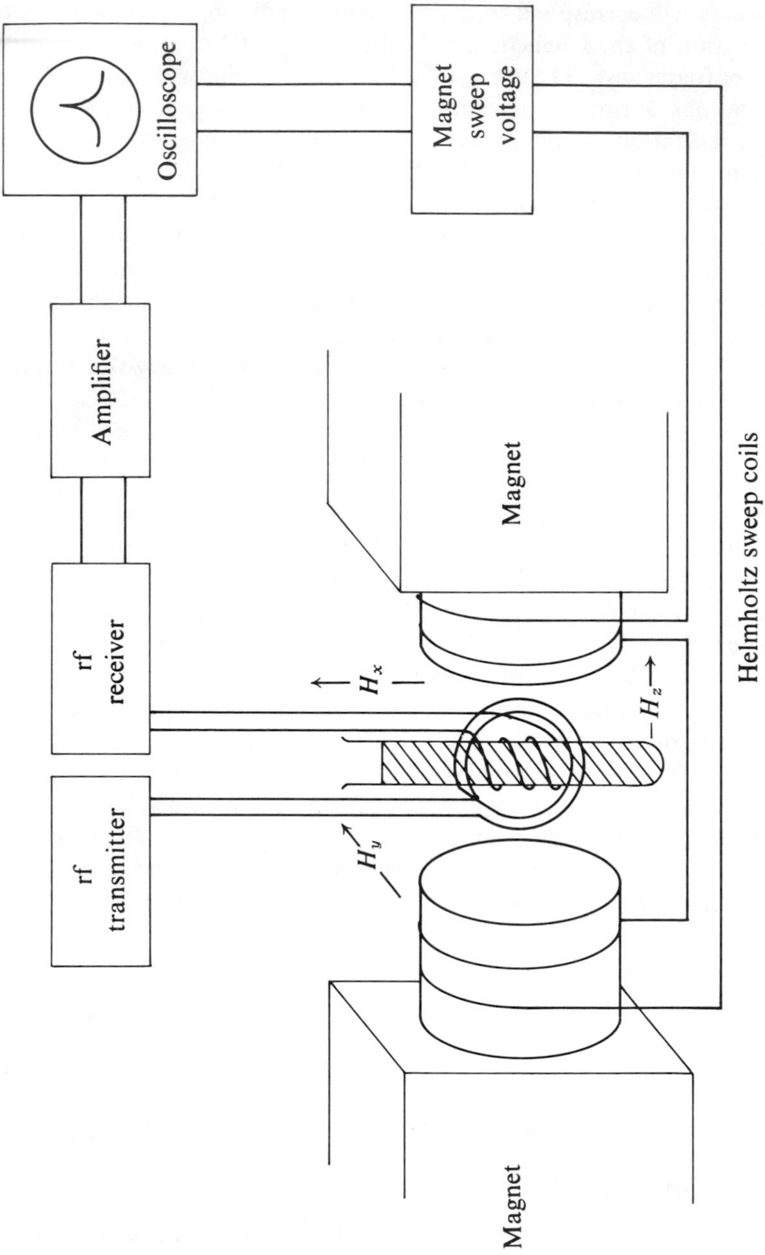

FIGURE 8-3 Instrumental arrangement of the basic nuclear magnetic induction experiment.

In this case, an external magnetic field H_z is applied to the sample, resulting in the splitting of the degenerate nuclear levels. The nuclear magnetic moments precess about this external field at the Larmor frequency. To excite transitions between these field-split levels, an oscillator coil is wrapped about the sample perpendicular to the external field. Using normally attainable external magnetic fields, the oscillating perpendicular field (H_x) required for proton resonance is of radiofrequency $\sim$60 MHz. According to Eq. (8-28a), the resonance condition can be achieved by varying either this oscillating field or the external field. Since it is more difficult to construct a highly stable variable-frequency oscillator, the external field is varied in order to achieve resonance. In practice, the external magnetic field is tuned to near resonance of the sample; then a superimposable finely tuned field of a few gauss, generated by varying the current of a pair of Helmholtz sweep coils, is used to scan the absorption region. During resonance, the energy generated by the oscillating circuit is decreased in intensity at the detector as a result of absorption by the sample. This decrease in magnetic intensity from the rf source is detected, amplified, and fed into the vertical deflection plates of an oscilloscope, so that what we observe is the familiar signal vs frequency dip due to absorption.

In the absorption experiment, depending on the particular sample, difficulties are experienced as a result of the low signal-to-noise (S/N) ratio. Although these problems have largely been overcome by using bridge circuits, lock-in amplifiers, and more recently, Fourier-transform signal-averaging techniques, there is an alternative NMR technique that has been developed simultaneously with the direct absorption technique; this is nuclear resonance induction. In the induction method, an additional coil is situated normal to both the external field (z axis) and the field (x axis) generated by the coil about the sample. In this arrangement, the additional coil (y axis) acts as a transmitting magnetic field. When this coil achieves resonance, the sample nuclei become magnetized and precess about the static field H_z at the Larmor frequency. This precessional motion, having x and y components, induces a voltage in the x-directed coil (which now performs as a receiver), which is amplified and fed to an oscilloscope for display. A nuclear magnetic resonance induction experimental setup is shown in Figure 8-3.

2. Chemical Shifts and Low-Resolution NMR

The low-resolution NMR spectra of acetaldehyde, acetic acid, and ethanol shown in Figure 8-4 illustrate the most important single parameter derived from this spectroscopic technique, the chemical shift. Instead

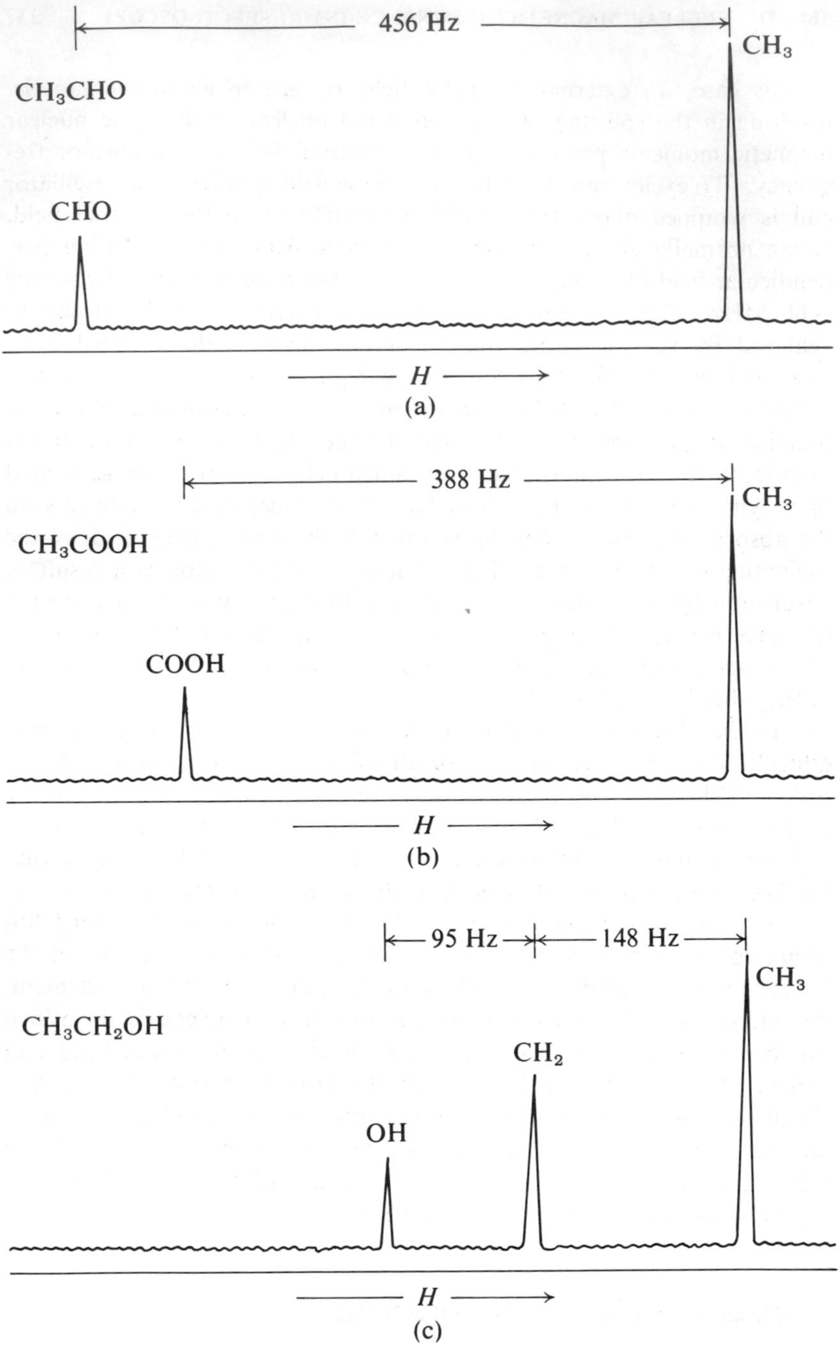

FIGURE 8-4 Low-resolution NMR spectra of (a) acetaldehyde, (b) acetic acid, and (c) ethanol. The chemical shift δ is related to the resonant peak differences $\Delta\nu_{ij}$ by the relation $\Delta\nu_{ij} = \delta\nu_0$, where ν_0 is the fixed frequency of the oscillating magnetic field.

of obtaining a single proton resonance peak for each of these compounds, the spectra clearly indicate that the various protons experience resonance at slightly different magnetic fields. We must assume that the constituent protons experience different magnetic fields at their nuclei as a result of the differing electronic environments. On further examination of these low-resolution spectra, we can easily identify each peak with types of protons, since the relative areas of the absorptions are proportional to the ratio of the types of constituent protons. The ratio of the two areas displayed in the acetic acid spectrum is 1:3, and these peaks are easily identified with COOH and CH_3 protons. A similar ratio and interpretation are obtained for the CHO and CH_3 protons of acetaldehyde. For ethanol, the three peaks in the ratio of 1:2:3 are again easily identified with OH, CH_2, and CH_3 protons. Nuclei of a given compound that come into resonance at the same externally applied magnetic field are defined as *chemically equivalent*; in these examples, the methylene (CH_2) and methyl (CH_3) protons are chemically equivalent.

These differences in magnetic field required to bring about different proton resonances are not altogether surprising to us, since we discussed (Section 8A) the local diamagnetic and paramagnetic fields resulting from the constituent electrons. These local fields will either reinforce or oppose the externally applied field. Since most stable substances are diamagnetic, the opposing field generated will have the net effect of shielding the nuclei of interest. This effect is expressed quantitatively as

$$H_i = H_0(1 - \sigma_i), \qquad \textbf{(8-38)}$$

where H_i is the magnetic field at the nucleus i, H_0 is the externally applied magnetic field, and σ_i is the *shielding constant*. Thus, chemically equivalent nuclei have identical shielding constants.

The difference in resonance line positions in a spectrum due to the difference in the shielding constants for nuclei in different electronic environments is defined as the *chemical shift*, δ. Since the differences in shielding constants are of the order of 10^{-6}, it is necessary to achieve a stability of parts per million in control of the magnetic field, and parts per billion for high-resolution NMR. Fortunately we have instruments capable of varying and measuring external field differences of the order of a few milligauss, corresponding to the observed differences. Although the resonance condition is achieved in these experiments by sweeping the external magnetic field, the actual chemical shifts are obtained directly as frequency (Hz) differences. This choice is based on the so-called sideband method, which provides an extremely convenient calibration of the NMR spectrum. Briefly described, if either the H_1 or the H_z (external field) magnetic field is modulated by introduction of an audiofrequency current through coils whose axis coincides with either field, then additional lines appear on both sides of each of the spectral absorptions. These sidebands are symmetrically disposed about a given absorption, and the spacing between them on either side of an absorption line (called the centerband) is equal to the modulating, or audio, frequency. Since this frequency can be accurately measured by an electronic counter, we can use this linear difference as a calibration of the spectrum. This method of displaying the magnetic field scan presents no difficulty, since the measured frequency difference $\nu_0\delta$ can be easily converted to magnetic field units (milligauss) by Eq. (8-29). For example, the frequency difference between the methylene protons and the acetylenic proton of $HC{\equiv}CCH_2OH$ is $\sim$111 Hz. The corresponding magnetic field difference is (Eq. (8-29)),

$$\Delta H = \frac{2\pi\Delta\nu_n}{\gamma_p} = \frac{(2)(3.14)(111)}{(2.68 \times 10^4)} = 26.01 \text{ milligauss,} \qquad \textbf{(8-39)}$$

where $\gamma_p = 2.675 \times 10^4$ rad/sec-G.

To avoid confusion in reporting chemical shifts in the scientific literature, there appears to be a general agreement to define δ as a field-independent (dimensionless) parameter relative to tetramethylsilane (TMS) as a proton reference compound,

$$\delta = (\sigma_r - \sigma_i) \times 10^6 = \frac{H_i - H_r}{H_0} \times 10^6. \qquad \textbf{(8-40)}$$

Each of the magnetic fields, H_i at the nucleus of interest and H_r at the nucleus of the reference compound, corresponds to its resonance condition at a fixed frequency of the oscillating field. The field H_0 is the static external field that is essentially equal to both H_i and H_r since $\delta \times 10^{-6}$ is so small. Since chemical shifts are obtained from experimental measurements in frequency units, we use Eq. (8-29) to convert Eq. (8-40) to

$$\delta = \frac{\nu_i - \nu_r}{\nu_0} \times 10^6. \qquad \textbf{(8-41)}$$

The choice of TMS as the internal reference compound is based on several facts: one, it is relatively stable in many liquids; two, it has a single resonance peak since all twelve protons are equivalent; and three, the resonance frequency is higher than those of most proton resonances since its protons are so highly shielded.

Since the resonance frequency of TMS, ν_r, is higher than the frequencies of most protons, δ is generally a negative number. To avoid having negative δ values, an additional chemical shift τ is defined:

$$\tau = 10.00 + \delta, \qquad \textbf{(8-42)}$$

where both τ and δ are expressed in parts per million (ppm). Some characteristic proton chemical shifts are shown in Table 8-1. The

TABLE 8-1. Typical Proton Chemical Shifts

Compound	Shift τ (ppm)
Methyl Protons	
$(CH_3)_4Si$	10.000
$CH_3(CH_2)_3CH_3$	9.15
$(CH_3)_4C$	9.08
CH_3CH_2OH	8.83
CH_3CH_2Cl	8.60
CH_3CH_2Br	8.34
$(CH_3)_2C{=}CH_2$	8.299
CH_3CN	8.026
$(CH_3)_2S$	7.942
CH_3COOH	7.915
CH_3I	7.84
$CH_3C_6H_5$	7.66
CH_3Br	7.38
CH_3Cl	7.00
$(CH_3)_2O$	6.73
CH_3OH	6.62
$CH_3OC_6H_5$	6.27
CH_3F	5.70
CH_3NO_2	5.72
Methylene Protons	
Cyclopropane	9.78
$CH_3(CH_2)_4CH_3$	8.75
Cyclohexane	8.56
Cyclopentane	8.49
Bicyclo-2,2,1-hepta-2,5-diene	8.05
Cyclopentanone	7.98
1,3-Cyclohexadiene	7.74
$(CH_3CH_2)_2CO$	7.61
$(CH_3CH_2)_2N$	7.58
$CH_3COCH_2COOCH_3$	6.52
$(CH_3CH_2)_2O$	6.64
$CH_3COCH_2COCH_3$	6.45
CH_3CH_2OH	6.41
Tetrahydrofuran	6.37
$HC{\equiv}CCH_2Cl$	5.91
$HC{\equiv}CCH_2OH$	5.82
$C_6H_5CH_2OH$	5.61
Methine Protons	
Chlorocyclopropane	7.05
$(CH_3)_2CHNH_2$	7.05
Chlorocyclohexane	6.08
$(CH_3)_2CHOH$	6.05
$(CH_3)_2CHCl$	5.88
$(CH_3)_2CHBr$	5.83
$(CH_3)CCHCH\ Br_2$	8.20
Bicyclo-2,2,1-heptane	7.81
Bicyclo-2,2,1-hepta-2,5-diene	6.53
Olefinic Protons	
$(CH_3)_2C{=}CH_2$	5.4
$(CH_3)_2C{=}CHCH_3$	4.79
1-Methyl cyclohexene	4.70
$(C_6H_5)_2C{=}CH_2$	4.60
Cyclohexene	4.43
Cyclohexa-1,3-diene	4.22
$CH_3CH{=}CHCHO$	3.95
Cyclopentadiene	3.58
$Cl_2C{=}CHCl$	3.55
Bicyclo-2,2,1-hepta-2,5-diene	3.35
cis-Stilbene	3.51
trans-Stilbene	3.01
Acetylenic Protons	
$HOCH_2C{\equiv}CH$	7.67
$ClCH_2C{\equiv}CH$	7.60
$C_6H_5C{\equiv}CH$	7.07
$CH_3COC{\equiv}CH$	6.83
Aromatic Protons	
Pyrrole (β)	3.93
Furan (β)	3.72
Pyrrole (α)	3.47
Mesitylene	3.36
Thiophene (β)	2.94
Toluene	2.91
Thiophene (α)	2.83

TABLE 8-1 (Continued)

Compound	Shift τ (ppm)	Compound	Shift τ (ppm)
Aromatic Protons		Aldehydic Protons	
Benzene	2.73	$(CH_3)_2N—CHO$	2.16
Furan (α)	2.64	CH_3OCHO	1.97
C_6H_5CN	2.46	$(CH_3)_2CHCHO$	0.44
Naphthalene	2.27	$C_6H_5CH{=}CHCHO$	0.37
Pyridine (γ)	2.64	CH_3CHO	0.284
Pyridine (β)	3.015	p-$CH_3OC_6H_4CHO$	0.199
Pyridine (α)	1.50	C_6H_5CHO	0.035

SOURCE: Davis, Jeff C., Jr. *Advanced Physical Chemistry*. New York: The Ronald Press Co., 1965. Reference 8-3, by permission.

chemical shifts summarized in Table 8-1 occur in certain ranges for specific types of atoms and groups. Such information is used as a powerful structural tool, and like other spectroscopic techniques, becomes more definitive when structural information is provided by some additional source (synergistic effect). The low-resolution NMR spectra of a variety of compounds are shown in Figure 8-5. The association of absorption areas with equivalent protons provides straightforward assignments in these cases.

In addition to proton magnetic resonance, there have also been a considerable number of studies involving the resonances of other magnetic nuclei, notable of which is ^{19}F. Typical chemical shifts in Hz ($\nu_0\delta$) for ^{19}F, ^{13}C, ^{14}N, and ^{31}P are shown in Figure 8-6. As we can see, the shifts for these nuclei are quite large compared with the proton shifts we have been examining. Both ^{19}F and ^{13}C compounds have been studied in some detail even though ^{19}F resonances occur over a considerable radiofrequency range and ^{13}C, with a natural abundance of 1.1%, is very difficult to detect. Of the other two magnetic nuclei, ^{14}N resonances are broadened by the coupling of the nuclear spin moment with the nuclear quadrupole moment, and ^{31}P NMR experiments have been most useful in the structural determination of organic phosphorus compounds.

3. High-Resolution NMR

a. Electron-Coupled Spin-Spin Interaction. As a result of the development of electromagnets and superconducting magnets capable of attaining highly stable (one part in 10^9) and relatively large magnetic fields (20

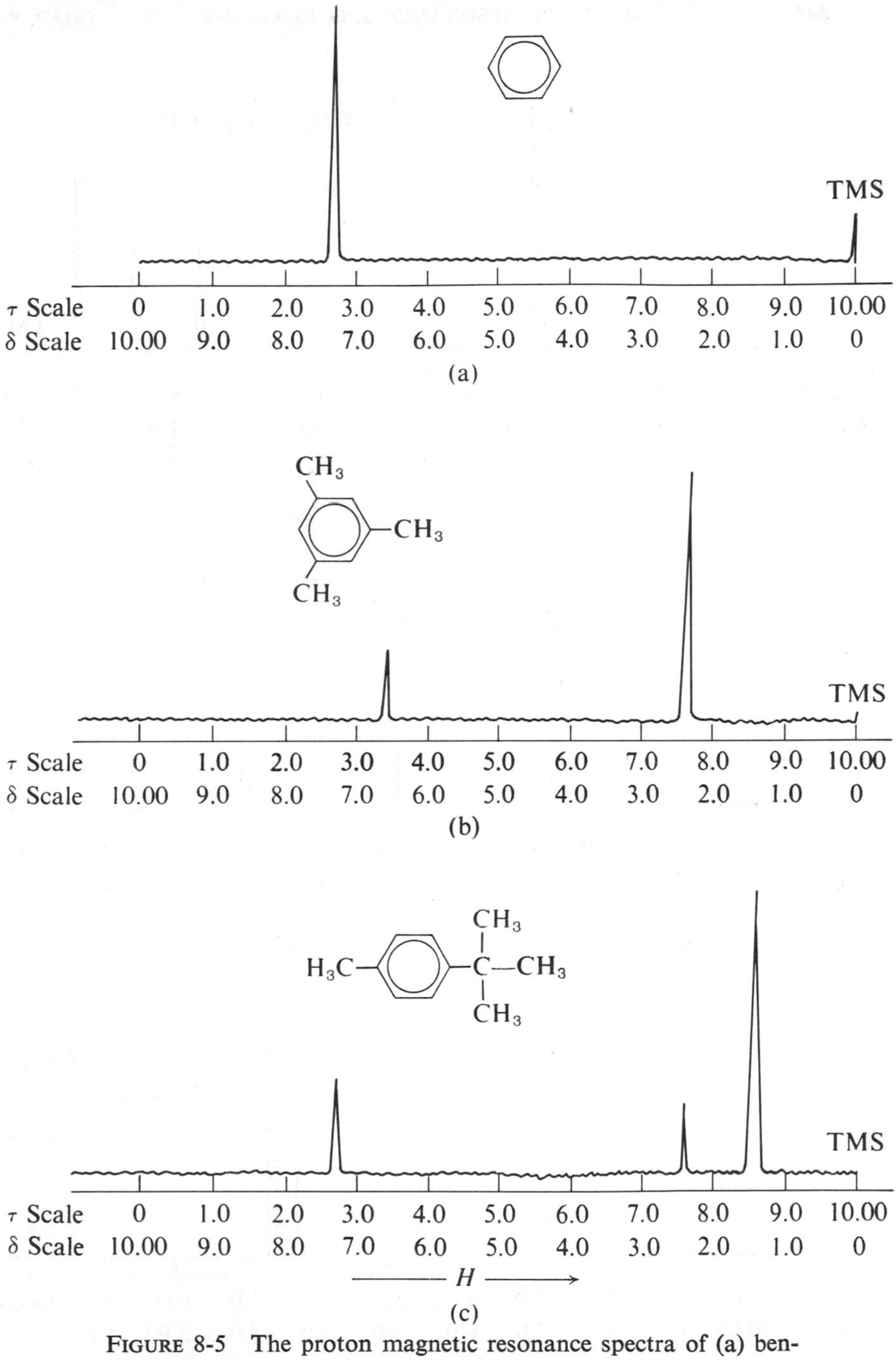

FIGURE 8-5 The proton magnetic resonance spectra of (a) benzene (b) mesitylene, (c) *p*-tert-butyltoluene, (d) *n*-propylbenzene, (e) 1,2-dibromo-1-phenylethane, and (f) *N*,*N*-bis(cyanomethyl)-benzylamine at 60 MHz. The chemical shifts are recorded using the τ and δ scales with TMS as the internal standard.

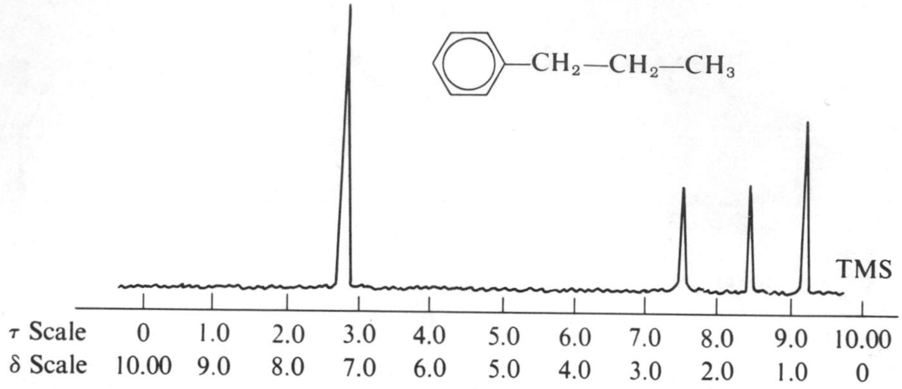

—CH₂—CH₂—CH₃
TMS
τ Scale 0 1.0 2.0 3.0 4.0 5.0 6.0 7.0 8.0 9.0 10.00
δ Scale 10.00 9.0 8.0 7.0 6.0 5.0 4.0 3.0 2.0 1.0 0

(d)

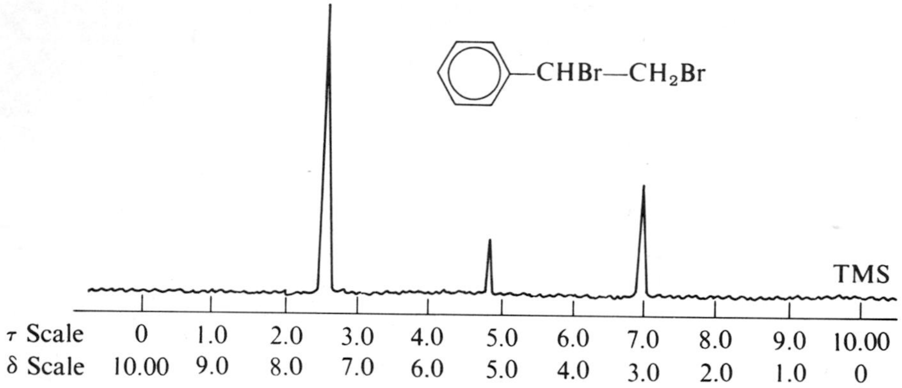

—CHBr—CH₂Br
TMS
τ Scale 0 1.0 2.0 3.0 4.0 5.0 6.0 7.0 8.0 9.0 10.00
δ Scale 10.00 9.0 8.0 7.0 6.0 5.0 4.0 3.0 2.0 1.0 0

(e)

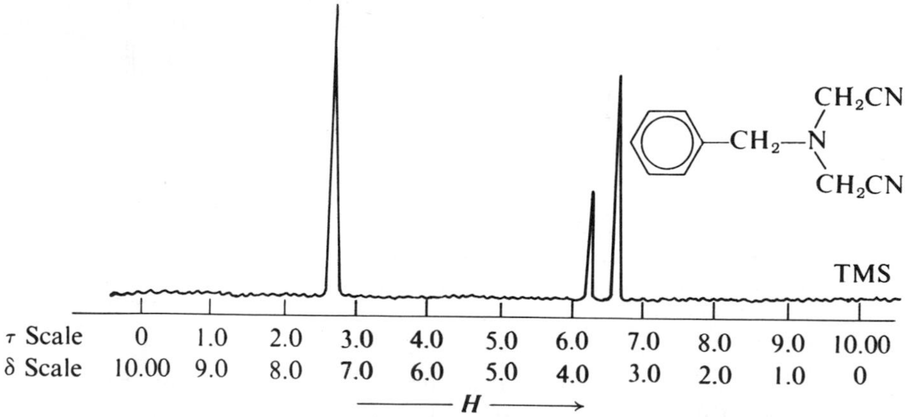

CH₂CN
—CH₂—N
CH₂CN
TMS
τ Scale 0 1.0 2.0 3.0 4.0 5.0 6.0 7.0 8.0 9.0 10.00
δ Scale 10.00 9.0 8.0 7.0 6.0 5.0 4.0 3.0 2.0 1.0 0
H

(f)

FIGURE 8-5 (Continued)

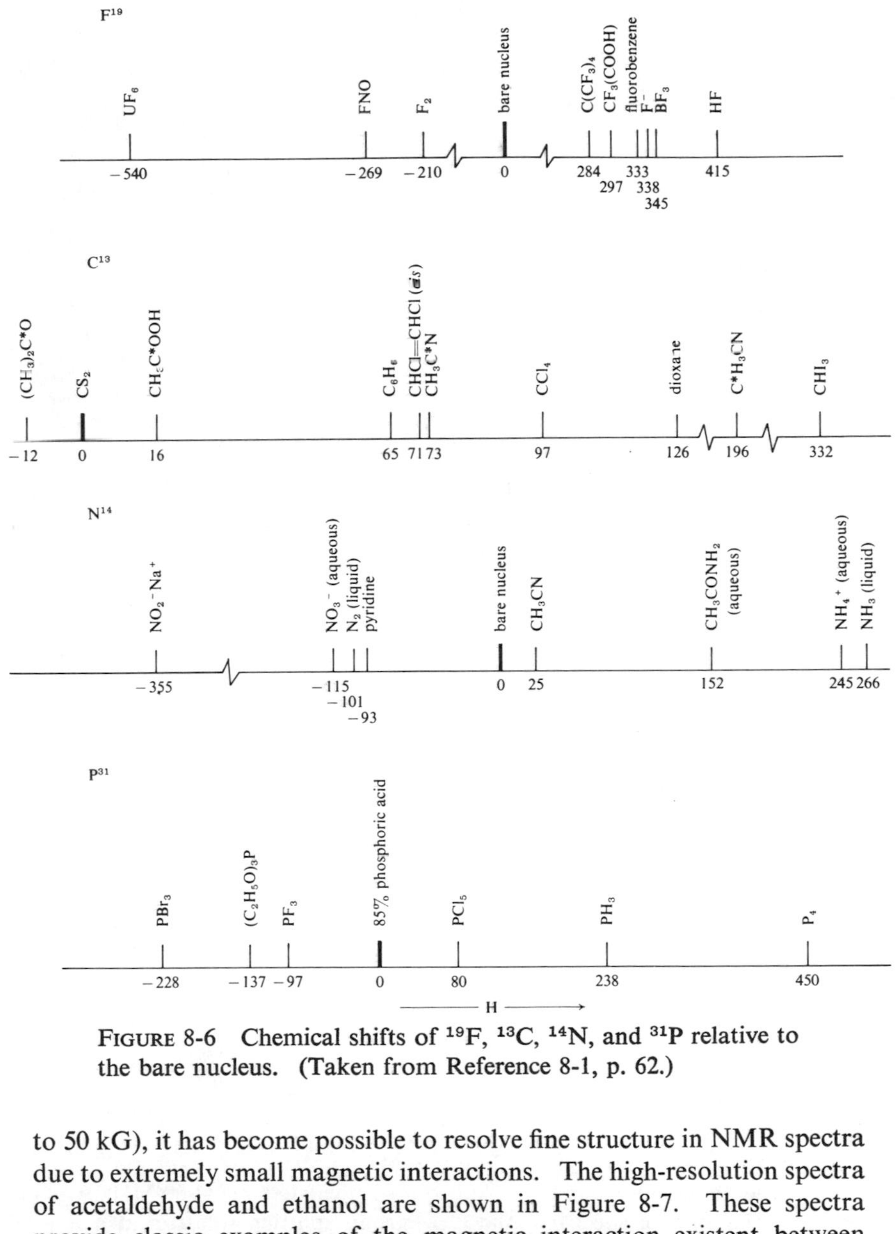

FIGURE 8-6 Chemical shifts of ^{19}F, ^{13}C, ^{14}N, and ^{31}P relative to the bare nucleus. (Taken from Reference 8-1, p. 62.)

to 50 kG), it has become possible to resolve fine structure in NMR spectra due to extremely small magnetic interactions. The high-resolution spectra of acetaldehyde and ethanol are shown in Figure 8-7. These spectra provide classic examples of the magnetic interaction existent between chemically nonequivalent neighboring nuclear spins. In the case of CH_3CHO, the aldehydic proton (CHO) is split into four peaks with intensity ratios of 1:3:3:1, whereas the methyl proton is split into a doublet of equal intensity. Although the high-resolution spectrum requires

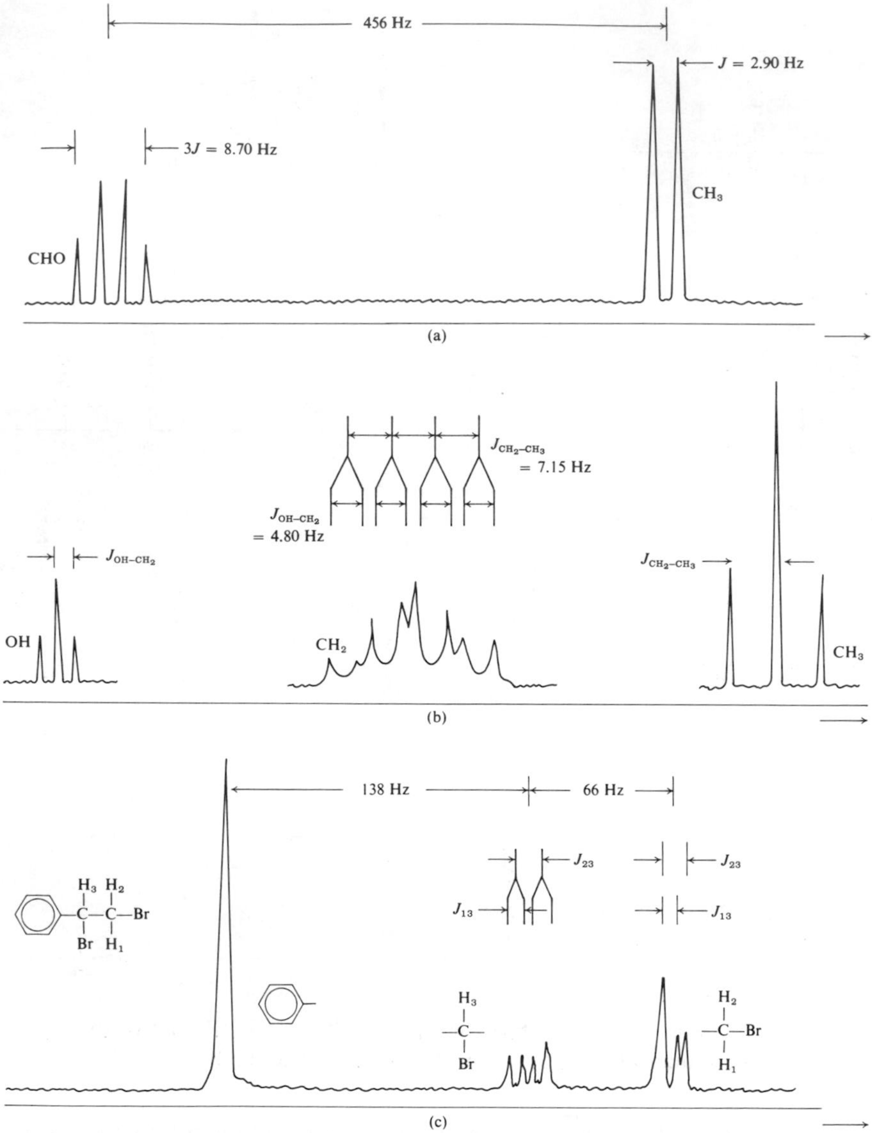

FIGURE 8-7 The high-resolution NMR spectra of (a) acetaldehyde, (b) ethanol, and (c) 1,2-dibromo-1-phenylethane at 60 MHz. In the ethanol spectrum, the CH_2 group splitting was run at a slower scanning rate so that it could be easily compared with the theoretical splitting pattern shown above. Although these spin-split spectra are drawn in a perfectly symmetrical manner for pedagogical purposes, we should note that actual spectra are not as symmetrical.

additional thought in terms of our interpretation, the ratio of the integrated areas under the two sets of peaks is still 1:3. The splitting (2.90 Hz) between both sets of peaks is observed to be independent of temperature and external magnetic field. We must conclude therefore that the magnetic interaction giving rise to this effect is of an internal nature. Furthermore, it can be shown theoretically that this splitting does not result from the interaction of chemically similar nuclei (CH_3, CH_2, CF_3, etc.), but between nuclei of chemically different neighboring groups. Nuclei in the former class are described as chemically and magnetically equivalent. Thus, we rationalize the CH_3CHO splitting by assuming that the CHO and CH_3 protons "see" each other's resultant nuclear magnetic dipole vectors. The CH_3 group will have resultant vectors $-\frac{3}{2}$, $-\frac{1}{2}$, $+\frac{1}{2}$, $+\frac{3}{2}$, in the statistical ratio 1:3:3:1, since each proton has spin $I = \frac{1}{2}$. The interaction of these magnetic vectors with the vector of the aldehydic proton gives rise to its observed splitting. The interaction is presumably transmitted via the bonding electrons between the two spin systems, and is known as *electron-coupled spin-spin multiplet splitting*. Although the detailed mechanism of this interaction has not been experimentally proved, it is believed to proceed via the stepwise sequence of interactions, nucleus (1)–electron (1), electron (1)–electron (2), . . . , electron (n)–nucleus (2). In a like manner, the CH_3 magnetic vector corresponding to the resonance frequency "sees" two orientations of the aldehydic proton ($I = +\frac{1}{2}$ and $I = -\frac{1}{2}$), and is split into a doublet of equal intensity. The splittings between both sets of peaks are equivalent, and the magnitude is defined as the *nuclear spin–spin coupling constant*. The second term of Eq. (8-13) characterizes this interaction, and the quantity J_{ij} (in energy, Hz, or G) is the coupling constant.

The high-resolution NMR spectrum of CH_3CH_2OH shown in Figure 8-7b is more complicated than the spectrum of acetaldehyde. The methyl peak is split into three components having an intensity ratio 1:2:1. This observation is easily rationalized as resulting from the three magnetic vectors generated by the adjacent methylene group. For two equivalent protons, the spin vectors are -1, 0, $+1$, with corresponding intensity ratio 1:2:1. In a like manner, the OH absorption peak is split into three components with intensity ratio 1:2:1, as a result of the magnetic vectors (spin orientations) of the methylene group. The multiplet splitting of the CH_2 absorption is considerably more complicated (partly because of resolution) than either of the two previously considered groups. In this case, we might assume that the CH_2 resonance vector sees the magnetic vectors generated by both the OH proton ($+\frac{1}{2}$ and $-\frac{1}{2}$) and the CH_3 protons ($-\frac{3}{2}$, $-\frac{1}{2}$, $+\frac{1}{2}$, $+\frac{3}{2}$). As a result, it can theoretically be split into four components by the CH_3 group and each of these components split into doublets by the OH group, thus producing a total of eight components. The actual observation of such a spectrum, however, depends on the relative magnitudes of the coupling constants and the spectral resolution obtainable. In this case, the J_{OH-CH_2} and $J_{CH_2-CH_3}$ coupling constants are not significantly different in magnitude. Thus, while the CH_2 splitting pattern does approximate this theoretical eight-component pattern, there is obvious superposition of some of the absorptions. In spite of the apparent agreement of this qualitative first-order perturbation approach, under very high resolution the observed spectrum is significantly more complicated (contains more lines of varying intensities); and it is more adequately calculated by second-order perturbation theory. This observation is true for the high-resolution spectrum not only of ethanol, but also of many molecules. Of further interest is that first-order coupling between the OH and CH_3 protons does not occur to any significant extent, which is consistent with the general observation that electron-coupled spin-spin interactions decrease fairly rapidly with increased distance between the nuclei of interest.

A final point concerning spin-spin coupling interactions is illustrated by the high-resolution NMR spectrum of 1,2-dibromo-1-phenylethane shown in Figure 8-7c. In Figure 8-5e, the low-resolution spectrum of this compound gives a single resolvable peak for the —CH_2Br protons, implying chemical equivalency (practically identical chemical shifts). Under high resolution, however, there is no discernible coupling between these two protons (H_1 and H_2), but we do observe separate coupling with the adjacent —CHBr— proton, indicating chemical equivalency but magnetic inequivalency of the —CH_2Br protons. The important point is that the chemical and magnetic equivalency of two or more nuclei must be *experimentally* established, in spite of what the low-resolution spectrum or presumed structure might imply. This property of dual equivalency generally occurs as a result of the inherent symmetry of the molecule (for example, $Si(CH_3)_4$) or from the averaging effect of intramolecular motion. For ethanol, the individual protons of the CH_2 and CH_3 groups are considered to be chemically and magnetically equivalent as a result of free rotation about the two C—C bonds. The —CHBr— proton (H_3) gives the expected quartet of approximately equal intensities as a result of the cumulative splitting by J_{23} and J_{13}. The phenyl group protons, which are not adjacent to the alkyl protons, do not show any noticeable spin-spin splitting, and thus we conclude that information concerning the existence of these magnetic vectors is not effectively transmitted via the ring carbon attached to the alkyl group. Actually, this non-spin-coupling interaction between ring and side-chain protons in alkylbenzenes is not an uncommon phenomenon.

The general approach outlined above for interpreting NMR fine structure in a given spectrum is justifiable solely where $\nu_0\delta \gg J_{ij}$. This will practically always be the case for the coupling of dissimilar nuclei (Problem 8-4), such as the molecule $^{31}P\ ^{19}F_3$. In the situation where the chemical shift in Hz ($\nu_0\delta$) is comparable to the coupling constant, then the resulting spectrum is significantly more complicated—not only from the overlapping of the expected simple patterns, but also from the breakdown of degenerate spin states (when $\nu_0\delta \gg J_{ij}$) via mixing induced by the

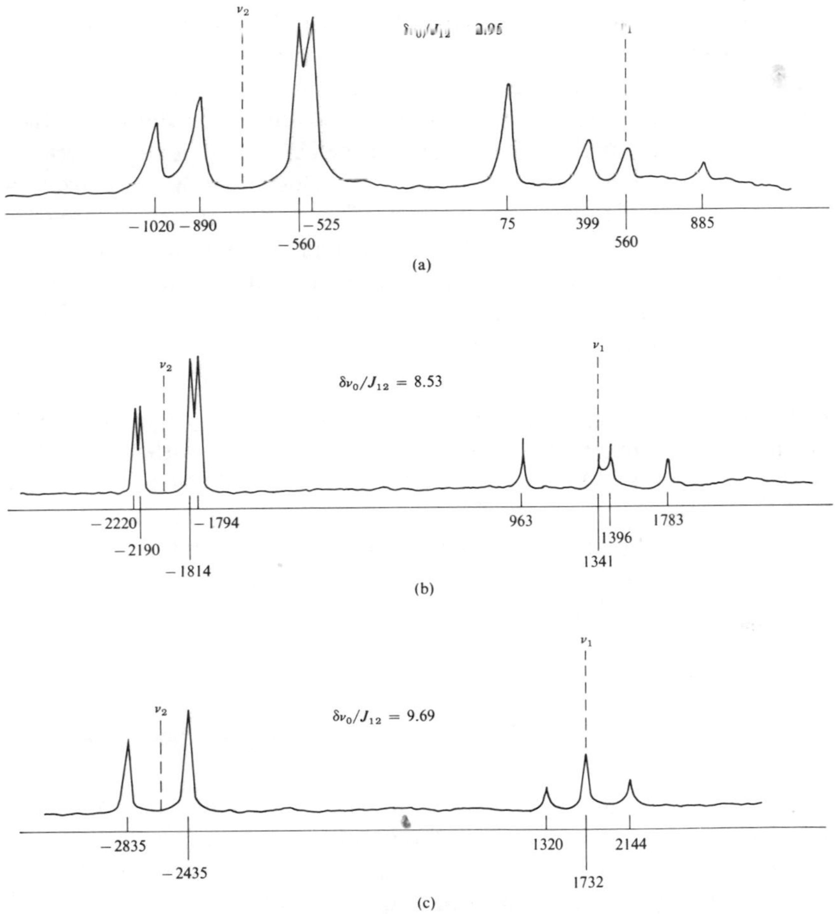

FIGURE 8-8 Fluorine 19 spectrum of ClF_3 at oscillating field frequency of (a) 10 MHz, (b) 30 MHz, (c) 40 MHz. All spectra were taken at -60 °C. Signal shifts are shown in MHz relative to the reference signal of SF_6. Here, $\delta\nu_0$ is the chemical shift in MHz between the two types of fluorine atoms, F_1 and F_2. (Taken from Pople, Schneider, and Bernstein [Reference 8-7, p. 97], by permission.)

external magnetic field. This breakdown of spin degeneracy increases the number of absorptions and also causes anomalous intensities in the observed spectrum. An excellent example of such a case is the ^{19}F NMR spectrum of ClF_3 at 10 MHz, discussed in Pople, Schneider, and Bernstein [Reference 8-7, pp. 96–98]. Chlorine trifluoride is *T*-shaped (Table 1-2) having two like Cl—F bonds and one unlike. Since ^{19}F has a spin $I = \frac{1}{2}$, we might expect the spectrum to consist of a doublet of equal intensity and a well-separated triplet in the ratio 1:2:1. The spectrum shown in Figure 8-8a at an oscillating field of 10 Hz consists of eight lines with no simple discernible intensity pattern. In this case $\delta\nu_0/J_{F_2-F_1} = 2.95$. If we take advantage of the fact that the chemical shift, $\delta\nu_0$, is a function of the applied static field while the coupling constant is not, then by increasing the applied field, we should be able to gradually generate a spectrum corresponding to $\delta\nu_0 > J_{F_2-F_1}$. This situation is realized in the spectrum of Figure 8-8c at 40 MHz, from which the $\delta\nu_0 = 4167$ Hz and $J_{F_2-F_1} \simeq 412$ Hz. Therefore, the most important factor in interpreting a high-resolution NMR spectrum is knowing the ratio $\delta\nu_0/J_{ij}$. The spectra obtained as a function of the range of this ratio for a two-spin ($I = \frac{1}{2}$, $I' = \frac{1}{2}$) system is discussed below.

b. NMR Spectrum of an AB System. A so-called AB system in NMR is one in which two nuclei (A and B) are coupled in such a way that $J_{AB} \sim \delta\nu_0$. In the cases of CH_3CHO, CH_3CH_2OH, and ClF_3 at 40 MHz (previously discussed), $\delta\nu_0 \gg J_{ij}$. According to convention, systems having large chemical shifts compared with the spin coupling constants have nuclear designations A and X; for instance, for CH_3CHO the designation is A_3X, whereas ClF_3 at 10 MHz is AB_2.

The Hamiltonian for an AB system according to the first two terms of Eq. (8-13) is

$$\hat{H} = -\{g_{n_A}\mu_N \hat{\mathbf{I}}_A \cdot \mathbf{H}_A + g_{n_B}\mu_N \hat{\mathbf{I}}_B \cdot \mathbf{H}_B + hJ_{AB}\hat{\mathbf{I}}_A \cdot \hat{\mathbf{I}}_B\} \text{ erg,} \qquad \textbf{(8-43)}$$

where H_A and H_B are the respective magnetic fields at nuclei A and B. They are in turn related to the static external field H_0 by Eq. (8-38). Substituting Eq. (8-38) for $\mathbf{H}_i$, and $(I_z)_i h/2\pi$ for $\hat{\mathbf{I}}_i$, and dividing through by h, we obtain the Hamiltonian in frequency units:

$$\hat{H} = -\left\{\left(\frac{\gamma H_0}{2\pi}\right)[(1 - \sigma_A)(I_z)_A + (1 - \sigma_B)(I_z)_B] + J_{AB}\hat{\mathbf{I}}_A \cdot \hat{\mathbf{I}}_B\right\} \text{ Hz,} \qquad \textbf{(8-44)}$$

where $(\gamma H_0/2\pi) = \nu_0$ is the frequency of the rf oscillating field at which resonance occurs for a bare unshielded nucleus of the A or the B type. Since there are two orientations with respect to the external field possible for each nucleus of this two-spin system, there will be four discrete energy levels. An appropriate set of basis functions is

$$\begin{aligned} \psi_1 &= \alpha(A)\alpha(B) \\ \psi_2 &= \alpha(A)\beta(B) \\ \psi_3 &= \beta(A)\alpha(B) \\ \psi_4 &= \beta(A)\beta(B), \end{aligned} \tag{8-45}$$

where α and β are respectively associated with the spin states $M_I = +\frac{1}{2}$ and $M_I = -\frac{1}{2}$. The corresponding eigenvalues for this system using standard quantum mechanical procedures are

$$\begin{aligned} \nu_1 &= \frac{E_1}{h} = -\frac{1}{2}(\nu_A + \nu_B) + \frac{1}{4}J_{AB} \\ \nu_2 &= \frac{E_2}{h} = -C - \frac{1}{4}J_{AB} \\ \nu_3 &= \frac{E_3}{h} = C - \frac{1}{4}J_{AB} \\ \nu_4 &= \frac{E_4}{h} = \frac{1}{2}(\nu_A + \nu_B) + \frac{1}{4}J_{AB}, \end{aligned} \tag{8-46}$$

where

$$C = \tfrac{1}{2}\sqrt{J_{AB}{}^2 + (\delta\nu_0)^2} \tag{8-47}$$

and $\delta\nu_0 = \nu_A - \nu_B$, the chemical shift in Hz.[4] In Eqs. (8-46), $\nu_A = (\gamma/2\pi)H_0(1 - \sigma_A)$; it represents the resonance frequency of nucleus A, assuming no coupling to nucleus B. A similar relation is true for ν_B. These energy levels and the allowed transitions ($\Delta M_I = \pm 1$) corresponding to $\delta\nu_0 \sim J_{AB}$ are shown schematically in Figure 8-9. The corresponding transition frequencies are

$$\begin{aligned} \nu_{21} &= \tfrac{1}{2}(\nu_A + \nu_B) - C - \tfrac{1}{2}J_{AB} \\ \nu_{43} &= \tfrac{1}{2}(\nu_A + \nu_B) - C + \tfrac{1}{2}J_{AB} \\ \nu_{31} &= \tfrac{1}{2}(\nu_A + \nu_B) + C - \tfrac{1}{2}J_{AB} \\ \nu_{42} &= \tfrac{1}{2}(\nu_A + \nu_B) + C + \tfrac{1}{2}J_{AB}. \end{aligned} \tag{8-48}$$

We can now predict theoretically the qualitative nature of the NMR spectrum of an AB system as a function of the $\delta\nu_0/J_{AB}$ ratio. These are illustrated schematically in Figure 8-10 and correspond to the following:

(*i*) In the limit $J_{AB} = 0$, we simply obtain two lines separated by the chemical shift $\delta\nu_0$. According to Eq. (8-48), $\nu_{21} = \nu_{43}$ and $\nu_{31} = \nu_{42}$, where

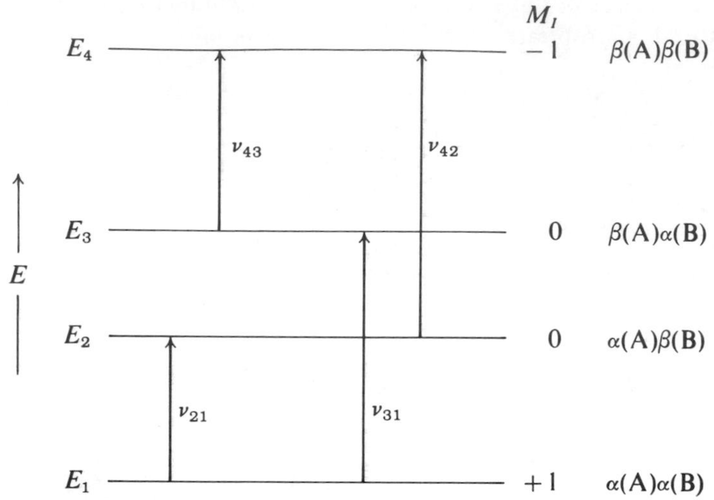

FIGURE 8-9 The energy levels and transitions ($\Delta M_I = \pm 1$) corresponding to $\delta\nu_0 \sim J_{AB}$ for an AB system. These particular transitions correspond to the spectrum shown in Figure 8-10c.

both lines occur equidistant ($\frac{1}{2}\delta\nu_0$) from the so-called *average Zeeman frequency*, $\frac{1}{2}(\nu_A + \nu_B)$ (Figure 8-10a).

(*ii*) In the case for which the spin-spin coupling is small compared with the chemical shift, $\delta\nu_0 \gg J_{AB}$, we obtain the spectrum shown schematically in Figure 8-10b. In this case, we assume $\sigma_A > \sigma_B$; then the high and low field doublets are essentially transitions associated with nucleus A (ν_{31} and ν_{42}) and nucleus B (ν_{21} and ν_{43}), respectively. In addition, the equal doublet splittings are equal to the coupling constant J_{AB}.

(*iii*) In the intermediate case, in which $\delta\nu_0 \sim J_{AB}$, the coupling constant is again the doublet splitting, as shown in Figure 8-10c. The difference frequency corresponding to $2C$, also shown in Figure 8-10c, provides a means of calculating the chemical shift via Eq. (8-47).

(*iv*) For $\delta\nu_0 \ll J_{AB}$, there are two close, very intense lines equidistant and opposite in direction from the average Zeeman frequency, as shown in Figure 8-10d. Their approximate separation in Hz is $(\delta\nu_0)^2/2J_{AB}$. There are also two weak lines that are symmetrically situated about the average Zeeman frequency, but considerably shifted relative to the other patterns from their doublet counterparts.

(*v*) In the limit, $\delta\nu_0 = 0$, the two strong lines of case (*iv*) merge into a strong single line corresponding to the average Zeeman frequency. Physically, we have a case of two identical nuclei, so that the states E_2 and E_3 of Eq. (8-46) and Figure 8-9 are now degenerate. The resulting transitions of Figure 8-9 for this three-level system are also degenerate and give rise to the superimposed single line described above (Figure 8-10e).

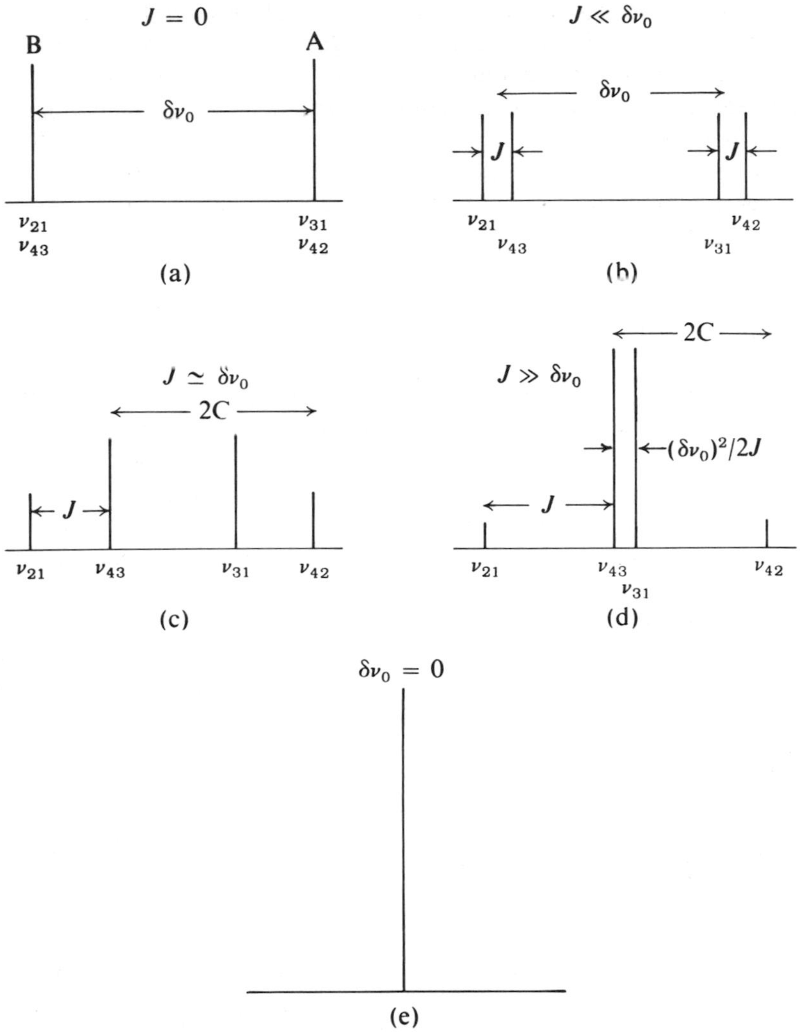

FIGURE 8-10 Qualitative NMR spectrum of an AB system as a function of the ratio $\delta\nu_0/J_{AB}$.

E. ELECTRON SPIN RESONANCE (ESR) SPECTROSCOPY

The possession of one or more unpaired electrons by species is a necessary requirement for a system to exhibit electron spin resonance. Even though most species in their ground states are singlets, there are numerous applications in which this technique has been extremely valuable in determining electronic structure. Systems which have been studied include organic and inorganic free radicals in the gaseous, liquid, or solid states, radiation-induced fragments and site defects in crystals and solids, and paramagnetic transition-metal and rare-earth ions. In examining the basic principles of ESR spectroscopy, we shall primarily analyze systems that are independent of magnetic field orientation (isotropic systems), and only briefly involve systems that are magnetic-field-dependent (anisotropic).

1. Experimental

The experimental apparatus necessary to detect transitions between electronic spin-split levels is similar to that shown in Figure 4-10, since these transitions also correspond to microwave frequencies (Example 8-1). A schematic diagram of an ESR spectrometer is illustrated in Figure 8-11. The source of the microwave radiation is a Klystron; a Klystron is a vacuum tube capable of producing highly monochromatic radiation as a function of the voltage applied to the tube. The radiation generated is propagated along either a cylindrical or a rectangular tube into a wavemeter. The calibrated wavemeter is used to identify the frequency (Hz) of the microwave radiation. The microwaves are then propagated through an attenuator, which allows adjusting the power level incident on the sample. Depending on the nature of the sample, either an X-band or a Q-band waveguide is used for most effectively propagating the radiation into the sample region. The X-band waveguide is most appropriate for the region 8.2 to 12.4 GHz, whereas the Q-band operates most efficiently over the range 33.0 to 50.0 GHz. In general, liquid samples are run using the former, whereas single crystals and other solid samples are more advantageously run with the latter. The source radiation is propagated into the resonant cavity that contains the sample. Ideally, the cavity is designed to maximize the radiation density, to provide coincidence of the sample with the H_1 field, and to have H_1 normal to the external magnetic field, H_z. The magnet system that produces the spin-level splittings is similar to that shown in Figure 8-3, except that the magnet sweep voltage is additionally modulated. Consequently, the attenuated signal, due to sample absorption that is propagated out of the resonant cavity and received by the crystal detector, is modulated. This modulated signal, which is fed to a phase-sensitive detector and then amplified, achieves a greater S/N (compared with a static field experiment) in the same way that was previously described for a microwave spectrometer (Section 4G-1). Again, the modulated external magnetic field H_z, is swept in order to achieve resonance. The amplified signal is displayed

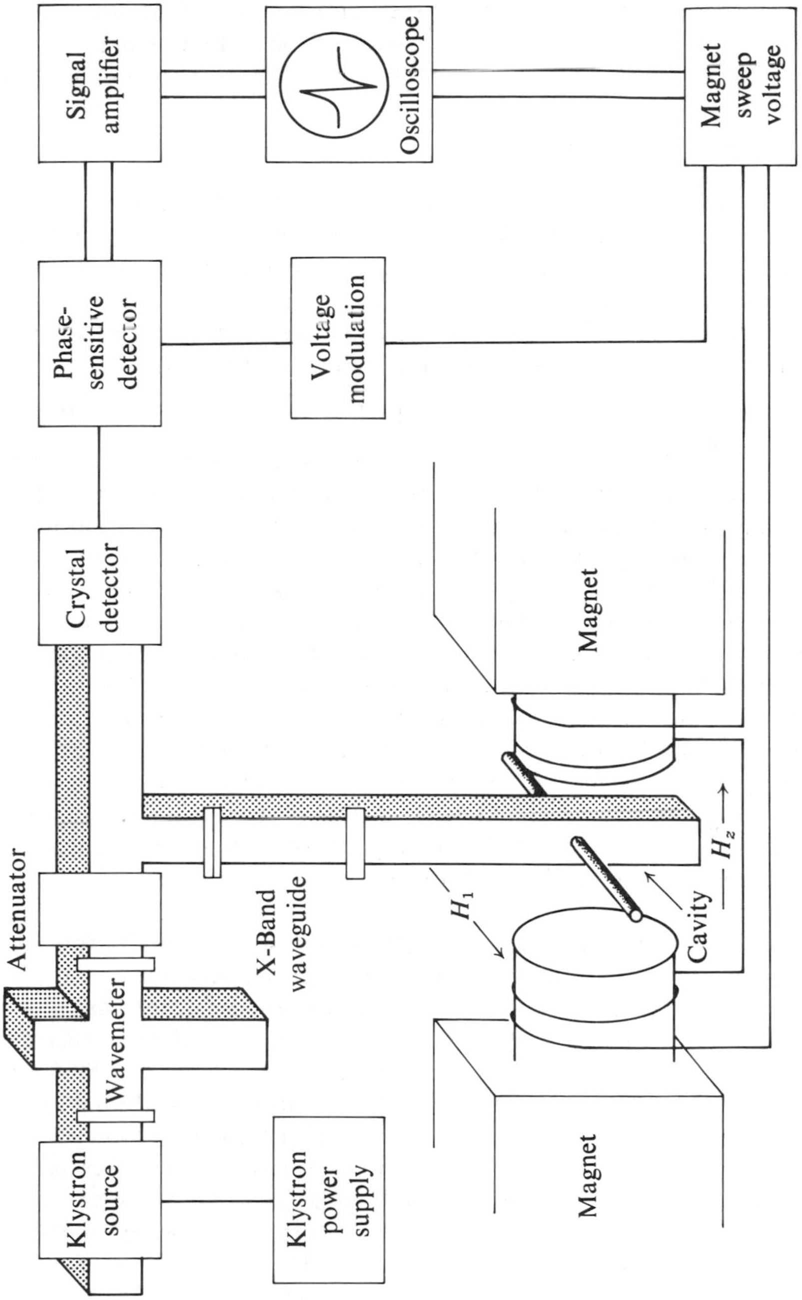

FIGURE 8-11 Schematic diagram of the basic components of an ESR spectrometer.

as the y axis and the varied magnetic field as the x axis on an oscilloscope or a recorder or both. As a result of the phase handling of the absorption signal, it is displayed as the (first) derivative of the first harmonic.

2. Nuclear Hyperfine Interaction

In much the same way that differing electronic environments about various nuclei give rise to differing NMR resonances, the magnetic field satisfying the resonance condition of Eq. (8-21a) will in turn be affected by neighboring nuclear magnetic dipoles. These magnetic dipoles generate local magnetic fields H_{loc}, which add vectorially to the external resonance field H_{er}, to produce observed resonance fields H_{r},

$$H_{\text{r}} = H_{\text{er}} + H_{\text{loc}}. \tag{8-49}$$

The term H_{er} is defined as the resonance field for a free electron at a given microwave frequency ($H_{\text{loc}} = 0$). The magnitude of the local fields H_{loc} generated by the nuclear magnetic dipoles is directly proportional to the nuclear-electron spin interaction. This interaction between an unpaired electron and a magnetic nucleus, first introduced by Fermi to account for the hyperfine splitting in atomic spectra, is called the *nuclear hyperfine interaction*. In general, this interaction may occur in such a manner that it is independent of the external field **H**, in which case it is called isotropic hyperfine coupling. In the case where the interaction depends on the **H** orientation, it is referred to as anisotropic hyperfine coupling. The net effect of this interaction is to cause a further splitting of each of the M_s states shown in Figure (8-1c). The magnitude and extent of this splitting depends critically on the nature of the interacting magnetic dipole or dipoles (to be discussed below).

a. Isotropic Hyperfine Coupling. Systems for which the electronic g factor of Eq. (8-21a) is independent of the magnetic field orientation are defined as isotropic. Those that are field-dependent are defined as anisotropic, and the electronic Zeeman term in this case is $\mu_\beta \mathbf{H}\cdot\mathbf{g}\cdot\mathbf{S}$, where $\mathbf{g}$ is now a tensor similar to the polarizability tensor of Eq. (5-32). Systems having spherical symmetry, such as a hydrogen atom, or octahedral symmetry, such as a trapped electron at the center of a regular octahedron of cations, are obvious examples of isotropic systems. On the other hand, low-viscosity solutions of paramagnetic ions or organic radicals are described as magnetically isotropic. The isotropic behavior in these cases results from the rapid tumbling and random reorientation of these species in such a way that the measured g factor is simply considered the average of the trace of the g tensor, that is, $\frac{1}{3}(g_{xx} + g_{yy} + g_{zz})$.

i. The Hydrogen Atom ($S = \frac{1}{2}$ and $I = \frac{1}{2}$). The simplest system exhibiting isotropic hyperfine coupling is the hydrogen atom. The interaction in this case is simply an unpaired electron with a nucleus $I = \frac{1}{2}$. The Hamiltonian for this system summed over the last three terms of Eq. (8-13) is

$$\hat{H} = g_e\mu_\beta\hat{\mathbf{S}}\cdot\mathbf{H} + hA\hat{\mathbf{S}}\cdot\hat{\mathbf{I}}, \tag{8-50}$$

where $H_{ss} = 0$ for a single spin system. For the $\hat{\mathbf{S}}$ projection along the z axis (Eq. (8-13)),

$$\hat{H} = g_e\mu_\beta H\hat{S}_z + hA\hat{S}_z\hat{I}_z. \tag{8-50a}$$

The appropriate set of basis functions that allows for easy solution of the Schrödinger equation is

$$\begin{aligned} \psi_1 &= \alpha_e\alpha_n \\ \psi_2 &= \alpha_e\beta_n \\ \psi_3 &= \beta_e\alpha_n \\ \psi_4 &= \beta_e\beta_n, \end{aligned} \tag{8-51}$$

where α is again associated with the spin state $+\frac{1}{2}$ and β with $-\frac{1}{2}$.[5] The eigenvalues of the electron Zeeman splitting are just those given by Eq. (8-20). The diagonal matrix elements generated by the second term of Eq. (50a) are

$$\begin{aligned} \langle\alpha_e\alpha_n|\hat{S}_z\hat{I}_z|\alpha_e\alpha_n\rangle &= +\tfrac{1}{4}hA \qquad \langle\beta_e\alpha_n|\hat{S}_z\hat{I}_z|\beta_e\alpha_n\rangle = -\tfrac{1}{4}hA \\ \langle\alpha_e\beta_n|\hat{S}_z\hat{I}_z|\alpha_e\beta_n\rangle &= -\tfrac{1}{4}hA \qquad \langle\beta_e\beta_n|\hat{S}_z\hat{I}_z|\beta_e\beta_n\rangle = +\tfrac{1}{4}hA. \end{aligned} \tag{8-52}$$

The resulting energy states (eigenvalues) are

$$\begin{aligned} \nu_{\alpha_e\alpha_n} &= \frac{E_{\alpha_e\alpha_n}}{h} = +\frac{1}{2}\frac{g_e\mu_\beta H}{h} + \frac{1}{4}A \\ \nu_{\alpha_e\beta_n} &= \frac{E_{\alpha_e\beta_n}}{h} = +\frac{1}{2}\frac{g_e\mu_\beta H}{h} - \frac{1}{4}A \\ \nu_{\beta_e\beta_n} &= \frac{E_{\beta_e\beta_n}}{h} = -\frac{1}{2}\frac{g_e\mu_\beta H}{h} + \frac{1}{4}A \\ \nu_{\beta_e\alpha_n} &= \frac{E_{\beta_e\alpha_n}}{h} = -\frac{1}{2}\frac{g_e\mu_\beta H}{h} - \frac{1}{4}A, \end{aligned} \tag{8-53}$$

where A is called the isotropic hyperfine coupling constant. These energy states are shown in Figure 8-12. The electronic transition probability between these states is again given by Eq. (8-33), except that this expression will also be multiplied by the nuclear spin functions $\langle\alpha_n|\alpha_n\rangle$, $\langle\beta_n|\beta_n\rangle, \ldots$. As a result, the nonzero matrix elements will be those corresponding to $\Delta M_s = \pm 1$ and those conserving nuclear spin during the electronic

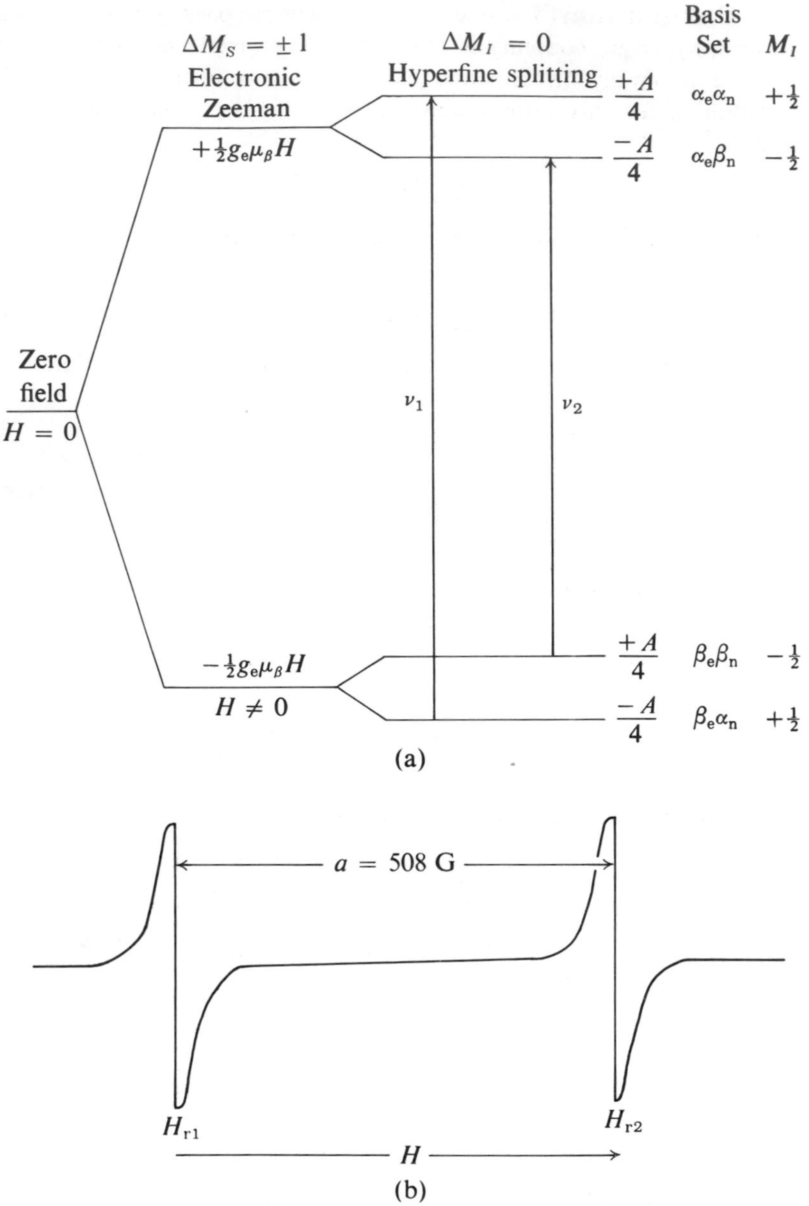

FIGURE 8-12 (a) Energy-level splitting of the hydrogen atom due to the electronic Zeeman and isotropic hyperfine terms. The symbol A (MHz) is the isotropic hyperfine coupling constant and a (Gauss) is the hyperfine splitting constant, $a = hA/g_e\mu_\beta$. (b) First-derivative hyperfine splitting spectrum caused by a hydrogen atom ($M_I = \frac{1}{2}$).

transitions, $\Delta M_I = 0$. The corresponding transition frequencies for this system are

$$\nu_1 = \nu_{\alpha_e\alpha_n} - \nu_{\beta_e\alpha_n} = \frac{g_e\mu_\beta H}{h} + \frac{1}{2}A$$

$$\nu_2 = \nu_{\alpha_e\beta_n} - \nu_{\beta_e\beta_n} = \frac{g_e\mu_\beta H}{h} - \frac{1}{2}A. \tag{8-54}$$

These transitions and the corresponding first derivative spectrum are shown in Figure 8-12. If we define the magnetic fields that bring about resonance for the two transitions of Eq. (8-54) as H_{r1} and H_{r2}, substituting and solving for these fields at a fixed microwave frequency ν_0, we obtain

$$H_{r1} = \frac{h\nu_0}{g_e\mu_\beta} - \frac{1}{2}a$$

$$H_{r2} = \frac{h\nu_0}{g_e\mu_\beta} + \frac{1}{2}a, \tag{8-55}$$

where $a = hA/g_e\mu_\beta$ (in gauss), defined as the hyperfine splitting constant, is simply the difference in the two absorption lines. The local magnetic field (H_{loc}) in this example is just $\frac{1}{2}a$. As a result of the magnetic-field-vectorial addition of Eq. (8-55), the higher-frequency transition ν_1 occurs at a lower magnetic field and vice versa for the lower frequency transition ν_2.

ii. Systems Having $S = \frac{1}{2}$ and Three Equivalent Nuclei. The energy-level scheme and splittings for systems of this nature may be obtained by the successive splitting of the initial electronic Zeeman levels, resulting from the interaction of $S = \frac{1}{2}$ with the external magnetic field. Considering the effect of the first nucleus, the $M_S = \pm\frac{1}{2}$ levels are split into a doublet. These are in turn further split by the second nucleus to give energy levels having degeneracies 1:2:1. Final splitting by the third nucleus results in energy level degeneracies of 1:3:3:1. We should note that these degeneracies occur because the three equivalent protons cause equal hyperfine splitting, and thus overlapping energy levels. The selection rules for transitions between these levels are again $\Delta M_s = \pm 1$ and $\Delta M_I = 0$. These hyperfine energy levels and the four resulting transitions at a fixed magnetic field are shown in Figure 8-13a.

As we discussed in the experimental section above, the actual ESR experiment is performed by varying the magnetic field at a fixed microwave frequency in order to bring about the various resonances. The expected pattern and relative intensities (resulting from level degeneracies) for this system are shown in Figure 8-13b. Since all three protons cause equal splitting, the absorption separations are all equivalent, and equal

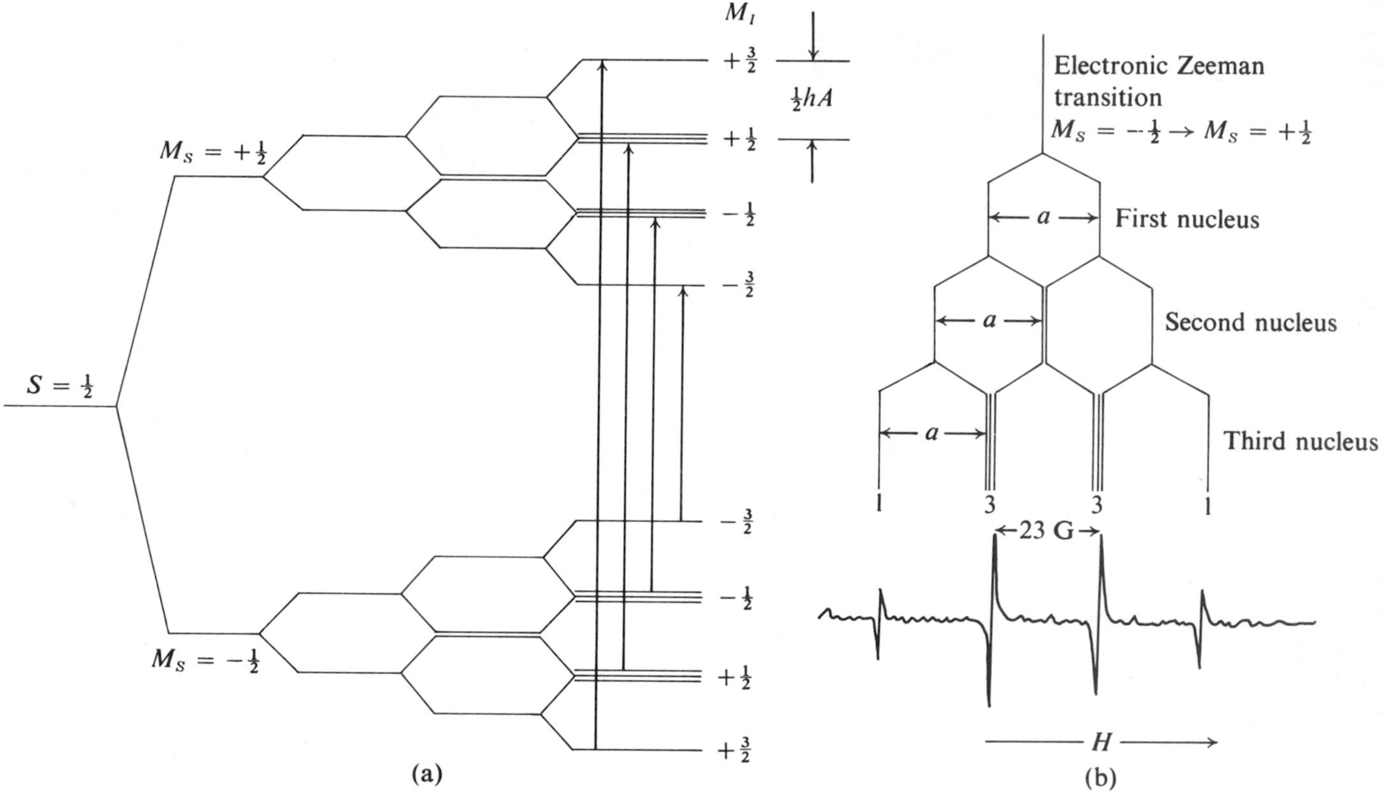

FIGURE 8-13 (a) Energy-level splittings and transitions of a system having a single unpaired electron interacting with three equivalent protons in a fixed magnetic field. (b) Transition pattern and relative intensities for the system shown as a function of the magnetic field. The ESR spectrum of the methyl radical ($\cdot CH_3$) is shown directly below the hyperfine pattern.

to a, the hyperfine splitting constant. In order to obtain the parameters of interest (a, A, and g_e) from this system, we can see from Figure 8-13a that the lowest magnetic field transition will have a frequency

$$\nu_1 = \frac{g_e \mu_\beta H}{h} + \frac{3A}{2}. \tag{8-56}$$

At a fixed microwave cavity frequency ν_0, the resonant magnetic field is given as

$$H_{r1} = \frac{h\nu_0}{g_e \mu_\beta} - \frac{3hA}{2g_e \mu_\beta} = \frac{h\nu_0}{g_e \mu_\beta} - \frac{3a}{2}, \tag{8-57}$$

where a is obtained directly from the spectrum, ν_0 is the known microwave frequency, and H_{r1} is the known magnetic field at which resonance occurs. Substituting these quantities into Eq. (8-57) we can obtain the electronic g_e factor. Finally, the hyperfine coupling constant A can be calculated by the relation $A = a g_e \mu_\beta / h$. Note that both a and A are independent of the external magnetic field (like J_{ij} in NMR), but dependent on the electronic g_e factor.

An example of this system is the methyl radical, $\cdot CH_3$. Its observed ESR spectrum is shown in Figure 8-13c.

Before concluding our discussion of systems having only equivalent magnetic nuclei, we should perhaps emphasize the generality of two points discussed in the specific examples above: one concerning the number of lines and their relative intensities in a spectrum for a given number of equivalent magnetic nuclei, and the other involving the magnetic fields at which the various resonances occur. On examining the intensity ratios for 1, 2, 3,... equivalent nuclei in the examples above, we note that they are 1:1, 1:2:1, 1:3:3:1.... These ratios are just the coefficients of the binomial expansion of $(1 + x)^n$, where n is the number of equivalent nuclei in a set. The coefficients for $n = 1$ through 8 equivalent nuclei are given by the so-called Pascal triangle, shown in Table 8-2.

TABLE 8-2. Pascal Binomial Triangle, Representing Coefficients of the Expansion of $(1 + x)^n$.

n									1								
1								1		1							
2							1		2		1						
3						1		3		3		1					
4					1		4		6		4		1				
5				1		5		10		10		5		1			
6			1		6		15		20		15		6		1		
7		1		7		21		35		35		21		7		1	
8	1		8		28		56		70		56		28		8		1

In the two examples discussed above, the resonant magnetic fields at fixed microwave frequency were illustrated by Eqs. (8-55) and (8-57). The first term in these equations corresponds simply to the resonant field for a free electron at a given microwave frequency. The second term, which is simply the local field, is observed to be proportional to M_I for a given transition. Furthermore, since M_I is conserved in these transitions, $H_{loc} = -M_I a$. The general expression for the resonant magnetic field corresponding to a specific transition is

$$H_{ri} = H_{er} + H_{loc} = H_{er} - M_I a, \qquad (8\text{-}58)$$

where a is the hyperfine splitting constant.

iii. Systems Having $S = \frac{1}{2}$ and Different Sets of Equivalent Nuclei. Analysis of systems that contain several sets of nuclei that are magnetically different involves again the stepwise splitting of nuclear spin states of a similar set. The procedure is to begin with the set having the largest hyperfine coupling constant A_1, proceeding as in the previous examples, until all the nuclei of the set have been considered. Each of these levels is in turn split by *each* of the nuclei in the next set having the second largest hyperfine coupling constant A_2. This procedure is continued until all sets have been accounted for.

EXAMPLE 8-2: Diagram the expected hyperfine energy splittings and transitions of the $\cdot CH_2—OH$ radical. Using this diagram, sketch the ESR spectrum where $a_1(CH_2) = 17.4$ G and $a_2(OH) = 1.15$ G. Calculate A_1 and A_2 assuming $g_e \sim 2.00$.

Solution: Since $A_i = a_i g_e \mu_\beta / h$, where $g_e \simeq 2.00$, $\mu_\beta = 9.274 \times 10^{-21}$ erg/G, and $h = 6.62 \times 10^{-27}$ erg-sec,

$$A_1 = \frac{(17.4\ \text{G})(2.00)(9.274 \times 10^{-21}\ \text{erg/G})}{(6.62 \times 10^{-27}\ \text{erg-sec})} = 48.75\ \text{MHz}$$

and

$$A_2 = \frac{(1.15\ \text{G})(2.00)(9.274 \times 10^{-21}\ \text{erg/G})}{(6.62 \times 10^{-27}\ \text{erg-sec})} = 3.22\ \text{MHz}$$

In energy units, $A_1 = hA_1 = 322.73 \times 10^{-21}$ erg/molecule and $A_2 = hA_2 = 21.33 \times 10^{-21}$ erg/molecule.

A more complicated radical ion illustrating the hyperfine splitting resulting from two sets of magnetically different protons is the naphthalene anion. The unpaired electron interacts with two sets of four protons each, as shown in Figure 8-14. By the procedure we have previously outlined, the first set corresponding to the larger coupling constant A_1 splits each of the Zeeman levels ($M_S = \pm\frac{1}{2}$) into 5 levels having degeneracies of 1:4:6:4:1 (Table 8-2). Each of these 5 levels is in turn split into

Diagram of Example (8–2)

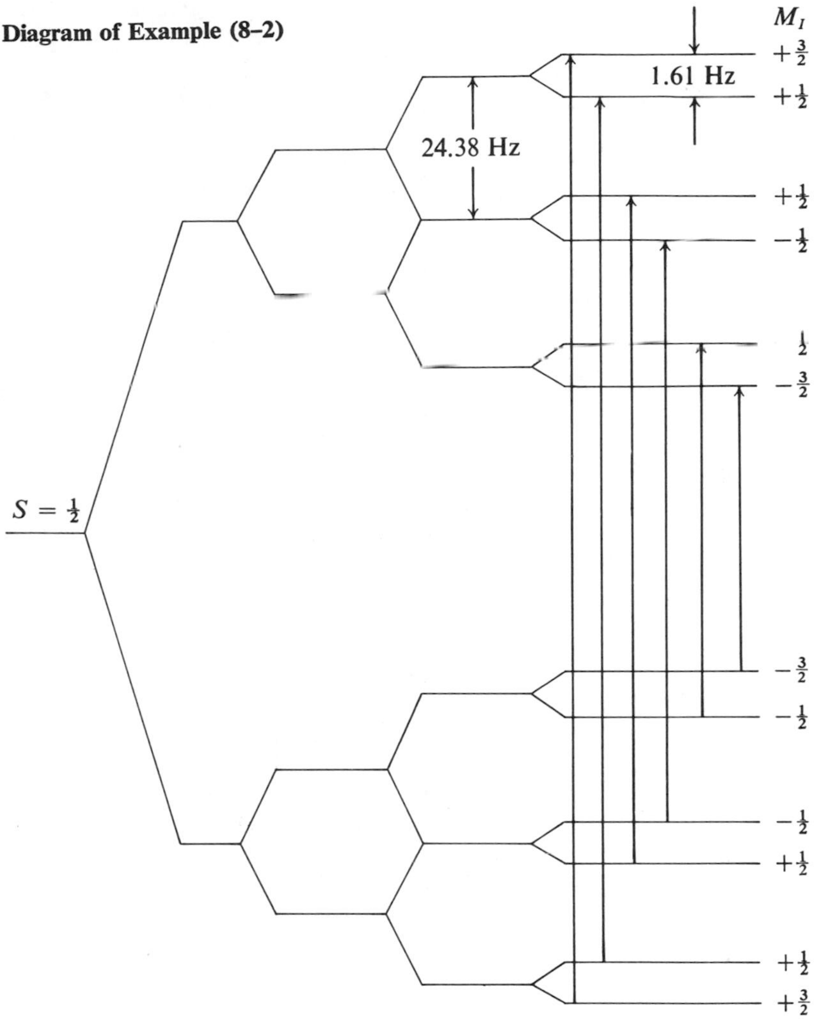

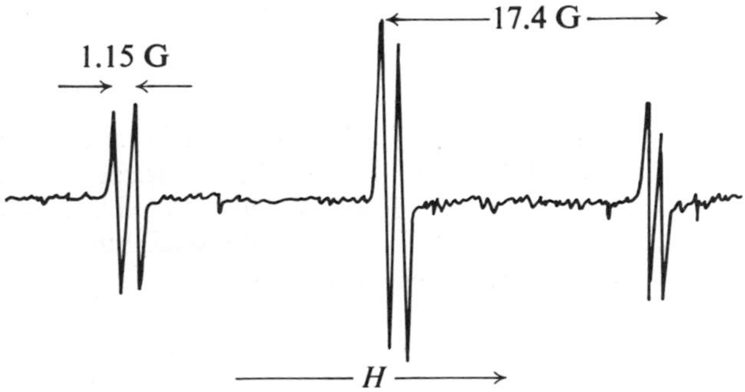

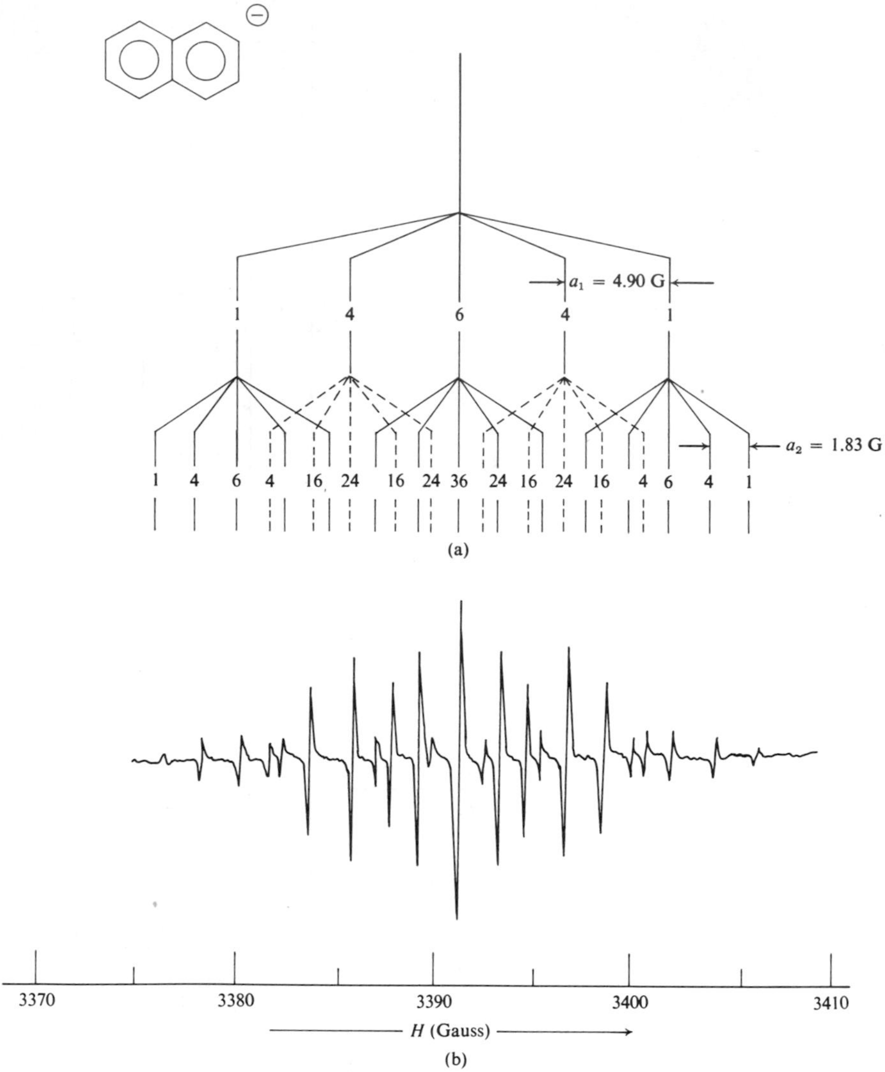

FIGURE 8-14 (a) Splittings resulting from the two sets of magnetically different protons of the naphthalene anion. The final split lines are divided into solid and dotted lines in order to avoid confusion. (b) ESR spectrum of the naphthalene anion matched to the expected intensity pattern of (a).

quintets by the second set of four protons. Each of the resulting Zeeman levels will be split into a total of 25 hyperfine levels. The ESR spectrum will therefore consist of 25 lines (transitions) having intensities corresponding to the degeneracies of the initial state. These statistical weights are shown in Figure 8-14a. The hyperfine spectrum of the naphthalene anion is shown in Figure 8-14b, from which we obtain $a_1 = 4.90$ G and $a_2 = 1.83$ G. This spectrum was recorded at a microwave frequency of 9503 MHz. Estimating the magnetic field corresponding to the strongest transition provides the remaining factor necessary for calculating the electronic g_e factor. The magnetic field corresponding to this transition is

$$H_{r3} = \frac{h\nu_0}{g_e \mu_\beta}, \tag{8-59}$$

where H_{r3} refers to the resonant field corresponding to transition 3 of 5. Substituting the factors $H_{r3} = 3391.5$ G, $\nu_0 = 9503$ MHz, and $\mu_\beta = 9.274 \times 10^{-21}$ erg/G, and rearranging Eq. (8-59), we obtain

$$g_e = \frac{h\nu_0}{H_{r3}\mu_\beta} = \frac{(6.62 \times 10^{-27})(9.503 \times 10^9)}{(3391.5)(9.274 \times 10^{-21})} = 2.00012,$$

compared with 2.0023 for a free electron. In this example, the splitting pattern occurs in such a way that we were able to calculate g_e without considering the contribution from the local field. In the case of Example 8-2 for the $\cdot CH_2OH$ radical, there is no line exactly at the center of the spectrum; consequently the field corresponding to a specific transition would be similar to Eq. (8-58). However, there will be local field contributions from two sets of equivalent protons. If we start at low magnetic field in labeling the six transitions of $\cdot CH_2OH$, the corresponding resonant fields will be

$$\begin{aligned} H_1 &= H_{er} - (a_1 + \tfrac{1}{2}a_2) & H_4 &= H_{er} - \tfrac{1}{2}a_2 \\ H_2 &= H_{er} - (a_1 - \tfrac{1}{2}a_2) & H_5 &= H_{er} + (a_1 - \tfrac{1}{2}a_2) \\ H_3 &= H_{er} + \tfrac{1}{2}a_2 & H_6 &= H_{er} + (a_1 + \tfrac{1}{2}a_2), \end{aligned} \tag{8-60}$$

where we have assumed the a_i values to be positive in order that the positive M_k values will occur at low field. These hyperfine splitting constants, however, may be positive or negative. Based on this illustration, Eq. (8-58) can be written for the more general case, where several sets of equivalent nuclei may contribute to the pattern, as

$$H_i = H_{er} - \sum_k M_k a_k, \tag{8-61}$$

where H_i is the resonant magnetic field corresponding to the ith line, H_{er} is the magnetic field at the center of the spectrum, and M_k corresponds to the M_Ith quantum number of the kth set.

The nuclear hyperfine splitting observed not only in the case of the naphthalene anion discussed above but also in numerous aromatic negative ions poses an interesting question concerning the molecular electronic structure of these radical anions. Presumably the isotropic hyperfine splitting constant measures the amount of s character in the unpaired electron wavefunction at a given magnetic nucleus. Since the unpaired electron in such systems is believed to be in a π molecular orbital (π MO) delocalized over the carbon atom framework, and the electron density at a given nucleus is significant only in the case of σ orbitals, how then do hydrogen 1s orbitals acquire the spin density necessary to account for the observed splittings? The obvious answer is in the inadequacy of the π-orbital wavefunctions, which illustrates the necessity for not only mixing σ and π MO's but also including excited state wavefunctions, as prescribed by experimental observations. These experimental results, which give a direct measure of electron densities in a molecule, are extremely valuable guides in constructing wavefunctions used in theoretical calculations. The combination of these experimental and theoretical efforts can be ultimately used to relate the electronic distribution to chemical and physical behavior.

b. Anisotropy and Electronic Spin-Spin Interaction. We have so far considered systems for which the effective g factor is independent of external magnetic field orientation—gases and low-viscosity solutions. On the other hand, systems in the solid or condensed state, which do not possess a high degree of symmetry (such as octahedral or spherical), will have resulting ESR spectra that are critically dependent on field orientation relative to a fixed crystalline orientation. This dependence on crystal–external field orientation is defined as the anisotropic effect. Typical systems include paramagnetic ions and point defects in single crystals and free radicals oriented in solids. For an anisotropic system having again a single unpaired electron, the Hamiltonian operator is given as

$$\hat{H} = \mu_\beta \mathbf{H}\cdot\mathbf{g}\cdot\hat{\mathbf{S}} + hA\hat{\mathbf{S}}\cdot\hat{\mathbf{I}} + h\hat{\mathbf{S}}\cdot\mathbf{T}\cdot\hat{\mathbf{I}}, \tag{8-62}$$

where the first term is the anisotropic electronic Zeeman splitting and the second and third terms are the isotropic and anisotropic hyperfine splittings.

In the first term of Eq. (8-62), **H** and **S** are vectors and **g** is a tensor. Thus, this term may be written as

$$\mu_\beta[\mathrm{H}_x, \mathrm{H}_y, \mathrm{H}_z]\begin{bmatrix} g_{xx} & g_{xy} & g_{xz} \\ g_{yx} & g_{yy} & g_{yz} \\ g_{zx} & g_{zy} & g_{zz} \end{bmatrix}\begin{bmatrix} \hat{S}_x \\ \hat{S}_y \\ \hat{S}_z \end{bmatrix}, \tag{8-63}$$

where x, y, and z are the orthogonal crystal fixed axes and the H_i's and S_i's are scalars of the corresponding vectors.

As in most cases, if the g tensor is symmetric ($g_{ij} = g_{ji}$), it can be diagonalized by an appropriate matrix transformation. The transformation matrices generally contain elements that relate the molecule-fixed axis system (X, Y, and Z) to the external crystal-fixed axis system (x, y, and z). The new principal axes of the diagonal matrix are g_{XX}, g_{YY}, and g_{ZZ}, which are determined from the experimental ESR spectra of the oriented species of interest in a fixed crystalline environment.

The second term of Eq. (8-62) is simply the isotropic hyperfine splitting discussed in detail above. In the third term, $\hat{\mathbf{S}}$ and $\hat{\mathbf{I}}$ are vectors and $\mathbf{T}$ is the magnetic dipolar tensor. This term arises from the magnetic coupling between the electron and nuclear magnetic moments, and for the classical analog is essentially a dipolar interaction between two bar magnets. For low-viscosity dilute solutions discussed previously, this interaction was averaged to zero, and only the isotropic hyperfine term remained. On the other hand, condensed phase–oriented ESR spectra do give rise to anisotropic hyperfine splitting. These hyperfine terms of Eq. (8-62) can be factored into

$$h\hat{\mathbf{S}}\cdot(A\mathbf{1} + \mathbf{T})\cdot\hat{\mathbf{I}}, \qquad \textbf{(8-64)}$$

where $\mathbf{1}$ is a unit tensor. The components of the hyperfine tensor ($A\mathbf{1} + \mathbf{T}$) are evaluated from the observed transitions between the hyperfine split levels. Thus we are able to obtain valuable information about the structure and orientation of paramagnetic ions in crystals.

Thus far in our discussion of ESR, we have been concerned with systems having a single unpaired electron. Consequently, the last term of Eq. (8-13), H_{ss}, has been zero in all these cases. For molecules having two or more unpaired electrons, magnetic interaction between these electrons gives rise to energy splittings correlated with various spin orientations, in both the presence and the absence of an external magnetic field. For systems with $S = 1$ (two unpaired electrons), when the triplet ($2S + 1 = 3$) degeneracy of this state is removed in the absence of a magnetic field, it is termed *zero-field splitting.*

The interaction that gives rise to the $\hat{H}_{ss}$ term for this system is a magnetic dipole-dipole spin interaction between the two unpaired electrons. Thus

$$\hat{H}_{ss} = \frac{\hat{\boldsymbol{\mu}}_{e1}\cdot\hat{\boldsymbol{\mu}}_{e2}}{r_{12}^{3}} - \frac{3(\hat{\boldsymbol{\mu}}_{e1}\cdot\mathbf{r}_{12})(\hat{\boldsymbol{\mu}}_{e2}\cdot\mathbf{r}_{12})}{r_{12}^{5}}, \qquad \textbf{(8-65)}$$

$\hat{\boldsymbol{\mu}}_{e1}$ are the magnetic moments generated by electrons 1 and 2. Substituting the appropriate spin operators, we obtain

$$\hat{H}_{ss} = g^2\mu_\beta^2\,\frac{\hat{\mathbf{S}}_1\cdot\hat{\mathbf{S}}_2}{r^3} - \frac{3(\hat{\mathbf{S}}_1\cdot\mathbf{r})(\hat{\mathbf{S}}_2\cdot\mathbf{r})}{r^5}, \qquad \textbf{(8-66)}$$

where $\mathbf{r}$ is the vector joining the two electrons, and $r^2 = x^2 + y^2 + z^2$.

Here again, x, y, and z refer to the external, or laboratory-fixed, axis system. Performing the appropriate nontrivial simplification of Eq. (8-66),[6] it can be expressed in terms of the total spin operator $\hat{\mathbf{S}}(=\hat{\mathbf{S}}_1 + \hat{\mathbf{S}}_2)$ as

$$\hat{H}_{ss} = \tfrac{1}{2}g^2\mu_\beta{}^2[\hat{S}_x, \hat{S}_y, \hat{S}_z]\begin{bmatrix} D_{xx} & D_{xy} & D_{xz} \\ D_{yx} & D_{yy} & D_{yz} \\ D_{zx} & D_{zy} & D_{zz} \end{bmatrix}\begin{bmatrix} \hat{S}_x \\ \hat{S}_y \\ \hat{S}_z \end{bmatrix}. \qquad \textbf{(8-67)}$$

$$\hat{H}_{ss} = \hat{\mathbf{S}}\cdot\mathbf{D}\cdot\hat{\mathbf{S}}, \qquad \textbf{(8-67a)}$$

where $\mathbf{D}$ is a second-rank tensor with a trace of zero which contains the term $g^2\mu^2{}_\beta/2$. As above, this tensor is diagonalized by matrices relating x, y, z to X, Y, Z and the resulting diagonal elements are D_{XX}, D_{YY}, and D_{ZZ}. Thus Eq. (8-67a) reduces to

$$\hat{H}_{ss} = D_{XX}\hat{S}_x{}^2 + D_{YY}\hat{S}_y{}^2 + D_{ZZ}\hat{S}_z{}^2, \qquad \textbf{(8-68)}$$

where $D_{XX} + D_{YY} + D_{ZZ} = 0$. These principal diagonal elements are also given as $\mathscr{X} = -D_{XX}$, $\mathscr{Y} = -D_{YY}$, $\mathscr{Z} = -D_{ZZ}$, where $\mathscr{X}$, $\mathscr{Y}$, and $\mathscr{Z}$ are the energies of the three spin states (formerly degenerate) relative to the zero splitting in a zero magnetic field (Figure 8-15). Therefore, the spin Hamiltonian for a system where $S \geqq 1$ is given as

$$\hat{H} = \mu_\beta\mathbf{H}\cdot\mathbf{g}\cdot\hat{\mathbf{S}} + \hat{\mathbf{S}}\cdot\mathbf{D}\cdot\hat{\mathbf{S}}. \qquad \textbf{(8-69)}$$

In the case where the g tensor anisotropy is small (g assumed isotropic), Eq. (8-69) can be approximated:

$$\hat{H} = g\mu_\beta\mathbf{H}\cdot\hat{\mathbf{S}} - \mathscr{X}\hat{S}_x{}^2 - \mathscr{Y}\hat{S}_y{}^2 - \mathscr{Z}\hat{S}_z{}^2. \qquad \textbf{(8-69a)}$$

Using an appropriate set of spin matrices or spin eigenfunctions, we find that the energy levels for the triplet state with the magnetic field parallel to Z are

$$E_Z = \mathscr{Z} \quad \text{and} \quad E_{X,Y} = \tfrac{1}{2}(\mathscr{X} + \mathscr{Y}) \pm \sqrt{g^2\mu_\beta{}^2H_z{}^2 + \tfrac{1}{4}(\mathscr{X} - \mathscr{Y})^2}. \qquad \textbf{(8-70)}$$

Recalling the fact that the D tensor is traceless $\mathscr{X} + \mathscr{Y} = -\mathscr{Z}$, we obtain for the zero magnetic field ($H_z = 0$) splitting ($\mathscr{X} \neq \mathscr{Y}$)

$$E_Z = \mathscr{Z} = -\frac{2D}{3}$$

$$E_X = \mathscr{X} = \frac{D}{3} - E \qquad \textbf{(8-71)}$$

$$E_Y = \mathscr{Y} = \frac{D}{3} + E,$$

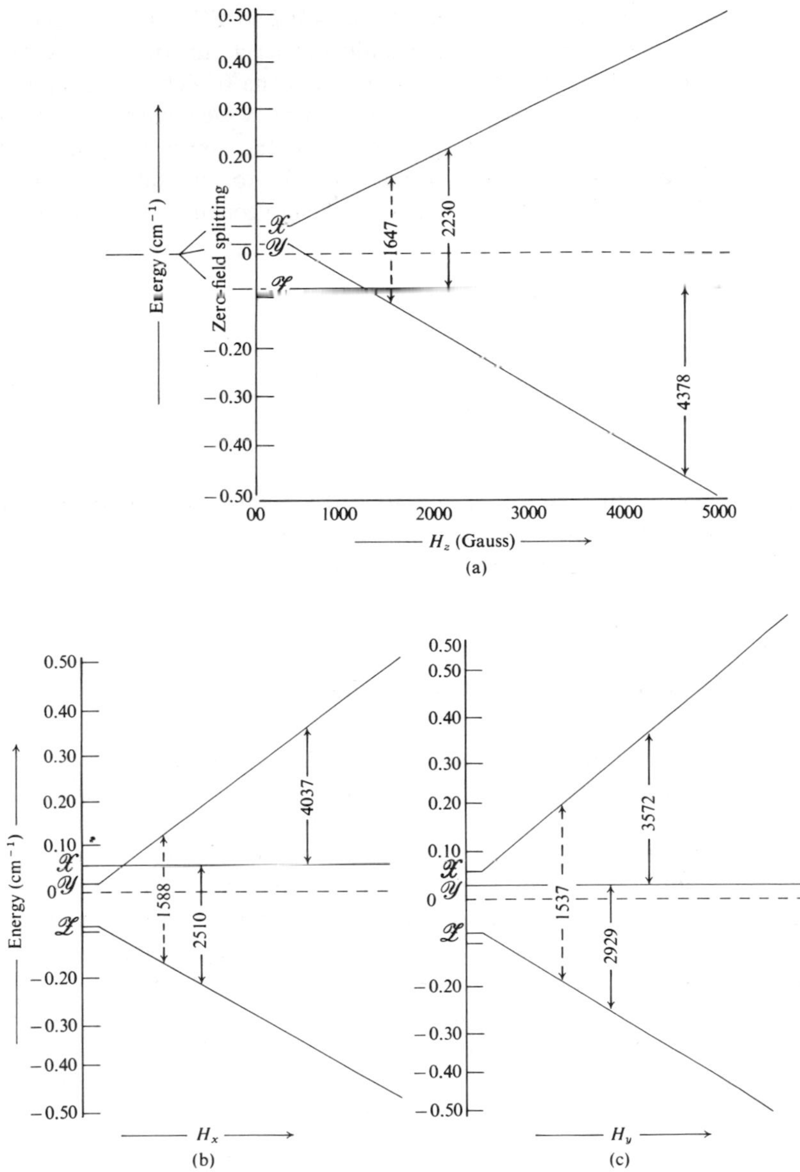

FIGURE 8-15 Zero-field and electronic Zeeman splittings for naphthalene in its lowest triplet state. The transitions $\Delta M_S = \pm 1$ (solid lines) and $\Delta M_S = \pm 2$ (dotted lines) correspond to the fixed microwave magnetic field (9.272 GHz) perpendicular and parallel to the static field, respectively. The transition numbers correspond to the magnetic fields at which resonance occurs. (a) $H_Z \| Z$; (b) $H_X \| X$; (c) $H_Y \| Y$.

where D is defined as $-3\mathscr{Z}/2$ and E as $-\frac{1}{2}(\mathscr{X} - \mathscr{Y})$. The zero-field splittings and the electronic Zeeman splittings as a function of the H_z field are shown in Figure 8-15a for the naphthalene triplet. Also shown are the transitions for $\Delta M_S = \pm 1$ (solid lines), which corresponds to the microwave magnetic field perpendicular to the static field, and for $\Delta M_S = \pm 2$ (dotted lines), which corresponds to the magnetic field parallel to the static field. In this example, the molecular axes correspond to

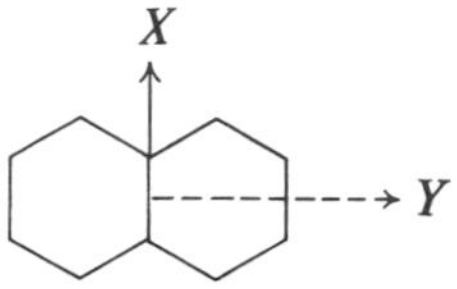

with the Z axis perpendicular to the molecular plane. It is interesting to note in this example that the zero-field splitting is of the order of 0.05 cm^{-1} and the electronic Zeeman splitting, of 0.40 cm^{-1}.

3. Electron-Nuclear Double Resonance (ENDOR)

Electron-nuclear double resonance (ENDOR) is a specialized technique designed to obtain very precise hyperfine coupling constants ($\sim$10 kHz) that are either unresolved or poorly resolved in ESR experiments. ENDOR also precisely determines g_n for a particular hyperfine splitting, and as a result a practically unequivocal identification of the particular nucleus responsible for the hyperfine effect. This technique is being applied with increasing frequency to systems involving organic and biological radicals, particularly those having proton interactions.

To describe this technique, we consider the case of a solid or a condensed-state radical having a single unpaired electron ($S = \frac{1}{2}$) interacting with a single proton ($I = \frac{1}{2}$). The spin Hamiltonian for this system is given by a combination of Eqs. (8-26) and (8-62),

$$\hat{H} = \mu_\beta \mathbf{H}\cdot\mathbf{g}\cdot\hat{\mathbf{S}} + hA\hat{\mathbf{S}}\cdot\hat{\mathbf{I}} + h\hat{\mathbf{S}}\cdot\mathbf{T}\cdot\hat{\mathbf{I}} - g_n\mu_N\hat{\mathbf{I}}\cdot\mathbf{H}, \tag{8-72}$$

for which all terms have been defined previously. For a fixed magnetic-field orientation, g may be taken as approximately isotropic, and the first three terms of Eq. (8-72) are exactly the same as Eq. (8-50); thus

$$\hat{H} = \mu_\beta g\mathbf{H}\cdot\hat{\mathbf{S}} + hA\hat{\mathbf{S}}\cdot\hat{\mathbf{I}} - g_n\mu_N\hat{\mathbf{I}}\cdot\mathbf{H}. \tag{8-73}$$

The resulting energy levels (Hz) are given by a combination of Eqs. (8-27) and (8-53) as

$$\frac{E_{\alpha_e\alpha_n}}{h} = +\frac{1}{2}\frac{g\mu_\beta H}{h} + \frac{1}{4}A - \frac{1}{2}\frac{g_n\mu_N H}{h}$$

$$\frac{E_{\alpha_e\beta_n}}{h} = +\frac{1}{2}\frac{g\mu_\beta H}{h} - \frac{1}{4}A + \frac{1}{2}\frac{g_n\mu_N H}{h}$$

$$\frac{E_{\beta_e\beta_n}}{h} = -\frac{1}{2}\frac{g\mu_\beta H}{h} + \frac{1}{4}A + \frac{1}{2}\frac{g_n\mu_N H}{h} \tag{8-74}$$

$$\frac{E_{\beta_e\alpha_n}}{h} = -\frac{1}{2}\frac{g\mu_\beta H}{h} - \frac{1}{4}A - \frac{1}{2}\frac{g_n\mu_N H}{h}$$

These energy levels are schematically shown in Figure 8-16a. The ESR transitions are shown by the heavy lines and correspond to the selection rules $\Delta M_S = \pm 1$ and $\Delta M_I = 0$. Those corresponding to the ENDOR transitions are shown by the light lines and correspond to the selection rules $\Delta M_S = 0$ and $\Delta M_I = \pm 1$.

The ENDOR experiment is conducted by first setting the dc external field to the ESR resonance condition. The corresponding fixed-frequency microwave source is adjusted to an intensity slightly less than what is necessary for total saturation (partial saturation). This intensity will obviously be critically dependent on the relaxation processes depleting states $\alpha_e\alpha_n$ and $\alpha_e\beta_n$. A radiofrequency generator of relatively wide range is used to scan the frequency region corresponding to ν_{n1} and ν_{n2}. These frequencies correspond to the transitions

$$\frac{E_{\alpha_e\beta_n} - E_{\alpha_e\alpha_n}}{h} = \nu_{n1} = \frac{g_n\mu_N H}{h} - \frac{1}{2}A$$

$$\frac{E_{\beta_e\beta_n} - E_{\beta_e\alpha_n}}{h} = \nu_{n2} = \frac{g_n\mu_N H}{h} + \frac{1}{2}A \tag{8-75}$$

where a single fixed dc field H may or may not be sufficient for observation of both ν_{n1} and ν_{n2}, depending on the rates of the various relaxation processes (to be discussed below).[7] When resonance is achieved at either ν_{n1} or ν_{n2}, the near equal populations (as a result of partial ESR saturation) of $\alpha_e\alpha_n$ and $\beta_e\alpha_n$ in one case and $\alpha_e\beta_n$ and $\beta_e\beta_n$ in the other are significantly changed in such a manner that *absorption* occurs in either of the ESR transitions in an attempt to reestablish the condition of partial saturation. This phenomenon is termed *enhancement* of the ESR transition intensity. Therefore, the ENDOR spectrum consists of the change in intensity of the partially saturated ESR absorption (y axis) as a function of the radiofrequency (x axis) over the region including ν_{n1} and ν_{n2}. These first-derivative spectra are shown in Figure 8-16b.

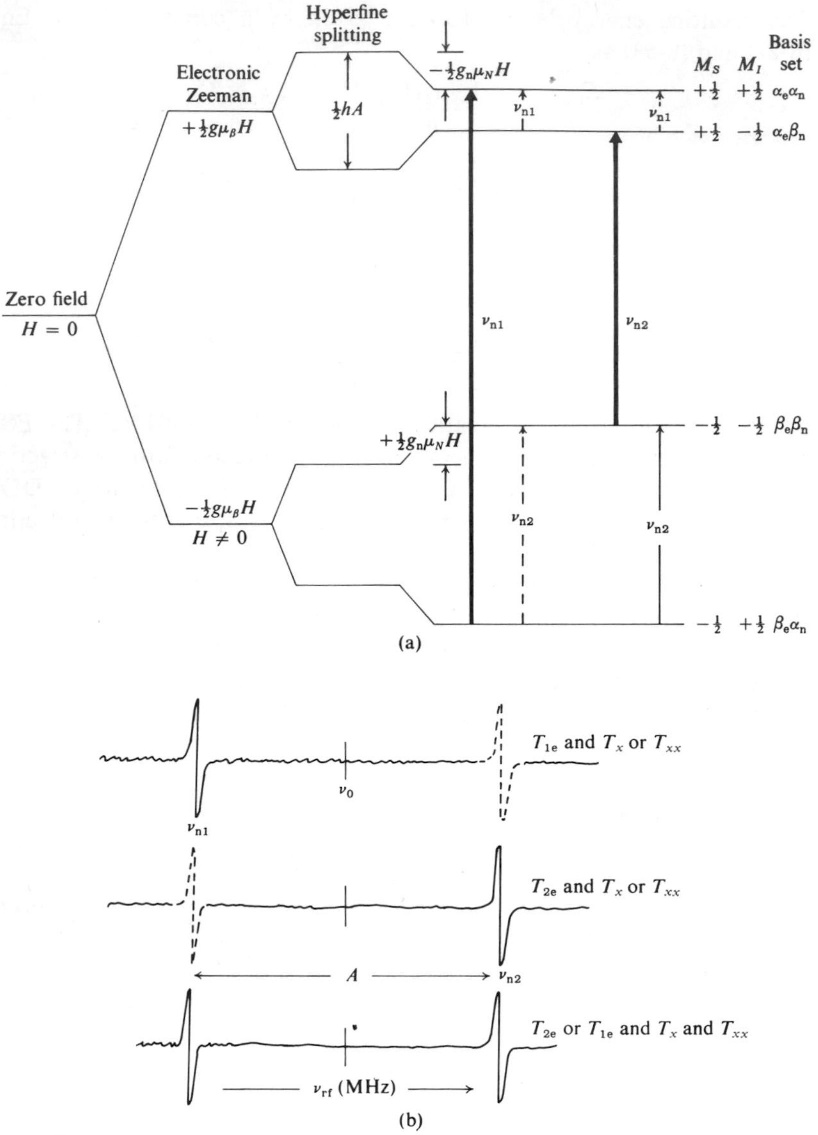

FIGURE 8-16 ENDOR (a) Energy-level splittings due to three terms of Eq. (8-74). The heavy lines correspond to the microwave saturation transitions $\Delta M_S = \pm 1$, $\Delta M_I = 0$. The other lines corresponding to the rf nuclear transitions ν_{n1} and ν_{n2} are the ENDOR lines for $\Delta M_S = 0$, $\Delta M_I = \pm 1$. (b) First-derivative spectra resulting from the effectiveness of the various "cross-relaxation" processes T_x, $\Delta(M_S + M_I) = 0$, and T_{xx}, $\Delta(M_S + M_I) = 2$. The dotted absorption trace indicates the absence of that peak.

The exact spectrum observed at fixed magnetic fields corresponding to the partially saturated ESR transitions ν_{e1} and ν_{e2} depends on the effectiveness of the various relaxation processes. These relaxation processes are shown schematically in Figure 8-17. The electron spin-lattice relaxation processes T_{1e} and T_{2e} are extremely short ($\sim 10^{-5}$ sec), and determine the ESR intensity necessary to maintain partial saturation. The nuclear spin-lattice relaxation processes T_{1n} and T_{2n} are generally orders of magnitude longer than T_{1e} and T_{2e}, and essentially play no role in the ENDOR relaxation processes. The "cross-relaxation" processes T_x and T_{xx}, involving mutual spin flips in the case of the former, $\Delta(M_S + M_I) = 0$, and concurrent spin flips in the case of the latter, $\Delta(M_S + M_I) = 2$ (Figure 8-17), provide alternative paths of relaxation, resulting in the significant reduction of $\alpha_e\alpha_n$ and $\alpha_e\beta_n$. Generally, the relative relaxation times are $T_{1e} \sim T_{2e} \ll T_x \simeq T_{xx} \ll T_{1n} \sim T_{2n}$. When the magnetic field

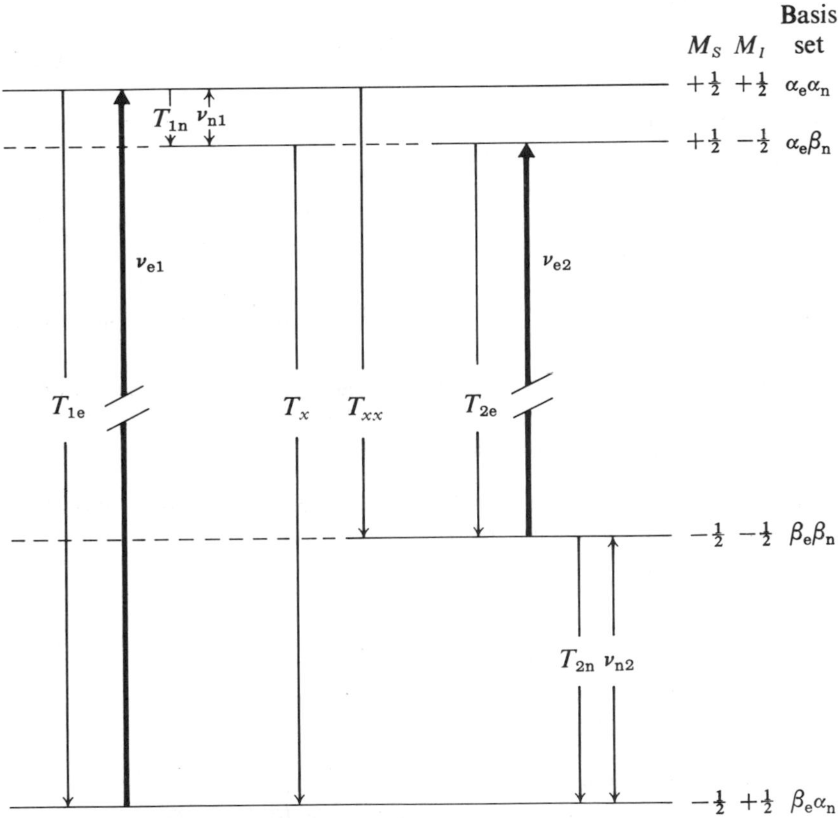

FIGURE 8-17 Schematic diagram of the various relaxation processes possible in the ENDOR experiment.

is set to resonate on the ESR line and only one of the cross-relaxation processes T_x or T_{xx} is effective in controlling the ENDOR behavior, then only the nuclear transition ν_{n1} is observed, as shown in the top trace of Figure 8-16b. Alternatively, when the field is set to resonate on the ν_{e2} transition, only the ν_{n2} line is observed for a single cross-relaxation process T_x or T_{xx} (shown in the middle spectrum of Figure 8-16b). When both T_x and T_{xx} are effective relaxation paths, both ENDOR absorptions occur with either the ν_{e1} or ν_{e2} saturating source, as shown in the bottom spectrum of Figure 8-16b.

The algebraic difference between ν_{n2} and ν_{n1} according to Eq. (8-75) is simply the hyperfine coupling constant A,

$$\nu_{n2} - \nu_{n1} = A. \qquad \textbf{(8-76)}$$

The algebraic sum provides a means of evaluating g_n for the particular nucleus causing the hyperfine splitting,

$$\nu_{n2} + \nu_{n1} = \frac{2g_n\mu_N H}{h}. \qquad \textbf{(8-77)}$$

The two ENDOR absorptions are equally shifted (by $\frac{1}{2}A$) in opposite directions from the central frequency ν_0, where

$$\nu_0 = \frac{\nu_{n2} + \nu_{n1}}{2} = \frac{g_n\mu_N H}{h}, \qquad \textbf{(8-78)}$$

which is the NMR resonance frequency (Eq. 8-28a) of the nucleus responsible for the splitting in the magnetic field at which ESR saturation occurs.

EXAMPLE 8-3: Estimate the ENDOR frequencies for the interaction of an unpaired electron with proton at a fixed microwave frequency $\nu_0 = 9.4176$ GHz. Assume $g_e = 2.0001$ and $a = 5.0$ G.

Solution: According to Eq. (8-55), the low field transition ν_1 shown in Figure 8-12a has a resonance dc field of

$$\begin{aligned} H_{r1} &= \frac{h\nu_0}{g_e\mu_\beta} - \frac{a}{2} \\ &= \frac{(6.6262 \times 10^{-27}\text{ erg-sec})(9.4176 \times 10^9\text{ sec}^{-1})}{(2.0001)(9.2741 \times 10^{-21}\text{ erg/G})} - \frac{5.0\text{ G}}{2} \\ &= 3364.2 - 2.5\text{ G} \\ &= 3361.7\text{ G.} \end{aligned}$$

The hyperfine coupling constant is

$$\begin{aligned} A &= \frac{a g_e\mu_\beta}{h} = \frac{(5.0\text{ G})(2.00)(9.27 \times 10^{-21}\text{ erg/G})}{(6.62 \times 10^{-27}\text{ erg-sec})} \\ &= 14.0\text{ MHz.} \end{aligned}$$

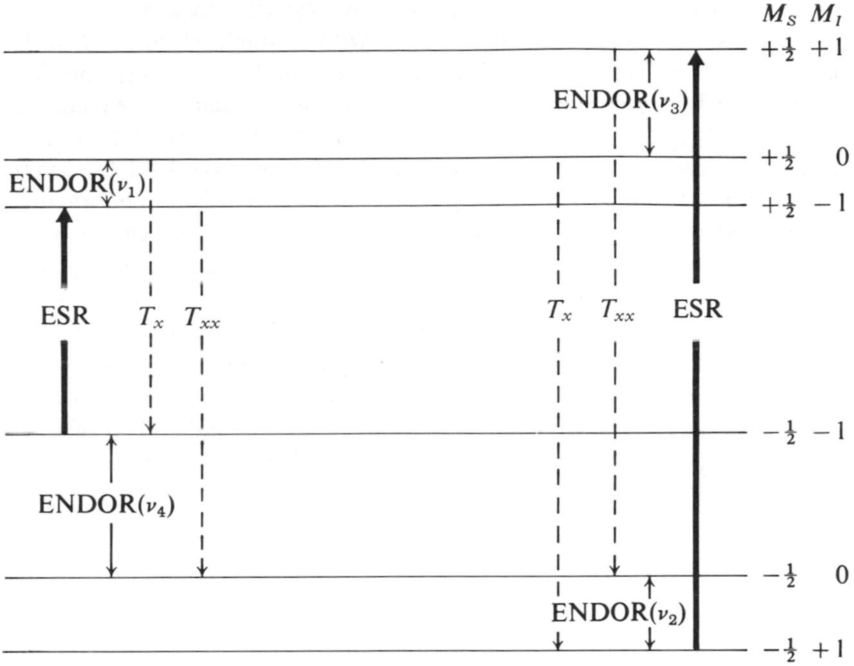

FIGURE 8-18 Energy-level diagram for the interaction of an $S = \frac{1}{2}$, $I = 1$ system (^{14}N with a single unpaired electron). The ESR, ENDOR, and relaxation transitions are separately shown by the heavy, light, and broken lines.

Using the nuclear g_n value for a proton, we obtain for the high-frequency and low-frequency ENDOR transitions (Eq. (8-75))

$$\nu_{n1} = \frac{g_n \mu_N H}{h} - \frac{1}{2}A$$

$$= \frac{(5.585)(5.0509 \times 10^{-24} \text{ erg/G})(3361.7 \text{ G})}{(6.62 \times 10^{-27} \text{ erg-sec})}$$

$$= 14.3 - 7.0 \text{ MHz} = 7.3 \text{ MHz}$$

and

$$\nu_{n2} = 21.3 \text{ MHz}.$$

The application of ENDOR to radicals involving $I \geqslant 1$ will have an additional term in Eq. (8-72), corresponding to the nuclear electric quadrupole coupling, $h\hat{\mathbf{I}}\cdot\mathbf{Q}\cdot\hat{\mathbf{I}}$. For systems in which the quadrupole interaction tensor $\mathbf{Q}$ has axial symmetry, this term reduces to one involving

hQ, the quadrupole interaction energy. Application to a nucleus with $I = 1$, ^{14}N, for example, that interacts with a single electron ($S = \frac{1}{2}$) gives rise to a characteristic four-line spectrum having transition frequencies at $\frac{1}{2}A_\perp \pm \nu_0 \pm Q$, where Q is defined as the quadrupole coupling constant; $A_\perp$ is the hyperfine coupling constant perpendicular to a symmetry axis, and ν_0 is the NMR resonance frequency in the ENDOR magnetic field. Examples of such systems include powders, nonoriented solids, and in favorable cases, single-crystal spectra for which the axial hyperfine interaction is small. The energy-level diagram of this system is shown in Figure 8-18 along with the relevant transitions and relaxation processes. The highest (ν_4) and lowest (ν_1) rf (ENDOR) transitions are observed for saturation of the low-field ESR transition on the left of Figure 8-18. The two intermediate rf (ENDOR) transitions are observed for saturation of the high-field ESR transition on the right of Figure 8-18. The characteristic four-line spectrum corresponds to the transitions

$$\begin{aligned} \nu_1 &= \tfrac{1}{2}A_\perp - \nu_0 - Q \\ \nu_2 &= \tfrac{1}{2}A_\perp - \nu_0 + Q \\ \nu_3 &= \tfrac{1}{2}A_\perp + \nu_0 - Q \\ \nu_4 &= \tfrac{1}{2}A_\perp + \nu_0 + Q. \end{aligned} \tag{8-79}$$

From the four-line spectrum corresponding to ν_1, ν_2, ν_3, and ν_4, we are able to determine $A_\perp$, ν_0, and Q.

SELECTED BIBLIOGRAPHY

8-1. Carrington, Alan, and McLachlan, Andrew D. *Introduction to Magnetic Resonance.* New York: Harper & Row, 1967.

8-2. Daniels, Farrington, Williams, J. W., Bender, Paul, Aberty, Robert A., Cornwell, C. Daniel, and Harriman, John E. *Experimental Physical Chemistry.* 7th ed. New York: McGraw-Hill Book Co., 1970.

8-3. Davis, Jeff C., Jr. *Advanced Physical Chemistry.* New York: Ronald Press Co., 1965.

8-4. Laszlo, Pierre, and Stang, Peter. *Organic Spectroscopy.* New York: Harper & Row, 1971.

8-5. Pake, George E. *Paramagnetic Resonance.* New York: W. A. Benjamin, 1962.

8-6. Poole, Charles P., Jr., and Farach, Horacio A. *The Theory of Magnetic Resonance.* New York: Wiley-Interscience, 1972.

8-7. Pople, J. A., Schneider, W. G., and Bernstein, H. J. *High Resolution Nuclear Magnetic Resonance.* New York: McGraw-Hill Book Co., 1959.

8-8. Wertz, John E., and Bolton, James R. *Electron Spin Resonance.* New York: McGraw-Hill Book Co., 1972.

ENDNOTES

1. $e^x = 1 + x \ldots$.
2. The time-dependent part of $\mathbf{H}_x$, separated initially, actually gives rise to the Dirac delta function $\delta(\omega_{mk} - \omega)$, requiring the resonance condition.
3. For transitions parallel to the static (external) magnetic field, the selection rules are $\Delta M_S = 0$ and $\Delta M_I = 0$.
4. Pople, Schneider and Bernstein [Reference 8-7, p. 120–21].
5. Since the eigenvalues of S_z and I_z are $M_s = \pm\frac{1}{2}$ and $M_I = \pm\frac{1}{2}$.
6. Wertz and Bolton [Reference 8-8, p. 224–26] and Carrington and McLachlan [Reference 8-1, p. 116–18].
7. Although we realize that A may also be negative, we shall in this discussion assume it is positive.
8. W. Low, *Paramagnetic Resonance in Solids*, Solid State Physics, Supplement II (New York: Academic Press, 1960), pp. 53 and 60.

PROBLEMS

8-1. Using the expression for the mean square radius of a hydrogenlike orbit, derive the expression for molar atomic susceptibility χ_M.

$$\bar{r}^2 = \frac{a_0{}^2 n^4}{z^2}\left[1 + \frac{3}{2}\left\{1 - \frac{\ell(\ell+1) - 1/3}{n^2}\right\}\right].$$

Calculate χ_M for H and Li.

8-2. Calculate the electronic g factor for a paramagnetic ion subjected to an external field of 1630.00 G (gauss) and resonant frequency 9.44 GHz. For ions having g_e factors of this magnitude, what interpretation is given to the electronic mobility?

8-3. Using operator mechanics, prove that the matrix element $\hat{S}_x$ of Eq. (8-1) is zero unless $m = k \pm 1$. Show also that for orientation of the oscillating magnetic field along the static field axis $m = k$.

8-4. For an external static field of 10,000 G, calculate the frequency of the resonance condition for a typical ^{19}F nucleus. $\mu(^{19}\text{F}) = 2.6273\ \mu_N$. Compare with a typical proton resonance frequency.

8-5. Predict and draw the spin-spin high-resolution NMR spectrum of HD.

8-6. Draw the hypothetical first-order spin-spin splitting pattern expected for a three-spin system ($I_A = \frac{1}{2}, I_B = \frac{1}{2}, I_C = \frac{1}{2}$), where $\nu_A > \nu_B > \nu_C$ and $J_{AB} > J_{BC} > J_{AC}$. Assume $\nu_0\delta \gg J_{ij}$ in all cases.

8-7. Calculate the hyperfine coupling constant A for the methyl radical, assuming $g_e \sim 2.00$.

***8-8.** In the text by Low, the fine structure formula for the angular dependence of the ESR spectrum for axial symmetry is given as[8]

$$h\nu(E_{M_S} \to E_{M_{S-1}}) = g\beta H + D\left(M_S - \frac{1}{2}\right)\left[\frac{3g_{\|}^2}{g^2}\cos^2\theta - 1\right]$$

$$- \left[\frac{Dg_{\|}g_{\perp}\cos\theta\sin\theta}{g^2}\right]^2\left[\frac{4S(S+1) + 24M_S(M_S-1) - 9}{2g\beta H_0}\right]$$

$$+ \left[\frac{(Dg_{\perp}^2\sin^2\theta)}{g^2}\right]^2\left[\frac{2S(S+1) - 6M_S(M_S-1) - 3}{8g\beta H_0}\right],$$

where $g_{ZZ} = g_{\|}$, $A_Z = A_{\|}$, $A_X = A_Y = A_{\perp}$, and $g_{XX} = g_{YY} = g_{\perp}$, and $g\beta H_0$ is a constant. In the presence of hyperfine interaction, the transition $\Delta M_S = -1$, $\Delta M_I = 0$ is obtained by adding to the above formula the following:

$$KM_I + \frac{A_{\perp}^2}{4g\beta H_0}\left[\frac{A_{\|}^2 + K^2}{K^2}\right][I(I+1) - M_I^2] + \frac{A_{\perp}^2}{2g\beta H_0}\left(\frac{A_{\|}^2}{K}\right)$$

$$\times (2M_S - 1)M_I + \frac{1}{2g\beta H_0}\left[\frac{A_{\|}^2 + A_{\perp}^2}{K^2}\right]\left[\frac{g_{\|}^2 g_{\perp}^2}{g^2}\right]\sin^2\theta\cos^2\theta\, M_I^2,$$

where $g^2 = g_{\|}^2\cos^2\theta + g_{\perp}^2\sin^2\theta$, and $K^2 = A_{\|}^2\cos^2\theta + A_{\perp}^2\sin^2\theta$, and θ is the angle between the external field and the symmetry axis.

Consider the limiting cases of $\theta = 0°$ and $\theta = 90°$. What are the expressions for spacing between the fine structure transitions at these angles?

What are the expressions for the spacing of the hyperfine transitions at $\theta = 0°$ and $\theta = 90°$?

Which spacing is closest to $A_{\|}$ and $A_{\perp}$, when $S = \frac{3}{2}$ and $I = \frac{3}{2}$?

Answers to Selected Problems

CHAPTER 1

1-2. $R_d = 6.06$ cc/mole
1-4. $\mu_{\text{trans}} = 1.14$ D
1-6. 83° from the principal axis
1-9. $\mu = 0.18$ D
1-11. $\mu_{\text{P—Cl}} = 1.67$ D
1-13. $\mu_{\text{—NO}_2} = 2.9$ D
1-16. $i(\text{KCl}) = 96.2\%$, $i(\text{HBr}) = 34\%$

CHAPTER 2

2-4. $(\mu)_{mk} = 5.21 \times 10^{-38}$ erg-cm,^{3} $D_{mk} = 2.27 \times 10^{-19}$ cm^2, $A_{km} = 1.69 \times 10^6$ sec^{-1}, $\tau = 5.9 \times 10^{-7}$ sec
2-5. $f = 0.53$
2-6. $Z = 3.4 \times 10^6$ collisions
2-8. $\Sigma^+ \leftrightarrow \Sigma^-$, $g \leftrightarrow g$, $\Delta S = 0$

CHAPTER 3

3-1. $^3\text{P}_{2,1,0}$, inverted ordering
3-7. $^1\text{P}_1 \leftarrow {}^1\text{S}_0$ (ground state), 3 lines of equal intensity
3-9. ^4D, ^2D, ^2D
3-11. $\nu_\text{L} = 1.409$ GHz, $\Delta E = 0.070$ cm^{-1}, $\text{H}_z = 4 \times 10^4$ gauss
3-13. $\omega_\text{L} \simeq 0.200$ cm^{-1}, microwave

CHAPTER 4

4-1. LiF, 0.11%; CsBr, 0.0025%

4-3. $B_0 = 97{,}535.14$ Hz, $\alpha_e = 1822$ MHz, $r_0 = 1.617$ Å

4-11. $r_{N-F} = 1.365$ Å; $\theta_{FNF} = 102°22'$

4-13. For 1_{10}, $\epsilon = 51{,}887.6$ MHz; 1_{11}, $\epsilon = 43{,}859.4$ MHz; 1_{01}, $\epsilon = 35{,}619.7$ MHz

4-15. $\Delta\nu^{(2)} = 144.8$ MHz

4-16. $\Delta\nu^{(1)} = -40.72$ Hz

4-18. 6×10^{-4} %, $\Delta\omega_p = 0.362$ MHz

4-20. $U_0 = 5.175$ kcal/mole

CHAPTER 5

5-1. $\{C_6, C_6'\}$, $\{C_3, C_3'\}$, $\{C_2\}$, $\{3C_2'\}$, $\{3C_2''\}$

5-3. *a*, *b*, *c*, and *d* commute.

5-5. (b) C_s; (d) $D_{\infty h}$; (f) C_{4v}

5-8. D_{2h}

5-10. ν_3 and ν_4 IR-active; ν_1, ν_2, ν_3, and ν_4 Raman-active; 2 IR absorptions, 4 Raman-active frequencies

CHAPTER 6

6-1. 1049.22 cm^{-1}, 1562.34 cm^{-1}, 2067.80 cm^{-1}

6-3. $\omega_{C=C} \simeq 1661$ cm^{-1}

6-4. $\omega_{DCl} \simeq 2143$ cm^{-1}

6-7. For NF_3; $\omega_1 = 1032$ cm^{-1}, $\omega_2 = 647$ cm^{-1}, $\omega_3 = 907$ cm^{-1}, $\omega_4 = 492$ cm^{-1}

6-9. Mechanical or electrical anharmonicity, or both

6-13. $\xi_3 = 0.042$ and $\xi_4 = 0.498$

6-16. For A_1: $S_1 = (1/\sqrt{3})(\Delta r_1 + \Delta r_2 + \Delta r_3)$, $S_2 = (1/\sqrt{3})(\Delta\theta_1 + \Delta\theta_2 + \Delta\theta_3)$; and for E: $S_{3a} = (1/\sqrt{6})(2\Delta r_1 - \Delta r_2 - \Delta r_3)$, $S_{3b} = (1/\sqrt{2})(\Delta r_2 - \Delta r_3)$, $S_{4a} = (1/\sqrt{6})(2\Delta\theta_1 - \Delta\theta_2 - \Delta\theta_3)$, $S_{4b} = (1/\sqrt{2})(\Delta\theta_2 - \Delta\theta_3)$

CHAPTER 7

7-1. $\xi = 3680$ cm^{-1}

7-3. ${}^4\Delta_r$, ${}^2\Delta$, ${}^2\Delta$

7-5. $^3\Sigma_u^+$
7-8. CH_2; $^3\Sigma_g^-$, $^3\Pi_u$
7-9. $^1A_1$, ^1E, $^3A_2$
7-12. $\Delta E \simeq 5.45 \times 10^5\ \text{cm}^{-1}$

CHAPTER 8

8-1. For H, $\chi_M = -2.37 \times 10^{-6}$ mole^{-1}. For Li, $\chi_M = 4.04 \times 10^{-6}$ mole^{-1}
8-2. $g = 4.13$
8-4. 110 MHz
8-7. $A = 64$ MHz
8-8. At $\theta = 0°$, $\dfrac{2D}{g_\parallel \beta}$; at $\theta = 90°$, $\dfrac{D - [D^2 g_\perp^2 (12 M_S)/8 g\beta H_0]}{g_\perp \beta}$. At

$\theta = 0°$, $\dfrac{A_\parallel - [(A_\perp^2/2g\beta H_0)(2M_I - 1)] + [(A_\perp^2/2g\beta H_0)(2M_S - 1)]}{g_\parallel \beta}$;

at $\theta = 90°$,

$$\frac{A_\perp - [(A_\parallel^2 + A_\perp^2/4g\beta H_0)(2M_I - 1)] + [(A_\parallel A_\perp/2g\beta H_0)(2M_S - 1)]}{g_\perp \beta}.$$

At $\theta = 0°$, $M_S = M_I$; at $\theta = 90°$, $M_S = \frac{1}{2}$, $M_I = \frac{1}{2}$.

Appendix I

Force Exerted at Center of Sphere Due to Surface Charge Density

We assume a sphere of radius $\mathbf{r}$, cut out of the dielectric medium shown in Figure 1-3. The electric polarization vector $\mathbf{P}$ is related to the component P along the electric field axis z by the polar angle θ. According to a

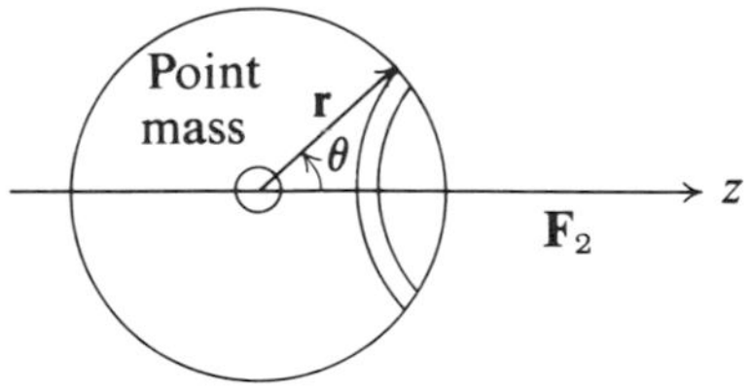

general theorem in electrostatics, the surface density of induced charge is $\sigma_c = P \cos \theta$. Since the area of a ring at angle θ on the surface of the sphere is $dA = 2\pi\mathbf{r}^2 \sin\theta \, d\theta$, the corresponding charge density on the ring is

$$\sigma_c \, dA = 2\pi P\mathbf{r}^2 \cos\theta \sin\theta \, d\theta. \tag{I-1}$$

This charge density produces a force at the center of the sphere whose differential component parallel to $\mathbf{F}_2$ is given by

$$d\mathbf{F}_2 = \frac{2\pi P\mathbf{r}^2 \cos^2\theta \sin\theta \, d\theta}{\mathbf{r}^2}. \tag{I-2}$$

Thus, the total charge on the sphere produces a force at the center equal to

$$\begin{aligned}\mathbf{F}_2 &= 2\pi P \int_0^{\pi} \cos^2\theta \sin\theta \, d\theta \\ &= -2\pi P\tfrac{1}{3}[\cos^3\theta]_0^{\pi} = 2\pi P(\tfrac{2}{3}) \\ &= \frac{4\pi}{3} P.\end{aligned} \tag{I-3}$$

Appendix II

Normalized Hydrogenlike Wavefunctions

$$\Psi_{n\ell m}(r, \theta, \phi) = \psi_{n\ell}(r)\psi_{\ell m}(\theta)\psi_m(\phi)$$

n	ℓ	m	$\psi_{n\ell}(r)$	$\psi_{\ell m}(\theta)$
1	0	0	$2a_0\left(\frac{Z}{a_0}\right)^{3/2} e^{-Zr/a_0}$	$(2)^{-1/2}$
2	0	0	$(8)^{-1/2}\left(\frac{Z}{a_0}\right)^{3/2}\left(2 - \frac{Zr}{a_0}\right)e^{-Zr/2a_0}$	$(2)^{-1/2}$
2	1	0	$(24)^{-1/2}\left(\frac{Z}{a_0}\right)^{3/2}\left(\frac{Zr}{a_0}\right)e^{-Zr/2a_0}$	$\frac{\sqrt{6}}{2}\cos\theta$
2	1	+1	$(24)^{-1/2}\left(\frac{Z}{a_0}\right)^{3/2}\left(\frac{Zr}{a_0}\right)e^{-Zr/2a_0}$	$\frac{\sqrt{3}}{2}\sin\theta$
2	1	−1	$(24)^{-1/2}\left(\frac{Z}{a_0}\right)^{3/2}\left(\frac{Zr}{a_0}\right)e^{\ Zr/2a_0}$	$\frac{\sqrt{3}}{2}\sin\theta$
3	0	0	$2(81)^{-1}(3)^{-1/2}\left(\frac{Z}{a_0}\right)^{3/2} \times \left[27 - \frac{18Zr}{a_0} + 2\left(\frac{Zr}{a_0}\right)^2\right]e^{-Zr/3a_0}$	$(2)^{-1/2}$
3	1	0	$4(81)^{-1}6^{-1/2}(Z/a_0)^{3/2} \times \left[\frac{6Zr}{a_0} - \left(\frac{Zr}{a_0}\right)^2\right]e^{-Zr/3a_0}$	$\frac{\sqrt{6}}{2}\cos\theta$

$$\Psi_{n\ell m}(r, \theta, \phi) = \psi_{n\ell}(r)\psi_{\ell m}(\theta)\psi_m(\phi)$$

n	ℓ	m	$\psi_{n\ell}(r)$	$\psi_{\ell m}(\theta)$
3	1	+1	$4(81)^{-1}6^{-1/2}(Z/a_0)^{3/2} \times \left[\frac{6Zr}{a_0} - \left(\frac{Zr}{a_0}\right)^2\right]e^{-Zr/3a_0}$	$\frac{\sqrt{3}}{2}\sin\theta$
3	1	−1	$4(81)^{-1}6^{-1/2}(Z/a_0)^{3/2} \times \left[\frac{6Zr}{a_0} - \left(\frac{Zr}{a_0}\right)^2\right]e^{-Zr/3a_0}$	$\frac{\sqrt{3}}{2}\sin\theta$
3	2	0	$4(81)^{-1}(30)^{-1/2}\left(\frac{Z}{a_0}\right)^{3/2} \times \left(\frac{Zr}{a_0}\right)^2 e^{-Zr/3a_0}$	$\frac{\sqrt{10}}{4}(3\cos^2\theta - 1)$
3	2	+1	$4(81)^{-1}(30)^{-1/2}\left(\frac{Z}{a_0}\right)^{3/2} \times \left(\frac{Zr}{a_0}\right)^2 e^{-Zr/3a_0}$	$\frac{\sqrt{15}}{2}\sin\theta\cos\theta$
3	2	−1	$4(81)^{-1}(30)^{-1/2}\left(\frac{Z}{a_0}\right)^{3/2} \times \left(\frac{Zr}{a_0}\right)^2 e^{-Zr/3a_0}$	$\frac{\sqrt{15}}{2}\sin\theta\cos\theta$
3	2	+2	$4(81)^{-1}(30)^{-1/2}\left(\frac{Z}{a_0}\right)^{3/2} \times \left(\frac{Zr}{a_0}\right)^2 e^{-Zr/3a_0}$	$\frac{\sqrt{15}}{4}\sin^2\theta$
3	2	−2	$4(81)^{-1}(30)^{-1/2}\left(\frac{Z}{a_0}\right)^{3/2} \times \left(\frac{Zr}{a_0}\right)^2 e^{-Zr/3a_0}$	$\frac{\sqrt{15}}{4}\sin^2\theta$

n ℓ m	$\psi_m(\phi)$	
0	$(2\pi)^{-1/2}$	$(2\pi)^{-1/2}$
1	$(\pi)^{-1/2}\cos\phi$	$(2\pi)^{-1/2}e^{i\phi}$
−1	$(\pi)^{-1/2}\sin\phi$	$(2\pi)^{-1/2}e^{-i\phi}$
2	$(\pi)^{-1/2}\cos 2\phi$	$(2\pi)^{-1/2}e^{2i\phi}$
−2	$(\pi)^{-1/2}\sin 2\phi$	$(2\pi)^{-1/2}e^{-2i\phi}$

Appendix III

Point Group Character Tables

1. THE NONAXIAL GROUPS

C_1	E
A	1

C_s	E	σ_h		
A'	1	1	x, y, R_z	x^2, y^2, z^2, xy
A''	1	-1	z, R_x, R_y	yz, xz

C_i	E	i		
A_g	1	1	R_x, R_y, R_z	$x^2, y^2, z^2,$ xy, xz, yz
A_u	1	-1	x, y, z	

2. THE C_n GROUPS

C_2	E	C_2		
A	1	1	z, R_z	x^2, y^2, z^2, xy
B	1	-1	x, y, R_x, R_y	yz, xz

$\epsilon = \exp(2\pi i/3)$

C_3	E	C_3	C_3^2		
A	1	1	1	z, R_z	$x^2 + y^2, z^2$
E	$\left\{\begin{matrix} 1 \\ 1 \end{matrix}\right.$	$\begin{matrix} \epsilon \\ \epsilon^* \end{matrix}$	$\left.\begin{matrix} \epsilon^* \\ \epsilon \end{matrix}\right\}$	$(x, y)(R_x, R_y)$	$(x^2 - y^2, xy)(yz, xz)$

C_4	E	C_4	C_2	C_4^3		
A	1	1	1	1	z, R_z	$x^2 + y^2, z^2$
B	1	-1	1	-1		$x^2 - y^2, xy$
E	1	i	-1	$-i$	$(x, y)(R_x, R_y)$	(yz, xz)
	1	$-i$	-1	i		

C_5	E	C_5	C_5^2	C_5^3	C_5^4		$\epsilon = \exp(2\pi i/5)$
A	1	1	1	1	1	z, R_z	$x^2 + y^2, z^2$
E_1	1	ϵ	ϵ^2	ϵ^{2*}	ϵ^*	$(x, y)(R_x, R_y)$	(yz, xz)
	1	ϵ^*	ϵ^{2*}	ϵ^2	ϵ		
E_2	1	ϵ^2	ϵ^*	ϵ	ϵ^{2*}		$(x^2 - y^2, xy)$
	1	ϵ^{2*}	ϵ	ϵ^*	ϵ^2		

C_6	E	C_6	C_3	C_2	C_3^2	C_6^5		$\epsilon = \exp(2\pi i/6)$
A	1	1	1	1	1	1	z, R_z	$x^2 + y^2, z^2$
B	1	-1	1	-1	1	-1		
E_1	1	ϵ	$-\epsilon^*$	-1	$-\epsilon$	ϵ^*	(x, y)	(xz, yz)
	1	ϵ^*	$-\epsilon$	-1	$-\epsilon^*$	ϵ	(R_x, R_y)	
E_2	1	$-\epsilon^*$	$-\epsilon$	1	$-\epsilon^*$	$-\epsilon$		$(x^2 - y^2, xy)$
	1	$-\epsilon$	$-\epsilon^*$	1	$-\epsilon$	$-\epsilon^*$		

C_7	E	C_7	C_7^2	C_7^3	C_7^4	C_7^5	C_7^6		$\epsilon = \exp(2\pi i/7)$
A	1	1	1	1	1	1	1	z, R_z	$x^2 + y^2, z^2$
E_1	1	ϵ	ϵ^2	ϵ^3	ϵ^{3*}	ϵ^{2*}	ϵ^*	$(x, y)(R_x, R_y)$	(xz, yz)
	1	ϵ^*	ϵ^{2*}	ϵ^{3*}	ϵ^3	ϵ^2	ϵ		
E_2	1	ϵ^2	ϵ^{3*}	ϵ^*	ϵ	ϵ^3	ϵ^{2*}		$(x^2 - y^2, xy)$
	1	ϵ^{2*}	ϵ^3	ϵ	ϵ^*	ϵ^{3*}	ϵ^2		
E_3	1	ϵ^2	ϵ^*	ϵ^2	ϵ^{2*}	ϵ	ϵ^{3*}		
	1	ϵ^{2*}	ϵ	ϵ^{2*}	ϵ^2	ϵ^*	ϵ^3		

C_8	E	C_8	C_4	C_2	C_4^3	C_8^3	C_8^5	C_8^7		$\epsilon = \exp(2\pi i/8)$
A	1	1	1	1	1	1	1	1	z, R_z	$x^2 + y^2, z^2$
B	1	-1	1	1	1	-1	-1	-1		
E_1	1	ϵ	i	-1	$-i$	$-\epsilon^*$	$-\epsilon$	ϵ^*	(x, y)	(xz, yz)
	1	ϵ^*	$-i$	-1	i	$-\epsilon$	$-\epsilon^*$	ϵ	(R_x, R_y)	
E_2	1	i	-1	1	-1	$-i$	i	$-i$		$(x^2 - y^2, xy)$
	1	$-i$	-1	1	-1	i	$-i$	i		
E_3	1	$-\epsilon$	i	-1	$-i$	ϵ^*	ϵ	$-\epsilon^*$		
	1	$-\epsilon^*$	$-i$	-1	i	ϵ	ϵ^*	$-\epsilon$		

3. THE D_n GROUPS

D_2	E	$C_2(z)$	$C_2(y)$	$C_2(x)$		
A	1	1	1	1		x^2, y^2, z^2
B_1	1	1	-1	-1	z, R_z	xy
B_2	1	-1	1	-1	y, R_y	xz
B_3	1	-1	-1	1	x, R_x	yz

D_3	E	$2C_3$	$3C_2$		
A_1	1	1	1		$x^2 + y^2, z^2$
A_2	1	1	-1	z, R_z	
E	2	-1	0	$(x, y)(R_x, R_y)$	$(x^2 - y^2, xy)(xz, yz)$

D_4	E	$2C_4$	$C_2(=C_4^2)$	$2C_2'$	$2C_2''$		
A_1	1	1	1	1	1		$x^2 + y^2, z^2$
A_2	1	1	1	-1	-1	z, R_z	
B_1	1	-1	1	1	-1		$x^2 - y^2$
B_2	1	-1	1	-1	1		xy
E	2	0	-2	0	0	$(x, y)(R_x, R_y)$	(xz, yz)

D_5	E	$2C_5$	$2C_5^2$	$5C_2$		
A_1	1	1	1	1		$x^2 + y^2, z^2$
A_2	1	1	1	-1	z, R_z	
E_1	2	$2\cos 72°$	$2\cos 144°$	0	$(x, y)(R_x, R_y)$	(xz, yz)
E_2	2	$2\cos 144°$	$2\cos 72°$	0		$(x^2 - y^2, xy)$

D_6	E	$2C_6$	$2C_3$	C_2	$3C_2'$	$3C_2''$		
A_1	1	1	1	1	1	1		$x^2 + y^2, z^2$
A_2	1	1	1	1	-1	-1	z, R_z	
B_1	1	-1	1	-1	1	-1		
B_2	1	-1	1	-1	-1	1		
E_1	2	1	-1	-2	0	0	$(x, y)(R_x, R_y)$	(xz, yz)
E_2	2	-1	-1	2	0	0		$(x^2 - y^2, xy)$

4. THE C_{nv} GROUPS

C_{2v}	E	C_2	$\sigma_v(xz)$	$\sigma_v'(yz)$		
A_1	1	1	1	1	z	x^2, y^2, z^2
A_2	1	1	−1	−1	R_z	xy
B_1	1	−1	1	−1	x, R_y	xz
B_2	1	−1	−1	1	y, R_x	yz

C_{3v}	E	$2C_3$	$3\sigma_v$		
A_1	1	1	1	z	$x^2 + y^2, z^2$
A_2	1	1	−1	R_z	
E	2	−1	0	$(x, y)(R_x, R_y)$	$(x^2 - y^2, xy)(xz, yz)$

C_{4v}	E	$2C_4$	C_2	$2\sigma_v$	$2\sigma_d$		
A_1	1	1	1	1	1	z	$x^2 + y^2, z^2$
A_2	1	1	1	−1	−1	R_z	
B_1	1	−1	1	1	−1		$x^2 - y^2$
B_2	1	−1	1	−1	1		xy
E	2	0	−2	0	0	$(x, y)(R_x, R_y)$	(xz, yz)

C_{5v}	E	$2C_5$	$2C_5^2$	$5\sigma_v$		
A_1	1	1	1	1	z	$x^2 + y^2, z^2$
A_2	1	1	1	−1	R_z	
E_1	2	2 cos 72°	2 cos 144°	0	$(x, y)(R_x, R_y)$	(xz, yz)
E_2	2	2 cos 144°	2 cos 72°	0		$(x^2 - y^2, xy)$

C_{6v}	E	$2C_6$	$2C_3$	C_2	$3\sigma_v$	$3\sigma_d$		
A_1	1	1	1	1	1	1	z	$x^2 + y^2, z^2$
A_2	1	1	1	1	−1	−1	R_z	
B_1	1	−1	1	−1	1	−1		
B_2	1	−1	1	−1	−1	1		
E_1	2	1	−1	−2	0	0	$(x, y)(R_x, R_y)$	(xz, yz)
E_2	2	−1	−1	2	0	0		$(x^2 - y^2, xy)$

5. THE C_{nh} GROUPS

C_{2h}	E	C_2	i	σ_h		
A_g	1	1	1	1	R_z	x^2, y^2, z^2, xy
B_g	1	−1	1	−1	R_x, R_y	xz, yz
A_u	1	1	−1	−1	z	
B_u	1	−1	−1	1	x, y	

C_{3h}	E	C_3	C_3^2	σ_h	S_3	S_3^5		$\epsilon = \exp(2\pi i/3)$
A'	1	1	1	1	1	1	R_z	$x^2 + y^2, z^2$
E'	$\begin{cases}1 \\ 1\end{cases}$	ϵ ϵ^*	ϵ^* ϵ	1 1	ϵ ϵ^*	ϵ^* ϵ	(x, y)	$(x^2 - y^2, xy)$
A''	1	1	1	−1	−1	−1	z	
E''	$\begin{cases}1 \\ 1\end{cases}$	ϵ ϵ^*	ϵ^* ϵ	−1 −1	$-\epsilon$ $-\epsilon^*$	$-\epsilon^*$ $-\epsilon$	(R_x, R_y)	(xz, yz)

C_{4h}	E	C_4	C_2	C_4^3	i	S_4^3	σ_h	S_4		
A_g	1	1	1	1	1	1	1	1	R_z	$x^2 + y^2, z^2$
B_g	1	−1	1	−1	1	−1	1	−1		$x^2 - y^2, xy$
E_g	$\begin{cases}1 \\ 1\end{cases}$	i $-i$	−1 −1	$-i$ i	1 1	i $-i$	−1 −1	$-i$ i	(R_x, R_y)	(xz, yz)
A_u	1	1	1	1	−1	−1	−1	−1	z	
B_u	1	−1	1	−1	−1	1	−1	1		
E_u	$\begin{cases}1 \\ 1\end{cases}$	i $-i$	−1 −1	$-i$ i	−1 −1	$-i$ i	1 1	i $-i$	(x, y)	

C_{5h}	E	C_5	C_5^2	C_5^3	C_5^4	σ_h	S_5	S_5^7	S_5^3	S_5^9		$\epsilon = \exp(2\pi i/5)$
A'	1	1	1	1	1	1	1	1	1	1	R_z	$x^2 + y^2, z^2$
E_1'	$\begin{cases}1 \\ 1\end{cases}$	ϵ ϵ^*	ϵ^2 ϵ^{2*}	ϵ^{2*} ϵ^2	ϵ^* ϵ	1 1	ϵ ϵ^*	ϵ^2 ϵ^{2*}	ϵ^{2*} ϵ^2	ϵ^* ϵ	(x, y)	
E_2'	$\begin{cases}1 \\ 1\end{cases}$	ϵ^2 ϵ^{2*}	ϵ^* ϵ	ϵ ϵ^*	ϵ^{2*} ϵ^2	1 1	ϵ^2 ϵ^{2*}	ϵ^* ϵ	ϵ ϵ^*	ϵ^{2*} ϵ^2		$(x^2 - y^2, xy)$
A''	1	1	1	1	−1	−1	−1	−1	−1	−1	z	
E_1''	$\begin{cases}1 \\ 1\end{cases}$	ϵ ϵ^*	ϵ^2 ϵ^{2*}	ϵ^{2*} ϵ^2	ϵ^* ϵ	−1 −1	$-\epsilon$ $-\epsilon^*$	$-\epsilon^2$ $-\epsilon^{2*}$	$-\epsilon^{2*}$ $-\epsilon^2$	$-\epsilon^*$ $-\epsilon$	(R_x, R_y)	(xz, yz)
E_2''	$\begin{cases}1 \\ 1\end{cases}$	ϵ^2 ϵ^{2*}	ϵ^* ϵ	ϵ ϵ^*	ϵ^{2*} ϵ^2	−1 −1	$-\epsilon^2$ $-\epsilon^{2*}$	$-\epsilon^*$ $-\epsilon$	$-\epsilon$ $-\epsilon^*$	$-\epsilon^{2*}$ $-\epsilon^2$		

C_{6h}	E	C_6	C_3	C_2	C_3^2	C_6^5	i	S_3^5	S_6^5	σ_h	S_6	S_3		$\epsilon = \exp(2\pi i/6)$
A_g	1	1	1	1	1	1	1	1	1	1	1	1	R_z	$x^2 + y^2, z^2$
B_g	1	-1	1	-1	1	-1	1	-1	1	-1	1	-1		
E_{1g}	1	ϵ	$-\epsilon^*$	-1	$-\epsilon$	ϵ^*	1	ϵ	$-\epsilon^*$	-1	$-\epsilon$	ϵ^*	(R_x, R_y)	(xz, yz)
	1	ϵ^*	$-\epsilon$	-1	$-\epsilon^*$	ϵ	1	ϵ^*	$-\epsilon$	-1	$-\epsilon^*$	ϵ		
E_{2g}	1	$-\epsilon^*$	$-\epsilon$	1	$-\epsilon^*$	$-\epsilon$	1	$-\epsilon^*$	$-\epsilon$	1	$-\epsilon^*$	$-\epsilon$		$(x^2 - y^2, xy)$
	1	$-\epsilon$	$-\epsilon^*$	1	$-\epsilon$	$-\epsilon^*$	1	$-\epsilon$	$-\epsilon^*$	1	$-\epsilon$	$-\epsilon^*$		
A_u	1	1	1	1	1	1	-1	-1	-1	-1	-1	-1	z	
B_u	1	-1	1	-1	1	-1	-1	1	-1	1	-1	1		
E_{1u}	1	ϵ	$-\epsilon^*$	-1	$-\epsilon$	ϵ^*	-1	$-\epsilon$	ϵ^*	1	ϵ	$-\epsilon^*$	(x, y)	
	1	ϵ^*	$-\epsilon$	-1	$-\epsilon^*$	ϵ	-1	$-\epsilon^*$	ϵ	1	ϵ^*	$-\epsilon$		
E_{2u}	1	$-\epsilon^*$	$-\epsilon$	1	$-\epsilon^*$	$-\epsilon$	-1	ϵ^*	ϵ	-1	ϵ^*	ϵ		
	1	$-\epsilon$	$-\epsilon^*$	1	$-\epsilon$	$-\epsilon^*$	-1	ϵ	ϵ^*	-1	ϵ	ϵ^*		

6. THE D_{nh} GROUPS

D_{2h}	E	$C_2(z)$	$C_2(y)$	$C_2(x)$	i	$\sigma(xy)$	$\sigma(xz)$	$\sigma(yz)$		
A_g	1	1	1	1	1	1	1	1		x^2, y^2, z^2
B_{1g}	1	1	−1	−1	1	1	−1	−1	R_z	xy
B_{2g}	1	−1	1	−1	1	−1	1	−1	R_y	xz
B_{3g}	1	−1	−1	1	1	−1	−1	1	R_x	yz
A_u	1	1	1	1	−1	−1	−1	−1		
B_{1u}	1	1	−1	−1	−1	−1	1	1	z	
B_{2u}	1	−1	1	−1	−1	1	−1	1	y	
B_{3u}	1	−1	−1	1	−1	1	1	−1	x	

D_{3h}	E	$2C_3$	$3C_2$	σ_h	$2S_3$	$3\sigma_v$		
A_1'	1	1	1	1	1	1		$x^2 + y^2, z^2$
A_2'	1	1	−1	1	1	−1	R_z	
E'	2	−1	0	2	−1	0	(x, y)	$(x^2 - y^2, xy)$
A_1''	1	1	1	−1	−1	−1		
A_2''	1	1	−1	−1	−1	1	z	
E''	2	−1	0	−2	1	0	(R_x, R_y)	(xz, yz)

D_{4h}	E	$2C_4$	C_2	$2C_2'$	$2C_2''$	i	$2S_4$	σ_h	$2\sigma_v$	$2\sigma_d$		
A_{1g}	1	1	1	1	1	1	1	1	1	1		$x^2 + y^2, z^2$
A_{2g}	1	1	1	−1	−1	1	1	1	−1	−1	R_z	
B_{1g}	1	−1	1	1	−1	1	−1	1	1	−1		$x^2 - y^2$
B_{2g}	1	−1	1	−1	1	1	−1	1	−1	1		xy
E_g	2	0	−2	0	0	2	0	−2	0	0	(R_x, R_y)	(xz, yz)
A_{1u}	1	1	1	1	1	−1	−1	−1	−1	−1		
A_{2u}	1	1	1	−1	−1	−1	−1	−1	1	1	z	
B_{1u}	1	−1	1	1	−1	−1	1	−1	−1	1		
B_{2u}	1	−1	1	−1	1	−1	1	−1	1	−1		
E_u	2	0	−2	0	0	−2	0	2	0	0	(x, y)	

D_{5h}	E	$2C_5$	$2C_5^2$	$5C_2$	σ_h	$2S_5$	$2S_5^3$	$5\sigma_v$		
A_1'	1	1	1	1	1	1	1	1		$x^2 + y^2, z^2$
A_2'	1	1	1	−1	1	1	1	−1	R_z	
E_1'	2	2 cos 72°	2 cos 144°	0	2	2 cos 72°	2 cos 144°	0	(x, y)	
E_2'	2	2 cos 144°	2 cos 72°	0	2	2 cos 144°	2 cos 72°	0		$(x^2 - y^2, xy)$
A_1''	1	1	1	1	−1	−1	−1	−1		
A_2''	1	1	1	−1	−1	−1	−1	1	z	
E_1''	2	2 cos 72°	2 cos 144°	0	−2	−2 cos 72°	−2 cos 144°	0	(R_x, R_y)	(xz, yz)
E_2''	2	2 cos 144°	2 cos 72°	0	−2	−2 cos 144°	−2 cos 72°	0		

D_{6h}	E	$2C_6$	$2C_3$	C_2	$3C_2'$	$3C_2''$	i	$2S_3$	$2S_6$	σ_h	$3\sigma_d$	$3\sigma_v$		
A_{1g}	1	1	1	1	1	1	1	1	1	1	1	1		$x^2 + y^2, z^2$
A_{2g}	1	1	1	1	−1	−1	1	1	1	1	−1	−1	R_z	
B_{1g}	1	−1	1	−1	1	−1	1	−1	1	−1	1	−1		
B_{2g}	1	−1	1	−1	−1	1	1	−1	1	−1	−1	1		
E_{1g}	2	1	−1	−2	0	0	2	1	−1	−2	0	0	(R_x, R_y)	(xz, yz)
E_{2g}	2	−1	−1	2	0	0	2	−1	−1	2	0	0		$(x^2 - y^2, xy)$
A_{1u}	1	1	1	1	1	1	−1	−1	−1	−1	−1	−1		
A_{2u}	1	1	1	1	−1	−1	−1	−1	−1	−1	1	1	z	
B_{1u}	1	−1	1	−1	1	−1	−1	1	−1	1	−1	1		
B_{2u}	1	−1	1	−1	−1	1	−1	1	−1	1	1	−1		
E_{1u}	2	1	−1	−2	0	0	−2	−1	1	2	0	0	(x, y)	
E_{2u}	2	−1	−1	2	0	0	−2	1	1	−2	0	0		

7. THE D_{nd} GROUPS

D_{2d}	E	$2S_4$	C_2	$2C_2'$	$2\sigma_d$		
A_1	1	1	1	1	1		$x^2 + y^2, z^2$
A_2	1	1	1	−1	−1	R_z	
B_1	1	−1	1	1	−1		$x^2 - y^2$
B_2	1	−1	1	−1	1	z	xy
E	2	0	−2	0	0	$(x, y)(R_x, R_y)$	(xz, yz)

D_{3d}	E	$2C_3$	$3C_2$	i	$2S_6$	$3\sigma_d$		
A_{1g}	1	1	1	1	1	1		$x^2 + y^2, z^2$
A_{2g}	1	1	−1	1	1	−1	R_z	
E_g	2	−1	0	2	−1	0	(R_x, R_y)	$(x^2 - y^2, xy), (xz, yz)$
A_{1u}	1	1	1	−1	−1	−1		
A_{2u}	1	1	−1	−1	−1	1	z	
E_u	2	−1	0	−2	1	0	(x, y)	

D_{4d}	E	$2S_8$	$2C_4$	$2S_8^3$	C_2	$4C_2'$	$4\sigma_d$		
A_1	1	1	1	1	1	1	1		$x^2 + y^2, z^2$
A_2	1	1	1	1	1	−1	−1	R_z	
B_1	1	−1	1	−1	1	1	−1		
B_2	1	−1	1	−1	1	−1	1	z	
E_1	2	$\sqrt{2}$	0	$-\sqrt{2}$	−2	0	0	(x, y)	
E_2	2	0	−2	0	2	0	0		$(x^2 - y^2, xy)$
E_3	2	$-\sqrt{2}$	0	$\sqrt{2}$	−2	0	0	(R_x, R_y)	$(xz, yz$

D_{5d}	E	$2C_5$	$2C_5^2$	$5C_2$	i	$2S_{10}^3$	$2S_{10}$	$5\sigma_d$		
A_{1g}	1	1	1	1	1	1	1	1		$x^2 + y^2, z^2$
A_{2g}	1	1	1	−1	1	1	1	−1	R_z	
E_{1g}	2	2 cos 72°	2 cos 144°	0	2	2 cos 72°	2 cos 144°	0	(R_x, R_y)	(xz, yz)
E_{2g}	2	2 cos 144°	2 cos 72°	0	2	2 cos 144°	2 cos 72°	0		$(x^2 - y^2, xy)$
A_{1u}	1	1	1	1	−1	−1	−1	−1		
A_{2u}	1	1	1	−1	−1	−1	−1	1	z	
E_{1u}	2	2 cos 72°	2 cos 144°	0	−2	−2 cos 72°	−2 cos 144°	0	(x, y)	
E_{2u}	2	2 cos 144°	2 cos 72°	0	−2	−2 cos 144°	−2 cos 72°	0		

D_{6d}	E	$2S_{12}$	$2C_6$	$2S_4$	$2C_3$	$2S_{12}^5$	C_2	$6C_2'$	$6\sigma_d$		
A_1	1	1	1	1	1	1	1	1	1		x^2+y^2, z^2
A_2	1	1	1	1	1	1	1	−1	−1	R_z	
B_1	1	−1	1	−1	1	−1	1	1	−1		
B_2	1	−1	1	−1	1	−1	1	−1	1	z	
E_1	2	$\sqrt{3}$	1	0	−1	$-\sqrt{3}$	−2	0	0	(x, y)	
E_2	2	1	−1	−2	−1	1	2	0	0		(x^2-y^2, xy)
E_3	2	0	−2	0	2	0	−2	0	0		
E_4	2	−1	−1	2	−1	−1	2	0	0		
E_5	2	$-\sqrt{3}$	1	0	−1	$\sqrt{3}$	−2	0	0	(R_x, R_y)	(xz, yz)

8. THE S_n GROUPS

S_4	E	S_4	C_2	S_4^3		
A	1	1	1	1	R_z	x^2+y^2, z^2
B	1	−1	1	−1	z	x^2-y^2, xy
E	$\begin{cases}1 \\ 1\end{cases}$	$\begin{matrix} i \\ -i\end{matrix}$	$\begin{matrix}-1 \\ -1\end{matrix}$	$\left.\begin{matrix}-i \\ i\end{matrix}\right\}$	$(x, y); (R_x, R_y)$	(xz, yz)

S_6	E	C_3	C_3^2	i	S_6^5	S_6		$\epsilon = \exp(2\pi i/3)$
A_g	1	1	1	1	1	1	R_z	x^2+y^2, z^2
E_g	$\begin{cases}1 \\ 1\end{cases}$	$\begin{matrix}\epsilon \\ \epsilon^*\end{matrix}$	$\begin{matrix}\epsilon^* \\ \epsilon\end{matrix}$	$\begin{matrix}1 \\ 1\end{matrix}$	$\begin{matrix}\epsilon \\ \epsilon^*\end{matrix}$	$\left.\begin{matrix}\epsilon^* \\ \epsilon\end{matrix}\right\}$	(R_x, R_y)	(x^2-y^2, xy); (xz, yz)
A_u	1	1	1	−1	−1	−1	z	
E_u	$\begin{cases}1 \\ 1\end{cases}$	$\begin{matrix}\epsilon \\ \epsilon^*\end{matrix}$	$\begin{matrix}\epsilon^* \\ \epsilon\end{matrix}$	$\begin{matrix}-1 \\ -1\end{matrix}$	$\begin{matrix}-\epsilon \\ -\epsilon^*\end{matrix}$	$\left.\begin{matrix}-\epsilon^* \\ -\epsilon\end{matrix}\right\}$	(x, y)	

S_8	E	S_8	C_4	S_8^3	C_2	S_8^5	C_4^3	S_8^7		$\epsilon = \exp(2\pi i/8)$
A	1	1	1	1	1	1	1	1	R_z	x^2+y^2, z^2
B	1	−1	1	−1	1	−1	1	−1	z	
E_1	$\begin{cases}1 \\ 1\end{cases}$	$\begin{matrix}\epsilon \\ \epsilon^*\end{matrix}$	$\begin{matrix}i \\ -i\end{matrix}$	$\begin{matrix}-\epsilon^* \\ -\epsilon\end{matrix}$	$\begin{matrix}-1 \\ -1\end{matrix}$	$\begin{matrix}-\epsilon \\ -\epsilon^*\end{matrix}$	$\begin{matrix}-i \\ i\end{matrix}$	$\left.\begin{matrix}\epsilon^* \\ \epsilon\end{matrix}\right\}$	(x, y); (R_x, R_y)	
E_2	$\begin{cases}1 \\ 1\end{cases}$	$\begin{matrix}i \\ -i\end{matrix}$	$\begin{matrix}-1 \\ -1\end{matrix}$	$\begin{matrix}-i \\ i\end{matrix}$	$\begin{matrix}1 \\ 1\end{matrix}$	$\begin{matrix}i \\ -i\end{matrix}$	$\begin{matrix}-1 \\ -1\end{matrix}$	$\left.\begin{matrix}-i \\ i\end{matrix}\right\}$		(x^2-y^2, xy)
E_3	$\begin{cases}1 \\ 1\end{cases}$	$\begin{matrix}-\epsilon^* \\ -\epsilon\end{matrix}$	$\begin{matrix}-i \\ i\end{matrix}$	$\begin{matrix}\epsilon \\ \epsilon^*\end{matrix}$	$\begin{matrix}-1 \\ -1\end{matrix}$	$\begin{matrix}\epsilon^* \\ \epsilon\end{matrix}$	$\begin{matrix}i \\ -i\end{matrix}$	$\left.\begin{matrix}-\epsilon \\ -\epsilon^*\end{matrix}\right\}$		(xz, yz)

9. THE CUBIC GROUPS

T_d	E	$8C_3$	$3C_2$	$6S_4$	$6\sigma_d$		
A_1	1	1	1	1	1		$x^2 + y^2 + z^2$
A_2	1	1	1	-1	-1		
E	2	-1	2	0	0		$(2z^2 - x^2 - y^2, x^2 - y^2)$
T_1	3	0	-1	1	-1	(R_x, R_y, R_z)	
T_2	3	0	-1	-1	1	(x, y, z)	(xy, xz, yz)

O_h	E	$8C_3$	$6C_2$	$6C_4$	$3C_2(=C_4^2)$	i	$6S_4$	$8S_6$	$3\sigma_h$	$6\sigma_d$		
A_{1g}	1	1	1	1	1	1	1	1	1	1		$x^2 + y^2 + z^2$
A_{2g}	1	1	-1	-1	1	1	-1	1	1	-1		
E_g	2	-1	0	0	2	2	0	-1	2	0		$(2z^2 - x^2 - y^2, x^2 - y^2)$
T_{1g}	3	0	-1	1	-1	3	1	0	-1	-1	(R_x, R_y, R_z)	
T_{2g}	3	0	1	-1	-1	3	-1	0	-1	1		(xz, yz, xy)
A_{1u}	1	1	1	1	1	-1	-1	-1	-1	-1		
A_{2u}	1	1	-1	-1	1	-1	1	-1	-1	1		
E_u	2	-1	0	0	2	-2	0	1	-2	0		
T_{1u}	3	0	-1	1	-1	-3	-1	0	1	1	(x, y, z)	
T_{2u}	3	0	1	-1	-1	-3	1	0	1	-1		

10. THE GROUPS $C_{\infty v}$ AND $D_{\infty h}$

$C_{\infty v}$	E	$2C_\infty^\phi$	...	$\infty\sigma_v$		
$A_1 \equiv \Sigma^+$	1	1	...	1	z	$x^2 + y^2, z^2$
$A_2 \equiv \Sigma^-$	1	1	...	-1	R_z	
$E_1 \equiv \Pi$	2	$2\cos\phi$	...	0	$(x, y); (R_x, R_y)$	(xz, yz)
$E_2 \equiv \Delta$	2	$2\cos 2\phi$	...	0		$(x^2 - y^2, xy)$
$E_3 \equiv \Phi$	2	$2\cos 3\phi$	...	0		
...	...	...	...	...		

$D_{\infty h}$	E	$2C_\infty^\phi$	...	$\infty\sigma_v$	i	$2S_\infty^\phi$	...	∞C_2		
Σ_g^+	1	1	...	1	1	1	...	1		$x^2 + y^2, z^2$
Σ_g^-	1	1	...	-1	1	1	...	-1	R_z	
Π_g	2	$2\cos\phi$	...	0	2	$-2\cos\phi$	...	0	(R_x, R_y)	(xz, yz)
Δ_g	2	$2\cos 2\phi$	...	0	2	$2\cos 2\phi$	...	0		$(x^2 - y^2, xy)$
...	...	...	...	...	...	...	...	...		
Σ_u^+	1	1	...	1	-1	-1	...	-1	z	
Σ_u^-	1	1	...	-1	-1	-1	...	1		
Π_u	2	$2\cos\phi$	...	0	-2	$2\cos\phi$	...	0	(x, y)	
Δ_u	2	$2\cos 2\phi$	...	0	-2	$-2\cos 2\phi$	...	0		
...	...	...	...	...	...	...	...	...		

Appendix IV

Table of Hermite Polynomials and Normalizing Constants

$H_v(\alpha),\ \alpha = \gamma^{1/2}q$	$N_v = \left[\left(\frac{\gamma}{\pi}\right)^{1/2} \frac{1}{2^v v!}\right]^{1/2}$
$H_0(\alpha) = 1$	$N_0 = \left(\frac{\gamma}{\pi}\right)^{1/4}$
$H_1(\alpha) = 2\alpha$	$N_1 = \left[\left(\frac{\gamma}{\pi}\right)^{1/2}\left(\frac{1}{2}\right)\right]^{1/2}$
$H_2(\alpha) = 4\alpha^2 - 2$	$N_2 = \left[\left(\frac{\gamma}{\pi}\right)^{1/2}\left(\frac{1}{8}\right)\right]^{1/2}$
$H_3(\alpha) = 8\alpha^3 - 12\alpha$	$N_3 = \left[\left(\frac{\gamma}{\pi}\right)^{1/2}\left(\frac{1}{48}\right)\right]^{1/2}$
$H_4(\alpha) = 16\alpha^4 - 48\alpha^2 + 12$	$N_4 = \left[\left(\frac{\gamma}{\pi}\right)^{1/2}\left(\frac{1}{384}\right)\right]^{1/2}$
$H_5(\alpha) = 32\alpha^5 - 160\alpha^3 + 120\alpha$	$N_5 = \left[\left(\frac{\gamma}{\pi}\right)^{1/2}\left(\frac{1}{3840}\right)\right]^{1/2}$
$H_6(\alpha) = 64\alpha^6 - 480\alpha^4 + 720\alpha^2 - 120$	$N_6 = \left[\left(\frac{\gamma}{\pi}\right)^{1/2}\left(\frac{1}{46080}\right)\right]^{1/2}$

The total generalized wavefunction for single vibrational mode is given as:

$$\psi_v = H_v(\alpha) N_v \exp(-\tfrac{1}{2}\gamma q^2).$$

And the first three levels:

$$\psi_0 = \left(\frac{\gamma}{\pi}\right)^{1/4} \exp(-\tfrac{1}{2}\gamma q^2).$$

$$\psi_1 = \left(\frac{\gamma}{4\pi}\right)^{1/4} 2\gamma^{1/2} q \exp(-\tfrac{1}{2}\gamma q^2).$$

$$\psi_2 = \left(\frac{\gamma}{64\pi}\right)^{1/4} (4\gamma q^2 - 2) \exp(-\tfrac{1}{2}\gamma q^2).$$

Appendix V

Useful Mathematical Relations

$$\sin x = \frac{1}{2i}(e^{ix} - e^{-ix}),\ e^{\pm ix} = \cos x \pm i \sin x$$

$$\cos x = \frac{e^{ix} + e^{-ix}}{2},\ \int \sin x \cos x\, dx = \tfrac{1}{2}\sin^2 x$$

$$\int \cos x\, dx = \sin x,\ \int \sin^m x \cos x\, dx = \frac{\sin^{m+1} x}{m+1}$$

$$\int \sin x\, dx = -\cos x,\ \int \sin mx \cos nx\, dx = \frac{\cos(m-n)x}{2(m-n)} - \frac{\cos(m+n)x}{2(m+n)};$$

$$m^2 \neq n^2$$

$$\int_{-\infty}^{+\infty} e^{-\mathbf{a}x^2}\, dx = \left(\frac{\pi}{\mathbf{a}}\right)^{1/2},\ \int_{-\infty}^{+\infty} x^2 e^{-\mathbf{a}x^2}\, dx = \frac{1}{2\mathbf{a}}\left(\frac{\pi}{\mathbf{a}}\right)^{1/2},$$

$$\int_{\infty}^{+\infty} x^4 e^{-\mathbf{a}x^2}\, dx = \frac{3}{4\mathbf{a}^2}\left(\frac{\pi}{\mathbf{a}}\right)^{1/2}$$

$$\int_0^{\infty} x e^{-\mathbf{a}x^2}\, dx = \frac{1}{2\mathbf{a}},\ \int_0^{\infty} x^3 e^{-\mathbf{a}x^3}\, dx = \frac{1}{2\mathbf{a}^2},\ \int_0^{\infty} \frac{\sin^2 x\, dx}{x^2} = \frac{\pi}{2}$$

$$\int_{-\infty}^{+\infty} \sin x \cos x\, dx = 0,\ \int \sin^2 x\, dx = \frac{x}{2} - \frac{1}{4}(\sin 2x)$$

Law of cosines: $a^2 = b^2 + c^2 - 2cb \cos A$,
where a is the side opposite the angle A.

Index

NOTE: (f) figure, (t) table